African linguistics on the prairie

Selected papers from the 45th Annual Conference on African Linguistics

Edited by

Jason Kandybowicz

Travis Major

Harold Torrence

Philip T. Duncan

language
science
press

Jason Kandybowicz, Travis Major, Harold Torrence & Philip T. Duncan (ed.). 2018.
African linguistics on the prairie: Selected papers from the 45th Annual Conference on African Linguistics (Contemporary African Linguistics 3). Berlin: Language Science Press.

This title can be downloaded at:
http://langsci-press.org/catalog/book/120
© 2018, the authors
Published under the Creative Commons Attribution 4.0 Licence (CC BY 4.0):
http://creativecommons.org/licenses/by/4.0/
ISBN: 978-3-96110-036-1 (Digital)
   978-3-96110-037-8 (Hardcover)

ISSN: 2511-7726
DOI:10.5281/zenodo.1219141
Source code available from www.github.com/langsci/120
Collaborative reading: paperhive.org/documents/remote?type=langsci&id=120

Cover and concept of design: Ulrike Harbort
Typesetting: Birgit Jänen, Felix Kopecky, Iana Stefanova, Phil Duncan, Sebastian Nordhoff
Proofreading: Alexis Michaud, Amr Zawawy, Andreas Hölzl, Bev Erasmus, Brett Reynolds, Christian Döhler, Eitan Grossman, Elizabeth Bogal Allbritten, Evans Gesure, Gerald Delahunty, Jean Nitzke, Jonathan Brindle, Ka Yau Lai, Ken Manson, M Lotta Aunio, Maria Isabel Maldonado, Martin Haspelmath, Paulson Skerrit, Richard Griscom, Rosey Billington, Steven Kaye
Fonts: Linux Libertine, Libertinus Math, Arimo, DejaVu Sans Mono
Typesetting software: X⅂LATEX

Language Science Press
Unter den Linden 6
10099 Berlin, Germany
langsci-press.org

Storage and cataloguing done by FU Berlin

Freie Universität Berlin

Contents

Contents

V Semantics and pragmatics

Part I

General linguistics

Chapter 1

Linguistic complexity: A case study from Swahili

Kyle Jerro
University of Essex

This paper addresses the question of linguistic complexity in Swahili, a Bantu language spoken in East and Central Africa. Literature on linguistic complexity in other languages has argued that high levels of second-language learning affect linguistic complexity over time. Swahili serves as an ideal case study for this question because it has been used as a lingua franca for several centuries. I compare the phonological and morphological systems in Swahili to five other related Bantu languages, as well as compare all six languages to the original Proto-Bantu systems. The results of the study show that there is no decrease in phonological or morphological complexity in (standard) Swahili when compared to other closely related Bantu languages, though the grammar has strongly diverged from the other related languages.

1 Introduction: the question of linguistic complexity

It is generally assumed by linguists that all languages share the same level of complexity, with "simpler" areas of grammar being compensated by more complexity elsewhere. Some researchers take this as a core design feature of language (cf. work from the generative perspective, such as Pinker & Bloom 1990; Pinker 1994; Baker 2003), though this has tacitly pervaded most linguistic thought.

Recently, however, work by various linguistic typologists has put this assumption into question, investigating several linguistic domains (see Miestamo 2008; Sampson 2009 and Givón & Shibatani 2009 for overviews of the literature on complexity). A core area of the research in this field is simply how to answer such a question (Nichols 2009; Sampson 2009; Miestamo et al. 2008). For example, Nichols (2009) compares various features of languages, such size of phoneme inventory, number of inflectional categories on a basic verb, number of alignments in a single language, etc. Other work situates linguistic complexity within a social context. One claim is that older languages tend to be more complex that new ones (e.g. Creoles), cf. McWhorter (2008) and Trudgill (2009).

Kyle Jerro. Linguistic complexity: A case study from Swahili. In Jason Kandybowicz, Travis Major, Harold Torrence & Philip T. Duncan (eds.), *African linguistics on the prairie: Selected papers from the 45th Annual Conference on African Linguistics*, 3–19. Berlin: Language Science Press. DOI:10.5281/zenodo.1251708

Another claim is that population size relates to linguistic complexity (Trudgill 2004; Hay & Bauer 2007; Nichols 2009).

Another vein of this literature – and the topic of this paper – has investigated the interaction of complexity and language contact, claiming that high amounts of second-language learning, including the use as a lingua franca, affects linguistic complexity and increases the rate of language change (Kusters 2003a,b; Trudgill 2009; McWhorter 2008; 2011; Trudgill 2011). Trudgill (2011) claims that that the specific effect on complexity is contingent upon the nature of second-language learning: while large amounts of second-language learning by adult speakers may result in net decomplexification, learning by children (e.g. through prolonged contact between two languages) may lead to *increased* complexity. This paper tests the affects of language contact on complexity in Swahili, used as a lingua franca throughout much of East and Central Africa. I compare Standard Swahili to neighboring Bantu languages in their synchronic morphological and phonological features as well as their divergence from Proto-Bantu.

To test this claim, I employ similar metrics of complexity to those used by Kusters and McWhorter (i.e morphology, see §5), comparing different aspects of Swahili morphology to the grammar of five sister languages. In addition, I discuss the phonological inventories of the languages, a component absent from Kusters' and McWhorter's studies, but discussed at length by others (Hay & Bauer 2007; Trudgill 2011). From the comparisons, I conclude that Swahili does not exhibit any systematic decomplexification in comparison to the other languages, though it shows several grammatical differences from related languages. This situation is predicted from the framework proposed in Trudgill (2011), where long-term bilingualism (here, between Swahili and Arabic) may lead to the rapid change of a contact language.

The remainder of this paper is organized as follows: in §2, I summarize the claims of the decomplexification hypothesis. I then outline the linguistic and sociolinguistic situations of five Bantu languages from East Africa chosen to serve as comparison cases. Sections 4-5 use phonological and morphological metrics, respectively, in order to compare the complexity of Swahili to the comparison languages. Section 6 discusses the findings and their relation to the the decomplexification hypothesis.

2 Contact and (de-)complexification

In research on complexity, two opposite effects on complexity have been found, depending on the nature of the linguistic community. Languages in prolonged contact regions tend to develop high amounts of linguistic complexity (Heine & Kuteva 2005; Dahl 2004; Givón 1984). On the other hand, situations with high numbers of sudden second-language learners result in simplification of linguistic structure. As discussed in Trudgill (2011), the crucial divide between the two groups is the critical period of language acquisition: adult learners are not as adept as children at acquiring a (second) language. In a situation where adult speakers are acquiring a language, this "sub-optimal acquisition" (a term from Dahl 2004) results in the reduction of ornamental or non-obligatory elements of grammar.

As Kusters (2003b) states, "the more second-language learning has taken place in a speech community, the more internal dialect contact and migrations occurred, and the less prestige a language has, the more *transparent* and *economic* the verbal inflection will become" (275, emphasis in original). For Kusters, an inflectional system is more economic if it makes fewer category distinctions. In order to test the prediction of the decomplexification hypothesis, lingua francas that have been used by many second-language learners can be compared to sister languages or varieties that have not been used as lingua francas.

Kusters (2003b,a) provides several case studies in contact languages that have undergone decomplexification, tracing the changes from an older stage of the language to various modern sister languages. For example, one case study comes from three descendants of Old Norse: Icelandic, Faroese, and Standard Norwegian. He argues that the varieties that are more insular have maintained complexity that is absent in metropolitan varieties (i.e. the dialect of the capital city of the Faroese Islands, Tórshavn). As an example, consider the data in Table 1, with the verb forms for the verb 'to awake' in Old Norse and three descendant languages (Kusters 2003b: 285, Table 5).

Table 1: Verbal tense in Old Norse and descendant languages

	Old Norse	Icelandic	Faroese	Tórshavn
1sg	vakn-a	vakn-a	vakn-i	(-′)
2sg	vakn-ar	vakn-ar	vakn-ar	(-′r)
3sg	vakn-ar	vakn-ar	vakn-ar	(-′r)
1pl	vakn-um	vökn-um	vakn-a	(-′)
2pl	vakn- i_	vakn-ið	vakn-a	(-′)
3pl	vakn-a	vakn-a	vakn-a	(-′)

He argues that Faroese, a variant that has been in prolonged contact with Danish, has reduced morphological complexity from the Old Norse, and Tórshavn has undergone further reduction, having only stress as a indicator of tense. The only person marking is the marking of second- and third-singular, to the exclusion of all other persons and numbers. In addition, the Tórshavn dialect has completely neutralized certain inflectional categories, like past indicative and present subjunctive.

McWhorter (2011; 2008) makes the stronger claim that second-language learning is the *only* factor that drives overall simplification in a language. Namely, sweeping loss of complexity in a language is impossible without the influence of second-language learning. The argument works in the opposite direction from Kusters'; when you find an instance of decomplexification, it is predicted that this must have come from a situation of high second-language learning. McWhorter's metrics of complexity are similar to those of Kusters (2003b). For example, in his 2008 paper, he compares two varieties of the Tetun language spoken in Timor. The first, Tetun Dili, is used as a lingua franca by two-thirds of the island; the other, Tetun Terik, is only spoken on the southern coastline. McWhorter predicts that because Tetun Dili is a lingua franca, it has a simpler grammar than Tetun Terik. He presents several instances where the Dili variety is more economical in the number of morphological categories it has. For example, while Terik has three verbal affixes, Dili has two; Tetun has six numeral classifiers while Dili only has four (and those four are used optionally); Tetun has an overt marker for definiteness, while Dili uses context to indicate this; Tetun has three copulas, while Dili has only one; etc. In short, the variety that is used as a lingua franca is systematically simpler than a sister variety without the same level of second-language use.

When two languages are in prolonged contact, and the acquirers of a second language are mostly children, the opposite effect is found: over time, more complexity is found, often by the additive borrowing from the neighboring language. For example, Comrie (2008) and Trudgill (2011) cite the example of Michif, a mixed language from contact between Cree and French (Bakker 1997). Michif, from prolonged multilingualism with French and Cree, developed an elaborate grammar, taking grammatical elements from both Cree and French, with verbal structure inherited from the former and nominal structure from the latter. The result is that Michif employs elaborate verbal and morphological categories found in neither French nor Cree.

In short, work on contact and complexity has found three related effects of contact: first, language contact increases the rate of language change; second, second-language learning by adults often leads to reduction in complexity via imperfect acquisition; and, third, prolonged contact between two languages often results in complexification as forms are taken from one and added into the other. In this paper, I tease apart the level of complexity of standard Swahili, comparing it to five related Bantu languages that have not had parallel situations of language contact.

3 Swahili and the five comparison languages

Swahili serves as another ideal case study in fleshing out the claims of the decomplexification hypothesis. Swahili is spoken as a native language along the Indian Ocean coast of Kenya and Tanzania and in the Zanzibari archipelago. It is also used as an official language and lingua franca in Kenya, Tanzania and the Democratic Republic of the Congo (DRC) in addition to a language of business and commerce at different points in history in Uganda, Rwanda, and Burundi. Because of this widespread use as a lingua franca, nearly 140 million people use Swahili as a second language, while only 5 million speak it natively. Given the overwhelming predominance of second-language speakers of the language, the decomplexification hypothesis predicts that Swahili should be systematically less complex than related languages with little or no use by second-language speakers.

I have chosen five languages spoken in the countries where Swahili is or has been routinely used as a lingua franca. I have chosen one language from each country, and the languages are all part of the Northeastern branch of the Bantu family (with the exception of Lingala).[1] The comparison languages are Gikuyu (Kenya, E.51), Lingala (DRC, C.30B), Haya (Tanzania, JE.22), Kinyarwanda (Rwanda, DJ.61), and Luganda (Uganda, JE.15).

Gikuyu is spoken in Central Kenya by the Gikuyu people, numbering at approximately 7 million. Lingala is a language spoken by approximately 2 million people in the Republic of Congo, the Democratic Republic of Congo, and parts of the Central African Republic. Haya is spoken in Northwestern Tanzania, near the shores of Lake Victoria (Byarushengo et al. 1977). There are approximately 1 million speakers of the language. Luganda is spoken by approximately 4 million people in Southern Uganda. Though used mostly by the Baganda people, it is also used as a second language by approximately 1 million people in Uganda (Ethnologue 2013). Although the use of Luganda by second-language learners is not ideal as a comparison case in the current study, the situation of Luganda is different from Swahili in that the majority of speakers use Luganda as a first language. Swahili on the other hand, is used overwhelmingly as a second language. Kinyarwanda is spoken by somewhere around 12 million people in Rwanda, Burundi, and parts of Uganda and DRC.

4 Phonological complexity

The first metric I use to compare the relative complexity among these languages is their phonological inventories. Phonological complexity did not figure in Kusters' and McWhorter's discussions, though several other works have used phonological inventory as a metric for calculating complexity (Hay & Bauer 2007; Nichols 2009). The decomplexification hypothesis as outlined above predicts that Swahili will have the smallest inventory of phonemes; over time, imperfect learning by second-language speakers would result in the reduction of phoneme contrasts not found in their first languages. Over time, this reduced vowel inventory becomes the standard inventory of the language.

4.1 Vowel complexity

4.1.1 Vowel inventory

Bantu languages generally have between five and seven vowels in their inventory, and they generally include tonal and length distinctions (Hyman 2003; Maddieson 2003). Proto-Bantu has been reconstructed to have seven vowels with high and low tone contrasts. Table 2 indicates the number of different vowels (based on quality) in each of the languages in the test set as well as whether each language makes a distinction between long and short vowels and between tones.

Numerically, Swahili has a simpler vowel inventory than the other languages; it has two fewer vowels than Proto-Bantu. Furthermore, Swahili has lost the tone and length

---

[1]A better comparison set may be languages that are more closely related to Swahili genetically than the five chosen here. Accessibility to resources was a major factor in linguistic choice, though the localization of these languages to East Africa is intentionally aimed at keeping to languages that are more similar to Swahili.

Table 2: Size of vowel inventories

Language	Vowels	Tone	Length	Source
Proto-Bantu	7	+	+	Maddieson (2003)
Swahili	5	–	–	Ashton (1966)
Gikyuyu	7	+	+	Barlow (1960)
Lingala	7	+	+	Guthrie (1966)
Haya	5	+	+	Byarushengo et al. (1977)
Kinyarwanda	5	+	+	Myers & Crowhurst (2006)
Luganda	5	+	+	Kirwan & Gore (1951)

contrasts in Proto-Bantu, while the other languages have retained these features. This is the kind of inventory reduction expected by the decomplexification hypothesis.

4.1.2 Other kinds of vowel complexity

Although the size of vowel inventories indicates a lower level of complexity in Swahili, another possible metric is linguistic markedness (cf. McWhorter 2008; 2011). Swahili, unlike its sister languages, shows three linguistically marked phonological processes that are absent in the other languages. These processes include the permission of syllabic consonants, an irregular stress system, and vowel hiatus. Unlike a numerical metric like phoneme inventory, however, phonological operations in a language are not as easily quantifiable. However, I argue here that the quantitatively fewer phonemic vowel contrasts in Swahili are counteracted by the complexity that ensues with respect to its vowel system.

First, Swahili has syllabic nasal consonants (Ashton 1966). This is present on words such as *mtoto* [m.toto] 'child,' *mtu* [m.tu] 'person,' and *mlango* [m.lango] 'door.' Of the sister languages, only Haya permits syllabic consonants; all maintain a minimal (C)CV syllable structure (cf. the cited grammars). Interestingly, Hyman (2003) assumes this is a natural change, derived from the loss of [u] in *mu-* nominal prefixes.

A further noteworthy difference between Swahili to the exclusion of the other languages is that Swahili permits vowel hiatus, with juxtaposed vowels serving as nuclei of separate syllables. For example, *chui* 'leopard' is syllabified as [tʃu.i], and *paa* 'gazelle' as [pa.a]. The other languages do not permit vowel hiatus; Kinyarwanda, for example, deletes one of any two adjacent vowels, even between word boundaries. For example, the sentence *uri umwana* 'you are a child' is pronounced [u.ru.mɲa.na], with the word-final [i] in *uri* being deleted.

Finally, unlike the other languages of the study, Swahili has several cases of irregular lexical stress.[2] In most Bantu languages, stress falls on the penultimate syllable. In Swahili, however, there are cases where Arabic loanwords carry stress on the antepenul-

---

[2] Thanks to Scott Myers for suggesting this point.

timate syllable, in words such as *nusura* ['nu.su.ra] 'almost,' *ratili* ['ra.ti.li] 'pound,' and *thumuni* ['tʰu.mu.ni] 'an eighth' (Ashton 1966). Here, contact with Arabic is the obvious influence of the complexification of the Swahili stress system.

These three examples show that despite the smaller phonemic inventory, Swahili has elements of complexity that are absent in the other languages. These features, however, are difficult to quantify, and their inclusion in metrics of complexity vary. My conclusion from the data in this section is that there is no clear reduction in complexity in the vowel system of Swahili.

4.2 Consonant inventory

Although the number of vowels in Swahili is quite low, the consonant inventory is noticeably larger than the inventories of the comparison languages.[3]

Table 3: Size of consonant inventories

Language	Consonants
Proto-Bantu	11
Swahili	30
Gikuyu	14
Lingala	15
Haya	19
Kinyarwanda	22
Luganda	18

The consonant inventory in Swahili is striking larger than the other languages under discussion, being over two times larger than the consonant inventory of Gikuyu and Proto-Bantu.[4] The larger inventory in Swahili comes in part from having both voiced and voiceless stops and fricatives for bilabial, alveolar, and velar places of articulation. Many languages lack a subset of these sounds, often having only the voiced or voiceless counterpart. Gikuyu, for example, lacks the voiceless bilabial stop, the voiceless velar fricative, and the voiced alveolar fricative that are found in Swahili.

A further difference is that Swahili is the only language in the group with the aspirated stops and fricatives [pʰ tʰ tʃʰ kʰ] (Ashton 1966; Engstrand & Lodhi 1985). Aspiration is also found in various other Bantu languages, such as Zulu, Swati, Makua, Doko, Chicheŵa, and Kongo. It has been argued that aspiration is a possible outgrowth

---

[3]The inventories in Table 3 come from the same sources as in Table 2, save for the number for Proto-Bantu, which comes from Hyman (2003).

[4]Nasalized consonants were not counted for any of the languages, as the descriptions of them were not satisfactorily convincing that these were indeed separate phonemes. The inclusion of these sounds in the data would not affect the trend, however, since they are also a class of sounds reported in Swahili.

of a consonant followed by the Proto-Bantu high vowels (Hyman 2003) or from an earlier voiceless pre nasalized stop (Maddieson 2003). Regardless of the origin of phonemic aspiration, the presence of aspiration results in a notable increase in the phonemic inventory of Swahili, resulting in a larger inventory than the comparison languages, as well as an innovation since Proto-Bantu.

Another interesting feature of the Swahili consonant system is that all voiced stops are implosives. Swahili has four of these phonemes: [ɓ ɗ ʄ ɠ]. Implosive stops are not found in any of the comparison languages from East Africa, though implosive stops are documented in the southern Bantu languages, with Maddieson (2003) treating implosives in the Bantu family as a natural development in some daughter languages.

4.3 Discussion

The decomplexification hypothesis predicts that Swahili should have a noticeably smaller phoneme inventory than the comparison languages. Although this is true with vowel inventory, the consonant inventory in Swahili is markedly larger than any of the other comparison languages. Importantly, the Swahili consonant system is nearly three times larger than in Proto-Bantu, suggesting considerable innovation during the evolution of Swahili.

5 Morphological complexity

The next domain of investigation is the morphological (dis)similarity between Swahili and the other Bantu languages. If the decomplexification hypothesis is correct, it is expected that Swahili will make fewer distinctions and that morphemes will be more phonologically reduced than the other languages. I investigate the domains of noun class morphology, valency-changing morphology, and tense/aspect/mood morphology, which are all three morphological domains that are found in each of the languages.

5.1 Gender classes on nominals

Bantu languages are well known for their rich noun class morphology. The noun classes for Swahili, Haya, Kinyarwanda, Luganda, and Lingala are provided in Table 4, as well as the reconstructions of the Proto-Bantu inventory (Meeussen 1967; Schadeberg 2003a).[5] Given then decomplexification hypothesis, it is expected that Swahili should be more economic in its morphological forms, either in the phonological shape of the morphemes or in the number of semantic distinctions.

Swahili has a comparable number of category distinctions to the other languages; although it is reduced from Proto-Bantu, only one of the other languages retains the number of category distinctions found in Proto-Bantu (i.e. Luganda). Clearly, the prediction

---

[5]The source for Gikuyu did not include enough detail for this comparison. The sources for the modern languages in Table 4 are: Swahili (Ashton 1966), Haya (Byarushengo et al. 1977), Kinyarwanda (kinyarwanda.net), Luganda (Kirwan & Gore 1951), and Lingala (Guthrie & Carrington 1988).

Table 4: Comparison of noun class morphology

Class	Swahili	Haya	Kinyarwanda	Luganda	Lingala	PB
1	m(u)-	mu-	umu-	(o)mu-	mo-	*mu-
2	wa-	ba-	aba-	(a)ba-	ba-	*ba-
3	m(u)-	mu-	umu-	(o)mu-	mo-	*mu-
4	mi-	mi-	imi-	(e)mi-	mi-	*mi-
5	ji-	li-	iri-	li-, eri-	li-	*ị-
6	ma-	ma-	ama-	(a)ma-	ma-	*ma-
7	ki-	ki-	iki-	(e)ki-	e-	*ki-
8	vi-	bi-	ibi-	(e)bi-	bi-	*bị-
9	n-	n-	i(n)-	(e)n-	N-	*n-
10	n-	n-	i(n)-	(e)n-	N-	*n-
11	u-	lu-	uru-	(o)lu-	lo-	*du-
12	n-	ka-	aka-	(a)ka-	bo-	*ka-
13	-	tu-	utu-	(o)tu-	-	*tu-
14	-	bu-	ubu-	(o)bu-	bo-	*bu-
15	ku-	ku-	uku-	(o)ku-	ko-	*ku-
16	pa-	-	aha-	wa-	-	*pa-
17	ku-	-	-	ku-	-	*ku-
18	mu-	-	-	mu-	-	*mu-
19	-	-	-	-	-	*pị-
20	-	-	-	(o)gu-	-	-
21	-	-	-	-	-	-
22	-	-	-	(a)ga-	-	-
23	-	-	-	e-	-	*ị-
	16	15	16	21	14	21

that Swahili exhibit a noteworthy reduction in the number category distinctions is not borne out in this comparison.

As for the phonological shape of the morphemes, Swahili lacks the pre-prefix that is found in Luganda and Rwanda. At a first glance, this could be argued to be an instance of phonological reduction in Swahili. However, it has been argued in the literature that these pre-prefixes were not present in Proto-Bantu (Katamba 2003), suggesting that the pre-prefix in languages that have it is an innovation.

Support for this point is that the use of the pre-prefix varies drastically in the languages which use it. In Luganda, a variety of features converge to predict the presence of the pre-prefix, such as whether the noun is a dependent or main clause, appears in the affirmative or negative, etc. (Hyman & Katamba 1991; 1993). In Zulu, it has been argued that the pre prefix is a case marker for nominals that lack structural case (Halpert 2012). Zerbian & Krifka (2008) show that features such as genericity, specificity, and definiteness are present in various languages which utilize the pre-prefix, such as Xhosa, Bemba, and Kinande. Crucially, it is assumed that the pre-prefix is a later innovation from Proto-Bantu, perhaps being a reanalysis of cliticized pronouns onto the main noun (Bleek 1869).

The lack of a pre-prefix in the Proto-Bantu stems, as well as the semantic nature of pre-prefixes in the languages which have them, suggests that the reduced phonological shape of class morphology in Swahili is not driven by phonological reduction due to second-language learning. Instead, Swahili has retained the original shape of Proto-Bantu stems.

5.2 Valency-changing morphology

Bantu languages utilize morphology to indicate valency changes to the argument structure of a verb. Both argument-adding (applicatives and causatives) and argument-reducing (stative, reciprocal, passive) morphology is employed by these languages. If the decomplexification hypothesis is correct, it is expected that valency-changing morphology in Swahili is simpler than in the comparison languages – be it phonologically reduced or with fewer morphological category distinctions.

Table 5 gives the morphological forms for different valency-changing morphology in Swahili (Russell 2003), Lingala (Guthrie 1966), Kinyarwanda[6] (Jerro 2015), Haya (Byarushengo et al. 1977), and the reconstructed forms in Proto-Bantu (Schadeberg 2003b).[7]

Table 5: Comparison of valency-changing morphology

Type	Swahili	Lingala	Kinyarwanda	Haya	PB
Benefactive	-(l)e /-(l)i	-el	-ir/-er	-il/-el	*-ɪl
Instrumental	-(l)e /-(l)i	-	-ish/-esh	-is/-es	*-ɪl
Locative	-(l)e /-(l)i	-	-ir/-er	-il/-el	*-ɪl
Causative	-ish/-esh	-is	-ish/-esh	-is/-es	*-i/-ici
Stative	-ik/-ek	-an	-ik/-ek	-ek	*-ɪk
Reciprocal	-an	-an	-an	-aŋgan	*-an
Passive	-(li)w/-(le)w	-	-w	-w	*-ʊ/-ɪbʊ

The first three types of morphology are applicatives, which add a new object to the valency of a verb. Reciprocals, statives, and passives all decrease the valency of a verb by one: reciprocals link the action back to the subject, i.e. the subject does the action to him or herself; passives demote the subject to an oblique position and promote the object to subject position; and statives describe the result state of a transitive verb.

---

[6] Those familiar with Kimenyi (1980) will notice that the locative applicative morpheme for Kinyarwanda in Table 5 differs from Kimenyi's description. Jerro (2015) describes a different locative applicative form for his speakers, who find Kimenyi's locative applicatives ungrammatical.

[7] The resources for Gikuyu and Luganda do not explicitly discuss valency-changing morphology.

Contrary to the decomplexification hypothesis, the data in Table 5 show that Swahili does not have a simpler system of valency-changing morphology. From the perspective of the number of category distinctions, it has a comparable number to the other languages, and has lost no form reconstructed for Proto-Bantu.

From the perspective of the phonological shape of the morphemes, there is no evidence that Swahili is simpler than the other languages. Many of the valency-changing forms in Bantu undergo vowel harmony with the nearest stem on the vowel, and Swahili is not an exception to this; it employs vowel harmony on valency-changing morphology in the same way as its sister languages.

In fact, if any argument were to be made regarding the complexity of valency-changing morphemes, Swahili is more complex in the phonological shape of its passive morpheme, which varies by context depending on the phonological shape of the verb to which it is applied (Russell 2003). The most productive form of the Swahili passive is *–w*, as in *fung–w–a* from *funga* 'fasten' and *tumi–w–a* from *tumia* 'use.' When the verb stem ends in [o] or [e], the form *–lew* is used. If the verb stem ends in [a] or [u], the form *–liw* is used, as in *za–liw–a* from *zaa* 'give birth' and *fu–liw–a* from *fua* 'wash clothes'. Russell (2003) also notes that the passive forms *–ew* and *–iw* are used with verbs of Arabic origin, such as *sameh–ew–a* from *samehe* 'forgive' and *hitaj–iw–a* from *hitaji* 'need.' In short, to form a passive in Swahili, there are complex factors that determine the phonological shape of the passive morpheme, and these factors are not present in the comparison languages.

In Kinyarwanda and Haya, for example, the passive form is *–w* for all verbs, and Lingala lacks a separate passive morpheme altogether (Guthrie 1966). This is evidence that valency-changing morphology in Swahili is not simpler than the sister languages, and in the domain of the passive, Swahili is actually more complex than the other forms.

5.3 Tense, aspect, and mood

Bantu languages have rich systems of tense, aspect, and mood (TAM). From the view of complexity, there are two ways in which a language may be simpler than the others with respect to TAM morphology. The language could make fewer distinctions in its tense, aspect, and mood categories, leaving TAM information to pragmatics. Another indication of decomplexification is if the language shows phonological reduction of the forms compared to other languages or from the protolanguage.

In Bantu languages, aspect and mood morphology generally appears as a prefix before the verb stem, but after the agreement subject marker. Aspect, on the other hand, appears as a suffix after the verb stem. If a language marks subjunctive or indicative, this appears in the aspect slot. The general template for TAM on a verb in Bantu is given in (1) (cf. Meeussen 1967; Nurse 2003).

(1)   Subject Marker – Tense – STEM – Aspect/Subjunctive

Table 6 includes data for five different kinds of TAM that are prevalent in Bantu languages: tense, indicative/subjunctive, aspect, negation, and idiosyncratic TAM morphology that does not fit consistently with the other categories.[8]

---

[8]Data from Lingala and Haya are not included due to a paucity of description of the tense/aspect systems in those languages.

Table 6: Comparison of tense, aspect, and mood morphology

Type	Swahili	Luganda	Gikuyu	Rwanda
Present	na-	∅	∅	∅
Present II	a-	-	-	-
Pres. Continuous	-	-	ra-	ra-
Recent Past	li-	a-	∅	a-
Distant Past	-	MS	a-...-ire	ara-
Perfect	me-	-	-a	-
Past Perfect	-	-	-ite	-
Immediate Future	ta-	naa-	kũ-	za-
Near Future	-	li-	ka-	-
Distant Future	-	-	rĩ-	-
Imperative	-e	-e	-e	-e
Subjunctive	-e	-e	-e/-(n)i	-e
Indicative	-a	-	-	-
Imperfective	-	-	-ga	-a(ga)
Perfective	-	-	-a	-(y)e
Negation	hu-/si-	si-	ti-	si-
Conditional	nge-/ngali-	andi-	ngĩ-	ni-
Habitual	hu-	-	ga-	-
Narrative	ka-	ne-	-	-
'not yet'	ji-	naa-	-	-
'even if'	japo-	-	-	-
'if'	ki-	-	-	-
'still'	-	kya-	-	-
optative	-	-	ro-	-
'also'	-	-	-	na-
	15	12	17	12

The first section shows various tense morphemes: variants of past, present, and future. For some languages (such as Gikuyu and Kinyarwanda) there are various past and future tenses, depending on the temporal proximity to the speech event. For languages with only one distinction for a particular tense, the form is listed in the tense closest to the present. For example Swahili only has one past tense, which is listed in the "Recent Past" row. The abbreviation MS for Luganda, indicates that a "modified stem" is used to indicate the distant past, formed by a lexically-determined set of stem-changing operations. In Gikuyu, the distant past is marked by the combination of a prefix and suffix, indicated by *a-...-ire*. In Swahili, the present *na-* can also be used for present continuous.

The second category covers indicative, subjunctive, and imperative morphology, found consistently among all of the languages. For Swahili, the final vowel *-a* is used as a general indicative mood marker.

The third category is aspect. Kinyarwanda and Gikuyu both have a distinction between perfective and imperfective, while Swahili and Luganda do not have morphology for these aspectual distinctions.

All of the languages share cognate morphology for negation.

Other mood distinctions are covered in the final section of Table 6. This is reserved for mood categories that are highly idiosyncratic meanings in particular languages, such as morphology for meanings such as 'not yet' and 'still' in Swahili and Luganda, respectively. Another is the "optative" in Gikuyu, used for blessings and curses (Barlow 1960). The narrative morpheme is used for verbs that are in a series during a narration of events.

There is no clear indication that any of these languages has a notably simpler system of TAM morphology. Summing the number of morphological category distinctions made in the four languages, it is clear that the inventory of distinctions is quite comparable for all the languages, and Swahili is not noticeably less complex than any other language. It is important to note the heterogeneity among the languages' TAM morphology; few morphemes are cognate, which makes it impossible to compare the phonological reduction among the languages, meaning that the phonological reduction of forms cannot be measured for complexity.

6 Discussion: complexity and language contact

Data comparing the phonological inventory and morphological systems among Swahili, Gikuyu, Kinyarwanda, Lingala, Haya, and, Luganda – as well as a comparison with Proto-Bantu – show that there is no instance where clear decomplexification has occurred in Swahili. In fact, in some instances, such as in consonant inventory, Swahili shows more complexity that the other languages. In nearly all of the grammatical properties discussed, Swahili is highly divergent from the other languages, with notable differences in phonological inventory, such as a larger consonant inventory, a smaller vowel inventory, and irregularities with respect to stress and syllabification. Crucially, all phonological changes that have occurred have happened via natural sound changes, but at a faster rate that than the other languages, i.e. Swahili is less similar to Proto-Bantu than the other languages.

This grammatical situation fits neatly within recent studies of the typological and sociolinguistic literature on contact: language contact results in an increased rate of change, and prolonged contact between two languages moves towards more linguistic complexity (Trudgill 2011). Prolonged contact with Arabic via the Omanis' presence in Zanzibar since the 13th century result in a strong change in the grammar of the language in comparison to other Bantu languages; however, it never blended with Arabic and became a pidgin or creole. Mufwene (2001) and Mufwene (2003) also notes the divergent behavior of Swahili when compared to other contact languages in Africa, showing that the exogamous use of Swahili has led to its adoption by the local population, which resulted in a relatively consistent use of Swahili. From this perspective, Swahili's divergence from the other languages is attributable to the specific contact situation of prolonged bilingualism with Arabic. Crucially, none of the comparison languages have engaged in this kind of long-term bilingualism, accounting for grammatical differences between them and Swahili.

In this paper, I have compared Standard Swahili as described in Ashton (1966) to the standard varieties of several other varieties of East African Bantu languages. As just noted, standard coastal Swahili has been in long-term contact with Arabic since the 13th century, and this contact resulting in expedited change (and, at times, complexification) of several grammatical features of the standard variety. Another prediction from the literature on linguistic complexity is that simplification of grammar occurs when adult learners attempt to learn a second language. Kusters (2003a) fleshes out this claim, comparing Standard Swahili (the variety discussed in the present paper) to two other varieties of Swahili that are used as lingua francas in areas where several adult speakers of the languages speak it regularly, specifically, inland Kenyan Swahili and the Swahili spoken in the trade town of Lubumbashi in the Katanga region of the Democratic Republic of the Congo. Crucially, both of these varieties have less prestige than the coastal standard.

Kusters' findings fit the typological pattern predicted: these two lingua franca languages show several reductions in category distinctions, morphophonological complexity and a reduction of inflectional information. For reasons of space, I refer the reader to Kusters' work, but the crucial point for the current discussion is that the three varieties of Swahili are clear examples of the two kinds of second-language learning in contact areas. Standard Swahili exemplifies the effects of long-term language contact, with acquisition by young children: it has a radically divergent and at times more complex grammar than related non-contact Bantu languages. Two other varieties of Swahili that have largely been used as lingua francas by adult second-language speakers show systemic reduction in grammatical structure when compared with standard Swahili (Kusters 2003a).

Acknowledgements

I am indebted to Tony Woodbury, Pattie Epps, Peter Trudgill, and the anonymous reviews for their invaluable comments during the development of this paper. I would also like to thank the audience of the 45th Annual Conference on African Linguistics for their input and suggestions. All errors remain the fault of the author.

Abbreviations

1	first person	ASP	aspect	SG	singular
2	second person	BEN	benefactive applicative		
3	third person	PL	plural		

References

Ashton, Ethel O. 1966. *Swahili grammar*. London: Longmans.

Baker, Mark C. 2003. Linguistic differences and language design. *Trends in Cognitive Science* 7. 349–353.

Bakker, Peter. 1997. *A language of our own: The genesis of Michif, a mixed Cree-French language of the Candadian Métis*. Oxford: Oxford University Press.

Barlow, A. Ruffel. 1960. *Studies in Kikuyu grammar and idiom*. Edinburgh: William Blackwood & Sons, Ltd.

Bleek, Wilhelm. 1869. *A comparative grammar of South African languages*. London: Trübner.

Byarushengo, Ernest Rugwa, Alessandro Duranti & Larry M. Hyman. 1977. *Haya grammatical structure*. Los Angeles: University of Southern California Press.

Comrie, Bernard. 2008. Inflectional morphology and language contact, with special reference to mixed languages. In Peter Siemund & Noemi Kintana (eds.), *Language contact and contact languages*, 15–32. Amsterdam: John Benjamins.

Dahl, Östen. 2004. *The growth and maintenance of linguistic complexity*. Amsterdam: John Benjamins.

Engstrand, Olle & Abdulaziz Y Lodhi. 1985. On aspiration in Swahili: Hypotheses, field observations, and an instrumental analysis. *Phonetica* 42. 175–185.

Givón, Talmy. 1984. *Syntax: A functional-typological introduction*. Amsterdam: John Benjamins.

Givón, Talmy & Masayoshi Shibatani (eds.). 2009. *Syntactic complexity: Diachrony, acquisition, neuro-cognition, evolution*. Amsterdam: John Benjamins.

Guthrie, Malcom. 1966. *Grammaire et dictionnaire de Lingala*. Westmead, England: Gregg Press Ltd.

Guthrie, Malcom & John F Carrington. 1988. *Lingala grammar and dictionary: English–Lingala, Lingala–English*. London: Baptist Missionary Society.

Halpert, Claire. 2012. *Argument licensing and agreement in Zulu*. MIT dissertation.

Hay, Jennifer & Laurie Bauer. 2007. Phoneme inventory size and population size. *Language* 83. 388–400.

Heine, Bernd & Tania Kuteva. 2005. *Language contact and grammatical change*. Cambridge: Cambridge University Press.

Hyman, Larry M. 2003. Segmental phonology. In Derek Nurse & Gerard Philippson (eds.), *The Bantu languages*, 42–58. New York: Routledge.

Hyman, Larry M. & Francis X. Katamba. 1991. Augment in Luganda tonology. *Journal of African Languages and Linguistics* 12. 1–46.

Hyman, Larry M. & Francis X. Katamba. 1993. The augment in Luganda: Syntax or pragmatics? In Sam Mchombo (ed.), *Theoretical aspects of Bantu grammar 1*, 209–256. Stanford: CSLI.

Jerro, Kyle. 2015. Revisiting object symmetry in Bantu. In *The Selected Proceedings of the 44th Annual Conference on African Linguistics*, 130–145. Somerville, MA: Cascadilla Proceedings Project.

Katamba, Francis X. 2003. Bantu nominal morphology. In Derek Nurse & Gerard Phillippson (eds.), *The Bantu languages*, 103–120. London: Routledge.

Kimenyi, Alexandre. 1980. *A relational grammar of Kinyarwanda*. Los Angeles: University of California Press.

Kirwan, Brian Edmond Renshaw & Peter A. Gore. 1951. *Elementary Luganda*. Kampala:
Uganda Bookshop.

Kusters, Wouter. 2003a. Linguistic Complexity: The Influence of Social Change on Verbal
Inflection dissertation.

Kusters, Wouter. 2003b. The fate of complex languages: Classical Arabic and Old Norse
in the age of globalisation. *Nordlyd* 31. 275–289.

Maddieson, Ian. 2003. The sounds of the Bantu languages. In Derek Nurse & Gerard
Philippson (eds.), *The Bantu languages*, 15–41. New York: Routledge.

McWhorter, John. 2008. Why does a language undress? Strange cases in Indonesia. In
Matti Miestamo, Kaius Sinnemäki & Fred Karlsson (eds.), *Language complexity: Typology, contact, change*, 167–190. Amsterdam: John Benjamins.

McWhorter, John. 2011. *Linguistic simplicity and complexity: Why do languages undress?*
Berlin: Mouton de Gruyter.

Meeussen, Achille Emile. 1967. Bantu grammatical reconstructions. *Africana Linguistica*
3. 80–122.

Miestamo, Matti. 2008. Grammatical complexity in a cross-linguistic perspective. In
Matti Miestamo, Kaius Sinnemäki & Fred Karlsson (eds.), *Language complexity: Typology, contact, change*, 23–42. Amsterdam: John Benjamins.

Miestamo, Matti, Kaius Sinnemäki & Fred Karlsson (eds.). 2008. *Language complexity:
Typology, contact, change*. Amsterdam: John Benjamins.

Mufwene, Salikoko S. 2001. *The ecology of language evolution*. Cambridge: Cambridge
University Press.

Mufwene, Salikoko S. 2003. Contact languages in the Bantu area. In Derek Nurse & Gerard Philippson (eds.), *The Bantu languages*, 195–208. New York: Routledge.

Myers, Scott & Megan Crowhurst. 2006. *Phonology: Case studies*. http://www.laits.utexas.
edu/phonology/.

Nichols, Johanna. 2009. Linguistic complexity: A comprehensive definition and survey.
In Geoffrey Sampson, David Gil & Peter Trudgill (eds.), *Language complexity as an
evolving variable*, 110–125. Oxford: Oxford University Press.

Nurse, Derek. 2003. Aspect and tense in Bantu languages. In Derek Nurse & Gerard
Philippson (eds.), *The Bantu languages*, 90–102. New York: Routledge.

Pinker, Steven. 1994. *The language instinct*. New York: W. Morrow.

Pinker, Steven & Paul Bloom. 1990. Natural language and natural selection. *Behavioral
and Brain Sciences* 13. 707–726.

Russell, Joan. 2003. *Teach yourself Swahili*. Chicago: McGraw-Hill Companies, Incorporated.

Sampson, Geoffrey. 2009. A linguistic axiom challenged. In Geoffrey Sampson, David
Gil & Peter Trudgill (eds.), *Language complexity as an evolving variable*, 1–18. Oxford:
Oxford University Press.

Schadeberg, Thilo C. 2003a. Derivation. In Derek Nurse & Gerard Philippson (eds.), *The Bantu languages*, 71–89. New York: Routledge.

Schadeberg, Thilo C. 2003b. Historical linguistics. In Derek Nurse & Gerard Philippson (eds.), *The Bantu languages*, 143–163. New York: Routledge.

Trudgill, Peter. 2004. Linguistic and social typology: The Austronesian migrations and phoneme inventories. *Linguistic Typology* 8. 305–320.

Trudgill, Peter. 2009. Sociolinguistic typology and complexification. In Geoffrey Sampson, David Gil & Peter Trudgill (eds.), *Language complexity as and evolving variable*, 98–109. Oxford: Oxford University Press.

Trudgill, Peter. 2011. *Sociolinguistic typology: Social determinants of linguistic complexity*. Oxford: Oxford University Press.

Zerbian, Sabine & Manfred Krifka. 2008. Quantification across Bantu languages. In Lisa Matthewson (ed.), *Quantification: A cross-linguistic perspective*, 383–415. Bingley: Emerald Publishing Group.

Chapter 2

Inter-party insults in political discourse in Ghana: A critical discourse analysis

Emmanuel Amo Ofori

University of Florida/University of Cape Coast

In recent times, politics in Ghana has become the politics of personal attack, vilification, and insults. Various attempts have been made to stop this brand of politics, including one spearheaded by the Media Foundation for West Africa, which releases a weekly report to the general public aimed at shaming politicians who are involved in the politics of insults. If a country could go to the extent of shaming politicians involved in politics of insults, then it shows how the issue of intemperate language has become entrenched in Ghanaian political discourse. Thus, there is a need to conduct a thorough analysis of the realization of insults in Ghanaian political discussion. Utilizing a Critical Discourse Analysis approach, this paper analyzes the underlying ideologies in the representation of insults in pro-New Patriotic Party (NPP) and National Democratic Congress (NDC) newspapers. It further compares and contrasts the use of insults in the newspapers.

1 Introduction

Ghana is a democratic country, and this has earned the West African country enviable recognition in the world. Ghana experienced her stable democratic dispensation in 1992 after a series of military take-overs/coup d'états from the period of independence until 1992 (4th republic). The democratic practices in Ghana are still in the infant stages and therefore it could be considered as an emerging democratic state. Since 1993, political discussions in Ghana have centered on various topics, such as the economy, social policies, employment, youth development, education, national security, and health. However, in recent years, Ghanaian political discourse has become a discourse of personal attack, vilification, and insults. Many have argued that the surge of insults in Ghanaian political discussions is due to the liberalization of the media in Ghana (Owusu 2012; Marfo 2014). This stems from the fact that before 1992, Ghana did not have many radio and television stations, newspapers and online websites. Currently, there are numerous radio stations and newspapers in Ghana, and most of the insults emanate from politicians through the various media outlets. These outlets have their own interest in promoting certain

Emmanuel Amo Ofori. Inter-party insults in political discourse in Ghana: A critical discourse analysis. In Jason Kandybowicz, Travis Major, Harold Torrence & Philip T. Duncan (eds.), *African linguistics on the prairie: Selected papers from the 45th Annual Conference on African Linguistics*, 21–35. Berlin: Language Science Press. DOI:10.5281/zenodo.1251710

ideologies and political positions. This is seen in how the media present their audience with "a steady supply of problems and crisis, and it may be their interest to exaggerate a problem, fostering the impression that there is a crisis and not just business as usual" (Cameron 2012: 83). It may seem that they are alerting the public to the surge of intemperate language; however, it is a subtle way of promoting an ideology or political position. Therefore the representation of insults from opponents is publicized or foregrounded not to alert the public about the problem of insults, but to put a political spin on it. The *us* versus *them* dichotomy was seen in media reportage of insults in pro-NPP and NDC newspapers. Thus, van Dijk's (1998) concept of ideological square, which is expressed in terms of emphasizing the positive actions of what a media institution considers the in-group and deemphasizing its negative actions, while, on the other hand, deemphasizing the positive actions of the outgroup, and emphasizing its negative actions, is applied in the analysis of the use of insults in Ghanaian political discourse.

In Ghana, politicians own some of the radio stations and newspapers as the means to disseminate the ideology and philosophy of their respective political parties. This is an attempt on the part of the political parties to control the media. Different groups compete in order to control the media as an instrument of social power, or an Ideological State Apparatus (ISA) in the sense of Althusser (1971), to legitimate and naturalize their ideologies, beliefs, and values (van Dijk 1995). Anyone who controls the media, to some extent, controls the minds of its listeners. This is because the media is seen as a major source of information. Therefore, this paper analyzes the underlying ideologies in the representation of insults in pro-New Patriotic Party (NPP) and National Democratic Congress (NDC) newspapers. It further compares and contrasts the use of insults in newspapers.

1.1 NPP and NDC

Ninsin (2006) observed that when the ban on political parties was lifted in May 1992, by November the same year 13 political parties had been formed and registered. However, the two dominant parties that have survived since 1992 are the National Democratic Congress (NDC) and the New Patriotic Party (NPP).

The NPP, the current party in opposition, emerged from an old political tradition dating back to the United Gold Coast Convention (UGCC) and United Party (UP) of the Danquah-Busia tradition. They fought for independence with Dr. Kwame Nkrumah's Conventions Peoples Party (CPP). The UGCC and the UP metamorphosed into the NPP in 1992 when the country returned to civilian rule after 11 years of military rule, in order to contest the 1992 December elections. Their political ideology is founded on capitalism, and they believe in privitalization, rule of law, and democracy. In short, they see the private sector as an engine of growth. The NPP lost both the presidential and parliamentary elections in 1992 and 1996. They won the 2000 and 2004 elections, and lost to the NDC in 2008 and 2012 in one of the most closely contested presidential elections in Ghana's history. The NPP lost by a margin of 0.46% in 2008.

The NDC, the current government in power, is one of the newest parties in Ghanaian politics. It was formed in 1992 from the Provincial National Defence Council (PNDC) military regime with Flt. Lt. Jerry John Rawlings as its leader. The PNDC overthrew a constitutionally elected government, the People's National Party (PNP), which ruled Ghana from 1979 to 31st December 1981, and ruled Ghana from 1981 to 1992. During the return to civilian rule, the PNDC metamorphosed into the NDC. The NDC won both the 1992 and 1996 elections. They then lost to the NPP in 2000 and 2004, and won the 2008 and 2012 elections. The political ideology of the NDC is founded on social democracy.

1.2 Data collection

The data for this study were obtained from reports in pro-NPP and NDC newspapers. The newspapers are *Daily Guide*, *The Daily Searchlight*, *The New Statesman*, and *The Chronicle* (pro-NPP newspapers); *The Informer*, *The Democrat*, *The Palaver*, *The Al-Hajji*, *The National Democrat*, *The Catalyst*, *The New Voice*, *Daily Post*, *Daily Heritage*, *Radio Gold online* (pro-NDC newspapers). In all, a total of 78 news articles were gathered from 2012 to February 2014. The articles were sampled and analyzed, using Fairclough's discourse-as-text (1989, 1992a, 1995a,b, 2000, 2003) and van Dijk's (1998) concept of ideological square.

1.3 Definition of insult

There are various definitions of insult. According to Aristotle, "insult is belittlement. For an insult consists of doing or saying such things as involve shame for the victim, not for some advantage to oneself other than these have been done but for the fun of it" (Aristotle Rhetoric cited in Yiannis 1998). Aristotle's definition of insult focuses on shame, for the fun of it, and it is a form of belittling the target.

In this paper, the working definition of insult adopted is a modification of Yiannis's (1998: 3) social psychology definition of insults, which considers insult as "a behavior or discourse, oral or written, which is perceived, experienced, constructed and at all times intended as slighting, humiliating, or offensive. Insult can also be verbal, consisting of mocking invective, cutting remarks, negative stereotypes rudeness or straight swearing".

I therefore define insult as "a behavior or discourse, oral or written, direct or indirect, gestural or non-gestural, which is perceived, experienced and most of the time intended as slighting, humiliating, or offensive, which has the potential of psychologically affecting not only the addressee or target but also his/her associates." This definition should not be taken as universal because there is no universal measure of insults. The yardstick to measure insults differs from society to society and also from culture to culture.

2 Critical Discourse Analysis (CDA)

The revolving idea of CDA is power, and it analyzes opaque as well as transparent structural relationships of dominance, discrimination, power and control as manifested in language (Wodak 2001: 2). van Dijk (2001: 96) also postulates that CDA focuses on social problems, especially on the role of discourse in the production and reproduction of power abuse or domination. This means that it focuses not only on linguistic elements per se, but also complex social phenomena that have semiotic dimensions (Wodak & Meyer 2009). In effect, the overall aim of CDA is linking linguistic analysis to social analysis (Wood & Kroger 2000: 206). CDA aims at making visible and transparent the instrument of power, which is of increasing importance in the contemporary world. It is very critical of the relationship between language, discourse, speech, and social structure. As the dimensions of CDA include "the object of moral and political evaluation, analyzing them should have effects on society by empowering the powerless, giving voices to the voiceless, exposing power abuse, and mobilizing people to remedy social wrongs" (Blommaert 2005: 25). These are the main concerns in analyzing insults in Ghanaian public political discourse: Who has access to the media? Who controls the media? What are the ideological standpoints of the media in Ghana? Whose agenda are they propagating? These are some of the questions that CDA tries to uncover in contemporary societies that relate directly to the present study.

The media discourse in Ghana has changed drastically in that before 2001 it was very difficult for media personnel to operate. This was due to the various laws governing media practices in Ghana. Even the ones that existed were so polarized that they were divided into two distinct genres: state press and private press (Hasty 2005). The state press were praise singers of the government. They published stories that projected the development, inspirational rhetoric and policies of the government. The private press was sometimes the opposite of the state press. They revealed the profligate spending, abuse of power, and social inequality attributed to the government. In analyzing the underlying ideologies in the representation of insults in pro-NPP and NDC newspapers, these developments must be taken into consideration. The two CDA approaches applied in this paper are Fairclough's discourse-as-text and van Dijk's ideological square.

2.1 Fairclough's discourse-as-text

Fairclough situates his theory of social-discoursal approach in Halliday's Systemic Functional Linguistics (SFL) and also draws on critical social theories, such as Foucault's concept of order of discourse, Gramsci'S concept of hegemony, Habermas' concept of colonization of discourses and many others. To fully understand the interconnectedness between languages, social and political thought, Fairclough proposes a three-dimensional approach to analyzing discourse. These are: discourse-as-text, discourse-as-discursive-practice and discourse-as-social practice. Since the analysis in this paper is based on discourse-as-text, I elaborate on it below (for detailed discussions on the other two dimensions see Fairclough 1989, 1995).

Discourse-as-text involves the analysis of the way propositions are structured and the way they are combined and sequenced (Fairclough 1995). Here, the analyst examines the text in terms of what is present and what could have been present but is not. The text, and some aspects of it, is the result of choice, that is, the choice to describe a person, an action or a process over another; the choice to use one way of constructing a sentence over an alternative; the choice to include a particular fact or argument over another. According to Fairclough (1995: 57), choice in text "... covers traditional forms of linguistic analysis-analysis of vocabulary and semantics, the grammar of sentences and smaller units, and the sound system (phonology) and writing system. But it also includes analysis of textual organization above the sentence, including the ways in which sentences are connected (cohesion) and aspects like the organization of turn-taking in interviews or the overall structure of a newspaper article". The application of textual analysis in CDA does not mean just focusing on the linguistic form and content; rather, it is the function that such elements play in their use in the text. Hence, the traditional forms of linguistic analysis should be analyzed in relation to their direct or indirect involvement in reproducing or resisting the systems of ideology and social power (Richardson 2007).

2.2 Van Dijk's concept of ideological square

One prominent feature of van Dijk's socio-cognitive approach is the concept of ideological square. It is about how different social groups project themselves positively and represent others negatively. The structures of ideologies are represented along the lines of an *us* verses *them* dichotomy, in which members of one social group present themselves in positive terms, and others in negative terms. There is polarization of how media institutions emphasize the positive actions of ingroup members and deemphasize its negative action on one hand, and deemphasize the positive action of the outgroup while emphasizing its negative actions. The ideological square consists of four moves: (1) express/emphasize information that is 'positive' about *us*; (2) express/emphasize information that is 'negative' about *them*; (3) suppress/deemphasize the information that is 'positive' about *them*; and (4) suppress/deemphasize information that is 'negative' about *us*. Any property of discourse that expresses, establishes, confirms or emphasizes a self interested group opinion, perspective or position, especially in a broader socio-political context of social struggle, is a candidate for special attention in ideological analysis (van Dijk 1998).

2.3 Ideology

Ideology is defined as systems of ideas, beliefs, practices, and representations, which work in the interest of a social class or cultural group. Gramsci sees ideology as "tied to action, and ideologies are judged in terms of their social effects rather than their truth-values" (Fairclough 1995: 76). Ideology has the potential to become a way of creating and maintaining unequal power relations, which is of central concern to discourse analysts who take a "particular interest in the ways in which language mediates ideology in a variety of social institutions" (Wodak 2001: 10). van Dijk (1998: 3) also defines ideology as political or social systems of ideas, values or prescriptions of a group that have the function of organizing or legitimating the actions of the group. The use of language reflects a person's philosophical, cultural, religious, social, and political ideology. Hence, ideology affects the way one talks, argues, and reacts.

3 Textual analysis

Textual analysis is Fairclough's first dimension of his three dimensional framework. The linguistic tools employed under this dimension in the analysis are lexicalization and predication, presupposition and verbal process.

3.1 Lexicalization and predication

Lexicalization involves the choice or selection and the meanings of words used to refer to social actors. A typical lexical analysis looks at the denotation (the literal or primary meaning of words) and connotation (the various senses that a word invokes in addition to its literal or primary meaning). This type of analysis is important because "words convey the imprint of society and of value judgments in particular" (Richardson 2007: 47). There is a strong relationship between lexicalization and ideology, as in the use of expressions such as 'terrorist' versus 'freedom fighter' for example. This suggests that language users have several choices of words to refer to the same persons, groups, social relations or issues, and in most or all cases these carry heavy semantic and ideological loads. The words in a text that communicate messages about subjects or themes in newspapers are framed ideologically. Thus "vocabulary encodes ideology, systems of beliefs about the way the world is organized" (Fowler 1987: 69).

The paper also analyzes predication. Wodak & Meyer (2009: 27) define predication strategies as terms or phrases that "appear in stereotypical, evaluative attribution of positive or negative traits and implicit or explicit predicates". Reisigl & Wodak (2001: 54) also see predicational strategies as "the very basic process and result of linguistically assigning qualities to persons, animals, objects, events, actions and social phenomena". Predicational strategies are not used arbitrarily: there are hidden ideologies in the various forms or phases. It also reveals the 'Us' versus 'Them' dichotomy that shows positive predications for the ingroup and negative predications for the outgroup. Indeed, "predication is used to criticize, undermine and vilify certain social actors, sometimes with potential dangerous consequences" (Richardson 2007: 53).

NPP newspapers reported insults with lexicalization and predication from people they considered as ingroup members targeted at the outgroup members. These included:

(1) Specialist in lies and propaganda shouldn't be managing our economy - Bawumia Daily searchlight, October 2, 2012

(2) J. J. tainted with blood - Daily Guide, December 5, 2013

(3) Greedy bastards and babies with sharp teeth - Rawlings The New Statesman, April 3, 2014

(4) Thieving Mahama caught - Daily Searchlight, October 2, 2012

The insult in (1) is a quote from Dr. Bawumia, a running mate to the presidential candidate of the main opposition party in Ghana. He has a PhD in economics and believes that the NPP has the experts to manage the economy. However, he believes that those managing the economy do not have the requisite expertise to manage it; they rely only on *lies* and *propaganda*, meaning they are not being truthful with the true state of the economy. Looking at the background of Dr. Bawumia, it would be difficult for the public to scrutinize his comment and it may not be possible for readers to understand that this is an attempt to convince the electorate that if the NPP is voted into power they will make the economy better. The underlying idea behind the report of this insult is that the ingroup has the experts to manage the economy better than the outgroup. Therefore, the newspaper reports the insults from the ingroup member seeking to negatively portray the outgroup as people who do not have the technical know-how to manage the economy.

Example (2) is a predication that projects the founder of the NDC (an outgroup member) as a killer. J. J. Rawlings has been accused several times of being responsible for the killing of the three Heads of State and three Supreme Court judges in Ghana. Therefore, the report of this insult from the NPP newspaper is a way to remind the public that the founder of the NDC is a known killer. Thus, the underlying idea behind the report of this insult is to negatively portray the outgroup member as a killer and not worth listening to.

The predicational insult in (3), *greedy bastards and babies with sharp teeth* was a comment made by the former President Rawlings to his own party members vilifying him. Expanding on this insult, it can be analyzed in two ways: first, it is used to describe the activities of the NDC with regards to corruption. Secondly, the second part of the insult, *babies with sharp teeth*, is a metaphor that describes the behavior of the young ones in the NDC. Rawlings made this comment at a time when most of the youth in the NDC were insulting him. So, his metaphor *babies with sharp teeth* refers to these youth who have the penchant toward behavior of vilifying and insulting people. Within the Ghanaian culture, kids or babies are not supposed to engage in adult communication, let alone to insult adults. This metaphor portrays the young people within the NDC as having outgrown their wings and vilifying the adults in the party. Therefore, pro-NPP newspapers reported this insult among others to expose the confusion within the camp of the outgroup, and to show that they are not the only people saying the outgroup members are corrupt; the founder of their party and members of their party concur with them.

In (4), the *Daily Searchlight* paper describes the president of Ghana, John Mahama, as a *thief*, for stealing the 2012 presidential election, which the NPP contested in court and lost. Calling the president a thief was to bring to the attention of the NPP supporters that the party won the 2012 elections, and that their loss was a typical case of a stolen verdict. Therefore, the insult was aimed at satisfying the aggrieved ingroup members and portraying the outgroup as thieves.

Similarly, pro-NDC newspapers used lexicalization and predicational strategy to report insults from the ingroup members targeted at the outgroup members.

(5)   No 'patapaa' President Mahama warns losers in December election - Ghana
      Palaver, September 14–16, 2012

(6) Arrogant Kan Dapaah running a one man show - Ghana Palaver, July 20, 2012

(7) Akuffo-Addo is wicked and not worth dying for - Ghana Palaver, June 20, 2012

(8) "Tɛ Ni" can't govern us. - The Al-Hajj, August 16, 2012

The lexical item *patapaa* in example (5) was uttered by the current president of Ghana, John Mahama, to advise all losers of the 2012 election, and this was reported by the *Ghana Palaver* newspaper. *Patapaa* is an Akan word, which means "a person who is violent or a violent behavior". It was used to describe the losers in the December elections. Though the word was part of a comment made to advise all losers, knowing that Ghana's election is a contest between the NDC and NPP, this insult was directed at the doorsteps of the main opposition party and most importantly to the 2012 presidential candidate of the NPP, Nana Akuffo-Addo. Because he was alleged to have said prior to the 2012 elections that the elections would be "all die be die", he was criticized for warmongering. Thus, the report of the president's insult is to negatively present the outgroup member, the NPP presidential candidate, as a violent person who would not accept the 2012 election results and would plunge the country into chaos if he lost; by extension, it is implied he is not even qualified to be a president.

In (6), the *Ghana Palaver* newspaper reports insults from NDC members of the Public Accounts Committee (PAC) of Parliament that were tasked to investigate financial malfeasance in the public service. Parliamentary regulations provide the opportunity for an MP from the opposition party to chair the (PAC) so that there is a fair investigation of government officials. The NDC members accused the chairman of the committee, Albert Kan Dapaah, an outgroup member, of being *arrogant* and *running a one-man show* because he threatened to cause the arrest of an ingroup member, Alfred Agbesi Woyome. The newspaper reports this predicational insult from the NDC members of the committee to negatively portray the outgroup member as someone who does not consult them before making decisions, and has therefore taken an arrogant posture. The publication of the insult is clearly meant to discredit the outgroup member.

The *Ghana Palaver's* predicational insult in (7) is targeted at Nana Akuffo-Addo, the NPP presidential candidate for 2008 and 2012 elections when he continued with his campaign at a time when the late former Vice President, Aliu Mahama, was admitted to the hospital. Akuffo-Addo was accused of not showing enough compassion and abandoning the former Vice President to die. The ingroup candidate is reported to have asked for prayers for the late vice president from Ghanaians. Therefore, the paper described Akuffo-Addo negatively as *wicked* and not qualified to be president of Ghana. The ingroup candidate is preferred over the outgroup candidate, revealing a group polarization between NPP and NDC newspapers.

The *Al-Hajj* newspaper reported the insult in (8) from a taxi driver who claimed to have heard some Akans using the lexical item "tɛ ni" to insult the president. This word needs elaboration. The correct spelling of the word is "tani," an Akan term used to insult people from the Northern part of Ghana. Recall that the NDC presidential candidate, John Mahama is a Northerner, and the NPP is perceived as an Akan dominated party.

So, for this term to surface on the front page of an NDC paper is a way of turning the people of the North against the NPP. The paper portrays to readers that the outgroup is presenting the ingroup presidential candidate as someone who is ethnically unfit to lead the country. This portrays the outgroup negatively for using tribal and ethnic sentiments against the ingroup candidate, while the ingroup is implicitly presented positively for not whipping up ethnic sentiments.

3.2 Presupposition

Presupposition is a "taken-for-granted, implicit claim embedded within the explicit meaning of a text or utterance" (Richardson 2007: 63). Wodak (2007: 214) provides a broader picture of presupposition: "presupposed content is, under ordinary circumstances, unless there is a cautious interpretive attitude on the part of the hearer, accepted without (much) critical attention (whereas the asserted content and evident implicatures are normally subject to some level of evaluation)". The claims are not critically evaluated and are generally considered to be true regardless of whether the sentence is true. It is a useful strategy in political discourse because it makes it difficult for the audience to identify or reject views communicated in this way. That is, it persuades people to take for granted something which is actually open to debate (Bayram 2010).

Pro-NPP and NDC newspapers utilized presupposition strategy using the authorial voice and non-politicians to describe people they considered to be outgroup members. Below are examples from pro-NPP papers:

(9) In his usual propaganda style - The Chronicle, July 19, 2012

(10) Send people who can make intellectual debate daily - Daily Guide, December 12, 2013

(11) Former President Jerry John Rawlings has suddenly found his voice - Daily Guide, December 10, 2010

The *Chronicle* paper used the presupposition in (9) to report an insult hurled on one of their reporters by Deputy Minister for Information, James Agyenim Boateng when he asked a question on whether the Constitutional Review Committee (CRC) was considering putting a clause in the constitution about health status of presidents and presidential candidates. Recall that it was during this time that the late president Mills was alleged to have been taken ill. The paper therefore presented members of the outgroup as people fond of using propaganda. Employing the lexical item *usual* by *The Chronicle* paper indicates that the outgroup member is noted for his habitual propaganda style.

In (10), the presupposition was reported from a source that presented the outgroup negatively. Fiifi Banson, a broadcast journalist with *Peace FM*, a radio station in Accra, is reported by the *Daily Guide* paper to have uttered that presupposition. He is presented as "an award winning Ghanaian broadcaster" to portray the genuineness of the presupposition. The meaning behind the presupposition is that the crop of panelists sent by the NDC to *Peace FM* are not astute enough to present the agenda of the party.

The former President Rawlings is also presented in the *Daily Guide* paper in (11) as suddenly finding his voice when he insulted former president Kufuor as an "autocratic thief". The use of *sudden* presupposes that Rawlings has been quiet for sometime and was now speaking. His sudden voice, however, was directed at an ingroup member not the outgroup, which the paper believes is noted for corruption. Therefore, the use of this presupposition is to negatively present the former president, an outgroup member, as directing his attention towards the wrong person. In sum, pro-NPP newspapers presented the outgroup members negatively using presupposition from both the authorial voice (depicting the ideology of the papers) and other sources.

Pro-NDC newspapers also employed presupposition strategy to present the outgroup negatively. They used presuppositions from the authorial voice and members in the ingroup. Some of the presuppositions included:

(12)   Loose-talking 'Genocide' MP on the loose again - The Catalyst, September 7, 2012

(13)   NPP turned Ghana into a cocaine country - Felix Kwakye-Ofosu country radiogold.com, June 7, 2013

(14)   True NPP old evil Dwarfs at work - Ghana Palaver, July 20, 2012

The Catalyst reported this presupposition in (12), using the authorial voice, to represent Kennedy Agyapong, the outgroup MP, negatively for insulting the President, John Mahama, the entire membership of NDC and the police service. The use of the lexical item *again* in the report presupposes that the MP's loose talking is not the first time. That is, the MP is known for his habitual loose talk. He is even described as a *genocide MP*, a term which negatively portrays the MP. Thus, the presupposition and the description are used to negatively present the outgroup member.

Radio Gold reported the presupposition in (13) from a deputy minster for information, Felix Ofosu Kwakye who described as unfortunate attempts by the NPP to link the arrest of the Managing Director of SOHIN Security in the United States for drug trafficking to the Mahama administration. The word *turned* presupposes that before the NPP came to power there was nothing like cocaine in Ghana; therefore, the NPP are responsible for turning Ghana into a cocaine country. The ingroup's administration is implicitly presented positively for not being responsible for the cocaine business in the country.

The *Ghana Palaver* paper employed the presupposition in (14) to insult the outgroup. The former President Rawlings was the first person to use the description *old evil dwarfs* to refer to some members of the NDC. For an NDC newspaper to use this same description with the adjective *true* to refer to the outgroup is interesting. The adjective *true* is used to qualify the noun phrase *NPP old evil dwarfs*. Richardson (2007) indicates that the use of nouns and adjectives to modify noun phrases trigger presuppositions he calls nominal presuppositions. So, *true NPP old evil dwarfs* is a nominal presupposition meant to present the outgroup negatively. *True* presupposes that the NPP are indeed the real or actual *old evil dwarfs*, not the NDC. Therefore, the nominal presupposition was used to present the outgroup negatively. In sum, pro-NDC newspapers employed presuppositions, using authorial voice and the ingroup to present the outgroup negatively.

3.3 Verbal process

Verbal process is "any kind of symbolic exchange of meaning" as well as predicates of communication (Halliday 1985). This means that they represent the action of talking, saying and communicating. Journalists use verbal processes to introduce the speech of people they are reporting on, and this can reveal the feelings and the attitudes of the journalists towards the people they consider important whose words or actions they report. Such reportage can be used to marginalize others and focus readers' attention towards the direction of the reporter. Thus, "choosing certain verbal process rather than others, the producer of a text is able to foreground certain meanings in discourse while others are suppressed" (Chen 2005: 34).

Chen (2005), following Halliday's analysis of verbal process, proposed three sub-categories of verbal process. The first is negative verbal process, which demonstrates a certain negative feeling on the part of the writer towards the person whose words the verbal process is used to introduce. Examples of such verbs are 'insisted', 'denied', 'claimed', 'admitted', 'complained'. The second is positive verbal process, which is used to promote in a reader the feeling that the person whose words are being reported is wise, authoritative, benign or in some other sense positive. Examples are 'pointed out', 'announced', 'explained', 'declared', 'indicated', and 'urged'. The last is neutral verbal process, where the writer's choice of verb does not indicate an endorsement or disparagement of what the person being reported is saying. Examples include 'said', 'told', 'described', 'asked', 'commented'.

Pro-NPP and NDC newspapers employed different verbal processes to report insults from people they considered ingroup positively and those they considered outgroup negatively. The analysis of the data showed that pro-NPP newspapers employed negative and neutral verbs to report insults directed at the outgroup. However, NDC newspapers adopted positive, negative and neutral verbs to report insults directed at the outgroup.

Table 1 sums up all the verbal processes employed by both NPP and NDC Newspapers.

Table 1: NPP and NDC verbal process.

newspapers	positive	negative	neutral
NPP		lashed out Jabbed blasted accused	describe challenge say
NDC	explain Confirm	warn blast lashed-out condemned	describe say

In sum, positive verbal processes were not very common; they only appeared in the reports of pro-NDC newspapers, showing that positive ingroup representation was more common in pro-NDC newspapers compared to NPP newspapers. However, negative other-representation manifested in both NPP and NDC newspapers.

4 Discussion

In this section, I expatiate on the textual analysis to investigate the broader sociopolitical and sociocultural context. Drawing on van Dijk's (1995) ideological square, I discuss the various ideological structures utilized by both pro-NPP and NDC newspapers on the textual analysis to represent the ingroup positively and the outgroup negatively (group polarization), paying particular attention to the sociopolitical context that necessitated this polarization. The two ideological structures employed by pro-NPP and NDC newspapers are negative lexicalization and predications and detailed description. These revealed group polarization between the two dominant political parties in Ghana.

In the first place, the lexical forms that are used to describe the political opponents show *Us* verses *Them* dichotomy. Pro-NPP newspapers for example employed the lexical item "propaganda" from Dr. Bawumia to refer to the managers of the Ghanaian economy. According to the United States Institute for Propaganda Analysis (USIPA) (2001), the word propaganda "is an expression of opinion or action by an individuals or groups deliberately designed to influence opinions or actions of individuals with reference to predetermined ends". They further state that the main idea of a propagandist is to put something across, either good or bad. The USIPA provides a list of seven propaganda devises. These are: (1) name calling, (2) glittering generalities, (3) transfer, (4) testimonial, (5) plain folks, (6) card stacking, and (7) band wagon (for detailed discussion of these devises, see USPIA 2001). The pro-NPP newspapers, therefore, published this lexical item for ideological purposes, that is, to present the outgroup as: (1) not giving the true state of the economy and (2) bad handlers of the economy. However, they portrayed to the reader that the NPP would be transparent and have the needed expertise to manage the economy better than the outgroup. This reveals group polarization, in that, the ingroup is presented positively as transparent and good managers of the economy while the outgroup is presented negatively as liars and bad handlers of the economy.

Pro-NDC newspapers also employed lexical items "patapaa" and "tani". The current president of Ghana, John Mahama prior to the 2012 general elections, used the word "patapaa", which means "a violent person or violent behavior or a thug". The meaning can be extended to "someone who uses force to claim what does not belong to him/her". This word was uttered to advise all losers of 2012 elections. However, this was an insult directed at the presidential candidate of the NPP, describing him as violent, adopting a "patapaa" stance to win the elections. NDC newspapers reported this negative lexicalization from the president to present the presidential candidate of the outgroup as violent while maintaining that the ingroup candidate is peaceful and not violent.

NDC newspapers employed the term "tani", an Akan word that is normally uttered to insult those from the Northern part of Ghana. There is no consensus as to the meaning of this word. While Agyekum (2010) argues that it is a derogatory term for people who move in pairs (*ntafoɔ*-twins and *tani*-one of the twins), reference is made to immigrants from the Northern part of Ghana; others have the understanding that it is an insult which makes reference to people from the northern part of Ghana as "dirty people". The common idea out of the two meanings is that it is not a good term to use for Northerners. Interestingly, this term surfaced on the front page of an NDC newspaper "*tani can't govern us*". Take note of the fact that the 2012 presidential candidate of the NDC and the current President is a Northerner. Also, it is important to recall that the NPP has long been perceived as an Akan or Ashanti dominated party, and historically Northerners were considered as servants of the Akans. Putting all these facts in context, the pro-NDC newspaper pitches an old ideological battle between the ingroup and the outgroup. The outgroup is presented negatively as insulting and marginalizing people from the North, consequently raising ethnic tension between people from the North and the outgroup, that is, turning the people from the North against the NPP. According to van Dijk (2001), ethnic prejudice and ideologies are not innate; rather, they are acquired and learned through communication, that is, through text and talk.

Secondly, with regard to detailed description, pro-NPP newspapers employed detailed positive descriptions to describe ingroup members as well as non-politicians insulting the outgroup. For example, the *Daily Searchlight* paper described Mr. Mohammed Ameen Adams, who accused the deputy energy minster, Alhaji Inusah Fuseini of being eco-nomical with truth concerning the energy crisis in the country as "an energy expert or economist". Similarly, the *Daily Guide* paper described Fiifi Banson, a broadcast journal-ist, as "an award winning Ghanaian broadcaster" when he criticized the outgroup for not sending people who can make an intellectual debates. The paper, however, referred to former President Rawlings as "founder of the ruling NDC" when he insulted the party he founded. Negative descriptions were also used to refer to outgroup members for insult-ing the ingroup. For example, the former President Rawlings was described by the *Daily Guide* paper as "see no evil" for calling former President Kufour an "autocratic thief".

NDC newspapers, on the other hand, employed honorifics and official titles to de-scribe ingroup members who insulted the outgroup. For example, the *Voice* newspaper described Hamza Abugri, the Bantama constituency organizer of the NDC, as "honor-able" for insulting the chairman of the NPP as "ignorant". This is very interesting be-cause "honorable" is a title given to Ministers of state, MPs, Metropolitan, Municipal and District Chief executives (MMDCE), and assembly members but not leaders of political parties. Members of the outgroup who insulted the outgroup were given more detailed descriptions such as "leading member of NPP" (*Daily Post*), "senior member of NPP" (Ra-dio Gold), and "a stalwart of the opposition" (*Informer*), to report such insults as credible. Negative descriptions were also used to refer to outgroup members' insults targeted at the in-group. For example, "genocide MP" and "loose talking MP" (*The Catalyst*).

van Dijk (1995) aptly states that one of the structures used to present the ingroup pos-itively is detailed description. This is supported by Blommaert (2005), who points out that members of the ingroup employ indexical meaning such as terms of politeness to elevate them to a particular social status. It is however important to note that, in this paper, it has been revealed that positive descriptions were used to describe the outgroup members who insulted their own party to portray to readers that the source of the insult or information is credible and authentic. Though the opposing group members are presented positively, it gives an impression to readers that there is confusion at the camp of the outgroup, which eventually presents them negatively.

In sum, the two important ideological structures used were negative lexicalization and predication as well as detailed description. A detailed analysis of these structures revealed group polarization between the pro-NPP and NDC newspapers.

5 Conclusion

Utilizing Fairclough's textual analysis and van Dijk's concept of ideological square, this paper has revealed the Us/Them representation of insults between the NPP and NDC newspapers. That is to say, the actions of the ingroup were presented positively while those of the outgroup were presented negatively. The ideological differences and political spin in the representation of insults showed a clear group polarization between NPP and NDC newspapers. The various lexicalizations and predications employed by both NPP and NDC newspapers revealed the Us/Them dichotomy between these two dominant political parties in Ghana. Using the authorial voice and other sources, the presuppositions also showed the ideological differences between the papers. Finally, verbal processes employed by NPP and NDC papers clearly manifested the positive ingroup representation in NDC papers as compared to NPP paper. Negative other representation was a common trait in both papers.

References

Agyekum, Kofi. 2010. *Akan verbal taboos in the context of ethnography of communication.* Accra: Ghana Universities Press.

Althusser, Louis. 1971. Ideology and ideological state apparatuses. In Louis Althusser (ed.), *Lenin and philosophy and other essays*, 121–173. London: New Left Books.

Bayram, Fatih. 2010. Ideology and political discourse: A critical discourse analysis of Edorgan's political speech. *ORECLS* 7. 23–40.

Blommaert, Jan. 2005. *Discourse: A critical introduction.* Cambridge: Cambridge University Press.

Cameron, Deborah. 2012. *Verbal hygiene.* New York: Routledge.

Chen, Lily. 2005. Transitivity in media texts: Negative verbal process sub-functions and narrator bias. *IRAL* 43. 33–51.

Fairclough, Norman. 1989. *Language and power.* New York: Longman.

Fairclough, Norman. 1995. *Media discourse.* London: Arnold.

Fowler, Roger. 1987. The intervention of the media in the reproduction of power. In Myriam Díaz-Diocaretz, Teun A. van Dijk & Iris M. Zavala (eds.), *Approaches to discourse, poetics and psychiatry*, 67–80. Amsterdam: Benjamins.

Gramsci, Antonio. 1971. *Selections from the prison notebooks of Antonio Gramsci.* New York: International Publishers.

Halliday, Michael. 1985. *An introduction to functional grammar*. London: Arnold.

Hasty, Jennifer. 2005. *The press and political culture in Ghana*.

Marfo, Samuel. 2014. Thinking of peace, democracy and politics of insults in Ghana: The paradox of freedom and culture of violence. *Online Journal of African Affairs* 3. 139–144.

Ninsin, Kwame. 2006. *Political parties and political participation in Ghana*. Accra: Konrad Adenauer Foundation.

Owusu, William. 2012. *The ghanaian media landscape: How unethical practices of journalists undermine progress*. Oxford: no publisher. Unpublished Masters thesis.

Reisigl, Martin & Ruth Wodak. 2001. *Discourse and discrimination: Rhetorics of racism and antisemitism*. London: Routledge.

Richardson, John. 2007. *Analyzing newspapers: An approach from critical discourse analysis*. Houndmills: Palgrave.

van Dijk, Teun. 1995. Discourse analysis as ideology analysis. In Christina Schaffner & Anita Wenden (eds.), *Language and peace*, 17–33. Dartmouth: Dartmouth Publishing Company Limited.

van Dijk, Teun. 1998. Opinions and ideologies in the press. In Allan Bell & Peter Garret (eds.), *Approaches to media discourse*, 21–63. Oxford: Blackwell.

van Dijk, Teun. 2001. Critical discourse analysis. In Deborah Schiffrin, Deborah Tannen & Heidi Hamilton (eds.), *The handbook of discourse analysis*, 352–371. Oxford: Blackwell.

Wodak, Ruth. 2001. What CDA is about - A summary of its history, important concepts, and its developments. In Ruth Wodak & Michael Meyer (eds.), *Methods of critical discourse analysis*, 1–13. London: Sage.

Wodak, Ruth. 2007. Pragmatics and critical discourse analysis: A cross-disciplinary inquiry. *Pragmatics & Cognition* 15(1). 203–225.

Wodak, Ruth & Michael Meyer. 2009. Critical discourse analysis: History, agenda, theory, and methodology. In Ruth Wodak & Michael Meyer (eds.), *Methods of critical discourse analysis*, 1–33. London: Sage.

Wood, Linda A & Rolf O Kroger. 2000. *Doing discourse analysis: Methods for studying action in talk and text*. London: Sage.

Yiannis, Gabriel. 1998. An introduction to the social psychology of insults in organizations. *Human Relations* 51. 1329–1354.

Chapter 3

Classification of Guébie within Kru

Hannah Leigh Sande

Guébie, a Kru language spoken in Côte d'Ivoire, is currently doubly classified within Eastern Kru according to Ethnologue (Lewis et al. 2013). It is listed as a dialect of two distinct subgroups, Bété and Dida. This double classification is clearly problematic, and this paper provides the initial work towards addressing the correct classification of the language. Here I compare the phonological and syntactic properties of Guébie with surrounding Bété and Dida languages in order to determine its relatedness to each subgroup. I conclude that Guébie is more closely related to Vata, a Dida language, than to Bété.

1 Introduction

Kru is a branch of Niger-Congo languages spoken in Côte d'Ivoire and Liberia. There are two major subdivisions of Kru languages: Eastern and Western Kru (Marchese 1979); however, there has been very little work done on the internal classification of those two branches. Many 'languages' classified as either Eastern or Western Kru are in fact subgroups of related languages. For this reason, many Kru languages are grouped together as a single language for classification purposes, sometimes for empirical reasons and sometimes for political or geographic ones, leading to linguistic misclassifications and inadequate descriptions of individual Kru varieties. In this paper I address one such case, that of Guébie, an Eastern Kru language spoken in southwest Côte d'Ivoire. I attempt to provide an initial classification of this particular Kru language.

Guébie is a particularly interesting case of misclassification. It is currently classified twice in Ethnologue (Lewis et al. 2013),[1] and I argue here that neither classification is accurate. Lewis et al. (2013) calls Guébie both a dialect of Bété-Gagnoa (btg), and an alternative name for Dida-Lakota (dic). Bété-Gagnoa has 150,000 speakers according to Ethnologue (Lewis et al. 2013), and Dida-Lakota (dic) has 94,000 speakers. Based on my own observations during fieldtrips along with estimates from consultants, I estimate that Guébie, the language in question, has only 7,000 remaining speakers. Thus, classifying Guébie as a dialect of Bété-Gagnoa or an alternative name for Dida-Lakota is incredibly misleading in terms of the number of remaining speakers and vitality of the language.

---

[1]The revised version of this chapter was completed in 2015. The version of Ethnologue cited throughout this paper is the 2013 edition, which was the most recent at the time of writing.

Hannah Leigh Sande. Classification of Guébie within Kru. In Jason Kandybowicz, Travis Major, Harold Torrence & Philip T. Duncan (eds.), *African linguistics on the prairie: Selected papers from the 45th Annual Conference on African Linguistics*, 37–49. Berlin: Language Science Press. DOI:10.5281/zenodo.1251712

The goal of this paper is to determine the appropriate classification of Guébie and advocate that it be classified separately from both Bété-Gagnoa and Dida-Lakota. I will demonstrate based on original Guébie data that Guébie is more closely related to Vata, a dialect of Dida-Lakota, than to Gbadi, a dialect of Bété-Gagnoa. I choose these two particular varieties as standards of comparison because there is more data available for Vata and Gbadi than for other Dida and Bété languages. I conclude based on this initial study that Guébie is more closely related to Dida languages than Bété ones, and further, that it is distinct from Vata (Dida-Lakota), thus it should be classified as a distinct Dida language.

I begin in §2 with background information on Guébie and its current classification within Kru. I turn in §3 to the methodology used here to determine relatedness of languages. In §4 I discuss the somewhat limited phonetic and phonological evidence that Guébie is more closely related to Dida-Lakota than to Bété-Gagnoa, and in §5 I discuss the more readily available syntactic data which supports the conclusion that Guébie is a Dida language, but is distinct from Dida-Lakota. I conclude in §6 with the implications and conclusions of the present study, arguing that Guébie be classified as distinct from both Bété-Gagnoa and Dida-Lakota, contra the current Ethnologue classification (Lewis et al. 2013).

2 Background: The current classification of Guébie

The current literature agrees that Kru is a branch of Niger-Congo (cf. Marchese Zogbo 2012). However, there have been many other contradictory proposals in the past. There have been claims that Kru is related to Gur (Vogler 1974), Kwa (Greenberg 1963), and Mande (Bennett & Sterk 1977). Welmers (1977) put forth the proposal that Kru is a distinct branch of Niger-Congo, and that has been corroborated by Marchese (1979) and later work. There are two major branches of Kru languages, Eastern and Western, which are geographically split near the country boarder of Côte d'Ivoire and Liberia. Guébie is an undescribed Eastern Kru language spoken in seven small villages in southwest Côte d'Ivoire about 30 kilometers southwest of Gagnoa and 30 kilometers east of Lakota. The largest of these villages, Gnagbodougnoa, has a population of 1000, about two thirds of whom are Guébie-speaking. The remaining third are Lobi speakers who were displaced during the national crisis of Côte d'Ivoire in the 1990s. Since Guébie is spoken in just seven villages, the largest of which has a population of 1000, I estimate that Guébie has at most 7000 speakers.

The data presented in this paper comes from original work with native speakers of Guébie. For eight months I worked with a native speaker temporarily living in Berkeley, California. This was followed by fieldwork in Gnagbodougnoa, Côte d'Ivoire in the summer of 2014. My consultants are five in number, include both men and women, and range in age from 19–76. This paper presents the first published documentation and description of Guébie.

Guébie villages are situated amidst a dense rainforest where temperatures are high year-round and there are two rainy seasons, one in June and the other in December.

The community of Guébie speakers are subsistence farmers who grow cassava, rice, and plantains. Rarely are these plants farmed for profit. A small percentage of Guébie people farm and sell cacao and coffee. Only one third of children attend school, while the others work on their family's farm. There is only one known monolingual speaker, my consultant Serikpa Emil, who is 76 years old. The rest of the Guébie-speaking population is bilingual in French. Children are still learning Guébie, however within a single generation, I predict that children will no longer learn Guébie as a first language.

The Eastern Kru family tree in Figure 1 is adapted from Ethnologue (Lewis et al. 2013).

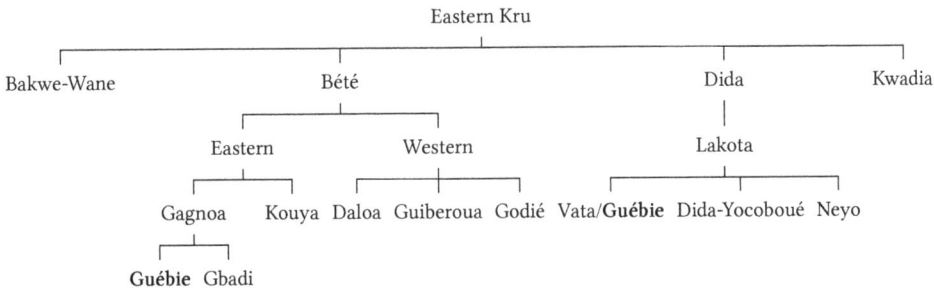

Figure 1: Eastern Kru family tree

Guébie, bolded in the tree above, is currently classified twice, as part of two distince Eastern Kru varieties. Due to geographic, historical, and possibly ethnic reasons, Guébie has been called a dialect of Bété-Gagnoa, spoken by about 150,000 people (Lewis et al. 2013). Due to linguistic similarity, Guébie is also listed as a second name for Dida-Lakota, an Eastern Kru language spoken by about 94,000 people in the city of Lakota, east of the Guébie-speaking area.

3 Methodology

The most widely accepted means of establishing genetic relationship between languages is the Comparative Method (cf. Bloomfield 1933 chapter 18, among others), which determines whether sound correspondences across languages are regular, thus the result of regular sound change. For the Comparative Method to be of use requires dictionaries or lists of lexical items in the languages in question to be used for comparison.

Ideally, we would compare sound correspondences across cognates in the lexicon of Guébie with the lexicon of Bété-Gbadi and Vata (Dida-Lakota) in order to determine relatedness. However, there has not been enough thorough documentation across Bété and Dida languages for comparing sound correspondences to be informative. The available resources for Guébie include only my own data elicted from September 2013 to July 2014. For Bété-Gbadi, there is a dictionary written by a native speaker linguist (Zogbo 2005). For Vata there is a small list of lexical items compiled from various works on the phonology and syntax of the language (Marchese 1979; Kaye 1981; Koopman 1984).

Amongst these resources, I have found fewer than 100 cognates to compare across the three languages. This number of cognates is not enough to determine relatedness based on sound change; however, I will present what minimal data exists in §4.

For each of the languages in question, Guébie, Bété-Gbadi, and Vata, there is some not insignificant amount of syntactic description in the literature. Basing genetic relationship on syntactic correspondences is less widely accepted than on sound correspondences and morphological paradigms (Garrett 2012; Ringe & Eska 2014, and citations therein). However, since there are no available lexicon lists for most Kru languages, I propose that we examine syntactic features of Bété and Dida languages, comparing them with Guébie to determine how these languages are related.

Lexical items are likely to be borrowed heavily from neighboring languages, and morphosyntactic correspondences are more likely to be conservative or undergo change less rapidly over time. Thus, if we can find convincing syntactic similarities between two languages, A and B (say, Guébie and Vata), but not between two others, A and C (say, Guébie and Bété-Gbadi), we may be able to tentatively say that the first two languages, A and B, are more closely related than the latter two. Comparing morphosyntactic features of languages has been crucial in determining the relatedness of Proto-Anatolian languages (Melchert 2013), and the place of Armenian within Indo-European (Hübschmann 1875). Thus, it is possible, however rare, for morphosyntactic similarity to influence decisions about language classification.

In the following two sections I compare the linguistic properties of Guébie with its two geographically closest documented neighbors, Bété-Gbadi and Vata. Bété-Gbadi is spoken in just north of the Guébie-speaking villages. The Bété-Gbadi data here comes from Marchese (1979); Zogbo (2005); Koopman (1984). Vata is a Dida language spoken east of the Guébie-speaking villages. The data here comes from Marchese (1979); Kaye (1981; 1982); Koopman (1984). Vata is a dialect of Dida-Lakota spoken slightly northeast of Lakota. Ideally we would compare Guébie with Dida-Lakota spoken in the city of Lakota; however, there is very little work on the Dida spoken in Lakota. Vata is slightly geographically further from Guébie; however, since it is a well documented and closely related to Dida-Lakota, I compare Vata, not the Dida of Lakota, with Guébie.

I demonstrate throughout the remainder of this paper that the linguistic properties of Guébie and Vata are too similar to be due to chance, and that Guébie is less closely related to Bété-Gbadi than to Vata. The words and sounds that do correspond in Guébie and Bété must be due to borrowing, or must have been present in Proto-Eastern-Kru. There is very little evidence that Bété and Guébie underwent any regular changes that other Eastern Kru languages did not undergo. Any assumptions made here about the features of Proto-Kru or Proto-Eastern-Kru come from Marchese (1979) and Marchese Zogbo (2012).

4 Phonetic and phonological evidence

There is very little, if any, phonetic or phonological evidence that can concretely determine the classification of Guébie as Bété or Dida. I present here some basic similarities and differences between Bété-Gbadi and Guébie, and Vata and Guébie.

4.1 Tone

The data in (1) shows that there are four contrastive tonal heights in Guébie. The words in (1a) are segmentally identical and are distinguished only by the height of their level tone. The data in (2) shows that Guébie also makes use of contrastive contour tones. There are two distinct rising tones and three distinct falling tones in Guébie.

(1) **Four contrastive tone heights in Guébie**
 a. ko^1 'line/row' ko^2 'pestle' ko^3 'skin' ko^4 'cadavre'
 b. no^2 'beverage' no^4 'woman'
 c. $ʝe^1$ 'egg' $ʝe^3$ 'star' $ʝe^4$ 'number'

(2) **Contour examples**
 $ʝa^{31}$ 'coconuts'
 $vɔ^{13}$ 'horns'
 su^2 'tree'
 su^{13} 'to shove'

There are four contrastive tonal heights in Guébie. There are also four contrastive tonal heights in Vata (Marchese 1979; Kaye 1981; Koopman 1984). It is controversial whether there are three or four contrastive tonal heights in Bété-Gbadi. Zogbo (2005)'s dictionary lists four contrastive tones for Bété-Gbadi; however, Marchese (1979; 1989) says that the four tonal heights posited for Proto-Kru have collapsed into three heights in Bété. Tones throughout this paper are marked with numbers 1–4, where 4 is the highest tone and 1 is the lowest. A dot between tones separates syllables, and two numbers within a syllable signifies a contour tone.

4.2 Vowels

There are ten contrastive vowels in Guébie, distinguished by height, backness, rounding and ATR value. /ə/ is the +ATR counterpart of /a/ in Guébie.

(3) **Guébie vowel inventory**

$$
\begin{array}{ccc}
\text{i} & & \text{u} \\
& \text{ɪ} \quad \text{ʊ} & \\
\text{e} & & \text{o} \\
& \text{ə} & \\
\text{ɛ} & \quad \text{ɔ} & \\
& & \\
& \text{a} &
\end{array}
$$

There are also ten contrastive vowels in Vata, identical to those in the vowel inventory in the chart above. There are only seven contrastive vowels in Bété-Gbadi. Bété-Gbadi lacks an ATR distinction between the mid and low vowels. Marchese Zogbo (2012) posits seven contrastive vowels for Proto-Kru, which means that Vata and Guébie each separately underwent vowel splits resulting in a larger vowel inventory. Alternatively, Vata and Guébie share a common ancestor that Bété-Gbadi does not share, and that ancestor underwent regular phoneme splits, adding three vowels to the inventory. This ten-vowel inventory was then passed down to both Vata and Guébie. Without more information we cannot say for sure which path of development of these vowel systems is the correct one.

There are marginal nasal vowels in Guébie. The three vowels [ɛ̃, ɔ̃, ã] are found in a just a handful of words. Proto-Eastern-Kru did not have nasal vowels. However, nearby Kwa and Mande languages, frequently in contact with Kru languages, have these same three nasal vowels. This contact could have resulted in the borrowing of Kwa and Mande words into Guébie, so that the borrowed words but no native words contain nasal vowels in Guébie. The three Guébie words that I have found containing nasal vowels are given in (4).

(4) **Guébie nasal vowels**
    a.   kãɔ̃$^{4.2}$ 'spine'
    b.   ɟiɛ̃$^{3.1}$ 'sea'
    c.   kpãɛ̃$^{4.4}$ 'very, a lot'

In Bété-Gbadi, nasal vowels are also found in a few, likely non-native, words. One of these is the same word, kpãɛ̃ 'very', that contains a nasal vowel in Guébie. Because both Guébie and Bété-Gbadi have had contact with surrounding Kwa languages in the past, it seems likely that both languages borrowed words containing nasal vowels from those Kwa languages. Alternatively, one of the two, Guébie or Bété-Gbadi, could have borrowed the words in (4) and these words could have in turn been borrowed into the other. Either way, it seems unlikely that nasal vowels were an innovation via regular sound change shared by Guébie and Bété; borrowing seems like a more plausible option because there are so few words in each language that contain nasal vowels, and the words that do have nasal vowels overlap in Guébie and Bété-Gbadi.

Guébie has pervasive ATR harmony from roots to suffixes. Vata shares the same ATR harmony process, though Bété-Guébie does not (Koopman 1984). Guébie ATR harmony can be seen in (5) where the causative morpheme is a low vowel suffix on verbs. Verb roots that contain +ATR vowels take the +ATR causative suffix [-ə] while those containing -ATR vowels in the root take the -ATR causative suffix [-a]. The same process can be seen with the Vata definite marker, where +ATR root vowels result in +ATR suffix vowels. There is rounding harmony in the Vata data that does not occur in Guébie. The Gbadi data shows that +ATR roots do not result in +ATR suffixes. This is likely a factor of the limited vowel inventory of Gbadi, however, where only high vowels show an ATR distinction. There are no suffixes in Gbadi that contain high vowels, so we can not say for certain whether or not there would be ATR harmony between roots and suffixes in high vowels in Gbadi.

(5)   **Vowel harmony data**
    Guébie   ci-ə$^{3.1}$ 'to cause to learn'   jɛ-a$^{3.2}$ 'to cause to dance'
    Vata   sle-e$^{2.3}$ 'the house'   gbʊ-ɔ$^{2.3}$ 'the cause'
    Gbadi   li-a$^{2.2}$ 'to cause to eat'   jue-a$^{4.4.2}$ 'the children'

Without a high-vowel suffix in Bété-Gbadi, we cannot say for certain whether all three languages have ATR harmony, or whether only Vata and Guébie share this ATR harmony process. If the latter is true, either this harmony process arose separately in Vata and Guébie, or it was lost relatively recently in Gbadi. Alternatively, Vata and Guébie share a common ancestor that Bété does not share, and that ancestor acquired a harmony process that Bété did not. More data is needed to know for certain.

4.3 Consonants

There is too little lexical data available from documented Bété and Dida languages to show regular sound changes in consonants that led from a Proto-language to the currently spoken languages.

4.4 Summary

Until further data is collected, the existing phonological data on these languages do not tell us much about their genetic relationship. What we can conclude from the above is that there are no known shared changes between only Guébie and Bété-Gbadi. All of the features that Guébie shares with Bété are also present in Vata, or there is evidence that those features a result of borrowing (nasal vowels). In the following section I turn to syntactic evidence of relatedness.

5 Syntactic evidence

In this section I compare certain syntactic properties of Guébie with those of Bété-Gbadi and Vata (Dida). I am limited by the specific syntactic properties that have been described for all three languages in question, though there are numerous syntactic features of Gué-bie that more closely resemble Vata than Bété-Gbadi and other Bété dialects.

Before describing the differences, it is important to note that all three languages share S AUX O V alternating with SVO word order. I turn now to those properties that are not shared amongst all three languages.

5.1 Aspect marking

The two major aspectual distinctions in Guébie, imperfective and perfect, are distin-guished by tone. All imperfective verbs have tone one step lower on the four-tone scale than the corresponding perfect verb, (6).

(6) **Perfective vs Imperfective in Guébie**
   a. $\mathfrak{o}^3$ li^2 $\mathfrak{z}a^{31}$
       3.SG eat.IMPF coconuts
       'He eats coconuts'
   b. $\mathfrak{o}^3$ li^3 $\mathfrak{z}a^{31}$
       3.SG eat.PERF coconuts
       'He ate coconuts (recently)'

Vata (and Dida-Lakota, Kaye 1982) also distinguishes imperfective from perfective as-pect with tone.

Bété-Gbadi, on the other hand, distinguishes imperfective from perfective aspect with auxiliary particles, and the verb surfaces finally: S AUX O V.

(7) **Comparing aspect distinctions**

Language	Perfective	Imperfective
Guébie	Tonal	Tonal
Vata	Tonal	Tonal
Gbadi	Particle	Particle

This difference means that in Proto-Eastern-Kru there was either an aspect-marking auxiliary that was reduced to a tonal morpheme in Guébie and Vata, or there was histor-ically a tonal morpheme that was replaced by an auxiliary in Bété-Gbadi, but not in all Eastern Kru languages.

5.2 Causation

There are two methods of adding a causative meaning to a verb in Guébie. One of these is suffixal, shown in (8).

(8) **Guébie suffixal causative**
   a. ci^{31} 'to learn' $ci\text{-}\mathfrak{o}^{3.1}$ 'to cause to learn, to teach'
   b. $j\varepsilon^3$ 'to dance' $j\varepsilon\text{-}a^{3.2}$ 'to cause to dance'

The second means of causativization in Guébie is with a clausal construction meaning literally "X speaks and Y Zs," where X is the causer, and Y is the subject of the verb Z.

(9) **Clausal causative in Guébie**
 kɔgʊlɲɔ-wa$^{4.2.2.2.3}$ gba^2 ne^4 ju-wa$^{4.4}$ ɔ^3 li^2
 farmer-DEF speak and boy-DEF 3.SG eat.PERF
 'The farmer is making the boy eat'

The suffixal causative in (8) is present in both Vata and Bété-Gbadi as well. However, the clausal causative is only found in Vata and Guébie, not Bété-Gbadi.

(10) **Clausal causative in Vata**
 n^3 gba^2 le^3 yɔ-ɔ$^{3.3}$ li^2
 I speak and boy-def eat
 'I made the boy eat.'

It is possible that the clausal causative construction was borrowed into Guébie from Vata or vice versa; however, it is also possible that the two share a common ancestor that Bété does not share, and the clausal causative was innovated in that ancestor language, inherited into both Guébie and Vata. All we can say is that there is no commonality between Bété and Guébie that Vata does not also share.

5.3 WH-questions

Wh-questions in Guébie are formed with a clause-final question marker and a clause-initial question word meaning literally 'person, place, thing' for 'who, where, what,' respectively.

(11) **Wh-questions in Guébie**
 a. ɲɔkpa$^{3.3}$ touri$^{1.1.3}$ ji^3 lɛtrɪ$^{3.2}$ kɔpa$^{3.23}$ na^3
  who Touri.NAME will letter send Q
  'To whom will Touri send a letter?'
 b. bɛba$^{2.2}$ touri$^{1.1.3}$ ji^3 ɟaci$^{2.2}$ kɔpa$^{3.23}$ na^3
  what Touri.NAME will Djatchi.NAME send Q
  'What will Touri send to Djatchi?'

According to (Koopman 1984: 87), Wh-questions are formed in Bété-Gbadi with an initial Wh-word and a clause-medial question marker, while in Vata they are formed with an initial Wh-word and a final question marker. This means that once again the Vata construction (12) is identical to the Guébie construction, while the Bété construction is distinct. The chart in (13) shows the similarity between the Guébie and Vata but not the Guébie and Bété Wh-construction.

(12) **Wh-questions in Vata**
   alɔ$^{1.4}$ ɔ^1 le^2 saka$^{3.4}$ la^1
   who he eat rice WH
   'Who eats rice?'

(13) **Comparing Wh-constructions**

Language	Initial	Medial	Final
Guébie	Wh	–	+Q
Vata	Wh	–	+Q
Gbadi	Wh	+Q	–

Much like the causative construction in the previous section, we see a similarity between Guébie and Vata that could be the result of borrowing or common inheritance. More data, prefereably historical data, is needed to know for certain.

5.4 Gerunds

There are two types of gerund formation in Guébie. One form of the gerund is formed by reduplicating the verb and adding the suffix /-je/. The other is formed by adding the suffix /-li/ to the verb[2]. The former gerund construction is found in Bété-Gbadi and not Vata, while the latter gerund construction is found in Vata but not Bété-Gbadi (Koopman 1984).

(14) **Gerunds in Guébie**
  a. saka$^{3.3}$ la^2 li-li-je$^{2.2.1}$
    rice GEN eat-eat-NOM
    'Rice-eating'
  b. saka$^{3.3}$ la^2 pi-li$^{3.1}$
    rice GEN cook-NOM
    'Rice-preparing'

(15) **Gerunds in Vata**
   saka$^{3.4}$ la^2 pi-li$^{2.1}$
   rice GEN cook-NOM
   'Rice-preparing'

(16) **Gerunds in Bété-Gbadi**
   li-li-je$^{2.2.1}$
   eat-eat-NOM
   'Eating'

The Guébie construction in (14b) is identical to the Vata construction in (15). Likewise, the Guébie construction in (14a) is shared by Bété-Gbadi, as shown in (16). Without knowing which gerund formation strategy was present in the proto language, we cannot make

---

[2] The two gerund formation strategies described here have distinct distributions that I cannot yet cleanly define.

any conclusions about whether each of these gerund constructions was inherited or borrowed. Without further information, gerunds do not shed light on the classification of Guébie.

5.5 Summary

We have seen that Guébie syntax is similar to Vata in aspect marking, causation, and wh-question formation. It shares ones gerund construction with Vata and another with Gbadi. However, there are very few other syntactic similarities between Guébie and Bété-Gbadi. Vata and Guébie share further syntactic properties not presented here for purposes of space. For example, they have identical applicative constructions, similar negation marking, and they both can undergo long-distance wh-movement while Bété-Gbadi cannot.

The table in (17) below summarizes the phonological and syntactic features compared here in Guébie, Vata, and Bété-Gbadi.

(17) Summary table

Feature	Bété	Guébie	Vata
# of tones	3	4	4
# of vowels	7	10	10
Aspect	particle	tone	tone
Clausal causation	–	yes	yes
Wʜ-question particle	medial	final	final
Gerunds	verb-verb-je	verb-verb-je, verb-li	verb-li

The Vata and Guébie columns above are nearly identical. The two share the same number of contrastive tones and the same vowel inventory. They both mark aspect distinctions with tone, they have clausal causative constructions, they have final Wh-particles, and they share a gerund construction. Guébie shares gerund construction with Bété-Gbadi but in all other respects there are key differences between the two.

Based on the limited phonological and syntactic data available for Guébie, Vata, and Bété-Gbadi, it seems that Guébie shares far more features with Vata, a Dida language, than with Bété-Gbadi, a Bété language. In the following section I argue that we should classify Guébie as a distint language in the Dida subgroup of Eastern Kru.

6 Implications and conclusions

We have seen evidence from the phonological and prosodic systems, and the morphosyntax of Guébie, that it resembles Vata, a Dida language, more closely than Bété-Gbadi, a Bété langauge. Further research on Bété and Dida languages will allow for lexical and sound-correspondence comparison as well, which will confirm or deny the claims made here.

I return here to the problem defined in §1 of this paper: where within in Eastern Kru should Guébie be classified. We saw that in Ethnologue (Lewis et al. 2013) Guébie is currently classified twice, once as a dialect of Bété-Gagnoa, and once as an alternative name for Dida-Lakota. Dida and Bété are distinct subgroups of Eastern Kru with distinct histories and distinct lingusitic features. The goal of this paper is to make an initial step towards determining whether Guébie is a Bété or Dida language. No firm conclusions can be made without further research; however, Guébie is culturally distinct from both of its neighboring Bété and Dida languages, and I argue here that it is also linguistically distinct. Guébie should be classified as a distinct language, and based on the data presented throughout this paper, I tentatively conclude that Guébie is a Dida language, closely related to Dida-Lakota and Vata, though not synonymous with either of them. This conclusion is based on the fact that there are many phonological and syntactic features shared between Guébie and Vata that are not present in Bété-Gbadi. It seems unlikely that all of the similarities between Guébie and Vata are due to chance or borrowing; thus, inheritence is a more plausible history.

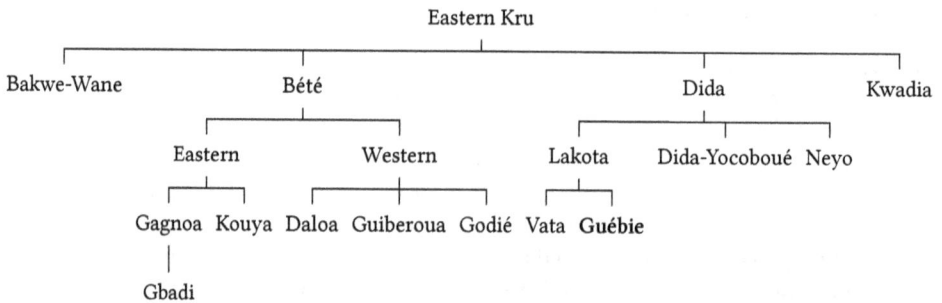

Figure 2: My proposed classification of Guébie within Kru

The tree in Figure 2 shows my proposed classification of Guébie, as a Dida-Lakota language related to but distinct from Vata. Crucially, I claim that Guébie is *not* a dialect of Bété-Gagnoa, and in fact it is not a Bété language at all.

Far more data is needed to prove the above classification and the further internal classification of Kru; however, this paper provides and initial step towards a more detailed understanding of the Kru languages and how they are related to each other. Arguing for the classification of Guébie at least provides a strong argument that can be argued for or against in future work when further data becomes available.

Finer grained classification than that shown in the tree above will require extensive further research. Comparative work such as Kaye (1982), "Les dialects dida," is a start toward this kind of comparative research in Kru.

References

Bennett, Patrick R. & Jan P Sterk. 1977. South central niger-congo: A reclassification. *Studies in African linguistics* 8. 241–273.

Bloomfield, Leonard. 1933. *Language.* New York: Henry Holt.

Garrett, Andrew. 2012. The historical syntax problem: Reanalysis and directionality. In Dianne Jonas, John Whitman & Andrew Garrett (eds.), *Grammatical change: Origins, nature, outcomes,* 52–72. Oxford: Oxford University Press.

Greenberg, Joseph H. 1963. Some universals of grammar with particular reference to the order of meaningful elements. In Joseph Greenberg (ed.), *Universals of language,* 73–113. Cambridge: MIT Press.

Hübschmann, Heinrich. 1875. Uber die stellung des armenischen im kreise der indogermanischen Sprachen. *Zeitschrift für Vergleichende Sprachforschung* 23. 5–42.

Kaye, Jonathan D. 1981. Las´election des formes pronominales en vata. *Revue qúebecoise de linguistique* 11. 117–135.

Kaye, Jonathan D. 1982. Les dialectes dida. In Jonathan D. Kaye, Hilda Koopman & Dominique Sportiche (eds.), *Projet sur les langues Kru,* 233–295. Montreal: Quebec University.

Koopman, Hilda. 1984. *The syntax of verbs.* Dordrecht: Foris Publications.

Lewis, M. Paul, F. Gary Simons & Charles D. Fenning (eds.). 2013. *Ethnologue: Languages of the world.* 17th edn. Dallas: SIL International.

Marchese Zogbo, Lynell. 2012. *Kru revisited, Kru revealed.*

Marchese, Lynell. 1979. *Atlas linguistique kru.* Abidjan: ILA.

Marchese, Lynell. 1989. Kru. In Bendor Samuel (ed.), *The Niger-Congo languages,* 119–213. Lanham: University Press of America Inc.

Melchert, H. Craig. 2013. The position of Anatolian. In Michael Weiss & Andrew Garrett (eds.), *Handbook of Indo-European studies,* 85–163. Oxford: Oxford University Press.

Ringe, Don & Joseph F. Eska. 2014. *Historical linguistics: Toward a twenty-first century integration.* Cambridge: Cambridge University Press.

Vogler, Pierre. 1974. Le problème linguistique kru, éléments de comparaison. *Journal de la Socíete des Africanistes* 44. 147–176.

Welmers, William E. 1977. The Kru languages: A progress report. In *Language and linguistic problems in Africa: Proceedings of the Seventh Conference on African Linguistics,* 353–62. Columbia, SC: Hornbeam.

Zogbo, Raymond Gnoleba. 2005. *Dictionnaire bété-français.* Abidjan: Editions du CERAP.

Chapter 4

What about Southern African story grammar? Promoting language specific macrostructures in educational settings

Heike Tappe

University of KwaZulu-Natal, Howard College Campus, Linguistics Programme

The current research is motivated by the assumption that the "canonical" story grammar (Stein & Glenn 1979) which is widely held to reflect universal story organisation (e.g. Mandler et al. 1980) may not be fully suited to assess the narrative potential of children with primary languages of non-European origin (e.g. Souto-Manning 2013). It thus juxtaposes the supposedly universal "canonical" story grammar with the idea of an as yet under-researched Southern African story grammar, which may represent common macro-structural features in Southern African storytelling.

The analysis of Southern African folktales from Lesotho, South Africa, Malawi and Zambia as well as narrative retellings produced by multilingual children in Malawi, whose dominant languages are Chichewa and English (Tappe & Hara 2013; Hara 2014), and in South Africa, whose dominant languages are isiZulu and English, provides evidence that Southern African narratives systematically deviate from the allegedly universal "canonical" story grammar (Anderson & Evans 1996; Stein & Glenn 1979). In both Southern African countries currently under investigation the "canonical" story grammar (CSG) is, however, promoted through the language of teaching and learning (English) and determines the assessment instruments used to measure the children's narrative skills.

Against this background the emancipation of Southern African ways of storytelling might be a crucial step in the fight against literacy in Southern African countries.

1 Introduction

Globally, education is conceptualized as a tool that serves the improvement of social justice and economic advancement. Accordingly, equal access to the full spectrum of the educational system was one major concern during protests against colonisation in all Southern African countries as the redistribution in social justice was widely equated with access to the kind of education that many term "quality education" (e.g. Tikly &

Heike Tappe. What about Southern African story grammar? Promoting language specific macrostructures in educational settings. In Jason Kandybowicz, Travis Major, Harold Torrence & Philip T. Duncan (eds.), *African linguistics on the prairie: Selected papers from the 45th Annual Conference on African Linguistics*, 51–64. Berlin: Language Science Press. DOI:10.5281/zenodo.1251714

Barrett 2011). Quality education can be conceptualised as education that enables learners to become "economically productive, healthy, secure and active citizens" (Tikly & Barrett 2011: 9).

However, in post-colonial Southern Africa "economically productive, healthy, secure and active citizens" are still predominantly of European descent, or have had access to education that is based on European curricula; hence the term "quality education" has become largely synonymous with European curricula taught in a European *language*.

A considerable number of empirical studies (e.g. Orman 2008; Nomlomo 2010; Nkosana 2011; Evans & Cleghorn 2014) provide evidence for this assessment as they observe that speakers of African languages constantly face the conundrum of cherishing their native language(s) on the one hand but wanting their children to be speakers of a European language (even if it is at the expense of their home language) on the other hand. Consequently, it has become a generally acknowledged common practise for schools in Southern Africa to offer instruction in a locally spoken, indigenous language for the first three to five years of schooling before an international language is introduced as a medium of instruction (e.g. Bloch 2006: 3).

Tragically, the negligence of children's native language(s) leads to great number of almost insurmountable problems and has been identified as one of the key factors in the literacy crisis in Southern Africa. Wagner (2000: 16) and many others report that a significant proportion of students in primary schools are illiterate in their native language(s). Moreover they do not necessarily succeed in attaining a sufficiently high competence in the second language either. Instead poor proficiency levels in the second language are the norm rather than the exception. Given that the second language (L2) is usually the language of instruction, low proficiency in L2 has been identified as a primary reason for low throughput and graduation rates at all levels of the educational system (primary, secondary and tertiary) with profound consequences for employment opportunities.

> It is widely acknowledged that, despite decades of literacy campaigns by UNESCO and others and efforts like Education for All (EFA) (Triebel 2001: 21), attempts to ensure that what is often referred to as the 'spread of literacy' in Africa have failed. (Bloch 2006: 3)

The current research project attempts to contribute to alleviating the literacy crisis in Southern Africa by suggesting that the acknowledgment of Southern African ways of storytelling might lead to the emancipation of African learners on a number of different levels and may contribute to an attitudinal change in speakers of African languages with respect to their primary language(s). In the outcome, it is anticipated that it might be possible to redefine the term "quality education" to mean education that integrates Southern African knowledge systems like Southern African storytelling. Such curricula reforms could in turn help to achieve quality education in Southern Africa as they might enable more learners to exit the educational system as economically productive, healthy, secure and active citizens.

2   Possible differences between the "canonical" story grammar and a Southern African Story Grammar

The "western" story grammar tradition suggests that a "canonical" story is comprised of a setting and an episode system and that stories basically share the same universal micro- and macro-structural features (Mandler et al. 1980). On a macro-structural level it is assumed that a "canonical" story encompasses all of the traditional story grammar elements as identified by Stein & Glenn (1979).[1] Table 1 presents these elements.

Table 1: Story grammar elements according to Stein & Glenn (1979)

Story grammar element	Definition
Setting	The spatial and/or temporal location where story events take place; the introduction of the main characters, the protagonist, and the spatio-temporal context.
Initiating event	An event which typically introduces a state-of-affairs that is 'out of the ordinary' for the protagonist, i.e. the occurrence that influences the main character to action.
Protagonist's internal response	An affective or emotive reaction to the initiating event. Indicates the thought(s), feeling(s) of the protagonist in response to the initiation event; may include an interpretation of the event, formulation of a goal and serves to motivate action.
Plan	A set of intentions formed in the mind of the person affected by the initiating event. Indicates the intended action of the protagonist (the announcement of the intended action).
Attempt	The protagonist's effort to execute the plan. Indicates the overt actions of the protagonist in pursuit of the goal.
Consequences or outcomes	The attainment or non-attainment of the goal, or other events that are the result of the attempt.
Resolution or outcome	Any emotional or evaluative response by the protagonist to the preceding chain of events.

However, an investigation of relevant literature (e.g. Canonici 1990; Makgamatha 1991; Motshwari 1998; Obiechina 1992) reveals that Southern African folktales from various

---

[1]These elements are summarized by Griffith et al. (1986: 541).

language groups differ both in the function and – importantly – terms of their macro- and microstructural features from this "universal" schema.

Against the background of these insights and a corpus analysis of popular folktales from Malawi and South Africa (Tappe et al. in preparation), we propose in Table 2 a first approximation to a Southern African story grammar. Importantly the elements *setting* and *internal response* of the CSG are demoted in our proposal of a Southern African Story Grammar, while the elements *traditional opening* and *traditional closing* are added.

Table 2: Story grammar elements of a proposed Southern African Story Grammar

Story grammar element	Definition
Traditional opening	The traditional opening initiates the dialogue between the story teller and the audience and reaffirms the readiness on both sides for the commencement of the story telling event.
Initiating event	An event which typically introduces a state-of-affairs that is 'out of the ordinary' for the protagonist, i.e. the occurrence that influences the main character to action.
Plan	A set of intentions formed in the mind of the person affected by the initiating event. Indicates the intended action of the protagonist (the announcement of the intended action).
Attempt	The protagonist's effort to execute the plan. Indicates the overt actions of the protagonist in pursuit of the goal. The description of the execution of the plan typically involves repetitions and dialogues which reflects the performative character of the storytelling.
Consequences or outcomes	The attainment or non-attainment of the goal, or other events that are the result of the attempt.
Resolution or outcome	Moral lesson(s) that emanate from the story and which are of general/communal significance.
Traditional ending	The story is concluded by a traditional formula which signals the return to the real world and binds any mystical creatures to the story realm.

The *setting* (i.e. the spatial and/or temporal location where story events take place, the introduction of the main characters, the protagonist, and the spatio-temporal context) seems to be demoted or absent in Southern African storytelling which places the emphasis on communal knowledge and universal applicability of the story. The second demoted element is the internal response of the protagonist to the initiating event: Thought(s) and feeling(s) are not necessarily ascribed to the protagonist by the story teller. This may be a function of the performative aspect of the storytelling where the feelings of the protagonist are enacted rather than verbalised; it may also reflect a taboo.[2] Moreover, the main characters seem to be conceptualised representatives of a particular type of person (e.g. a young man, a girl), rather than individuals, to allow for maximum identification with the protagonist. In line with the demotion of the internal response element, the protagonist's emotional or evaluative response to the chain of events as it unfolds in the story also seems to be demoted in Southern African storytelling, whereas the moral lesson(s) that may be gained from the story events seem(s) to be promoted. Importantly, the performative character of Southern African storytelling also implies the use of repetitions at various levels of granularity (word, phrase, and paragraph) and the inclusion of dialogues as a stylistic means in the main section of the story, i.e. *the attempt* (Canonici 1990; Makgamatha 1991; Motshwari 1998; Obiechina 1992; Tappe et al. in preparation).

3 The relevance of narratives for literacy development and the consequences of a misalignment between the "canonical" story grammar and language-specific story grammars

Bloch (1999: 46) highlights that storytelling – just like reading – exposes children to a special form of language which is holistic, rich and complex. In a later publication, she elaborates on this point; "[t]his allows them [the children] to tune into the rhythms and structures of language and broadens their conceptual worlds and their vocabulary to express themselves" (Bloch 2006: 11). Moreover, the repetitive and rhyming play with language that is characteristic for storytelling may aid in developing a child's phonological awareness, which has been acknowledged as a critical literacy skill by a number of researchers (e.g. Goswami & Bryant 1990; Duncan et al. 2013).

In addition, Bloch (2006: 13) emphasises the role that narratives play in identity building and in emotional development, which adds further weight to their significance in child development. Referencing authors like Meek (1992: 44) and Egan (2005: 10); Bloch points out that through narratives children learn to overcome "egocentric feelings" and develop a communal sense. This aspect of communal identity is a central aspect of traditional Southern African folktales, which are means to preserve and to express "the collective memories of a group, amassed over a long period of time" (Ntuli 2011: 65).

However, the questions that arise in the current context are: How can the benefits of the "holistic, rich and complex" nature of narratives be unlocked to further literacy development if said narratives are in a foreign language and – importantly – follow a foreign macro-structure? How can identity building happen if the narratives that children are exposed to and are required to reproduce in an educational setting do not follow

---

[2]In an informal survey, students and colleagues from Lesotho, Malawi, South Africa, Zambia and Zimbabwe suggested that it may be widely considered inappropriate to verbalise one's feelings and to ascribe feelings to others. This observation needs further research.

a child's story telling experiences at home? How "naturalistic and ecologically valid" is the assessment of children's narratives in Southern African educational systems, which seem to be deeply rooted in the "western" story grammar tradition and which do not seem to widely recognise the narrative traditions of the children's primary languages?

While many researchers emphasise that it is necessary for teachers to recognise the cultural contexts that learners originate from in order to be able to aid them in appropriate ways (e.g. Heath 1983; Michaels 1991; Bloch 2006; Souto-Manning 2013) and to do them justice in assessments, this insight does not seem to have widely filtered through into assessment tool development and curriculum design. On the contrary, research which addresses the question of how a misalignment between the indigenous narratives and "mainstream" narratives may affect literacy development in Southern African children is largely outstanding (see, however, e.g. Obiechina 1992 and Bloch 2006).

Research findings, e.g. from the United States of America, clearly indicate a need to rectify this oversight. Westby et al. (2002) analyse the situation of academically underperforming students from an original people's background in the USA, where more than 30% of all students are not Anglo-American, whereas the majority of teachers are whites of European descent. The authors emphasise that the indigenous narratives that the children are exposed to at home differ drastically form the narratives they hear in the media and at school. The task of reconciling the often conflicting demands of the two narrative traditions is left to the pupils, much to their disadvantage. Westby et al. (2002: 238) point out that research on the misalignment between narrative practises at school and narrative practises in the pupils' primary languages is predominantly available on US-American children from "African-American and Hispanic backgrounds (Gee 1989; Gutierrez-Clellen 1995; Hester 1996; Hyter & Westby 1996; Labov & Waletzky 1967; Shuman 1986), but very little is available on children from other cultural/linguistic backgrounds." Even though it seems as if an elaborate academic discourse about the cultural differences of students' schooling experiences and the significance of such differences is readily available, the dominant paradigm appears to be one where an assimilation to the mainstream is globally more highly prized than acknowledging multi-cultural diversity (see, e.g. Souto-Manning 2013 for an identical assessment of the situation).

4 The psycho-linguistic "reality" of a Southern African Story Grammar: Findings from case studies conducted in Malawi and South Africa

In order to provide evidence for the psycho-linguistic "reality" of a Southern African story grammar the author embarked on a research project that currently operates in Malawi and South Africa and is envisioned to bring together researchers and to include findings from as many sub-Saharan countries and languages as possible. To date our research has yielded a number of surprising results which suggest that despite the prevalence of modern media, urbanisation and the language hegemony of European languages, Southern African children are still aware of Southern African folktales and that these folktales and the underlying story grammar shape the children's ways of (re-)telling stories.

The research methodology that we use entails that children in the age range between 10 and 12 answer a language questionnaire to assess their language background and their experiences with different types of narratives (oral, written, in the form of films). Thereafter, we present the children either with a wordless picture book or we show them wordless video clips, which the children narrate first in their one dominant language, and after a period of about three weeks, in their other dominant language (i.e. currently an African language and English).[3] The children narrate their stories to an interlocutor who is a speaker of the target language and who (from the children's perspective) does not know the stimulus material.

In the first phase of the project we use stimulus material that is not culturally "adequate" for children from Southern Africa which reflects a common experience that they have in the educational setting; in the second phase we will use culturally adequate material and compare the findings from both phases.

Currently we have data from retellings of two non-verbal video clips[4] and four pre-recorded audio files which narrate the stories depicted in the video clips in either Chichewa or English. We also elicited narratives by employing the widely used wordless picture book "Frog where are you" (Mayer 1969). Some of the characters in the selected stories – land animals (mole, deer, gopher) as well as sea creatures (starfish, crab, seahorse) – and some of the objects used (a rocket) are alien to the children who participate in our investigation.

4.1 Exposure to indigenous story telling

Our questionnaire studies indicate that children in both Malawi and in South Africa may still be exposed to African folktales on a regular basis. Tappe & Hara (2013) found that 108 of the 127 Malawian children who participated in their investigation and who live in the city of Lilongwe in central Malawi heard Malawian folktales on a regular basis. Similarly, 35 out of 41 South African children from urban Durban who are currently participating in the project rated their exposure to isiZulu folktales on a Likert scale from 1 (I do not agree) to 5 (I totally agree) by choosing 5; while another three children chose 4. One child whose primary language is SiSwati chose 3 and two children, whose primary language is isiXhosa chose 1. In addition many of the children volunteered to tell us folktales and were very excited when they heard that we are interested in traditional storytelling. This is in stark contrast to the often heard assumption by parents, teachers and headmasters that children who grow up in the urban centres do not know and are not interested in indigenous folktales.

---

[3]The children who participate in our project are often multilingual. Most of them do have two dominant languages, however, one of which is an African language and the other is the language of teaching and learning (LOTL). For the Malawian and South African children in our current sample the LOLT is English.
[4]"The mole and the rocket" (Miler 1966, accessible at: http://www.veoh.com/watch/v74680117WxTgAWxp) and "The little mole and the radio" (Miler 1968 accessible at: http://www.veoh.com/watch/v74680119r3m6t4Rd).

4.2 The presence of a South African story grammar in the children's narratives

Overall, our results indicate that rather than producing stories that adhere to the "western"/ "canonical" story grammar (see Table 1) (Stein & Glenn 1979), the children produce narratives that reflect features prevalent in Southern African folktales and which are captured in our first approximation to a Southern African story grammar (Table 2).

The main differences between the two story grammars are reflected in the narratives that we elicited. As an illustration, Table 3 presents a summary of the findings from Tappe & Hara (2013) and Hara (2014) with respect to narratives of the Malawian children in our investigation. The most striking differences pertain to the "canonical" story grammar elements *setting* and *internal response*. We found that the children did not produce these in the frequency that one would have expected if the children followed the "canonical" story schema.

Table 3: The realization of story grammar elements in the Malawian narratives

Element	Western story grammar	African story grammar	Realised	
			Chichewa	English
Opening formula	–	✓	37%	39%
Setting	✓	–	23%	17%
Initiating event	✓	✓	✓	✓
Protagonist's internal response	✓	–	2.49%	5.25%
Plan	✓	✓	✓	✓
Attempt	✓	✓	✓	✓
Consequences or outcomes	✓	✓	✓	✓
Resolution or outcome	✓	✓	✓	✓
Closing formula	–	✓	33%	32%

In stark contrast to these percentages, Acker (2012)[5] who investigated South African monolingual English or Afrikaans speaking children between the ages of five to nine-and-a-half years old, found her participants predominantly inserted settings in their narratives elicited by a wordless picture book (Acker 2012: 80). In particular, 55% of the five to six year olds, 88% of the six to seven year olds and 100% of the eight-and-a-half to nine-and-a-half year olds in her sample started their narratives with a setting. Moreover, Acker (2012: 57) found that 50% of her five to six year olds, 65% of her six to seven year olds, and 68% of her eight-and-a-half to nine-and-a-half year olds described internal responses of the protagonist.

---

[5]There are no comparative data from monolingual Malawian children with a primary language of European origin available. We investigated in at a number of schools in Lilongwe whether they had any student enrolment that fits these criteria and received exclusively negative responses.

About 30% of the Malawian children inserted an opening and/or a closing formula as would be expected in traditional Southern African storytelling. The formulae that the children use are clearly no imitation from the stimulus material. Examples of such formulae are provided in Table 4.[6]

Table 4: Opening/closing formulae in the Malawian children's narratives

Chichewa opening formulae	Chichewa closing formulae
Padangokhala 'once upon a time'	*Nkhani yanga yathera pomwepo, nkhani yathera pomwepo* 'this is the end of the story'
Kalekale 'long time ago'	*Ndamaliza* 'I have finished'
Tsiku lina 'one day'	*Basi* 'That's all' or other similar versions.
Panali or *padali* or *kunali* or *kudali* 'There was (once)'	*Ndi zomwe ndinamvapo* 'That's how I heard it'

In addition to the elements already discussed, the children's narratives in our corpus appear to generally diverge from the stories presented to them as stimuli in that their narratives contain a greater number of repetitions and different repetitions than are present in the stimulus material. Such repetitions occur both at word, phrase and sentence level. Moreover, the children tend to insert lively dialogues into the stories that are also not part of the stimulus material. Both dialogues and repetitions are important stylistic elements of traditional Southern African story telling; see e.g. Obiechina (1992: 218) for the role of repetitions in Southern African folktales.

Our general observation so far is that children both in Malawi and in South Africa deviate from the stimulus material in that they have a tendency to both omit elements that were present in the stimulus material and to add elements that were not present in the stimulus material in a systematic way that reflects features of the proposed Southern African Story Grammar. We also find that the children who participate in our project sometimes try to "assimilate" the stimulus material to their background knowledge: In one narrative, e.g. the protagonist of the "frog where are you" book is placed on a farm and upon arriving in the forest he meets an "antelope" rather than a deer.

5 The relevance of our findings in an educational setting

Language related obstacles (extremely low literacy rates; insufficiently developed textual production skills; low levels of discourse/text comprehension skills) have been identified to be a major hindrance to educational success in the developing world where the "lack of literacy" appears to be paralysing the developing economies. Indeed national and international efforts to measure literacy in Southern African countries have consistently

---

[6]Compare Hara 2014: 247 and 250.

returned devastatingly bad figures over a number of years and across a number of different countries. Smith & Barrett (2011: 23) report on the Progress in International Reading Literacy Study (PIRLS) 2006 survey, which found that "less than 22% of Grade 4 students in South Africa [...] achieved the "lowest international benchmark" compared to more than 95% in North American and Western countries (for more detail see Mullis et al. 2007: 69)."

Successful intervention is thus largely overdue. The integration of African storytelling into Southern African school curricula may be one very powerful intervention. Past and current attempts to promote Southern African languages at school level seem to have mainly focussed on terminology development to transform the Southern African languages into languages of academic learning and writing (which – due to budget constraints – has been a very slow process). However, I want to argue that the mere translation of existing teaching materials into the African languages does not solve the problem that narratives (and maybe other text types, too) may have different macro-structural features in the European and in the African languages. Hence a translated text may still not alleviate the misalignment between the "canonical" story grammar that is currently required in the educational setting and a Southern African story grammar that is acquired during pre-school socialisation.

Tragically, however, we do not seem to acknowledge that the Southern African languages have a particular value in the educational setting, which is in part the legacy of colonial education acts (like the "Bantu education act"[7] in South Africa). The outcome seems to be a "rhetoric of deficiency" with dire consequences for the majority of learners in Southern African countries. They seem to enter school feeling doubly undervalued. Sentiments like: "My primary language is neither a language of teaching and learning nor a language of prestige" and "My primary language does not have any value in academia; it still has to be developed" seem to be prevalent among speakers of African languages. However the perception that one's abilities are valuable has been found to be tightly linked with achievement motivation (e.g. Hardré 2007; Hardré et al. 2007). Achievement motivation is one of the key ingredients of academic success (e.g. Beck 2004; Hidi & Harackiewicz 2000; Schunk et al. 1996).

Hence the acknowledgment of existing indigenous narrative language skills could strengthen the self-worth and the achievement motivation of Southern African children. Narratives have been identified as means of "self-presentation" because "identity work" is "being accomplished by the narrating subject" (Baynham 2000: 100). If we were to strengthen and nourish the narrative skills that Southern African children have in their native languages, we could amplify their academic skills development in two ways: First, indirectly, by strengthening their achievement motivation (as explained above) and second, directly, through promoting their narrative skills themselves. Narrative skills have consistently been found to be closely linked to academic success (O'Neill et al. 2004) and to reading comprehension development (Cain 2003; Oakhill & Cain 2012). Fostering narrative growth in the early years is hence of utmost important to academic achievement

---

[7]The major provision of the Bantu Education Act (Act No. 47 of 1953; later renamed the Black Education Act, 1953) was enforcing racially separated educational facilities.

and alleviating illiteracy. In conclusion the current paper proposes that bringing stories that the majority of our children may be able to relate to into the classrooms across Southern Africa may be a powerful tool to encourage children to engage with language and with each other across linguistic and cultural divides. Such a reform would help to alleviate learner frustration and might bolster learner motivation which are essential prerequisites for successful learning.

Acknowledgements

The researcher is grateful for an ACAL45 travel grant which facilitated her conference attendance in Lawrence, Kansas. Suggestions and comments from the conference audience and two anonymous reviewers aided enhancing the current contribution. Remaining shortcomings are the author's sole responsibility. I would also like to thank the children who participate in our project as well as my co-workers, Agness Hara, Mandisa Ndlovu, Thandeka Maphumulo, Mbali Mntungwa and Megan Govender. Funding from the South African Research Foundation (NRF) for the funding period 2015–2017 is gratefully acknowledged (CSUR93632: *Southern African text and discourse structures and their relevance for education*).

References

Acker, Twanette. 2012. *The patterns of development in generated narratives of a group of typically developing South African children aged 5 to 9 years.* Stellenbosch MA thesis.

Anderson, Kimberley & Cay Evans. 1996. The development of the canonical story grammar model and its use in the analysis of beginning reading computer stories. *Reading Improvement* 33. 2–15.

Baynham, Mike. 2000. Narrative as evidence in literacy research. *Linguistics and Education* 11(2). 99–117.

Beck, Robert C. 2004. *Motivation: Theories and principles (5th ed.)* Upper Saddle River, NJ: Prentice.

Bloch, Carole. 1999. Literacy in the early years: Teaching and learning in multilingual early childhood classrooms. *International Journal of Early Years Education* 7(1). 39–59.

Bloch, Carole. 2006. *Theory and strategy of early literacy in contemporary Africa with special reference to South Africa.* Oldenburg (Germany): University of Oldenburg. (Doctoral thesis).

Cain, Kate. 2003. Text comprehension and its relation to coherence and cohesion in children's fictional narratives. *British Journal of Developmental Psychology* 21. 335–351.

Canonici, Noverino N. 1990. *Oral studies in South Africa.* Durban. (Master's thesis).

Duncan, Lynne G., São Luís Castro, Sylvia Defior, Philip H. K. Seymour, Sheila Baillie, Jacqueline Leybaert, Philippe Mousty, Nathalie Genard, Menelaos Sarris, Costas D. Porpodas, Rannveig Lund, Baldur Sigurðsson, Anna S. Þráinsdóttir, Ana Sucena & Francisca Serrano. 2013. Phonological development in relation to native language and literacy: Variations on a theme in six alphabetic orthographies. *Cognition* 127. 398–419.

Egan, Kieran. 2005. *An imaginative approach to teaching*. San Francisco: Jossey-Bass.

Evans, Rinelle & Ailie Cleghorn. 2014. Parental perceptions: A case study of school choice amidst language waves. *South African Journal of Education* 34(2). 1–19.

Gee, James Paul. 1989. Two styles of narrative construction and their linguistic and educational implications. *Discourse Processes* 12(3). 287–307.

Goswami, Ursula & Peter E. Bryant. 1990. *Phonological skills and learning to read*. Hillsdale NJ: Laurence Erlbaum Associates.

Griffith, Penny L., Danielle N. Ripich & Sondra L. Dastoli. 1986. Story structure, cohesion, and propositions in story recalls by learning disabled and non-disabled children. *Journal of Psycholinguistic Research* 15(6). 539–549.

Gutierrez-Clellen, Vera F. 1995. Narrative development and disorders in Spanish-speaking children: Implications for the bilingual interventionist. In Hortencia Kayser (ed.), *Bilingual speech-language pathology: An Hispanic focus*, 97–128. San Diego, CA: Singular Publishing Group.

Hara, Agness. 2014. *Text comprehension in multilingual children: Mental representation and narrative text structure*. Durban (South Africa): University of KwaZulu-Natal. (Unpublished Doctoral Dissertation).

Hardré, Patricia L. 2007. Preventing motivational dropout: A systemic analysis in four rural high schools. *Leadership and Policy in Schools* 6(3). 231–265.

Hardré, Patricia L., Michael H. Crowson, Teresa K. Debacker & Deborah White. 2007. Predicting the academic motivation of rural high school students. *The Journal of Experimental Education* 75(4). 247–267.

Heath, Shirley Brice. 1983. *Ways with words: Language, life and work in communities and classrooms*. Cambridge: Cambridge University Press.

Hester, Eva Jackson. 1996. Narratives of young African American children. In Alan Kamhi, Karen E. Pollock & Joyce L. Harris (eds.), *Communication development and disorders in African American children*, 227–245. Baltimore, MD: Paul H. Brookes Publishing.

Hidi, Suzanne & Judith M. Harackiewicz. 2000. Motivating the academically unmotivated: A critical issue for the 21st century. *Review of Educational Research* 70. 151–179.

Hyter, Yvette D. & Carol E. Westby. 1996. Using oral narratives to assess communicative competence. In Alan Kamhi, Karen E. Pollock & Joyce L. Harris (eds.), *Communication development and disorders in African American children*, 247–284. Baltimore, MD: Paul H. Brookes Publishing.

Labov, William & Joshua Waletzky. 1967. Narrative analysis: Oral versions of personal experience. In June Helm (ed.), *Essays on the verbal and visual arts*, 12–44. Seattle: University of Washington Press.

Makgamatha, Phaka Moffat. 1991. *Characteristics of the Northern Sotho folktales: Their form and structure*. Johannesburg & Cape Town: Perskor.

Mandler, Jean M., Sylvia Scribner, Michael Cole & Marsha De Forest. 1980. Cross-cultural invariance in story recall. *Child Development* 51. 19–26.

Mayer, Mercer. 1969. *Frog where are you?* New York: Dial Press.

Meek, Margaret. 1992. Literacy: Redescribing reading. In Keith Kimberley, Margaret Meek & Jane Miller (eds.), *New readings: Contributions to an understanding of literacy*, 224–234. London: A & C Black.

Michaels, Sarah. 1991. Hearing the connections in children's oral and written discourse. *The Journal of Education* 167(1). 36–56.

Miler, Zdenek. 1966. *The mole and the rocket.* London: Golden Pleasure Books.

Miler, Zdenek. 1968. *The mole and the radio.*

Motshwari, Julia Jakoentle. 1998. *Magic and its significance in Tswana folktales.* Johannesburg. (Master's thesis).

Mullis, Ina V. S., Michael O. Martin, Ann M. Kennedy & Pierre Foy. 2007. *PIRLs 2006 international report: IEA's progress in international reading literacy study in primary schools in 40 countries.* Chestnut Hill, MA: TIMSS & PIRLS International Study Center, Lynch School of Eduation, Boston College.

Nkosana, Leonard B. M. 2011. Language policy and planning in Botswana. *The African Symposium* 11(1). 129–137.

Nomlomo, Sylvia Vuyokazi. 2010. Parents' choice of the medium of instruction in Science: A case study of one primary school in the Western Cape, South Africa. In Birgit Brock-Utne, Zubeida Desai, Martha A. S. Qorro & Alan Pitman (eds.), *Language of instruction in Tanzania and South Africa—Highlights from a project*, 1–2. Rotterdam: Sense Publishers.

Ntuli, Cynthia D. 2011. The transmission and reproduction of folktales with special reference to Nanana Bosele. *Southern African Journal for Folklore Studies* 21(2). 63–75.

Oakhill, Jane V. & Kate Cain. 2012. The precursors of reading ability in young readers: Evidence from a four-year longitudinal study. *Scientific Studies of Reading* 16. 91–121.

Obiechina, Emmanuel. 1992. Narrative proverbs in the African novel. *Oral Tradition* 7(2). 197–230.

O'Neill, Daniela K., Michelle J. Pearce & Jennifer L. Pick. 2004. Preschool children's narratives and performance on the Peabody Individualized Achievement Test Revised: Evidence of a relation between early narrative and later mathematical ability. *First Language* 24. 149–183.

Orman, Jon. 2008. *Language Policy and nation building in post-apartheid South Africa.* Berlin & New York: Springer.

Schunk, Dale H., Judith R. Meece & Paul R. Pintrich. 1996. *Motivation in education: Theory, research, and applications.* Englewood Cliffs, NJ: Prentice.

Shuman, Amy. 1986. *Storytelling rights: The uses of oral and written texts by urban adolescents.* Cambridge: Cambridge University Press.

Smith, Michèle & Angeline M. Barrett. 2011. Capabilities for learning to read: An investigation of social and economic effects for Grade 6 learners in Southern and East Africa. *International Journal of Educational Development* 31. 23–36.

Souto-Manning, Mariana. 2013. Competence as linguistic alignment: Linguistic diversities, affinity groups, and the politics of educational success. *Linguistics and Education* 24. 305–315.

Stein, Nancy L. & Christine G. Glenn. 1979. An analysis of story comprehension in elementary school children. In Roy Freedle (ed.), *New directions in discourse processing*, 53–120. Norwood, NJ: Ablex.

Tappe, Heike & Agness Hara. 2013. Language specific narrative text structure elements in multilingual children. *Stellenbosch Papers in Linguistics (SPIL)* 42. 297–331.

Tappe, Heike, Mbali Mntungwa & Agness Hara. in preparation. *The presence of a Southern African story grammar in selected folktales from Malawi and South Africa.*

Tikly, Leon & Angeline M. Barrett. 2011. Social justice, capabilities and the quality of education in low income countries. *International Journal of Educational Development* 27. 3–14.

Triebel, Armin. 2001. The roles of literacy practices in the activities and institutions of developed and developing countries. In David R. Olsen & Nancy Torrance (eds.), *The making of literate societies*, 19–53. Oxford: Blackwell Publishers.

Wagner, Daniel A. 2000. *Thematic studies: Literacy and adult education. UNESCO World Education Forum: Education for All 2000. Paris: UNESCO.* http://unesdoc.unesco.org/images/0012/001233/123333e.pdf, accessed 2014-05-10.

Westby, Carol E., Celia Moore & Rosario Roman. 2002. Reinventing the enemy's language: Developing narratives in Native American children. *Linguistics and Education* 13(2). 235–269.

Chapter 5

How multilingual policies can fail: Language politics among Ethiopian political parties

Mehari Zemelak Worku

Addis Ababa University

Because language has instrumental as well as symbolic values, the issue of language will always have a political aspect (Smith 2008). Often, the choice of language and its use is construed as one of the central traits to people's definition of themselves. Besides, any given state must decide or determine the language that it deems appropriate to carry out its development and to generate, disseminate and enrich the knowledge necessary for such development. However, the case grows problematic when it comes to Sub-Saharan Africa where "every language carries a distinct and weighty baggage" of identity (Obeng & Purvis 1999). The decision was not easy for different regimes in Ethiopia, home of more than 80 ethnic groups (CSA 2008). The three consecutive regimes which have ruled the country for the last 75 years followed different paths in addressing this diversity management question. The reframing of the country under ethnic federalism, which legislates Amharic as the working language of the federal government (hereafter WL) and guarantees the right of each ethnic state to decide its own WL, is the recent attempt to respond to the same politics of recognition. However, dissatisfied voices regarding the current language policy (hereafter LP) can still be heard among political groups. Some see it as 'not enough' while others see it as Balkanization. Despite a few research efforts and publications on the LPs of the consecutive governments of Ethiopia, there has been no research done on the alternative policies and options available among the political parties or their relative value as LPs. Thus, the grand objective of this study is to survey, analyze and evaluate the linguistic proposals of Ethiopian political parties in government, education, and endangered languages.

Mehari Zemelak Worku. How multilingual policies can fail: Language politics among Ethiopian political parties. In Jason Kandybowicz, Travis Major, Harold Torrence & Philip T. Duncan (eds.), *African linguistics on the prairie: Selected papers from the 45th Annual Conference on African Linguistics*, 65–83. Berlin: Language Science Press. DOI:10.5281/zenodo.1251716

1 Language politics in Ethiopia: Historical overview

In this section I will briefly discuss the issue of language throughout Ethiopian political history.[1] A compact version of the history will be presented with a focus on three sections: pre-1974 (before the outbreak of the student-led Ethiopian Revolution), 1974–1991 (the time where the military junta called the "därg" stayed in power) and post-1991, the era of the incumbent EPRDF.

1.1 Pre-1974: Language in imperial Ethiopia

"In the historical, political and literary fields, two languages have dominated Ethiopian Studies: Amharic and Geez" (Bender 1976). Along with their dominant status in the field of Ethiopian Studies, Bender's words can be extended to show how overriding the two languages were in the overall social life of Ethiopia. As the antiquities from the Axumite Dynasty indicate, Geez was the official indigenous language of the Axumite Dynasty (Philipson 2012). This official domain had been kept to Geez until Amharic took over as ləsanä nəgus 'the language of the king' some time during the reign of the Zagwe Dynasty in the 11th–13th centuries (Awgchew 2009). We do not have any document to answer why and how Geez took over the higher domains as the official language in that time. Nevertheless, we can say it can be one of the two cogent reasons given by Cooper (1976): as a result of government-implemented official LP or as a consequence of societal dynamics among speakers of different languages, or maybe both.

Irrespective of efforts by evangelists to reduce other Ethiopian languages into writing like Onesimos Nesib, an Oromo missionary who translated the Holy Bible into Affan Oromo[2] using the Ethiopic script in the early 20th century, Amharic and Geez continued to confluence dominantly in the educational, religious and political domains of the region until the 20th century, when western education stepped in to the country with the complete support of emperor Menilik II (ኃይለሥላሴ 2008). The policy of the Ethiopian kingdom regarding other languages was only to be found in the indigenous traditional collection of religious and secular laws known as the Fətha Nägäst (law of kings). The code has been used in the country for several centuries and contains legal provisions for speakers of other indigenous languages to have judges speaking their native tongues (Tzadua 1968 cited in Cooper 1976).

The boost of modern education and its legacy during the reign of emperor Haile Selassie I created a new domain for Amharic and Geez. Meanwhile other indigenous languages, regardless of their powers in numerical terms, were kept only to non-official domains. The education arena, in its early stages, was generally a field for the learning

---

[1]In this regard the works of Cooper (1976); McNab (1990); Bulcha (1998); Getachew & Ado (2006); Heugh et al. (2007); Smith (2008); Zemelak (2011) and Leyew (2012) are worth reading for a more detailed discussion on the typology of the LPs of different regimes in Ethiopia. Even though it is not going to be confined to their outlooks, the timing frame of the discussion in this paper is basically sketched out by the marked works.

[2]Cobarrubias (1983) wrongly writes "Gallah [sic] in Ethiopia" (Galah is a derogatory reference to mean Oromo) as an example for a language "without a writing system." But, by the time Cobarrubias' article was published, Afan Oromo speakers had been using the Afan Oromo Bible for about 90 years.

of foreign languages. Remarkably, it was a stage of competition between French and English, as the envoys of both neighboring colonial powers vied for swift influence over the Ethiopian crown. Initially, the French were more successful than their British contenders in retaining a positive attitude of the oligarchy towards French. However, this lasted briefly, only up to 1935 when Fascist Italy declared war on the Ethiopian Empire and invaded to avenge the humiliating defeat it suffered at the battle of Adowa in 1896. Bowen & Horn (1976: 610) note that during the Italian occupation, which lasted until 1941, the burgeoning educational efforts of Ethiopia were interrupted and most schools were closed. The mission of the few functioning schools was altered from training indigenous children to be citizens defending the country's interest in all possible domains, to educating the colonial masters' Italian children to keep them in touch with their European "mother civilization." This offered them a corner of the earth where they could enjoy 'sun bathing', to use Mussolini's terms. Ethiopians were obliged to stay confined to primary level education.

With the implementation of the age-old *divide et impera* policy of oppressors, the Italians divided the country into six regions according to major ethnic lines. They also ordered, without any deliberate effort to capacitate the languages in corpus planning, each of the major indigenous languages to be used in native schools in the respective regions. In addition, the Governor- General of each province had the authority to establish any other language as additional instructional medium in the schools (Pankhurst 1976: 322, cited in Bowen & Horn 1976; Zewde 2002).

Table 1: Administrative regions and languages of instruction during the Italian occupation (1935–1941).
* This term is used by the Italians to refer to the Oromo people. However, the Oromo people do not refer themselves with this word and is considered offensive.

No.	Regions named by the Italians	Languages proclaimed to be media of instruction
1	Eritrea and Tigray	Tigrinya and Arabic
2	Amhara	Amharic
3	Addis Ababa	Amharic and Oromifa
4	Harar	Harari and Oromifa
5	Galla* and Sidama	Oromifa and Kafficho
6	Somalia	Somali

This LP, nevertheless, was not put into full effect except in Eritrea, which had been a colony of Italy for about fifty years after the battle of Adowa in 1896. First, the policy was understood by the natives as a separatist movement to dissuade the country's noble men and gentry in to ethnic division to enervate the patriotic movements. Second, during the Italian occupation the education system was barely functioning. Third, as a result of the multitude of patriotic movements against them, the Italian Fascists did not have enough time to establish a lasting educational system. Nonetheless, this time is remarkable because of the deliberate abandonment of any effort in the education sector to promote a common indigenous language of communication among the variegated linguistic groups of Ethiopia. The LP of the occupiers came to an end when the Italians were ousted by the coalition of Ethiopian patriotic forces and the British troops from eastern Africa in 1941.

After the Italians, the British took their shot at attempting to influence the crown. Since then 'the British way' of doing things came to be accepted as the better way in alignment with His Imperial Majesty Haile Selassie's I aspirations for a strong, modernized nation. This was particularly reflected when gradually English took away the education domain that French occupied.[3]

Amharic had also reclaimed its former dominance over all indigenous languages as Haile Selassie I aspired to build a unified modern empire under one crown and one dominant language. In the revised constitution of Ethiopia it was stated explicitly that "the official language of the empire is Amharic." (Revised Constitution of Ethiopia: 125). It was a must that new laws be published in Amharic and English in the official gazette of Ethiopia. The statutes of domestic companies were required to be filled in Amharic or English. Foreigners were also required to write and speak Amharic 'perfectly', in order to attain Ethiopian citizenship. According to the regulation decreed in 1944 concerning missionary activities in Ethiopia, missionaries also were obliged to learn Amharic to pursue their mission for it was outlawed to use other indigenous languages except at the early stages of the missionary activity. The credo insists on both the missionary and the pupil to have a working knowledge of the "official language of the empire" (Cited in Cooper 1976). Such proclamations, charters and codes vividly display the dominant status Amharic had in the state.

In the 1960s, as a result of external and internal political pressure exacerbating through time, the state-owned broadcast media had shown some signs of a more relaxed stance towards embracing indigenous languages other than Amharic. The languages that were introduced to the government-owned broadcasting radio stations were Afar, Somali, Tigrinya and Tigre (Smith 2008). However, the time allotment for them was extremely scanty when compared with the time allotment to Amharic. The imperial administration did not have the political will to abandon the counterproductive effort of unifying a multilingual country under one language and a unitary state.

---

[3] According to Bowen & Horn (1976) the erosion, nevertheless, began in the 1930s before the Italians stepped in to the Ethiopian soil. Aleme Eshete (cited in Bowen & Horn 1976) points at one person's influence on the crown, Dr. Workneh Eshete, who was taken to India, a British colony by then, and studied medicine. As Aleme remarks, because of this man's beliefs in the British system and conviction to make the country as strong as the Great Britain, a group of 18 Indians were brought to Ethiopia in the 1930 to serve as technicians, doctors, teachers and other badly needed specialists. Since Indians were not well versed in French, if not oblivious at all, it was necessary for the students to become literate in English to exploit the available expatriate resource. However, a few exceptions can be mentioned in relation to the use of local languages in the Ethiopian primary education. For example, in Swedish and American missionary schools, mother tongues were used before European languages at the primary level (McNab 1988, cited in Heugh et al. 2007: 45).

1.2 1974–1991: The Ethiopian Student Movement and the därg on the language issue

Amharic as an established state language was challenged with the increase in influence of modern education in the country's social, economic, and political domains. University students who were becoming increasingly political espoused strong criticisms against the regime. The imperial regime did not have the administrative ability among its agents to undertake any successful amendment to appease the public demand (Zewde 2002).

Left wing Marxism became the dominant ideology among the students. Immediate recognition of "the oppressed identities of nations and nationalities" [4] was one of the main demands of the students. The issue reached a boiling point when the Lenin/Stalin-Fanon inspired Wallelign Mekonen published an article entitled "On the Question of Nationalities" on 17th November, 1969 in the Haile Selassie I University student publication, *Struggle*. Walelign merged the Leninist/Stalinist idea of *the nation* with Frantz Fanon's justification of violence against colonial oppression. His argument was that Ethiopia was not a nation; rather it was a collection of nations (Gurage, Somali, Oromo, etc.) that had been subdued by the "Amhara-Tigre (two of the dominant ethnic groups) hegemony." These oppressed nations, he explained, can only reclaim their freedom through "revolutionary armed struggle" (Mekonen 1969). [5] Since then, the language issue has clung to Ethiopian politics as a symbol of identity recognition for ethno-linguistic groups in the country.

The imperial regime was toppled in 1974 by a revolution rooted in the student movement, and abetted by the distraught military personnel of the regime. In the wake of the victorious revolution, a sense of euphoria spread with the prevailing idea of creating a modernized and prosperous Ethiopia, where all people, irrespective of their linguistic identity, would be treated equally. The trajectory of ethnic equality spilled over to language, as every linguistic group in the country was to be recognized as equals (Zewde 2002; Gudina 2006; Balsvik 2007).

Consequently, the military council, [6] which hijacked the revolution, [7] waged a literacy campaign across the country using 16 indigenous languages as media of instruction for basic literacy. This was in direct contrast to the former overtly monolingual education policy. The 1976 political program of the National Democratic Revolution of Ethiopia overtly proclaimed the right of nationalities as the following:

---

[4]It is at this particular time where ethnic groups of the country started to be referred as "nations and nationalities" in the political discourse of the country.

[5]For Stalin (1913) one of the defining characteristics of a nation is speaking one common language. After defining the nation as "a historically constituted, stable community of people, formed on the basis of a common language, territory, economic life, and psychological make-up manifested in a common culture," he asserts that "it is sufficient for a single one of these characteristics to be lacking and the nation ceases to be a nation." Wallelign's denial of the existence of the "Ethiopian nation" as one nation seems to be based on influence from his Marxist tendency.

[6]Often called "the därg," a word derived from Geez to mean 'committee' or 'council'.

[7]The aim of the campaign had two aims: to show the military council's intention to the linguistic equality and empowerment of all Ethiopians, to weaken the voice of the students, who were calling for the establishment of civilian administration, by dispersing them in the rural parts of the country as teachers in the literacy campaign (Balsvik 2007).

> The right of self-determination of all nationalities will be recognized and fully respected. No nationality will dominate another one since the history, culture, language, and religion of each nationality will have equal recognition in accordance with the spirit of socialism.... Given Ethiopia's existing situation, the problem of nationalities can be resolved if each nationality is accorded full rights of self-government. This means that each nationality will have regional autonomy to decide on matters concerning its internal affairs. Within its environs, it has the right to determine the contents of its political, economic, and social life use its own languages and elect its own leaders and administrators to head its own internal organs (Ethiopian Government Programme (1976) cited in McNab 1990).

Despite the overflowing rhetoric, the centralist ideology of the military regime and its ambition to create a unified Ethiopia was uncompromising to the idea of transferring power to a civilian government. It did not take much longer for the politics of recognition and autonomy to ascend to the dome of political discourse as an unanswered question. Because of its extremely repressive politics the military junta forced most of the leftwing socialists and ethnic liberation groups, some of whom were already guerilla fighters, to armed struggle. Later, the military council unsuccessfully tried to transform itself into a civilian government. In 1987 it promulgated a new constitution, which renamed the country as the Peoples' Democratic Republic of Ethiopia. All indigenous languages were guaranteed equal recognition as languages of the country. Amharic lost its status as the national language but maintained its degree of dominance as the constitution declared it as the official Working Language (hereafter WL) of the government.

Under this constitution the country was reframed under 14 autonomous provinces as way to appease the guerilla fighting ethnic rebel groups. It was too late! The rebels disparaged the transformation attempt as a theatre to cover all the cantankerous and assimilationist natures of the dictator Mengistu Hailemariam to pen in the rebels, but they did not give in.

1.3 Post-1991: Language in the country of "Nations, Nationalities, and Peoples"

The military regime's LP was essentially a *de jure* claim of equal status of all languages in the country, while the *de facto* LP was merely a preservation of the imperial LP which prescribed Amharic for all educational and official domains at the expense of other indigenous languages. Research done by the Ministry of Education in 1986, proves the language policy of the military regime was merely the extension of the imperial policy, jeopardized the enrolment and efficacy of students whose mother tongue was not Amharic (cited in Heugh et al. 2007.

On May 28th 1991 the coalition of ethnic cored armed groups under the umbrella of EPRDF took control of the capital Addis Abäba, ousting the military regime. The questions of autonomy and recognition of linguistic identity were reinvigorated. In July, 1991 a conference was held for the plethora of newly formed as well as old, but highly enervated, political parties. At the conference a charter, which served as a foundation for the forthcoming constitution, was provided. That was the stance where the political arena, which used to be entirely occupied by a military junta, officially proclaimed to embrace several parties to give sufficient significance for all the voices of cultural and political groups (Zewde 2008; Berhanu 2003). The question of language appeared to be a subject of notability to the political agendas held by most of the political groups. The historian Bahru Zewde recalls an event from the conference:

> The first order of business in the course of the eventful deliberations of that conference was the determination of the working language. In view of the difficulty getting interpreters for the multiplicity of languages represented by the ethnonationalist organizations attending the conference, it was decided to adopt Amharic and English. However, organizations that brought their own interpreters could use their language. The EPLF leader, Issayas Afeworki, took the latter option and addressed the conference in his native Tegreñña. But what is of particular interest to this investigation is the ire that he visibly demonstrated at what he felt was a less than adequate Amharic rendering of his delivery, showing that his Amharic was as good as, if no better than, his designated interpreter. The spokesman of OLF, also understandably, addressed the conference in his native Oromo language. But it was translated not in to Amharic but into English, there by leaving the overwhelming majority of the national audience in the dark (Zewde 2008: 77).

This is a self-explanatory situation to portray the linguistic sensitivity of the post 1991 political system. In 1992 the new Transitional Government of Ethiopia first proclaimed the rights of every ethnic group of Ethiopia to use and develop its languages and culture. This was further strengthened and confirmed in the 1995 Ethiopian Constitution.

In contrast to the 1987 constitution which starts with the phrase "We, the working people of Ethiopia", the preamble of the 1991 constitution begins with "We, the Nations, Nationalities and Peoples of Ethiopia." [8] The constitution also divides the country into nine autonomous ethnic states each with its own constitution, flag and the right to self-determination including and up to secession (Article 39). This took nobody by surprise since most of the political players who had a greater role in writing the constitution were members of the student movement. In the retention of Amharic as the WL of the government and the egalitarian approach to all languages in the country, the new constitution follows in the footsteps of the 1987 constitution (Article 5: 2). Audaciously supporting the ethnic cause, the new constitution gives member ethnic states of the federation unsurpassable right to determine their respective WL by law (Article5: 3). Subsequently, indigenous languages became widely used in primary education, media, administrative and judiciary systems. In 1994 the Ministry of Education of Ethiopia proclaimed a new

---

[8]However, the constitution doesn't give a single hint, let alone definition, to state the difference between these three terms is. Rather, it defines all the three terms as follows: "Nation, Nationality or People for the purpose of this Constitution, is a group of people who have or share large measure of a common culture or similar customs, mutual intelligibility of language, belief in a common or related identities, a common psychological make-up, and who inhabit an identifiable, predominantly contiguous territory" (Article 39: 4). Hence, in the current political discourse of Ethiopia any linguistic group is considered as a "nation/nationality" (Vaughan 2006).

Education and Training Policy, which declares: "Cognizant of the pedagogical advantage of the child learning in mother tongue and the rights of nationalities to promote the use of their languages, primary education will be given in nationality languages" (FDRE 1994). The existing language in education policy frames the entire system as indicated by the following table.

Table 2: The Existing Language in Education Framework.

No.	Languages	Level of education	Function
1	Mother tongues/ Nationality languages	Primary	Medium of instruction
2	Amharic	Primary up to secondary level education	As a subject and language of country wide communication
3	English	From grade 1	As a subject
4	English	Secondary and higher education	As a medium of instruction
5	One more nationality and foreign language	All levels	As subjects for intercultural and international communication
6	Mother tongues/ Nationality languages	Teachers training for primary level education	Medium of Instruction

Currently, there are twenty five indigenous languages used as media of instruction. Most regions selected indigenous languages spoken by the 'majority' of the denizens of that particular area. It is about twenty years now since this LP favoring indigenous languages has been implemented, and there is a sizeable amount of research reckoning the effects of this policy. However, it is still considered by the EPRDF government as one of its achievements from both the linguistic rights as well as pedagogical point of view. There are political groups who consider the current system as 'The Answer' for all questions on linguistic rights. On the other hand, there are others who criticize the system as Balkanization and enhancing deadly ethnic conflicts. These voices have representations in the political discourse of the country through political parties which suggest options through their political programs and manifestos. In the next part of this paper I will try to expound what policy proposals are forwarded by these political groups of the country.

2 Sampling methodology and conceptual tools

Scarcity of resources would not allow this study to include all the National Electoral Board of Ethiopia recognized (hereafter NEBE) 79 political parties, since most of them are regional parties (Board 2009). Particularly the number of regional parties, 63, and their scattered location all over the country is unmanageable to be taken as a whole. Hence, this study is done by taking representative samples. According to the NEBE, there are 79 National[9] and Regional Political Parties. Out of these 19 are categorized by the NEBE as National Political Parties while the remaining 60 are labeled as regional. Out of the 19 parties labeled as national 10 were selected randomly.[10] The same was done to the parties categorized as regional. Fourteen regional parties were selected randomly.[11] This enabled the sample to include about 30.4 % of the entire party population. The size of the sample was intentionally expanded to include parties from different ethnic and ideological bases. Moreover, it is worth mentioning that the distribution of regional parties is extremely uneven throughout the regional states of the country. Among the regional parties there were those which reported to NEBE not to be functioning anymore and thus excluded from the sampling.

The conceptual tools used in this descriptive study to analyze the types of the LPs as well as the motivations and ideologies beneath the LPs are garnered eclectically from Fishman (1972); Cobarrubias (1983); Schiffman (1996) and Patten (2001).

3 Language politics among the functioning political parties of Ethiopia

In this section an overall assessment of the LPs of the political parties is presented first. Then, I will deal with the proposals of the political parties about the language that should take the status of the WL of the federal government. The next focus of the analysis is the proposals about language in education. Through the analysis besides providing typology of the LPs motivations and ideologies of the proposals are inferred.

3.1 Overall assessment of the political parties' LPs

Although the need for a thoroughly thought-out and well planned LP for a multilingual country such as Ethiopia is unquestionable, out of the 24 political parties included in this study only seven[12] have put relatively clear and implementation orientated LPs. It is only these seven parties which explicitly propose to legislate, if they are voted to power, what the federal WL should be or how it should be selected, and what the language use in education shall be. Moreover, they also suggest establishment and expansion of

---

[9]According to the Board (2009), national political parties are those whose campaigns are not limited to a certain ethnic state. In contrast, parties which run only in a certain ethnic state are called regional parties.

[10]GSPP, EDP, EPRDF, Forum, EJDFF, AEUP, EPAP, ERaeiP, UEDF, AEDP.

[11]ONC, OPDU, DDQPDU, DDDP, OLP, WPDF, HNL, GPRDF, KPC, ANDO, ARDUF, BMPDO, BGDUF, WSDP.

[12]EDP, AEDP, EPRDF, OLP, Forum, GPRDF and ONC.

language research centers and the deployment of resources by the federal government to the corpus development of the languages. Out of the remaining 17 parties 16 of them do not give detailed and implementation oriented LPs. The remaining one party[13] proposes nothing about the language issue.

Depending on the broadness or narrowness of their LPs, the 16 parties without detailed LPs can also be divided into two sub-categories. First,[14] there are ten parties which present a **too-broad** and highly generalized claim to ensure the recognition of the languages and cultures, history and identities ethnic groups. Even though these parties have not offered any detailed implementation frame work, they have displayed support to mother tongue education at primary level. The second group holds five[15] parties, all of them regional parties, which provided **too-narrow** LPs in their political programs such as, language X shall be included in schools as a subject. The proposals in this group neither tell what the medium of instruction at the schools shall be nor what is to be done in the development of the languages they suggest to be included in the education system; nor do they say anything about the linguistic rights of other linguistic groups in the area where these parties aim to gain legitimacy.

3.2 Issue of the federal WL

Out of the seven parties that give relatively detailed and implementation orientated LPs, two[16] propose the promotion of Afan Oromo, to have the WL status beside Amharic. The reason for such legislation, the two parties forward, is the numerical muscle Afan Oromo have.[17] Three[18] parties from this group propose the adoption of an additional WL beside Amharic without mentioning a particular language. One[19] of these three parties forwarded that the additional WL should be chosen from the indigenous languages based on its numerical muscle; while the other two[20] preferred the selection to be on the basis of "facilitating science, technology and market exchange." On the other hand, two[21] of these seven parties stand in peculiarity by not mentioning the promotion of any specific language overtly; rather they propose egalitarian preservation, usage and development to all languages in the country. All[22] the proposals from the parties grouped under the non- detailed LPs have the same stand. All propose the preservation of 'all languages' in the country.

As described above, the LPs from these two parties are overt and dedicated to the promotion of Afan Oromo to be the federal state's WL. As the language they propose is

---

[13]DDPDO.

[14]HNL, AEUP, GSPP, WPDF, DDQPDO, UEDF, EJDFF, OPDU, EPAP, ERaeiP.

[15]ARDUF, WSDP, ANDO, BMPDO, KPC.

[16]OLP and ONC.

[17]Oromo is the largest ethnic group in Ethiopia (CSA 2008).

[18]EDP, AEDP, and FORUM.

[19]FORUM.

[20]EDP and AEDP.

[21]EPRDF and GPRDF.

[22]DDQPDO, WSDP, ANDO, HNL, WPDF, BGDUF, BMPDO, OPDU, ARDUF, EPAP, ERaeiP, AEUP, UEDF, EJDFF, GSPP, KPC.

an indigenous one, they are endoglossic LPs. Besides, these overt and promotion LPs of the parties can be said to follow the Language Maintenance model to formulate their LPs for the following reasons. First, the aspiration is to preserve and promote the language and the identity represented by the language through making the language the WL of the FDRE. This provides a better opportunity to the language and speakers of the language to preserve their language and identity as something worth preserving as it opens access to higher domains of state business and economic benefit. In other words, the parties aspire to win symbolic affirmation and identity preservation simultaneously. However, because none of the policies proposed by the political parties have explicitly included anything about the economic, social, cultural and/or political benefits to be gained by making the language they propose the WL of FDRE, the motivation can be argued to be sentiment and authentication. The only points the LPs mention to justify the need for Afan Oromo to be the national language is the numerical muscle the language has and as part of the "emancipation" of Oromo identity from the "cultural oppression" perceived by the parties.

The second group is constituted from three parties[23] which follow linguistic rationalization model and overtly propose the adoption of an additional WL besides Amharic. One of the parties in this group proposes the numerical muscle of the language to be the rationale for selection. The remaining two[24] parties, forward that the selection should be based on "the people's will" and suitability for science, technology and market exchange. As all the parties in this group favor the selection and promotion to be from the languages of the nationalities of the country their LPs can be labeled as endoglossic and promoting. On the other hand, from the point of view of the model provided by Patten (2001), the policies of these political parties always confirm that all the languages and identities of nationalities shall be respected and allowed to flourish. With this their proposals show a major feature of the official multilingualism model.

The third group holds two[25] of the detailed and all of the non- detailed parties. These parties propose nothing as a precise answer to the question of the WL of the federal government. Instead, they propose the equal preservation and cultivation of languages and linguistic identities.

Because the parties in this group have no explicitly stated language proposal about the WL of the federal government, it will be ambiguous to point their sway exactly whether they have agreed with the status quo or not. This makes their LPs regarding the WL of the federal government to be a covert one. However, it is also worth mentioning that they have an overtly stated proposal for an egalitarian preservation of all languages in the country. Besides, since their policies affirm the preservation and cultivation of the languages of the "nations, nationalities and peoples" of Ethiopia, it can be said that as a trajectory they lean towards the indigenous languages. Although all the parties in this group do not explicitly promote any particular language, their proposals for the dedication of the state towards full support to the development and preservation of the

---

[23]EDP, AEDP and FORUM.
[24]AEDP and EDP.
[25]EPRDF and GPRDF.

indigenous languages makes them holders of the promoting and official multilingualism models. Yet, there are two[26] parties in this group that presented the value of recognition of the indigenous languages from an angle of political participation and democratic rights as follows:

> Unless the people are using their own language they would not be able to sufficiently participate in the political system through interpreters. Unless citizens use their language to express about their culture and history it is impossible to them to exercise their right to freedom of expression (Press and Audio Visual Directorate/ EPRDF 2002).

The motivations behind the LP proposals of this group can be said to be both sentimental and instrumental. Those who propose the preservation and recognition of the languages for the sake of identity preservation are the ones with a sentimental motivation and those that propose the recognition and preservation of the languages to be used by the respective people emphasize the political benefits to be reaped from using one's own language as an instrument for communication.

The fourth group is constituted from one regional party[27] with no language proposal at all. This party has suggested no proposal regarding the WL of the federal government. Yet, it is still possible to argue that the party hasn't mentioned the language issue in its political programs may be because, it has a covert LP that is comfortable with the current LP of the country.

3.3 Language in education

From the parties that presented relatively expatiated language proposals,[28] two parties[29] explicitly propose one particular language to be used as medium of instruction. These parties overtly state Afan Oromo to be used as medium of instruction in schools. However, no instrumental benefit that is to be gained from using the language as medium of instruction in this multilingual country is pointed out by the parties. It can be argued that such LPs covertly marginalize other languages from being used as instructional media within the Oromia ethnic state itself since other ethnic groups also live there. In the proposals from these parties there is no mentioned space in education to other languages of the country. Since the LP is aimed at promoting the language and the linguistic identity the ideology beneath can be supposed to be vernacularization. The motivation behind can be, thus, inferred as authentication of the Oromo identity. However, one can contend that there is an assimilationist and hegemonic tendency in this policy because it tries to impose a particular language over "all schools" in the vicinity to be ruled by the party. Such a policy does not seem to look how imposing one's language in a multilingual arena would certainly contradict with the economic development and political participation of

---

[26]EPRDF and WPDF.
[27]DDPDO.
[28]FORUM, GPRDF, EPRDF, EDP, AEDP, ONC and OLP.
[29]ONC and OLP.

minority groups. This in turn can result resentment from other ethno-linguistic groups. At the worst case scenario, it could invite a total discordance in a region.

From the non- detailed group, two parties[30] in the **too-narrow** sub-group share common feature that they mention a language to be used in education. For instance, the social program of the ARDUF suggests that "Afar language shall be included in the school curriculum as a subject." The social program from the KPC also suggests that "Kambata language shall be introduced and taught." In the proposals from these parties, there is nothing stated about the other indigenous languages in the region. In addition, the proposals do not seem to push beyond making the languages they mention to be included in the school curriculum as a subject. They also do not justify their suggestions based on the benefits that the policies will bring to the people. Nor they give any additional policy about developing the languages to sustain their use in education.

The remaining five[31] parties in the detailed group, one[32] of the parties from the **too-narrow** and all the parties in the **too-broad** subgroups accede with one axiom: mother tongue education at the primary level. Particularly at the primary level education all of them consent that the medium of instruction shall be the mother tongues of the students. None of the policies of these parties restrict any indigenous language from being used as medium of instruction. However, it is worth mentioning that two[33] parties in this group propose to take special consideration towards metropolitan cities in the implementation of mother tongue education. With such policies the two parties have shown special consideration and a peculiar treatment of the metropolitan cities of the country that are practically variegated in ethnic composition. This gives space to the interest of people from different ethnic groups as their children probably pick the ethnic language of their parents as mother tongue. There is also the possibility for the children to assume the dominant language of the city as their native language. Besides, in addition to promoting the indigenous languages to be used as media of instruction, such policies also show caution from imposition of one language over another linguistic community without the interest and consent of the latter.

On the other hand, from the parties that offered relatively detailed LP, three[34] of them which are among parties that proposed the selection of additional language(s) to the status of the federal WL, affirm that, after selection of the additional language the selected language(s) of the federal government shall be taught as (a) subject(s) in the entire schools of the country; and shall also serve as media of instruction depending on the need. They also have conferred the responsibility onto the shoulders of the government to implement the teaching of the selected language(s) in the regular education system. Unification is the major motive at play in such LPs because teaching the federal WL in all schools of the regional states is basically to facilitate communication and social mobility among different language speakers of the federation as one political society. Since these LPs confer the authority to the regional states to select their respective WLs and

---

[30]KPC and ARDUF.
[31]EDP, EPRDF, AEDP, FORUM, and GPRDF.
[32]ANDO.
[33]EDP and AEDP.
[34]EDP, AEDP, and FORUM.

use them as media of instruction in schools located in the region, there will be no space for the oppressive assimilationist ideology.

Except for one[35] party none of the parties included in this study have proposed an LP regarding the language to be used as a medium of instruction beyond the primary level education. On the other hand, except for the above pointed one party and the parties that propose the maintenance of the selected additional WL of the federal government, none of the political parties have articulated anything about the medium of instruction after the primary level education or on second or foreign language choice. It might be conjectured that they are either comfortable with the status quo, i.e. using English as medium of instruction, or that they have no alternative policy to offer the public in this regard.

4 Conclusions and recommendations

Although there exists no political party that overtly proposes the adoption of a mono-lingual LP, none of the parties can take pride in having a thoughtful, all-encompassing and strategically implementable LP. These policies have failed in addressing burning linguistic issues in Ethiopia.

The failure of the LPs to address the issue of language beyond primary language education is one instance. Notwithstanding the necessity of language of wider communication (LWC), the best communicative medium in education is the best known language by both the learners and the teacher: in most of the cases the mothertongue. However, in Ethiopia, English -a language barely known by the overwhelming majority- takes the secondary and tertiary level education dominantly as the only official medium of instruction. The reality in Ethiopian schools as well as researches investigating the effectiveness of this policy, nevertheless, indicate that English, a foreign tongue for both the teachers and the students, has become the "medium of obstruction" in classes (Stoddart 1986 cited in Bogale 2009). It is ironic to see none of the political parties addressing this very critical issue! The other point where all the political parties have failed to address is the issue of language endangerment in the country. According to UNESCO (2015), 28 Ethiopian languages are endangered. The numerical muscle of most of Ethiopian languages is in hundreds and a few thousands. I argue that none of the current multilingual LPs of the political parties discussed above will benefit these languages. Putting an LP which treats all languages as equals can by no means be beneficial to these endangered languages, no matter how endoglossic it is. Equality should not mean treating the advantaged and the disadvantaged in the same way. Rather, it is supporting the disadvantaged without diminishing the advantaged unfairly. LPs cannot benefit their respective societies just because they appear to be proponents of multilingualism. Without well thought and strategically well designed LPs neither empowerment of indigenous languages nor preservation of endangered languages can happen.

---

[35] OLP.

Since Ethiopia is a multilingual state, with all the centuries old squabbling between elites of different ethno-linguistic groups, any societal development plan should always consider language as an issue to be thought thoroughly in planning economic development as well as regional tranquility. Hence, all the political parties should try to work in cooperation with the concerned academia for a well detailed discussion of the pros and cons of LPs.[36] In addition, beyond the promotion of ethnic identities, parties should look for policies that will have a positive effect on durable regional stability, since imposing one's language over the other will inevitably ostracize the latter from easily accessing economic development and political participation.

Furthermore, as there is a sizeable number of parties that are calling for an additional WL of the federal government, all of the people in the political business and stake holders of the language issue, such as researchers and consultants of policy makers, should begin to deeply look at the economics of such LP from the perspective of language economics (Grin 1994; Chiswick 2008). Any proposal regarding the WL of the federal government should not be a result of incessant lobbying from the political entrepreneurs. A thorough cost benefit analysis that carefully considers the ethnographic and economic realities of the country is the only best way to design an effective LP.

Acknowledgments

I would like to say the age old adage "thank you" for the ACAL45 conference organizers at KU, particularly Dr. Jason Kandybowicz, for the travel grant I was awarded to participate in ACAL45. My heartfelt gratitude also goes to my colleagues Biniam Jembere and Haile Gezae, both from Addis Ababa University, for their valuable comments and suggestions on this paper.

---

[36] At least, the three language model forwarded by Wodajo (2014), the replacement of Amharic by English as the sole WL suggested by Gebreselassie (2015), etc., should all be considered, discussed and evaluated by political groups to come up with better LPs with well-designed implementation strategies.

Abbreviations

AEDP	All Ethiopian Democratic Party	GSPP	Geda System Proponents Party
AEUP	All Ethiopian Unity Party	HNL	Harari National League
ANDO	Argoba Nation's Democratic Front	KPC	Kembata People's Congress
ARDUF	Afar Revolutionary Democratic Unity Front	MEISON	All Ethiopian Socialist Movement
BGDUF	Benishangul Gumuz Democratic Front	OLF	Oromo Liberation Front
BMPDO	Bahrworq Mesmes People's Democratic Organization	OLP	Oromo Liberation Party
DDPDP	Dubie and Degeni People Democratic Party	ONC	Oromo National Congress
DDQPDO	Denta, Dubamo Qinchilchila People's Democratic Organization	OPDU	Omo People Democratic Unity
EDP	Ethiopian Democratic Party	PDRE	People's Democratic Republic of Ethiopia
EJDFF	Ethiopian Justice and Democratic Forces Front	PMAC	Provisionary Military Administrative Council
EPAP	Ethiopian Pan-Africanist Party	SNNPR	Southern Nations Nationalities and People's Region
EPLF	Eritrean People Liberation Front	TPLF	Tigray People's Liberation Front
EPRDF	Ethiopian People's Revolutionary Democratic Front	UEDF	United Ethiopian Democratic Forces
EPRP	Ethiopian People's Revolutionary Party	UJDP	Unity for Justice and Democracy
ERAEIP	Ethiopian Vision Party	WPDF	Wolaita People Democratic Front
FDRE	Federal Democratic Republic of Ethiopia	WPE	Workers' Party of Ethiopia
FORUM	Forum for Federalist Democratic Unity of Ethiopia	WSDP	Western Somalia Democratic Party
GPRDF	Gambella People's Revolutionary Democratic Front		

References

Awgchew, Girma. 2009. *The origin of Amharic*. Addis Ababa: Addis Ababa University Press.

Balsvik, Randi Ronning. 2007. *The quest for expression: State and University in Ethiopia under Three Regimes, 1952- 2005*. Addis Ababa: Addis Ababa University Press.

Bender, M. Lionel. 1976. Introduction. In M. Lionel Bender (ed.), *The non-Semitic languages of ethiopia*, 1–24. East Lansing: Michigan State University in Cooperation with Southern Illinois University.

Berhanu, Kassahun. 2003. Political culture and party politics in Ethiopia. In Mohammed Salih (ed.), *African political parties: Evolution institutionalization and governance*, 1–2. London: Pluto Press.

Board, National Electoral. 2009. *Political parties for election 2010*. http://www.NEBE.net. et, accessed 2011-09-11.

Bogale, Berhanu. 2009. Language determination in Ethiopia: What medium of instruction? In Svein Ege, Harald Aspen, Birhanu Tefarra & Shiferaw Bekele (eds.), *Proceedings of the 16th International Conference of Ethiopian Studies*, 1089–1101. Trondheim: Norwegian University of Science & Technology.

Bowen, Donald & Nancy Horn. 1976. Language education. In Lionel Bender (ed.), *The non-Semitic languages of Ethiopia*, 608–634. East Lansing: African Studies Center Michigan state University.

Bulcha, Mekuria. 1998. The politics of linguistic homogenization in Ethiopia: Trends in the development of the oromo language. In Kwesi Kwaa Prah (ed.), *Between distinction and extinction*, 1–2. Johannesburg: Witwatersrand University Press.

Chiswick, Barry. 2008. *The economics of language: An introduction and overview*. Chicago: Institute for the Study of Labor.

Cobarrubias, Juan. 1983. Ethical issues in status planning. In Joshua A. Fishman & Juan Cobarrubias (eds.), *Progress in language planning: International perspectives*. 41–87. Berlin: Walter de Gruyter.

Cooper, Robert L. 1976. Government language policy. In M. L. Bender, J. D. Bowen, R. L. Cooper & C. A. Ferguson (eds.), *Language in Ethiopia*, 187–190. Oxford: Oxford University Press.

FDRE. 1994. *Education and training policy*. Addis Ababa.

Fishman, Joshua A. 1972. *Language in sociocultural change*. Stanford: Stanford University Press.

Gebreselassie, Fisseha. 2015. *Choosing a working language in mutilingual nations: Rethinking Ethiopia's working language policy*. no address: no publisher. http://www. aigaforum.com/articles/Paper-on-Ethiopia-Language-Policy.pdf, accessed 2015-06-25.

Getachew, Anteneh & Derib Ado. 2006. History and current trends. *Ethiopian Journal of Education and Sciences* 2. 37–60.

Grin, Francois. 1994. The economics of language: Match or mismatch? *International Political Science Review* 15(1). 25–42.

Gudina, Merera. 2006. Contradictory interpretations of the ethiopian history. In David Turton (ed.), *Ethnic federalism: The ethiopian experience in comparative perspective*, 119–131. Addis Ababa: Addis Ababa University Press.

Heugh, Kathleen, Carol Benson, Berhanu Bogale & Mekonnen Alemu Gebre Yohannes. 2007. *Final report study on medium of instruction in primary schools in Ethiopia*. Addis Ababa: MOE.

Leyew, Zelealem. 2012. A historical and typological overview. *Ethiopian Journal of Languages and Literature* 12(2). 1–59.

McNab, Christine. 1988. *Language policy and language practice: Implementation dilemmas in Ethiopian education*. University of Stockholm dissertation.

McNab, Christine. 1990. Language policy and language practice: Implementing multilingual literacy education in Ethiopia. *African Studies Review: Special Issue for the International Year of Literacy* 33(3). 65–82.

Mekonen, Walelign. 1969. *On the question of nationalities in Ethiopia*. no publisher. http://www.walelignfordemocracia.com/onationalqu.pdf, accessed 2014-11-09.

Obeng, G. Samuel & M. Tristan Purvis. 1999. Sub-Saharan africa. In Joshua A. Fishman (ed.), *The handbook of language and ethnic identity*, 334–390. Oxford: Oxford University Press.

Pankhurst, Richard. 1976. Historical background of education in Ethiopia. In Lionel Bender (ed.), *The non-Semitic languages of ethiopia*, 305–323. East Lansing: Michigan State University in Cooperation with Southern Illinois University.

Patten, Allan. 2001. Political theory and language policy. *Political Theory* 29. 691–715.

Philipson, David. 2012. *Foundations of an African civilization: Aksum & the northern horn, 1000 BC-AD 1300*. Addis Ababa: Addis Ababa University Press.

Revised Constitution of Ethiopia. 1955. Addis Ababa.

Schiffman, Harold. 1996. *Linguistic culture and language policy*. London: Routledge.

Smith, Lahra. 2008. The politics of contemporary language politics in Ethiopia. *Journal of Developing Societies* 24. 207–243.

Stalin, Joseph. 1913. *Marxism and the national question*. http://www.marxists.org, accessed 2014-11-09.

Stoddart, John. 1986. *The use and study of English in ethiopian schools*. Addis Ababa.

Tzadua, Paulos. 1968. Foreward. In Peter L Strauss & Paulos Tzadua (eds.), *The fetha nagast: The law of the kings*, xv–xxix. Addis Adaba: Faculty of Law, Haile Sellassie I University.

UNESCO. 2015. *Interactive atlas of the world's languages in danger*. no address. http://www.unesco.org/languages-atlas/index.php, accessed 2015-06-25.

Vaughan, Sarah. 2006. Responses to ethnic federalism in Ethiopia's Southern Region. In David Turton (ed.), *Ethnic federalism: The Ethiopian experience in comparative perspective*, 181–207. Addis Ababa: Addis Ababa University Press.

Wodajo, Mesfin. 2014. Sociolinguistic challenges of the Post-1991 Ethiopian Language Policy. *Journal of Languages and Cultures* 5(2). 17–23. http://www.academicjournals.org, accessed 2015-06-25.

Zemelak, Mehari. 2011. *The language issue among Ethiopian political parties.* Addis Ababa. MA thesis unpublished.

Zewde, Bahru. 2002. *A history of Modern Ethiopia, 1855-1991.* Addis Ababa: Addis Ababa University Press.

Zewde, Bahru. 2008. The changing fortunes of the Amharic language: Lingua franca or instrument of domination? In *Society, state and history: Selected essays,* 77–95. Addis Ababa: Addis Ababa University Press.

Part II

Language endangerment

Chapter 6

Linguistic imperialism and language decolonisation in Africa through documentation and preservation

Kofi Agyekum
The University of Kansas

This paper addresses the politics of language use in African nations and societies. It highlights the role of power and economics in the choice of language. It discusses linguistic imperialism and language shift, and how they lead to language endangerment. The paper also discusses linguistic decolonization whereby societies resist linguistic domination and endangerment and embark on language maintenance. It touches on the methods employed in language decolonisation, namely language revitalisation, resistance, maintenance, documentation and preservation. Attention will be on lexicology, terminology and the role of radio and TV. We argue that as a society tries to redeem itself from linguistic imperialism through decolonisation, certain stronger politico-economic factors push it back into linguistic imperialism. We will find out that some of the indigenous people themselves kick against language decolonisation. The paper hinges on the theoretical base of language endangerment. Examples are taken from African and Ghanaian languages with emphasis on Akan.

1 Introduction and definition of linguistic imperialism

According to Phillipson (2009: 780) "linguistic imperialism is the notion that certain languages dominate internationally on others. It is the way nation-states privileged one language, and often sought actively to eradicate others, forcing their speakers to shift to the dominant language." The expressions, *actively* eradicating and *forcing* speakers are too strong because despite the policies employed by the colonial masters in their former colonies, they cannot be said to be actively seeking to eradicate African languages. According to Mous (2003: 158) "Contrary to the situation in Latin America, in Africa, colonial languages are not a major factor in language loss." In the context of this paper, our working definition and conception of linguistic imperialism is "a linguistic situation where the indigenous people are gradually conscientised to shun their indigenous languages and adopt foreign languages because of the benefits they expect to derive from

Kofi Agyekum. Linguistic imperialism and language decolonisation in Africa through documentation and preservation. In Jason Kandybowicz, Travis Major, Harold Torrence & Philip T. Duncan (eds.), *African linguistics on the prairie: Selected papers from the 45th Annual Conference on African Linguistics*, 87–104. Berlin: Language Science Press. DOI:10.5281/zenodo.1251718

them. They are made to believe that their languages cannot be used in any transaction in education, economics, science and technology but instead a foreign language is the best.

In linguistic imperialism, there is a greater relationship between political and economic dependence. Even though many African and Asian countries have won political independence, there is still economic reliance and dependence on the developed and industrial world. This has culminated in linguistic and economic neo-colonialism. The European languages are still the dominant languages in science and technology, medicine, engineering and ICT. The linguistic dominance of the English language in science and technology has marginalized other languages in this field.

Phillipson (2009: 780) further argues that "linguistic imperialism entails unequal resource allocation and communicative rights between people, defined in terms of their competence in specific languages, with unequal benefits as a result." Linguistic imperialism has deepened in African countries to the extent that many families in the cities communicate with their children in English, French, Portuguese and Arabic, and the children cannot speak their mother tongue. People bear western names and have shelved their African names. Attitudes towards African languages in school and at home are very negative, and people are ashamed of speaking their languages.

Linguistic imperialism shows that language is one of the manifestations of European imperial expansion in Africa, Asia and Latin America. After the European Struggle and Partition of Africa, new languages of communication emerged patterned on the colonial masters' languages. Linguistic imperialistic ideologies glorify the dominant languages like Arabic, French, Hebrew, Latin, English, as the languages of religion and civilization.[1]

2 Language shift and language endangerment

This section discusses the theoretical notions of language shift and language endangerment. In language contact, language imperialism leads to language shift, whereby a community of speakers effectively abandons one language and shifts to another (Garret 2006: 63).[2] Language shift is the gradual replacement of the communicative functions of one language by another which the user considers to serve the maximum linguistic, political and social benefits (see Agyekum 2009). The basic determining factor in language shift relates to particular benefits to be derived from the use of the target language; especially economic benefits (see Mufwene 2006, 2002: 175, Mous 2003: 160). Mufwene (2006: 116) states that "English is spreading around the world because there are more and more people who hope to find better jobs, to travel, to distant places, to be read by more and more scholars, etc." In language shift, the functions of the minority language diminishes

---

[1]Phillipson (2009: 782) posits that linguistic imperialism is the maintenance of injustice and inequality by means of language policies, and it is strongly connected to policies in commerce, science, international affairs, education, culture and the media.

[2]O'Shannessy (2011: 83) states that "in language shift, members of the community stop speaking the pre-contact language habitually and mostly speak the post-contact language, which comes to be the language of the next generation."

in relation to the more "prestigious and politically powerful language" whose functions become expanded to cater for previous functions of the minor language. Speakers find the dominant languages more advantageous in all spheres of their lives. We can say that language shift comes from two sources (1) linguistic imperialism involving forcing or conscientisation, and (2) speakers making the change from the indigenous language to another language whether a foreign or a major indigenous language for socio-economic benefits.

Pandharipande (2002: 213–214) adopts the term *functional load* and asserts that the higher the functional load, the more powerful the language is perceived to be. An increase in the functional load implies the promotion and sustenance of the dominant language (colonial or national language) while the trend of "linguistic diminishing returns" in the functional load is serious. An uncontrolled language shift can lead to language decay, endangerment, extinction and death or attrition. Derhemi (2002a: 151) avers that "An endangered language is a language that may soon vanish, ceasing to be used as a vehicle of communication, perhaps even disappearing completely from human history." In Ghana, the Togo-Mountain languages can be considered as examples of endangered languages.

Language shift and death are engineered by globalization, language ideologies, language policies, language attitudes and everyday communicative practices in bilingual or multilingual communities. Theoretically, communities that have positive attitudes about their own language and community try to embark on language revitalisation and maintenance. In looking at the positive attitude towards language survival and maintenance Adegbija (2001: 307) posits that " As long as speakers of a language have a deep stake in its survival and a high emotional involvement and commitment to its existence, all the language shift agents and triggers in this world will not be able to kill their resolve." By contrast, negative attitude to one's language results in language shift, culminating into language death. Minority languages can die when their speakers are indifferent and lack the effective interventional means to protect them (see Derhemi 2002a: 249).

The other major causes of language shift and endangerment are social status of the language, educational and cultural factors, power relations of the languages that are in contact, economic, migratory and settlement patterns, exogamous marriages, religion, language policies and globalisation (Austin & Sallabank 2011: 5–6).

2.1 Language shift based on globalisation and international language policies

Some language shifts are caused by globalisation while some are based on language policies coming from colonial masters or national governments.

2.1.1 Globalisation

Globalisation is one of the key factors of language endangerment (see Austin & Sallabank 2011: 21). In language shift within the context of globalisation, very few languages benefit from international trade and international exchange. Brenzinger (2009: 446) asserts that

"The international exchange of knowledge and world trade are conducted in only a few world languages, and some scholars, seem to expect that, given this tendency, a world culture, based on one common language will finally emerge from these development." In the language of globalisation, the selected languages have wider communication and they are also easily accessed (see Bamgbose 2011: 5).

Some imperial languages are used as supra-regional or global languages of communication in international organisations like UN, Council of Europe, NATO, EU, AU, and ECOWAS. Imperial languages are used in negotiations between two or more states, languages of diplomacy, international agreements and pacts. English is increasingly becoming the world's international lingua franca.[3] Mous (2003: 160) records that "In Nigeria there is the rebirth of Nigerian Pidgin English as a consequence of globalisation. Other examples of language rebirth under globalisation in Africa are cases of urban slang losing its stigma and serving the function of bridging ethnicity and taking over all communication situations in the big city." Examples are Iscamto in Johannesburg, South Africa, and the use of Ghanaian Pidgin English in secondary schools, universities and public work places in Ghana.

Linguistic imperialism and education, and the expansion of the English language have provided a market and economic force for the teaching of English as a second language for foreigners. The English Language Teaching and Learning business is a major pillar for the British economy. [4] English language has become a global commodity sold in the international market. The socio-economic factors in language shift to a language like English for economic integration, cultural shifts, international networks and employment makes language a more marketable commodity than a marker of identity (see Austin & Sallabank 2011: 21). At the University of Ghana, students from Equatorial Guinea are sponsored heavily by their government to learn English at the Language Centre. At the department of Linguistics, Legon, a full-fee Sandwich Masters programme in TESL is oversubscribed. The situation is different for an MA sandwich in Ghanaian Languages at the University of Education Winneba. Very few students are ready to pay full-fees to study Ghanaian languages. The Presbyterian University of Ghana has a Ghanaian languages department but has not been able to enroll a single student to pay full fees.

2.1.2 Language policies

In some cases legislation is passed declaring that a language is the only one that individuals are allowed to use in both public and non-public domains (see Lewis 2013: 677). Some aspects of language shift deals with language of official communication. Most African countries use the former colonial masters' languages as the official languages in national administration, governance, education, legislation, judiciary, media, etc. Politically, very few of the masses in African countries speak the colonial languages; it is limited to the

---

[3]The integration of the new European Union member states accelerates the spread of English as the European lingua franca.

[4]Phillipson (2009: 781) records that the British economy benefits by £11billion directly and a further £11billion indirectly from their intake of foreign students in Higher education. He continues that over half a million foreign students attend language schools in Britain each year, spending time in learning English.

few elites. For instance, in Ghana, the official parliamentary language is English and nobody can become an MP without speaking English. Undoubtedly, no matter how brilliant one is, if s/he cannot communicate in English s/he cannot take part in any serious and meaningful political deliberations, and cannot be a parliamentarian. What happens in parliament is an evidence of disenfranchising of the masses by a few small classes of educated elites (Bamgbose 2000). In Ghana, all formal and official interactions at the governmental levels are done in English. The constitution and public documents are all in English.

Within the same nation, some languages are instrumentalised by governments, and they receive official and national support and recognition. In North Africa, Arabic varieties are expanding very fast. Kiswahili is established as a nationwide language for communication in Tanzania, and is threatening more than 130 other Tanzanian languages (see Mous 2003: 159). The same phenomenon prevails in Botswana where Setswana language is dominating about 30 other languages in the country.

2.2 Education and language shift

Language shift occurs due to the type of language policy in education (see Agyekum 2009). Where a different language (colonial or African) is the language of education there is a shift from the indigenous languages. In some schools in the urban centres in Ghana, children from other indigenous languages have no option but to use, study and pass in the local language. For example, all pupils who attend school in the Ashanti region study Asante Twi for their Basic Education Certificate Examination (BECE). In the schools in Accra, the capital city of Ghana, pupils are exposed to only three languages, namely Twi, Ewe and Ga. Here too, the Twi language dominates and most children from the three northern territories are forced to study Twi. This is *subtractive bilingualism* and can lead to loss of self-confidence and lower achievements (see Austin & Sallabank 2011: 9).

In Ghana, one cannot enter any high school or tertiary institution without passing English language. Many families thus forbid their children to learn or communicate in the Ghanaian languages even at home so as to be fluent in English. Most private basic schools prohibit their pupils from speaking any of the Ghanaian languages apart from having them as courses on the timetable. Pupils who flout this rule are punished. Teachers hang placards around pupils' necks reading, "I have spoken vernacular", or "Vernacular is prohibited". These trample on the pupils' linguistic human rights and freedom of speech.[5]

2.3 Media and language shift

Linguistic imperialism goes with media imperialism. Many news agencies in Africa carry their information mostly in English, French or Portuguese. Politically, the world's infor-

---

[5] Adegbija (2001: 285) records that "Ex-colonial languages have been functionally placed on a pedestal, being attitudinally extolled and being seen as inevitable both at the individual and societal levels." He further stated that "In Nigeria, Ghana, Uganda, Kenya and many other African countries colonized by the British, for instance, to be educated is virtually synonymous with knowing and being able to use English."

mation channels are dominated by these few languages, and to follow the global trends of information, one needs to know one or more of these languages.[6] Most programmes, classified advertisements on jobs, funeral announcement, conferences and other important announcements in the print media, radio and TV are mainly in the colonial languages.

There is a social stratification based on the degree of access to communication where speakers of the indigenous languages are not able to use their own *languages in broadcasting*. They are compelled to use the dominant languages, and this shift can lead to language endangerment and marginalisation of the masses. In Ghana, after independence, there were a few newspapers in the local languages, including, Nkwantabisa in Asante Twi and Ewe. Unfortunately, there is not a single newspaper printed in any Ghanaian language now, The Daily Graphic, the most widely circulated Ghanaian newspaper tried a pull up in its Tuesday edition and captioned it *Ghana Nsɛmpa* 'Ghana's Good News' but it did not go well so they have stopped. Until the proliferation of many FM radio stations that broadcast in the local languages, many people who listened to Ghana Broadcasting Corporation (GBC), BBC, and VOA were elites. The current use of indigenous languages in radio and TV is a situation of language decolonisation where the media shields the local languages from linguistic imperialism. In Accra most FM radio stations broadcast in Akan, and the local language Ga, was succumbing to the Akan language until the government established Ogbonu FM that broadcasts only in Ga to shield the Ga language.

2.4 Religion and language shift

Every religion has a political undertone especially when it is a foreign religion. It can change the ideology and attitude of the adherents. Adherents to new religious faiths must learn the language associated with it, and shift from their indigenous languages during worship (Brenzinger 2009: 447–448). For example, Arabic, Hausa and Dyula languages have spread in West Africa along with Islam. All good Moslems, especially the Sheiks, are expected to be proficient and knowledgeable in the Arabic language and culture.[7]

2.5 Economic occupational and migratory language shift

Economic and occupational survival are crucial factors in language learning and shift either from a minority to a majority language or vice versa (see Salzmann 2004: 194, Holmes 2001: 58).[8] Africans in Europe, Asia and American learn the host language so as to be employed. Theoretically, notwithstanding how strongly people are attached to their languages and cultures, the socio-economic pressures in modern global world make it

---

[6] Unequal benefits in language also lead to cultural imperialism where one society spreads its culture unto others such that they will throw away their cultures. Most African countries have fallen into this trap.

[7] According to the literature, Arabic was strongly attached to the widespread of Islam because people firmly believed that it was very difficult if not impossible to translate the Quran into another language (see Saville-Troike 1989: 208). This myth of the intranslatability of the Quran has now been broken since there are English and Akan versions of the Quran.

[8] Philips (2006: 485–486) asserts that 'The political economic position of a group determines its attitude towards the codes in a group's multilingual repertoire, the group's code choices, and the ultimate survival of the codes being spoken. The inequality of languages originates in economic equality.'

difficult for them to glue themselves to ancestral languages and culture, they have to shift to another language (see Mufwene 2002: 190). Lack of language and cultural practices gradually lead to language attrition and death.

Economic factors can raise a language to the status of a lingua franca and many non-native speakers will have the urge and zeal to learn and speak it. This supports an assertion by Mufwene (2006: 130) that "A particular language can be preferred because it functions both as vernacular and as a lingua franca, or because it is associated with money- making or better paying jobs, or because it affords its speakers a better social status, or because it is more widely spoken demographically and/or geographically."

Adegbija (2001: 286) asserts that "The more powerful and functionally the dominant language, the more pressing its attraction and pull and the greater the tendency to shift towards it given the fact that the pressure for social vertical mobility is virtually irresistible." In view of this notion, many dominant languages in Africa are replacing the smaller ones. Examples are the spread of the Somali language in Somali, Bamana or Jula in Mali, and Burkina Faso, Hausa in Nigeria and Niger, Yoruba and Igbo in Nigeria, Lingala in Congo, and Wolof in Senegal, Kikuyu in Kenya, Akan and Ewe in Ghana. These replacement are normally based on urbanisation, economic benefits and prestige (see Mous 2003: 160, Adegbija 2001: 286)

In Ghana, the Akan language is dominating the other indigenous languages very fast.[9] Non-Akan speakers naturally find it more advantageous to learn Akan so as to operate easily and extensively in Ghana. It is used mostly in the non-Akan cities and major towns like Accra, Bolgatanga, Yendi, Tamale, Navrongo, Wa, as the preferred lingua franca in religion, trade and commerce, music and the arts, artisanship and many aspects of the society. The same situation prevails in the Volta region where most of the Togo Mountain minority languages are being dominated by the Ewe language. In the Akan and Ewe examples, we can argue that the language shift from the minority languages is not caused by Indo-European languages but by African languages that the groups choose based on socio-political benefits (see Mous 2003, Brenzinger 1998, Lüpke & Storch 2013).

Social mobility, migration and settlement patterns result in language contact and language shift (see Agyekum 2009). Some people move to urban centres and abandon their languages for the 'so-called' prestigious ones. However, large groups of immigrants often manage to preserve their languages.

3 Language decolonisation

The term *language decolonisation* is derived from colonisation and decolonisation. Jaffe (2009: 534) states that

> Linguistic decolonisation (LD) describes both the actions taken in postcolonial contexts to undo the social, political, and cultural effects of the dominance of colonial

---

[9]In Ghana, Akan is spoken in six out of the ten regions and by 47.5% of the entire population as native speakers and also by 44% of the remaining Ghanaians as non-native speakers.

languages and a philosophical challenge to the Western language ideologies that underpinned the colonial project and that have persisted in the postcolonial period.

3.1 Strategies and tools for language decolonisation

Language decolonisers employ documentary approaches, sociological, ideological and pragmatic concepts to fight against language shift, endangerment, extinction and death. In language decolonisation, states and societies take nationalist interventions, efforts and action plans to legitimate their languages and identities that have been suppressed by linguistic imperialism.

They use multifaceted avenues and tools for language revitalization, and maintenance. These include educational curriculum, literacy and awareness of language death, media, especially radio, linguistic pluralism, language documentation and preservation. Language decolonisation, documentary projects and interventions redress the linguistic inequality, manipulation, repression and cultural oppression created by the replacement of the functions of their language by the majority and colonial languages.

3.2 Language decolonisation through radio, TV and pop-culture

The media can be a strong tool for language decolonisation; it serves as a platform for the use, documentation and development of the endangered languages.[10] To Moriarty (2011: 447) "Endangered media and pop-culture can help raise the status of the relevant language, aid corpus planning through the dissemination of new terminology, and encourage language acquisition by increasing language exposure in both the public and private domains." In Ghana, the mass media, especially radio record most of their programmes in the Ghanaian languages. Mass media serves as a mechanism for the storage of expressions, reservoirs and reference points for the circulation of words, phrases and discourse, proverbs and other aspects of Ghanaian language and popular culture (see Debra 2001: 96). The media as a tool for language decolonization and language maintenance serves as an unplanned and surest area where language changes and practical language policies can be employed spontaneously by the speech community (see Agyekum 2010, Derhemi 2002b: 158, Moriarty 2011: 447).

3.3 Recycling, recontextualisation and reinterpretation of media discourse

Oral media discourse in Africa is an essential aspect of the people's life and a new social interconnection across socio-structural, ethnic, religious, professional and party groupings. African societies have public and private FM stations that have adopted African languages policy. Some do 50%, 70% and even 100% African languages programmes. In Ghana, examples are Ogbonu FM in Tema (Ga), Ada FM (Ada), Peace FM. Nhyira, Adom,

---

[10]Debra (2001: 95) records that "there are several cases in which phrases and discourse styles are extracted from radio broadcasting and then recycled and reanimated in everyday usage outside of the contexts of radio listening".

Oman, and FM, (Akan). These policies are means of revitalising, maintaining, preserving and documenting their languages as part of the process of language decolonisation.

3.4 Linguistic impact

Linguistically, African language programmes on radio and TV have immensely contributed in African societies. Listeners learn a lot of things on language such as new vocabularies for modern concepts in politics, medicine, health, education, administration, economics and science from African programmes. They get new terms, idiomatic expressions, etymologies of words, proverbs, archaisms, appellations, etc. of indigenous languages (see Agyekum 2010 on radio).

One of the major functions of the African language programmes on RADIO AND TV TALK-SHOWS is language modernization, development and elaboration of terms to cater for most aspects of human life. Radio is one of the most powerful tools in the dissemination, interpretation and recontextualisation of discourse (see Agyekum 2000, 2010). Coined terms and phrases commonly used on African language radio programmes are picked up by the people and accepted for use outside radio. Below are some Akan (Ghana) terms popularly used, they include:

(1) dumsɔ is from dum, 'to switch off' and sɔ, 'switch on', implying 'power outage'.[11]

(2) *ɔmampanin*, is made up of *ɔman*, 'state', *panin*, 'elder' and hence 'president'.

(3) *ɔsoafoɔ*, 'minister' is made up of *soa*, 'to carry' and agentive prefix *ɔ*- and suffix *-foɔ*. The minister is the carrier of the "load" and responsibility of the ministry.

(4) *mmarahyɛbadwa*, 'parliament', the components are mmara, 'laws', *hyɛ*, 'to fix' and *badwa*, a gathering of people who are tasked to make laws.

(5) *ankoreankorɛ kyɛpɛn*, for 'human rights' the adjective *korɛ* means singular and the derived compound *ankoreankorɛ* means individuals, *kyɛpɛn* is made up of *kyɛ*, 'to share' and *pɛn* means level or equal. The composite term thus means equal distribution of entities to people (see Agyekum 2006 for other terms).

African oral literature genres appear on radio because they are less available in urbanized areas where the heterogeneous nature of the society is making people lose their cultural heritage. The radio and TV are becoming repositories (and innovators) for African languages especially in areas of orality. Radio culture is gradually replacing the traditional "village" oral traditions that were provided by the elders. Until the advent of the missionaries, the African languages were purely oral. Storytelling and proverb sections that were earlier on provided by the elders in the villages are now done effectively on African radio and TV programmes for a wider audience (see Agyekum 2000). The air waves allow us to reach "the villages", the radio is wider than the reach of the village oral literature sessions.

---

[11]Dumsɔ, 'power outage' has gained international recognition and has been used in Wikipedia and in Google.

3.5 Linguistic pluralism and official multilingualism as language decolonisation

One of the surest theoretical approaches to language maintenance and decolonization in African multilingual societies is the policy of *linguistic pluralism and official multilingualism* whereby various languages are decolonised and liberated from language imperialism and endangerment. Linguistic pluralism or official multilingualism is a system that promotes the coexistence of different languages and allows them to operate on equitable basis. The same opportunity for development and usage are given to more languages irrespective of their number of speakers. Linguistic pluralism is a democratic way of dealing with linguistic varieties in a multilingual nation.

Eritrea is one of the recognised linguistic pluralistic nations in Africa that gives all the nine indigenous languages the same opportunity in the mass media and in schools.[12] Societies that practise *official multilingualism* include Canada (French, English) Switzerland (French, Swiss, and German) and South Africa (11 languages).[13]

The most obvious problem with linguistic pluralism is economic, we use more money for printing books, training personnel, employing examiners, etc. A cost benefit analysis will prove that money spent in operating linguistic pluralism would be far less than money spent in peacekeeping if conflicts and wars emerge out of linguistic imposition and imperialism.

3.6 Language resistance and maintenance

Let us continue our discussion with language resistance and maintenance as tools of language decolonisation. It is possible for a community to undertake language revitalization and maintenance during the time that the shift is taking place. This happens in a situation where the speakers of the language undergoing a shift are loyal to their language and are bent on maintaining it. Nahir (2003) states that

> Language maintenance is the preservation of the use of a group's native language, as a first or even as a second language, where political, social, economic, educational, or other pressures threaten or cause (or are perceived to threaten or cause) a decline in the status of the language as a means of communication, a cultural medium, or a symbol of group or national identity. (Nahir 2003: 439).

Lewis (2013: 673) also posits "Language maintenance is the effort to arrest and reverse the process of language shift: an effort is made to ensure that a vulnerable language does not decline and eventually disappear, but rather it continues to be spoken by a sustainable community of people." Language maintenance is the situation where a language group that is bound to shift to other languages and become endangered under linguistic

---

[12] The nine languages used in Eritrea are Afar, Arabic, Beja, Blin, Kunama, Nara, Saho, Tigre and Tigrinya. Ghana embarks on partial linguistic pluralism, and offers eleven languages in schools at the Junior High School (JHS), Senior High School (SHS) and universities.

[13] The South Africa 1996 Constitution has a new language policy that accords official status to eleven languages also referred to as 'de facto' national languages spoken by major populations within the country. The aim is to avoid linguistic conflicts.

imperialistic circumstances, rather holds to their language and expands its functional load (see Coulmas 2005: 157).

Most Africans adhere to various practical ways to maintain their languages and culture. Culture and language are inextricably interwoven. The loss of a language through language shift and endangerment logically results in the loss or reduction of cultural practices (Derhemi 2002b: 153). These include oral literature genres like proverbs, folktales, myths, legends, historical narratives, folk songs and poetry (see Crystal 2000). There are good reasons to protect languages and cultures from dying.

Speakers of a particular language group themselves can maintain their language instead of shifting to the dominant language. An extended form of this type of language maintenance is found in African communities in Europe and North America. African ethnic groups congregate from different parts of the cities in which they live to meet regularly and chat in their languages, eat African food, and wear African clothes. They have African musical groups that meet occasionally to perform. They have chiefs, queens and sub-chiefs, and they continue to practice their cultures and languages. They have established African churches where the worship is conducted in African languages and they sometimes invite African pastors from Africa to preach. These types of gatherings help to promote African languages and cultures in the developed world.

4 Language documentation

This section discusses basic concepts, techniques, and challenges of language documentation.

4.1 Basic concepts about language documentation and preservation

Let us finally look at decolonising language through documentation and preservation of aspects of the language including the phonology, syntax, semantics, ethnography, culture, and oral literature.

To salvage situations of language death and endangerment, linguists counteract language death through *language preservation, revitalization* and *documentation*. The linguistic documentation of dying languages is sometimes labelled as "salvage linguistics" (Craig 1997: 257). The documentation of language and oral art is the major technique that acts as the catalyst for its preservation and language decolonization, because it is a way for putting out materials in the form of books, CD Rom, and all kinds of electronic forms. These sources can be consulted for specific aspects of language teaching, learning and research.

Language documentation is a proactive process and involves actions that are meant to record, maintain and preserve a language for the future; it is also geared towards protecting it from language shift and death (see Agyekum 2012). From this standpoint, language documentation precedes preservation.[14] To Himmelmann (2006: 1), "Language

---

[14] Trilsbeek & Wittenburg (2006: 3140) identify three agents in the archiving of language and these are (a) the depositors, (b) the users, and (c) the archivists. The depositors record, and create different sorts of material and hand these over to the archivists (documentation). The users are those who use the materials, and the archivists solve the long-term preservation problems (preservation).

documentation is a lasting, multipurpose record of language." The researcher should rely on the *linguistic knowledge* of the native speakers on flora and fauna, kinship systems, artefacts, food items, religion, narratives and oral literature genres, etc. If native speakers are actively involved in the creation of the document, the researcher gets firsthand information about the language, and this increases the authenticity of the information for documentation and preservation.

Before independence, language documentation in Ghana was carried out by missionaries like the Presbyterian and the Methodist who also translated the Bible into Twi, Fante, Ewe and Ga. Since independence, documentation in the country has been undertaken by the Bureau of Ghanaian Languages, Ghana Publishing Corporation and Ghana Institute of Literacy and Bible Translation. The Linguistic and Ghanaian language departments of the universities research into Ghanaian languages by producing long essays, theses, dissertations, primers, dictionaries and journal articles (see Agyekum 2012).

4.2 Techniques in language documentation

The major strategies of language documentation are the recording, processing, preservation and dissemination of the primary data (see Woodbury 2011: 159). It involves audio and/or video recording of all communicative events such as folktales, myths, proverbs, folksongs, dirges, appellations, ordinary conversations and all other observable linguistic behaviour. In documentation, we collect the language materials and put them into archival database, and disseminate the information for public use (see Salffner 2006: 106). The scope of language documentation covers a large set of primary data that provides strong evidence of language use in their natural sociocultural settings such as funerals, traditional rituals, greetings, requests, apology, thanking, political discourse and chieftaincy (see Agyekum 2012). The language documenter elicits information from people and takes notes from earlier documents like literature books, history and religion or recorded court proceedings and notes from the Bible where they exist.

Language documentation should include many varied records and everything that is related to language. To Himmelmann (2006: 3), "The goal of language documentation is to create a record of language in the sense of a *comprehensive corpus of the primary data* which leaves nothing to be desired by later generations wanting to explore whatever aspect of the language they are interested in." No matter how thoroughly we record and document it, there would be areas that are undocumented.

In specific subject language documentation, the researcher could set some limits based on his focus and needs. There is the danger of producing what Himmelmann (2006: 4) calls *"data graveyards"*. This refers to large heaps of data with little or no use to anyone. However, if we collect very limited data, the documented information may not reflect the real nature and state of the language under study (see Agyekum 2012).

Data is of no importance if it is not well formatted and catalogued for easy accessibility (see Agyekum 2012: 26). Any data should be accessible to the compilers of the document, and also be user friendly and accessible to a broad range of users including children, researchers, and foreigners who want to learn the language in future.[15]

4.3 Factors militating against language decolonisation and documentation:

Most linguistic decolonisers do not have the requisite resources and materials needed to develop and raise their languages to the levels that can replace the status and functions of the colonial languages in all domains. The colonial masters are politically and economically powerful, and their languages resist the challenges of decolonization, and they embark on official monolingualism (see Lewis 2013). Fishman (2001: 13) states that "the resources available to threatened languages are often quite meager and constantly fewer than those available to their Big Brother rivals and competitors.... Threatened languages often have no *outside support of any optimal significance* to fall back upon." For instance, at the University of Ghana, most of the funds for research are granted to the sciences and social sciences and not to Linguistics, Languages and Performing arts.

Another reason for the resistance to Language Decolonisation is that language planning policies favour foreign languages and majority national languages; this phenomenon makes language decolonisation difficult. This unfortunate situation prevails in Ghana where the official language policy states that the medium of instruction for the first three years should be the indigenous Ghanaian languages, but the "international and preparatory" schools in the urban areas rather use the English language as the medium from day one especially when the pupils come from diverse linguistic backgrounds.

The development of the national and the minority languages for education and other modern domains creates a division between the pure and mixed codes of the various languages (see Jaffe 2009: 534). If the minority and threatened languages are only taught as school subjects and not used in homes there is a disconnection, and that retards the progress of the language. This is what normally happens in the urban centres, where the minority language becomes a second language (see also Fishman 2001: 14–15). The use of the colonial languages brings about elitism and social stratification that help the elite to lord over the non-elite. They therefore want to do everything possible to thwart the efforts of the linguistic decolonisers.[16]

Some scholars argue that language preservation and documentation are very costly and not cost effective. Mufwene (2002: 162, 191) asserts that language development should take a natural path. The changes occurring in linguistic behaviour of speakers are simply an adaptation to changes in the socio-economic conditions of the speech communities

---

[15] The documents should provide information about; participants, purpose, setting (when and where the data was recorded), contents, structure and quality of the data, general information about the speech community and the language, the data collection methods, links and references to other resources (books and articles), (Himmelmann 2006: 11–12). The materials should be stored in hardcopy, softcopy, backup, pen drives, CDs, DVD, CD Roms, e-mail accounts, etc.

[16] Jaffe (2009: 535) concludes that "Postcolonial linguistic agents are often faced with a double-bind: if they use the colonial language, they are seen as traitors to their cultural/ethnic group; if they use the dominated language, their voice has a more limited power and reach."

driven by interests related to costs and profits that come along with language use, and therefore must be respected. Theoretically, language shift, endangerment and death are all part of language evolution and must be allowed to take their natural path based on human behaviour.

Generally, if speakers of an endangered language have more pressing socio-economic concerns and prospects to think about, they are less worried about the fates of their languages and how to salvage them from linguistic imperialism. Despite this conundrum facing Language decolonisation, it is prudent to forge ahead since linguistic imperialism tramples on peoples' "linguistic human rights", and language endangerment is a machine that drives languages into the morgue.

Problems that militate against research, documentation, and publication of indigenous languages include lack of cooperation from the informants, especially on issues relating to the secret elements of oral art, filming materials or the performance itself. Translating oral literature materials is not an easy task, many words and concepts are archaic and obsolete, some flora, fauna and particular names are untranslatable.

Many African universities have a negative attitude towards teaching and research in African languages, oral literature and cultural studies, and will not provide funds to promote the development of African languages. There are difficulties in finding outlets and funds for publication of research materials in oral literature, lexicology and other aspects of African languages.

4.4 Recommendations for the development of African languages

All languages should be given the opportunity to survive so as to maintain their cultural heritage (see also Adegbija 2001: 305–306). Based on the points raised in this paper, we make the following recommendations and conclusions for the promotion, development and decolonisation of African languages.

- The provision of vocabulary and appropriate terminology for the teaching and learning of African languages should be made an important aspect of language development. To cope with language modernisation and elaboration, lexicology and terminology should be integral parts of the language curriculum at the teachers' training colleges, language centres and the linguistics departments of our universities. This will help us to produce word lists, terms and special dictionaries, glossary books on all aspects of African linguistics, English- African reference books for African language students, broadcasters, translators, etc.

- We must develop and elevate the status of the African languages and literatures to be used in education to teach our languages, mathematics, science, and technology in all our schools, universities and technical institutions.

- At the training colleges, the teaching and research into African languages should be intensified to produce well-trained knowledgeable and adequately qualified teachers to teach our African languages (see Prah 1993: 9, Adegbija 2001: 305).

- More books and articles should be written on African languages. The more we document and preserve the language, the better we are able to revitalise, maintain and decolonize our African languages from linguistic imperialism. We could translate some of the African, Caribbean, and Western literature into the African languages to expand our textbooks and supplementary readers (see Agyekum 2003).

- A branch of language planning and modernisation should be established within the Academy of Arts and Sciences in African countries. Our departments of languages at the universities should teach courses on language planning and policies especially, MTE.

- African languages, linguistics and literature institutes should establish language planning branches. We should also have national interdisciplinary lexicographical and terminological centres to deal with language documentation in the various African languages. Africans should have explicit, practicable, implementable and firm language policies and planning on MTE rather than the theory and "skip-hopping policies".

- We should establish language media; radio, TV and newspapers and popular culture domains that the youth will be involved in and enjoy. The media can shape and change their negative attitudes and ideologies about African indigenous languages.

- African agencies like the AU, ECOWAS and zonal groups should equip Bureaux of African Languages in our countries with personnel, technical know-how, and funds to develop our own languages (see Agyekum 2012, 2003). The 21st century should be dubbed "Afrolingual Independence and Development". We should be proactive to develop our mother tongues and decolonise them from linguistic imperialism, language endangerment and death. The overall result of positive linguistic intervention will help our social, economic, religious, political, scientific, and technological development.

5 Conclusions

In this paper, we have seen that language shift is part of language and politics and it is found in language policy, politics, language of education, religion, media, economics, immigration and settlement patterns. Naturally, a language with limited instrumental utility to catch up with modernisation and globalisation is replaced with the one that serves the current needs of the people. The international exchanges of knowledge and world trade are conducted in only a few world languages. We opined that language imperialism occurs in two folds (a) conscientisation of a people to gradually shift from their language, and (2) shift of a language for socio-economic and political benefits.

We paid attention to Linguistic decolonisation as a process where a society reinstates its language status and reverses language shift. Decolonising agencies in African redeem and maintain their languages across geographical frontiers. Unfortunately, while language decolonisers work very hard, globalisation, language attitude by some elites, modernisation and technological influence, borrowing and diffusion hamper their progress. Problems relating to the collection, documentation and publication include the uncooperative and negative attitude of informants and speakers, lack of funds, problems of translation, and difficulty in finding publishers (see Bamgbose 2011: 5).

Theoretically, every language can become a vehicle of modern civilization to meet the demands of her people. The non-use of a language in both informal and formal set ups contribute to language shift, endangerment, decay and loss, and restricts its functional usage, but the documentation of a language is a big step in the process of language survival and restoration (see Derhemi 2002a: 256).

The survival of every language theoretically depends on whether it is appropriate to be used for all contexts of communication identified by the society such as marketing, occupation, religion, music, etc. A language begins to lose its prestige and eventually decays if its functional load is restricted to only informal usage. Our languages should be integrated into ICT. It is only when our languages are able to cope with most of our societal needs that Africa's independence can be said to be complete.

Finally, the paper has argued that if we develop African languages, it will have a corresponding impact on African culture, art, politics, economics, agriculture, industrialisation, technology, medicine, primary health, commerce and trade, environmental studies, media and education. If the modern ideas and information are disseminated in the indigenous African languages, their impact will be greater and help the majority of the masses to understand them better. *Political independence without linguistic independence is partial independence.* In such a situation, our pace in modernisation will be slow, and we will still be under linguistic imperialism and language endangerment (Agyekum 2003).

References

Adegbija, E. 2001. Saving threatened languages in Africa: A case study of oko. In Joshua A. Fishman (ed.), *Can threatened languages be saved? Reversing language shift, revisited: A 21st century perspective*, 284–308. Clevedon: Multilingual Matters.

Agyekum, Kofi. 2000. Aspects of akan oral literature in the media. *Research Review* 16(2). 1–18.

Agyekum, Kofi. 2003. *Akan linguistics: Metalanguage and terminology.* Legon: University of Ghana dissertation.

Agyekum, Kofi. 2006. Lexical expansion and elaboration in akan: Afisem and the media. *Issues in Political Discourse Analysis* 1. 71–85.

Agyekum, Kofi. 2009. Language shift: A case study of Ghana. *Sociolinguistics Studies* 3(3). 381–403.

Agyekum, Kofi. 2010. Ghanaian radio and the Akan language: Unplanned language planning and development. *Issues in Political Discourse Analysis* 3(2). 141–161.

Agyekum, Kofi. 2012. Documentation and preservation of the akan language. *Basic Research Journal of Education Research and Review* 1(2). 23–37.

Austin, Peter K. & Julia Sallabank. 2011. Introduction. In Peter K. Austin & Julia Sallabank (eds.), *The Cambridge handbook of endangered languages*, 1–24. Cambridge: Cambridge University Press.

Bamgbose, Ayo. 2000. *Language and exclusion: The consequences of language policies in Africa.* Munster: LIT Verlag.

Bamgbose, Ayo. 2011. African languages today: The challenge of and prospects for empowerment under globalization. In Eyamba G. Bokamba, Ryan K. Shosted & Bezza Tesfaw Ayalew (eds.), *Selected proceedings of the 40th Annual Conference on African Linguistics*, 1–14.

Brenzinger, Matthias (ed.). 1998. *Endangered languages in Africa.* Köln: Rüdiger Köppe.

Brenzinger, Matthias. 2009. Language maintenance and shift. In Jacob L. Mey (ed.), *Concise encyclopedia of pragmatics*, 2nd edn., 444–452. Amsterdam: Elsevier Ltd.

Coulmas, Florian. 2005. *Sociolinguistics: The study of speakers' choices.* Cambridge: Cambridge University Press.

Craig, Colette Grinevald. 1997. Language contact and language degeneration. In Florian Coulmas (ed.), *The handbook of sociolinguistics*, 257–270. Oxford: Blackwell.

Crystal, David. 2000. *Language death.* Cambridge: Cambridge University Press.

Debra, Spitulnik. 2001. The social circulation of media discourse and the mediation of communities. In Alessandro Duranti (ed.), *A companion to linguistic anthropology*, 95–118. Malden: Blackwell Publishers.

Derhemi, Eda. 2002a. The endangered arbesh language and the importance of standardized writing for its survival: The case of piani degli albanesi, sicily. *International Journal of Multicultural Societies* 4(2). 248–269.

Derhemi, Eda. 2002b. Thematic introduction: Protecting endangered minority languages: Sociolinguistic perspectives. *International Journal of Multicultural Societies* 4(2). 150–161.

Fishman, Joshua A. 2001. Why is it hard to save a threatened language? In Joshua A. Fishman (ed.), *Can threatened languages be saved? Reversing language shift, revisited: A 21st century perspective*, 1–22. Clevedon: Multilingual Matters.

Garret, Paul B. 2006. Language contact and contact languages. In Alessandro Duranti (ed.), *A companion to linguistic anthropology*, 46–72. Malden: Blackwell Publishers.

Himmelmann, Nikolaus P. 2006. Language documentation: What is it and what is it good for? In Jost Gippert, Nikolaus P. Himmelmann & Ulrike Mose (eds.), *Essentials of language documentation*, 1–30. Berlin: Mouton de Gruyter.

Holmes, Janet. 2001. *An introduction to sociolinguistics.* 2nd edn. Harlow, England: Longman Publishers.

Jaffe, Alexandra. 2009. Linguistic decolonialization. In Jacob L. Mey (ed.), *Concise encyclopedia of pragmatics*, 2nd edn., 534–535. Amsterdam: Elsevier Ltd.

Lewis, Huw. 2013. Language maintenance: A liberal-egalitarian approach. *Journal of Multilingual and Multicultural Development* 34(7). 672–689.

Lüpke, Friederike & Anne Storch. 2013. *Repertoires and choices in African languages.* Berlin: de Gruyter.

Moriarty, Máiréad. 2011. New roles for endangered languages. In Peter K. Austin & Julia Sallabank (eds.), *The Cambridge handbook of endangered languages*, 446–458. Cambridge: Cambridge University Press.

Mous, Maarten. 2003. Loss of linguistic diversity in Africa. In Mark Janse & Sijmen Tol (eds.), *Language death and language maintenance: Theoretical, practical and descriptive approaches*, 157–170. Amsterdam/Philadelphia: John Benjamins.

Mufwene, Salikoko S. 2002. Colonisation, globalisation, and the future of languages in the twenty-first century. *International Journal of Multicultural Societies* 4(2). 162–193.

Mufwene, Salikoko S. 2006. Language endangerment: An embarrassment for linguistics. *Proceedings from the Parasessions of the Forty-second Meeting of the Chicago Linguistic Society* 42(2). 111–140.

Nahir, Moshe. 2003. Language planning goals: A classification. In Christina Bratt Paulston & G. Richard Tucker (eds.), *Sociolinguistics: The essential readings*, 423–448. Malden: Blackwell Publishers.

O'Shannessy, Carmel. 2011. Language contact and change in endangered languages. In Peter K. Austin & Julia Sallabank (eds.), *The Cambridge handbook of endangered languages*, 78–99. Cambridge: Cambridge University Press.

Pandharipande, Rajeshwari V. 2002. Minority matters: Issues in minority languages in India. *International Journal of Multicultural Societies* 4(2). 213–234.

Philips, Susan U. 2006. Language and social inequality. In Alessandro Duranti (ed.), *A companion to linguistic anthropology*, 474–495. Malden: Blackwell Publishers.

Phillipson, Robert. 2009. Linguistic imperialism. In Jacob L. Mey (ed.), *Concise encyclopedia of pragmatics*, 2nd edn., 780–782. Amsterdam: Elsevier Ltd.

Prah, Kwesi Kwaa. 1993. *Mother tongue for scientific and technological development in Africa*. Cape Town: University of the Western Cape.

Salffner, Sophie. 2006. Learning endangered languages. A linguistic frame of reference for modelling readers. In Francis Ogbokhare (ed.), *Globalization and the future of African languages*, 104–116. Ibadan, Nigeria: Ibadan Cultural Studies Group.

Salzmann, Zdeněk. 2004. *Language, culture and society: An introduction to linguistic anthropology*, 3rd edn. Oxford: Westview Press.

Saville-Troike, Muriel. 1989. *The ethnography of communication: An introduction*. 2nd edn. Oxford: Blackwell.

Trilsbeek, Paul & Peter Wittenburg. 2006. Archiving challenges. In Jost Gippert, Nikolaus P. Himmelmann & Ulrike Mosel (eds.), *Essentials of language documentation*, 311–335. Berlin: Mouton de Gruyter.

Woodbury, Anthony. 2011. Language documentation. In Peter K. Austin & Julia Sallabank (eds.), *The Cambridge handbook of endangered languages*, 159–186. Cambridge: Cambridge University Press.

Chapter 7

Dictionary Day: A community-driven approach to dictionary compilation

Bryan D. Gelles
University of Florida

A common component of language documentation is the compilation of a small dictionary. The method of compilation has changed very little in the last century: most documentarians elicit individual lexical items from a speaker and check the item through both translation and backtranslation with other speakers. Two major problems with this method are the absence of larger community engagement and idiosyncratic problems that come from lexical item elicitation.

Animere is an endangered language spoken by around thirty speakers all aged over forty years. The speech community is located in Kecheibi, northern Volta Region, Ghana. Over a five month period I began the initial documentation of Animere with funds provided by a Small Grant from the Endangered Languages Documentation Programme, integrating Dictionary Day, one day a week when members of the community would gather to discuss lexical items. This method proved highly successful: I saved time and funds by making use of the speech community's intuition while obtaining valuable folk linguistic information when there was disagreement. Furthermore, the speech community was not only engaged but agentive, allowing for genuine consultation between the linguist and the speech community. The major drawback, however, is lack of synergy among documentarians and other linguists when excluding prescribed data collection methods.

1 Introduction

From the time of the Structuralists to the present, a language documentation at minimum consists of the Boasian trilogy: a grammar, a collection of texts, and a dictionary. The method for eliciting lexical items for a dictionary has also not changed much since the introduction of the Swadesh list (Swadesh 1955): most frequently a single linguist, using a Swadesh list, will elicit individual lexical items from a single speaker. As noted by Chelliah & de Reuse (2011) the dictionary has often been ignored by field linguists possibly due to limitations on time in the field and the linguist's research interests. Modern linguistic field methods and language documentation handbooks, however, devote

Bryan D. Gelles. Dictionary Day: A community-driven approach to dictionary compilation. In Jason Kandybowicz, Travis Major, Harold Torrence & Philip T. Duncan (eds.), *African linguistics on the prairie: Selected papers from the 45th Annual Conference on African Linguistics*, 105–116. Berlin: Language Science Press. DOI:10.5281/zenodo.1251720

an entire chapter on doing ethical fieldwork, focusing on collaboration with the speech community as well as encouraging linguists to give back to the speech community whenever possible, most frequently in the form of a tangible item such as a sketch grammar or dictionary.[1] During my own research, the first thing the speech community asked for was a dictionary of the language I was documenting. The compilation of a dictionary, regardless of its exhaustiveness, is one of the most straightforward ways of giving the community a physical manifestation of a documentation. Furthermore, Hill (2012) recounts a tumultuous field setting where the creation of a dictionary provided positive benefits to the speech community in the form of recognition of the language and the building of self-esteem in the community. A dictionary, thus, is not only a book of definitions but is a cultural icon for the speech community.

The question, however, is whether the method of compilation affects the type of lexical data is collected, whether for crosslinguistic comparison or theoretical application. If so, what methodological approaches should be used in order to strike a balance between the linguist's (and the larger linguistic community's) own goals and the desire to conduct an ethical documentation. Furthermore, the linguist must consider whether the status of the language affects what methodological approach should be taken. First I will discuss the current methods employed in the field for dictionary compilation as well as the implications for the wider linguistic community and the problems that come with it. Then I will present an alternative method I used when compiling a dictionary of a highly endangered language spoken in rural Ghana as well as discussing its implications and drawbacks. Finally I will offer concluding remarks.[2]

2 Current methodology

The current methodology for eliciting lexical items for a dictionary is mostly the same across fieldwork guides. Since Swadesh (1955), common practice has been for the linguist to elicit individual lexical items from members of the speech community. At one end of the extreme, Vaux et al. (2007) advocates for the lexical items to either come from a Swadesh list or a frequency list from a related language.

I	this	what	many	big
you	that	not	one	long
we	who	all	two	small

Figure 1: Sample portion of a Swadesh list

Mosel (2004), however, notes that a predetermined list such as the Swadesh list may present problems such as the absence of the lexical item in the speech community. For this reason, Mosel (2004) advocates for 'active eliciting' whereby the linguist asks for

---

[1]Among others Bowern (2008); Chelliah & de Reuse (2011), and Vaux et al. (2007).

[2]It should be noted the discussion itself is limited to lexical item elicitation and not specifically lexicography. A good summary of lexicography's own idiosyncratic problems can be found in Haviland (2006).

words related to a topic chosen by the linguist (for example, items in the home). Bowern (2008) also suggests allowing the community members to have limited agency by having the linguist ask them to do things like show them around the house and name items. The linguist, in all situations, records the lexical item for the dictionary. The linguist then must confirm the data with other speakers of the language through translation and backtranslation to account for inconsistencies throughout the speech community as well as to account for mistakes made on both the part of the linguist and individual community members. The data is then compiled into a dictionary.

Another way of eliciting data is by using field guides such as those found at the Max Planck Institute for Evolutionary Anthropology.[3] These stimulus kits consist mainly of pictures that the linguist points to, hopefully eliciting a lexical response as well as questionnaires. The linguist then records the data and uses it to compile a dictionary.

Figure 2: Example of topological relations stimuli (Bowerman & Pederson 1992).

Current language documentation methodology focuses on the audiovisual documentation of interactions with the speech community. At minimum, a microphone should capture the audio signal of both the speaker and the linguist to not only account for the lexical item but also the prompt (an invaluable resource when there are discrepancies among speakers). There should also be a video recording of the interaction to account for visual cues that may aid in spontaneous elicitations (the linguist may forget what exactly a given stimulus was for a lexical item whereas a recording will not). Dense metadata is compiled for each speaker and each interaction to account for not only foreseen circumstances (possible age, gender, dialect distinctions, etc.) but also for unforeseen circumstances (anything the linguist is currently unaware of about the community that may eventually play a factor in language differences across the community). The audiovisual component may capture those things that the linguist may either miss or misconstrue while gathering lexical items.

---

[3]http://www.eva.mpg.de/lingua/tools-at-lingboard/tools.php

In all of these instances, the linguist supplies the theme if not the individual items themselves, and (hopefully) the speech community provides a lexical item. After translating and backtranslating across multiple speakers, the linguist records what he or she believes is the consensus across the speech community. This data is compiled into a dictionary of the language with the necessary caveats in place regarding exhaustiveness.

3 Implications

It is not a coincidence that most linguists rely on a Swadesh list for gathering lexical items. The use of cognates to establish the genetic relationship between languages using the Comparative Method predates the Swadesh list, but the advent of the Swadesh list made this work much easier by codifying the list of words used for elicitation: since linguists were using (roughly) the same set of words in the field, typologists could use the data collected for direct comparison between languages. Also, by focusing on such things as numbers and color terms in a language, typologists are able to compare across multiple languages and language families relying on field linguists to gather this data during individual documentations. It is not uncommon for typologists to contact field linguists in order to see whether their documentations have such data necessary for typological work, an example of the synergy between typologist and field linguist that only a shared resource such as a Swadesh list can provide.

Stimulus materials are also used for crosslinguistic analysis by relying on the field linguist to gather very specific data the typologists and theorists cannot gather themselves due to logistical constraints. One example of this is the Pear Story, a student-made film that has grown to become a resource for analyzing crosslinguistic strategies for storytelling (Chafe 1980). Much like the Swadesh list, by having multiple field linguists use the same stimulus materials, typologists and theorists can analyze a specific type of data across languages without having to enter each speech community individually themselves, saving both time and finite resources.

4 Problems

There are several problems with these methods, however. As noted in Mosel (2004), the Swadesh list may not line up isomorphically with the language being discussed leading to inconsistencies: not only is it possible for an item on the Swadesh list to not be specific or general enough for the language in question (for example, a language that does not distinguish between the hand or the arm of a person), but it is possible that the item does not have a correlate in the language leading to an embarrassed speech community member who feels he or she is not up to the task at hand.[4] Though the former seems like a straightforward situation that will be easily noted by the linguist, other subtler lexical distinctions could be lost due to strict adherence to a predetermined list. The Swadesh

---

[4]During my own research, one community member, after not knowing a lexical item, checked every word with a family member during the rest of the session.

List (or a frequency list) thus may inherently fail to capture the semantic boundaries of the language while also possibly discouraging community members in the process.

The most problematic result of both using lists as well as 'active eliciting' is the difficulty in capturing cultural patterns due to working with individual speakers. The most common issue facing field linguists wishing to elicit lexical items is what to do with items that speakers disagree on. It is common in the field for one speaker to state that the lexical item is one thing, whereas a different speaker will insist that the first speaker has no idea what they are talking about and that the 'real' lexical item is something else entirely. In many cases, this may simply be due to dialectal differences between speakers, but if the linguist is unaware of such differences, this generalization may be lost and simply reduced to one speaker being incorrect. Furthermore, several speakers may differ from other speakers of the language. If the linguist discovers such a difference exists, he or she may deduce a generalization exists, but if the linguist only encounters a few members of the speech community and they all agree due to a small random sampling, this generalization is lost. In short, by only eliciting, translating, and backtranslating one speaker at a time, the linguist must assume the few speakers that were consulted were prototypical of the entire speech community, a flawed assumption statistically.

Another major problem with the Swadesh list specifically is how to elicit the items themselves. As can be seen in Figure 1 above, the Swadesh contains not only flora and fauna (which again may not exist in field site) but also items such as personal pronouns. Although the Swadesh list is suggested by field manuals, there is no explanation for how to actually elicit these items. As any linguist who has ever tried to elicit personal pronouns can attest, such lexical items are tricky at best to elicit. Furthermore, without any practical elicitation strategy to work from, each linguist creates their own method for elicitation often having to learn by trial and error what works and potentially misconstruing the data in the process. Although the list itself is codified, the way for eliciting it is not potentially leading to mistakes on the part of the linguist.

The linguist has also taken the majority of the agency of the documentation. The speech community, at best, has a choice among prescribed topics and at worst must merely translate from a list the linguist chooses. In this way the speaker is no longer a consultant who works with the linguist to document the language but is merely an informant who does the linguist's bidding. If the documentation is indeed a collaborative effort (a major emphasis from an ethical standpoint), it is disconcerting that the linguist is making decisions without the speech community's input in regards as to what lexical items comprise the language's dictionary. Literally, the linguist is telling the speech community what is appropriate for a dictionary that the linguist is partially using as justification that he or she is giving back to the community. In this power dynamic, the linguist has all the power, and the speech community is merely a group that has the data the linguist wants.

From a practical position, working with individual speakers is also a waste of time and resources. There is limited time in the field, and the linguist must manage this time wisely in order to accomplish as much possible. Working with individual speakers and then translating and backtranslating across individual speakers uses up not only time but the resources the linguist is allocating for working with speakers of the community (compensation in whatever form the linguist deems appropriate). These resources could be used for other things that further the documentation as a whole instead of using primarily for the gathering of lexical items.

For these reasons, the current methods for gathering lexical items are insufficient. There is, however, another way to gather lexical items in a way that emphasizes collaboration while making differences among speakers clearer to the linguist. The question, though, is whether too much is then lost in terms of synergistic activities with typological and theoretical linguists.

5 Dictionary Day

From December 2012 until May 2013 I began the initial documentation of Animere, a Kwa language spoken in the rural northern Volta Region of Ghana. Previous contact with the community produced a sociolinguistic profile as well as a short wordlist used for comparative purposes (Ring 2006). The language is highly endangered, numbering around thirty speakers in one isolated village. The community consisted of cocoa farmers who work every day except for one day a week when the local market was held. On the morning of this day, all of the speech community was invited to participate in 'Dictionary Day',[5] a two hour period to discuss lexical items before they went to the market. Since the community determined it wanted a dictionary of their language, we agreed that I would use my linguistic resources to transcribe those items they deemed appropriate for their dictionary. They would decide on a topic for the day (or I would suggest a topic if they were at a loss for where to begin), and I would transcribe what they told me was appropriate for their dictionary. As this is a moribund language, it was common for the children of the speakers to come and watch the commotion, since Dictionary Day had a tendency to become rather lively at times due to disagreements. The dictionary that is being compiled of this language is organized based on the topics that the community (and sometimes myself) chose, including flaura, fauna, and traditional occupations. At the suggestion of one speaker, their dictionary includes useful phrases in the language as well. The dictionary, thus, is mostly their own work with the linguist performing the role of linguistic consultant as opposed to the guider of the elicitation.

6 Methodology

As opposed to the other methods for gathering lexical items, Dictionary Day is an attempt to gather the entire speech community at one time.[6] For reasons that are obvious this is not feasible in most field situations but is fully possible when the entire speech

---

[5]The name and the basic idea was first suggested by Dr. Jack Martin based on his collaboration with an American Indian speech community.

[6]It should be mentioned that Bowern (2008) states in passing that working in small groups was beneficial for collaborative reasons I will also mention for a larger group setting.

community is both small and local to the field site, and as will be seen this presents unique benefits that cannot be gained in much larger speech communities. The speech community is arranged in a circle, allowing each member full access to the conversation. The linguist is also a part of this circle as both physically and symbolically an equal part of the collaboration.

Figure 3: Dictionary Day

If the speech community meets one day a week, they are given the entire week to think about and discuss among themselves what they would like to be a part of their dictionary. By the time the linguist arrives on Dictionary Day, the topic will usually be selected already by the community. If this is not the case, the linguist can suggest topics that are appropriate to the speech community, allowing the community to determine whether they would like to proceed with the topic suggested.

Once a topic is suggested, the community members are asked to spontaneously suggest items for the dictionary. This will only have to be done once: the community will not need much prodding to suggest items in the future. With each topic the community members will discuss among themselves not only the appropriateness of the lexical item but also what forms to include in the dictionary. The linguist will then transcribe this form and use their linguistic expertise to identify relevant information about it for the sake of the dictionary, fulfilling their prescribed role of linguistic consultant.

An additional list of lexical items should be kept by the linguist with the community's permission. In this dictionary will be all the items that were controversial, noting the controversy surrounding the item and later, with help of the audiovisual record, what led to the disagreement. It will be this information that will shed light on the folklinguistics of the speech community as will be discussed further below.

All sessions should be recorded audio-visually, preferably from at least two angles if possible to capture all the community members. The audio component will rely on microphones with wide ranges in order to capture the spontaneous speech of the community members. For this reason microphone stands are essential: not only will the community start to speak more spontaneously without the constant reminder of a microphone that a linguist pointing at them would entail, but it is also impossible for a linguist to use a single microphone to capture all of the spontaneous interactions of the speech community. Although the linguist will be transcribing the dictionary on the spot and writing dense metadata about the session, it is these recordings that will reveal some of the missing cultural information the speaker does not know about the language ecology of the field site as will be explained below.

7 Implications

From an ethical standpoint, this method is ideal. The problem with the other methodologies is that they rely on the linguist to make all of the important decisions regarding what will go into the dictionary. As discussed above, if the linguist uses a predetermined list, the dictionary in effect becomes his or her work with the speech community only serving as informants rather than consultants of the project. Since current ethical guidelines call for a collaborative effort, the collaboration should not only extend to working *with* community members but also where possible to essentially work *for* them as well. It is worth stating that the majority of a language documentation has traditionally been to the benefit of the linguist as opposed to the speech community. This is one small way that the community itself is able to direct the documentation of their own language.

From a purely linguistic perspective, this method also alleviates most of the problems of the aforementioned methods. The question of how to elicit lexical items thus becomes moot. Instead of wondering how to elicit such items from the Swadesh list as 'louse' or 'I', the speech community will suggest items, negating any need for the linguist to invent idiosyncratic ways to elicit lexical items. Also, the problem of speakers not knowing a lexical item is no longer relevant as well. As Bowern (2008) notes, having multiple speakers during a session is beneficial in that speakers will be able to prompt each other on certain items that are little known among the speech community. This will alleviate the pressure on the speakers to perform for the linguist and will instead merely require the speaker to speak when comfortable, thus not endangering the linguist's relationship with individual speakers.

Another added benefit of this method is that disagreements among speakers are no longer in the hands of the linguist. As mentioned above, navigating discrepancies among speakers using a prescribed list falls on the linguist, since the linguist is meeting speakers one at a time. Thus, if one speaker disagrees with another, the linguist must determine which speaker's item is suitable for the dictionary. This could cause a rift between the linguist and those speakers' items that were left out of the dictionary, since it is the linguist who determines the veracity of each item. If the decision is left to the community, this no longer becomes a problem. From a practical standpoint, it is also incumbent on the linguist working with individual speakers to determine what constitutes a representative sample. Field manuals mention translating and backtranslating as a way of policing data, but they fail to mention just how many times it is required before an item is acceptable to add to the dictionary, leaving the choice to each individual linguist. Such an unsystematic approach could lead to idiosyncratic data, a situation often found when dealing with older language data. This linguistic policing of data is no longer the job of the linguist but falls onto the speech community, the group that has a better knowledge of the language and the idiosyncrasies that come with it.

Disagreements, however, are also important for linguistic information that is normally unavailable to a linguist working with a new speech community one member at a time. Through disagreements among the speech community, the linguist can glean sociolinguistic information about the language. During a heated debate during Dictionary Day, two groups formed, arguing about which lexical item was most appropriate for the language. Both sides claimed the other was wrong, and neither was willing to give any ground. Through mediation among other members of the speech community, a form was selected for their dictionary. My dictionary of the language, however, has both, because the two groups that were arguing belonged to different age groups: the age-mates of one group were arguing with the age-mates of the other. Though currently unprovable, this suggests that there may be a generational difference linguistically that I may have not seen if I had approached each member one at a time. During another session, the leader of the speech community suggested an item, and everyone automatically supported the item due to the speaker's prestige. One speaker, however, disagreed, telling me privately that another form was preferable. This form turned out to be an extension of a morphological pattern that I had not seen previously. Without this quiet reaction from a member normally not vocal, I would not have seen the pattern. In this way, through various spontaneous disagreements over otherwise uninteresting lexical items, I was able to discover both sociolinguistic data as well as a linguistic pattern I would not have been able to see previously.

One major benefit of Dictionary Day that has thus far been assumed is the idea of consensus among speakers. Using traditional methods, consensus is a matter of the linguist determining just how many members are necessary to constitute a representation of the entire language. When working with a small speech community, this can be done by speaking to each community member individually, but, as mentioned, disagreements must be navigated somehow by the linguist. By bringing the entire community together, however, consensus can be built among the community itself. By discussing items individually among themselves, they are literally forming a consensus for each item one by one. Verification is done on the spot without any need to recheck most items individually. When a major dispute occurs, however, it becomes necessary to approach individual members of the community to determine what constitutes speaker differences. This, however, is only limited to major disputes, whereas the traditional method requires rechecking every item. In short, actual consensus among the community can be reached by having the entire community present at one time as opposed to choosing a number of speakers to individually confirm lexical items.

Finally, from a practical standpoint, Dictionary Day saves both time and resources. Instead of having to allocate the beginning of each day to checking and rechecking various lexical items speaker by speaker, the linguist can use one day a week to go over the same amount of words while freeing up the rest of the week to work on other things. Since each lexical item is verified at the time of its suggestion, no additional time is required, and more lexical items can be elicited quickly and efficiently. Also, whatever the linguist deems appropriate in terms of compensation to the community will be used towards other things besides gathering lexical items, a boon to the linguist who may have personal goals in mind in the field.

Dictionary Day thus solves the problems presented by the traditional method of gathering lexical items. Through real collaboration with the speech community, the linguist is not only ethically interacting with the community but also doing it in a way that that benefits his or her own research goals by freeing up additional resources. More importantly, the idiosyncrasies of the data can be worked out in a group setting without the linguist becoming the arbitrator. The linguist may also discover language patterns that would not be visible when speaking to only a single member of the community, a help to the field linguist who is documenting a language that has not been analyzed previously.

8 Problems

When compared to methods that require the linguist to choose topics that speakers then supply lexical items for, Dictionary Day is preferable in all respects. However, when compared to the use of prescribed lists or stimulus kits, Dictionary Day has a major drawback, namely synergy among theorists, typologists, and field linguists. As previously mentioned, by using a Swadesh list, field linguists are supplying comparative linguists with data that they themselves cannot obtain. Also, by using stimulus kits, the field linguist is no longer supplying theorists and typologists with the same kind of crosslinguistic data. Although language documentation is itself becoming an independent field with its own goals, it is still preferable for documentarians to work with other linguists rather than isolate themselves in their subfield. A common refrain among documentarians is that it is not their job to orient their documentation around prescribed data collection methods by theorists and typologists. It is also a common refrain among documentarians of understudied languages that their work is often ignored by those same theorists and typologists that they themselves refuse to work with. By building a documentation collaboratively with the speech community, the data gathered becomes idiosyncratic in that it may not fulfill any needs of other linguists due to the random sampling of data in the field. In this way, Dictionary Day further exacerbates this problem by not only not limiting the data to prescribed areas of interest to other linguists but also by possibly failing to address such areas at all.

It is, however, worth noting that many field linguists choose to use a Swadesh list not due to any concern with other linguists' interests but due to not contemplating an alternative, and it is very common for fieldwork to go unnoticed regardless of the field linguist's intentions to the contrary. These are much larger problems than one methodology could possibly address, but it is worth mentioning those areas where the methodology fails to bridge the gap between documentarians and other linguists. For this reason, Dictionary Day should be used in collaboration with more traditional methods. A simple way of addressing this issue is to add Swadesh list items whenever possible to Dictionary Day itself when the community allows. Stimulus kits could also be added, though practically it seems out of place in the context of lexical item elicitation. Whenever possible, both traditional methods and Dictionary Day should be used side-by-side in order to not only address the problems of the former but also to account for the problems with latter. In this way, the documentarian can work with other linguists while not compromising the collaborative goals of the documentation.

9 Conclusion

Dictionary Day is a way for a field linguist to work collaboratively with a speech community as a whole in situations where such a collaboration is feasible. Considering the concern of documentarians with the ethics of fieldwork, such a speech community-driven collaboration is preferable, since it gives the agency to the community as opposed to the linguist who has traditionally not only had all of the power but mostly uses such power to guide the documentation in the direction of his or her own research interests. Although direct elicitation is making a comeback (Matthewson 2004), allowing speakers to spontaneously suggest lexical items reduces the problems of elicitation such as data reliability. It also benefits the data collection by not only offering a different mechanism for dealing with disputes among community members but also using such moments to gain insights into the language itself. Consensus is thus built among the entire speech community and not left to the linguist to determine what arbitrary number constitutes speech community consensus. Practically, it also saves time in the field for furthering the documentation in other ways while the linguist is in the field.

Problematically, though, Dictionary Day fails to account for linguists who need cross-linguistic data. By focusing solely on what the community chooses to do, the field linguist is not feeding more new and interesting data into the comparative, theoretical, and typological discussion that a Swadesh list or stimulus kit would. For this reason, Dictionary Day should be used in collaboration with other methods whenever possible. The community's wishes must come first, but the linguist still has an obligation to the field if he or she hopes to address such issues as the absence of understudied languages in linguistic theory. Although documentarians and other linguists sometimes have disputes about the exhaustiveness of linguistic typology and theory, the impetus is on the documentarian to enter the discussion as well. By combining both methods, the field linguist can find a way to bridge the divide between documentation and theory.

Bryan D. Gelles

Acknowledgements

This research was made possible by a grant from the Endangered Languages Documentation Programme (SG0199).

References

Bowerman, Melissa & Eric Pederson. 1992. Topological relations picture series. In Stephen C. Levinson (ed.), *Space stimuli kit 1.2*, 51. Nijmegen: Max Planck Institute for Psycholinguistics.

Bowern, Claire. 2008. *Linguistic fieldwork: A practical guide.* New York: Palgrave.

Chafe, Wallace L. (ed.). 1980. *The pear stories: Cognitive, cultural, and linguistic aspect of narrative production (Advances in discourse processes).* Santa Barbara: Praeger.

Chelliah, Shobhana & Willem de Reuse. 2011. *Handbook of descriptive linguistic fieldwork.* New York: Springer.

Haviland, John Beard. 2006. Documenting lexical knowledge. In Jost Gippert, Nikolaus P. Himmelmann & Ulrike Mosel (eds.), *Essentials of language documentation*, 129–162. Berlin: Mouton de Gruyter.

Hill, Deborah. 2012. One community's post-conflict response to a dictionary project. *Language Documentation and Conservation* 6. 273–281.

Matthewson, Lisa. 2004. On the methodology of semantic fieldwork. *International Journal of American Linguistics* 70. 369–415.

Mosel, Ulrike. 2004. Dictionary making in endangered speech communities. In Peter Austin (ed.), *Language documentation and description, Endangered Languages Project*, 39–54. London: School of Oriental & African Studies.

Ring, J. Andrew. 2006. *We have no one to sing our songs: Concerns of an African elder.* Presented at the International Workshop on the Documentation and Description of GTM Languages.

Swadesh, Morris. 1955. Towards greater accuracy in lexicostatistic dating. *International Journal of American Linguistics* 21. 121–137.

Vaux, Bert, Justin Cooper & Emily Tucker. 2007. *Linguistic field methods.* Eugene: Wipf & Stock.

Chapter 8

Language endangerment in Southwestern Burkina: A tale of two Tiefos

Abbie Hangtan-Sonko

Most of the thirty or so small-population languages of southwestern Burkina Faso are still reasonably viable in spite of the spread of Jula as the dominant regional vernacular. An unusual case is Tiefo, which is really two distinct but closely related and geographically contiguous Gur languages. One, here dubbed Tiefo-N, was spoken in the villages of Noumoudara and Gnanfongo (Nyafogo). The other, Tiefo-D, was spoken in the nearby village cluster of Dramandougou. Several other ethnically Tiefo villages in the zone had already been completely Jula-ised by the mid-20th Century. Tiefo-N is moribund (a handful of ageing semi-speakers in Gnanfogo, none in Noumoudara), the villagers having gone over to Jula. By contrast, Tiefo-D is in a relatively comfortable bilingual relationship to Jula and is still spoken to some extent even by children, though everyone also speaks Jula. This paper clarifies the relationship between Tiefo-N and Tiefo-D and addresses the question why the two languages have had such different fates.

1 Tiefo

Tiefo (pronounced [čɛfɔ]) is an important ethnic group in southwestern Burkina Faso. There are some 20 villages that still consider themselves ethnically Tiefo. The core is constituted by the villages of Noumoudara, Gnanfogo, and Dramandougou,[1] the latter two being really clusters of several distinct physical settlements. This core is located directly on (in the case of Noumoudara) or to the east of the highway from Bobo Dioulasso to Banfora. There are other Tiefo villages scattered around, including one to the west of Bobo Dioulasso (on the road to Orodara) and others east and southeast of the core.[2]

Tiefo belongs to the large Gur language family, which dominates much of Burkina Faso (including the large-population Mooré language of the Mossi ethnicity) and spreads westward into parts of Ghana, Niger, Togo, Benin, and Nigeria. Manessy (1982), who

---

[1]Alternative spellings are Numudara, Nyafogo, and Daramandougou or Daramandugu.
[2]The village of Tiefora, east of Banfora on the road to Sideradougou and Gaouwa, is not far from Dramandougou, but in spite of its name it is apparently not Tiefo ethnically.

Abbie Hangtan-Sonko. Language endangerment in Southwestern Burkina: A tale of two Tiefos. In Jason Kandybowicz, Travis Major, Harold Torrence & Philip T. Duncan (eds.), *African linguistics on the prairie: Selected papers from the 45th Annual Conference on African Linguistics*, 117–132. Berlin: Language Science Press. DOI:10.5281/zenodo.1251722

worked out the genetic sub-groupings within Gur, examined unpublished Tiefo data from André Prost and concluded that Tiefo constituted its own subgroup, with no especially close relatives.

The published descriptive material on Tiefo primarily includes Kerstin Winkelmann's invaluable monograph (in German) on Tiefo-D Winkelmann 1998). It consists of a descriptive reference grammar (emphasising phonology and morphology) and a basic lexicon. Winkelmann was part of a German-staffed project on Gur languages and cultures that was active in the 1990's but has now disappeared due to retirements of senior personnel and career switches by Winkelmann and others. Her fieldwork was carried out in Dramandougou, but she also did brief survey work (core lexicon and a little morphology) on Tiefo-N.

Winkelmann commented that Tiefo-N, even during her fieldwork period (1990–94), was at a much more advanced state of decline than Tiefo-D. She was able to elicit a little data from two elderly men in Noumoudara and somewhat more from semi-speakers in Gnanfogo. The Tiefo-N lexical material was included, alongside Tiefo-D data, in her lexicon. She calculated cognate counts for the Swadesh 100-word list between Dramandougou and either Noumoudara or Gnafongo in the 75–77 percentage range, with cognates partially disguised by sound changes and grammatical differences. She stated flatly that Tiefo-D was not understood in either of the Tiefo-N communities.[3] On the other hand, there was good inter-comprehension between Noumoudara and Gnafongo. A reasonable conclusion is that Tiefo-D and Tiefo-N are distinct languages using normal linguistic (as opposed to political) criteria.

Given Winkelmann's description of the dire language situation in Gnanfogo in the early 1990's, I was rather surprised to find some speakers in Tiefo-N in that village when I arrived in the Bobo Dioulasso area about a decade later in 2012. In retrospect, it may be that Winkelmann slightly underestimated the state of Tiefo-N in Gnafongo during her brief stay there, in part because of a misunderstanding of nominal plural formation. She stated that Gnafongo informants had difficulties producing such plurals, which a reader could understand as implying that the language was only imperfectly remembered by a few semi-speakers. It turns out, however, that Tiefo-N pluralises many nouns by lengthening the final vowel, i.e. singular ...Cv1 becomes ...Cv1v1. This corresponds to the productive Tiefo-D plural with -r followed by a copy of the stem-final vowel, i.e. ...Cv1 becomes ...Cv1-rv1. Evidently Gnafongo Tiefo-N lost the *r and the remaining identical vowels coalesced into a long vowel, a phonetically subtle pluralisation process that could be missed during short-term fieldwork by a linguist who was not primed to look for it.

Given the urgency of the language situation and the lack of substantial documentation of Tiefo-N, I did some 5 months fieldwork with elderly Gnafongo speakers between August 2013 and the following January. Subsequently, Jeffrey Heath collected flora-fauna terminology for Tiefo-N and local Jula in Gnafongo.[4] In order to illustrate some of the

---

[3] "Die in den beiden weiteren untersuchten Dörfern gesprochenen Cɛfɔ-Dialekte weichen ganz erheblich von dem von Daramandugu ab. Weder in Nyafogo noch in Numudara ist das Daramandugu-Cɛfɔ verstehbar" (Winkelmann 1998: 5).

[4] Aminata Ouattara, a Burkina linguistics student of ethnic Tiefo origin, was also continuing fieldwork on Tiefo-N as of early 2015.

true consequences of language contact, a greatly misunderstood phenomenon in West Africa, I show the examples of two varieties of one moribund language. I argue that our methodology is no longer data driven, and that because we have a certain set of ideals in place as to what happens when one language comes into contact with another, we are blind to the real circumstances. Instead of mourning so-called "language death" (Nettle & Romaine 2000; Price 1984), we should be celebrating the diversity of new mixed languages which are born when speakers come into contact with one another. Through an examination of different sociological, historical, and geographic paths, we see that one language has become in fact two. However, without an interdisciplinary methodology that starts from the ground up, our theoretical footing will be unsound and vice versa. In order to illustrate the differences between the presently existing Tiefo varieties, and because there has been such little attention paid to Tiefo-N, I present an overview and comparison of the major grammatical features of Tiefo-N and Tiefo-D. The main phonological features are illustrated in §2 and the morphology in §3. §3.4 discusses the differences in the pronominal (which in turn is related to the tense/aspect) systems of the two varieties, discussed in the following section, 3.5.

Then, §5 provides an exploration of the reasons thus far provided in the literature concerning the different fates of the Tiefo villages. While geographical and sociolinguistic reasons have been referenced in the past, the current discussion explores the historical causes of the divergent dialects.

2 Phonology

Tiefo-N and Tiefo-D have similar consonant inventories: stops plus palatal affricates /p b t d tʃ dʒ k g kp gb/, nasals /m n ɲ ŋ ŋm/, fricatives /f s ɣ ʕ/, glottal /ʔ/, and nonnasal sonorants /w l r j/. Note the distinction between the voiced pharyngeal /ʕ/ (cf. Arabic) and glottal /ʔ/.

Table 1: Tiefo consonantal inventory.

	Labial	Alveolar	Palatal	Velar	Pharyngeal	Glottal
Plosive	p b	t d		k g		ʔ
Nasal	m ŋm	n	ɲ	ŋ		
Fricative	f	s	(ʃ)	ɣ	ʕ	
Affricate	kp gb	c j				
Approximant	w	l	y			
Trill/tap		r				

Absent from the consonantal inventory of both languages are several consonants reconstructed for Proto-Gur (Naden 1989): voiced implosives /ɓ ɗ ʄ/, voiced palatal stop /ɟ/, voiced affricate /dʒ/, and labiodental fricative /v/.

Tiefo-N and Tiefo-D likewise have similar vowel inventories, which are shared with other languages of the zone. There are seven vowel qualities, including high /i u/, low /a/, and two pairs of mid-height vowels, [+ATR] /e o/ and [-ATR] /ɛ ɔ/. The high and low vowels are ATR-neutral and may combine with either type of mid-height vowel. In Tiefo-D (Winkelmann 1998: 20, 23) but not Tiefo-N, phonemes /i u/ have optional [-ATR] phonetic variants in words with a following [-ATR] mid-height vowel. Proto-Gur is reconstructed with a ten-vowel system, including [±ATR] distinctions in high and low as well as mid-height vowels.

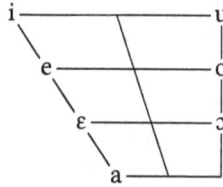

Figure 1: Tiefo vocalic inventory.

Tiefo-N and Tiefo-D also have the same three tone levels. High tones are marked by an acute accent [á], low tones by a grave accent [à]. Mid tones are written either without an accent (Winkelmann 1998) or more explicitly with a macron [ā].

In spite of the nearly identical phonemic inventories between the two languages, many actual pairs of Tiefo-N and Tiefo-D cognate words are disguised by phonological differences. Some examples are in Table 2, which pools data from Winkelmann (KW) and myself (AH). Correspondences that occur in more than one set even in this small corpus are Tiefo-D glottal stop or zero for Tiefo-N medial [g], Tiefo-D [c] for Tiefo-N [s], and Tiefo-D [d] for Tiefo-N [ʒ, j].

Table 2: Tiefo cognates.

Tiefo-D (KW)	Tiefo-N (KW)	Tiefo-N (AH)	Gloss
blaʔa ~ bla	bárágà ~ bálágà	bārāʔá	'river'
dráⁿ	dáragá	dárá	'home'
brà(ʔà)	bàgàle, bàrài	bàɣàʔè	'hair'
buɔⁿ	bɔʔɔⁿ, bɔɔⁿ	būɔ ⁿ	'dog'
ceʔe	serege	sérííⁿ	'skin'
cicí	sisiu	ʃíʃíʔĩ	'urine'
cùru	suru	sūsúⁿ	'millet cake'
dè	ʒàga, yèà	jéjāʔā	'sun'
dɛ	ʒɔ	ndɛ	'elder brother'

3 Morphology

Morphological features found in Tiefo-N but not in Tiefo-D are a definite prefix (§3.1), a specific set of plural suffixes (Section3.2), and an ablaut-like system of adjective-noun agreement (§3.3).

3.1 Definite prefix

The dialect of Tiefo-N in Gnafongo has what I will call a definite prefix (but see below for qualms about this categorisation). It has three variants depending on the dominant vowel of the stem: [e-] before nouns with an [e] vowel in the stem, [o-] before nouns with a back vowel [o ɔ u], and [a-] before nouns with [a] or [ɛ] vowel in the stem. Examples are in Table 3. The stem 'moon' irregularly has [a-] instead of expected [e-].

Table 3: Tiefo definite.

Noun (Tiefo-N, Def-Sg)	Gloss
è-kḗʔē̄ⁿ	'spoon'
è-jōē̄ⁿ	'neck'
ē-sāè	'ground'
ò-ŋōʕō	'mosquito'
ō-fláɲō	'baobab'
ò-sīɔ̄ⁿ	'salt'
ò-ɲū	'water'
à-bītɛ́ʔɛ̀	'leaf'
à-fērēé	'moon'
ā-kɛ́rɛ̄ ɛ̄	'hand'
ā-fīyāʕā	'field'

The definite marker is generally optional in the singular but in some cases is obligatory in the plural. However, when the noun is followed by a quantifier or by an adjective, the definite prefix is omitted. This suggests that the "definite" prefix functions in part to indicate that the noun is free of modifiers.

This is more clearly the case in Tiefo-D. (Winkelmann 1998: 132) describes the Tiefo-D prefix [e-], infrequently [o-], as obligatory in citation forms. She confirms for Tiefo-D that it vanishes in the presence of a determiner (possessor, demonstrative).

3.2 Plural suffixes

Proto-Gur has been reconstructed as having a complex system of noun class markers in the form of paired singular-plural combinations Naden (1989), along the lines of other Niger-Congo families including Bantu. Many extant Gur languages still have class suffixes, and some have prefixes as well (Miehe et al. 2012).

In addition to lengthening of the final vowel (mentioned above), a number of other singular/plural relationships occur in Tiefo-N. Examples are shown in Table 4.

Table 4: Tiefo-N plural suffixes.

	Singular	Plural	Gloss
a.	nāmi	ō-nāmī-jō	'child'
	yō nāmí	yō nāmí-jō	'fruit'
	ɲō	ō-ɲí-jō	'person'
	bī	bī-jō	'baby'
	ŋmāʕa bí	ŋmāʕa bí-jō	'star'
b.	cómī-ī	ɲ̄ -cómī	'bird'
	ɲómī-ī	ɛ̄ -ɲómī	'toe'
c.	yē	yē-ʔé	'year'
	jāá bɔ̄ ^{n}	jāá bɔ̄ -ɔ̄ ^{n}	'girl'
d.	gbé-ē^n	gbē	'stool'
e.	ʒɔ́wē ^{n}	ɛ́-ʒɔ́wī^n	'neck'
f.	fēreʔé	fērē ʔē	'moon'
g.	dɔ̄ -jɛ̄	dɔ̄ -rɔ̄	'man'

There are also some nouns that appear to have no singular-plural difference, such as [búgúnɛ] 'beans (variety)', either because of recent morphological loss or because these nouns do not lend themselves to individuation.

Winkelman reported a Tiefo-D plural /-O/ (by which she indicates an archiphoneme representing either for [o] or [ɔ] depending on the [ATR] class of the stem), though for animates only. This corresponds to the [-jō] (always after i) in (4a), though often not in the same words across the Tiefo varieties. Some of the Tiefo-N glosses in (4a) are inanimate ('star', 'fruit'), but these are compounds including 'child' or 'baby', e.g. 'tree-child' = 'fruit'. The stem 'man', (4g) is a rare case where Tiefo-N has a plural [-rV] (with copied vowel quality), the productive plural in Tiefo-D. Other Tiefo-N singular/plural patterns (4b-f) lack known Tiefo-D matches, and are difficult to connect to reconstructed inventories of Proto-Gur noun class markers listed by Naden (1989).

3.3 Adjectival harmony

In Tiefo-N, the final vowels of certain adjectives harmonise with the vowel of the definite prefix of the modified noun. Consider the forms for harmonising 'black' in examples (1-2) and for nonharmonising 'big' (2-4). The vowel quality of the prefixes on 'house' and 'man' match that of the final-vowel of 'black'. This may reflect an archaic suffixal agreement pattern, creating a construction of the type *[CLASS-noun adjective-CLASS]. Synchronically it could be described as a terminal ablaut (i.e. mutation of the final vowel into another quality). There is no similar mutation of the adjective 'big', which has an invariant shape in (2-4).

(1) wà-wūʕú jōb-á
DEF   hut   black

'the black house'

(2) ò-dɔ̀ɛ̀ jób-ō
DEF   man black

'the black man'

(3) à-wūʕú sãg⁻ bānāʔà
DEF   hut big

'the big house'

(4) ò-dɔ̀ɛ̀ sãg⁻ bānāʔà
DEF   man big

'the big man'

3.4 Pronouns

The subject personal pronouns of Tiefo-N are those in Table 5. The singular but not plural forms vary depending on the aspect (perfective/imperfective) of the clause (imperfective includes progressive). The basic Tiefo-D forms (Winkelmann 1998: 140) are shown for comparison; specifically imperfective ('present') and negative Tiefo-D combinations are omitted. Tiefo-D distinguishes animacy in the 3SG, and also has uses the distant demonstrative [bó] as a discourse-anaphoric 3SG pronoun.

Table 5: Tiefo pronouns.

	Tiefo-N Imperfective	Perfective	Tiefo-D
1SG	ɲí	ān	no
1PL	é	é	ʔejuò
2SG	mì	m	mo
3PL	nā	nā	buò
3SG	kā ō	n ō	ʔɔ̃ⁿ (anim), ʔà (inan), bó (anaph) ʔò
3PL	ɲí	ān	no

For Tiefo-N, 1SG subject is exemplified examples (5-6), 1PL in (7-8).

(5) ɲí   wɔʕɔ bè kú
    1SG.IPFV PROG come today
    'I am coming today.'

(6) n bàʔ jànā
    1SG come yesterday
    'I came yesterday.'

(7) é wɔʕɔ bè kú
    1PL PROG come today
    'We are coming today.'

(8) é bàʔ jànā
    1PL come yesterday
    'We came yesterday.'

Unlike Tiefo-D, Tiefo-N does not currently distinguish animacy or anaphoricity (e.g. reflexives) in the 3SG pronoun. This might be due to recent grammatical simplification, and the occasional use of Jula 3SG pronouns shows that language contact has impacted the pronominal system.

3.5 Verbal aspectual inflection

Verbal aspectual morphology in Tiefo-N is more intricate than nominal or pronominal morphology. The main opposition is between imperfective and perfective (sometimes called 'continuous' and 'neutral', respectively).

In one verb class, the imperfective is unsuffixed while the perfective is marked by a low- or mid-toned suffix -ra ~-la Table 6. It can be nasalised to -na, see 'arrive' (Table 6, row (d)).

Table 6: Tiefo aspectual affixation.

	Imperfective	Perfective	Gloss
a.	jē̄	jé-rā̄	'enter'
b.	jè	jē̄-rà	'walk'
c.	bĭέ	bĭέ̄ -rà	'farm'
d.	dā̃	dā-nà	'arrive'
e.	dīò	dīō-là	'sell'

Several other verbs show ablaut-like vocalic mutations, in some cases along with other internal changes or affixes. Two multiply attested patterns are vowel to [a] (row (a) in Table 7) and [a] to [e/ε] (row (b) in Table 7). Mutation types attested once are in (row (c) in Table 7).

Table 7: Tiefo aspectual mutation.

	Imperfective	Perfective	Gloss
a.	sè	sá	leave/go
	bè	bāʔ	come
	bē	b-là	tire
	díʔī	díā	eat
	dōʔò	dāà	plant
	dōrōʕò	dárāʕā	buy
b.	ɲānā	ɲéné	stop/stand
	náʔā	nɛ́nɛ̄	wash (clothing)
	dárāà	dɛ̄ rɛ̀ɛ̀	rip
	bārá	bɛ̄rɛ̀	sweep
	jāʕà	jɛ̄ gɛ̀	break
c.	ɲ-à	ɲ-ū	drink
	bó	bwɛ̄	tie

An important difference between the two Tiefo varieties is that Tiefo-N has a preverbal morpheme wɔ ʕɔ that marks progressive aspect. No similar preverbal progressive or imperfective morpheme is reported for Tiefo-D. It is possible, however, that the Tiefo-N form is archaic, reflecting a proto-form *bo 'be' Manessy (1982).

4 Influence from Jula

The data in 6 consist of verbs which are suffixed with [-rV] or allomorphs [l]~[n] in an aspectual form known as 'neutral' or perfective. The suffix may be a borrowing from Jula since the perfective suffix in Jula is [-ra] with allomorph [-la]. An example illustrating the [-rV/lV] suffix in Gnanfongo Tiefo is the verb 'hide', borrowed directly from Jula as [dūgū], 'hidden' [dūgū-là]. Many of the verbs in this category are probable borrowings from Jula, even though a neutral suffix [-da/ra/ta] is attested in other Gur languages. However, according to Naden (1989), most verbal markers are treated as particles rather than affixes in other Gur languages. The most widely marked inflectional category in Gur languages is expressed through a contrast between the continuous (imperfective) and a form described as 'neutral'. Therefore, the neutral suffix in Tiefo is likely related to the particle found in other Gur languages, but possibly has been reanalysed in Gnanfongo Tiefo as a perfective suffix on Jula borrowings.

According to lexical comparisons between Tiefo and other Gur languages by Manessy (1982), there is but a mere 28 out of 435 correspondence, 20 percent. With sample correspondences shown in Table 8, between the data gathered by the author from Gnanfongo Manessy's (1982) from Dramandougou and surrounding Gur languages, we do see, however limited, some strong evidence for a a related source.

Table 8: Correspondences between Tiefo and Gur languages (Manessy 1982: 146)

Tiefo (AH)	Tiefo (GM)	Viemo	Doyose	Gan	Lobi	Dyan	Kulango	Loron	Gloss
pĩí	pini	pinyɔ	pĩíse				pĩí	pinigu, pininyu	'excrement'
kãʕà	kaʔa	kaasɔ	kaase	kasa					'meat'
sáã́	sãã	saasi	-sãã	-sãã			-sãã, -sãzi	-sã	'three'
ɲĕréẽ	ɲinde			ɲɛɲɛ	ɲeɲa	ɲeɲa	ɲugo		'breast'
fẽrẽʕé	feregi			ferge	filiki				'moon'
nãfaʕɔ́	donu			doni	doɳko				'slave'
ɲã̃	ɲã						ɲã		'give'
yãá	ya						yɛrɛ		'woman'
sãʕè	sari				siru			sáákɔ	'earth'
bẽʕé	bẽ				bɔnə			bẽ	'wilderness'
káʕá ɲĩn	kaane	kannɔ							'tooth'
ɡbã̃ á	bɔ, baa	baawɔ		bana					'sheep'

Manessy gives three hypotheses for how non-Gur roots are found in Tiefo: Tiefo should be placed within a separate branch of Gur, certain words are borrowed from an unknown Gur language, or the source of the borrowing is non-Gur, possibly Mande. If language contact from Jula were the dividing factor, one would expect there to be clear borrowings from Jula into Tiefo. If the Jula language is an influence, it would be apparent in the lexicon.

Among plant names, we find evidence for a sustained symbiosis between Jula and even Tiefo-N. For example, Heath recently recorded flora-fauna terms in Gnanfogo, both in Tiefo-N and in the local Jula. Quite a few of these terms are phrasal, and the Tiefo-N and local Jula often share the phrasing. Some plant names are in Table 9.

These correspondences, though limited to natural species terms, are indicative of a broader pattern of calquing, the effect of which is develop a local Tiefo-ized Jula. Outside the core Tiefo area, this must have the same general sociolinguistic function of marking speakers as Tiefo, as we observe with familiar ethnically-tinged English varieties (Yinglish, Spanglish, and the like).

While we do see some evidence of borrowing from Jula in both dialects of Tiefo in the Table 10, according to comparisons between my data and Winkelmann's shown in Table 11, most are like the second table, with 87 out of 185 core lexical items do not bear any resemblance between the two dialects, nor to Jula (based on my knowledge of Jula).

The evidence presented from the lexicon shows that Jula has not influenced either variety of Tiefo to the point that one would expect if the majority language were to be blamed for the loss of the minority language. Considering the long term contact of Jula with Tiefo, one would expect more of an influence on the lexicon than what is found. Further, the lexical differences between the two dialects, for the most part, cannot be

Table 9: Tiefo plant names.

Tiefo	Jula	Identification	Literal
sòy-pûŋ	lè-bíí^n	Acanthospermum hispidum	'pig-herb'
pô:ŋ-sà:^{n}-wi	bí:ŋ-ŋwání-tígi	Amaranthus spinosus	'herb-thorn-owner'
bàwá^n-sāní	sàmà-ŋwánì	Asparagus africanus	'elephant-thorn'
cò:-kú:^{n}	sùlà-fí^{n}sá^n	Cola cordifolia	'monkey-cashew.apple'
bàwá^n-dùrté	sàmá-tìsékàà-bé	Combretum nigricans	'elephant can't knock it down'
nàfɔ́yɔ́^{n}-bàkó-èllè-wí	jààtìgì-fáyá	Ficus thonningii	'host-kill'
blákè-póróŋ	sándé^n-wɔ̀rɔ̀sɔ́	Heeria insignis	'rain-sickle'
nɔ̀yɔ̀sì-dúy	nɔ̀yɔ̀sì-kúú	Heliotropium indicum	'chameleon-tail'
kà^{n}kóó^n-tòè	sòfàlì-túló	Leptadenia hastate	'donkey-ear'
bě y^n-jùsú^n	kòŋó-jèsé	Securidaca longepedunculata	'outback-wire'
só^n-bà^{n}flà-glá-yò	sò-tìgí-bà^{n}flà-bɔ	Senegalia macrostachya	'horseman-hat-take.off'
sèsèré-dúy	bàsà^n-kúù	Stachytarpheta indica	'agama-tail'
blákέ-flɔ̄	sándé^n-sìrà-yírí	Sterculia setigera	'hare's baobab fruit'
wámbíí-ʃìnàà	fárátá-débέ	Uapaca togolensis	'orphan-mat'
sìsàyà-dúrúŋ-tè-pô:ŋ	kámmélé-kóróbóo	clumpy grass sp.	'young.man-test-grass'

attributed to influence from Jula on either end of the dialect spectrum. The cause of the divergences within Tiefo and within Gur must have been triggered by another source, but it remains unknown.

Table 10: Potential borrowings from Jula into Tiefo.

Tiefo Dramandougou	Tiefo Gnanfongo	Jula	Gloss
gūglīká	kērē kīté	kɔtɛ	'snail'
blanà(-nɔ)	míɔ̃ nɔ̃	mali	'hippopotamus'
nāklɔ̃	mīɔ̃ nɔ̃	malo	'rice'
po-jenɔ̃ , poka	ō-dòsō	donso	'hunter'
ɲã	sɔ̃ ʕɔ́	so	'horse'
jũwéʔaɛ́	gānāʕà	galaji	'indigo'
dɔ̌	náfāʕō	jɔn	'slave'
jɔ̃ , jɔ̃ -rɔ̃	bíkā	jo	'fetish'
wòrò	dōʕōbíyō	wòro	'kola nuts'

Table 11: Cross-dialectal lexical non-concordance not due to Jula influence.

Tiefo Dramandougou	Tiefo Gnanfongo	Jula	Gloss
sú	dúrú	ɲinan	'mouse'
sègè	dúwī	dimi	'hurt'
sɔ́ʔɔ́, séʔɛ́	dūwɔ̌	cin	'sting'
sīglòʔó -ro	fáʕláī	suruku	'hyena'
ɠbɛ bà	fĩyāá	lana	'take'
pū́ɔ̃, poʔo	fĩyāʕā	kungo	'wilderness'
dè, bɛ-tɔʕɔ	fĩyáʕā	foro	'field'
diɛ̀	fĩyɔ̃	bugu	'multiply'
baʕa	fĩʕī	tɔmɔ	'pick up'
jũwéʔaɛ́	gānāʕà	galaji	'indigo'
sàk͡pè	kā kɔ́	fali	'donkey'

5 Why different fates?

The preceding discussion demonstrates that Tiefo-N and Tiefo-D are two distinct, though closely related languages. Why have they suffered such different fates?

Isolation? Perhaps Dramandougou (Tiefo-D) is more isolated than Gnanfongo and Noumoudara (Tiefo-N). Well, it is true that Noumoudara is directly on the Bobo Diolasso to Banfora highway, and this may have been the coup de grace factor for Tiefo-N in that village. But Gnanfongo and Dramadougou are both located in the same lowlands area southeast of a long escarpment that cuts them off from the highway. Both are reached from the highway with some difficulty, by 4x4 or a motorcycle, either by taking a southern route that avoids the cliffs or by winding one's way down a circuitous descent in a relatively benign part of the escarpment between Noumoudara and Gnanfongo. Government institutions (schools, clinics) are present in Gnanfongo and Dramandougou to about the same extent. They are equally "isolated".

Perhaps a vigorously expanding regional language had a more direct line of sight on Gnafongo than on Dramandougou due to some geographical quirk? The two candidates for "killer" languages (Nettle & Romaine 2000; Price 1984) would be French and Jula. Indeed it was once feared that French and English would give the same scorched earth treatment to African languages as English has given to the indigenous languages of Australia and North America. This has now been broadly debunked by Batibo (2005) and Mufwene (2009). In West Africa, even in sophisticated and heavily Gallicized coastal megalopolises like Dakar and Abidjan, French has developed symbiotic relationships with other languages rather than eliminating them, and new synthetic formations such as Nouchi and Urban Wolof are emerging. In villages far from the coast like Gnanfongo and Dramandougou, French is a minor factor in the sociolinguistic equation. Naden (1989: 141) makes the point that southwestern Burkina has historically been a "backwater" relatively unaffected by the outside world, from the late medieval Saharan trade routes to the present.

Jula is another matter. Southwestern Burkina is a linguistic mosaic of ancient Gur languages (Tiefo, Lobi, Viemo, Dogose, Turka, and others) with interspersed Mande languages like Bobo and Zuungo that date to the Mande expansion of the late Middle Ages. The Bambara-Jula-Mandinke dialect group, which is also Mande genetically, has become the linguistic juggernaut throughout southern Mali (Bamako, Segou), southwestern Burkina, and northern Cote d'Ivoire. Its spread in Burkina was spearheaded by merchants who made it into the lingua franca in markets and then in urban concentrations. The name of the biggest city southwestern Burkina, Bobo Dioulasso (i.e. Bobo-Jula-So), attests to the coexistence of Jula with other indigenous languages. If there is a killer language in the area, it is clearly Jula, not French.

However, there is no obvious geographical reason why Jula should have targeted Tiefo-N for extinction any more than Tiefo-D. Jula is the dominant interethnic vernacular in the entire region, extending deeply into neighbouring Cote d'Ivoire. If Dramandougou were more isolated than Gnanfongo, Jula might have had a more powerful foothold in the latter. But Dramandougou is no more isolated than Gnanfongo. Jula is spoken at least as second language by everyone in Dramandougou as well as Gnanfongo.

What about strategic self-interest as an explanation? An SIL-sponsored survey of the local situation does state that "Most Tiefo have abandoned their language in favour of Jula ... presumably as a result of a perceived social advantage to be gained by using Jula" (Berthelette & Berthelette 2001: 5). But self-interest should be just as pertinent to Tiefo-D as to Tiefo-N. As Showalter (2008) states in his survey of the languages of Burkina Faso, only two communities in the entire country replaced their languages with Jula, one being Tiefo-N and Lüpke & Storch counter such simplistic reasoning: "there is no evidence of which we are aware where the shift to another language (as opposed to maintaining it as a language in a multilingual repertoire) has yielded real socio-economic advantages" (Lüpke & Storch 2013: 286).

What about differential "prestige" as an explanation? Aside from the elusiveness of this concept,[5] the fact is that Tiefo ethnic pride is if anything stronger in the Tiefo-N than Tiefo-D area, and perhaps stronger there than in the other small-population ethnicities in the area between the proud, larger-population Bobo and Lobi. The background to this is that the Tiefo tribe was a feared military power until the turn of the 20th Century. To this day there is a Tiefo "chef de guerre" in Noumoudara, distinct from the regular political chief. He commands no battalions, but he does supervise a small military museum dedicated to the memory of an early chief named Amoro Ouattara. In this museum, visitors get guided tours recounting the great battles of the past and demonstrating (gently) the uses of the traditional weapons, shields, and torture equipment that are on display. It is not large, but it is more than the other small-population ethnicities in the area have.

In Africa and elsewhere, language coexistence (multilingualism) is the norm, not the exception. There is no zero-sum fight to the death among languages. Again (Mufwene 2009: 76): "Such a practice of language alternation is traditional to Africa and has sustained multilingualism, so much so that it takes a natural disaster to force whole villages to move and find themselves in situations where they have to shift to the host population's language."

The cataclysmic event that accelerated the decline of Tiefo was the military victory of the Jula leader Samori Touré over the Tiefo, followed by the slaughter of many Tiefo people in 1897. This is cited as the key event in the demise of the language by Hébert (1958), Le Moal (1980: 31), and Winkelmann (1998: 2). It is likely that the Tiefo-N villages who commanded the Tiefo forces were the principal victims.

Dramandougou, on the periphery and not centrally involved in military activity, appears to have already reached an accommodation with the Jula, resulting in a less confrontational relation, at the time of those hostilities. For that reason it was spared the brunt of the reprisals.

6 Conclusion

Despite the fact that there are only five speakers in the village of Gnanfongo, all in their 70's and 80's, the dialect of Tiefo differs from the neighbouring village, particularly in the lexicon. The differences between the two dialects of Tiefo cannot be due to Jula alone. In fact then, language contact, in addition to not "killing" a language, may not have as much influence as we think.

Languages, differing from the metaphors we like to invoke of species, rarely simply die out without a trace, rather, they converge into and diverge from one another. Speakers do not suddenly one day wake up and decide it will be advantageous to being speaking another language. The history of many countries in Africa and the world is volatile, with environmental and political factors influencing language to a greater degree than we may account for. The example of the Tiefo serves not only to illustrate that we are

---

[5]In the early days of American sociolinguistics, the core idea was that lower middle-class individuals sought to emulate the speech of the highest local socioeconomic class. But the data eventually forced recognition of, first, a kind of prestige in the lower echelons, and then another kind of prestige in the middle.

missing pieces in the history of the people, but also that we are ill equipped to gather those pieces given the framework we have been using.

Although the cause of the loss of the Tiefo language can with a fair amount of certainly be attributed to Samori Toure and his army of invaders, beyond that, the discrepancies between the existing Tiefo dialects which cannot be attributed to Jula remains a mystery. In summary, Tiefo shares some features of geographically neighbouring Gur languages but does not fit into any known branch of Gur. Further, the variety of Tiefo that remains in the lives of the five elderly speakers in Gnanfongo differs significantly from the more robust version of the language spoken in neighbouring Dramandougou.

Acknowledgements

This research is conducted as part of the project "Investigating the interaction of tone and syntax in the Bangime and the Dogon languages of Mali and Burkina Faso", funded by BCS-1263150 (2013–16), PI Jeffrey Heath. I am grateful to Jeffrey Heath, Friederike Lüpke, Marieke Martin, and Sophie Salffner for their contributions and support throughout the writing of this paper. I would also like to thank the two anonymous referees for their helpful comments.

References

Batibo, Herman M. 2005. *Language decline and death in Africa: Causes, consequences and challenges.* Clevedon: Multilingual Matters.

Berthelette, John & Carol Berthelette. 2001. *Sociolinguistic survey report for the Tíefo language.* Tech. rep. SIL International.

Hébert, Jean R. P. 1958. Une page d'histoire voltaïque: Amoro, chef des Tiefo. *Bulletin de l'I.F.A.N B* 20. 377–405.

Le Moal, Guy. 1980. *Nature et fonction des masques.*

Lüpke, Friederike & Anne Storch. 2013. *Repertoires and choices in African languages.* Berlin: Mouton De Gruyter.

Manessy, Gabriel. 1982. Materiaux linguistiques pour servir à l'histoire des populations du sud-ouest de la Haute Volta. *Sprache und Geschichte in Afrika* 4. 95–164.

Miehe, Gudrun, Ulrich Kleinewillinghöfer, Manfred von Roncador & Kerstin Winkelmann. 2012. Overview of noun classes in Gur (II)(revised and enlarged version). In Gudrun Miehe, Brigitte Reineke & Kerstin Winkelmann (eds.), *Noun class systems in Gur languages*, vol. 2, 5–37. Köln: Rüdiger Köppe.

Mufwene, Salikoko S. 2009. What Africa can contribute to understanding language vitality, endangerment, and loss. In Matthias Brenzinger & Anne-Maria Fehn (eds.), *Proceedings of the 6th World Congress of African Linguistics, Cologne, 17-21 August 2009*, 69–80. Cologne: Rüdiger Köppe Verlag.

Naden, Anthony J. 1989. Gur. In John Bendor-Samuel & Rhonda L. Hartell (eds.), *The Niger-Congo languages: A classification and description of Africa's largest language family*, 140–168. New York: University Press of America.

Nettle, Daniel & Suzanne Romaine. 2000. *Vanishing voices: The extinction of the world's languages*. Oxford: Oxford University Press.

Price, Glanville. 1984. *The language of Britain*. London: Edward Arnold.

Showalter, Stuart D. 2008. *Un profil du bilinguisme en dioula au sud-ouest du Burkina Faso*. Technical report, SIL International.

Winkelmann, Kerstin. 1998. *Die Sprache der Cefo von Daramandugu (Burkina Faso)*. Sonderforschungsbereich 268 an der JW Goethe-Universität.

Part III

Morphology and phonology

Chapter 9

Consonant substitution in child language (Ikwere)

Roseline I. C. Alerechi

University of Port Harcourt

The Ikwere language is spoken in four out of the twenty-three Local Government Areas (LGAs) of Rivers State of Nigeria, namely, Port Harcourt, Obio/Akpor, Emohua and Ikwerre LGAs. Like Kana, Kalabari and Ekpeye, it is one of the major languages of Rivers State of Nigeria used in broadcasting in the electronic media. The Ikwere language is classified as an Igboid language of the West Benue-Congo family of the Niger-Congo phylum of languages (Williamson 1988: 67, 71, Williamson & Blench 2000: 31). This paper treats consonant substitution in the speech of the Ikwere child. It demonstrates that children use of a language can contribute to the divergent nature of that language as they always strive for simplification of the target language. Using simple descriptive method of data analysis, the paper identifies the various substitutions of consonant sounds, which characterize the Ikwere children's utterances. It stresses that the substitutions are regular and rule governed and hence implies the operation of some phonological processes. Some of the processes are strengthening and weakening of consonants, loss of suction of labial implosives causing them to become labial plosives, devoicing of voiced consonants, etc. While some of these processes are identical with the adult language, others are peculiar to children, demonstrating the relationships between the phonological processes in both forms of speech. It is worthy of note that highlighting the relationships and differences will make for effective communication between children and adults.

1 Introduction

The Ikwere language is spoken in four out of the twenty-three Local Government Areas (LGAs) of Rivers State of Nigeria, namely, Port Harcourt, Obio/Akpor, Emohua and Ikwerre LGAs. Like Kana, Kalabari and Ekpeye, it is one of the major languages of Rivers State used in broadcasting in the electronic media (Alerechi 2007a: 1). Williamson (1988: 67, 71) classifies Ikwere as one of the Igboid group of languages as well as Igbo, Ekpeye, ogba, Echie, to mention but a few. Williamson & Blench (2000: 31) locate Igboid under the node of West Benue-Congo family of Niger-Congo phylum of languages. The

Roseline I. C. Alerechi. Consonant substitution in child language (Ikwere). In Jason Kandybowicz, Travis Major, Harold Torrence & Philip T. Duncan (eds.), *African linguistics on the prairie: Selected papers from the 45th Annual Conference on African Linguistics*, 135–155. Berlin: Language Science Press. DOI:10.5281/zenodo.1251724

Ikwere language comprises twenty-four divergent dialects, which are mutually intelligible. It is yet to develop a standard dialect. However, there are published works such as Donwa-Ifode & Ekwulo's (1987) *Ikwere Orthography, Tẹsitament Iikne* (a translated New Testament Bible), and some recent scholarly works in the language.

Some of the works like Williamson (1980), Donwa-Ifode & Faraclas (2001), among others, observe different realization of some phonological segments in Ikwere. In fact, Alerechi (2007a) specifically identified some phonological processes responsible for the different realizations of segments, which may have contributed to the divergent nature of the Ikwere language. Some of such processes are loss of suction of labial implosives causing them to become labial plosives, the spirantization (weakening) of labial and alveolar plosives to labial and alveolar fricatives, respectively, the voicing of alveolar fricatives, etc.

It is interesting to note that these studies are focused on the adult use of the Ikwere language to the neglect of the area concerning child language. This serves as a motivation for this paper. Given that the general trend for children is to change the sounds of the language in an attempt to use them, this paper is aimed at identifying such changes and consequently the phonological processes characteristic of Ikwere children aged 3 to 4 years. Following the assertion of Fromkin et al. (2003a: 358) that early phonological rules generally reflect natural phonological processes that occur in the adult (target) language, this paper further investigates if the phonological processes in child language are identical with those of the adult (target language).

This paper focuses on Ọdeegnu (Odgn), Ẹmowha (Emwh), Akpo, Aluu and Omuanwa (Omnw) dialects of Ikwere, an Igboid language spoken in Rivers State of Nigeria. Even though the sound substitution in child language involves both consonants and vowels, this paper specifically focuses on the substitution of consonants of the target language for those characteristic of the child's language.

1.1 Literature review

This section gives a brief review of literature in child language acquisition. It specifically treats the phonological development, phonological processes and outlining the target sounds.

1.2 Phonological development

Communication is a natural phenomenon to every human being. Thus, to enable children to communicate with others in their environment, they need to acquire the language. O'Grady et al. (2011: 361) state that the ability of children to produce speech sounds begins to emerge at around six months with the onset of babbling. Babbling enables the children to experiment with and begin to gain control over their vocal apparatus. It increases in frequency until the age of about twelve months, when the children begin to produce their first understandable words.

Scholars have investigated the order of acquisition of sounds by the children and some observed that among the earlier sounds are the back velar sounds [k]and [g], and front vowels like [a], [i] and [e]. Others recognize the bilabials [m], [p] and the alveolar sounds [n] and [d] demonstrated in such sequences as ma, pa, di (Bolinger 1975: 283; Labarba 1981: 344; Ojukwu & Alerechi 2011: 69). There is a contrary view that children acquire velar consonants before the bilabials and alveolars (Anthony et al. 1971: 45). In line with this view, Alerechi & Awala (2012: 257) observe that Ekpeye children below age three replace the velar plosives [k] or [g] with the alveolar plosives [t] or [d], respectively. This implies that despite the similarity observed in the order in which children acquire speech sounds, individual differences still abound. In fact, each child develops his own systematic way of producing adult forms within his limited scope of sound sequences (Menn 1992: 813).

In spite of a good deal of variation observed from one child to the other in terms of the order of mastering sounds in production and perception, the general tendencies as outlined by O'Grady et al. (2011: 362) seem to exist. Based on the manner of articulation (stricture), stops tend to be acquired before other consonants. In terms of place of articulation, labials are often acquired first followed (with some variation) by alveolars, velars, alveopalatals.

Realizing that sounds do not exist in isolation but in sequences to form morphemes or words, such sequences comprise vowel and consonant. Thus, vowel and consonant occur in a sequence to make up syllable structure and children tend to simplify the syllable or word structure of the target language. Children structures are mainly CV, CVCV (Akpan 2004: 25). This implies that in the acquisition of the adult speech by the children certain phonological processes are in operation.

1.3 Phonological processes

Phonological processes are those changes which segments undergo that result in the various phonetic realizations of the underlying phonological segments (Yul-Ifode 1999: 144) Children adopt certain phonological processes to attain to the adult sounds. According to Akpan (2004: 26), phonological processes in children are short-cut processes that operate on the child's speech in his attempt to attain the adult target. As the child's chronological age increases, the phonological processes decrease to conform to the phonological system of the language. Akpan (2004: 27) further notes three major classifications of the phonological processes: substitution, assimilatory and syllable structure processes. In addition to these major classifications, Yul-Ifode (2003: 2) recognizes dissimilation (intervocalic consonant devoicing) as a fourth major process. Of the four major phonological processes identified in the literature, the present paper focuses on consonant substitution in children speech.

Substitution is the systematic replacement of one linguistic feature for another or one phoneme for another that the child finds easier to articulate (Fromkin et al. 2003b: 357; Akmajian et al. 2008: 491; O'Grady et al. 2011: 365. O'Grady et al. (2011: 365) identified common substitution processes to include stopping, the replacement of a fricative by a corresponding stop; fronting, the moving forward of a place of articulation; gliding, the replacement of a liquid by a glide; and denasalization, the replacement of a nasal stop by a non-nasal counterpart. Scholars like Akmajian et al. (2008), Akpan (2008), David (2009), Akpan (2010), Alerechi & Ojukwu (2010) and Ojukwu & Alerechi (2011) have equally identified various forms of sound substitution in child language in different languages. The present paper treats the consonant substitution in Ikwere.

1.4 The target sounds

There are nine phonetic oral vowels [i ɪ e ɛ a o ɔ u ʊ], and eight phonetic nasalized vowels [ĩ ɪ̃ ẽ ã õ ɔ̃ ũ ʊ̃] in Ikwere (Donwa-Ifode & Ekwulo 1987: 42–43; Alerechi 2007a). They are summarized in the vowel charts on Figure 1 and Figure 2 respectively.

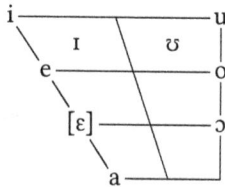

Figure 1: The Ikwere phonetic oral vowels.

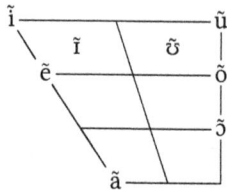

Figure 2: The Ikwere phonetic nasalized vowel.

Contrary to Donwa-Ifode & Ekwulo (1987: 42–43), which see [e] and [ɛ] as the allophonic variants of the phoneme /e/ in Ikwere, Alerechi (2007a: 65) observed that the vowel [ɛ] contrasts with other vowels in some dialects and is an allophonic variant of /e/ in some other dialects. It is also noted that beside the distinctive nasal vowels recorded in the language, vowels in the environment of nasal consonant may or may not be nasalized.

On the other hand, Ikwere records thirty-one phonetic consonants as shown in Table 1. There is no long consonant in the language.

Of the thirty-one consonants recorded in the language twenty-eight of them are phonemic. Following Alerechi (2007a: 98), the number of the phonemic consonants in each of the dialects, however, varies. It ranges from twenty-six to twenty-eight.

All the sounds in parentheses in Table 2 occur in Ọgkr. Whereas one or more of these sounds are allophone(s) in some dialects, and do not exist in others. Alerechi (2007a: 99)

Table 1: The phonetic consonants of Ikwere (adapted from Donwa-Ifode & Ek-wulo 1987).

Manner of articulation	Place of articulation						
	Labial	Alveolar	Palatal	Velar	Labialized velar	Labial-velar	Glottal
Nasal	m	n	ɲ	ŋ	ŋʷ		
Plosives	p b	t d		k g kʷ		gʷ	ʔ
Implosives	ɸ ɓ						
Affricatives			tʃ dʒ				
Fricatives	f v	s z	ʃ ʒ		ɥ hʷ		h
Tap		ɾ					
Central approximants			j			w	
Lateral approximant		l					

Table 2: The phonemic consonants of Ikwere.

Manner of articulation	Place of articulation						
	Labial	Alveolar	Palatal	Velar	Labialized velar	Labial-velar	Glottal
Nasal	m	n	ɲ	ŋ	ŋʷ		
Plosives	(p) (b)	t d		k g kʷ		gʷ	
Implosives	ɸ ɓ						
Affricatives			tʃ dʒ				
Fricatives	(f) (v)	s z			ɥ hʷ		h
Tap		ɾ					
Central approximants			j			w	
Lateral approximant		l					

gives clear picture of the occurrence of [p b f v] in the dialects of Ikwere as shown in Table 3 - Table 7.

Table 3 shows that /p b f v/ are phonemic in Ọgkr.

Table 3: Ọgkr.

p	b
f	v

Table 4 records /p b v/ as phonemes in the above dialects.

Table 4: Ozha, Ọmnw, Ubma, Akpb, Egbd, Elle, Omdg, Ubmn Omrl and Apni.

p	b
–	v

Table 5 illustrates that /b f v/ are phonemic in Ẹmwh.

Table 5: Ẹmwh.

–	b
f	v

The dialects in Table 6 record only /p b/ as phonemes.

Table 6: Akpọ , Obio, Alụu, Igwr Omgw, Iskp, Ipo and Omdm.

p	b
–	–

Table 7 is the reverse of Table 6 as only /f v/ are phonemic in the four dialects.

Table 7: Rmkp, Rndl, Ọdgn and Ib/Ob.

–	–
f	v

The foregoing Table 3 - Table 7 demonstrate the occurrence the consonants /p b f v/ in the various dialects of Ikwere. The present study, therefore, intends to find out among other things, if children from the dialects without any of these sounds would manifest such in course of acquiring the language.

1.5 Methodology

The wordlist used in collecting data from the subjects was drawn from the wordlist collected by Alerechi (2007b) for treating labial variation in Ikwere. It contains seventy-two words of everyday life obtainable in the environment of the subjects. The words contain different sounds of the language and are made up of monosyllabic, disyllabic and polysyllabic structures, giving such structures as V, CV, VCV, VCVCV, etc. The data were collected from each of the subjects by imitation and object pointing methods at their residence. The visit to each subject's residence during the period of data collection was about two to three times in order to elicit the accurate forms of the subject's speech. The subjects' speech forms were recorded manually and finally transcribed for analysis. The study adopts a descriptive approach in analyzing the data. It focuses on identifying and analyzing the substitution patterns and processes of consonants in the speech of the Ikwere children. The data was also analyzed using SPSS. Descriptive statistics was carried out to describe the performance of the subjects. The different occurrence of the consonants produced by the adult and subject in each dialect, were converted to quantitative data which was presented as percentages using Bar Charts.

1.6 The subjects

The subjects consulted during the period of data collection are seven; however, five of them were selected for the analysis because a comparison of the speech forms of two subjects from the same dialect area showed a replication of the other. The five subjects comprise three female and two male and fall within the age range of 3 to 4 years (3, 3, 3 ½, 3 ½ , 4). They were selected from Odeegnu, Emowha, Akpo, Aluu and Omuanwa so as to investigate if in the course of sound change, a child from a particular area would manifest forms typical of those of other area(s) or not. Table 8 summarizes details of the subjects.

Table 8: Data on the subjects.

Subject	1. VN	2. MA	3. EE	4. IN	5. GW
Gender	Female	Male	Female	Female	Male
Age	3 years	3 years	3 ½ years	3 ½ years	4 years
Village	Rumuodogo	Elibarada	Rumuolumini	Omuokiri	Ubordu
Dialect	Odeegnu	Emowha	Akpo	Aluu	Omuanwa

1.7 Consonant substitution

There are twenty-eight phonemic consonants /m n ɲ ŋ ŋʷ p b t d k g kʷ gʷ ɸ ɓ ʧ ʤ f v s z ɥ hʷ h r j w l/in Ikwere. Some of these consonants are replaced with some others in child language. The pattern of substitution reflects those involving different states of the glottis, places of articulation and manners of articulation. The pattern reflecting different states of the glottis sometimes overlap with those of places of articulation. I, therefore, present the various substitutions based on manner of articulation.

1.7.1 Substitution according to manners of articulation

The different manners of articulation observed in the data involve the plosives, fricatives, affricates, implosives, approximants, etc.

1.7.2 Substitution of plosive with plosive

The substitutions here reflect those involving states of the glottis or places of articulation. Hyman (1975: 16) observed that the general tendencies in child language include the learning of voiceless stops before voiced stops. This phenomenon is identified in this paper in the utterances of children above the age of 3 to 4. Thus, where the target language records the voiced stops [b] or [d], the tendency is for the children above age 3 to 4 to replace them with their voiceless counterparts [p] or [t], respectively. Table 9 is, therefore, strong evidence that Ikwere children are not left out in first acquiring voiceless consonants and subsequently revert to the target forms. The table shows the Odgn subject replacing the voiceless velar plosive [k] with the voiceless alveolar plosive [t] of the target.

Table 9: d → t: b → p, k → t.

Odeegnu		Emowha		Akpo		Aluu		Omuanwa		Gloss
Target	VN 3yrs	Target	MA 3½yrs	Target	EE 3½yrs	Target	IN 3½yrs	Target	GW 4yrs	
m̀ɓòró ákâ	m̀pòtó átà	m̀ɓòró áká	m̀pèrè-áká	m̀ɓèré-áká		ìsíní ákâ	ìpèní á·kâ	m̀ɓèré ákâ	ípèlé á·kâ	'elbow'
àɓà	àɓà	àɓà	àɓà	àɓǎ	àbà	àɓà	àɓà	àɓà	àpà	'jaw'
zì	dʒì	zì	zì	zì		zɪ	zɪ	dɪ	tè	'is'
àkítì	àtítì	àkɪdɪ	àkɪdɪ	àkídì		àkísì	àkítì	àkɪdɪ	àkʷà	Beans (brown)

There is also the tendency of the Ikwere subjects replacing complex articulated (labialized) sounds with those of simple articulation (single segments). This phenomenon is predominant in the speech form of the Odgn child, even though children from other dialect areas manifest traces of this phenomenon. Consider the data in Table 10. Note that the data include the simplifying of labialized fricative and nasal.

1.7.3 Substitution of plosive with fricative

The pattern of substitution treated in this section reflects those involving [v] with [b], and vice versa, and that of [s] with [t]. While children from Emwh and Akpo show preference for [b] instead of [v] of the target language, they, conversely, replace [v] with

Table 10: kw → k; kw → t; gw → g; hw → w, ŋw → m.

Odeegnu		Emowha		Akpo		Aluu		Omuanwa		Gloss
Target	VN 3yrs	Target	MA 3½yrs	Target	EE 3½yrs	Target	IN 3½yrs	Target	GW 4yrs	
vékʷū̄	vétù	békʷū̄	békʷū̄	békʷū̄	békʷū̄	békʷū̄	békʷū̄	ákʷá	békù	Greet
ɛkʷá	ɛtá	ɛkʷá	áŋkʷá	àkʷá	àká	àkʷá	ŋ́ká	ákʷá	ákʷá	Cry
ɛkʷâ	àtâ	ɛkʷâ	ɛkʷâ	àkʷá	àká	àkʷâ	á˩kʷâ	àkʷâ	àkʷâ	Egg
ɛŋʷʊ	ɛmʊ	ɛŋʷʊ	ɛmʊ	àŋʷʊ	àŋʷʊ	àŋʷʊ	áŋʷʊ	áŋʷʊ	áwʊ	Death
ɛkʷà	àtà	ɛkʷà	àkʷà	àkʷà	àkʷà	àkʷà	àkʷà	àkʷà	àkʷà	Bush fowl
ɛ˩ŋʷâ	ámà	ɔ˩ŋʷâ	ɛŋʷâ	ɔ˩ŋʷâ	ɔ˩má	ɔ˩ŋʷâ	ɔ˩ŋʷâ	ɔ˩ŋʷâ	ɔ˩ŋʷâ	Moon
ɛhî̀	ɛjɪ	ɛhî̀	àjî	ɛhí	àhɪ	àhʷʊ	àwʊ	àhʷʊ	àwʊ	Body
ʤɪ	ʤɪ	ʤɪ-	ʤɪ	ʤɪ	ʤɪ	gʷʊ	gɔ	gʷʊ	gʷʊ	Given (name)
ɔʧɪ	ɔʧɪ	ɔʧɪ	ɔʧɪ	ɔʧɪ	ɔʧɪ	ɔkʷʊ	ɔkʊ	ɔkʷʊ	ɔkʷʊ	Leg

[b] as demonstrated in Table 11. The data further show the children in the choice of [t] for [s] of Aluu. The substitution in this section agrees with the observation of Crystal (1997: 242) that the replacement of fricatives with stops is one of the possible trends for children in language acquisition. It is worthy of note that this substitution seem peculiar to children that are above age 3 to 4.

Table 11: s → t; v →b; b → v.

Odeegnu		Emowha		Akpo		Aluu		Omuanwa		Gloss
Target	VN 3yrs	Target	MA 3½yrs	Target	EE 3½yrs	Target	IN 3½yrs	Target	GW 4yrs	
tó-	tɔ-	tòɾú	tòɾú	só	tʃó	só	só	tò	tòɾú	'follow'
óvírízí	óvílìʤì	óbírízí	óbíjíz	óbírízí	óbílízí	óbírízí	óvírízí	óbúrúzù	óbúlúsù	'sympathy'
èvùlù	àvùlù	èvùlù	èvùlù	èvùlù	èbùlù	èbùlù	èbùrù	m̀fùlù	èvùlù	'ram'
dívjà	-	dívjà	dívjà	díbjà	-	díbjà	díbjà	díbjà	díbjà	'doctor'
tó	ʤɔ	tó	tó	só	-	só	só	tó	tó	'grow'
m̀vɔ	m̀vɔ	m̀vɔ	m̀bú	m̀bɔ	m̀bɔ	m̄˩bɔ	m̄˩bɔ	m̄˩vɔ	m̄˩fɔ	'comb (in)'
ɔvɔʧɪ	ɔvɔʧɪ	ɔvɔʧɪ	ɔbɔʧɪ	ɔbɔʧɪ	ɔbɔʧɪ	ɔbɔʧɪ	ɔbɔʧɪ	ɔbɔʧɪ	ɔbɔʧɪ	'day'
òvèʤè	òvèʤì	òbèʤè	èvèʤè	òbòʤò	òbòjò	òbèʤè	òbòʤè	òbèʤè	òbòʤò	'mudskipper'
àkítì	àtítì	àkɪdɪ	àkɪdɪ	àkídì	-	àkísì	àkítì	ákɪdɪ	àkwà	Beans (brown)

1.7.4 Substitution of fricative with fricative

In addition to substituting voiced stops with their voiceless counterparts, Table 12 further proves that the replacement of voiced consonants with their voiceless counterparts extends to the fricatives. The substitution is, however, predominant in the speech of an Omnw child of 4years old than those of Odgn of 3years and Akpo of 3¹/₂ yrs as the data demonstrate. Thus, the children replace [v] and [z] of the target language with [f] and [v], respectively. Our data show that the changes occur both word-initially and word-medially indicating that there is no conditioning factor for the change. The data further demonstrate the tendency of the child from Omnw replacing some of the vowels in initial position with a syllabic nasal. This additional peculiarity observed in the speech of the Omnw child, further strengthens the claim of the presence of a slight speech problem in this child's language. This, however, requires further investigation in other to confirm our claim.

Table 12: v → f, z → s.

Odeegnu		Emowha		Akpo		Aluu		Omuanwa		Gloss
Target	VN 3yrs	Target	MA 3½yrs	Target	EE 3½yrs	Target	IN 3½yrs	Target	GW 4yrs	
sá	sá	sá	sá	zá	-	zá	zá	zá	sá	'imitate'
ú⁺sʊ̂	údʒù	ú⁺sʊ̂	ń⁺sʊ̂	í⁺zú	ɪʧu	í⁺zú	í⁺dʒû	ú⁺zú	ń⁺sʊ̂	'corpse'
sʊ́	ʧʊ́	sʊ́	sʊ́	Zú	zú	zú	dʒú	zú	sú	'steal'
ɔsʊ̌	ɔʧʊ	ɔsʊ̌	àsʊ̌	àzʊ́	àzʊ́	àzʊ̌	àdʒû	àzʊ̌	àsʊ̌	'back'
ɔ⁺sʊ̌	ɔʧʊ	ɔsʊ̌	ɔsʊ̌	ázʊ̀	áʧʊ	ázʊ̀	ádʒʊ	ázʊ̀	ásʊ̌	'fish'
zʊ	dʒʊ	zʊ	zʊ	zʊ	sʊ	zʊ	dʒʊ	zʊ	sʊ	'buy'
zɔ	dʒɔ	zɔ	zɔ	zɔ	dʒɔ	zɔ	zɔ	zɔ	sɔ	'step on'
ézè	-	ézè	ézè	ézè		ézè	édʒè	ézè	ésè	'king'
-	ɪvú	ɪvù	ɪvú	ɪvù	ɪvú	ɪbû	ɪ⁺bû	ívû	m̀fû	'load'
ɔɲì	ɪvǔ	ɪvù	ɪvù	ɪvù	ɪvù	ɪbù	ɪbù	ɪvù	m̀fù	'fat'
èvùlù	àvùlù	èvùlù	èvùnù	èvùlù	èbùlù	èbùlù	èbùrù	m̀fùlù	èvùlù	'ram'
ɔzà	ádʒà	ɔzʊzà	àzʊzà	ɔzʊzà	ɔsìsà	ɔzìzà	ɔdʒìzà	ɔzìzà	ɔsìsà	'broom'
vǎ	fǎ	vǎ	vǎ	bǎ-	bǎ	bá	bǎ	bǎ	bà	'enter'

1.7.5 Substitution of fricative with affricate

There is also the substitution of the alveolar fricatives [s] and [z] of the adult utterance with the palato-alveolar affricates [ʧ]and [dʒ], respectively, in children pronunciation. Thus, where Odgn, Akpo and Aluu adult articulate [s] or [z], the choice for the children is [ʧ] or [dʒ], respectively, indicating the affrication of these fricatives. Occasionally, the children substitute [s] for [dʒ] or [z] for [ʧ] as demonstrated in Table 13. The substitution

Table 13: Fricative versus affricate: s → ʧ; z → ʧ, z → dʒ.

Odeegnu		Emowha		Akpo		Aluu		Omuanwa		Gloss
Target	VN 3yrs	Target	MA 3½yrs	Target	EE 3½yrs	Target	IN 3½yrs	Target	GW 4yrs	
ú⁺sʊ̂	údʒù	ú⁺sʊ̂	ń⁺sʊ̂	í⁺zú	ɪʧu	í⁺zú	í⁺dʒû	ú⁺zú	ń⁺sʊ̂	'corpse'
sʊ̂	ʧʊ́	sʊ̂	sʊ̂	Zú	zú	zú	dʒú	zú	sú	'steal'
ɔsʊ̌	ɔʧʊ	ɔsʊ̌	àsʊ̌	àzʊ́	àzʊ́	àzʊ̌	àdʒû	àzʊ̌	àsʊ̌	'back'
ɔ⁺sʊ̌	ɔʧʊ	ɔsʊ̌	ɔsʊ̌	ázʊ̀	áʧʊ	ázʊ̀	ádʒʊ	ázʊ̀	ásʊ̌	'fish'
zʊ	dʒʊ	zʊ	zʊ	zʊ	sʊ	zʊ	dʒʊ	zʊ	sʊ	'buy'
zɔ	dʒɔ	zɔ	zɔ	zɔ	dʒɔ	zɔ	zɔ	zɔ	sɔ	'step on'
ó⁺sʊ̂	óʧù	ó⁺sʊ̂	ósú	ó⁺sú	ó⁺sú	é⁺sú	é⁺ʧû	é⁺sʊ̂	ń⁺sʊ̂	'millipede'
sʊ	ʧʊ	sʊ	sʊ	sʊ	ʧʊ	sʊ	ʧʊ	sʊ	sʊ́	'pound (yam)'
sʊ́	ʧʊ́	sʊ́	sʊ́	sʊ́	ʧʊ́	sʊ́	sú	sʊ́	sʊ́	'wash'
ɔsʊ	ɔʧʊ	ɔsʊ	ɔsʊ́	ɔsʊ	ɔʧʊ	ɔsʊ	ɔsʊ	ɔsʊ	ɔsʊ	'bat'
sɔ	ʧɔ	sɔ	sɔ	sɔ	ʧɔ	sɔ	sɔ	sɔ	sɔ	Forbid or respect
tɔ̌-	tɔ	tɔ̌	tò-	sɔ̌	ʧɔ́	sɔ̌	só	sɔ̌	tò-	Follow
zɪ	dʒɪ	zì	zì	zì	-	zɪ	zɪ	dɪ	tè	'is'
ǹzí	ǹdʒì	ǹzí	ǹzí	ǹzí	ǹzí	ǹzí	ǹdʒí	ǹdí	ìdí	'husband'
óvírízí	óvílìdʒì	óbírízí	óbíjíz	óbírízí	óbílízí	óbírízí	óvírízí	óbúrúzù	óbúlúsù	'sympathy'

of alveolar fricatives with palato-alveolar affricates is restricted to the child of 3years, whereas the replacement of the voiced alveolar fricative with the voiceless counterpart seems peculiar to the child of 4. This phenomenon, though, geographically determined is observed in the adult speech, the impression of this paper is that it may be a case of speech impediment in the utterance of this 4 year old child.

1.7.6 Substitution of fricative with approximant/null

The majority of the children have not acquired the glottal fricative [h]. The data in Table 14 demonstrate that they either delete it wherever it occurs in the target form or replace it with [j]. See Table 14.

Table 14: h → j, h →∅.

Odeegnu		Emowha		Akpo		Aluu		Omuanwa		Gloss
Target	VN 3yrs	Target	MA 3½yrs	Target	EE 3½yrs	Target	IN 3½yrs	Target	GW 4yrs	
há	á	-	-	ɓĕ	pĕ	-		ɓé	pè	Peel (orange)
úhjé	újeá	úhjé	újé	ɪhjé	ɪjé	ɪhjé	ɪjé	úhjí	újé	Red
ɛhî	ɛjɪ	ɛhî	àjî	ɛhí	àhɪ	àhʷʊ	àwʊ	àhʷʊ	àwʊ	Body

1.7.7 Substitution of tap with lateral or nasal

The tendency is also recorded of Ikwere children to use the alveolar lateral approximant instead of tap or nasal. Thus, where the adult use the alveolar[r], the children show preference for the alveolar lateral [l] or the alveolar nasal [n]. This substitution is characteristic of children that cut across ages 3 to 4 as shown in Table 15.

Table 15: r →l, l → r.

Odeegnu		Emowha		Akpo		Aluu		Omuanwa		Gloss
Target	VN 3yrs	Target	MA 3½yrs	Target	EE 3½yrs	Target	IN 3½yrs	Target	GW 4yrs	
ɛɓárá	ɔpálá	ɔɓárá	ɔpálá	ɔɓárá	ɔpárá	ɔɓárá	ɔpáná	ɔɓárá	ɔpálá	'first son'
óvírízí	óvílìdì	óbírízí	óbíjíz	óbírízí	óbílízí	óbírízí	óvírízí	óbúrúzù	óbúlúsù	'sympathy'
m̀pòró ákâ	m̀pòtó átà	m̀pòró ákâ	m̀pèrè-áká	m̀pèrè-áká		ìsíní ákâ	ìpèní á·kâ	m̀pèrè ákâ	ìpèlé á·kâ	'elbow'
ùrì	ùlì	ùrì	ùlì	ìrì	ìlì	ìrì	ùlì	ùrì	ùlì	'indigo'
rí	-	rí	rí	rí	-	rí	lí	rí	lí	'eat'
ŋʷɔ	-	ŋʷɔ	ŋʷɔ̃	ŋʷɔ	-	rí	wɔ	rí	lí/lílí	'drink'
ɔ·lô	ɔrɔ	ó·lô	ó·rô	ó·lô	ɔ·rɔ	é·lô	á·rɔ	é·lô	é·lô	'antelope'

1.7.8 Substitution of implosive with plosive

The replacement of the labial implosive [ɓ] of the target language with the labial plosive [p] serves as another trend in the speech of Ikwere children. Thus, where the choice in the target language is [ɓ], the children use [p] as demonstrated in Table 16. The data show that the substitution of [ɓ] with [p] cuts across ages 3 to 4. A similar trend is observed with the voiced counterparts [ɓ] and [b]. This implies that the acquisition of [ɸ] and [ɓ] is a later development in the language of children.

Table 16: ɸ → p, ɓ → b.

Odeegnu		Emowha		Akpo		Aluu		Omuanwa		Gloss
Target	VN 3yrs	Target	MA 3½yrs	Target	EE 3½yrs	Target	IN 3½yrs	Target	GW 4yrs	
eɓárá	ɔpálá	ɔɓárá	ɔpálá	ɔɓárá	ɔpárá	ɔɓárá	ɔpáná	ɔɓárá	ɔpálá	First son
m̀ɓòró ákâ	m̀pòtó átà	m̀ɓòró ákâ	m̀pèrè-ákâ	m̀ɓèrè-ákâ		ìsíní ákâ	ìpèní áꞌkâ	m̀ɓèré ákâ	ípèlé áꞌkâ	Elbow
ɓʊ́	-	ɓʊ́	pé	ɓʊ́		ɓʊ́	pé	ɓʊ́	pè	Scrape
ɓó	-	ɓŏ	pó	ɓŏ	Pó	ɓŏ	pŏ	ɓŏ	pó	Pack waste
há	á	-	-	ɓĕ	pĕ	-	-	ɓé	pè	Peel (orange)
-	-	vŏ	vú	ɓŏ	Pó	bŏ	bó	bŏ	bó	Accuse
àɓà	àbà	àɓà	àbà	àɓă	àbà	àbà	àbà	àbà	àpà	Jaw

The data in this paper demonstrate that sound substitution in child language also involves the vowels. From the data, however, the replacement of sounds involving vowel are not as recurrent as those of the consonants. This agrees with previous studies that vowels are acquired earlier by children than consonants. By the age of 3 years most vowels sounds would have been established hence, no need for much substitution. Tonal substitution in the language is not significant in children speech as sown in most of the data.

1.8 Substitution processes

The various substitution patterns observed in this paper give additional evidence of the simplification of adult (target) language by children. It is observed that as children develop, the substituted sounds are dropped to conform to the adult forms when they have gained greater articulatory control. Recalling that the substitutions are not haphazard but rule governed, an interesting question would be what rules do children impose to simplify the adult language? In other words, what are the phonological processes operating to relate the child utterances with the target forms? Considering the divergent nature of the Ikwere language, Alerechi (2007a) identified a number of phonological processes relating one form of speech of a particular geographical location with the form of the others, one of which is the reflex of the proto-form, while others are likely innovations. Thus this section does not only identify the phonological processes in operation, but also draws attention to the processes that are identical with those of the adults as in the speech of different geographical areas and those that are typical of child language. The following subsections discuss the phonological processes observed in this paper.

1.9 Strengthening and spirantization (weakening)

Bearing in mind the replacement of plosives with fricatives and vice versa, I observed the processes of strengthening and spirantization (weakening), respectively, in Table 11. Alerechi (2007a: 262) earlier observed the spirantization (weakening) of [b] of some dialects to [v] in some other dialects but not the strengthening of [v] to [b]. In child language, however, there is an addition of the phonological process of strengthening of [v] of the adult form to [b] showing that the process reflecting the change of [v] to [b] is typical of children in Ikwere, whereas that involving the change of [b] to [v] is identical with the adult speech.

1.10 Loss of suction and a shift to plosive

Concerning the substitution of [ɓ] with [p], we note a loss of suction of labial implosive of the adult language and a shift to labial plosive in child language. Alerechi (2007a: 260) recognized this phonological process in Ikwere. Here children from the dialect areas with the preponderant use of [ɓ] show preference for [p] of some other dialect areas. This change does not only reveal that the phonological process in child language is identical with the adult language, it also proves that phonological substitution characteristic of child language is rule governed.

1.11 (Successive) affrication (and (de)voicing)

For the change of fricatives with affricates, two phonological processes are in operation. One is the affrication of [s] to [ʧ] and [z] to [ʤ] depending on voicing. Another is the successive affrication and voicing or devoicing of fricatives as in [s] changing to [ʤ] and [z] changing to [ʧ]. Even though Alerechi (2007a: 261) observed affrication in adult language, this affrication is different as it reflects [s] and [ʧ] or [z] and [ʤ] and not [t], [ʧ], [ʃ] and [s] as in the adult language.

1.12 De-labialization

De-labialization is a process whereby the feature of lip rounding on the primary stricture is lost. In Table 10, it is observed that all the subjects replaced the main stricture in either one or more of these changes [kʷ→ k; kʷ→ t; gʷ→ g; hʷ→ w, ŋʷ→ m]. Even though a child may have produced any of the labialized sounds accurately, labialized sounds are among the difficult consonants for the children to acquire since all the subjects manifested de-labialization process.

1.13 Gliding

Gliding in child phonology is a process whereby any consonant is realized as a glide (Yul-Ifode 2008: 255). In addition to producing accurately [j] as in the target form, the Odeegnu and Emowha subjects produce [h] as [j] intervocalically, indicating that [j] is among the early sounds in child language acquisition.

1.14 Denasalization

Even though this paper focuses on consonants, we observed a preponderance loss of nasalization of nasalized vowels in child language in our data especially in Table 16. Thus the phonological process of denasalization of certain vowel segments of the target language is evident of child language. Though Alerechi (2007a: 249) observed denasalization in the adult language, it is not as predominant as that in child language, showing that loss of nasalization is one of the ways children actually simplify their pronunciation. In fact nasalizing a vowel segment requires extra energy or force and more natural for children to neglect it than the adults. This explains why we record a preponderance loss of nasalization in children speech forms more than those of the adults.

2 Interpretations

The foregoing substitutions of segments in the language of Ikwere children are evidence of simplification of items of the target pronunciation of the Ikwere consonants. In an attempt to articulate the sounds of the language, Ikwere children, like other children, change the sounds when trying to attain the target form thus, resulting in imperfect rendering of some of the target sounds. The imperfect representations of the adult sounds generate ambiguous forms and this contributes significantly to the communication gap existing between children and adults. While the children understand the adults, but find it difficult to communicate effectively, the adults, on the other hand, have achieved greater articulatory control of the target language, but cannot grasp fully the intentions of the children. This could create serious problems such as frustration on the part of the adults, particularly, the impatient ones and dissatisfaction, resentment and most likely, seclusion on the part of the children if the gap is not bridged as the adult may not reach their needs. However, it is the parents that understand their children better than any other person.

The various phonological processes observed in §1.5, which demonstrate that the processes in both adults and children's forms of speech are to a great extent identical with slight differences also has implication. The similarities indicate that the gap in communication existing between adults and children could be bridgedparticularly if the adults are conversant with the forms of the varieties spoken in other geographical locations. For the forms peculiar to children, an exposure to what should be expected could facilitate communication and reduce communication gap to the barest minimum.

2.1 Performance scores of consonants

Table 17 represents the phonetic consonants of Ikwere observed in the data. It shows the articulatory activity of each subject. The total occurrence of each consonant is obtained by counting the number of occurrences of the sound in the words elicited from both the target and the subjects. These were converted to quantitative data and presented as percentages using bar charts. The bar charts displaying the performance of the children from Odeegnu, Emowha, Akpo, Aluu and Omuanwa are represented in Figure 3 to Figure 7. It should be noted that twenty-three (23) consonants were observed in the data collected. Due to dialectal difference all the consonants did not manifested in the target of all the dialects. Thus Odeegnu records 17; Emowha and Akpo have 19 consonants each, while Aluu and Omuanwa used 21 and 23, respectively.

2.2 Consonants in Odeegnu

Table 17 and Figure 3 show that the Odeegnu subject aged 3 years scored 100% in the production of [ʧ] and [ʤ]. It could be that the number of these sounds is limited or that the child has mastered them completely. The subject has acquired [v f t l d j] to a reasonable extent but not completely. The table and figure also show that the subject could not produce [ŋʷg kʷ ɓ z r] and had difficulty in pronouncing [k]. The total performance of the subject in the production of the target consonants is 43.2%, which is below the average.

2.3 Consonants in Emowha

From Table 17 and Figure 4, it is observed that the Emowha male subject of 3 ½ years produced [t d k g ʧ ʤ f s z j] accurately and above the average in [kʷ v ŋʷ]. He, however, scored zero percent in the production of [β ɓ h]. This subject seems to have acquired most of target sounds as against those that are yet to be included in his inventory. Table 17 puts the total performance of the Emowha subject in the production of target consonants at 75.6%.

2.4 Consonants in Akpo

From Table 17 and Figure 5, the Akpo female subject of 3 ½ years scored 100% in the production of [p b t d k g ʧ f j], above average in [ʤ v kʷ] and has attained average score in [ŋʷ h l]. On the other hand, she scored zero percent in the production of [β] and less than average in [r s z]. Table 17 also shows that the subject has acquired 64.3% in the production all the target sounds.

2.5 Consonants in Aluu

Table 17 and Figure 6 show the Aluu male subject of 3 ½ years with 100% score in the production of the consonants [ŋʷ p t d k g ɓ ʧ ʤ j], 93.8% in [b] and above the average in [s kʷ]. However, the subject scored zero percent in the production of [gʷ β h hʷ w], and 14.3% and 25% performance scores in [r] and [l], respectively. The total percentage for the production of all the target consonants is 64.4%, indicating above average mastery of the target sounds.

Table 17: Frequency of occurrence for consonants.

Sound	Odeegnu			Emowha			Akpo			Aluu			Omuanwa		
	T	1	%	T	2	%	T	3	%	T	4	%	T	5	%
ŋʷ	3	0	0	3	2	66.7	2	1	50	2	2	100	2	1	50
p	–			–			1	1	100	3	3	100	2	2	100
b	–			4	2	50	9	9	100	16	15	93.8	12	11	91.7
t	4	3	75	4	4	100	2	2	100	2	2	100	2	2	100
d	3	2	66.7	4	4	100	2	2	100	3	3	100	6	4	66.7
k	3	1	33.3	4	4	100	1	1	100	3	3	100	4	3	75
g	1	0	0	2	2	100	1	1	100	3	3	100	2	2	100
kʷ	4	0	0	4	3	75	5	3	60	5	3	60	7	6	85.7
gʷ	–			–			–			1	0	0	1	1	100
ɓ	2	0	0	5	0	0	3	0	0	4	0	0	5	1	20
ƥ	–			2	0	0	–			1	1	100	1	0	0
ƒ	2	2	100	4	4	100	4	4	100	1	1	100	1	1	100
ʤ	4	4	100	4	4	100	4	3	75	2	2	100	2	2	100
f	5	4	80	4	4	100	1	1	100	–			2	2	100
v	10	9	90	10	7	70	4	3	75	–			4	0	0
s	11	2	18.2	11	11	100	7	2	28.6	9	6	66.7	8	6	75
z	6	0	0	8	8	100	10	4	40	13	5	38.5	11	0	0
h	3	0	0	2	0	0	2	1	50	1	0	0	1	0	0
hʷ	–			–			–			1	0	0	1	0	0
r	6	0	0	7	3	42.9	4	1	25	7	1	14.3	8	0	0
j	3	2	66.7	4	4	100	4	4	100	5	5	100	5	5	100
w	–			–			–			1	0	0	1	0	0
l	4	3	75	4	2	50	4	2	50	4	1	25	4	3	75
Total	74	32	43.2	90	68	75.6	70	45	64.3	87	56	64.4	92	52	56.5

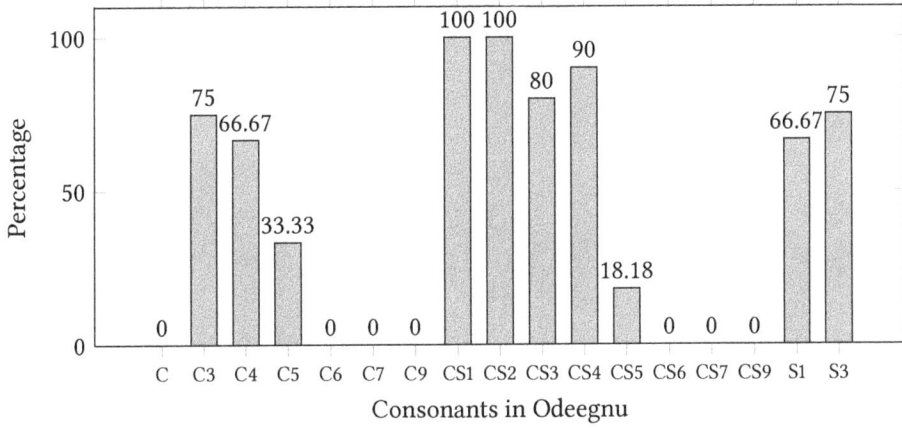

Figure 3: The Odeegnu subject performance in consonants.

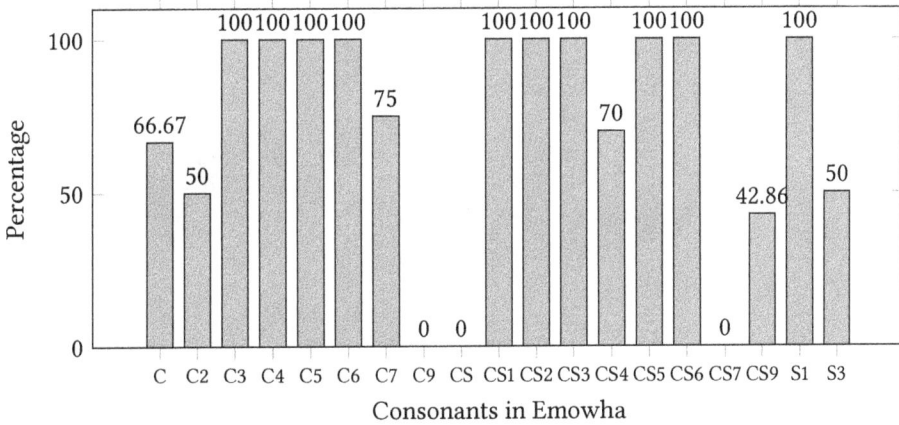

Figure 4: The Emowha subject performance in consonants.

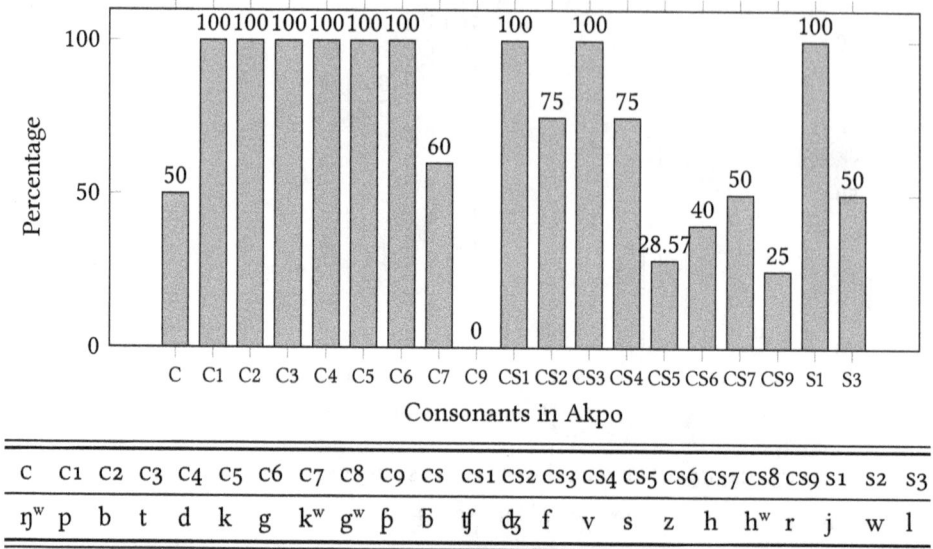

Figure 5: The Akpo subject performance in consonants.

C	C1	C2	C3	C4	C5	C6	C7	C8	C9	CS	CS1	CS2	CS3	CS4	CS5	CS6	CS7	CS8	CS9	S1	S2	S3
ŋʷ	p	b	t	d	k	g	kʷ	gʷ	ɓ	ɓ	tʃ	dʒ	f	v	s	z	h	hʷ	r	j	w	l

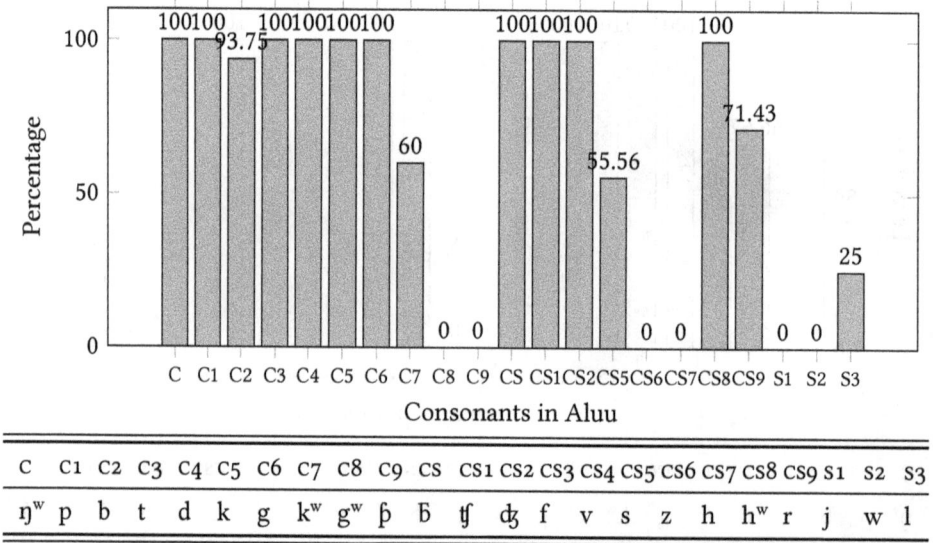

Figure 6: The Aluu subject performance in consonants.

C	C1	C2	C3	C4	C5	C6	C7	C8	C9	CS	CS1	CS2	CS3	CS4	CS5	CS6	CS7	CS8	CS9	S1	S2	S3
ŋʷ	p	b	t	d	k	g	kʷ	gʷ	ɓ	ɓ	tʃ	dʒ	f	v	s	z	h	hʷ	r	j	w	l

152

2.6 Consonants in Omuanwa

The Omuanwa male subject of 4 years scored 100% in the production of [p t g gʷ ʧ ʤ f j]; 91.7% and 85.7% in [b] and [kʷ], respectively, and 75% in [k s l]. For the difficult sounds, the subject obtained zero percent score for [ɓ v z h hʷ r w] and 20% for [β]. The total performance of this subject in the production of all the consonants is 56.5% of the target. These are shown in Table 17 and Figure 7.

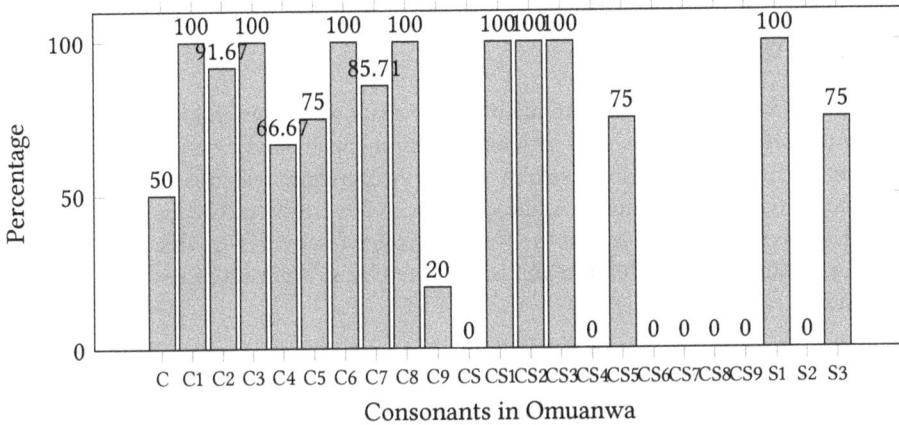

C	C1	C2	C3	C4	C5	C6	C7	C8	C9	CS	CS1	CS2	CS3	CS4	CS5	CS6	CS7	CS8	CS9	S1	S2	S3
ŋʷ	p	b	t	d	k	g	kʷ	gʷ	β	ɓ	ʧ	ʤ	f	v	s	z	h	hʷ	r	j	w	l

Figure 7: The Omuanwa subject performance in consonants.

3 Discussion

A close look at the performance of the subjects demonstrates that the majority of the subjects recorded 100% accuracy in the production of 9 to 10 consonants, except the Odeegnu subject that recorded only 2 consonants as shown in Table 17 and Figure 3 to Figure 7.

Comparing the total performance of target sounds by the subjects, therefore, it is observed that the Emowha subject has acquired a greater percentage of 75.6 of the adult sounds, followed by the percentage scores of 64.4 and 64.3 by the Aluu and Akpo subjects, respectively. The Omuanwa subject scored 56.5% and Odeegnu scored below average of 43.2%. While the reason for the low performance of the Odeegnu subject could be attributed to age factor (3 years) that of the Omuanwa subject may be due to delayed acquisition of the target or slight speech disorders. This, of course, requires further investigation before conclusion could be drawn.

Having noted the performance of individual subject in the target consonant, one may say that the easy sounds for Ikwere subjects generally are [p t k g d b ʧ ʤ f j] particularly if they occur in the target speech. On the other hand, [β r h hʷ] appear more problematic than other consonants. Some others not listed as either easy or difficult may be easy or difficult based on the unique articulatory performance of the subject. Thus, the plosives, affricates, fricatives and approximants seem not to constitute areas of difficulty, whereas the implosives, tap and glottal fricatives do.

4 Conclusions

Inthis paper, we have been able to identify the various changes children impose on the Ikwere (target) language as they articulate certain consonants. Some of these changes conform to the forms used by speakers of different geographical areas, while others are characteristic of child language. Adult speakers of Ikwere should be aware of the existing varieties of the language and the forms peculiar to children as this could facilitate communication between children and adults, thereby, preventing problems engendered by communication gap.

References

Akmajian, Adrian, Richard A. Demers, Ann K. Farmer & Robert M. Harnish. 2008. *Linguistics: An introduction to language and communication*. 5th edn. New Delhi: Prentice-Hall of India.

Akpan, Ekaete E. 2004. *Topics in developmental psycholinguistics*. Calabar: Paico Press & Books.

Akpan, Ekaete E. 2008. Vowel processes in the ibibio 2½ to 4½ years old monolingual children. In Shirley Yul-Ifode & Rotimi Badejo (eds.), *Reading on child language and communication disorders in Nigeria*, 239–250. Choba: University of Port Harcourt Press.

Akpan, Ekaete E. 2010. A study of the segmental phonology of Ibibio children. *Journal of Child Development and Communication Disorders* 2. 151–170.

Alerechi, Roseline I. C. 2007a. *A dialect survey of Ikwere: A phonological perspective*. Choba: University of Port Harcourt Doctoral dissertation.

Alerechi, Roseline I. C. 2007b. Labial variation in Ikwere. In Ozo-Mekuri Ndimele (ed.), *Convergence: English and nigerian languages*, 347–369. Port Harcourt: Mand J Grand Orbit Communication Ltd. & Emaih Press.

Alerechi, Roseline I. C. & G. Awala. 2012. Consonant substitution in the speech of the Ekpeye child. *Journal of Child Development and Communication Disorders* 4. 249–260.

Alerechi, Roseline I. C. & Obed Ojukwu. 2010. Vowel processes in the speech of Ikwere child. *Journal of Child Development and Communication Disorders* 2. 44–53.

Anthony, A., A. Bogle, Thomas T. S. Ingram & M. W. McIsaac. 1971. *Edinburgh articulation test*. London: Longman Group.

Bolinger, Dwight. 1975. *Aspects of language*. New York: Harcourt Brace Jovanich.

Crystal, David. 1997. *The Cambridge encyclopedia of language.* Cambridge: Cambridge University Press.

David, Stephen O. 2009. A cognitive perspective on language development of the Nigerian child. *Journal of Child Development and Communication Disorders* 10. 104–117.

Donwa-Ifode, Shirley O. & S. A. Ekwulo. 1987. Ikwere orthography. In Rebecca N. Agheyisi (ed.), *Orthographies of Nigerian languages: Manual v.* Lagos: National Language Centre, Federal Ministry of Education.

Donwa-Ifode, Shirley O. & Nicholas Faraclas. 2001. *A dialect atlas of Ikwere.* Coba: Port Harcourt University Press.

Fromkin, Victoria, Robert Rodman & Nina Hyams. 2003a. *An introduction to language.* Australia: Thompson Wardsworth.

Fromkin, Victoria, Robert Rodman & Nina Hyams. 2003b. *An introduction to language.* Australia: Thompson Wardsworth.

Hyman, Larry M. 1975. *Phonology: Theory and analysis.* New York: Holt, Reinhart & Winston.

Labarba, Richard C. 1981. *Foundations of developmental psychology.* New York: Academic Press.

Menn, Lise. 1992. Acquisition of language: Phonology. In William Bright (ed.), *International encyclopedia of linguistics 1.* 12–16. New York: Oxford University Press.

O'Grady, William, John Archibald & Francis Katamba. 2011. *Contemporary linguistics: An introduction.* Harlow: Pearson Education Limited.

Ojukwu, Obed & Roseline I. C. Alerechi. 2011. A process account of child phonological system: Insights from Ohuhu-igbo. *Journal of Child Development and Communication Disorders* 3. 65–76.

Williamson, Kay. 1980. *Reading and writing Ikwere.* Port Harcourt: Rivers Readers Project.

Williamson, Kay. 1988. Linguistic evidence for the prehistory of the Niger-Delta. In Ebiegberi J. Alagoa, Frederick N. Anozie & Nzewunwa Nzenwa (eds.), *The early history of the Niger Delta*, 65–119. Hamburg: Burske.

Williamson, Kay & Rogger Blench. 2000. Niger-congo. In Bernd Heine & Derek Nurse (eds.), *African languages: An introduction*, 11–42. Cambridge: Cambridge University Press.

Yul-Ifode, Shirley. 1999. *A course in phonology.* Choba: University of Port Harcourt Press.

Yul-Ifode, Shirley. 2003. *Aspects of the phonology of six normally developing Ibibio children.* Poster presented at the symposium on research in child language disorders, University of Wisconsin, Madison, USA, June 5th to 7th 2003.

Yul-Ifode, Shirley. 2008. The relation between language acquisition and language change (evidence from Southern nigeria). In Shirley Yul-Ifode & Rotimi Badejo (eds.), *Reading on child language and communication disorders in Nigeria*, 251–265. Choba: University of Port Harcourt Press.

Chapter 10

A morphosyntactic analysis of adjectives in two Kwa languages: Ga and Dangme

Regina Oforiwah Caesar
University of Education, Winneba, Ghana

Yvonne A. A. Ollennu
University of Education, Winneba, Ghana

The adjective category normally serves as attribute for the nouns in languages that do have them. The paper investigates the morphosyntactic properties of adjectives in two Kwa languages, Ga and Dangme. Both languages have derived and non-derived adjectives. The paper which is mainly descriptive, examines the similarities and differences that exist between these two Kwa languages in terms of their morphological and syntactic features. The paper reveals that though similarities exist in the occurrence of adjectives syntactically, there exist differences in their morphological properties. On the other hand, Ga and Dangme show agreement in terms of number with the head noun for all adjectives used attributively. The paper concludes that in both languages, adjective occur after the head noun in attributive position. Predication of adjectives can occur in nominal forms and the verbal equivalence is also employed in both languages. Plural marking in adjectives is through reduplication and affixation in Ga while in Dangme, it is only through affixation. Data for this paper were collected from both primary and secondary sources.

1 Introduction

Adjectives as one of the subclasses of modifiers have been studied in Ghanaian languages by several linguists (e.g., Osam 2003; Ameka 2003; Otoo 2005; Adjei 2007; Amfo et al. 2007; Danti 2007; Dzameshie 2007; Naden 2007; Pokuaa et al. 2007; Caesar 2013, a.o.). This study investigates the morpho-syntactic properties of adjectives in Ga and Dangme. Ga and Dangme belong to the Kwa group of languages from the Niger Congo family. Ga is a two tone language whiles Dangme is a three tone language. Ga has twenty six letters in its alphabet whiles Dangme has thirty letters of the alphabet. Both languages have seven oral vowels and five nasal vowels.

Regina Oforiwah Caesar & Yvonne A. A. Ollennu. A morphosyntactic analysis of adjectives in two Kwa languages: Ga and Dangme. In Jason Kandybowicz, Travis Major, Harold Torrence & Philip T. Duncan (eds.), *African linguistics on the prairie: Selected papers from the 45th Annual Conference on African Linguistics*, 157–173. Berlin: Language Science Press.
DOI:10.5281/zenodo.1251726

Ga is spoken along the coastal area in Accra. These areas include Ga Mashi, Osu, La, Teshi, Nungua, Tema, Oyibi, Bawaleshi, and its surrounding villages. The area stretches to the foot of the Akwapim hills, the Nyanam hill up to Ninobi, and then to the south-wards of Langma hill in the southern part of Kasoa, whiles Dangme is spoken in two regions of Ghana: Eastern and Greater Accra mainly in South-Eastern Ghana along the coastal belt and the forest areas. Dangme speakers thus, inhabit the coastal area of the Greater Accra Region, east of Accra and part of Eastern Region of Ghana. Dangme has seven dialects while Ga has no dialects but there may be vocabulary differences geo-graphically in terms of pronunciation. The seven dialects of Dangme include: Ada, Nugo, Kpone, Gbugblaa/Prampram, Osudoku, Sɛ and Krobo (Yilo and Manya). There are sev-eral small communities east of the Volta Region that trace their origins to Dangme land; most of these have shifted to Ewe as a language of daily life but others have not (Dakubu 1966, Sprigge 1969 cited in Ameka & Kropp Dakubu 2008). Patches of speakers are also found in Togo land for instance, Nyetoe and Gatsi. Data used for this study were col-lected from some native speakers of Ga and Dangme and were cross-checked with other native speakers. Data were also drawn from books (Ablorh-Odjidjah 1961; Kropp Dakubu 1987; 2000; Adams 1999; 2000; Amfo et al. 2007; Adi 2003; Odonkor 2004; Otoo 2005; and Caesar 2013). The aim of this paper is to find out how similar or different the usage of adjectives in these two languages looks like. It is said that a concept in a language may be expressed in another, using a word from a particular word class but the same concept may be expressed in another language using a word from a different word class (Dixon 1977; 1982; 2004). The theoretical framework is based on Dixon's (2004) classification of adjectives.

1.1 Theoretical framework

Dixon (2004) identifies a set of semantic types of property concepts that are encoded by the adjective class in languages that have them. There are thirteen classes in his recent work, which are:

- DIMENSION e.g. big, small, long, deep, etc
- PHYSICAL PROPERTY, e.g. hard, strong, sweet, cheap, etc
- SPEED, e.g. fast, quick, rapid, etc
- AGE, e.g. new, old young, modern, etc
- COLOUR, e.g. black, white, golden, etc
- VALUE, e.g. good, bad, lovely, pretty, etc
- DIFFICULTY, e.g. easy, tough, hard, simple, etc
- VOLITION, e.g accidental, purposeful, deliberate, etc
- QUALIFICATION, (this has subtypes) e.g. true, obvious, normal, right, etc
- HUMAN PROPENSITY, (this also has subtypes), e.g. angry, jealous, clever, sad, etc
- SIMILARITY, e.g. different, equal (to) analogous (to), etc

- QUANTIFICATION, e. g. many, few, plenty, little, etc
- POSITION, e.g. high, low, etc.

For the purpose of this study, we use examples from the following classes: dimension, colour, value, age and physical property. This is because the adjectives in these two Kwa languages are mostly found in these groups. Other semantic groupings will be investigated in future.

2 Sources of adjectives

Linguistic scholars (Kropp Dakubu 1987; Adi 2003; Adams 1999; 2000; Odonkor 2004; Amfo et al. 2007; Caesar 2013) have identified that Ga and Dangme have both deep level and derived adjectives. Deep level adjectives are monomorphemic, that is, they cannot be segmented into morphemes to be meaningful. Examples of deep level are found below in (1).

(1) **Ga:**   **Dangme:**
    agbo 'big'   *yumu* 'black'
    kpitioo 'short'   *kpiti* 'short'
    kpakpa 'good'   *kpakpa* 'good'
    kakadaŋŋ 'long'   *wayoo* 'small'
    gojoo 'huge'   *gojoo* 'huge'

2.1 Adjectives derived from verbs

Adjectives in Dangme could also be derived from verbs through either total or partial reduplication. When adjectives are derived through total reduplication in Dangme, the reduplicant takes an additional segment base on the vowel of the verbs stem, that is, verb stems that end in {u, o, or ɔ} take {i, e or ɛ} to arrive at the adjective. Two processes occur in partial reduplication: the deletion of a consonant and a rise in tongue high level of the vowel of the reduplicant morpheme. Consider the following examples in Dangme:

(2) **Dangme:**
    Verb   **Reduplicated form**
    bla 'to join'   *ba~blɛ* 'joint'
    ngla 'to burn'   *nga~nglɛ* 'burnt
    sa 'to spoil'   *sa~sɛ* 'rotten'
    tsu 'to redden'   *tsu~tsu* 'red'
    gbo 'to die'   *gbo~gboe* 'dead'
    pɔ 'to wet'   *pɔ~pɔe* 'wet'
    fi 'to tie'   *fi~fii* 'tried'
    si 'to fry'   *si~sii* 'fried'
    ngma 'to write'   *ngma~ngmɛɛ* 'written'

The lateral /l/ is elided in the base of the reduplicated forms *bablɛ* 'joint' and *nganglɛ* 'burnt' and there is a rise in tongue height. That is, the low front vowel /a/, has changed to the low mid vowel /ɛ/ as exemplified in the first two examples of (2) above. From the data, it is observed also that reduplicated adjectives in Dangme can be formed by copying the whole of the base and by adding a vowel to the reduplicated part of the verb as shown in the last five examples of (2) above.

Adjectives could also be derived from verbs in Ga through affixation and reduplication. Affixation is characterised with the suffixation of {-ŋ}, {-ru} and {-ra} to the base form of some verbs to form adjectives. {-ŋ} is attached to verb stems that end in /i, ɛ/. {-ru} is suffixed to verb stems that end in /u/, and {-ra} is attached to root forms that end in /a/. Consider the Ga examples below:

(3) **Ga:**

Verb	**Adjective**
gbi 'to dry'	*gbi-ŋ* 'dried'
di 'to blacken'	*di-ŋ* 'black'
yɛ 'to whiten'	*yɛ-ŋ* 'white'
tsu 'to ripe'	*tsu-ru* 'red'
sha 'to spoil'	*sha-ra* 'spoilt'

The Ga examples in (3) above have adjectives formed from verbs through affixation. The illustrations below also show the reduplication process. The verb is either suffixed with a segment or morpheme before reduplicated, or it is reduplicated and then suffixed with the /i/ segment as in (4) below:

(4) **Ga:**

boda 'to be bent'	*boda~bodai* 'crooked'
kwɔ 'to be deep'	*kwɔŋ~kwɔŋ* 'deep'
nyaŋe 'to shun/despise'	*nyaŋemɔ~nyaŋemɔ* 'disgusting'

In complete reduplication in Ga, the segment /i/ is attached to the reduplicated part of some verbs as in *boda-boda-i* 'crooked'. However, a verb such as *kwɔ* 'to be deep' is suffixed with the velar nasal /ŋ/ to become *kwɔŋ* before it is reduplicated as *kwɔŋkwɔŋ* 'deep'. It is realised that the velar nasal, /ŋ/ is attached to the base as well as the reduplicated part of the adjective. Similarly, the verb root, *nyaŋe* 'to shun/despise' has been suffixed with {-mɔ} to become *nyaŋemɔ* before it is reduplicated as *nyaŋemɔnyaŋemɔ* 'disgusting'. This class of verbs is limited in Ga.

2.2 Adjectives derived from nouns

The stock of Dangme and Ga adjectives could also be added to through reduplication of nouns. In Ga, the nouns are mostly pluralised first and then reduplicated. In Dangme, however, some of the nouns just go through a total reduplication while others are pluralised as in Ga before they are reduplicated to derive adjectives. Consider the Dangme examples below:

(5) **Dangme:**

Noun	Reduplicated form (Adjective)
zu 'sand'	*zu~zu* 'sandy'
mamu 'powder'	*mamu~mamu* 'powdery'
nyu 'water'	*nyu~nyu* 'watery'
zɔ 'oil'	*zɔ~zɔ* 'oily'
tso 'tree'	*tsohi~tsohi* 'spongy'
tɛ 'stone'	*tɛhi~tɛhi* 'rocky'
wu 'bone'	*wuhi~wuhi* 'bony'
kpɔ 'lump'	*kpɔhi~kpɔhi* 'lumpy'

It is observed in the Dangme examples in (5) that the first four examples of the redu-plicated nouns have not taken on any affix after the reduplication. However, the last three have attached the plural marker for common nouns, {-hi}, to indicate that they are countable.

(6) **Ga:**

Noun	Reduplicated form (Adjective)
tɛ 'stone'	*tɛi~tɛi* 'stony/rocky'
tso 'tree	*tsei~tsei* 'spongy'
nu 'water'	*nui~nui* 'watery'
shia 'sand'	*shia~shiai* 'sandy'
kpaa 'rope'	*kpaa~kpai* 'knotty'
kpɔ 'lump'	*kpɔi~kpɔi* 'lumpy'
wu 'bone'	*wui~wui* 'bony'

Ga generally attaches the plural suffix {–i} to count nouns while Dangme adds {-hi} to common count nouns to form its plural. It is observed from the data on Ga that unlike Dangme which pluralises only the count nouns, Ga pluralises the count and some non-count nouns by attaching the morpheme {-i} to the base and the reduplicated forms of the word in many cases like *nu* 'water' becoming *nu-i-nu-i* 'watery'. It is however observed that the base form of the noun, *shia* 'sand' has not been pluralised in the reduplicated form *shia-shia-i* 'sandy'. A few of the nouns however, do not add the {-i} segment to the nouns to form adjectives in Ga. See some examples in Ga below:

(7) *ŋmɔtɔ* 'mud'   *ŋmɔtɔ~ŋmɔtɔ* 'muddy'
     kotsa 'sponge'   *kotsa~kotsa* 'spongy'
     ŋoo 'salt'   *ŋoo~ŋoo* 'salty'

3 Morphosyntactic properties

This section discusses the morphological process of number agreement and reduplication of adjectives in these two Kwa Languages. Adjectives in Ga and Dangme can inflect for number (Kropp Dakubu 1987; 2000; Adams 1999; 2000). The Ga adjective is marked overtly to indicate plurality to show agreement with the head noun it modifies. However, in Dangme, adjectives are not marked morphologically to show number agreement in the constructions when the definite article is present in the NP. The number agreement is marked on the definite article to indicate plurality and therefore has scope over the entire noun phrase.

3.1 Plural formation in adjectives in Ga and Dangme

In Ga and Dangme, the plural affix of a noun, is either attached to the adjective that qualifies the preceding noun or follows the NP. The adjective suffixes in Ga include {-i. -ji. -bii} and the zero morpheme in few instances. Dangme also has noun plural suffixes {-hi, -mɛ, -bi, -wi, -li}. The animate or human nouns in Dangme are what are marked morphologically for plural in Dangme. In noun phrases where adjectives are present, the adjectives select the {-hi} plural marker. {-mɛ} however, is attached to definite and indefinite articles, such as {ɔ, a or ko}, to form the plural of the articles. The plural marking on any of the articles scopes over the entire noun phrase. Consider the examples in Dangme below:

(8) **Dangme:**
Bo   **tsutsu-hi** ngɛ daka a   mi.
cloth red-PL   are box DEF in

'There are red cloths in the box.'

(9) Mangoo **mumu ɔ-mɛ**   sa.
mango fresh   DEF-PL rotten.

'The fresh mangoes are rotten.'

(10) Duku **futa** **a-mɛ** sɛ mu.
scarf white DEF-PL dirty.

'The white scarves are dirty.'

In example (8), the adjective *tsutsu-hi* 'red.PL' has taken the plural marker of the noun *bo* 'cloth' which is {-hi} retaining the noun in its singular form in the clause. In example (9), the adjective *mumu* 'fresh' comes in between the subject noun *mangoo* 'mango' and the definite plural marker *'ɔmɛ'* in the morphology. Similarly in example (10), the adjective *futaa* 'white' comes in between the subject noun *duku* 'scarf' and the definite plural marker, *amɛ*.

In Dangme we observe that to show number agreement in a noun phrase, it is the plural form of the definite or indefinite articles that is used. The definite or indefinite article informs us that the noun and adjective are in their plural forms even though the nouns are not marked morphologically as in (8-10) above. Consider the Ga examples in (11-13).

(11) **Ga:**
Wo-ji **he-i**   lɛ   dara.
book-PL new-PL DEF big.ITER
'The new books are big.'

(12) Atade-i **fɛɛfɛ-ji**   lɛ   elaaje.
dress-PL beautiful-PL DEF lost
'The beautiful dresses are lost.'

(13) Tse-i **kakada-ji** lɛ   kumɔ.
tree-PL long-PL   DEF broke.ITER
'The tall trees broke.'

On the other hand, Ga has a suffix on both the nouns *wo-ji* 'books' *atade-i* 'dresses' and adjectives *he-i* 'new', *fɛɛfɛ-ji* 'beautiful.PL', *tse-i* 'tress', and *kakada-ji* 'tall ones' to show number agreement. The definite article however, is not marked as it has no plural form in Ga. Another observation from the above Ga example is that the definite article retains its shape for both the singular and the plural forms of the nouns. Some adjectives are also reduplicated in Ga and Dangme to express plural number in the entity named as in (14-17) below:

(14) **Ga:**
E-he   **shikpɔŋ lɛkɛtɛɛ.**
3SG-buy land   wide
'He/she bought a wide land.'

(15) E-he   **shikpɔ-ji lɛkɛtɛ~lɛkɛtɛɛ.**
3SG-buy land-PL   wide~RED
'He/she bought wide lands.'

(16) **Dangme:** E   jua   **blodo daka.**
3SG sell.AOR bread box
'He/she sold a box full of bread.'

(17) E   juaa   **blodo daka~daka.**
3SG sell.AOR bread box~RED
'He/she sold boxes of bread.'

The Ga example *lɛkɛtɛɛ* 'wide' in (14) denotes a singular number. On the other hand, *lɛkɛtɛ-lɛkɛtɛɛ* 'wide-wide', denotes plurality in the plural noun, *shikpɔ-ji* it qualifies in (15). But in Dangme, the mere reduplication of the adjective does denote plurality. Plural marking affixes are however, not expressed on the noun being modified as exemplified in (16-17).

3.2 Reduplication of adjectives

Ga and Dangme adjectives can also be reduplicated. Normally when an adjective is reduplicated, it shows intensity. As in the NPs, the reduplicated adjectives are pluralised in both their base and the reduplicant parts. Below are examples to illustrate:

(18) **Ga:**
   wulu 'big'   *wuji~wuji* 'big'
   kpitioo 'short'   *kpitibii~kpitibii* 'short'
   bibioo 'small'   *bibii~bibii* 'small'
   wamaa 'large'   *wamaa~wamaa* 'large'

(19) **Dangme:**
   agbo 'big'   *agbo~agbo* 'big'
   nyafi 'small'   *nyafi~nyafi* 'small'
   yumu 'black'   *yumu~yumu* 'blackened'
   tsutsu 'red'   *tsutsu~utsu* 'reddish'

The reduplication process can be total or partial. This is demonstrated in example (19) where *tsutsu* 'red' becomes *tsutsuutsu* 'reddish'. The reduplication process in Dangme is total whereas in Ga, there is generally the suffixation of {-i, -bii, -jii} as plural affixes to adjectives and nouns. With the exception of few adjectives such as *wamaa –wamawamaa*, all other nouns and adjectives take any of the three suffixes above. Their conditioning is not discussed in this paper. See below how some of these reduplicated forms of adjectives can occur in sentences.

(20) **Ga:**
   Gbekɛ **bibioo** lɛ   e-wɔ.
   child small DEF PERF-sleep
   'The little child is asleep.'

(21) Gbekɛbii **bibii~bibii** lɛ   e-wɔ.
   child-PL small~very DEF .PERF-sleep
   'The little children are asleep.'

(22) **Dangme:**
   Tade **yumu** ɔ   gba.
   dress black DEF tear.AOR
   'The black dress is torn.'

(23) Tade **yumu~yumu** ɔ   ngɛ tsu   ɔ   mi.
   dress black~very DEF is room DEF inside
   'The very black dress is in the room.'

In the Ga examples in (20-21), it is observed that the reduplicated form of *bibioo* 'a small...' is *bibiibii* 'very small ones'. *Bibioo* expresses singularity in the entity being discussed while *bibiibii* expresses intensity and plurality. In the Dangme examples in (22-23), it is observed that *yumu* 'black' has been reduplicated as *yumuyumu* 'very black'. The reduplicated form, *yumuyumu*, shows the intensity of the colour *yumu*, 'black'.

Both Ga and Dangme nominalise the adjective to be the head of an NP and also to be a subject of a sentence. To nominalise an adjective in Ga and Dangme, the prefix {e-} is attached to certain class of adjectives. However some of these adjectives are not attached with the prefix but remain in the same form as nominals. The prefix {e-} nominalises a class of adjectives that denotes colour and age of objects. For instance, in Ga, *yɛŋ* 'white' becomes *e-yɛŋ* 'white one', *diŋ* 'black' becomes *e-diŋ* 'black one', *tsuru* 'red' becomes *e-tsuru* 'red one', *hee* 'new' becomes *e-hee* 'new/new one', *momo* 'old' becomes *e-momo* 'old one', *ŋmɔŋ* 'fresh' becomes *e-ŋmɔŋ* 'fresh one'. Likewise, in Dangme, *ku* 'male' becomes *ku-e-ku* 'male one', *yo* 'female' becomes *e-yo* 'female', *he* 'new' becomes *e-he* 'new one', *agbo* 'big' becomes *e-agbo* 'big one', *wayoo* 'small' becomes *e-wayoo* 'small one'. The conditioning for the zero allomorph is yet to be investigated.

4 Functions of adjectives

Dixon (2004) asserts that adjectives typically fill two roles in the grammar of a language. These two roles are the attributive and predicative use of adjectives. In addition to these roles, the adjective can occur in comparative constructions. When an adjective plays the attributive role, it serves as a modifier to the head noun. When the adjective is used predicatively, it occurs as a copula complement in most languages. Dixon (2004) notes however that these two roles, attributive and predicative may not occur for all adjectives in all languages. In certain instances, only one of these roles may be found. Such adjectives can occur within sentences as exemplified below. We begin with adjectives in attributive position.

4.1 Adjectives in attributive position

Dangme adjectives as well as Ga adjectives that qualify nouns have the reversal structure as compared to English. Such adjectives come after the nouns they qualify in a phrase, clause or of any kind. Consider the following examples in Dangme and Ga:

(24) **Dangme:**
Womi **he** ɔ ka.
book new DEF be.long
'The new book is long.'

(25) Bɔɔlu **momo** ɔ pɛ.
ball old DEF burst
'The old ball is burst.'

(26) Kɔɔpoo **agbo** ɔ   hyi.
cup   big   DEF be.full
'The big cup is full.'

(27) E   juaa   blodo **bɔdɔɔ**.
he/she sell.HAB bread soft
'He/she sells soft bread.'

(28) **Ga:**
Nuu **agbo** lɛ   wɔ   vii.
man big   DEF sleep. PST deeply
'The big man slept soundly/deeply.'

(29) Wolo **hee** lɛ   da.
book new DEF be big
'The new book is big.'

(30) Atade **momo** lɛ   e-tsere.
dress old   DEF 3SG-tear
'The old dresses are torn.'

(31) Blodo **bɔdɔɔ** e-hɔ-ɔ.
bread soft   3SG-sell-HAB
'He/she sells soft bread.'

In examples (24-25) in Dangme, *he* 'new' and *momo* 'old' are expressing age. *Agbo* 'big' indicates dimension in (26) and *bɔdɔɔ* 'soft' shows physical property. All these adjectives come after the nouns, *womi* 'book', *boolu* 'ball', *kɔɔpoo* 'cup' and *blodo* 'bread' in (27) they respectively qualify. In example (28-31) on Ga, it is realised also that *agbo* 'big', *bɔdɔɔ* 'soft', *hee* 'new' and *momo* 'old' express dimension, physical property, and age as in the Dangme examples in (24-27). These adjectives in Ga, are preceded by the head nouns *nuu*, 'man', *wolo* 'book', *atade* 'dress' and *blodo* 'bread'. From the above examples in (24-27) in Dangme and (28-31) in Ga, we see the adjectives occurring after the nouns they modify, followed by the definite article, if present in the clause. Thus, the adjective comes in between the noun and the definite or indefinite article as in other Ghanaian languages.

The adjective for 'beautiful' in Ga is *fɛɛfɛo*. In example (32), *fɛɛfɛo* is used attributively in a clause. Dangme on the other hand, employs a whole phrase such as *'he ngɛ fɛu'* or *'kɛ e he fɛu'* in other to express the attributive use of the adjective, 'beautiful' as in example (33) below:

(32) **Ga:**
Asupaatere **fɛɛfɛo** lɛ   etse.
shoe/sandals beautiful DEF tear.PST
'The beautiful pair of shoes is torn.'

(33) **Dangme:**
Tokota   **kɛ   e   he fɛu** ɔ   hia.
shoe/sandal with 3SG.POSS part beauty DEF tear.AOR

'The beautiful pair of shoes is torn.'

4.2 More than one adjective in attributive position

The paper also investigates when more than one adjective is used attributively for a noun.
In Ga, it is observed that sometimes the last adjective used in a sequence is prefixed with
{e-}. Consider the Ga examples (34-37) below:

(34) **Ga:**
Tɛ   **bibioo e-hee**   ko   ka jɛmɛ.
stone little NMLZ-new DEF lie there.

'There is a new small stone lying there.'

(35) Gbee **agbo kpitioo** lɛ   gbo.
dog big   short   DEF die.PST

'The big short dog is dead.'

(36) Mi-he   shia **fɛɛfɛo   agbo** ko.
1SG-buy.PST house beautiful big   certain.

'I bought a certain big beautiful house.'

(37) Gbe-i **agbo-i e-di-ji**   lɛ   egbo.
dog-PL big-PL NMLZ-black-PL DEF PERF.die

'The big black dogs are dead.'

In the Ga examples in (34-37), the adjectives are *bibioo* 'small' and *ehee* 'new', *agbo*
'big' and *kpitioo* 'short', *fɛɛfɛo* 'beautiful' and *agbo* 'big', *agbo-i* 'big ones' and *edi-ji* 'black
ones' have respectively occurred in a sequence. In Dangme, the category of age, value or
colour may precede those with physical or dimension properties. Those from the physical
property and human property tend to be used in copula complement function. Sentences
(38-41) present some examples of adjective sequencing in Dangme.

(38) **Dangme:**
Mangoo **ngmlikiti gaga** nɔ si.
mangoo ripe.NEG   long fall down.

'The unripe oval shaped mango has fallen down.'

(39) To   **futa agbo** kɛ   e   nane gagaaga a   laa.
sheep/goat white big   with 3SG.POSS leg long.RED DEF lost

'The white fat sheep/goat with the long legs is lost.'

(40) Sɛ   **yumu nyafii** ngɛ sukuu tsu   ɔ   mi.
      Stool/chair black DIM   is   school room DEF inside

      'The black small stool/chair is in the classroom.'

(41) Lo   **momo sasɛ** ɔmɛ   ngɛ tso   goga   a   mi.
      fish/meat old   rotten DEF.PL at   wood bucket DEF inside

      'The little rotten old meat/fish is in the wooden bucket.'

4.3 Predicative use of the adjective

The paper now examines whether the adjective can function predicatively in the two languages. Dixon (2004: 106) asserts that adjectives function as copula complement usually referred to as predicative adjectives. A predicatively used adjective is one kind of subject complement. It is an adjective that modifies the subject of the sentence. In addition, they function as adjectives usually to qualify the NPs they occur with within sentences as exemplified below:

(42) **Ga:**
      Asapaatere lɛ yɛ   fɛo.
      Shoe/sandals DEF possess beauty

      'The pair of shoe/sandals is beautiful.'

(43) **Dangme:**
      Tokota   a   ngɛ   fɛu.
      Shoe/sandals DEF possess beauty.

      'The pair of shoe/sandals is beautiful.'

In the examples (42) and (43) the use of the adjectives in complement position are normally nominalised. The copula verb *yɛ* and *ngɛ* are used respectively in Ga and Dangme. The adjective, *fɛo* in (42) and *fɛu* in (43) are the nominal forms of the adjectives in Ga and Dangme. The Ga adjective normally does not occur in predicate position except when prefixed with {e-} or remains in the same form (zero morpheme). Sometimes adjectives which have verbal equivalents are used by native speakers of both Ga anad Dangme languages. The constructions below indicate this phenomenon:

(44) **Dangme:**
      Siadeyo ka.
      Siadeyo be.tall

      'Siadeyo is tall.'

(45) Bo   ɔ   pɔ.
      cloth DEF be.wet

      'The cloth is wet.'

(46) Tso ɔ   gbli.
      tree DEF be.dry

      'The tree is dried.'

(47) **Ga:**
      Aku **kwɔ**.
      Aku be.tall

      'Aku is tall.'

(48) Atade lɛ   **e-fɔ**.
      dress DEF PERF-wet

      'The dress is wet.'

(49) Tso lɛ   **gbi**.
      tree DEF PERF.dry

      'The tree is dry.'

Examples (44-46) are intransitive clauses with one core argument each in the subject position. The morphemes in bold print are intransitive predicates with their heads being verbs. All verbs which denote adjectival meanings in sentence (44-46) occupy the predicative position but modify the noun *Siadeyo* 'a personal name', *bo* 'cloth' and *tso* 'tree' in the Dangme clauses. In a similar way, *kwɔ* 'be tall', *fɔ* 'wet' and *gbi* 'dry' modify the nouns *Aku,* 'a personal name', *atade* 'dress' and *tso* 'tree' in the Ga examples in (47-49) above.

From the examples in (44-49), it was realised that some of these adjectives when used predicatively make use of verbs when there are equivalence in Ga and Dangme. It was also noted that in Ga, when the verb equivalence is absent, there is the copula construction and the nominalised form of the adjective is used. When the adjectives are from the human propensity class they normally tend to be nouns. Relative clauses are also sometimes used in both languages. Below are some other verbs that could be used to express adjectival meanings.

(50) **Dangme:**   (51) **Ga:**
      tí ' to be thick'   *ti* 'to be thick'
      fú 'to be ripe'   *tsu* 'to be ripe'
      gbó 'to die'   *gbo* 'to die'
      kle 'to be big'   *da* 'to be big'
      hì 'to be good'   *hi* 'to be good'

These are verbs as they take all aspect and tense markers like other verbs. Dixon (2004) refers to such adjectives as verbal adjectives. These can be negated as shown in (52) and (53). In Ga and Dangme, each of these takes a negative suffix. For instance:

(52) **Dangme:**
    ti we 'not thicken'
    fu-i 'not ripe'
    gbo we 'not dead'
    klee we 'not big'

(53) **Ga:**
    tii-i 'not thicken'
    tsuu-u 'not ripe'
    gboo-o 'not dead'
    daa-a 'not big'

In Ga, there are two verb classes, one class takes circumfixes most often to mark negativity and aspect and the other class employs suffixes. These have shown up in (53) where the affirmative forms of the verbs are either suffixed or circumfixed with the negative marker(s). That is, verbs of this category can also take on the full range of tense/aspect markers just like any other verb in Ga and Dangme. According to Dixon (2004: 19), when an adjective occurs as an intransitive predicate, it may take some or all the morphological processes available to verbs in the slot, thus, tense, aspects, mood, polarity, etc. An adjective in Dangme functions directly as a modifier of a noun in a noun phrase, acting as a copula complement and shows morphological categories similar to those of nouns especially those related to numbers.

5 Similarities and differences

Ga and Dangme both have deep level adjectives which are monomorphemic. Both languages have derived adjectives from verbs and nouns which are obtained through total or partial reduplication and an addition of a segment. In the process of reduplication, Dangme attaches {-i, -e, or -ɛ} to verb stems that end in {-u, -o or -ɔ} while Ga attaches {-ŋ, -ru, -ra} to verb stems that end in {-i, -ɛ, -u, -a} to derive adjectives. We found that in the process of deriving adjectives from nouns in Ga and Dangme involves two processes. That is, either the root noun goes through a complete reduplication only, or reduplicates completely and then attaches a plural marker to both the root noun and the reduplicated parts of the noun. Dangme attaches the {-hi} plural marker while in Ga, {-i} is attached as discussed in examples (5-7). It is to be noted that whilst in Dangme, non-countable nouns are not pluralised either in a part or in all the morphemes of the reduplicated form of the noun, Ga does attach a plural affix, {-i} to each of the free forms of countable and non-countable nouns reduplicated to form an adjective, with the exception of a few that do not pluralise the root noun of the reduplicated word as in *shia-shia-i* 'sandy'. Adjectives can also be reduplicated to show intensity and express plural number in both languages.

Adjectives in Ga and Dangme function attributively. It is to be noted that just as it occurs in other Ghanaian languages such as Akan, Ewe, Gurene, Dagbani and the like, Ga and Dangme adjectives and nouns have a reversed structure in the NP as compared to English, i.e. the adjective occurs after the noun it qualifies. It is also to be noted that while Ga has lexical nominal forms of adjectives such as *fɛɛfɛo* for the English word 'beautiful', Dangme on the other hand employs phrases such as '...*he ngɛ fɛu*' or '*kɛ e he fɛu*'.

It was realised that plural adjectives are marked morphologically on the adjective and not on the noun stem in Dangme when the definite article is absent in a phrase, a clause or a sentence. It is also noted that, where determiners come into play, the adjectives come in between the noun and the determiner. However, the definite article in Ga does not take any plural affix whiles the definite article in Dangme have plural form. The definite article denotes number concord in the noun and adjective in Ga and Dangme. When there is more than one adjective in a construction in Ga, they are all marked to express plurality. In Dangme however, it is only the final adjective that takes the plural suffix.

The study has identified that predicative adjectives are preceded by copula verbs in both languages. While Ga employs the copula verb, *yɛ*, Dangme uses *ngɛ*. In Ga, when the adjective is used predicatively, it is prefixed with {e-} or may occur in the same form. Sometimes, verbs which denote adjectival meanings are used. Where there is no verbal equivalence, the construction becomes a copula one.

6 Conclusion

This paper has examined certain morphological and syntactic features of adjectives in Ga and Dangme, two Kwa languages spoken in Ghana. It considered the similarities and differences between adjectives in Ga and Dangme, It was observed that the membership for the adjective class in these two languages is increased by deriving adjectives from other sources such as reduplication and the derivation of nouns and verbs. Although, Ga and Dangme employ these three ways of forming adjectives, some of the processes vary. When adjectives are derived through total reduplication, the reduplication template takes an additional segment base on the vowel of the verbs stem to express adjectival properties in Ga and Dangme. It was identified that the two languages have the potential of using reduplicated verbs and nouns as adjectives to modify other nouns in the language. Adjectives can also be reduplicated to show intensity as in other languages of the world. In dealing with categories of adjectives, one can see that adjectives in Ga and Dangme help differentiate one nominal from the other as in other languages.

The study established that even though Ga and Dangme are related to a large extent in the area of adjectives, there are identifiable differences in their morphological and syntactic properties of adjectives as discussed under the similarities and differences in §5. It is hoped that this study will add to the typological study on adjectives universally.

Abbreviations

1	first person	NP	noun phrase
3	third person	PERF	perfective
AOR	aorist	PL	plural
DEF	definite article	POSS	possessive
HAB	habitual	PST	past tense
NMLZ	nominalizer	SG	singular

Regina Oforiwah Caesar & Yvonne A. A. Ollennu

Acknowledgements

We are grateful to Management of the University of Education, Winneba for permitting us to attend and present this paper at ACAL45 in Kansas, USA.

References

Ablorh-Odjidjah, J. R. 1961. *Ga wiemɔ ekomɛi a nitsumɔi.* Accra: Presby.

Adams, George. 1999. *Aspectuals in Ga.* Accra: University of Ghana. Unpublished thesis.

Adams, George. 2000. *Nominalization processes in Ga.* Accra: University of Ghana. Unpublished thesis.

Adi, Daniel B. 2003. *Animosa sua.* Winneba: Teye-Ngua Publications.

Adjei, Francisca A. 2007. Adjectives in Siyase (Avatime). In George Dakubu Mary Esther Kroppand Akanlig-Pare, Emmanuel K. Osam & Kofi K. Saah (eds.), *Proceedings of the annual colloquium of the Legon-Trondheim linguistics project, 2005* (Studies in the languages of the Volta basin 4), 122–134. Accra: University of Ghana Department of Linguistics.

Ameka, Felix. 2003. *The adjective class in Ewe: Its strata and emergent nature.* Unpublished manuscript.

Ameka, Felix K. & Mary Esther Kropp Dakubu. 2008. *Aspect and modality in Kwa languages.* Amsterdam: John Benjamins Publishing Company.

Amfo, Nana Aba, Stella Boateng & Yvonne A. Otoo. 2007. A comparative study of the morphosyntactic properties of adjectives in three Kwa languages. In George Dakubu Mary Esther Kroppand Akanlig-Pare, Emmanuel K. Osam & Kofi K. Saah (eds.), *Proceedings of the annual colloquium of the Legon-Trondheim linguistics project, 2005* (Studies in the languages of the Volta basin 4), 60–71. Accra: University of Ghana Department of Linguistics.

Caesar, Regina O. 2013. Adjectives in Dangme. In Felix A. Fabunmi & Akeem S. Salawu (eds.), *Readings in African dialectology and applied linguistics,* 39–50. München: Lincom.

Danti, Alexis. 2007. The Kasem adjective phrase structure. In George Dakubu Mary Esther Kroppand Akanlig-Pare, Emmanuel K. Osam & Kofi K. Saah (eds.), *Proceedings of the annual colloquium of the Legon-Trondheim linguistics project, 2005* (Studies in the languages of the Volta basin 4), 116–126.

Dixon, R. M. W. 1977. Where have all the adjectives gone? *Studies in Language* 1. 19–80.

Dixon, R. M. W. 1982. *Where have all the adjectives gone and other essays in semantics.* Berlin: Mouton.

Dixon, R. M. W. 2004. Adjective classes in typological perspective. In R. M. W. Dixon & Alexandra Y. Aikenvald (eds.), *Adjective classes: A cross linguistic typology,* 1–49. Oxford: Oxford University Press.

Dzameshie, Alex. 2007. A comparative study of adjectives in Ewe and Akan. In George Dakubu Mary Esther Kroppand Akanlig-Pare, Emmanuel K. Osam & Kofi K. Saah (eds.), *Proceedings of the annual colloquium of the Legon-Trondheim linguistics project, 2005* (Studies in the languages of the Volta basin 4), 72–84.

Kropp Dakubu, Mary Esther. 1987. *The Dangme language.* Accra: Unimax Publishers Limited.

Kropp Dakubu, Mary Esther. 2000. *The Ga nominal phrase.* Unpublished manuscript.

Naden, Tony. 2007. Descriptives: Adjectives in Mampruli. In George Dakubu Mary Esther Kroppand Akanlig-Pare, Emmanuel K. Osam & Kofi K. Saah (eds.), *Proceedings of the annual colloquium of the Legon-Trondheim linguistics project, 2005* (Studies in the languages of the Volta basin 4), 85–99. Accra: University of Ghana Department of Linguistics.

Odonkor, Padi. 2004. *An introduction to the grammar of Dangme: A linguistics approach.* Accra: Adjwensa Publishers.

Osam, Emmanuel Kweku. 2003. An introduction to the verbal and multiverbal system of Akan. In Martha Larsen, Dorothee Beermann & Lars Hellan (eds.), *Proceedings of the Workshop on Multi-Verb Constructions.* Trondheim: Norwegian University of Science & Technology.

Otoo, Yvonne A. 2005. *Aspects of Ga syntax: Adjectives.* Trondheim: University of Trondheim dissertation.

Pokuaa, Christiana, E. Kweku Osam & Kofi K. Saah. 2007. Adjective sequencing in Akan: A preliminary investigation. In George Dakubu Mary Esther Kroppand Akanlig-Pare, Emmanuel K. Osam & Kofi K. Saah (eds.), *Proceedings of the annual colloquium of the Legon-Trondheim linguistics project, 2005* (Studies in the languages of the Volta basin 4), 140–149.

Chapter 11

Towards a unified theory of morphological productivity in the Bantu languages: A corpus analysis of nominalization patterns in Swahili

Nick Kloehn

University of Arizona

Models arguing for a connection between morphological productivity and relative morpheme frequency have focused on languages with relatively low average morpheme to word ratios. Typologically synthetic languages like Swahili which have relatively high average morpheme to word ratios present a challenge for such models. This study investigates the process of agentive nominalization from the perspective of the Dual Route Model. The findings suggest that all agentive nominal forms should decompose when accessed and thus that speakers of Swahili should include these morphemes in their lexical inventory apart from root morphemes. This process appears to not be influence by noun classification, or verbal derivation.

1 Introduction

Within the realm of MORPHOLOGICAL PROCESSING in LEXICAL ACCESS, a growing body of research has been conducted with the aim of developing a quantitative theory of MORPHOLOGICAL PRODUCTIVITY. The central notion of this body of research is the proposition that a morpheme's tendency to productively affix to a novel word-form is determined by whether existing words containing said affix undergo MORPHOLOGICAL DECOMPOSITION when accessed in the lexicon (Bybee 1995, Hay 2002, Hay & Baayen 2002). However, studies supporting these findings have been conducted in Indo-European languages which contain relatively low average morpheme per word ratios compared to the Bantu Languages.[1] This study aims to kick start a vein of research investigating the quantitative

---

[1]2.55 morphemes per word for Swahili versus 1.68 morphemes per word for Modern English (Greenberg 1959).

Nick Kloehn. Towards a unified theory of morphological productivity in the Bantu languages: A corpus analysis of nominalization patterns in Swahili. In Jason Kandybowicz, Travis Major, Harold Torrence & Philip T. Duncan (eds.), *African linguistics on the prairie: Selected papers from the 45th Annual Conference on African Linguistics*, 175–190. Berlin: Language Science Press. DOI:10.5281/zenodo.1251728

determinants of morpheme productivity in a group of languages which have higher average morpheme to word ratios than those previously studied. This first step is made by analyzing the process of nominalization in Swahili from the perspective of THE DUAL ROUTE MODEL (Baayen 1992) (Henceforth, DRM) in order to determine whether derived nominal morphology is predicted to be productive. The derivational process of nominalization is chosen by virtue of being analogous to the sorts of derivational patterns in English used as evidence to support DRM. However unlike English, nominalization in Swahili interacts both with noun classification and verbal derivation. This study touches upon the interaction of these morphological systems to illustrate the complexity of the issue of productivity in synthetic language. These systems are reviewed in §1.1 and §1.2. The study is contextualized with a discussion of the relevant Lexical Access literature in §1.3 as well as models of morphological productivity in §1.4 The history of morphological processing in synthetic languages, and the motivation for the current study is outline in §1.5. In §2 the paper outlines two corpus study designed to investigate the degree of predicted productivity of derived nominals in Swahili and the degree to which they interact with noun classification. In §3 the degree to whether or not productivity interacts with presence and number verbal extensions is evaluated. Finally, the results of these studies are discussed and future research is suggested in §4.

1.1 Nominal and verbal derivation in Swahili

One of the primary features common to all members of the Bantu language subgroup of the Niger-Congo language family is the presence of a rich noun class system (Heine 1982). In Swahili, noun class membership is indicated by a word initial prefix with little exception. These prefixes determine the grammatical number and semantic distinction of the nominal forms to which they are affixed. All nominals in Swahili must occur in some noun class even when the noun class is not signaled by a prefix. Regardless of whether the prefix is present, class membership can be determined by agreement patterns of agreeing prepositions, verbal inflection, nominal phrase constituents, and relativizers (Mohamed 2001). Example (1) gives the morphological breakdown for three nominals in Swahili each corresponding to a different noun class. The degree to which noun classification can be considered derivational or inflectional is debatable, but from the purposes of the present study it is only important to note that the process of noun classification has both inflectional properties (bound and obligatory) and derivational properties (changes meaning and category).

(1)   (Swahili noun classes (Mohamed 2001, TUKI 2001))

        a. mi-parachichi
            CL4-avocados
            'avocado trees'

        b. vi-atu
            CL11-shoe
            'shoes'

   c. u-nywele

      CL8-hair

      'hair'

Another morphological process that is present in Swahili is the system of verbal extensions. These suffixes denote a type of derivation that alters the semantic denotation of a verb and often the adicity of the verb undergoing this process.[2] Henceforth, a verb lacking a verbal extension will be described as simplex, and one which contains a verbal extension will be described as complex. Swahili takes advantage of its morphological system to represent semantically complex verbal environments in the form of morphologically complex verbs, whereas languages like English denote functionally analogous environments by both morphological and non-morphological means. For example, verbs that are semantically analogous in English to those derived through the process described in Example (2) must either (i) undergo the addition of derivational morphology (e.g. *lock - un-lock*), (ii) undergo the addition of inflectional morphology (e.g. *pay - paid*), (iii) introduce a phonologically and morphologically unrelated lexical item (e.g. *close - grasp*), or (iv) require a bi-clausal structure (e.g. *cook - make cook*). Furthermore, verbal extensions may occur multiple times forming multimorphemic complex verbs such as Causative-Applicatives.[3] Example (2) gives the derivation of two complex verbs (right of the arrow) and their simplex counterparts (left of arrow).

(2)   (Complex verb derivations (Mohamed 2001, TUKI 2001, Seidl & Dimitriadis 2003))

     a. yunj-a ↔ yunj-ik-a

        break-FV break-STAT-FV

        'break' 'be broken'

     b. song-a ↔ song-o-a

        press-FV press-AUG-FV

        'press' 'press out'

Given that nominals in Swahili are mostly derived from verbs, the presence of verbal extensions affects the amount of morphology contained within many nominal forms. In other words, since nominals can be derived from both simplex and complex verb forms, the issue of whether a verb is simplex or complex is relevant to any investigation of nominalization. Regardless of whether a nominalized form is simplex or complex, the nominal will obligatorily be classified in a given noun class.

1.2 Nominalization in Swahili

In addition to the noun class prefix and optional verbal extension, the derivation of deverbal nouns requires the addition of one of three word final suffixes denoting nomi-

---

[2] I.e. some extensions (e.g. Causative) require the addition of an argument of the verb and others (e.g. Reciprocal) require the subtraction of an argument of the verb.

[3] E.g. *anz-il-isha* start-APPL-CAUS 'initiate'

nalization (Katamba 2003). In Swahili, nominalizing suffixes denote the relationship of the derived noun to the verb as either agentive or instrumental. Critically, agentive and instrumental forms are limited in the noun class prefixes which it may take,[4] as seen in Table 1.[5]

In addition, Table 1 shows that deverbal nouns may be formed from both simplex and complex verbs, and that they may also undergo both agentive and instrumental nominalization. Unfortunately, this paradigm does not cover the whole story. There also exist deverbal nouns for which there is a morphological variant suffix -*i*. [6] However, the current research limits the domain of inquiry to the suffix denoting agentive nominalization -*aji* which is loosely equivalent to the English suffix -*er* indicating the doer of an action.

1.3 Morphological processing in Lexical Access

The aim of the current subsection is to contextualize this study by reviewing the literature on how morphologically complex words are accessed. Research in the area of Lexical Access is able to rely upon the fact that frequent words are accessed in the lexicon faster than infrequent words. This WORD FREQUENCY EFFECT (Broadbent 1967) has been used to study morphological complexity as a methodology for determining whether affixed words are stored together or separately in the lexicon. Taft (1979) found in a VISUAL WORD RECOGNITION task that when multi-morphemic words of a constant frequency vary in the frequency of their stem morpheme, there was an asymmetry in time it took to access these words. Specifically, a word like size-d, which contains a stem of high frequency (*size*) was accessed faster than a word which has an identical surface frequency (*rake-d*), but which contain a less frequent stem (*rake*). This suggests, Taft concludes, that words containing a given stem are stored together in the lexicon (i.e. *size* is stored with *sized*, *sizable*, *sizing*, etc.). Similarly, it has been suggested that stems that occur with more non-inflectional affixes (e.g. *calculate: calculable, calculation, calculator, calculus, incalculable, incalculably, miscalculate, and miscalculation*) are accessed faster than those co-occurring with only few non-inflectional affixes (*roar: uproar*). This line of research has shown that reaction times in Visual Lexical Decision tasks are faster for nouns having a higher number of morphological neighbors for both mono-morphemic (Baayen et al. 2007, De Jong IV et al. 2000), and multi-morphemic nouns (Bertram et al. 2000)

Another vein of research has suggested that whether or not a complex word (e.g. *happiness*) is stored as one unit (*happiness*) or as multiple units (*happy+ness*) has to do with whether or not the component morphemes are parsed in perception (Baayen 1992 and Hay 2002). If one actively decomposes these forms during perception, then both units will be stored in the lexicon (as *happy* and -*ness*), and if one does not actively decompose them, then the form will be stored as a single unit (as *happiness*). Crucially, they claim that parsing is a function of the frequency ratio of the individual units. Specifically, parsing occurs when the frequency of the stem (*happy*) is greater than the frequency of the

---

[4]Class 3/4 may only occur with Instrumental Nominalization, and Class 1/2 may only occur with Agentive Nominalization.

[5]The associated verb is listed to the left.

[6]E.g. *mw-anz-il-ish-i* CL1-start-APPL-CAUS-AGENT_NOM 'founder'

Table 1: List of complex and simplex verbs and their corresponding deverbal nominal. These forms are divided by whether they are agentive or instrumentive nominals, and vary in their noun class. (Mohamed 2001,TUKI 2001, Katamba 2003).

Simplex Verb		Deverbal Nouns	
		Singular	Plural
cheza 'play'	Agentive Nominalization of Class 1/2	m-chez-aji CL1-*play*-AGENT_NOM 'player'	wa-chez-aji CL2-*play*-AGENT_NOM 'players'
	Instrumentive Nominalization of Class 3/4	m-chez-o CL3-*play*-INST_NOM 'game'	mi-chez-o CL4-*play*-INST_NOM 'games'
pepe 'fan'	Agentive Nominalization of Class 11	u-pepe-aji CL11-*fan*-AGENT_NOM 'fanning, waving'	—
	Instrumentive Nominalization of Class 11	u-pep-o CL11-*fan*-INST_NOM 'wind'	—

Complex Verb			
piga-na 'hit-RECIP'	Agentive Nominalization of Class 1/2	m-pig-an-aji CL1-*hit*-RECIP-AGENT_NOM 'fighter'	wa-pig-an-aji CL2-*hit*-RECIP-AGENT_NOM 'fighters'
	Instrumentive Nominalization of Class 3/4	m-pig-an-o CL3-*hit*-RECIP-INST_NOM 'battle'	mi-pig-an-o CL4-*hit*-RECIP-INST_NOM 'battles'
piga-na 'hit-RECIP'	Agentive Nominalization of Class 11	u-pig-an-aji CL11-*hit*-RECIP-AGENT_-NOM 'rivalry'	—
	Instrumentive Nominalization of Class 11	u-pig-an-o CL11-*hit*-RECIP-INST_NOM 'contest'	—

complex form (*happiness*), and does not occur when the ratio is the reverse. The model encompassing these concepts has been termed 'The Dual Route Model.' This tendency to parse has been argued to be hierarchically ordered from more separable units, which can freely attach to a base or stem (*-ness*), to less separable affixes which may only attach to a base (*-th*) (Hay & Plag 2004, Plag & Baayen 2009) pending semantic or syntactic selectional restrictions.

However, subsequent research has argued against this model by suggesting that morphological decomposition must occur in all cases (Taft 2004), that an information theoretical analysis will outperform the frequency accounts described above in predicting reaction times in a Visual Lexical Decision task (del Prado Martín et al. 2004) and that complex word-form frequency is a better predictor of decomposition overall (Baayen et al. 2007). So far, this research suggests that words are stored near their morphological neighbors, and are arguably stored in either morphologically complex or simplex forms.

1.4 Morphological productivity

The aim of this section is to describe the line that has been drawn from the status multi-morphemic word storage (as one unit or as multiple units) to claims about morpheme productivity. Morpheme productivity is defined as the ability of a morpheme to occur in new environments, or to occur with novel words. For example, in English re- is qualitatively more productive than *en-*, because it can occur with words new to the language more readily (e.g. re-google: to google again versus #*engoogle*). Early research questioning the status of productivity has been qualitative (Schultink 1961) or as extremely difficult to measure (Aronoff 1976). However, newer models have attempted to categorize productivity as a consequence of word frequency. Bybee (1995) claims that token frequency (e.g. number of occurrences of *re+visit*) and type frequency (e.g. number of occurrences of *re+*STEM) are indicative of productivity. From this perspective, when a complex word-form has an individual token frequency that is relatively high, the word is more likely to be stored as a whole unit in one's mental lexicon and thus may not be decomposed. Words with a relatively low token frequency will tend to be novel, and if they are associated with a high type frequency then all of these words will be stored by each other in the lexicon. This storage, she argues, creates a stronger representation of the affix (e.g. *re-*). Bybee asserts that a stronger representation for a given morpheme should generally be associated with an increase in its productivity. Whereas Bybee's analysis does not make claims about a numeric threshold for this effect, Alegre & Gordon (1999) argue for a numeric threshold for a token frequency effect for complex forms above six per one million.

Baayen (1992) and Hay & Baayen (2002) claim that comparing token frequency (e.g. *re+visit*) and type frequency (e.g. *re+*STEM) alone is insufficient to account for productivity. Rather, the number of different decomposed forms acts as the predictor of productivity. They define decomposition as a function of the relationship between the derived form of a complex word (e.g. *re+visit*) and its underived or base (e.g. *visit*). If the derived form is lower than the base form, then the derived form will be parsed in perception. This is measured by looking at the underived versus derived frequency of forms containing the affix in question (Hay 2002). If enough of these forms that contain the given affix (e.g. all words that contain the affix *re-*) are parsed in perception, then the morpheme will have an autonomous representation in the lexicon, and will therefore be productive. Here, there is a direct line between parsing and production: if an affix is parsed more often than memorized, it is stored separate from the words it affixes to, and is therefore predicted to be productive.

1.5 Rationale for present study

The research described has evaluated the relationship between frequency and productivity in languages like Dutch, English, French and Spanish (Baayen 1992, Bybee 1997, and Hay & Baayen 2002) but little work of this form has been conducted in more synthetic languages like Swahili. One such example is a study in Finnish which found that words which have larger numbers of morphologically related words elicit correct responses in a visual lexical decision task faster than those who had have smaller number of related words (del Prado Martín et al. 2004). The researchers claim that when a word in Finnish is morphologically related to many derived or complex words, those words tend to be accessed faster as opposed to the overall number of morphologically similar words in the language as is the case in Dutch. In another study on Finnish, Lehtonen et al. (2006) used fMRI to test neural activation during the recognition of complex words. They found that words which were morphologically complex tended to elicit activation in the region associated with semantic and syntactic processing, and that this might be evidence for morphological decomposition in perception.

Besides Finnish, other research has been done on languages with higher degrees of synthesis than previous languages including work on the productivity of nominal morphemes in Japanese. One such example is a study which tested both aphasic and non-aphasic speakers of Japanese on how they processed two nominal suffixes which varied in their productivity (Hagiwara et al. 1999). They claim that most adjectives in Japanese may derive a nominal by co-occurring with the highly productive *-sa* (e.g. *takai* → *takasa* versus *kebai* → *kebasa*), but only a subset of adjectives may derive a nominal by co-occurring with the less productive *-mi* (e.g. *takai* → *takami* versus *kebai* → **kebami*). They found that the processing of the two suffixes coincided in the activation of two areas: Broca's area for the productive (*-sa*) morpheme and the left-middle and inferior temporal areas for the semi-productive morpheme (*-mi*). To them, the difference in activation provides evidence for the claim that these two morphemes vary in a qualitative degree of productivity.

Overall, the work on typologically synthetic languages has suggested a difference in how these languages are processed compared to less synthetic languages. Whereas the results in the Japanese seem to support the predictions made by the DRM, nothing has been down to evaluate productivity in a language with the degree of synthesis in Swahili. The only experiment on Lexical Access in Swahili has argued that morphologically related words are stored near each other in the lexicon for second language speakers. Foote et al. (2014) performed an experiment in Visual Masked Priming aimed at asking whether one can prime noun class prefixes within a semantic class (e.g. does *m-tu* 'CL1.SG-man' prime *wa-tu* 'CL2.PL-man'?) for L2 Swahili speakers. They found that when the primes were related by noun class (e.g. *vi-tanda* 'CL8.PL-bed'), there was an accelerated reaction time in accurately identifying the target word (e.g. *kitanda* 'CL.7-SG-bed'), but not to the same extent as to when the prime and target were identical (e.g. *kitanda - kitanda*). This suggests that words in the same noun class are stored in the same area in the mental lexicon for L2 speakers of Swahili. However, these findings are only a small step towards evaluating the relationship between productivity and word storage in Swahili. Therefore, this study evaluates the relative frequencies of nominal forms as outlined by the DRM in order to evaluate whether any asymmetry in productivity is predicted. This is performed by investigating the agent nominalizing affix *-aji* and the degree to which agentive nominalization interacts with the noun classification and verbal extension system. In order to see how often the suffix occurs (token frequency) and how many different word forms contain the suffix (type frequency) a frequency list is created from a corpus representing a sample population of Swahili words. In addition, token frequency is compared to type frequency and hypotheses are made to the likeliness of forms to be decomposed, and therefore the degree to which *-aji* may or may not be productive. Next, the log frequency of every instance of the morpheme (token derived frequency) is compared to the log underived frequency of each token in the same corpus (token underived frequency) in order to look at the overall trend in aggregate frequencies. Lastly, the number of morphemes per word is compared to the degree of predicted productivity of individual forms to determine whether a higher number of morphemes is correlated to a higher degree of predicted productivity.

2 Evaluating productivity

The aim of the current section is to describe a corpus analysis investigate that words that occur with the agentive nominalizing suffix *-aji*, and to answer whether the process can be described as productive based upon the models described above (Bybee 1995, Hay & Baayen 2002). The corpus study was performed using the the Helsinki Swahili Corpus of approximately 12.6 million words (HCS 2004) compiled from 12 news sources. The corpus of modern Swahili was used as a sample of the synchronic language present in speakers minds such that frequencies of word forms listed may very well reflect the frequency of occurrence of words contained in a speaker's lexicon. This commonly made behavioral inference leads us to the idea that frequency reflects the degree to which representations of a given word form has been accessed, and therefore will lead us to the idea ultimately of how productive these forms may be. In order to get around the issue as to whether complex verbs could be considered underived forms, all forms were included and controlled for in both analyses.[7]

---

[7]This issue could be a paper in itself. Hay & Baayen (2002) consciously limit their analysis to root forms and root+1 morpheme forms exactly because multiple affixation conflates the effect of relative frequency. Essentially, measuring the effect of underived versus derived frequencies get complicated when you have multiple affixation which themselves can denote both a derived and underived form relative to each other.

2.1 Measure 1: Token versus type frequency

The current subsection describes a Token versus Type frequency analysis of agentive deverbal nouns in Swahili. This was performed by using a regular expression to acquire all forms that ended in *-aji* along with the token frequency of each form. The regular expression used to obtain these words was unrestricted in order to include every possible token occurrence, and thus the resulting list required editing in order to filter out words that contained the word sequence *-aji* but were not related to the derivational suffix (e.g. *haji* 'pilgrim'; *jaji* 'judge') as well as words that were misspelled (e.g. **nitakusemaji* cf. *nitakusemaje* 'how I will tell you'). In order to obtain the type frequency (all occurrences of *-aji*), the token frequencies for each of the findings were summed. Each item was manually coded for whether it was simplex of complex,[8] and for its noun class. The resulting list was then analyzed in R, and a frequency table was made combining Noun Classes which vary only in number. Table 2 depicts the finding per Noun Class.

The data depicted in Table 2 demonstrate multiple important aspects of agentive nominalization in Swahili. First, there is a high tendency for nominalized forms to occur in 2 semantic fields (i.e. class 1/2 and class 11). Since class 1/2 denotes animates, and class 11 denotes abstract concepts the data show that there is a strong association of *-aji* with animacy, and with the abstract class. Second, the Token Frequency for each Noun Class (save for Class 5/6) is above the 6 per million threshold argued by Alegre & Gordon (1999) to be the minimum frequency for the parsing of complex forms. This indicated that for most of these forms, we would predict that the frequencies are not too low to exhibit

---

[8]Complex is divided into two groups: 1 verbal extension present or 2 verbal extensions present.

Table 2: Agentive deverbal nouns. Number of occurrences per million of tokens of the type STEM-aji in the Helsinki Swahili Corpus of 12,610,158 tokens. These tokens are divided by noun class ranging from the highest frequency to the lowest frequency occurrences per class. The Type Frequency column depicts how many unique words occur in each class per million, and the Token Frequency column depicts the raw number of words occurring in each class per million (given that many words have repeat occurrences this number is higher than the type frequency). The percentages highlight the proportion of total tokens that occur in a given noun class. The third columns shows that ratio of Type to Token occurrences per noun class.

Noun class	Type frequency (per million)		Token frequency (per million)		Type:Token
m-/wa- (1/2)	24.11	*47.28%*	876.03	*57.32%*	*0.0275*
u- (11/14)	23.39	*45.87%*	611.80	*40.04%*	*0.0382*
ki-/vi- (7/8)	1.98	*3.88%*	29.90	*1.96%*	*0.0662*
ji-/ma- (5/6)	0.95	*1.86%*	4.20	*0.27%*	*0.2262*
n-/n- (9/10)	0.56	*1.11%*	6.26	*0.41%*	*0.0895*
Total	50.99		1528.19		

parsing in perception. Lastly, and most relevant to productivity: the ratio of token and type frequencies are very similar between noun classes. A fair assertion to make here is that, given that the ratios are not wildly different, we would predict of similar degree of productivity across the classes if productivity is in fact a function of Type versus Token frequency. This would indicate that the tendency for tokens to occur in only two classes is a likely a semantic effect and not an effect of productivity.[9]

In order to determine whether productivity is predicted to occur equally in each noun class, a one-way ANOVA was used to test whether there has a correlation between noun class and the Type: Token ratio. Significance would suggest that if productivity were truly a function of Type:Token ratio, then we would predict asymmetries in productivity between noun classes, and non-significance would predict no productivity asymmetries between noun classes. Type:Token ratio did not significantly vary across the noun classes $F(1,574) = .767$, $p < .35$. This may indicate that agentive deverbal nominals will be equally productive across the noun classes, and that asymmetry in the overall frequency of these classes is conditioned by semantic restriction.

Collapsing across the classes, we can assess productivity from the perspective of Token versus Type frequencies by identifying the average number of occurrences for each type. According to Bybee, a productive morpheme would have many tokens that occur only a few times, as opposed to a few forms that occur many times. Figure 1 represents the token frequency for each Type as a histogram.

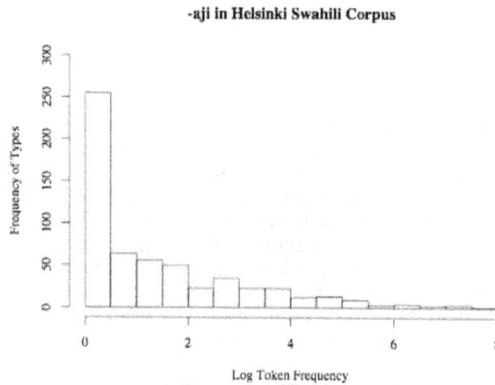

Figure 1: Histogram depicting the log of the Token Frequency along the x-axis, and the Frequency of Types occurring per log token frequency on the y-axis. This means that the bar furthest left depicts a group in which there are 250 tokens with a log frequency of zero (i.e. a frequency of 1, given that Log(1)=0).

---

[9] This notion stems from the idea that these noun classes are both semantically and functionally determined. Whereas class 1/2 and 11 have strong semantic distinctions, many others do not indicate semantic fields that are as consistently clear. In addition, most new words are put into class 9/10 (often unmarked) indicating a non-semantic classification, based on grammatical necessity of noun class membership in the language.

The histogram depicts data much like what Bybee's productive morpheme would resemble. There are around 250 type types with a log frequency occurrence of 0, moving right, there are over 400 types with a Log Token Frequency of less than 2, around 520 less than 4, and possibly only 50 types greater than 4. The result is clear: the majority of types have a relatively low token frequency, and only a few outliers represent the bulk of token frequency (more than 10 tokens).[10] The data show that one would predict productivity from the standpoint of a model that draws upon productivity from Token versus Type frequency analysis. If the relationship between Type and Token frequency is a cue for productivity, and not overall raw frequency, then one would predict a speaker to be equally accepting of a novel form in one noun class as opposed to another barring semantic ill-formedness.

2.2 Measure 2: Underived versus derived frequency

The aim of this subsection is to build on the analysis in the previous section in making a case for productivity by testing agentive deverbal nouns for the derived versus underived frequency. This was performed by using the list of all tokens from the previous analysis. A Perl regular expression was then used to strip all deverbal nouns of their noun class prefixes and agentive suffixes in order to find the underived forms. Given that verbs in Swahili may not occur without left peripheral inflectional prefixation, the underived words included verbs containing inflectional affixation.[11] No complete form of the Helsinki Swahili Corpus is openly available, and so frequency information may only be obtained by web query. Given the number of underived forms tested (574), the process was automated using a BASH cURL script which saved the returned token and frequency information in JAVA script. The results were concatenated into a single text file, and search and replace commands were used to transform the data into analyzable columns, to then be added to the data frame from the previous analysis.

In the vein Hay & Baayen (2002), the log frequencies of the underived (base) tokens were graphed against the log frequency of the derived tokens. Figure 2 demonstrates the relationship between base frequency (underived form) and derived frequency of each occurrence of -*aji* within the corpus. Within the DRM, whether or not a form is parsed is related to its position on this graph to an X=Y line. This is simply a line with a slope of 1, and a y-intercept of 0 that bisects points where the x and y measure are equivalent. In addition, they require that an r2 line describing the data should be significantly above the X=Y line in order for the morpheme to be productive. According to Hay & Baayen, this

---

[10]It is important to note here that forms that are derivationally related but vary in semantic noun class and not just number (e.g. word forms that occur in class 1 and 11) have not been combined into the same type category. An analysis combining the two or more types would gather together words that differ in in one derivational morpheme, but who share the same derivational root. Whether or not the frequency of one should effect the other will be left to future studies.

[11]Swahili verbs inflect as follows, with [] indicating obligatory inflection, and {} indicating optional inflection/derivation based upon the denotation of the proposition: [Subject]-[Tense/Aspect]-{Object}-Verb Stem-{Verbal Extension(s)}-Final Vowel *Chakula ki-na-ku-pik-i-w-a.* CL7.food CL7.AGR-PRES-2SG.OBJ-cook-APPL-PASS-FV 'The food is being cooked for you.'

relationship reveals whether we can predict that the morpheme in question has some sort of mental representation, and therefore occurs productively as seen in Figure 2.

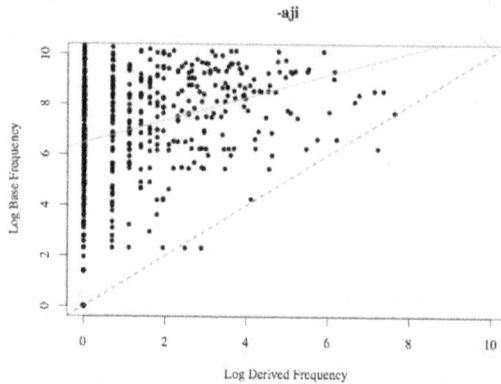

Figure 2: Log Derived Frequency pitted against Log Base Frequency. The blue dotted line represents that X=Y line. A data point on this line will have an equivalent derived and underived frequency. Points above this line have a higher Log Base Frequency than a Log Derived Frequency, and ones below have a higher Derived Frequency than Base Frequency. The green solid line represents the r2 line (p > .0001) which demonstrates the significant positive correlation between Base Frequency and Derived Frequency.

The Figure above shows data points that relate a single forms derived and underived frequencies. A data point below the line will not be parsed in perception according to the theory, and one above the line would be parsed. Clearly the bulk of the data is above the X=Y which means we would predict parsing in perception. The r^2 line describes this phenomenon mathematically. The relationship between the X=Y line and the r^2 line is significantly above the X=Y line, we can posit that the bulk of data points have a higher underived frequency than derived frequency. It is precisely this relationship that denotes productivity in the Dual Route Model.

The aim of this section was to strengthen a claim for productivity of the agentive nominal from the perspective of a dual processing route model. Both theories predict productivity of the affix. The next section aims to expand on this claim by analyzing morphological complexity within the nominal forms.

3 Morphological complexity and productivity

The aim of the current section is to analyze the relationship of the verbal extension system to the degree of how productive a given form is. We would predict that the presence of verbal extensions impacts productivity, then there will be an asymmetry in the predicted productivity of verbs containing verbal extension and those which do not. To do this, the residuals of the r^2 line from §2 (the distance from the line describing the distribution) are compared to the number of verbal extensions present in the forms.

3.1 Regression analysis

In order to test this relationship, morphological complexity was tested against the degree morphological productivity measure using the residuals. A residual of zero means that the data point is on the r^2 line, and points above and below are indicated by positive and negative integers respectively. The assertion here is that points with a negative residual, while still being parsed, are working against productivity, whereas a positive residual is working towards a higher level of productivity. The question then is, is there any correlation between this tendency and whether or not there is a verbal extension present?

3.2 Results

A one-way ANOVA was used to test whether morphological complexity influenced distance for the r^2 line. Given the unevenness of scores per group (300 in Simplex, 150 in 1 Complex, and 59 in 2 Complex) a random sample of data was taken from the two larger groups of equal number to the smallest group. The groups Distance from the r2 line do not vary significantly across the three groups, $F (1, 58) = 26.89$, $p > .2$. However, as the box plot in Figure 3 shows, the non-truncated data shows a trend toward significance in which there is an inverse relationship between morphological complexity and distance from the r2 line. However, a nonsignificant affect suggests that the predicted productivity of denominal verbs is not impacted by whether or not verbal extensions are present.

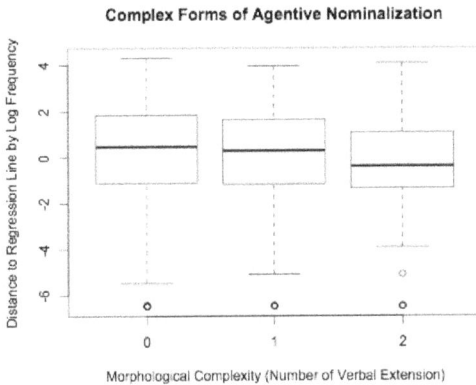

Figure 3: Box plot showing the three groups of morphological complexity on the x-axis (0 Verbal Extensions, 1 Verbal Extension, and 2 Verbal Extensions), and the distance to the regression line on the y-axis. The medians of the groups nonsignificantly decrease as the number of verbal extensions increase.

4 General discussion

Under each analysis given, one would predict that the affix -*aji* should be productive for both complex and simplex verb forms, and regardless of noun classification. The next question to be answered is whether or not all nominalized forms exhibit the same variation. For example, does the instrumental form -*o* exhibit the same degree of predicted productivity with no inhibition for the other morphological systems? A related question would be to isolate whether there are any morphological processes in Swahili that are non-productive. A corpus study on a much larger scale will be able to evaluate this by compare derived and underived forms of all verbs and nominals. If it is the case that these affixes are all predicted to be productive, then there is a testable prediction for a behavioral study investigating the ways in which Swahili speakers process complex words. Namely, the DRM would predict that all forms should be decomposed and therefore that there should be no significant asymmetry in reaction times between complex word forms beyond their base frequencies. The opposite result would indicate that speakers of Swahili may have different thresholds for parsing than speakers of more isolating languages like English. Such a finding would provide evidence for the idea that Lexical Access is ordered relative to the language you acquire. This would entail that some languages would make use of one route of processing more commonly than a language like English, or that these models are wide of the mark, demanding a reanalysis of the way in which human language is processed cross-linguistically.

Acknowledgements

The data in this paper were presented at The University of Arizona Graduate Student Showcase Feb 2014, and ACAL 45 at the University of Kansas. Thanks to all involved and to Mike Hammond, Heidi Harley, Adam Ussishkin and Andy Wedel for comments.

Abbreviations

Numbers in glosses indicate noun class prefixes and pre-prefixes. Abbreviations follow Leipzig glossing conventions, with the following exceptions:

AGENT_NOM	agentive nominalizer	FV	final vowel
AUG	augment	STAT	stative

References

Alegre, Maria & Peter Gordon. 1999. Frequency effects and the representational status of regular inflections. *Journal of Memory and Language* 40(1). 41–61.

Aronoff, Mark. 1976. Word formation in generative grammar. *Linguistic Inquiry Monographs* 1. 1–134.

Baayen, Harald R. 1992. Quantitative aspects of morphological productivity. In Geert Booij & Jaap van Marle (eds.), *Yearbook of morphology 1991*, 109–149. Netherlands: Springer.

Baayen, R. Harald, Lee H. Wurm & Joanna Aycock. 2007. Lexical dynamics for low-frequency complex words: A regression study across tasks and modalities. *The Mental Lexicon* 2(3). 419–463.

Bertram, Raymond, R. Harald Baayen & Robert Schreuder. 2000. Effects of family size for complex words. *Journal of memory and language* 42(3). 390–405.

Broadbent, Donald E. 1967. Word-frequency effect and response bias. *Psychological review* 74(1). 1.

Bybee, Joan L. 1995. Regular morphology and the lexicon. *Language and Cognitive Processes* 10(5). 425–455.

Bybee, Joan L. 1997. Semantic aspects of morphological typology. In Joan L. Bybee, John Haiman & Sandra A. Thompson (eds.), *Essays on language function and language type: Dedicated to t. Givón*, 25–37. Amsterdam: John Benjamins Publishing.

De Jong IV, Nivja H., Robert Schreuder & Harald R. Baayen. 2000. The morphological family size effect and morphology. *Language and Cognitive Processes* 15(4-5). 329–365.

del Prado Martín, Fermín Moscoso, Aleksandar Kostić & Harald R. Baayen. 2004. Putting the bits together: An information theoretical perspective on morphological processing. *Cognition* 94(1). 1–18.

Foote, Rebecca, Patti Spinner & Rose Mwasekaga. 2014. *Morphological decomposition in Swahili. Presentation at Linguistic Society of America 2014 Annual Meeting.*

Greenberg, Joseph H. 1959. Africa as a linguistic area. In William R. Bascom & Melville J. Herskovits (eds.), *Continuity and change in African cultures*, 15–27. Chicago: University of Chicago Press.

Hagiwara, Hiroko, Yoko Sugioka, Takane Ito, Mitsuru Kawamura & Jun I. Shiota. 1999. Neurolinguistic evidence for rule-based nominal suffixation. *Language* 75(4). 739–763.

Hay, Jennifer. 2002. From speech perception to morphology: Affix ordering revisited. *Language* 78(3). 527–555.

Hay, Jennifer & Harald R. Baayen. 2002. Parsing and productivity. In Geert Booij & Jaap van Marle (eds.), *Yearbook of morphology 2001*, 203–235. Netherlands: Springer.

Hay, Jennifer & Ingo Plag. 2004. What constrains possible suffix combinations? On the interaction of grammatical and processing restrictions in derivational morphology. *Natural Language and Linguistic Theory* 22(3). 565–596.

Heine, Bernd. 1982. African noun class systems. *Apprehension: das sprachliche Erfassen von Gegenstanden* 1. 189–216.

Katamba, Francis X. 2003. Bantu nominal morphology. In Derek Nurse & Gerard Phillippson (eds.), *The Bantu languages*, 103–120. London: Routledge.

Lehtonen, Minna, Victor A. Vorobyev, Kenneth Hugdahl, Terhi Tuokkola & Matti Laine. 2006. Neural correlates of morphological decomposition in a morphologically rich language: An fMRI study. *Brain and Language* 98(2). 182–193.

Mohamed, Mohamed Abdulla. 2001. *Modern Swahili grammar.* Nairobi: East African Publishers.

Plag, Ingo & Harald R. Baayen. 2009. Suffix ordering and morphological processing. *Language* 85(1). 109–152.

Schultink, Henk. 1961. Produktiviteit als morfologisch fenomeen. *Forum der letteren* 2. 110–125.

Seidl, Amanda & Alexis Dimitriadis. 2003. Statives and reciprocal morphology in Swahili. *Typologie des langues d'Afrique et universaux de la grammaire* 1. 239–284.

Taft, Marcus. 1979. Recognition of affixed words and the word frequency effect. *Memory & Cognition* 7(4). 263–272.

Taft, Marcus. 2004. Morphological decomposition and the reverse base frequency effect. *Quarterly Journal of Experimental Psychology Section A* 57(4). 745–765.

TUKI, The Institute of Swahili Research at the University of Dar es Salaam. 2001. *English - swahili dictionary - kamusi ya kiingerza-kiswahili.* Dar es Salaam: Laurier Books Ltd. ISBN 9976911297.

Chapter 12

The acoustic vowel space of Anyi in light of the cardinal vowel system and the Dispersion Focalization Theory

Ettien Koffi

St. Cloud State University

The Cardinal Vowel System (CVS) and the Dispersion Focalization Theory (DFT) make an important assumption about the inventory of vowels in world languages. The claim is that languages organize their vowels in a certain way in the auditory-perceptual space so as to maximize intelligibility. The vowel diagrams of African languages in influential publications such as Welmers (1973: 20–45) explicitly or implicitly reflect this assumption. However, persistent confusions between [ɪ] and [e] among Anyi Morofu speakers have aroused my curiosity and led me to investigate the matter acoustically. The findings reported here show that the vowel space of Anyi Morofu is in a between and betwixt state. The data indicates that this dialect is moving from a nine-vowel system to an eight-vowel system through the merger of [ɪ] and [e]. There are also signs of the impending merger of [ʊ] and [o].

1 Introduction

The Cardinal Vowel System (CVS) and the Dispersion Focalization Theory (DFT) agree on the principle that languages organize their vowel inventories in order to maximize intelligibility. The principle underlying both approaches is known as the Principle of Perceptual Separation (PPS). Ladefoged & Johnson (2015: 238) explain it as follows, "One of the forces acting on languages may be called the principle of sufficient perceptual separation, whereby the sounds of a language are kept acoustically distinct to make it easier for the listener to distinguish one from another." This important principle collides with how Anyi Morofu organizes its vowel inventory. Anyi Morofu is the biggest dialect of the Anyi language spoken in Côte d'Ivoire, West Africa. According to the 2000 census (outdated, but there is no other official census data to go by), this dialect is spoken by more than half of the 755,365 Anyi speakers in Côte d'Ivoire. Anyi belongs to the Akan family of languages. Before presenting the evidence for how Anyi Morofu runs counter to the core principle of CVS and DFT, let's acquaint ourselves briefly with these two phonetic frameworks. The goal here is not to review these two theories extensively, but

Ettien Koffi. The acoustic vowel space of Anyi in light of the cardinal vowel system and the Dispersion Focalization Theory. In Jason Kandybowicz, Travis Major, Harold Torrence & Philip T. Duncan (eds.), *African linguistics on the prairie: Selected papers from the 45th Annual Conference on African Linguistics*, 191–204. Berlin: Language Science Press. DOI:10.5281/zenodo.1251730

rather to use the data they provide to explain the perceptual confusion between [ɪ] and [e] and the signs announcing the upcoming merger of [ʊ] and [o].

1.1 A short history of the cardinal vowel system

On the occasion of Ladefoged's sixtieth birthday, Fromkin (1985) put together a collection of papers from influential phoneticians. In Abercrombie's article (1985:17), he gives us a glimpse of how CVS came about. His account is authoritative because he had a front row seat when Jones was designing his method. He was Jones' student and later became Ladefoged's teacher and mentor. He notes that for Jones, CVS was not a theory, but a technique. He describes this technique as follows:

> This way of teaching phonetics meant intensive training of the proprioceptive, i.e., the tactile and kinesthetic senses concerned with the organs of speech, something that is not valued very highly by many other schools of phonetics. The proprioceptive senses, in the view of phoneticians in the Jones tradition, play an important part in the analysis and description of unfamiliar sounds. The phonetician, having learnt to make a sound of the language he is working on to the complete satisfaction of his native informant, then examines what he himself is doing with his vocal organs, and infers the informant is doing the same.

Jones learned to produce a wide variety of vowels this way. Thomas (2011: 146) provides in Table 1 the formant frequencies of 18 vowels that Jones learned to produce.

For the purposes of this paper, the focus will be on nine vowels, [i, ɨ, e, ɛ, a, ɔ, o, ʉ, u], because Anyi also has nine vowels. According to Maddieson's (1984) UCLA Phonetic Segment Inventory Database (UPSID), 17 out the 266 languages in the database have nine vowels. Languages such as Anyi with a nine-vowel system represent only 6.39% of the total number of languages in UPSID. Furthermore, only seven of the 17 nine-vowel languages have a perfect symmetry of four front vowels and four back vowels and one low central vowel. The vowel system of these seven languages is similar to the one we find in Anyi. Jones' cardinal vowel system did not include [ɪ] and [ʊ] because [-ATR] vowels were not known at the time. Even so, the plotting of his vowels gives us a realistic picture of what a nine-vowel system looks like.[1]

A few cursory remarks need to be made. First and foremost, in the nine-vowel system produced by Jones, we see that the PPS obtains. No two vowels overlap in acoustic space. CVS has had a far-reaching impact on how the vowel inventories of African languages are plotted in Welmers (1973: 20–45), in *Atlas des Langues Kwa de Côte d'Ivoire, Tome 1*, and in countless other publications. Thomas (2011: 145–147) opines that Jones' original intention in proposing CVS was only to "standardize impressionistic transcription to make it more useful for interlanguage comparisons," not to idealize it as the acoustic vowel spaces for all languages. Koffi (2009) and all who have described the Anyi vowel quadrant have used this idealized system. This is the reason why the confusion between [ɪ] and [e] came as a surprise because under the idealized Anyi vowel quadrant, unintelligibility was not expected.

---

[1] The diagrams were produced using Norm, available at http://lingtools.uoregon.edu/norm/norm1.php.

Table 1: Jones' Vowels

N0	Vowels	F1	F2	F3
1.	[i]	266	2581	3627
2.	[ɨ]	312	2078	2544
3.	[ɯ]	337	1275	2180
4.	[u]	248	490	2512
5.	[y]	289	2231	2747
6.	[ʉ]	285	1487	2066
7.	[e]	376	2213	2652
8.	[ø]	353	1946	2375
9.	[ɤ]	569	1153	2282
10.	[o]	354	724	2348
11.	[ɛ]	588	1910	2328
12.	[œ]	554	1549	2158
13.	[ɶ]	722	1227	2180
14.	[ɒ]	582	769	2150
15.	[ʌ]	542	1145	2273
16.	[ɔ]	522	932	2180
17.	[ɑ]	650	940	2472
18.	[a]	929	1688	2354

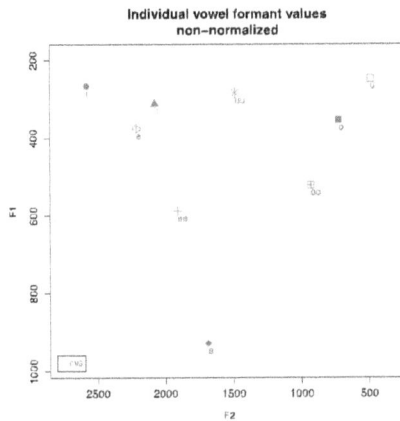

Figure 1: The Norm website does not recognize certain IPA symbols. The following legend is used <ii> = [ɨ], <uu> = [ʉ], <ee> = [ɛ], <oo> = [ɔ] instead.

1.2 A quick overview of the Dispersion Focalization Theory

PPS is also at the core of the Dispersion Focalization Theory (DFT) that Schwartz et al. (1997) put forth. However, Becker-Kristal (2010: 10) contends that "the idea that vowel inventories are structured in a manner that enhances contrast, by maximally dispersing vowels in the auditory-perceptual space, is as old as the intuition that vowel inventories follow universal structural patterns." It is worth stating clearly and unambiguously that the goal pursued in this paper is not to review, critique, or summarize DFT or the Dispersion Theory (DT) from which it sprang. Such an exercise would require us to make a long detour in the histories and developments of these two theories. It is not the theoretical claims of DFT that interest us as much as the impressive amount of formant frequency data provided for 22 "prototypical" vowels, as seen in Table 2. Aspects of this data will be used in Figure 2 to highlight the acoustic vowel space of a prototypical language with a nine-vowel system.

Table 2: Prototypical Vowel Frequencies

N0	Vowels	F1	F2	F3
1.	[i]	277	2208	3079
2.	[y]	277	1937	2232
3.	[ɨ]	277	1520	2310
4.	[ɯ]	277	1218	2500
5.	[u]	277	553	2420
6.	[ɪ]	344	2170	2660
7.	[y]	344	1770	2230
8.	[ʊ]	344	635	2413
9.	[e]	414	2065	2570
10.	[ø]	414	1608	2250
11.	[ə]	414	1516	2500
12.	[ɤ]	414	1248	2500
13.	[o]	414	721	2406
14.	[ɛ]	565	1819	2528
15.	[œ]	565	1520	2500
16.	[ɜ]	565	1462	2500
17.	[ʌ]	565	1258	2500
18.	[ɔ]	565	915	2373
19.	[æ]	648	1712	2490
20.	[ɐ]	648	1405	2500
21.	[ɑ]	735	1278	2500
22.	[a]	800	1228	2500

Nine of the prototypical vowels, [i, ɪ, e, ɛ, a, ɔ, o, ʊ, u], are also found in Anyi. They are plotted in Figure 2 to show how these prototypical vowels are organized in an acoustic space.

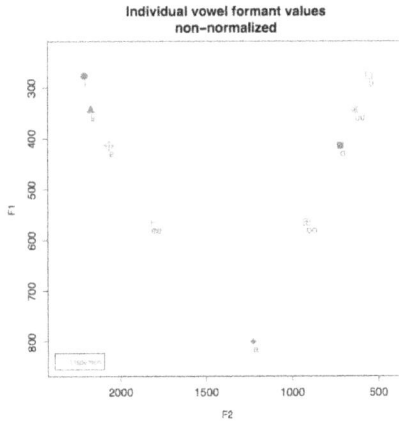

Figure 2: Vowel space of nine prototypical vowels
The Norm website does not recognize certain IPA symbols. The following legend is used for [-ATR] vowels: <ii> = [ɪ], <uu> = [ʊ], <ee> = [ɛ], <oo> = [ɔ].

The plotting shows that the claims of PPS hold here as they did in Figure 1. No vowel encroaches on the space of another vowel. Consequently, intelligibility is maximized. Let's now turn to the Anyi Morofu data and examine its vowel space in light of CVS and DFT.

2   Data collection and participants

Koffi (2009), Quaireau (1987: 27), Retord (1980: 96), to name only the three main researchers on Anyi, have all diagrammed the oral vowels of Anyi as shown in Figure 3:

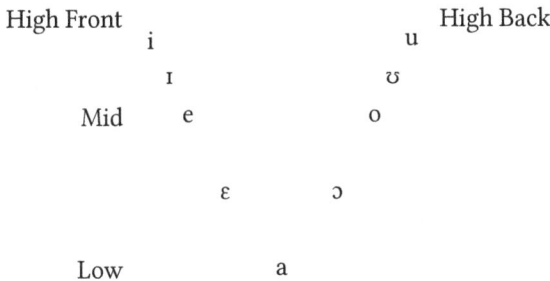

Figure 3: Anyi Morofu vowel diagram

Anyi also has seven nasal vowels: [ɪ, ĩ, ũ, ʊ, ɛ, ɔ, ã]. The vowels [ɛ] and [ɔ] are deemed unnasalizable in some Akan languages, but not in Morofu. The only vowels that are unnasalizable are [e] and [o] (Koffi 2004). Figure 3 may be an accurate representation of a

nine-vowel phonemic system in Anyi Morofu, but it is no longer an accurate representation of its contemporary phonetic vowel system. This became abundantly clear during
a literacy seminar in the summer of 2011. During the dictation task, teachers in training
confused [ɪ] with [e], and [e] with [ɪ] regardless of who was doing the dictation.[2] Test
takers would frequently stop to ask the reader whether he meant [e] or [ɪ] in instances
where the contextual cues were not enough to disambiguate the lexical items containing
these vowels. For example in a sentence such as, *ɔ'a hɪ nnaán* 'he trapped an animal',
some test takers wrote *ɔ'a he nnaán* 'he shared/gave away some of his meat'. The high
number of confusion incidences such as these caused me to wonder if a merger was
happening between these two vowels in the Morofu dialect spoken in the Bongouanou
area. Figure 4 shows this dialect in relation to the other Anyi dialects. As noted earlier,
Morofu has more speakers than all the other dialects of Anyi combined.

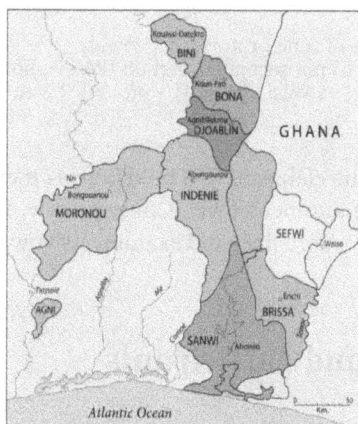

Figure 4: The Anyi dialect area

The matter was investigated further through data collection in the summers of 2012
and 2013 after securing the approval of the Institutional Review Board (IRB) from my
university. The same ten male adult literacy teachers were invited again. Female speakers
were not intentionally excluded. At that time, there were no female literacy teachers. The
situation has now changed and we have three female teachers. The lack of female data
does not affect the present analysis negatively because most of the various predictions
of DFT and DT are based on male speech (Becker-Kristal, 2010:31). The participants are
all bilingual in Anyi and French. They range in age from the 30s to 50s. Each participant
produced nine sentences, each containing one of the nine vowels under consideration:

(1)   a.   <ɔ'a hi> (he/she has refused to eat it)
      b.   <ɔ'a hɪ> (he/she has caught it)

---

[2] Ladefoged (2003: 126,130–131) tells a similar story about Banawa, a language of the Amazonian rain forest in
Brazil where there was confusion between [u] and [o] that led to strong disagreements in the orthography
of the language.

c. <ɔ'a he> (he/she has shared it)

d. <ɔ'a hɛ> (he/she is late)

e. <ɔ'a hu> (it has boiled)

f. <ɔ'a hʊ> (a nonsense word)

g. <ɔ'a ho> (he/she has dug a whole)

h. <ɔ'a hɔ> (he/she has left)

i. <ɔ'a ha> (he/she has bitten)

Each sentence was repeated three times, for a total of 30 repetitions. The data set consists of 270 items (9 x 3 x 10). The data was collected on an Olympus Digital Voice Recorder WS-710. The participants wore a Panasonic head-mounted, noise cancellation fixed microphone. The recording took place in a quiet room on the premises of the Anyi Literacy and Translation Center (CATA).

2.1 Methodology

The elicitation word in each sentence begins with /h/. These words were chosen intentionally in order to replicate Peterson and Barney's methodology as much as possible. Countless studies of vowels have followed this methodology. Ladefoged (1996: 112) explains the benefits of choosing /h/ in these kinds of acoustic phonetic studies as follows:

> As the positions of the articulators during the sound [h] are similar to those of the surrounding sounds, such as the adjacent vowels, the frequency components in [h] sounds have relative amplitudes similar to those in vowels; but the complex wave has a smaller amplitude and no fundamental frequency, as it is not generated by regular pulses from the vocal cords.

Since [h] exists in Anyi as an allophone of /k/, Peterson and Barney's methodology can be replicated without any problem. The entire duration of the vowel, from the onset to the offset, was measured. It was not deemed necessary for this study to take measurements at various points in the vowel because the environment in which the vowel occurred did not foster co-articulation. Furthermore, the methodology used by Peterson and Barney that is being replicated in this study did not sample vowels at multiple intervals. The onset of each vowel was easily identified because of the frication noise contained in [h]. However, it was more challenging to determine the offset of vowels. In annotating the offset, Thomas (2011: 142) proposes three options:

> ... The same problem crops up frequently with vowels before a pause. In these cases, you have another choice to make. One option is to look for a spot where the vocal fold vibrations become more or less unrecognizable or start looking more like staticky patterns of aspiration than the sharper pattern usually evident with vocal fold vibrations. Often, the best way to determine this spot is by moving the cursor to different spots and listening; after a certain point, all you hear is aspiration, and

that point is where you mark the offset. The other option is to mark the offset at the end of the recognizable aspiration, though this point may be quite difficult to define.

For this study, the offset of the vowel was determined by following the second option in Thomas' recommendation, that is, demarcating the offset right before the point at which aspiration is heard. The measurements for one speaker were done manually to ensure that the offsets of vowels are identified accurately. Once the pattern was well established, Ryan's (2005) Grid-maker script for Praat was used to annotate all the vowels produced by the rest of the speakers. Subsequently, Yoon's (2008) Stress-analysis script for Praat was employed to collect all the relevant information displayed in Tables 3 and 4.

Various statistical analyses can be run from the measurements in Tables 3 and 4. However, in this study they are used exclusively for the purpose of generating the acoustic vowel space in Figure 5 and for explaining why Anyi Morofu hearers have a problem distinguishing [ɪ] and [e] aurally.

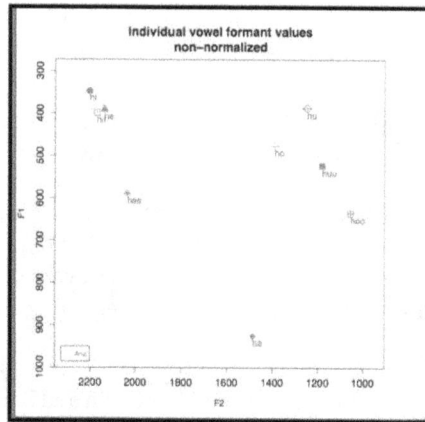

Figure 5: Anyi acoustic vowel space

2.2 The reason for the confusion

Figure 5 shows us visually why Anyi Morofu hearers confuse [ɪ] and [e] aurally. We see that they overlap in perceptual space. The measurements in Table 3 explain why. These two vowels mask each other aurally because [ɪ] (399 Hz) and [e] (392 Hz) are separated by only 7 Hz in the F1 domain. It is a well-known fact that a minimum of 20 Hz is needed for humans to perceive a difference between two sound segments (Ferrand 2007: 34). It is also well known that the lowest frequency at which a sound is intelligible on an eight-octave frequency band is 63 Hz. Auditory frequency measuring devices and many audio applications use this baseline as their reference level (Everest & Pohlmann 2015: 12–16). For acoustic phonetic analyses, this threshold has been rounded down to 60 Hz to make

Table 3: F1 Formant for all participants

F1	[i]	[ɪ]	[e]	[ɛ]	[u]	[ʊ]	[o]	[ɔ]	[a]
Speaker 1	325	368	355	556	423	539	481	624	942
Speaker 2	280	407	408	576	329	595	429	639	885
Speaker 3	307	435	408	623	345	431	414	653	983
Speaker 4	291	344	368	573	384	583	429	677	882
Speaker 5	291	415	361	601	396	510	469	639	980
Speaker 6	304	402	493	662	342	546	556	662	823
Speaker 7	338	378	381	536	473	506	544	634	981
Speaker 8	444	469	449	597	420	491	445	654	940
Speaker 9	255	360	350	584	365	545	544	628	815
Speaker 10	654	421	356	583	405	490	468	635	1028
Mean	348	399	392	589	388	523	477	635	925

Table 4: F2 Formant for all participants

F2	[i]	[ɪ]	[e]	[ɛ]	[u]	[ʊ]	[o]	[ɔ]	[a]
Speaker 1	2265	2167	2192	2068	1383	950	1694	896	1519
Speaker 2	2366	2085	2082	1960	856	859	839	1047	1525
Speaker 3	2298	2462	2350	2397	781	716	773	964	1551
Speaker 4	2202	2231	2211	2043	1216	1151	891	1171	1468
Speaker 5	2402	2534	2455	2192	1105	841	1041	946	1542
Speaker 6	1902	1746	1937	1745	918	1248	1754	1103	1382
Speaker 7	1911	1977	1931	1906	2103?	817	1429	829	1429
Speaker 8	2060	2067	2037	2069	1655	1206	1637	1053	1456
Speaker 9	2351	2208	2234	2026	1371	1804	1985	993	1538
Speaker 10	2304	2269	1985	1982	1960	2228	1885	1561	1455
Mean	2206	2174	2141	2038	1249	1182	1392	1056	1486

calculations simpler (Fry 1979: 68). Labov et al. (2006: 204–221) use it in *Atlas of North American English* (ANAE) to assess dialectal variations. Labov et al. (2013: 43) use it to assess vowel change in Philadelphia. The same 60 Hz threshold is used here to explain the confusion between [ɪ] and [e], and vice versa. Though F2 and F3 formants contribute to the overall perception of vowel quality, the calculations of vowel intelligibility are based on F1 because it alone contains 80% of the acoustic energy in the vowel (Ladefoged & Johnson 2015: 207).

The practical steps used to assess vowel intelligibility are as follows. On the F1 frequency band, if the acoustic distance between two contiguous front vowels or two contiguous back vowels is ≥ 60 Hz, the two vowels are perceived as distinct. However, if their acoustic distance falls between 59 and 21 Hz, intelligibility is compromised. If the acoustic distance between two vowels is ≤ 20 Hz, it means that a merger has taken place or is taking place. The reason for this is because human beings cannot perceive frequencies lower than 20 Hz. This is exactly what is going on with Anyi Morofu. Hearers in general have a hard time distinguishing [ɪ] from [e], and vice versa, because the mean acoustic distance between them is only 7 Hz. There are, however, small inter-speaker variations. The segments [ɪ] and [e] produced by Speakers 5, 6, and 10 are intelligible because the acoustic distances between them are respectively 54 Hz, 91 Hz, and 65 Hz. However, for seven of the speakers [ɪ] and [e] are aurally indistinguishable. For Speakers 1, 2, 7, 8, and 9 the two vowels mask each other because the acoustic distances between them are ≤ 20 Hz, as shown in Table 5:

Table 5: Inter-speaker variation

F1	[ɪ]	[e]	Distance
Speaker 1	368	355	13
Speaker 2	407	408	1
Speaker 3	435	408	27
Speaker 4	344	368	24
Speaker 5	415	361	54
Speaker 6	402	493	91
Speaker 7	378	381	3
Speaker 8	469	449	20
Speaker 9	360	350	10
Speaker 10	421	356	65
Mean	399	392	7
Standard Deviation	37	47	28

The situation in Anyi is similar in this respect to the merger between [ɑ] and [ɔ] that is going on in several dialects of American English. For Central Minnesota English, Koffi (2013: 5) reports that the merger between [ɑ] (855 Hz) and [ɔ] (851 Hz) is complete in the speech of female speakers because the acoustic distance between the two vowels is only 4 Hz.

Cross-linguistically, something is going on between [ɪ] and [e] that deserves further investigation. Ladefoged (1999: 41–42) displays the vowels of a southern California speaker whose [e] has risen above [ɪ]. Koffi's (2014:16–17) acoustic phonetic measurements of Central Minnesota English show that that [e] is higher than [ɪ] in male and female speech. In male speech, [e] (434 Hz) is higher than [ɪ] (542 Hz) by 108 Hz. In female speech, [e] (508 Hz) has risen above [ɪ] (573 Hz) by 65 Hz. In these examples, the raising of [e] above [ɪ] does not result in unintelligibility because the acoustic distance between them is still higher than the 60 Hz threshold. However, this is not so in the case of Anyi Morofu where only a mere 7 Hz separate these vowels. In the terminology that Schwartz et al. (1997) use to describe vowel systems, Anyi is an "atypical" nine-vowel system because it does not conform to the predicted patterns. Becker-Kristal (2010: 169) explains why:

> Across all analyses, inventories with ATR harmony often violate the principles of dispersion, in formant spans, in even vowel spacing and in phonetic adjustments in response to structural change. These deviations are understandable if such inventories are not treated as one large system but as two parallel smaller systems.

More acoustic phonetic data such as the one used to describe the confusion between [ɪ] and [e] is needed from other African languages with [±ATR] vowel systems to see if Anyi Morofu is really atypical or if this phenomenon is widespread. In the case of Anyi, it is the vowels [ɪ] and [e]. In other languages, it may be different pairs of vowels.

2.3 The future of the Anyi acoustic vowel space

What does the future hold for the phonemic inventory of Anyi vowels? How long before the acoustic vowel space is completely reduced to an eight-vowel system? Will the acoustic vowel space be reduced further to a seven-vowel system? Becker-Kristal (2010: 113) discusses a possible scenario that may be in store for Anyi:

> They [vowels] might fall closer to other vowels, which are repelled further, albeit by a smaller magnitude, and this process propagates as a push chain shift with gradual decay through other vowels until the entire system finds a new balance.

What will the new balance look like for Anyi? It is hard to predict the future. However, we can anticipate what the Anyi Morofu vowel space will look like in the near future by learning from the current state of vowels in some languages in the Akan family. Mensah (1983: 430) reports that Krobou, another Akan language, has reduced the number of its vowels from nine to eight. It no longer has the vowel [ɪ], which has been replaced by [e]. If Anyi finds a new balance in an eight-vowel system, this balance will be temporary because another shift is afoot. The data in Table 6 shows that the next vowel targeted for disappearance is [ʊ] (523Hz):

It will most likely be replaced by [o] (477 Hz). The acoustic distance between them is 46 Hz. This merger may take a little while, but it is inevitable. Only Speakers 2 and 4 mark a clear contrast between these two vowels. Intelligibility is compromised in the speech of Speakers 1, 5, and 8. A merger has already taken place in the pronunciation of Speakers 3,

Table 6: The Impending Merger of [ʊ] and [o]

F1	[ʊ]	[o]	Distance
Speaker 1	539	481	58
Speaker 2	595	429	166
Speaker 3	431	414	17
Speaker 4	583	429	154
Speaker 5	510	469	41
Speaker 6	546	556	10
Speaker 7	506	544	38
Speaker 8	491	445	46
Speaker 9	545	544	1
Speaker 10	490	468	22
Mean	523	477	46
Standard Deviation	48	52	57

6, and 9; and it is on the verge of happening for Speaker 10. The merger between [ʊ] and [o] has already taken place in Baule, which is closely related to Anyi. Kouadio (1983: 284) reports that Baule no longer has [ɪ] or [ʊ]. Other languages in the Akan family spoken in Côte d'Ivoire have a seven-vowel system instead of the nine traditionally associated with this language family. Hérault (1983: 262) reports that Avikam has lost both [ɪ] and [ʊ], and so has Ebrie (Bole-Richard 1983: 324). The acoustic vowel space of Anyi Morofu will achieve stability when the number of its vowels goes from nine to seven.

3 Summary

The vowel spaces of languages are always shifting. English underwent a major shift between 1400 and 1600 (Fromkin et al. 2014: 342)). This change has been nicknamed the Great Vowel Shift. Labov et al.'s (2006) voluminous *ANAE* shows that another shift known as the Northern Cities Shift is slowly but surely fanning across the Midwest. Since change is a language universal process, one would expect the vowels of Anyi to also shift. The vowel [e] is masking [ɪ] for now. How long will it take for [ɪ] to be swallowed up by [e]? It is hard to tell. However, the process that is underway is almost irreversible given what has taken place in other Akan languages that are closely related to Anyi Morofu. For now Anyi is following the same path as Krobou. In a not so distant future, the shift from [ʊ] to [o] will run its course, and Anyi will have seven vowels like Baule and other Akan languages spoken in Côte d'Ivoire. However, synchronically, Anyi is in a between and betwixt state which causes it to be atypical, that is, it does not conform to PPS as predicted by CVS and DFT.

References

Abercrombie, David. 1985. Daniel Jones' teaching. In Victoria Fromkin (ed.), *Phonetic linguistics: Essays in honor of Peter Ladefoged*, 15–24. Orlando: Academic Press.

Becker-Kristal, Roy. 2010. *Acoustic typology of vowel inventory and dispersion theory: Insights from a large cross-linguistic corpus*. Los Angeles, CA: UCLA Doctoral dissertation.

Bole-Richard, Remy. 1983. L'ebrie. In Georges Hérault (ed.), *Atlas des langues Kwa de Côte d'Ivoire*, vol. 1, 307–357. Abidjan, Côte d'Ivoire: Institut de Linguistique Appliquée.

Everest, Alton F. & Ken C. Pohlmann. 2015. *Master handbook of acoustics*. 6th edn. New York: McGraw Hill Education.

Ferrand, Carole T. 2007. *Speech science: An integrated approach to theory and clinical practice*. 2nd edn. New York: Allyn & Bacon.

Fromkin, Victoria. 1985. *Phonetic linguistics: Essays in honor of peter ladefoged*. Orlando: Academic Press.

Fromkin, Victoria, Robert Rodman Rodman & Nina Hyams. 2014. *An introduction to language*. 10th edn. New York: Wadsworth Cengage Learning.

Fry, Dennis Butler. 1979. *The physics of speech*. Cambridge: Cambridge University Press.

Hérault, Georges. 1983. L'Avikam. In Georges Hérault (ed.), *L'Avikam*, vol. 1, 255–276. Abidjan, Côte d'Ivoire: Institut de Linguistique Appliquée.

Koffi, Ettien N. 2004. Oral vowels in nasalization contexts in Anyi: Implications for orthography. *Trends in African Linguistics* 6. 163–170.

Koffi, Ettien N. 2009. *The interface between phonology and morpho(phono)logy in the standardization of Anyi orthography*. Bloomington, IN: Indiana University. http://orthographyclearinghouse.org/index.php/. Revised doctoral dissertation.

Koffi, Ettien N. 2013. The acoustic vowel space of Central Minnesota English: Focus on intelligibility. *Linguistic Portfolios* 2. 2–16.

Koffi, Ettien N. 2014. The acoustic vowel space of Central Minnesota English in light of the Northern cities shift. *Linguistic Portfolios* 3. 2–20.

Kouadio, Jérémie N. 1983. Le Baoule. In G. Hérault (ed.), *Atlas des langues kwa de côte d'ivoire tome*, vol. 1, 277–306. Abidjan, Côte d'Ivoire: Institut de Linguistique Appliquée.

Labov, William, Sharon Ash & Charles Boberg (eds.). 2006. *Atlas of North American English: Phonetics, phonology, and sound change*. New York: Mouton de Gruyter.

Labov, William, Ingrid Rosenfelder & Josef Fruehwadl. 2013. One hundred years of sound change in Philadelphia. *Language* 48. 30–65.

Ladefoged, Peter. 1996. *Elements of acoustic phonetics*. 2nd edn. Chicago: The University of Chicago Press.

Ladefoged, Peter. 1999. American english. In *Handbook of the international phonetic association: A guide to the use of the international phonetic alphabet*, 41–50. New York: Cambridge University Press.

Ladefoged, Peter. 2003. *Phonetic data analysis: An introduction to fieldwork and instrumental techniques*. Malden, MA: Blackwell Publishing.

Ladefoged, Peter & Keith Johnson. 2015. *A course in phonetics.* 7th edn. Stamford, CT: Cengage Learning.

Maddieson, Ian. 1984. *Patterns of sounds.* Cambridge University Press: New York.

Mensah, Emanuel N. A. 1983. Le Krobou. In Georges Hérault (ed.), *Atlas des langues Kwa de Côte d'Ivoire*, vol. 1, 425–463. Abidjan, Côte d'Ivoire: Institut de Linguistique Appliquée.

Quaireau, André. 1987. Description de l'Agni: Des Parlers Moronou, Ndénié et Bona: Université de Grenoble III Doctoral dissertation.

Retord, Georges L. A. 1980. *Etude radiocinématographique des articulations de l'Agni-Sanvi.* Paris Doctoral dissertation.

Ryan, Kevin. 2005. *Grid-maker. Praat.* no address: no publisher. http : / / phonetics . linguistics.ucla.edu/facilities/acoustic/praat.html.

Schwartz, Jean-Luc, Louis-Jean Boe, Nathalie Vallée & Christian Abry. 1997. The dispersion-focalization theory of vowel systems. *Journal of Phonetics* 25. 255–286.

Thomas, Erik R. 2011. *Sociophonetics: An introduction.* New York: Palgrave Macmillan.

Welmers, William E. 1973. *African Language Structures.* Paul F. A. Kotey & Haig Der-Houssikian (eds.). Los Angeles, CA: University of California Press.

Yoon, Tae-Jin. 2008. *Stress-analysis. Praat.* http://web.uvic.ca/~tyoon/resource/vq.praat.

Chapter 13

Gender instability in Maay

Mary Paster

Pomona College

This paper discusses variation in the gender of nouns in Maay, a language of Somalia. Languages of the Eastern Omo-Tana subgroup of East Cushitic (including Maay, Somali, Rendille, and Tunni) have gender systems wherein every noun is masculine or feminine. Masculine nouns take k-initial variants of suffixes including the definite marker, demonstratives, and possessive markers; these suffixes are *t*-initial with feminine nouns. As is now well known, gender in these languages is sensitive to plurality in various ways: in some languages, gender 'polarity' reverses the gender of nouns in the plural; in others, feminine nouns change to masculine when their plurals are formed with certain suffixes but not others. In Maay, plurals are all masculine regardless of how they are formed, but the gender of many singular nouns is inconsistent across individuals. The masculine plural pattern makes the gender of singular nouns unrecoverable from their plurals, so nouns that are frequently plural are susceptible to gender instability. If there is uncertainty about the gender of some nouns, speakers may be inclined to guess masculine, thereby producing more feminine to masculine changes than the reverse, due to the prevalence of masculine nouns in the Maay lexicon.

1 Introduction

The Maay language is known to exhibit significant inter-speaker variation in its phonology and morphology (Paster 2013). This paper describes variability in the gender assignment of Maay nouns and considers explanations for why gender is unstable for certain nouns in this language. I will argue that gender instability is connected to, and facilitated by, a regular pattern in the language where gender is neutralized to masculine in plural nouns.

The structure of the paper is as follows. First, in §2 I give some background on the Maay language and its classification. In §3, I explain the gender neutralization pattern in Maay plurals and discuss similar phenomena in related languages. §4 describes the problem of gender instability in Maay. In §5, I propose an explanation of gender instability that attributes the emergence of gender instability in part to gender neutralization in plurals; I also consider and reject a number of alternative explanations. §6 concludes the paper.

Mary Paster. Gender instability in Maay. In Jason Kandybowicz, Travis Major, Harold Torrence & Philip T. Duncan (eds.), *African linguistics on the prairie: Selected papers from the 45th Annual Conference on African Linguistics*, 205–218. Berlin: Language Science Press.
DOI:10.5281/zenodo.1251732

2 Background on Maay

Maay (also known as Af-Maay or MayMay; see Paster 2007; Comfort & Paster 2009; Paster 2010) is a Cushitic language spoken in Somalia that is related to, but not mutually intelligible with, Somali. It is classified as an East Cushitic language, for which a tree is given in (1).

(1)   East Cushitic (modified from Saeed 1999: 3)

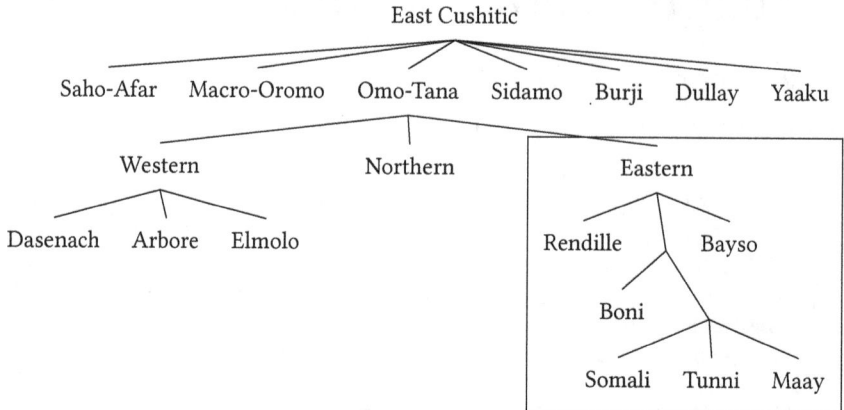

In this paper, I will be focusing on the Eastern Omo-Tana (EOT) subgroup of East Cushitic, marked in the tree above.

3 Gender in EOT languages

Cushitic studies often refer to the existence of three genders (masculine, feminine, and plural; cf. Corbett & Hayward 1987). In Maay, this is essentially how third person subject agreement works for verbs, as seen in four different tenses in (2) (data and tense/aspect category names are from Paster 2007).

(2)   a. **Simple Past**
         roor-i
         run-3SGM.PAST
         'he ran'

         roor-ti
         run-3SGF.PAST
         'she ran'

         roor-eena
         run-3PL.PAST
         'they ran'

      b. **Simple Present B**
         ɗeer-ya
         be.tall-3SGM.STATIVE
         'he is tall'

         ɗeer-ta
         be.tall-3SGF.STATIVE
         'she is tall'

         ɗeer-yena
         be.tall-3PL.STATIVE
         'they are tall'

c. **Immediate Future**

kooy-e
come-3SGM.FUTURE
'he will come'

kooy-ase
come-3SGF.FUTURE
'she will come'

kooy-ayeena
come-3PL.FUTURE
'they will come'

d. **Present Progressive**

aam-oy-e
eat-PRES.PROG-3SGM.PRESENT
'he is eating'

aam-oy-te
eat-PRES.PROG-3SGF.PRESENT
'she is eating'

aam-oy-eena
eat-PRES.PROG-3PL.PRESENT
'they are eating'

For purposes of noun morphology, however, there are only two genders in Maay: masculine and feminine. Masculine nouns (3a) take *k*-initial suffixes for definites, demonstratives, and most possessive markers, while these suffixes are *t*-initial with feminine nouns (3b).

(3) a. geet-ki   'the tree'   b. bilaan-ti   'the woman'
        geet-kaŋ   'this tree'   bilaan-taŋ   'this woman'
        geet-kas   'that tree'   bilaan-tas   'that woman'
        geet-kew   'which tree'   bilaan-tew   'which woman'
        geet-key   'my tree'   bilaan-tey   'my woman'
        geet-ka   'your tree'   bilaan-ta   'your woman'
        geet-'ye   'his/her tree'   bilaan-tis   'his woman'
                                        bilaan-tie   'her woman'
        geet-kaynu   'our tree'   bilaan-tayno   'our woman'
        geet-kiŋ   'your pl. tree'   bilaan-tiŋ   'your pl. woman'
        geet-'yo   'their tree'   bilaan-tio   'their woman'

For the purposes of this paper, I will focus on this type of gender agreement.

As has been documented elsewhere, gender in EOT languages is sensitive to plurality. This is broadly referred to as "gender polarity", but it sometimes manifests as neutralization rather than polarity *per se*. This varies from language to language; below I summarize the situation in a number of different EOT languages.

In Standard Somali (SS), according to Saeed (1999: 54–55), most plural nouns reverse their gender. There are multiple different plural suffixes, and several of them trigger gender polarity, as can be seen in (4a). However, plurals of masculine nouns formed by reduplication, as well as 'a subgroup of masculine suffixing nouns' retain their masculine gender in the plural, as seen in (4b).

(4) a. abtí (m)   'maternal uncle'   abti-yó (f)   'maternal uncles'
        túke (m)   'crow'   tuka-yáal (f) 'crows'
        káb (f)   'shoe'   kab-ó (m)   'shoes'
        galáb (f)   'afternoon'   galb-ó (m)   'afternoons'
     b. wán (m)   'ram'   wan-án (m)   'rams'
        béer (m)   'liver'   beer-ár (m)   'livers'
        dhéri (m)   'clay pot'   dhery-ó (m)   'clay pots'
        wáran (m)   'spear'   warm-ó (m)   'spears'

Thus, in SS, in the plural all feminine nouns become masculine, and some masculine nouns become feminine but some stay masculine.

Central Somali exhibits a different pattern, where plurals formed with the suffix -*o* exhibit polarity (5a), while plurals formed with -*(i)yaal* are masculine regardless of their gender in the singular (5b) (Saeed 1982: 11–12).

(5) a. fileer-taas (f)   'that arrow'   fileer-o-gaas (m)   'those arrows'
        laan-taas (f)   'that branch'   laam-o-gaas (m)   'those branches'
        shiid-kaas (m)   'that stone'   shiid-o-daas (f)   'those stones'
        eleeŋ-kaas (m)   'that ram'   eleem-o-daas (f)   'those rams'
     b. jeer-taas (f)   'that hippo'   jeer-iyaal-kaas (m)   'those hippos'
        shimbir-taas (f)   'that bird'   shimbir-iyaal-kaas (m)   'those birds'
        ba'iid-kaas (m)   'that oryx' ba'   iid-iyaal-kaas (m)   'those oryxes'
        weer-kaas (m)   'that jackal'   weer-iyaal-kaas (m)   'those jackals'

Lecarme's (2002) discussion of an unidentified Somali dialect (which appears to be distinct from both SS and CS) includes the observation that each of several different pluralization strategies tends to result in plural forms with a particular gender. For example, all plurals in -*o* (whose singulars are mostly feminine, but some masculine nouns also occur in this group) (6a) are masculine (Lecarme 2002: 118). Plurals in -*oyin* (whose singulars are always feminine) are always masculine (6b) (Lecarme 2002: 119). Plurals in -*yaal* (6c) (whose singulars can be masculine or feminine) are "masculine or feminine, depending on regional variation, and thus either polaric or not" (Lecarme 2002: 119) (though note that the only plural forms provided are feminine).

(6) a. fár (-ta) (f)   'finger'   far-ó (-á-ha) (m)   'fingers'
        náag (-ta) (f)   'women'   naag-ó (-á-ha) (m)   'women'
        maálin (-ka) (m)   'day'   maalm-ó (-á-ha) (m)   'days'
        wáran (-ka) (m)   'spear'   warm-ó (-á-ha) (m)   'spears'

b. hóoyo (-áda) (f)	'mother'	hooyo-óyin (-ka) (m)	'mothers'
eeddó (-áda) (f)	'paternal aunt'	eeddo-óyin (-ka) (m)	'paternal aunts'
magaaló (-áda) (f)	'town'	magaalo-óyin (-ka) (m)	'towns'
xeró (-áda) (f)	'enclosure'	xero-óyin (-ka) (m)	'enclosures'
c. maroodí (-ga) (m)	'elephant'	maroodi-yáal (-sha)	'elephants'
waraábe (-áha) (m)	'hyena'	waraaba-yáal (-sha) (f)	'hyenas'
áabbe (-áha) (m)	'father'	aaba-yáal (-sha) (f)	'fathers'
jáalé (-áha) (m)	'comrade'	jaala-yáal (-sha) (f)	'comrades'

Lecarme's analysis locates gender features in the various plural suffixes, explaining the connection between the gender changes and the use of each of the suffixes.

In Maay, plural nouns are masculine, regardless of whether the plural is formed with the suffix -o (7a), the suffix -yal (7b), or with both (7c) (Paster 2007; Comfort & Paster 2009; Paster 2010) (note that /k/ and /t/ lenite to [ɣ] and [ð] intervocalically).

(7)	a. ʤeer-tey (f)	'my hippo'	ʤeer-o-ɣey (m)	'my hippos'
	gewer-tey (f)	'my daughter'	gewer-o-ɣey (m)	'my daughters'
	walaal-key (m)	'my brother'	walaal-o-ɣey (m)	'my brothers/sisters'
	aʤir-key (m)	'my thigh'	aʤir-o-ɣey (m)	'my thighs'
	b. mindi-ðey (f)	'my knife'	mindi-yal-key (m)	'my knives'
	gaʔan-tey (f)	'my hand'	gaʔan-yal-key (m)	'my hands'
	bakeeri-ɣey (m)	'my cup'	bakeeri-yal-key (m)	'my cups'
	miis-key (m)	'my table'	miis-yal-key (m)	'my tables'
	c. ʤeer-tey (f)	'my hippo'	ʤeer-o-yal-key (m)	'my hippos'
	gaʔan-tey (f)	'my hand'	gaʔam-o-yal-key (m)	'my hands'
	aʤir-key (m)	'my thigh'	aʤir-o-yal-key (m)	'my thighs'
	miis-key (m)	'my table'	miis-o-yal-key (m)	'my tables'

In Tunni, the "gender-opposition is neutralized in Plural nouns, all of which are Masculine" (Tosco 1997: 43; no illustrative examples are provided). And finally, Rendille exhibits a complex pattern where some nouns appear to switch gender in the plural, while others take a separate set of plural-agreeing suffixes beginning with /h/ rather than feminine /t/ or masculine /k/ (see Oomen 1981 for much more detailed discussion).

Summing up, it can be observed that some EOT languages have true polarity and others have only masculine plurals. None of the languages (as far as I am aware) have only feminine plurals.[1] It seems likely that Proto-EOT did exhibit polarity, since polarity ex-

---

[1]A reviewer points out that K'abeena has feminine plurals. According to Mous (2008: 143), plurals "trigger masculine agreement in the demonstratives, [plural] agreement in the definite markers, but feminine agreement on the verb in external, clausal agreement." Since I am focusing on agreement with determiners, demonstratives, and possessors, for the present purposes I would not consider K'abeena to have feminine plurals.

ists in Cushitic languages outside of the EOT group as well, e.g., in Oromo (Andrzejewski 1960) and Burunge (Wolff 2014).

This background on gender phenomena in EOT will be relevant to the discussion of gender instability in §4, since I will argue that it is the masculine-plural pattern in Maay that provides the mechanism for the emergence of instability.

4 Gender instability in Maay

Wolff (2014) observes that "[a] notable historical feature [of Afro-Asiatic languages] is 'gender stability', meaning that words for common things tend to share the same gender across the languages of the Afro-Asiatic phylum, no matter whether or not the particular words are cognate across the specific languages in question" (the implication being that Afro-Asiatic exhibits a greater degree of gender stability than other families do). But as I will show below, there are exceptions to the 'gender stability' generalization within the Maay language itself.

Considering a sample of 55 common lexical items in Maay, each elicited from up to 6 speakers, I found 34 of them to be consistently masculine, shown in (8) (note that animals are deliberately excluded, for reasons to be explained below).

(8)　Consistently masculine nouns[2]

moos-ki	'the banana'	suŋ-ki	'the belt'
doŋ-ki	'the boat'	buug-i	'the book'[3]
baaka-ɣi	'the box'	kawaʃ-ki	'the cabbage'
hɛɛl-ki	'the cardamom'	kuraas-ki	'the chair'
belet-ki	'the city'	nardʒiŋ-ki	'the coconut'
hawuug-i	'the corn'	bakeri-ɣi	'the cup'
ilbap-ki	'the door'	dɛp-ki	'the fire'
ɛɛs-ki	'the grass'	maða-ɣi	'the head'
miniŋ-ki	'the house'	fur-ki	'the key'
nal-ki	'the light'	beer-ki	'the liver'
af-ki	'the mouth'	basal-ki	'the onion'
los-ki	'the peanut'	galaŋ-ki	'the pen'
biiŋ-ki	'the pin'	barit-ki	'the rice'
woβi-ɣi	'the river'	dʒit-ki	'the road'
haðag-i	'the rope'	kasab-ki	'the sugarcane'
miis-ki	'the table'	nyaanya-ɣi	'the tomato'
gɛɛt-ki	'the tree'	hidig-i	'the star'

---

[3]Masculine nouns ending in *k* appear to have the suffix *-i* rather than *-ki* because the /k/ of the stem and /k/ of the suffix reduce to a single /k/ and then optionally undergo intervocalic voicing. This stop does not undergo intervocalic lenition to [ɣ] because lenition applies before degemination. Paster (2007) provides a deeper discussion of Maay phonology.

Six nouns in the dataset were consistently feminine, shown in (9).

(9)   Consistently feminine nouns

saʔad-i	'the clock'[4]	dɛk-ti	'the ear'
far-ti	'the finger'	saan-ti	'the footprint'
luk-ti	'the leg'	suk-ti	'the market'

Interestingly, 15 nouns in the dataset showed inconsistent gender across speakers, as shown in (10).

(10)   Unstable nouns

ukun-ti ~ ukuŋ-ki	'the egg'	farketi-ði ~ farketi-ɣi	'the fork'
il-i ~ il-ki	'the eye'[5]	sun-ti ~ suŋ-ki	'the poison'
beer-ti ~ beer-ki	'the garden'	dariʃa-ði ~ dariʃa-ɣi	'the window'
gaʔan-ti ~ gaʔan-ki	'the hand'	siin-ti ~ siiŋ-ki	'the hip'
mindi-ði ~ mindi-ɣi	'the knife'	hambal-i ~ hambal-ki	'the leaf'
embe-ði ~ embe-ɣi	'the mango'	kaal-i ~ kaal-ki	'the spoon'
istaraʃa-ði ~ istaraʃa-ɣi	'the napkin'	baloon-ti ~ baloon-ki	'the ball'
irbid-i ~ irbit-ki	'the needle'		

In the following section, I will propose an analysis of the unstable nouns in (10), attempting to explain how their gender came to be ambiguous across speakers. I will suggest that the pattern of gender neutralization to masculine in Maay plurals creates ambiguity in the gender of singular nouns (particularly when the plural form is more familiar), leading speakers to sporadically reassign the gender of some nouns.

5 Analysis

To explain the unstable nouns, we could look at properties of both the speakers and the nouns themselves. Before presenting my proposed analysis that attributes the instability to gender neutralization in the plural, I consider a number of other factors that could potentially be relevant to gender instability, showing that none turns out to provide an explanation for the observed phenomenon.

To start, we might ask whether age, gender, region, or language use could explain the divide among the speakers. Table 1 provides some demographic and language use information for each of the Maay speakers consulted for this project.

---

[4]Feminine nouns ending in *t* appear to have the suffix *-i* due to degemination as with masculine nouns ending in *k*.

[5]Feminine nouns ending in *l* appear to have the suffix *-i* due to a regular phonological rule that deletes /t/ after /l/.

Table 1: Demographic and language use information

Speaker	Gender	Age	Origin	Languages
OM	M	33	Kowan (near Jamaame)	Zigua, Swahili, English
HJ	M	30s	Jamma; lived in Kenya	Zigua, English, Somali
JA	M	62	Jilib	Some English, some Somali
HM	M	42	Jamaame; grew up in Mogadishu	Somali, Zigua, English, Swahili
BM	F	48	Jamaame	Zigua, Somali, English, some Swahili
LJ	M	52	Jamaame	Zigua, Somali, English, Swahili, Italian, some Spanish
AM	M	27	Kismaayo; lived in Kenya	Zigua, Somali, English, Swahili, Turkana, Giryama
HA	F	30s	Jamaame; grew up in Kenya	Zigua, Swahili, English
MA	F	23	Jamaame	Zigua, Swahili, Somali, some English
KJ	F	50s	Jamaame; Kismaayo; lived in Kenya	Zigua, Somali, Swahili, some English

In Table 2, I give the gender of each noun according to the available data elicited from each speaker.

Considering the noun gender data by speaker, a few generalizations emerge. First, the available data from LJ indicate that he has assigned masculine gender to all of the nouns in question. Second, HA also has many of these nouns as masculine, and HJ has some masculine. All available instances of these 15 words from AM and OM were feminine.

In an attempt to align these observations with the speakers' demographic characteristics, it can be observed that LJ, HA, and HJ, who had more masculine forms of these nouns than other speakers did, are from the same area. However, OM and BM are also from the same region and had almost all of these nouns as feminine, so an explanation in terms of a geographically defined dialect feature is unlikely. The age of the speakers also does not seem to be a relevant factor, since the group of three speakers who produced the

Table 2: Noun gender by speaker

	LJ	HJ	HA	AM	OM	BM
ball			M	F	F	
egg			M	F		
eye		M	M	F	F	
fork		F	M			
garden			M	F		F
hand	M		F	F	F	
hip			M			F
knife	M	F	M		F	F
leaf		M	F	F	F	
mango	M	M	M			F
napkin	M		M		F	
needle		F	M	F		
poison		F	M			M
spoon		M	M	F	F	F
window	M				F	

most masculine forms includes one of the oldest speakers (LJ) and two of the youngest (HA and HJ). Gender seems irrelevant, since LJ and HJ are male while HA is female. And finally it can be observed that the two speakers who produced all feminine forms, OM and AM, are younger men, but HJ is also a younger man and produced several masculine forms. Thus, properties of the speakers themselves do not seem to provide any insight into the behavior of the unstable nouns.

It is possible that language experience and/or language attitudes play a role in determining which gender each speaker will assign to a given noun, but here again no clear explanation emerges. In language attitude surveys, HA and HJ, both of whom produced more masculine nouns in this set than other speakers, stated that they identify more with Zigua (a Bantu language spoken by many members of the community) than Maay as their mother tongue and that they speak Zigua at home. However, it is not clear what influence Zigua might have on the gender of their Maay nouns apart from general interference with regular Maay usage, since Zigua has noun classes rather than binary gender. No other details about any of the speakers' experiences with languages other than Maay appear to correlate with the data.

Having considered the possibility that the gender of the unstable nouns is a dialect feature relating to the geographic origin of, or other facts about, the speakers and finding none, we might consider whether there are properties of the nouns themselves that can shed light on why they are unstable across speakers.

One obvious potential factor could be the phonological form of the nouns, but a consideration of the nouns in (8-10) does not reveal any good candidates for a phonological property that might unify any set of nouns. The masculine nouns (8) and unstable nouns (10) end in either a consonant or a vowel, and they can have anywhere from one to three syllables (one unstable noun has four syllables). The feminine nouns in (9) all end in a consonant, and only one has more than one syllable, but there are stable masculine nouns and unstable nouns that also have these properties, so the shape of the six feminine nouns in (9) does not reflect a phonological natural class.

A second property of the nouns that could be considered is whether they are native or borrowed, and if borrowed, the source of the borrowing. But here again, there is no clear pattern. Table 3 gives the sources for four of the nouns in the unstable class that can be identified as borrowings.

Table 3: Sources of borrowed unstable nouns

Noun	Source
ball	Italian or English
fork	Italian
napkin	Italian
poison	Arabic

While it is true that two or three of the unstable nouns are Italian borrowings, one of them is from Arabic, and the remaining 11 unstable nouns are apparently native. Therefore once again no solid generalization can be made. The list stable masculine nouns in (8) also includes both native words and borrowings from English, Italian, and Arabic; the stable feminine class in (9) includes both native words and Arabic borrowings.

A third possibility is that the semantics of the unstable nouns might explain their behavior. At first this does not seem to be a likely source for an explanation, since nouns of many different semantic categories have unstable gender, including body parts, utensils, foods, and miscellaneous others. Recall that animals were deliberately omitted from this study. The reason is that if an animal noun exhibits gender variability, this could be attributed to a functional use of gender corresponding to the animal's sex. In fact, several animal nouns do show gender variability, as seen in (11).

(11) yahas-ti ~ yahas-ki   'the crocodile'
      mayoonda-ði ~ mayoonda-ɣi   'the (monkey sp.)'
      ʤeer-ti ~ ʤeer-ki   'the hippo'

When these forms were produced, it is possible that the speaker had an animal of a particular sex in mind, even if this was not necessarily indicated in the English translation, (e.g., even if the speaker did not specify 'a *male* crocodile' when giving the form *yahas-ki*).

Given this, the set of unstable nouns does not initially seem to form a semantic natural class. However, a closer look reveals a possible unifying property for several of the unstable nouns. It is instructive to compare the unstable nouns in Maay with the so-called 'double gender' nouns in Dutch, where Semplicini argues that "nouns whose referents are characterized by a high degree of individuation tend to trigger common agreement, while nouns with less individuated referents are more likely to trigger neuter agreement" (2012: 176). The notion of the "degree of individuation" may be relevant in Maay as well, since most of the unstable nouns in (10) are at least somewhat likely to occur frequently in the plural, and furthermore, some (especially paired body parts) probably occur much more often in the plural form than the singular. This observation about the unstable nouns is noteworthy because it links gender instability to the masculine-plural pattern in Maay: because the masculine-plural pattern makes the gender of singular nouns unrecoverable from their plurals, nouns that are frequently plural may be susceptible to gender instability.

Supposing that the gender of a noun's singular form is determined by analogy using the plural when the gender of the singular noun is unknown, speakers will arrive at different singular forms depending on which words they choose to form the analogy. For example, when a speaker tries to determine the singular form of 'hip' from the plural form *siim-o-yi* 'the hips', if he/she analogizes to *sum-o-yi* 'the belts' as in (12a), then the singular 'hip' will end up masculine. However, if the speaker instead analogizes to *saam-o-yi* 'the footprints' as in (12b), then the singular 'hip' will end up feminine.

(12) Two possible analogies for recovering the gender of a noun from its plural

a. sum-o-ɣi	'the belts'	(m.) : suŋ-ki 'the belt' (m.) ::	
siim-o-ɣi	'the hips'	(m.) : siiŋ-ki 'the hip' (m.)	
b. saam-o-ɣi	'the footprints'	(m.) : saan-ti 'the footprint' (f.) ::	
siim-o-ɣi	'the hips'	(m.) : siin-ti 'the hip' (f.)	

The analogy in (12a) may overapply relative to (12b) due to a preponderance of masculine nouns in the lexicon, since if a speaker selects a phonological neighbor to form the analogy, more often than not the neighbor will happen to be masculine. This would cause feminine nouns to shift to masculine more often than the reverse, although shifts could occur in either direction.[6]

6 Conclusion

A number of predictions follow from the hypothesis presented above. Four predictions are enumerated in (13); I will discuss each in more detail below, showing that the available evidence is consistent with the predictions.

---

[6] Note that my analysis does not hinge on the proposal that analogy is to phonological neighbors in particular. The analogy could instead be to semantic relatives, for example, and the same result would be predicted to emerge.

(13)   a. More unstable nouns should have feminine cognates in related languages than masculine cognates

      b. More speakers will have the unstable nouns as feminine than masculine

      c. Nouns that are frequently plural are most likely to change gender in languages with the masculine-plural pattern

      d. Languages with the masculine-plural pattern are more likely to have gender instability

The first prediction, that unstable nouns should have feminine cognates in related languages, follows from the observation made earlier that, given the scenario I have outlined for how singular forms are recovered from their gender-ambigious plural counterparts, the overall masculine skewing of the lexicon will cause more feminine nouns to shift to masculine than the reverse. Thus, the instability will more often affect historically feminine nouns. A look at cognates in EOT does appear to uphold this prediction, although the sample size is small. For example, in Central Somali, all of the cognates of the unstable nouns given by Saeed (1987) are feminine ('egg', 'eye', 'hand', and 'leaf'). None of the other nouns in the unstable class have Central Somali cognates provided ('knife' is also feminine in Central Somali, but it is not a cognate with the Maay form). Similarly, in Tunni (Tosco 1997), 'egg', 'eye', 'hand', 'knife', 'leaf' are all feminine (no other cognates are provided). Given the skewing of stable Maay nouns towards masculine, it is striking that all of the cognates that were found in Central Somali and Tunni for the unstable nouns are feminine. Thus, the prediction appears to be accurate, though a consideration of cognates in other EOT languages is warranted.[7]

The second prediction, that more speakers will have the unstable nouns as feminine than masculine, also relates to the idea that the analogical recovery of singular gender will tend to shift previously feminine forms into the masculine category. If this is indeed the mechanism producing the instability, we expect to see a recurring pattern where most speakers have a particular noun as feminine but one or more speakers innovates a masculine form. In that case we expect to see a recurring pattern where most speakers continue to treat a given noun as feminine, while a smaller number of speakers treat it as masculine. Again the data do appear to uphold this prediction, though again the sample is small. For all but two of the unstable nouns ('mango' and 'poison'), at least as many speakers have the noun as feminine as masculine. And in several cases the feminines outnumber the masculines by a ratio of at least three to one. 'Mango' and 'poison', while they do not uphold the predicted trend themselves, are still not problematic since the proposed mechanism does allow masculine nouns to shift to feminine. A finding that these

---

[7]Note that masculine nouns can also become unstable through the same mechanism; they are just posited to be less likely to do so than feminine nouns. Note also that a noun that is not more commonly attested in the plural form than in the singular can still become unstable if the speaker does not know its gender; in that case, rather than analogizing from a plural form, the speaker might just guess at the noun's gender. Thus, although I am suggesting that a feminine noun that is frequently used in the plural and rarely in the singular is the most likely type of noun to become unstable, other types of nouns may also become unstable.

two nouns have masculine cognates in EOT would add further weight to the conclusion that this second prediction is upheld in the data.

The third prediction was that nouns that are frequently plural are most likely to change gender in languages with the masculine-plural pattern. This is a cross-linguistic prediction that could not be tested within the scope of this study. Within the EOT group, Tunni is the other language that has a uniform masculine-plural pattern, so one might expect to find a similar pattern of noun gender instability in that language, whereas languages with true gender polarity (like Rendille) would not be as likely to have gender instability since the gender of the singular form is unambiguously recoverable (though reversed) from the plural. I am not aware of the existence of multi-speaker gender-marked noun datasets for these or other relevant languages that would allow us to test this prediction cross-linguistically at present, but as I have argued here, it does seem to be true for Maay.

The final prediction was that languages with the masculine-plural pattern are more likely to have gender instability than other languages are. As with the previous prediction, this is a cross-linguistic prediction that has yet to be tested, though I have argued that Maay is an example of a language upholding this prediction. It is possible that the lack of the Maay-type masculine-plural pattern elsewhere in Cushitic enables us to reconcile the gender instability in Maay with Wolff's assertion, cited at the beginning of this paper, that Afro-Asiatic in general exhibits gender stability, but this remains an empirical question to be tested by comparing Maay and other languages that have the masculine-plural pattern with those that do not.

As a whole, then, the explanation I have proposed for the gender instability in Maay nouns does find support within the language and tentatively within the EOT group. Its applicability outside of EOT and Cushitic in general remains to be tested.

A final observation is that a number of languages have genderless plurals, and this analysis of Maay does predict that such languages should be susceptible to gender instability.[8] It is possible that further research will reveal that gender polarity has indeed developed in such languages; it is also conceivable that there are additional factors that have facilitated its development in Maay that are not present in other languages. For example, because the speakers are refugees and live in a community where not everyone speaks Maay and where several other languages are used, the language as a whole could be considered somewhat unstable (which is also consistent with the high degree of inter-speaker variability discussed in Paster 2013). Perhaps the gender neutralization in the plural has combined with a generally unstable language situation to produce the phenomenon we observe in Maay. Further research is needed to determine how widespread the phenomenon is and what determines when and where it emerges.

Acknowledgements

Many thanks to the Somali Bantu Community of San Diego, to my fall 2012 Field Methods class at Pomona College, and to Rodrigo Ranero and Rebekah Cramerus for participating

---

[8]Thanks to an anonymous reviewer for raising this issue.

in this research. Thanks also to the audience at ACAL 45 and to the anonymous reviewers of this paper for helpful comments. This research was funded in part by an Arnold L. and Lois S. Graves Award and by a Wig Teaching Innovation Grant from Pomona College.

References

Andrzejewski, Bogumil. 1960. The categories of number in noun forms in the Borana dialect of Galla. *Africa* 30. 62–75.

Comfort, Jade & Mary Paster. 2009. Notes on Lower Jubba Maay. In Masangu Matondo, Fiona McLaughlin & Eric Potsdam (eds.), *Selected Proceedings of the 38th Annual Conference on African Linguistics*, 204–216. Somerville, Massachusetts: Cascadilla Proceedings Project.

Corbett, Greville G. & Richard J. Hayward. 1987. Gender and number in Bayso. *Lingua* 73. 1–28.

Lecarme, Jacqueline. 2002. Gender 'polarity': Theoretical aspects of Somali nominal morphology. In Paul Boucher & Marc Plénat (eds.), *Many morphologies*, 109–141. Somerville, Massachusetts: Cascadilla Press.

Mous, Maarten. 2008. Number as an exponent of gender in Cushitic. In Erin Shay & Zygmunt Frajzyngier (eds.), *Interaction of morphology and syntax: Case studies in Afroasiatic*, 137–160. Amsterdam: Benjamins.

Oomen, Antoinette. 1981. Gender and plurality in Rendille. *Afroasiatic Linguistics* 8(1). 35–75.

Paster, Mary. 2007. Aspects of Maay phonology and morphology. *Studies in African Linguistics* 35(1). 73–120.

Paster, Mary. 2010. Optional multiple plural marking in Maay. In Franz Rainer, Wolfgang U. Dressler, Dieter Kastovsky & Hans Christian Luschützky (eds.), *Variation and change in morphology* (Current Issues in Linguistic Theory 310), 177–192. Amsterdam: Benjamins.

Paster, Mary. 2013. *An I-Language approach to inter-speaker variation in Maay*. Lecture presented at the 44th Annual Conference on African Linguistics/Georgetown University Round Table on Languages and Linguistics, Georgetown University.

Saeed, John I. 1982. Central Somali: A grammatical outline. *Monographic Journals of the Near East: Afroasiatic Linguistics* 8(2). 77–119.

Saeed, John I. 1987. *Somali reference grammar*. Wheaton, Maryland: Dunwoody Press.

Saeed, John I. 1999. *Somali*. Amsterdam: John Benjamins Publishing Company.

Tosco, Mauro. 1997. *Af Tunni: Grammar, Texts, and Glossary of a Southern Somali Dialect*. Köln: Rüdiger Köppe Verlag.

Wolff, H. Ekkehard. 2014. *Afro-Asiatic languages*. Encyclopedia Brittanica, online edition. http://www.britannica.com/EBchecked/topic/8488/Afro-Asiatic-languages/, accessed 2014-04-03.

Chapter 14

Egyptian Arabic broken plurals in DATR

Lindley Winchester

Georgetown University

This paper examines plural inflectional processes in Egyptian Arabic, with specific focus on the complex broken plural system. The data used in this examination is a set of 114 lexemes from a dictionary of the Egyptian Arabic variety by Badawi & Hinds (1986) collected through comparison of singular to plural template correspondences proposed by Gadalla (2000). The theoretical side of this analysis builds upon Alain Kihm's realizational "Root-and-Site Hypothesis", which categorizes concatenative and non-concatenative morphological processes as approachable in the same manner when discussing inflection as not only represented in segments but also as "sites" where inflectional operations may take place (Kihm 2006: 69). To organize the data through a computational lens, I emulate Kihm's approach in DATR, a lexical knowledge representation language, to generate the grammatical forms for a set of both broken and regular plural nouns. The hierarchically-structured inheritance of DATR allows for default templates to be defined and overridden, permitting a wide scope of variation to be represented with little code content. Overall, the analysis reveals that complex morphological phenomena, such as the broken plural, can be accounted for through a combination of theoretical and computational approaches.

1 Introduction

Egyptian Arabic is a branch of the Arabic language and the national language of Egypt. Outside of Egypt, it is intelligible in other Arabic-speaking countries, such as Libya, Syria, and Yemen. It is defined characteristically as part of the central and south branch of the Afroasiatic language family and Semitic genus (Lewis 2009). The particular inflectional process in focus here occurs on the nominal forms of the language, which are inflected for plural number through one of two separate processes, a suffixal inflection and infixational inflection, both of which will be elaborated upon further in §2. The latter process will take the majority of the focus, analyzed through a pre-existing theoretical framework and formalized in the computational model, DATR. The purpose of this examination is to computationally model theory in the construction of broken plurals in Egyptian Arabic, seeking an analysis that encompasses a majority, if not all, of the complex forms in question.

Lindley Winchester. Egyptian Arabic broken plurals in DATR. in Jason Kandybowicz, Travis Major, Harold Torrence & Philip T. Duncan (eds.), *African linguistics on the prairie: Selected papers from the 45th Annual Conference on African Linguistics*, 219–231. Berlin: Language Science Press. DOI:10.5281/zenodo.1251734

2 Nominal inflection

Although nominals are inflected for definiteness, possession, number, and grammatical gender in Egyptian Arabic, the discussion here focuses on the language's singular and plural number inflection (Gadalla 2000: 129–130)[1]. While singular number is not overtly marked, the expression of plural number in the Arabic varieties is realizable through two different inflectional processes and therefore partitions the lexicon of the language into two groups according to which process they utilize. The group of words which employ the first process, called the sound plurals, add a suffix to the singular stem without changing its internal structure. This group is loosely analogous to the *dog/dog-s* number inflection in English. However, unlike English the suffixes which attach to the stem agree in gender.

The broken plural group (BPs from here) is characterized by internal stem modification through the infixation of interweaving vowels, which vary in both vowel quality, length, and position between the consonantal roots of the stem. These plurals are considerably less predictable than their suffixal counterparts, analogous to the irregular *man/men* inflections in English. An example of this group is the masculine singular noun *ʃaahid* 'witness', which does not attach the masculine suffix /-iin/ but becomes *ʃuhuud* in the plural. Unlike verbal derivation, the broken plural inflection cannot be associated with any one sequence of vowels (such as the -u-uu- format in *ʃuhuud*) and similarly can not be defined through the process of allomorphy. Rather, the vowel qualities of both the singular and plural forms are semi-regular at best, making it difficult to distinguish any one vowel as the plural marker and any one vowel as the singular (Kihm 2006: 70). Examples of BP inflectional variation can be seen in Table 1 below.[2]

Table 1: Examples of BP variation.

Singular	Broken Plural	Gloss
suura	suwar	'chapter of the Koran (331)'
taman	ʔatmaan	'price (137)'
ʃagaan	ʃuguun	'sorrow (453)'

In addition, plural patterns cannot be uniquely associated with any one singular form nor any singular with any one plural form. For example, the $C_1aC_2C_3$ singular templatic form is associated with multiple BP patterns as seen in Table 2 below.

---

[1]Egyptian Arabic, unlike Classical and Modern Standard Arabic, does not inflect for case through affixation (Gadalla 2000: 108).

[2]The numbers listed in parentheses after each gloss in this and the following tables refer to the page in Badawi & Hinds (1986) on which the respective example is found.

Table 2: Examples of inflectional variation between templates.

Singular	Plural	Gloss
garh $(C_1aC_2C_3)$	guruuħ, giraaħ $(C_1uC_2uuC_3, C_1iC_2aaC_3)$	'wound (153)'
raxw $(C_1aC_2C_3)$	raxaawi $(C_1aC_2aaC_3i)$	'whiplash (331)'

2.1 Broken plurals in theory

Currently in Arabic linguistics, morphological research has been divided into two camps by differing theoretical approaches. Previously, the field assumed a root-based approach used by traditional Arab grammarians in explaining Arabic morphology. In opposition to this traditional approach are the word or stem-based approaches (Ratcliffe 2013: 71–91). From the span of approaches used to analyze BPs,[3] I selected Kihm's (2006) analysis of BPs and verbal nouns within Classical Arabic to provide the main theoretical framework in this paper.[4] This decision was influenced heavily by Kihm's adherence to the traditional root-and-pattern approach to Arabic morphological studies in addition to its flexibility and adaptability to DATR.

The widely accepted approach on the opposing side, a prosodic approach by McCarthy & Prince (1990), would not satisfy the intended goal of this paper. In their analysis, the main focus is placed on the leftmost heavy syllable, or two moras, as the singular stem's minimal word within which the BP is formed (Ratcliffe 1998: 80; McCarthy & Prince 1990: 231). With this, they structure their analysis around developing BPs from lexemes' singular stems, replacing some material while utilizing portions of its structure as distinctive in developing the iambic plural structure. One such feature that is transferred from the singular to plural form is said to be the vowel length of the final syllable when the singular's first syllable is heavy (CVC or CVV). However, despite being the "most familiar of the non-root properties," it is not consistently maintained in EA data, as seen in the singular *ʃaahid* becoming plural *ʃuhuud* 'witnesses' (McCarthy & Prince 1990: 218; Badawi & Hinds 1986: 122). Though *ʃaahid* does contain an initial heavy syllable /ʃaa-/, the short vowel in the singular's final syllable /-hid/ is not maintained in the plural but rather is lengthened to a long vowel.[5] Though rules such as this do find some grounding in the EA data at hand, they are not consistent enough to develop wide sweeping generalizations.

Furthermore, McCarthy & Prince's analysis places a heavy emphasis on the iambic

---

[3]Namely, Hammond (1988), McCarthy & Prince (1990), Ratcliffe (1998), and Kihm (2006). This list is by no means exhaustive.

[4]With supplemental information from an array of his other publications, each of which assists in explaining the framework further.

[5]This is just one feature McCarthy & Prince (1990) discuss as transferrable from the singular stem to a BP. Refer to Kihm (2006) for a further elaboration on the issues with relying on singular forms in determining BPs.

plural, which they present as most productive in the Arabic lexicon. Though this may be true, the analysis presented is not easily adaptable to the remaining non-iambic forms in my data and therefore cannot serve for the purpose of this paper. The root-based assumptions used in Kihm's analysis allow for more flexibility in presenting a wider array of the type of BPs found in the data.

Finally, Kihm's theoretical adherence to the root-and-pattern approach also allows for an easy transition into DATR, which focuses on the lexeme, defined as the consonantal root for this paper, rather than the morpheme as the minimal sign in a morphological paradigm (Brown & Hippisley 2012: 5).

2.2 The Root-and-Site Hypothesis

Kihm's Root-and-Site Hypothesis (RSH) takes a realizational nonsegmental concatenative approach to the BP phenomenon in Classical Arabic based upon a HPSG-type lexicon (see Pollard & Sag 1994). He argues this and other non-concatenative morphological processes could be absorbed into the category of concatenative morphology, shared by the sound plural inflection, if not only segments but also abstract elements, which he names functional "sites," can act as the locations in which morphology can occur (Kihm 2006: 69). These locations can be both outside and inside the stem boundary.

The functional site designated for the nominal BP inflection is located within the stem, between the second and third consonants. Though root-based, this placement coincides well with the word/stem-based hypotheses from Ratcliffe (1998) and McCarthy & Prince (1990). This root internal site is thus associated with the feature bundle NUM(ber) and is realized by the insertion of a glide, designated as /I/ (which can surface as /i/ or /j/), /U/ (which can surface as /u/ or /w/) and /A/ (which can surface as /a/ or /ʔ/) (Kihm 2006: 80).

Once inserted, the featured glide can either remain or spread into a short or long vowel construction within the word form (Kihm 2006: 80). The determination of which form surfaces is dependent upon the type of location it is inserted into: a slot designated for consonants or vowels. It surfaces as a long vowel when inserted in a consonantal location, and a short vowel when in a vowel slot (Kihm 2006: 81). This short vowel occurrence accounts for the construction of non-iambic broken plurals (see McCarthy & Prince 1990) and forms the basis for the "No long vowel inflection" class in the organization of data for this research.

Defining the diversity of the glide's timbre and the location in which it is inserted (whether a consonant or vowel slot) as irreducible, Kihm posits that each lexical entry must therefore supply the timbre of the glide, the type of slot in which it will be inserted, and the consonantal roots (Kihm 2006: 81).

3 Methodology

The data collected for the purpose of this research is a summation of a comparative analysis between two written sources. Gadalla's (2000) comparative morphological analysis of Modern Standard Arabic and Egyptian Arabic supplies a complete list of singular to broken plural templates (as well as those apt to take the sound plural) for Egyptian Arabic, such as follows: $C_1aC_2C_3 \rightarrow C_1uC_2uuC_3$, $C_1iC_2aaC_3$, etc.[6] In order to collect a set of concrete wordforms for analysis, I matched the list of template correspondences to vocabulary entries listed in Badawi & Hinds (1986) *A Dictionary of Egyptian Arabic*, in a similar fashion to:

(1) $C_1aC_2C_3 \rightarrow garħ$; $C_1uC_2uuC_3 \rightarrow guruuħ$

The collection process resulted in 114 individual lexemes that form BPs. These sets are meant to exhibit the range of variation seen in the broken plural formation from singular stems in Egyptian Arabic and are not based upon type or token statistical frequency within the language. The lack of such statistics should be considered a limitation at this point as the data does not provide a picture of the more or less commonly used BP forms within the language. However, the purpose of this analysis is not to discuss the most frequent forms in comparison to their infrequent siblings but rather to encompass as much of the found variation as possible within the computational construction.

Coinciding with Kihm's theoretical approach, I have categorized the data into inflectional classes based on their inflection site (at this point assumed to be a long vowel) in the BP form. These classes are then further separated based on major alterations to the stem during the inflection process, such as the insertion of a glottal stop prefix or a non-root based glide. From the 114 sets of singular to plural forms collected, one representative set is selected for each inflection class and subclass, characterized by the placement of the BP inflection site (class), any modification to the stem (subclass), and number of consonantal roots. These categories are displayed in Table 3 below, containing examples from Badawi & Hinds (1986), which I have organized according to the site in which their inflection occurs.

4 DATR

DATR is a lexical knowledge representation language used to express default-inheritance networks. Its primary use is the "representation of lexical entries for natural language processing" (Evans & Gazdar 1989: 66). Therefore, in DATR's language, I am able to define connections between a lexical entry's informational content and various nodes, which contain separate collections of internally related grammatical information, to construct a representation of the singular and BP forms. My representation heavily relies on networks of inheritance and the specification of morphosyntactic features through attribute paths. To elaborate, attribute paths can be realized as values, as in an atom: <path1> == value, a separate path: <path2> == <path1>, or as a combination of the two: <path3> == <path1> a. This final example might represent the fact that some morphosyntactic

---

[6]In alignment with other researchers, Gadalla utilizes F-ʕ-L as markers of the consonantal roots in the Arabic languages, correlational to C_1-C_2-C_3. For the remainder of this paper, I will use the latter form of consonantal notation.

Table 3: Nouns covered by second DATR theory.

Designated Inflection class	Singular form	Plural form	Gloss
Triconsonantal Roots			
Inflected after C1	sajjid	saada	'male polite form of address (440)'
Inflected after C2	gabal	gibaal	'hill (148)'
	garħ	guruuħ	'wound (153)'
	ʃagaan	ʃuguun	'sorrow (453)'
→ with glottal stop prefix	taman	ʔatmaan	'price (137)'
→ with glide insertion	garħa	gawaariħ	'carnivore (153)'
→ previously defined "derived noun"	matgar	mataagir	'place of business (122)'
	marsa	maraasi	'harbor (337)'
Inflected after C3	ɣuraab	ɣirbaan	'crow (619)'
	sˤadiiq	ʔasˤdiqaaʔ	'friend (499)'
No long vowel inflection	dibb	dibab	'bear (275)'
Quadriconsonantal Roots			
Inflected after C2	tuzluk	tazaalik	'leather leggings (128)'
	zooraq	zawaariq	'small boat (386)'
No long vowel inflection	sˤajdali	sˤajadla	'pharmacist (516)'

feature, named path3, is realized as whatever form path1 realizes plus a word-final /-a/ suffix (Evans & Gazdar 1996: 167–168). For a concrete example, refer to the basic lexical entry for the noun, *gabal* 'hill/mountain' (*gibaal* 'hills/mountains' for the plural) below in (2).

(2) GABAL 'hill/mountain' lexical entry
```
GABAL:
        <syn_cat> == \isi{noun}
        <gender> == masc
        <gloss> == hill , or , mountain
        <vowel sg> == V2:<vowel>
        <vowel pl> == <vowel sg>
        <c 1> == g
        <c 2> == b
        <c 3> == l
        <stem sg> == SINGULAR:<stem sg 3>
        <stem pl> == INFLC2.
```

Here, I have designated the syntactic category for *gabal* as a noun, the gender as masculine, and so forth. The < > denote paths that are realized by the values following the == (Evans & Gazdar 1996: 169).

Following the conceptual purpose of the DATR language, which is to create wide-sweeping generalizations within language inflection while avoiding redundancy throughout the coding process, we see that the singular stem <stem sg> and plural stem <stem pl> values refer to a separate node and does not simply state the singular and plural stem (Evans & Gazdar 1996: 169). It would be contradictory to our purpose as well as DATR's to simply state <stem sg> == gabal and <stem pl> == gibaal. Rather, as seen in (2), we rely on networks of inheritance to form these for the lexical entry, and hopefully various others, by creating separate nodes called SINGULAR for the singular stem and INFLC2 for the plural. The paths that are realized by these two nodes can construct the singular and plural stems through the insertion of vowels and the consonantal root values specified within the lexical entry. This inheritance appears just as in Figure 1 below, where the lexical entry GABAL looks to the INFLC2 node searching for a path that matches its own <stem pl>. This <stem pl> within INFLC2 then yields a template in which GABAL inserts the values for its consonantal roots.

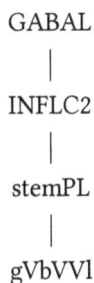

GABAL

|

INFLC2

|

stemPL

|

gVbVVl

Figure 1: GABAL inheritance visual representation.

Within the same lexical entry, the singular path is realized by a separate node titled SINGULAR, which itself contains a path designated as <stem sg 3>. Similar to the description above for Figure 1, to form GABAL's singular stem, it looks to a node called SINGULAR, finds a path within it named <stem sg 3>, inherits the template specified there and inserts its consonantal root values.

The coding within these two nodes can be seen below in (3).

(3) Singular and post-C_2 BP inflection coding

```
SINGULAR:
    <stem sg 3> == "<c 1>" "<vowel sg>" "<c 2>" "<vowel sg>" "<c 3>".
INFLC2:
    <stem pl> == "<c 1>" "<vowel pl 2>" "<c 2>" "<vowel pl>"
    "<vowel pl>" "<c 3>".
```

The question now is how to associate the appropriate vowel qualities within the <vowel sg> and <vowel pl> paths defined in the <stem pl> and <stem sg 3> templates. While it would be easy to simply place them within the templatic structures specified within the INFLC2 and SINGULAR nodes, allowing the lexical entry to inherit both the templatic form and vowel qualities together, the theory would no longer have the ability to account for words that have the same template but different vowels. An example of this is the singular *ʃagaan* 'sorrow' becoming the plural *ʃuguun* 'sorrows'. In the plural, *gibaal* and *ʃuguun* share the same template (C_1-V-C_2-V-V-C_3) but vary in vowels. In order for the lexical entries SHAGAAN and GABAL to both inherit from the same INFLC2 <stem pl>, the vowel qualities for the respective plural stems must simply be specified in a separate location where they can be inherited by the corresponding lexical entry. In SINGULAR's template, we see the vowels are both specified as some default singular vowel (<vowel sg>), whereas the vowels in INFLC2 are designated as a long default plural vowel in the second syllable (<vowel pl> <vowel pl>) and a non-default plural vowel in the first syllable (<vowel pl 2>). These specifications require that the lexical entry realize the paths: <vowel sg> and <vowel pl>. By having content from multiple nodes converge into one, the lexical entry, the result is called a multiple inheritance network (Evans & Gazdar 1996: 202–203). Since a <sg> and <pl> inheritance for the vowels is distinguished, the theory can link the values from separate vowel nodes to the appropriate singular and plural vowel paths specified in the templatic structures of the SINGULAR and INFLC2 nodes.

Referring back to GABAL's lexical entry, we see the singular vowels are to be assigned from the v2 node and any of its <vowel> path values. Looking at v2, we find the coding in (4).

(4) v2 node

```
V2:
<vowel> == a
<vowel 2> == i.
```

With this vowel value and DATR's use of multiple inheritance, we can now insert material into the <vowel sg> paths in <stem sg 3>'s template in (3) to create the full singular stem, g -*a-b-a-l* → *gabal*. Since <stem sg 3> does not call for a <vowel sg 2>, the information provided by <vowel 2> in v2 is ignored for now.

For the plural, the vowel values are assigned from the same node as the <vowel sg>'s path. Using the same procedure as above, DATR inserts this <vowel> value into the <vowel pl> path locations specified in INFLC2's <stem pl> template. Unlike the singular, the template now calls for a <vowel pl 2> value and therefore inserts the values specified for <vowel 2> within v2, creating g -*i-b-a-a-l* → *gibaal*. The full inheritance hierarchy for GABAL can be seen below in Figure 2.

Now let's expand our theory to account for SHAGAAN. Its lexical entry appears as below in (5).

GABAL

```
        VSG        VPL
         |          |
      SINGULAR   INFLC2
         |          |
      stemSG3    stemPL
         |          |
       gabal      gibaal
```

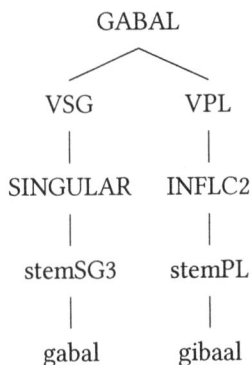

Figure 2: GABAL inheritance visual representation.

(5) SHAGAAN 'sorrow' lexical entry
    SHAGAAN:
        <syn_cat> == \isi{noun}
        <gender> == masc
        <gloss> == sorrow
        <vowel sg> == V1:<vowel>
        <vowel pl> == V6:<vowel>
        <c 1> == ʃ
        <c 2> == g
        <c 3> == n
        <stem sg> == SINGULAR:<stem sg 5>
        <stem pl> == INFLC2.

As with GABAL, the lines designating the syntactic category, gender, gloss, consonantal roots, and stem/vowel qualities for both the singular and plural stems are included. SHAGAAN follows the same procedure as GABAL in forming the plural, inheriting the same <stem pl> template from INFLC2 and plural vowels from a node named v6, which supplies the /u-uu/ vowel melody. The coding for v6 appears the same as v2, except specifying <vowel> == u in this instance.

The two lexical entries differ in their singular form and therefore inherit different templates within the SINGULAR node. Specifically, SHAGAAN inherits from a path named <stem sg 5>, with the number only distinguishing the different templates with no relation to hierarchy. The coding for the SINGULAR node now appears in (6), including both SHAGAAN and GABAL's singular stem formations.

(6) SINGULAR node coding

```
SINGULAR:
    <stem sg 3> == "<c 1>" "<vowel sg>" "<c 2>" "<vowel sg>" "<c 3>"
    <stem sg 5> == "<c 1>" "<vowel sg>" "<c 2>" "<vowel sg 2>"
    "<vowel sg 2>" "<c 3>".
```

The remainder of the inheritance remains the same as in GABAL. SHAGAAN inherits SINGULAR's <stem sg 5> and inserts its consonantal roots and the inherited vowel from the V1 node's <vowel>, the coding of which is seen below in (7).

(7) V1 node
```
V1:
    <vowel> == a.
```

These are then inserted into the appropriate slots in the singular stem's template (C_1-V-C_2-V-V-C_3), creating *ʃ-a-g-a-a-n → ʃagaan*. The redundancy we see in comparing nodes V1 and V2 is necessary in order to capture the vowel variation seen in stems like singular *gabal → plural gibaal, ʃagaan → ʃuguun*, and *matgar* 'place of business' → *mataagir* 'places of business'. Lexical entries for GABAL and MATGAR will inherit from V2 to achieve the /a-i/ or /i-a/ vowels in their plural while SHAGAAN inherits from V1 to achieve solely /a/ vowel insertion. Mimicking GABAL above, the tree representation for SHAGAAN can be seen in Figure 3 below.

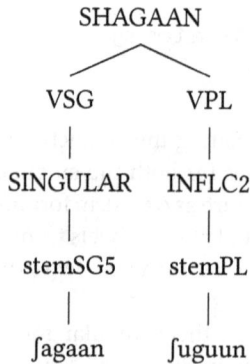

```
                    SHAGAAN
                   ⌒‾‾‾‾⌒
            VSG              VPL
             |                |
         SINGULAR          INFLC2
             |                |
          stemSG5          stemPL
             |                |
          ʃagaan           ʃuguun
```

Figure 3: SHAGAAN inheritance visual representation.

In addition to triconsonantal roots, the theory can also form quadriconsonantal singular and BP forms. An example of the lexical entry for such can be seen in (8) below.

(8) ZOORAQ 'small boat' lexical entry
     ZOORAQ:
        `<syn_cat> == \isi{noun}`
        `<gender> == masc`
        `<gloss> == small, boat`
        `<vowel sg> == V4:<vowel>`
        `<vowel pl> == V2:<vowel>`
        `<c 1> == z`
        `<c 2> == w`
        `<c 3> == r`
        `<c 4> == q`
        `<stem sg> == QUAD_SINGULAR:<stem sg 2>`
        `<stem pl> == QUAD_PL_INFLC2:<stem pl 2>.`

It appears the same as the two previous entries but with an additional consonant specified as <c 4>. This lexeme is particularly interesting for containing a glide as its second consonantal root. Within the data, medial glide root consonants sometimes surface as a long vowels within either the lexeme's singular or plural forms (such as the singular *sajjid* becoming the plural *saada* 'polite forms of address' with the root consonants /s-j-d/). Since ZOORAQ's weak medial root consonant, /w/, does not appear as a consonant in the singular but rather as the long vowel /oo/, it uses the value of <stem sg 2> in the QUAD_SINGULAR node to form a template. This template is structured by the coding in (9) below.

(9) Subset of QUAD_SINGULAR node

    QUAD_SINGULAR:
        `<stem sg 2> == "<c 1>" "<vowel sg>" "<vowel sg>" "<c 3>"`
        `"<vowel sg 2>" "<c 4>".`

As is necessary to output *zooraq*, the template is structured to place a long vowel after the first root consonant and does not call for a <c 2>. However, in the plural template, the glide value of <c 2> is required and therefore structured in QUAD_PL_INFLC2's <stem pl 2> value creating z-a-w-a-a-r-i-q → *zawaariq*.

The structure of these lexical entries simulates my intended adherence to Kihm's theoretical framework. Specifically, each stem forming node, such as INFLC2, provides a template for either a singular or plural form while the lexical entry defines the vowel timbre and consonantal roots.[7] The plural stem formation nodes are organized according to the occurrence of the long vowel (or lack thereof as in *dibb* → *dibab* 'bears'), with further variation for stems within each node. An example of this organization can be seen in (10) below.

---

[7] The inheritance defined between a lexical entry and the V(owel) nodes should be viewed as simply a selection process from the set of vowels permitted for this particular language. The purpose of separating them from the lexical entry itself was a foresight so the theory could be expanded further to encompass verbal and other derivations.

(10)   INFLC3 node coding

```
INFLC3:
    <stem pl> == "<c 1>" "<vowel pl 2>" "<c 2>" "<c 3>" "<vowel pl>"
    "<vowel pl>" n
    <stem pl 2> == ?a "<c 1>" "<c 2>" "<vowel pl 2>" "<c 3>"
    "<vowel pl>" "<vowel pl>" ?.
```

In this example, we see the plural templates for those words with long vowel inflection after the third root consonant. <stem pl> creates words such as *ɣuraab* 'crow' → *ɣirbaan* 'crows' while <stem pl 2> forms plurals such as *sˤadiiq* 'friend' → *ʔasˤdiqaaʔ* 'friends'.

A simplistic hierarchical representation of BP formation as it is constructed in the theory can be seen in Figure 4 below.

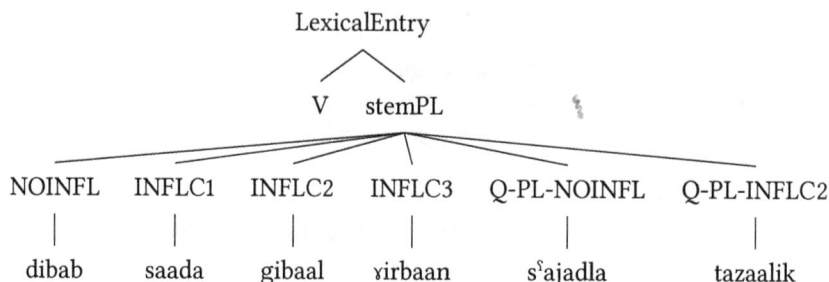

LexicalEntry

V   stemPL

NOINFL	INFLC1	INFLC2	INFLC3	Q-PL-NOINFL	Q-PL-INFLC2
dibab	saada	gibaal	ɣirbaan	sˤajadla	tazaalik

Figure 4: Inheritance network for plural formation.

Working from the bottom of the tree, examples of BPs from Table 3 are located under their corresponding stem formation nodes. From left to right we have a class for BPs with no apparent long vowel inflection (NOINFL), with long vowel inflection following the first consonantal root (INFLC1), following the second consonantal root (INFLC2), and following the third consonantal root (INFLC3). The two classes located at the far right of the tree are designed for quadriconsonantal roots. These are further divided by whether the quadriconsonantal BP shows long vowel inflection after the second root consonant (Q-PL-INFLC2) or not at all (Q-PL-NOINFL). Altogether, these plural stem formation nodes represent the fourteen distinct BP forms seen in Table 3 and exemplify the variation found in BPs across the language.

5 Conclusions

In an attempt to construct a wide array of complex broken plural forms in Egyptian Arabic, the fundamentals of Kihm's Root-and-Site Hypothesis can be integrated into DATR. Though encountering difficulties within the theoretical framework for portions of the data, the theory generates exemplary singular and plural forms for each of the designated inflection classes and subclasses into which the data has been organized. Therefore, it covers the extent of complex variation found within the data set through an extension of the theoretical framework. In this analysis, it has been shown that not only theoretical but computational approaches can be utilized in the representation of complex morphological phenomena like the broken plural.

References

Badawi, El-Said & Martin Hinds. 1986. *A dictionary of Egyptian Arabic*. Beirut: Librairie Du Liban.

Brown, Dunstan & Andrew Hippisley. 2012. *Network morphology: A defaults-based theory of word structure*. Vol. 133. Cambridge: Cambridge University Press.

Evans, Roger & Gerald Gazdar. 1989. Inference in DATR. In *Proceedings of the Fourth Conference on European Chapter of the Association for Computational Linguistics*, 66–71. Association for Computational Linguistics.

Evans, Roger & Gerald Gazdar. 1996. DATR: A language for lexical knowledge representation. *Computational Linguistics* 22(2). 167–216.

Gadalla, Hassan AH. 2000. *Comparative morphology of standard and egyptian arabic*. Vol. 5. Lincom Europa Munich.

Hammond, Michael. 1988. Templatic transfer in Arabic broken plurals. *Natural Language and Linguistic Theory* 6(2). 247–270.

Kihm, Alain. 2006. Nonsegmental concatenation: A study of Classical Arabic broken plurals and verbal nouns. *Morphology* 16. 69–105.

Lewis, M. Paul (ed.). 2009. *Ethnologue: Languages of the World, Sixteenth edition*. Dallas: SIL International.

McCarthy, John J. & Alan S. Prince. 1990. Foot and word in prosodic morphology: The Arabic broken plural. *Natural Language and Linguistic Theory* 8.2. 209–283.

Pollard, Carl & Ivan A. Sag. 1994. *Head-driven phrase structure grammar*. Chicago: University of Chicago Press & Stanford: CSLI Publications.

Ratcliffe, Robert R. 1998. *The broken plural problem in Arabic and comparative semitic: Allomorphy and analogy in non-concatenative morphology*. Amsterdam/Philadelphia: John Benjamins.

Ratcliffe, Robert R. 2013. Morphology. In Jonathan Owens (ed.), *The Oxford handbook of morphology*, 71–91. Oxford: Oxford University Press.

Part IV

Syntax

Chapter 15

Factive relative clauses in Pulaar

Ibrahima Ba

The University of Kansas

Drawing from Kayne (1994a), this chapter shows that Headed Relative Clauses and Factive Clauses in Pulaar are built from similar structures. Both display word order similarities, and in each case the complementizer, which is homophonous with the determiner, agrees with the (null or overt) head NP in Spec,CP. The verb form is also the same in Headed Relatives and Factive Relatives, and it undergoes the same agreement pattern. Furthermore, Headed Relatives and Factives in Pulaar both exhibit island constraints such that extraction out of either construction is impossible; this indicates that they all involve movement of some sort. The difference between these constructions is that the Headed Relative has an overt head noun whereas Factives have null head nouns.

1 Introduction

This paper investigates factive relative clauses in Pulaar, a West Atlantic language spoken in Senegal and other West African countries. The Pulaar variety described here is spoken in the southern part of Senegal. Specifically, the paper provides an analysis of two factive constructions in Pulaar, namely the verbal factive and the *ko*-factive, as (1a) and (1b) respectively: in (1a), the infinitive form of the verb is fronted and followed by the complementizer; in (1b), the particle *ko*[1] (glossed as a relative complementizer) always appears at the leftmost edge of the clause.[2]

(1) a. [**def-go** ngo **ndef**-mi ñebbe ngo] bettu   Hawaa.   Verbal Factive[3]
cook-INF C.REL cook-1SG beans CL.the surprise Hawaa

'The fact that I cooked beans surprised Hawaa.'
'The cooking that I cooked the beans surprised Hawaa.'

    b. [**ko ndef**-mi ñebbe ko]   bettu   Hawaa.   *ko*-Factive
C.REL cook-1SG beans CL.the surprise Hawaa

'The fact that I cooked beans surprised Hawaa.'

---

[1]*Ko* has a variety of meanings in Pulaar, most of which are not related semantically. I treat these various instances of *ko* as homophones, which have meanings/functions such as focus/topic (see Cover 2006), copula, noun class, complementizer, pronoun.

[2]The two meanings of (1a) are discussed in §3.2.

Ibrahima Ba. Factive relative clauses in Pulaar. In Jason Kandybowicz, Travis Major, Harold Torrence & Philip T. Duncan (eds.), *African linguistics on the prairie: Selected papers from the 45th Annual Conference on African Linguistics*, 235–251. Berlin: Language Science Press.
DOI:10.5281/zenodo.1251736

The main claim in this paper is that the constructions in (1) are relative clause constructions with a derivation similar to headed relative clauses in Pulaar, as in (2):

(2) Musa ñaam-ma [ñebbe ɗe   ndef-mi ɗe].
     Musa eat-PERF beans C.REL cook-1SG CL.the

     'Musa ate the beans that I cooked.'

I argue that headed relatives as well as factive relatives can be derived from the same underlying structure in (3) following Kayne (1994b). The structure in (3) is composed of a D and a CP complement.

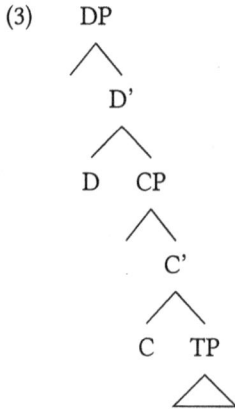

(3) DP

     D'

     D   CP

         C'

         C   TP

This is explicitly shown in the structures in (4) where we can see the different movement operations that occur in the derivation of the different clauses. Specifically, the entire CP moves to Spec, DP.

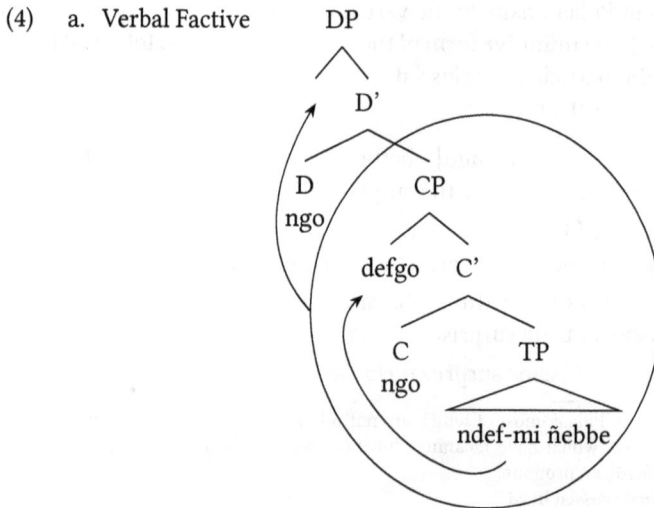

(4) a. Verbal Factive   DP

     D'

     D   CP
     ngo

          defgo   C'

               C   TP
               ngo
                    ndef-mi ñebbe

b. *Ko*-Factive

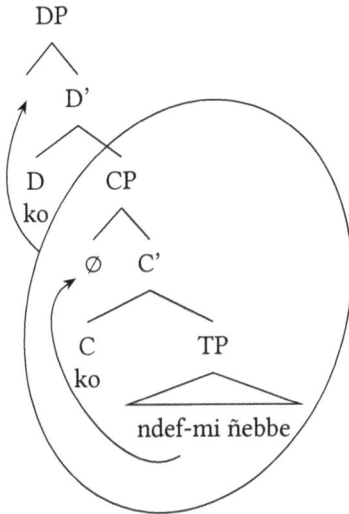

c. Headed RC

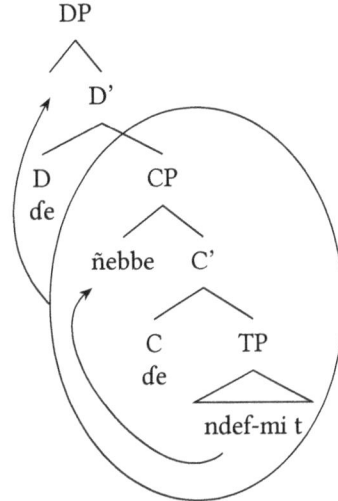

The remainder of this paper is structured as follows: §2 provides a short background on Pulaar which will include the basic word order, some properties of the noun and the agreement morphology. The distribution of factive clauses is laid out in §3. §4 deals with the structural similarities that exist between Headed Relatives and Factives in Pulaar. §5 demonstrates that both headed relatives and factives are islands and §6 shows the derivation of Headed Relatives and Factive clauses. §6 presents concluding remarks.

2 Background on Pulaar

Lewis (2009) states that Pulaar belongs to Atlantic branch of the Niger-Congo language family. There is a large number of Pulaar dialects with varying levels of mutual intelligibility, spoken from Senegal to Cameroon and Sudan and all the countries in-between. There are at least four dialects of Pulaar in Senegal: Futa Tooro region (north-east), Fula(kunda) spoken in the Kolda region (south), Pular (spelled with one 'a') spoken by people originally from Guinea Republic; and the dialect spoken in Kabaadaa (south and east of Kolda), also known as Toore, which this paper is based on.

2.1 Word order

Pulaar is used here as a general term to refer to the language. It is a Subject-Verb-Object (SVO), prepositional language, as shown in the sentence below.

(5) Taalibe mo   jangu-m   deft-are nde   les   lekki.
    student CL.the read-PERF.NEUT book-CL CL.the under tree
    'The student has read the book under a tree.'

Focus in Pulaar is generally encoded by the particle *ko* which precedes the focused phrase, as shown in the example below:

(6) a. (Ko) raandu ndu   Musaa yii-noo.   DP focus
         FOC dog.CL CL.the Musaa see-PAST

         'It's the dog that Musaa saw.'

     b. Musaa (ko) yii-no   raandu ndu.   Verb focus
         Musaa FOC see-PAST dog.CL the.CL

         'Musaa saw the dog (not heard it bark).'

The parentheses indicate that *ko* is optional. In the absence of *ko*, focus can still be interpreted from the verb ending. Long vowels indicate DP focus whereas short vowel indicate Verb focus, regardless of the presence or absence of of the focus particle *ko*. *Ko* is also used in Wh-questions, as in the following example:

(7) Ko   Musaa yii-**noo**?   Wh-question
     what Musaa see-past

     'What did Musaa see?'

2.2 Nouns in Pulaar

Pulaar is a noun class language. It has twenty-two noun classes and the noun class marker follows the noun (Sylla 1982: 34).

(8) a. raa-ndu ndu
         dog-CL CL.the

         'the dog'

     b. daa-ɗi ɗi
         dog-CL CL.the

         'the dogs'

The noun in (8a) can be analyzed as the root noun *raa* "dog" and a suffix *ndu*. Thus, the noun always occurs as a combination of the noun and the suffix, like *raandu* "a dog".

The infinitive in Pulaar is composed of the verb root and the infinitive suffix *go*, as seen in the examples in (9a-b). This infinitive form occurs in a variety of positions within a sentence. The examples below show the different positions that the infinitive can occupy.

(9) a. Mbiɗo yiɗi/foti   **def-go**   maaro.   Complement of V
         1SG   want/should cook-INF rice

         'I want to cook rice.'

     b. O ñoot-ma tuuba am ba   **ñoot-go** wesoo.   As a noun + adjective
         3SG sew-PERF pants my CL.the sew-INF beautiful

         'He has sewn my pants a beautiful sewing.'

(9b) shows that the infinitive in Pulaar can be modified by an adjective, which suggests that it behaves as a noun belonging to the *ngo* class. Table 1 shows the noun classes in Pulaar.

Table 1: Noun Classes in Pulaar.

	Noun class	example	gloss
1	mo	suko mo	the child
2	nde	hoore nde	the head
3	ndi	ngaari ndi	the ox
4	ndu	raandu ndu	the dog
5	nge	nagge nge	the cow
6	**ngo**	jungo ngo	the hand
7	ngu	pucuu ngu	the horse
8	nga	damnga nga	the door
9	ba	mbabba ba	the donkey
10	ka	laanaa ka	the plane, boat
11	ki	leɓii ki	the knife
12	**ko**	huuko ko	the grass
13	ɗum	ɓaleejum ɗum	the black thing
14	ɗam	ndiyam ɗam	the water
15	nge	laacee nge	the little tail
16	ka	leyka ka	the small land
17	ngi	damngii ngi	the huge door
18	nga	neɗɗaa nga	the huge person
19	ɓe	yimɓe ɓe	the people
20	ɗe	gite ɗe	the eyes
21	ɗi	babaaji ɗi	the donkeys
22	koñ	laanoñ koñ	the small boats

Noun classes 1 to 18 are singular and noun classes 19 to 22 are plural. The noun class 1 is used for humans and borrowed words. It has two plural forms: 19 for humans and 21 for borrowed words. However, while 19 relates specifically to humans, 21 is not only related to borrowed words; it is also the plural of other noun classes such as 3, 4, 5, 7 etc. The noun class 20 is also the plural of several noun classes such 8, 10, 2, etc. The noun class 22 is the plural for diminutives 15 and 16. The augmentative classes 17 and 18, however, have the regular plural class 20 even when the "augmented" noun denotes a human referent.

For the remainder of this paper, I will be spelling nouns as one single unit, for instance *raandu* instead of a split word *raa-ndu*.

Table 2: Singular/Plural Mapping of Noun Classes.

Singular	Plural
mo	ɓe (humans), ɗi (loanwords)
ndi, ndu, nge, ngu, ba, ko, ɗum, ɗam	ɗi
nde, ngo, ka, ki & the augmentatives nga, ngi	ɗe
nge, ka (diminutives)	koñ

2.3 Consonant mutation

Consonant mutation refers to the change of one consonant into another under certain conditions. According to Sylla (1982) and McLaughlin (2005), Pulaar exhibits consonant mutation, for instance the alternation between *y*, *g* and *s*, *c* below:

(10)　a.　yitare 'eye'
　　　 b.　gite 'eyes'

(11)　a.　sengo 'side'
　　　 b.　cengle 'sides'

Table 3 shows the alternation patterns that can be found in Pulaar.

Table 3: Mutating Initial Consonants.

Initial consonant of the verb	
Simple	Mutated
Ø[4], g	ŋg
f	p
h	k
b, w	mb
s	c
j, y	ñj
d, r	nd

Alternations like these occur in a variety of contexts such as subject agreement on the verb, singular/plural alternation on nouns, but also affixation. In what follows, I show an example of each of these alternations. In matrix clauses for instance, subject agreement is shown on the verb through the mutation of the initial consonant when the subject is plural.

---

[4]The symbol 'Ø' represents cases when the verb starts with a vowel. In such cases, [ŋg] becomes the mutated sound in the right context.

(12) a. mi/a/o   sood-ma   oto.   Singular
         I/you/he/she buy-PERF.NEUT car

         'I/you have bought a car.'

      b. En/on/ɓe   cood-ma   oto.   Plural
         We/you/they buy-PERF.NEUT car

         'We have bought a car.'

In (13a) the sentence has a singular subject and the verb 'buy' starts with [s]. In (13b), however, where the subject is plural the verb 'buy' begins with <c> and is pronounced [ʧ].

Consonant mutation may also occur in nominalization; that is when a verb is turned into a noun, as shown in the following examples:

(13)   Verb to Noun Alternations

       a. surku-go   → curki 'smoke'
          smoke-INF

          'to smoke'

       b. yim-go   → jimoo 'a song'
          sing-INF

          'to sing'

Note the alternations in examples (13a) and (13b) in which the initial consonant of the verb changes in the corresponding noun.

3 Distribution and semantic interpretations of factives

3.1 Distribution of factives

Both factive clause types occur as subjects and complements to factive predicates, i.e. predicates that presuppose the truth of their subjects or complements. For instance, the sentence in (14), from Kiparsky & Kiparsky (1970), involves the non-factive verb 'claim'. In other words, a claim may be proven either right or wrong, as shown in (14b-c):

(14)   a. John claims that he offended Mary.   Non-factive Predicate
       b. ... and in fact, he did.
       c. ... but in fact, he did not.

The example in (15), however, involves a factive verb. That means it refers to an event that has necessarily occurred, as shown in (15b-c):

(15)   a. John regrets that he offended Mary.   Factive Predicate
       b. ... and in fact, he did.
       c. # ... but in fact, he did not.

The examples in (16b) and (16c) respectively show verbal and *ko* factives as subjects:

(16) a. ɓe nguju-m deftare.   (input to (16b-c))
          3.PL steal-PERF book

          'They stole a book.'

      b. [wuju-go ngo ɓe nguj-i   deftare ngo] bettu-mii-m.   Verbal-Factive
          steal-INF C.REL 3.PL steal-PERF book   CL.the surprise-1SG-PERF

          'The fact that they stole the book surprised me.'

      c. [ko ɓe nguj-i   deftare ko]   bettu-mii-m.   *ko*-Factive
          C.REL 3.PL steal-PERF book   CL.the surprise-1SG-perf

          '(The fact) that they stole the book surprised me.'

In Pulaar, factive clauses occur as arguments of factive verbs like *bettugo* 'surprise', *loɓgo* 'to be angry', *ricitaago* 'to regret'. Factive clauses can, thus, be complements to factive verbs, as in the following examples where the verbal and the *ko* factive are objects of the verb *ricitaago* 'to regret':

(17) a. ɓe ndicit-iim [wuju-go ngo ɓe nguj-i   deftare ngo].   Verbal-Factive
          1PL regret-PERF steal-INF C.REL 3.PL steal-PERF book   CL.the

          'They regret the fact that they stole the book.'

      b. ɓe ndicit-iim [ko ɓe nguj-i   deftare ko].   *ko*-Factive
          1PL regret-PERF C.REL 3.PL steal-PERF book   CL.the

          'They regret (the fact) that they stole the book.'

Also, factive clauses do not occur as arguments of non-factive verbs like *siɓ-go* 'to doubt', as shown in the following examples:

(18) a. * Verbal-Factive
          mbiɗo siɓ-i   [wuju-go ngo ɓe nguj-i   deftare ngo].
          1SG   doubt-PERF steal-INF C.REL 3.PL steal-PERF book   CL.the

          Intended: 'I doubt the fact that they stole a book.'

      b. * *ko*-Factive
          mbiɗo siɓ-i   [ko ɓe nguj-i   deftare ko].
          1SG   doubt-PERF C.REL 3.PL steal-PERF book   CL.the

          Intended: 'I doubt that they stole a book.'

3.2 Semantic interpretations of Pulaar factive clauses

There are interpretive differences between the verbal factive and the *ko*-factive in Pulaar. In fact, whereas the verbal factive is ambiguous between an eventive and a manner readings, the *ko*-factive can be interpreted as an event.

(19) a. [**def-go** ngo **ndef**-mi ñebbe ngo] bettu   Hawaa.   Verbal-Factive
          cook-INF C.$_{REL}$ cook-1SG beans CL.the surprise Hawaa

          'The fact that I cooked beans surprised Hawaa.'
          'The cooking that I cooked the beans surprised Hawaa.'

     b. [**ko ndef**-mi ñebbe ko]   bettu   Hawaa   *ko*-Factive
          C.$_{REL}$ cook-1SG beans CL.the surprise Hawaa

          'The fact that I cooked beans surprised Hawaa.'

The example in (19a) can mean that Hawaa did not expect the speaker to cook the beans in the first place; maybe they agreed that the beans were for sale. In addition to this eventive reading, the verbal factive has a manner reading under which (19a) would mean that Hawaa expected the speaker to cook the beans but the cooking turned out to be either so good or so bad that Hawaa is somehow surprised.

As for the *ko*-factive, it only has an eventive reading. In (19b) for instance, Hawaa is surprised that the speaker cooked the beans. There may be a few reasons to this; Hawaa may not have expected or wanted the beans to be cooked or she may not have expected or wanted the speaker to cook the beans he/she does not like cooking or is a terrible cook, etc.

4 Pulaar relative clauses

In this section I show the morphological similarities between factive clauses and headed relative clauses. Specifically, I show that factive clauses are types of relative clauses. In addition to being head initial, these three constructions have agreeing complementizer, final determiner, similar placement for subject DP or pronoun. They also have the same agreement properties.

4.1 Clause structure of headed relative clauses

Pulaar has head-initial relative clauses. The relativizer (or complementizer) agrees with and follows the head noun. It is homophonous with the clausal determiner at the end of the clause which encodes definiteness. When it is omitted, the head noun is indefinite. The relative complementizer is obligatory.

(20) a. simis **mo** Hawaa loot-i   **mo**   Headed Relative Clause
          shirt C.$_{REL}$ Hawaa wash-PERF CL.the

          'the shirt that Hawaa washed'

     b. simis *(**mo**) Hawaa loot-i
          shirt C.$_{REL}$ Hawaa wash-PERF

          '(some) shirt that Hawaa washed'

(21) a. faɗoo **ngo** Hawaa watt-ii   **ngo**
         shoe C.REL Hawaa wear-PERF CL.the

      'The shoe that Hawaa is wearing'

   b. faɗoo *(**ngo**) Hawaa watt-ii
         shoe C.REL   Hawaa wash-PERF

      '(some) shoe that Hawaa is wearing'

The examples in 20 have all the same material, the only difference is that (20a) ends with a determiner which is missing in (20b). However, the complementizer in (20b) cannot be deleted. The same can be said (21) where the only difference is that (21b) is lacking the final determiner; and again the complementizer is mandatory.

Subject agreement is shown on the verb through consonant mutation for plural subjects, as in matrix clauses. This is shown in the examples below:

(22) a. ñebbe ɗe   Hawaa def-i   ɗe   3SG subject
         beans C.REL Hawaa cook-PERF CL.the

      'the beans that Hawaa cooked'

   b. ñebbe ɗe   ndef-mi ɗe   1SG subject
         beans C.REL cook-1SG CL.the

      'the beans that I cooked'

   c. ñebbe ɗe   rewɓe ɓe   ndef-i   ɗe   3PL subject
         beans C.REL women CL.the cook-PERF CL.the

      'the beans that the women cooked'

The initial consonant of the verb changes from [d] in (22a) to [nd] in (22b,c). DP subjects in relative clauses always precede the verb.

Table 4: Pulaar subject pronouns.

Singular	Plural
mi	min, en
a	on
o	ɓe

The word order of the headed object relative clauses in Pulaar is as follows:

(23) NP   C.REL   S   V   O_trace   DET.CL

4.2 Clause Structure of factive clauses

Verbal factives are so called because a form of the verb (the infinitive or gerundive) is treated as a noun heading the factive clause. In this clause, the nominalized form of the verb is followed by an agreeing relativizer which is homophonous with the determiner at the end of the clause. This can be seen in the examples below:

(24) loot-go **ngo** Hawaa loot-i wutte **ngo**   Verbal Factive
wash-INF C.$_{REL}$ Hawaa wash-PERF shirt CL.the

'the fact that Hawaa washed a shirt'

(25) **ko** Hawaa loot-i wutte **ko**
C.$_{REL}$ Hawaa wash-PERF shirt CL.the

'(the fact) that Hawaa washed a shirt'

When the determiner is omitted, the verbal noun is indefinite[5]. The relative complementizer is obligatory. This is shown in the following examples:

(26) Loot-go *(**ngo**) Hawaa loot-i wutte
wash-INF C.$_{REL}$ Hawaa wash-PERF shirt

'A/some washing that Hawaa washed a shirt'

(27) *ko Hawaa loot-i wutte[6]
C.$_{REL}$ Hawaa wash-PERF shirt

'the fact that Hawaa washed a shirt'

In verbal factive constructions, the verb appears to show some form of agreement. Subject agreement is shown on verb through consonant mutation for plural subjects, as in matrix clauses. However, singular subjects also trigger consonant mutation when they follow the verb. This is shown in the examples below:

(28) a. def-go ngo Hawaa **def**-i ñebbe ngo   3SG subject
cook-INF C.$_{REL}$ Hawaa cook-PERF beans CL.the

'the fact that Hawaa cooked beans'

b. def-go ngo **ndef**-mi ñebbe ngo   1SG subject
cook-INF C.$_{REL}$ cook-1SG beans CL.the

'the fact that I cooked beans'

c. def-go ngo 6e **ndef**-i ñebbe ngo   3PL subject
cook-INF C.$_{REL}$ SUBJ.pro cook-PERF beans CL.the

'the fact that they cooked beans'

---

[5]This is still interpreted as a factive. Structures like (26) and (27) can be answers to a question like: 'What is so and so mad about' where the person answering the question is not making it sound like their interlocutor knew about that specific event.

[6]This is just interpreted as a subject focus construction and means something along the lines: 'It's Hawaa who cooked/washed...'.

The initial consonant of the main clause verb changes from [d] in (28a) to [nd] in (28b,c). DP subjects in relative clauses always precede the verb, as in (28a). However, all subject pronouns, except 3SG/PL, have to follow the verb. In this case, the initial consonant of the verb mutates even when the subject pronoun is singular, as in (28b).

The word order in a verbal factive appears to be the following:

(29) V_{NOM} C.REL   S   V   O   DET.CL

I assume that the infinitive form of the relative verb (V_{NOM}) is moved to Spec,CP to fill in for a null noun 'fact' (which does not exist in Pulaar) along the lines of Collins (1994) and Tamba & Torrence (2013). Assuming that only the verb root has been moved, the presence of the infinitive suffix can be justified by the need for agreement; V_{NOM}, the complementizer and the determiner must all agree.

4.3 Clause structure of the ko-factive

With *ko* as a relativizer, the *ko*-factive is headless, or it is rather headed by a null noun. This is due to the fact that Pulaar does not have the word 'fact'. But one piece of evidence is also that this null noun is associated with an existing noun class *ko*. When the determiner is omitted, the structure cannot be interpreted as a factive. The relative complementizer is obligatory. This is shown in the following examples:

(30) *ko Hawaa loot-i wutte[7]
      C.REL Hawaa wash-PERF shirt
      'the fact that Hawaa washed a shirt'

(31) *ko Hawaa def-i   ñebbe
      C.REL Hawaa cook-PERF beans
      'the fact that Jeyla cooked beans'

Similar to verbal factive and headed relative constructions, the verb show of agreement morphology in *ko*-factives. Subject agreement is shown on verb through consonant mutation for plural subjects, as in matrix clauses. This is shown in the examples below:

(32) a. ko   Hawaa def-i   ñebbe ko   3SG subject
          C.REL Hawaa cook-PERF beans CL.the

          'the fact that Hawaa cooked beans'

      b. ko   ndef-mi ñebbe ko   1SG subject
          C.REL cook-SG beans CL.the

          'the fact that I cooked beans'

---

[7]This is just interpreted as a subject focus construction and means something along the lines: 'It's Hawaa who cooked/washed...'.

c. ko ɓe ndef-i ñebbe ko   3PL subject
    C.REL 3RD.PL cook-PERF beans CL.the

'the fact that they cooked beans'

The initial consonant of the verb changes from [d] in (32a) to [nd] in (32b,c). DP subjects always precede the verb. However, all subject pronouns, except 3SG/PL, have to follow the verb. In this case, the initial consonant of the verb mutates even when the subject pronoun is singular, as seen (32b).

The word order in a *ko*-factive appears to be the following:

(33) Ø_NP   C.REL   S   V   O   DET.CL

Based on the data presented here, the headed relative clause and factive relative clauses share a similar structural pattern, as shown below:

(34) a. NP   C.REL   S   V   O_trace   DET.CL   Headed relative
      b. V_NP   C.REL   S   V   O   DET.CL   Verbal factive
      c. Ø_NP   C.REL   S   V   O   DET.CL   *ko*-factive

Factive clauses involve a null noun for the *ko*-factive and a verb with nominal features for the verbal factive and both of these nominals agree with a specific complementizer and the corresponding homophonous determiner or noun class. I assume the presence of a null noun in the *ko*-factive due to the fact that it agrees with a noun class, but also there is no noun 'fact' in Pulaar.

The clear parallel that exist between the headed relative clause and factive relative clauses suggest that these constructions look like NP [CP] Det. I will follow Kayne (1994b) and analyze relative clauses as involving a D + CP, as in the structure in (35):

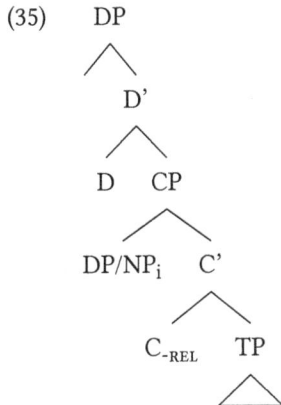

(35) DP

         D'

      D   CP

         DP/NP_i   C'

              C_-REL   TP

However, whether these constructions are all derivable from the same structure is dependent upon whether or not they all involve some type of movement.

The data below suggest that relativization and factivization involve movement. In fact, relativization or 'factivization' out of a relative clause is impossible in headed relatives as well as the verbal and *ko*-factive clauses. The examples below illustrate this fact:

(36) a. ɗa yiɗ-i   [suko mo   Isa tott-i   ñebbe mo.]
          2SG like-PERF child CL_REL Isa give-PERF beans CL.the

          'I like the boy that Isa gave beans'

   b. * ɗa yiɗ-i   [ñebbe ɗe   [suko mo Isa tott-i ___ mo].   RC
          2SG like-PERF [beans CL_rel [child CL_rel Isa give-PERF] CL.the

          'You like the beans that boy that Isa gave'

   c. * ɗa yiɗ-I   [tottu-go ngo [suko mo Isa tott-i]   ñebbe mo   ngo.
          2SG like-PERF [give-INF CL_rel [child CL_rel Isa give-PERF] beans CL.the CL.the

                                                                        VF

   d. * ɗa yiɗ-i   [ko [suko mo Isa tott-i]   mo   ko   ñebbe ɗe.
          2SG like-PERF [CL_rel [child CL_rel Isa give-PERF] CL.the CL.the beans CL.the

                                                                        Ko-F

The examples in (36b-d) show that it is impossible to relativize (or 'factivize') out of a relative clause. The examples (36b), (36c) and (36d) show, respectively, a relative clause, a verbal factive and a *ko*-factive. The impossibility of extracting out of a relative clause or relativizing out of a relative clause indicates that these constructions involve some type of movement and are islands.

5 Derivation of relative and factive clauses

In this section, I provide a unified analysis of RCs and factive clauses. Following Tamba & Torrence (2013), Torrence (2005) and Kayne (1994b), I assume that in Pulaar, headed relatives and factives can be derived from the same underlying structure which consists of a D and a CP complement. I argue that in this structure CP raises to Spec,DP.

I first analyze relative clauses like (35):

(37) wutte_i mo   Hawaa loot-i   t_i mo   Headed Relative Clause
      shirt CL.REL Hawaa wash-PERF   CL.the

      'The shirt that Hawaa washed'

In this construction, the head (object) NP moves to Spec,CP as shown in (38):

(38)

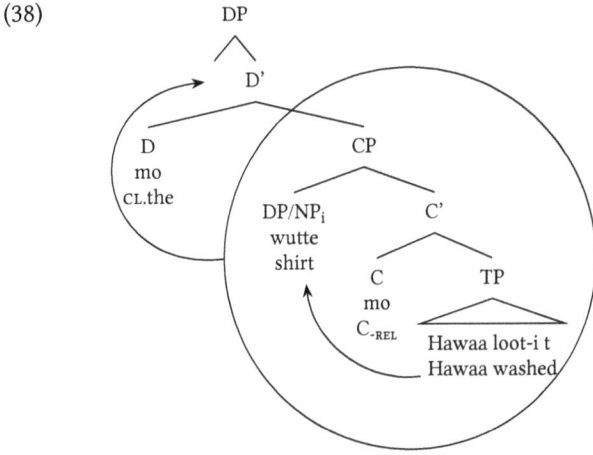

In the second step of the derivation, CP moves to Spec,DP to yield the surface structure, as it appears in (39).

Turning to verbal factives, along the lines of Tamba & Torrence (2013) and following Collins (1994) and Aboh (2005), I argue that in the Verbal Factive in (39a), a copy of the verb, which is relativized and carries the infinitival −*go*, is moved to Spec,CP. The complementizer agrees in noun class with the infinitival verb in Spec,CP. As have I have pointed out, the infinitive form the Pulaar verb exhibits nominal properties[8].

(39) a. loot-go **ngo** Hawaa loot-i wutte **ngo**
      Wash-INF C.REL Hawaa wash-PERF shirt CL.the

   'the fact that Hawaa washed a shirt'

b.

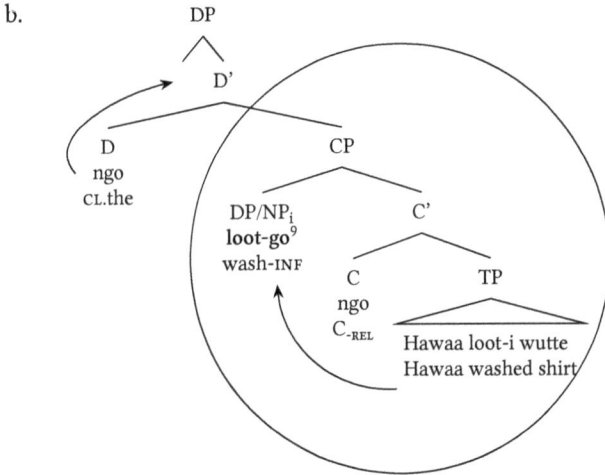

---

[8]See example (9b).

Once the infinitival verb has moved to Spec,CP, the whole CP node is then moved to Spec,DP generating the expected surface structure.

This analysis correctly derives the word order of the Verbal Factive construction in (39a) in a way similar to the derivation of the headed relative.

I now move to the *ko*-factive structure. The *ko*-Factive Relative is slightly different from the other relative types because it involves a null NP meaning 'fact'. But the presence of this null NP is signaled by its agreement with some noun class, in this case *ko*.

In order to derive a *ko*-Factive like the one in (40a), we can posit the movement of the null NP from inside the TP to Spec,CP. As a second step, the movement of CP to Spec,DP yields the surface word order along the lines of Headed Relatives and Verbal Factives, as we can see in (40b):

(40) a. ko Jeyla loot-i wutte ko
          C.REL Jeyla wash-PERF shirt CL.the

      '(the fact) that Jeyla washed a shirt'

  b.

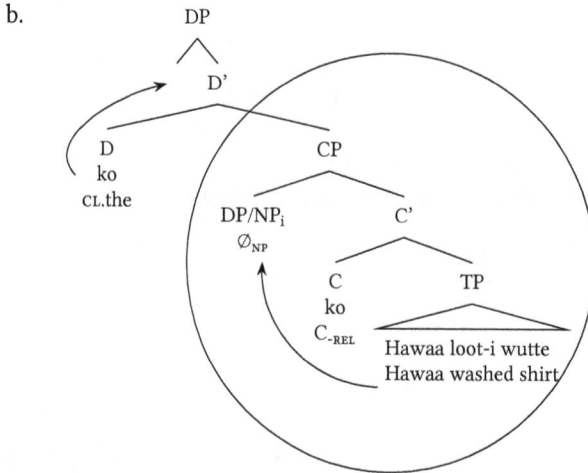

As the analysis has shown, Headed Relatives and Factive Relatives in Pulaar can all be derived from the same hierarchical structure in a relatively similar manner.

6 Concluding remarks

In this paper, I have argued that Headed Relatives and Factive Relatives have similar structure in sense that they have a similar word order and in all of them the complementizer agrees with the (null or overt) head NP in Spec,CP and is homophonous with the determiner.

---

[9] A reviewer notes that the fact the verb copy is infinitival indicates that there is more structure involved. I leave for future research the precise nature of the nominal constituent in Spec,CP and how a verb becomes nominalized.

In my analysis, the differences between the three types has to do with the material in Spec,CP. In headed RCs, it is a lexical noun. In the verbal factives, it is a nominalized copy of the verb, while in the *ko*-factives it is a null noun of the *ko* class.

References

Aboh, Enoch O. 2005. Deriving relative and factive contructions in Kwa. In Laura Brugè, Giuliana Giusti, Nicola Munaro, Walter Schweikert & Giuseppina Turano (eds.), *Contributions to the Thirtieth Incontro di Grammatica Generativa. Cafoscarina*, 265–285. Venice: Libreria Editrice Cafoscarina.

Collins, Chris. 1994. *The factive construction in Kwa*. New York: Cornell University. (Unpublished manuscript).

Cover, Rebecca. 2006. *Focus on ko: The syntax, semantics, and pragmatics of identificational focus in Pulaar*. Berkeley: University of California Berkeley dissertation.

Kayne, Richard S. 1994a. *The antisymmetry of syntax*. Cambridge, Massachusetts: MIT Press.

Kayne, Richard S. 1994b. *The antisymmetry of syntax*. Cambridge, MA: MIT Press.

Kiparsky, Paul & Carol Kiparsky. 1970. Fact. In Manfred Bierwisch & Karl Erich Heidolph (eds.), *Progress in linguistics*, 143–173. The Hague: Mouton.

Lewis, M. Paul (ed.). 2009. *Ethnologue: Languages of the World, Sixteenth edition*. Dallas: SIL International.

McLaughlin, Fiona. 2005. Reduplication and consonant mutation in the Northern Atlantic languages. In Bernhard Hurch (ed.), *Studies on reduplication*, 111–133. Berlin: Mouton de Gruyter.

Sylla, Yèro. 1982. *Grammaire moderne du Pulaar*. Dakar, Sénégal: Nouvelles Éditions Africaines.

Tamba, Khady & Harold Torrence. 2013. *Factive relative clauses in Wolof*. Annual Meeting of the Linguistic Society of America handout.

Torrence, Harold. 2005. A promotion analysis of relative clauses in Wolof. *Annual Meeting of the Berkeley Linguistics Society* 31(2). 107–118.

Chapter 16

Object suffixes as incorporated pronouns in Seereer

Nico Baier

In Seereer (Atlantic, Senegal), singular pronominal objects are obligatorily marked by an object suffix on the verb. This paper provides the first comprehensive description of this object suffixation pattern, a topic that has been only cursorily described in the extant literature on Seereer (cf. Renaudier 2012). In addition, I provide a preliminary theoretical account of the Seereer object suffix system. I argue that Seereer object suffixes are best analyzed as incorporated pronouns. Evidence for such an analysis comes from the following: (i) an object suffix may never occur with an in situ object DP; (ii) an object suffix may not double an extracted object in relative clauses, wh-questions, or focus constructions; (iii) there is only one object suffix allowed per clause; and (iv) an object suffix may reference either object in a double object construction. I argue that object suffixes raise to Spec-vP and are subsequently incorporated in the verb via m-merger (Matushansky 2006, Kramer 2014, Harizanov 2014). This analysis elegantly derives the behaviors listed above. Such an approach also allows us to integrate the Seereer object suffixation data into the broader understanding of cliticization patterns crosslinguistically, thereby enriching our understanding of object marking systems in verbs.

1 Introduction

In Seereer (Atlantic; Senegal), singular object pronouns are marked by a suffix on the verb, as shown in (1). Plural object pronouns are realized as a full pronominal DP (2).[1]

(1) **Singular Object Suffixes**

  a. Jegaan a naf-a-[xam].
      Jegaan 3 hit-DV-1SG.OBJ
      'Jegaan hit me.'

  b. Jegaan a naf-a-[ang].
      Jegaan 3 hit-DV-2SG.OBJ
      'Jegaan hit you.'

  c. Jegaan a naf-a-[an].
      Jegaan 3 hit-DV-3SG.OBJ
      'Jegaan hit him/her/it.'

---

[1]Plural object pronouns are preceded by the differential object marker *a*. This marker is required with objects that are pronouns or proper names. I will not discuss the differential object marker here.

Nico Baier. Object suffixes as incorporated pronouns in Seereer. In Jason Kandybowicz, Travis Major, Harold Torrence & Philip T. Duncan (eds.), *African linguistics on the prairie: Selected papers from the 45th Annual Conference on African Linguistics*, 253–268. Berlin: Language Science Press. DOI:10.5281/zenodo.1251738

(2) **Plural Object Pronouns**

    a. Jegaan a naf-a a   **in.**   c. Jegaan a naf-a a   **den.**
       Jegaan 3 hit-DV OBJ 1PL   Jegaan 3 hit-DV OBJ 3PL

       'Jegaan hit us.'   'Jegaan hit them.'

    b. Jegaan a naf-a a   **nuun.**
       Jegaan 3 hit-DV OBJ 2PL

       'Jegaan hit you guys.'

There are only singular object suffixes; no equivalent plural object suffixes exist in the language. Alongside the suffixes, Seereer has a full set of free pronouns for all person/ number combinations. The object suffixes and the free pronouns are shown below in Table 1:

Table 1: Object Suffixes vs. Free Pronouns

	1SG	2SG	3SG	1PL	2PL	3PL
Object Suffix	*-aam*	*-ong*	*-in*			
Free Pronoun	*mi*	*wo'*	*ten(o)*	*in*	*nun*	*den(o)*

In Table 1, the object suffixes are given in their underlying forms. In most cases, these underlying forms are obscured by morphophonological processes. For reasons of space I will not discuss these processes here.[2]

    Although there is a small amount of published work on Seereer (Faye 1982; McLaughlin 1994; 2000; Renaudier 2012), there is no comprehensive description of the object suffix system. This paper aims to fill this gap. I show that object suffixes are best analyzed as pronouns that are morphologically incorporated into the verb, rather than object agreement. I also sketch a preliminary analysis of the pronoun incorporation process. Building on analyses of pronominal clitics by Harizanov (2014) and Kramer (2014), I propose that object suffixes originate in an argument position as pronouns and undergo head movement to v^0.

    The structure of this paper is as follows. In §2, I show that the distribution of object suffixes is identical to the distributio of free object pronouns, and argue that this shows object suffixes to be incorporated pronouns. I then discuss constraints on object suffixation in §3. Based on these facts, I present my analysis in §4. Section §5 provides conclusions.

---

[2]Though see Renaudier (2012) for discussion of the morphophonology of object suffixes in a different Seereer dialect, Seereer-Marlodj.

2 Object suffixes are pronouns

In this section, I show that object suffixes have the same distribution as other object pronouns and are therefore best analyzed as incorporated pronouns. Evidence for this comes from the fact that object suffixes cannot double an *in situ* object DP; that they cannot co-occur with an Ā-moved object; and that they must resume a left-dislocated object.

2.1 Doubling of full NPs

In situ full DP objects can never co-occur with a coreferential object suffix on the verb, as shown by the pair of examples in (3a-b):

(3) a. Mataar a jaw-a   [$_{DP}$ **maalo fe**]
         Mataar 3 cook-DV   rice   DET

     'Mataar cooked the rice.'

     b. * Mataar a jaw-a-⎡**an**$_i$⎤   [$_{DP}$ **maalo fe**]$_i$
         Mataar 3 cook-DV-3SG.OBJ   rice   DET

         Intended: 'Mataar cooked the rice.'

In (3a), there is a single full, post-verbal full DP object, *maalo fe* 'the rice'. When a object suffix coreferential with *maalo fe* is added to the verb in (3b), the sentence becomes ungrammatical. Seereer is completely invariant with respect to this constraint. As shown in (4), an object suffix can never double any kind of full DP object:

(4) a. * Jegaan a bug-a-**an**$_i$ [$_{DP}$ **ya'**   **um**   **oxe**]$_i$.
         Jegaan 3 love-DV-3SG.OBJ   mother 3POSS DET

         Intended: 'Mataar loves his mother.'   Kinship term

     b. * Jegaan a ga'-a-**xam**$_i$ [$_{DP}$ **a**   **mi**]$_i$.
         Jegaan 3 see-DV-1SG.OBJ   OBJ 1SG

         Intended: 'Jegaan saw me.'   Free pronoun

     c. * Jegaan a ga'-a-**an**$_i$ [$_{DP}$ **okoor oxe**]$_i$.
         Jegaan 3 see-DV-3SG.OBJ   man   DET

         Intended: 'Jegaan saw the man.'   Human animate

     d. * Jegaan a ga'-a-**an**$_i$ [$_{DP}$ **muus ne**]$_i$.
         Jegaan 3 see-DV-3SG.OBJ   cat   DET

         Intended: 'Jegaan saw the cat.'   Non-human animate

     e. * Jegaan a jik-a-**an**$_i$ [$_{DP}$ **mbin ne**]$_i$
         Jegaan 3 buy-DV-3SG.OBJ   house DET

         Intended: 'Jegaan bought the house.'   Inanimate

So, the basic observation is that full, post-verbal DP objects are in complementary distribution with object suffixes. This observation is immediately explained if we assume that object suffixes and full DP objects occupy the same structural position at some point in the derivation. Thus, object suffixes and full DP objects compete for an argument position, as there can only be one argument per structural position. This, in turn, straightforwardly follows if we assume that object suffixes are pronouns that have been incorporated morphologically into the verb.

2.2 Object extraction contexts

Object suffixes are also in complementary distribution with an Ā-extracted object. This is true for all constructions that involve Ā-extraction in Seereer: *wh*-questions, focus clauses, and relative clauses.[3] First, an object suffix cannot co-occur with an extracted object *wh*-phrase, as shown in (5a-b):

(5) a. * **xar**$_i$ Ami a jik-u-$\boxed{\mathbf{n_i}}$?
      what Ami 3 buy-EXT-3SG.OBJ

      Intended: 'What did Ami buy?'   Inanimate *wh*-word

  b. * **an**$_i$ Ami a bug-u-$\boxed{\mathbf{n_i}}$?
      who Ami 3 love-EXT-3SG.OBJ

      Intended: 'Who does Ami love?'   Animate *wh*-word

This constraint is also active in object focus clauses, as shown in (6a-b):

(6) a. * **Jegaan**$_{iFOC}$ Ami a bug-u-$\boxed{\mathbf{n_i}}$.
      Jegaan   Ami 3 love-EXT-3SG.OBJ

      Intended: 'It's Jegaan that Ami loves.'   DP focus

  b. * (a) **wo'**$_{iFOC}$ Ami a bug-$\boxed{\mathbf{ong_i}}$.
      OBJ 2SG   Ami 3 love-2SG.OBJ.EXT

      Intended: 'It's you that Ami loves.'   Pronoun focus

Finally, in object relative clauses, an object suffix may not double the extracted DP, as seen in (7):

(7) * [$_N$ **maalo**]$_i$ [$_{CP}$ **ne**   Ami a ñam-uu-$\boxed{\mathbf{n_i}}$-a]
      rice   REL.DET Ami 3 eat-EXT-3SG.OBJ-REL

    Intended: 'the rice that Ami ate'

The data in (5)-(7) also follow from the idea that object suffixes are underlyingly pronouns that saturate argument positions. An Ā-extracted argument must be generated in an

---

[3]Evidence that these clauses involve Ā-extraction of the object comes from the fact that the verb takes the final suffix *-u*, which only occurs when Ā-movement has occurred in a clause within which the verb is contained. See Baier (2014) for extensive discussion.

argument position before it undergoes Ā-movement, and this blocks an object suffix from being generated in the same argument position. Note that plural object pronouns, which do not have a suffixal form, are also blocked from co-occuring with an extracted plural DP object:

(8) a. * **aniin**$_i$ Ami a bug-u   a   **den**$_i$?
       who.PL Ami 3 love-EXT OBJ 3PL

       Intended: 'Who all does Ami love?'   Plural *wh*-word

   b. * (a) **nuun**$_{iFOC}$ Ami a ga'-u   a   **nuun**$_i$.
       OBJ 2PL   Ami 3 see-EXT OBJ 2PL

       Intended: 'It's you all that Ami saw.'   Plural DP focus

So object suffixes have the exact same distribution as free, plural object pronouns in cases of object Ā-extraction. This is further evidence that object suffixes are pronouns that are incorporated into the verb.

2.3 Left dislocation contexts

Object suffixes must double a left-dislocated full DP object. As shown in (9), when the dislocated DP is singular, an object suffix is required on the verb:

(9) a. **maalo fe**, Mataar a jaw-a-[**an**].
       rice DET   Mataar 3 cook-DV-3SG.OBJ

       'The rice, Mataar cooked it.'   Suffix

   b. * **maalo fe**, Mataar a jaw-a-[Ø].
       rice DET   Mataar 3 cook-DV

       Intended: 'The rice, Mataar cooked it.'   No Suffix

Free singular object pronouns may also be dislocated. Resumption by an object suffix is also required in this case:

(10) a. (a) mi, Mataar a bug-a-*(**xam**).
       OBJ 1SG Mataar 3 cook-DV-1SG.OBJ

       Intended: 'Me, Mataar likes.'

   b. (a) wo', Mataar a bug-a-*(**ang**).
       OBJ 2SG Mataar 3 cook-DV-1SG.OBJ

       Intended: 'You, Mataar likes.'

Again, the behavior of object suffixes is the same as that of free plural object pronouns. When a plural object DP is left dislocated, a plural pronoun is required as a resumptive, (11a); lack of one results in ungrammaticality (11b):

(11) a. **goor we**, Mataar a ga'-a   a   [**den**].
       men DET   Mataar 3 see-DV OBJ 3PL

       'The men, Mataar saw them.'   Pronoun

   b. * **goor we**, Mataar a ga'-a $\boxed{\text{Ø}}$.
      men DET Mataar 3 see-DV

     Intended: 'The men, Mataar saw them.'   No Pronoun

Left dislocation in Seereer does not involve Ā-movement. Evidence for this comes from the fact that left dislocation does not trigger the presence of the Ā-sensitive final suffix *-u*.[4] Instead, left dislocation involves base generation of a DP in the left periphery and resumption in an argument position in the main part of the clause. Since resumptive elements are usually pronouns (McCloskey 2006), this supports the idea that object suffixes are themselves pronouns. Again, this idea is reinforced by the fact that they pattern identically to free plural pronouns in this construction.

3 Syntactic constraints on object suffixation

In the previous section, I presented distributional evidence that object suffixes are in fact pronouns that end up as a morphological subunit of the verb word. Following this line of thought, I assume that, as pronouns, object suffixes are generated as D heads in object position as the complement to V. This is shown in (12), where 'OS' stands for object suffix:

(12)   [$_{VP}$ V [$_D$ OS]]

Thus, object suffixes are simply generated in argument position like any other object and later become associated morphologically with the verb. But why do object suffixes incorporate into the verb? In this section, I present evidence that object suffixation is constrained by the syntactic structure of the clause and therefore object suffixation is a fundamentally syntactic process. The specific data are derived from the following contexts:

(13)   a. The obligatoriness of object suffixes

     b. Multiple object constructions: Ditransitives, applicatives, causatives

     c. Object suffixes in passive clauses

3.1 Obligatoriness

If there is only one singular object pronoun, it must *always* surface as a suffix, never as a free pronoun, as shown by (14).

(14)   a. Jegaan a fal-a-$\boxed{\textbf{ang}}$.
        Jegaan 3 kick-DV-2SG.OBJ

      'Jegaan kicked you.'   Object suffix

---

[4]For further discussion, see Baier (2014).

b. * Jegaan a fal-a (a) wo' .
  Jegaan 3 kick-DV OBJ 2SG

  Intended: 'Jegaan kicked you.' Free pronoun

Regardless of the presence of other post-verbal constituents, a singular object pronoun must be realized as a suffix. Consider (15), which shows that a free singular object pronoun is impossible in such contexts:

(15) a. Jegaan a fal-a-ang faak.
  Jegaan 3 kick-DV-2SG.OBJ yesterday

  'Jegaan kicked you yesterday.'

  b. * Jegaan a fal-a faak (a) wo'.
  Jegaan 3 kick-DV yesterday OBJ 2SG

  Intended: 'Jegaan kicked you yesterday.'

  c. * Jegaan a fal-a (a) wo' faak.
  Jegaan 3 kick-DV OBJ 2SG yesterday

  Intended: 'Jegaan kicked you yesterday.'

Note that, otherwise, objects are generally freely ordered with regards to other post-verbal constituents. As shown in (16), plural object pronouns and full DP objects may precede or follow an adverb such as *faak* 'yesterday':

(16) a. Jegaan a ga'-a (a nuun) faak (a nuun).
  Jegaan 3 kick-DV OBJ 2PL yesterday OBJ 2PL

  'Jegaan saw you guys yesterday.' Plural pronoun

  b. Jegaan a ga'-a (otew oxe) faak (otew oxe).
  Jegaan 3 kick-DV woman DET yesterday woman DET

  'Jegaan saw the woman yesterday.' Full DP

These data are important in that they show that object suffixation is insensitive to linear order. If object were sensitive to linear order, we would expect a clause like (14b), in which an adverbial intervenes between a singular object pronoun and the verb, to be grammatical (as the plural counterpart in (16a) is). However, this order is not possible. Since syntactic operations not sensitive to linear order, this points to a syntactic account of object suffixation.

3.2 Multiple object constructions

Seereer has several types of double object constructions (DOC). Such constructions occur with lexical ditransitive verbs, such as *ci'* 'give'; verbs bearing one of the applicative suffixes *-an* 'benefactive' and *-(i)t* 'instrumental/locative'; and causative verbs derived with the causative suffix *-noor*. Lexical ditransitive verbs and applicative verbs pattern together with regard to word order and object suffixation, while causative verbs pattern differently than the first two classes with regard to these diagnostics.

Ditransitive verbs and applicative verbs in Seereer are SYMMETRICAL double object constructions (following the terminology of Bresnan & Moshi 1990). When ditransitive and applicative verbs have two full DP arguments and both are post-verbal, these arguments are freely ordered. This is shown for ditransitives in (17) and for the benefacative applicative -*an* in (18). In the following examples, '↔' indicates that the bracketed constituents can be reversed in order:

(17) a. Jegaan a ci'-a   [DP okoor oxe]GOAL ↔ [DP atere le]THEME.
          Jegaan 3 give-DV   man   DET   book DET

          'Jegaan gave the man the book.'   ✓ GOAL < THEME / ✓ THEME < GOAL

(18) a. a jaw-an-a   [DP okoor oxe]BEN ↔ [DP maalo fe]THEME.
          3 cook-BEN-DV   man   DET   rice   DET

          'He cooked the rice for the man.'   ✓ BEN < THEME / ✓ THEME < BEN

When one of the objects of a ditransitive or applicative verb is a singular pronoun, it *must* be realized as a suffix, as shown for a ditransitive verb in (19).[5] This constraint holds regardless of order, as shown by (19b-c):

(19) a. Jegaan a ci'-a-|angGOAL| [DP atere le]THEME.
          Jegaan 3 give-DV-2SG.OBJ   book DET

          'Jegaan gave you the book.'   Object suffix

      b. * Jegaan a ci'-a   [DP a   wo']GOAL [DP atere le]THEME.
          Jegaan 3 give-DV   OBJ 2SG   book DET

          Intended: 'Jegaan gave the book to you.'   Free pronoun

      c. * Jegaan a ci'-a   [DP atere le]THEME [DP a   wo']GOAL.
          Jegaan 3 give-DV   book DET   OBJ 2SG

          Intended: 'Jegaan gave the book to you.'   Free pronoun

When a ditransitive or applicative verb takes two singular object pronouns, either argument may surface as a suffix, as shown in (20a-b).[6] However, there is a *maximum of one* object suffix per verb form; the verb cannot take multiple object suffixes, as shown by (20c):

(20) a. Jegaan a ci'-a-|angGOAL| [DP a   ten]THEME.
          Jegaan 3 give-DV-2SG.OBJ   OBJ 3SG

          'Jegaan gave you it.'   Goal suffix

---

[5]For reasons of space, I will use data only from lexical ditransitives for the remainder of this section. The judgements also apply to all applicatives.

[6]In cases where one object is a speech act participant and the other is not, my consultant showed a preference for suffixation of the SAP object. However, this is not a hard and fast constraint. Examples like (20a) are perfectly grammatical.

  b. Jegaan a ci'-a-$\boxed{\text{an}_{\text{THEME}}}$ [$_{DP}$ a wo']$_{\text{GOAL}}$.
   Jegaan 3 give-DV-3SG.OBJ OBJ 2SG

   'Jegaan gave it to you.'   Theme suffix

  c. * Jegaan a ci'-a-$\boxed{\text{ang}_{\text{GOAL}}\text{-in}_{\text{THEME}}}$.
   Jegaan 3 give-DV-2SG.OBJ-3SG.OBJ

   Intended: 'Jegaan gave you it.'   Two suffixes

So these particular multiple object constructions are symmetrical with regard to object suffixation, in that either object may be realized as an object suffix when they are both singular pronouns.

 On the other hand, causatives of transitive verbs derived with the suffix *-noor* are **asymmetrical** double object constructions. Such verbs take two objects: the subject of the caused event (the CAUSEE) and the underlying object of the caused event. With regard to word order, a full DP causee must *always* precede a full DP object, as shown in (21):

(21) a. Jegaan a fal-**noor**-a [$_{DP}$ okoor oxe]$_{\text{CAUSEE}}$ [$_{DP}$ naak le]$_{\text{OBJECT}}$.
    Jegaan 3 kick-CAUS-DV man DET cow DET

    'Jegaan made the man kick the cow.'   ✓CAUSEE < OBJECT

  b. * Jegaan a fal-**noor**-a [$_{DP}$ naak le]$_{\text{OBJECT}}$ [$_{DP}$ okoor oxe]$_{\text{CAUSEE}}$.
    Jegaan 3 kick-CAUS-DV cow DET man DET

    Intended: 'Jegaan made the man kick the cow.'   *OBJECT < CAUSEE

This is the opposite of what we saw for ditransitive and applicative verbs, where either ordering was licit. Also unlike ditransitive and applicative verbs, there is an asymmetry for causative verbs with regards to which argument is able to appear as an object suffix. The causee *must* be an object suffix if it is a singular pronoun, as shown by (22):

(22) a. Jegaan a fal-**noor**-a-$\boxed{\text{ang}_{\text{CAUSEE}}}$ [$_{DP}$ naak le]$_{\text{OBJECT}}$.
    Jegaan 3 kick-CAUS-DV-2SG.OBJ cow DET

    'Jegaan made you kick the cow.'   Object suffix

  b. * Jegaan a fal-**noor**-a [$_{DP}$ a wo']$_{\text{CAUSEE}}$ [$_{DP}$ naak le]$_{\text{OBJECT}}$.
    Jegaan 3 kick-CAUS-DV OBJ 2SG cow DET

    'Jegaan made you kick the the cow.'   Free pronoun

However, the object of the causative verb *cannot* be realized as an object suffix, even if it is the only singular object pronoun in the clause, as shown by (23a):

(23) a. Jegaan a fal-**noor**-a [$_{DP}$ okoor oxe]$_{\text{CAUSEE}}$ [$_{DP}$ a wo']$_{\text{OBJECT}}$.
    Jegaan 3 kick-CAUS-DV man DET OBJ 2SG

    'Jegaan made the man kick the cow.'   Free pronoun

  b. * Jegaan a fal-**noor**-a-$\boxed{\text{ang}_{\text{OBJECT}}}$ [$_{DP}$ okoor oxe]$_{\text{CAUSEE}}$.
    Jegaan 3 kick-CAUS-DV-2SG.OBJ man DET

    'Jegaan made the man kick you.'   Object suffix

Again, this is exactly the opposite of what we saw with ditransitives and applicatives. Like those verbs, however, it is also impossible for a causative verb to take two object suffixes, as shown by (24):

(24)　* Jegaan a fal-**noor**-a-$\boxed{\text{ang}_{\text{CAUSEE}}\text{-in}_{\text{OBJECT}}}$.
　　　Jegaan 3 kick-CAUS-DV-2SG.OBJ-3SG.OBJ

　　Intended: 'Jegaan made you kick it.'　　　　　　　　　　　　　　　Two suffixes

All of the facts just discussed are summarized in Table 2:

Table 2: Sereer double object constructions

Type	Word Order	Object Suffix	Multiple Suffixes
Ditransitive	SYM	SYM	✗
Applicative	SYM	SYM	✗
Causative	ASYM	ASYM	✗

The differences between symmetrical (ditransitive/applicative) and asymmetrical (causative) double object constructions are a convincing argument in favor of a syntactic account of object suffixation. As we will see below, these differences can be relativized to independent principles of locality in which causatives include a barrier to object suffixation of the internal argument of the causativized predicate, whereas ditransitives and applicatives do not.[7] A non-syntactic account would have to stipulate these differences.

　In addition, the general ban on multiple suffixes is an argument against approaches to object suffixation that do not take place in the syntax, as such accounts would have to posit a different set of weak pronouns that occur as suffixes, and a stipulation would be required to block these suffixes from co-occuring. A syntactic approach, on the other hand, can take advantage of the idea that the operation triggering incorporation of a pronoun into the verb only applies once per structure.

3.3 Passives

The final constraint on object suffixation concerns passives. When a ditransitive verb is passivized, one of the underlying objects is promoted to subject, while the other object is left behind in the post-verbal position and treated as an object. Either object may be promoted to subject, as shown in (25):

(25)　a.　[$_{\text{DP}}$ okoor oxe]$_{\text{GOAL}}$ a ci'-e　　[$_{\text{DP}}$ atere le]$_{\text{THEME}}$
　　　　　man　DET　3 give-PASS　book DET

　　　　'The man was given the book.'　　　　　　　　　　　　　　　Goal subject

---

[7]See Baker et al. (2012) for such an approach to similar data in Lubukusu.

b. [$_{\text{DP}}$ atere le]$_{\text{THEME}}$ a ci'-e   [$_{\text{DP}}$ okoor oxe]$_{\text{GOAL}}$
    book DET   3 give-PASS   man   DET

'The book was given to the man.'   Theme subject

In (25a), the goal argument is promoted to subject and the theme remains post-verbal as an object. In (25b), the theme is promoted to subject and the goal argument remains behind. When the object that remains post-verbal is a singular pronoun, it *cannot* be realized as a suffix. This is true regardless of which argument it refers to, as shown by (26):

(26)   a. * [$_{\text{DP}}$ okoor oxe]$_{\text{GOAL}}$ a ci'-e-[n]
         man   DET   3 give-PASS-3SG.OBJ

     Intended: 'The man was given it.'   Goal suffix

   b. * [$_{\text{DP}}$ atere le]$_{\text{THEME}}$ a ci'-e-[n]
         book DET   3 give-PASS-3SG.OBJ

     Intended: 'The book was given to him/her.'   Theme suffix

In (26a), the object suffix on the verb corresponds to the theme argument. In (26b), the object suffix on the verb refers to the goal argument. Both examples are ungrammatical. This ungrammaticality is avoided by realizing the pronominal object as a full, free pronoun.

(27)   a. [$_{\text{DP}}$ okoor oxe]$_{\text{GOAL}}$ a ci'-e   [$_{\text{DP}}$ a   ten]$_{\text{THEME}}$
         man   DET   3 give-PASS   OBJ 3SG

     'The man was given it.'

   b. [$_{\text{DP}}$ atere le]$_{\text{THEME}}$ a ci'-e   [$_{\text{DP}}$ a   ten]$_{\text{GOAL}}$
         book DET   3 give-PASS   OBJ 3SG

     'The book was given to him/her.'

As seen in (27), a post-verbal object in a ditransitive passive is grammatical, while a object suffix is not. This observation is another argument for a syntactic approach to object suffixation, as we expect different voice types to enforce different syntactic constraints. An account that locates object suffixation in a post-syntactic module of the grammar would have to appeal to a stipulation by stating that singular pronouns cannot be realized as suffixes in a structure with a passive. Alternatively, one could say that there is a templatic restriction banning incorporation into a passive verb. A syntactic analysis, on the other hand, can appeal to differences in the structure of active and passive sentences to account for the availability of object suffixation. For instance, perhaps object suffixation is triggered by a head present in the active that is not present in the passive. I now move on to sketching such an approach in section 4.

4 Towards an analysis

Before moving on to my analysis, I present a summary of the generalizations made above concerning object suffixation in (28):

(28) **Characteristics of Object Suffix**
      a. There are only singular object suffixes
      b. An object suffix may not co-occur with an *in situ* DP.
      c. An object suffix may not co-occur with an Ā-extracted object (focus/*wh*-relative)
      d. An object must co-occur with a topicalized object.
      e. There is a limit of one object suffix per verb.
      f. An object suffix is obligatory where possible.
      g. An object suffix may refer to either argument in a symmetrical DOC.
      h. An object suffix cannot refer to the theme of a causativized transitive verb.
      i. An object suffix cannot occur in a passive verb.

In this section, I sketch an analysis that aims to capture the generalizations given above.

The core idea of my analysis is that object suffixation involves head movement of a pronoun (D^0) to the head v^0, which causes it to be morphologically incorporated into the verb. This idea is schematized in (29):

(29) $[_{vP}$ V+v+OS $[_{VP}$ ~~V~~ $[_D$ ~~OS~~ $]]]$

There are two questions that must be answered with regards to the structure in (29). First, what triggers movement of a pronominal D^0 to v^0 and why does it only target singular pronouns? Second, why is the head movement impossible in some circumstances, such as when there are multiple objects or when the verb is passive?

Building on analyses of Bulgarian pronominal clitics by Harizanov (2014) and Amharic object suffixes by Kramer (2014), I suggest that incorporation of a pronoun into v^0 is motivated by the operation Agree which is triggered by a probe on v^0. Both Harizanov and Kramer and adopt the conception of head movement developed by Matushansky (2006) in which head movement is taken to be regular phrasal movement to a specifier followed by a special operation M-MERGER which fuses a specifier with its head. They argue that clitic doubling in Amharic and Bulgarian derives from movement of a DP to specifier of v, after which the DP m-merges with v^0. For Harizanov, m-merger of a XP reduces that projection to its label, yielding a complex head. This is shown in (30):

(30) a. $[_{vP}$ DP $[v [_{VP}$ V ~~DP~~ $]]]$ DP moves to Spec-vP
          $\underset{\text{MOVE}}{\underline{\qquad\qquad}}$

      b. $[_{vP}$ D+v $[_{VP}$ V ~~DP~~ P $]]]$ M-Merger of DP

Under this analysis, object suffixation in Seereer occurs because v^0 is equipped with a probe that causes a pronoun to move to its specifier. Later, that pronoun undergoes m-merger with v^0, resulting in morphological incorporation of the pronoun into the verb.

I propose that active v^0 in Seereer is equipped with a NUMBER PROBE ($[u\#]$) that triggers movement of an argument in VP to Spec-vP. I follow much work on the operation Agree in assuming that probes can be relativized to search for specific values of a feature (Béjar 2008; Béjar & Rezac 2009; Preminger 2011). In this case, I assume that the number probe on v^0 is relativized to search for singular features. I represent this as $[u\#_{SG}]$.

Assuming that the #-probe on v^0 is relativized to search only for singular features immediately derives the fact that only singular pronouns will incorporate into the verb in Seereer, yielding only singular object suffixes. But how do we derive the fact that no doubling of an in situ DP object is possible in Seereer? Recall that the head movement approach I am employing assumes that DPs can undergo m-merger to form a complex head with v^0. Thus, clitic doubling should, in principle, be possible.

I propose that the ability for XPs to undergo m-merger is subject to parametric variation. In languages like Bulgarian it is possible, and therefore clitic doubling occurs. In languages like Seereer, however, it is not possible, and therefore DPs can never be doubled by object suffixes, as these suffixes are impossible to generate. Thus, we have two situations in Seereer, given in (31) and (32).

(31) **Singular Pronoun = m-merger**

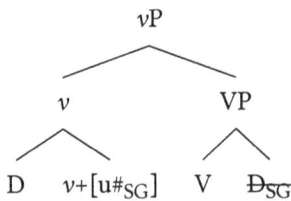

vP
  v   VP
 D v+$[u\#_{SG}]$ V ~~D~~$_{SG}$

(32) **Singular DP = no m-merger**

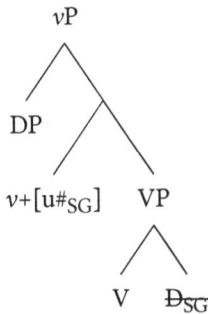

vP
 DP
  v+$[u\#_{SG}]$ VP
       V ~~D~~$_{SG}$

In (31), the complement of V is a singular pronoun, a minimal D^0, and therefore, object suffixation occurs. In (32), on the other hand, the complement of V is a singular DP. Therefore, m-merger of DP is not possible after it moves to Spec-vP and no object suffix surfaces. This derives the fact that there is no doubling of full DPs by object suffixes in Seereer.

A key characteristic of object suffixation in Seereer is that it is obligatory when it is possible, but when it is impossible, no ungrammaticality results. This is problematic for the idea that suffixation is triggered by Agree, as we would expect sentences without singular objects and active v to be ungrammatical. To alleviate this problem, I follow Preminger (2011) in assuming that the failure of a probe to find matching features does not result in crash. Therefore, a #-probe can be present on every active v, but derivations without a singular DP object will not crash. This derives the generalization that object suffixes are obligatory when there is a singular object pronoun, but when there is not one, the sentence is fine.[8]

Furthermore, because there is only one #-probe on v^0, only one object suffix is possible on any given verb. Thus, I assume that once the #-probe on v^0 has found a matching singular DP, it does not have to probe further, and is satisfied. Thus, when there are two singular object pronouns in the structure, as in a DOC, the higher object pronoun in the structure is found by the #-probe on v^0, and that pronoun incorporates. The other is left free:

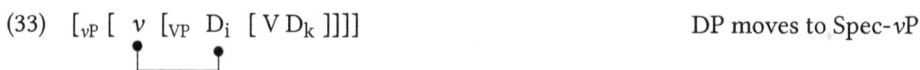

(33) $[_{vP} [\ v\ [_{VP}\ D_i\ [\ V\ D_k\ ]]]]$ DP moves to Spec-vP

In (33), the #-probe on v^0 finds the higher of two object pronouns, and thus that one is the only one that is incorporated.

Finally, this analysis is able to derive two further constraints on object suffixation. First, because v is responsible for encoding the voice of the clause, it is reasonable to assume that the #-probe is limited to certain v heads. Namely, passive v lacks the #-probe, and therefore, no object suffix is possible in passive structures. Second, the differences between symmetrical DOCs (ditransitives/applicatives) and asymmetrical DOCs (causatives) can be derived by appealing to Phase-based locality (Chomsky 2001; 2008). In causative DOCs, there is a phase boundary between the causee object and the theme object which blocks Agree with the theme. In symmetrical DOCs, on the other hand, there is no such boundary, and therefore both objects can occur as suffixes.

5 Conclusion

In this paper, I have presented a description of Seereer object suffixes, focusing on their distribution and syntactic behavior. On the basis of their distributional characteristics, I have argued that they are best analyzed as pronouns that are morphologically incorporated into the verb. I have further argued that this process of incorporation occurs in the syntax, in that it is constrained by syntactic structure. These constraints include the fact that object suffixation is obligatory; that it cannot occur more than once per verb; that it is sensitive to the voice of the clause; and that it is sensitive to the structure of double object constructions. I have also also sketched an implementation of the syntactic approach based on the idea that active v^0 in Seereer bears a #-probe relativized to search for singular DPs, and that this probe triggers head movement of pronouns to adjoin to v^0.

---

[8] An alternative would be to posit that the probe is only sometimes present on v^0. However, pursuing this line of thinking would require one to devise a way to enforce the probe's presence when there is at least one singular object pronoun in the structure. I will avoid this discussion here, and leave the comparison of the two analyses to future work.

Acknowledgments

I thank Peter Jenks and Line Mikkelsen for insightful comments, guidance, and discussion on this project, as well as the audience at ACAL 45 at the University of Kansas. I am also indebted to my consultant Malick Loum for taking the time to share his knowledge of Seereer with me. All data in this paper were gathered during the 2012–2013 UC Berkeley Field Methods class and subsequent follow-up work with John Merrill in 2013–2014.

Abbreviations

DET	determiner	REL	relative
DV	default vowel	SG	singular
EXT	extraction suffix	1	first person
INF	infinitive	2	second person
OBJ	object	3	third person
PL	plural		

References

Baier, Nico. 2014. *Spell-out, Chains, and Long Distance Wh-movement in Sereer*. Ms., UC Berkeley.

Baker, Mark C., Ken Safir & Justine Sikuku. 2012. Sources of (a)symmetry in Bantu double object constructions. MS: Rutgers.

Béjar, Susana. 2008. Conditions on Phi-Agree. In Daniel Harbour, David Adger & Susana Béjar (eds.), *Phi theory*, 130–154. Oxford: Oxford University Press.

Béjar, Susana & Milan Rezac. 2009. Cyclic agree. *Linguistic Inquiry* 40(1). 35–73.

Bresnan, Joan & Lioba Moshi. 1990. Object asymmetries in comparative Bantu syntax. *Linguistic Inquiry* 22(2). 147–186.

Chomsky, Noam. 2001. Derivation by phase. In Michael Kenstowicz (ed.), *Ken Hale: A life in linguistics*, 1–52. Cambridge, Massachusetts: MIT Press.

Chomsky, Noam. 2008. On phases. In Robert Freidin, Carlos Peregrín Otero & Maria Luisa Zubizarreta (eds.), *Foundational issues in linguistic theory: Essays in honor of jean-roger vergnaud* (Current Studies in Linguistics), 133–166. Cambridge, MA: MIT Press.

Faye, Souleymane. 1982. *Morphologie du verbe sérère*. Dakar: Centre de Linguistique Appliquée de Dakar.

Harizanov, Boris. 2014. Clitic doubling at the syntax-morphophonology interface: A-movement and morphological merger in Bulgarian. *Natural Language and Linguistic Theory* 32. 1033–1088.

Kramer, Ruth. 2014. Clitic doubling or object agreement: The view from Amharic. *Natural Language and Linguistic Theory* 32. 593–634.

Matushansky, Ora. 2006. Head movement in linguistic theory. *Linguistic Inquiry* 37(1). 69–109.

McCloskey, James. 2006. Resumption. In Martin Everaert & Henk van Riemsdijk (eds.), *Resumption*, vol. IV (The Blackwell Companion to Syntax), 94–117. Blackwell.

McLaughlin, Fiona. 1994. *Noun classification in Seereer-siin*. UT Austin dissertation.

McLaughlin, Fiona. 2000. Consonant mutation and reduplication in Seereer-siin. *Phonology* 17. 333–363.

Preminger, Omer. 2011. *Agreement as a fallible operation*. MIT dissertation.

Renaudier, Marie. 2012. *Dérivation et valence en Seereer*. Université Lumière Lyon 2 dissertation.

Chapter 17

Searching high and low for focus in Ibibio

Philip T. Duncan
University of Kansas

Travis Major
University of California, Los Angeles

Mfon Udoinyang
University of Kansas

This paper discusses two strategies in Ibibio for focusing verbs: contrastive verb focus and exhaustive verb focus. We demonstrate how these constructions differ crucially in the syntactic configurations and derivations that underlie each. Exhaustive verb focus is marked by the presence of the focus operator *kpɔ́t* 'only', which is base-generated high in the left periphery and triggers phrasal movement of the TP containing the focused verb via pied-piping. Contrastive verb focus is marked by verb doubling produced by head movement, and it invokes a low focus phrase situated in the middle field, somewhere at the boundary of the inflectional and verbal domains. Both types of verb focus in Ibibio are thus syntactically-driven, but the locus of each is split across the clausal spine, and each Foc head can probe independent of the other. Ibibio thus furnishes further evidence that multiple foci can occur in a single clause, and it also provides independent support for the existence of a low focus phrase.

1 Introduction

In this paper, we discuss morphosyntactic properties of two types of focus involving verbs in Ibibio: contrastive verb focus (1b) and exhaustive verb focus (1c).

(1) a. ékpê á-mà   á-kót   ŋ̀-wèt   (input to 1b,c)
       ekpe 3SG-PST 3SG-read NMLZ-write

       'Ekpe read a book.'

Philip T. Duncan, Travis Major & Mfon Udoinyang. Searching high and low for focus in Ibibio. In Jason Kandybowicz, Travis Major, Harold Torrence & Philip T. Duncan (eds.), *African linguistics on the prairie: Selected papers from the 45th Annual Conference on African Linguistics*, 269–288. Berlin: Language Science Press. DOI:10.5281/zenodo.1251740

   b. ékpê á-ké   á-kòó-kót   ŋ̀-wèt   Contrastive Verb Focus

       ekpe 3SG-PST.FOC 3SG-CON.FOC-read NMLZ-write

       'Ekpe READ the book (not, say, take it away).'

   c. ékpê á-ké   á-kót   ŋ̀-wèt   kpɔ́t   Exhaustive Verb Focus

       ekpe 3SG-PST.FOC 3SG-read NMLZ-write only

       'Ekpe only read the book.'

We motivate and explore two distinct focus positions corresponding to each construction, a high focus phrase (HFocP) in the C domain, and a low focus phrase (LFocP) in the inflectional domain. We also show that Ibibio has both syntactically and semantically distinct loci of verb focus. Exhaustive verb focus recruits structure high in the left periphery, and is derived by phrasal movement where the TP is pied-piped. On the other hand, contrastively focused verbs are situated much closer to VP and are generated by head movement, where V^0 is attracted to the lower focus head. Moreover, we discuss how these distinct structural configurations allow for double verb focus constructions. The structural superiority of the phrasal projection that houses the exhaustively focused verb triggers scope effects such that exhaustive focus takes wide scope over contrastive focus obligatorily.

    Ibibio thus provides independent evidence for multiple foci occurring in a single clause (Krifka 1992; Rizzi 1997; Kiss 1998) and further support for the existence of a low focus position (Belletti 2004). Our proposed analysis is given in (2), which shows the derivation for both exhaustive verb focus and contrastive verb focus:

(2)

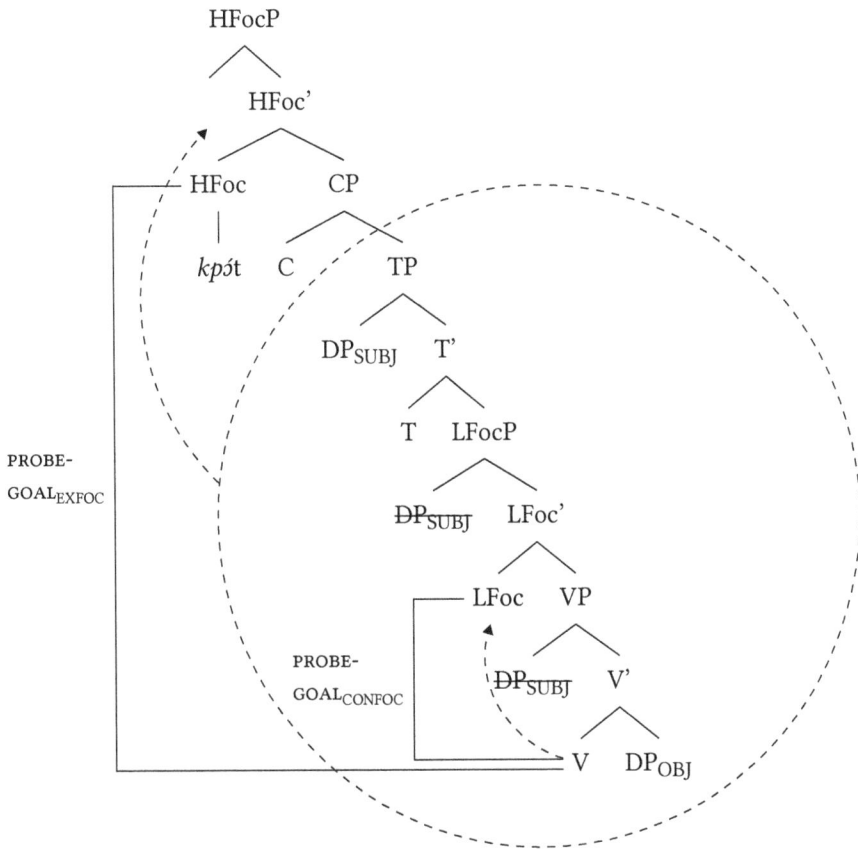

This derivation illustrates our analyses for contrastive and exhaustive verb focus, and it also demonstrates how both of these structurally distinct foci can be activated to generate double focus. In contrastive verb focus, LFoc^0 probes V^0 and triggers head raising. In exhaustive focus, HFoc^0 forms a probe-goal relation with V^0; instead of generating head movement, though, the TP is pied-piped to Spec,HFocP. When both foci are activated, ordering is critical: contrastive verb focus must be embedded under exhaustive focus for the derivation to be sustained.

This paper is organized as follows. In §2, we provide a basic background of Ibibio, focusing on word order and agreement, and motivating the existence of verb raising in the language. Following this, in §3 we turn to argument focus and *wh*-questions to provide a backdrop for understanding verb focus constructions. §4–6 provide our analyses of contrastive verb focus, exhaustive verb focus, and double verb focus, respectively. §7 concludes.

2 Background

2.1 Word order & agreement

Ibibio is a Lower Cross Niger-Congo language spoken in Akwa Ibom state in southeastern Nigeria. It is an SVO language with both subject agreement and object agreement (Essien 1990a; Baker & Willie 2010):

(3) a. èkà   á-mà   á-fát   áyín
         mother 3SG-PST 3SG-hug child

         'The mother hugged the child.'

     b. èkà   á-mà   á-ŋ́-fát   (míèn)
         mother 3SG-PST 3SG-1SG-hug 1SG

         'The mother hugged me.'

As seen in (3), subject agreement surfaces on both T^0 and V^0, leading to multiple subject agreement. Object agreement occurs on V^0 only, and is not always visible in the surface form.[1]

Ibibio matrix clauses project not only TP, but also a series of functional layers such as AspP and MoodP. Subject agreement has "no firm upper limit" and is present on "every verbal functional head" (Baker & Willie 2010: 110):

(4) ú-kpá   ú-ké   ú-sé   ú-màná-ké   ú-nám
     2SGS-COND 2SGS-PERF 2SGS-IMPF 2SGS-do.again-NEG 2SGS-do

     'You should not have been doing it again.' (Baker & Willie 2010: 118)

These facts yield the following word order in a standard declarative clause:

(5) DP_{SUBJ} Agr_{SUBJ}-T [...] Agr_{SUBJ}-/Agr_{OBJ}-V DP_{OBJ}

2.2 Verb raising

Verb movement occurs in several contexts in Ibibio. One of these is negation, illustrated below:

(6) a. òkón á-mà   á-tóŋŋó   Affirmative
         okon 3SG-PST 3SG-start

         'Okon had started.'

     b. òkón í-ké   í-tóŋŋó-ké   Negative
         okon 3SG-PST.FOC 3SG-start-NEG

         'Okon had not started.'

---

[1]Oftentimes because of phonological reasons (e.g. vowel hiatus resolution) object agreement is difficult to discern. All person markers in Ibibio are vowels except 1SG, which is a nasal that assimilates to the onset of the verb root. Thus, object marking always survives in cases involving 1sg objects because the nasal does not delete.

c. ímá á-mà   á-**dép**   Affirmative

   ima 3SG-PST 3SG-buy

   'Ima bought it.'

d. ímá í-ké   í-**dép-pé**   Negative

   ima 3SG-PST.FOC 3SG-buy-NEG

   'Ima didn't buy it.'

Note in these examples that negation surfaces as a CV suffix, which in these cases is either -*ké* (6b) or an assimilated suffix (6d).[2] These forms provide evidence for the order of Tense and Negation, as well as morphosyntactic consequences of V raising (Baker & Willie 2010).[3,4] The abbreviated tree in (7) shows the formation of the complex head in (6d):

(7)

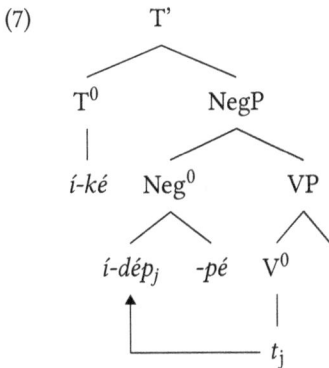

As in (7), NegP dominates VP, and V-to-Neg raising results in negation surfacing postverbally.[5]

Verb raising also occurs in reciprocal constructions, which are bipartite in Ibibio, producing a suffix that resembles negation. Reciprocal morphology is circumfixal, as in (8c), consisting of a *du*- prefix and a CV suffix[6]:

---

[2]There is also a third allomorph, -ɣV, which surfaces on monosyllabic verb roots. See Akinlabi & Urua (2002), who also treat the various allomorphs of the negative suffix to be "underlyingly /ké/" (Akinlabi & Urua 2002: 127).

[3]In agreement with Baker & Willie (2010), we believe that V raising is supported by the fact that negation surfaces preverbally as a separate word, ké, in small clause constructions (e.g. causatives) and subjunctives, which may lack the TP layer. We remain agnostic at present with respect to the possibility of V raising through Neg to T, though we feel this is a viable option (see Baker 2008).

[4]We discuss below our account for the change in tense markers.

[5]Alternatively, one reviewer points out, the negative suffix could result from V raising around Neg followed by Neg encliticizing onto V (see Pollock 1989, for French; Holmberg & Platzack 1995, for Scandinavian). For our purposes, though, either analysis predicts the same output, as we merely wish here to motivate the existence of verb raising in Ibibio independent of contrastive verb focus.

[6]As with the negative suffix, the reciprocal suffix form is assimilative and varies according to the syllable structure and phonetic form of the verb root.

(8) a. é-mà   é-kít   Affirmative
         3PL-PST 3PL-see

         'They saw.'

     b. í-ké   í-kít-té   Negation
         3PL-PST.FOC 3SG-see-NEG

         'They didn't see.'

     c. é-mà   é-dû-kìt-tè   Bipartite reciprocal
         3PL-PST 3PL-REC-see-REC

         'They saw each other.'

Negated reciprocals have stacked suffixes, as seen in (9), and negation appears farther away from the verb than the reciprocal suffix:[7]

(9) í-ké   í-dú-kìt-tè-kè   Reciprocal + Negation
     3PL-PST.FOC 3PL-REC-see-REC-NEG

     'They didn't see each other'

Ibibio verbs thus raise for structurally superior heads to surface postverbally (à la Baker's 1985 Mirror Principle). In (9), the bipartite reciprocal is formed prior to negation, and the ordering of the stacked suffixes gives insight into syntactic structure. The schematic in (10) shows the derivation based on the hierarchy we posit to derive the aforementioned properties of negatives and reciprocals:

---

[7]The semantics of negated reciprocals support our ordering where Neg >> Rec. Negation always takes wide scope over the reciprocal, which suggests that the reciprocal verb constitutes the input to negation. Additionally, negation can appear before a reciprocal verb in the effect clause of a causative:

(i) eno á-mà   á-nám   ɔmmɔ ké í-dú-kìt-tè
     eno 3SG-PST 3SG-make they NEG 3PL-REC-SEE-REC

     'Eno made them not see each other.'

Following Baker & Willie (2010) we take it that the preverbal negative particle in (i) is the morphological exponent of Neg^0 when the verb does not raise. Note, though, that the verb bears reciprocal morphology, which again suggests that the reciprocal suffix attaches to the verb before the negative suffix.

(10)
$$TP$$

```
(10)    TP
         /\
           T'
          /\
        T⁰  NegP
            /\
         Neg⁰  RecP
          |    /\
          └ Rec⁰  VP
              |   /\
              └ V⁰
```

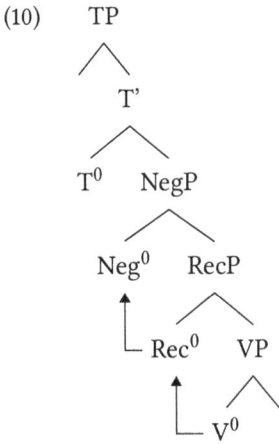

Thus, if RecP intervenes between NegP and VP, V raising ensures that the reciprocal suffix surfaces closest to the verb, since the verb head raises first to Rec^0. This forms a complex head that provides the input to Neg^0. As we argue below, verb raising and the architecture in (10) are significant for understanding contrastive verb focus, which also involves head movement.

3 Argument focus & *wh*-questions

When arguments are focused, the past tense marker -*mà* is replaced with -*ké*:[8]

(11) a. ànìyè (ówó) ké èkà   á-ké/*mà   á-fát   Object *wh*-question
         who   person COMP mother 3SG-PST.FOC/*PST 3SG-hug
         'Who did the mother hug?'
      b. (á-dò) áyín ké èkà   á-ké/*mà   á-fát   Object focus
         3SG-be child COMP mother 3SG-PST.FOC/*PST 3SG-hug
         'It was the child that the mother hugged.'

Thus, in past tense, -*mà* is incompatible with argument focus (Essien 1990a,b; Willie & Udoinyang 2012: 244). "Focus" -*ké* surfaces obligatorily in argument focus contexts (for past tense), as well as *wh*-questions (Note that the 1st *ké* in (11a–b) is the complementizer; the inflected *á-ké*—relevant for our discussion—is obligatory). Following Rizzi (1997), we take it that the landing site of focused constituents and *wh*-expressions is a focus phrase located in the C domain. In this paper, we call this projection HFocP to distinguish it from a second focus phrase that we argue projects rather low in the clausal spine. $HFoc^0$ bears a focus feature that draws a phrasal element to its specifier, presumably because such movement is induced by the need to satisfy a focus-criterion (Rizzi 1997).

---

[8]We here only present data in the past tense, though present and future tenses pattern similarly in this regard.

In contrast to object *wh*-questions and object focus, an overt C is illicit in subject *wh*-questions and subject focus. Moreover, past tense *-mà* cannot occur in these constructions, and the fact that *-mà* and "focus" *-ké* are in complementary distribution suggests that the *-ké* in (12a, c) is "focus" *-ké*, not the complementizer.

(12)   a.   àniyé í-ké/*mà   í-fát   áyín   Subject *wh*-question
            who 3SG-PST.FOC/*PST 3SG-hug child

            'Who hugged the child?'

       b. * àniyé ké   í-ké   í-fát   áyín
            who   COMP 3SG-PST.FOC 3SG-hug child

            (Intended: 'Who hugged the child?' or 'Who is it that hugged the child?')

       c.   (á-dò) èkà   á-ké/*mà   á-fát   áyín   Subject focus
            3SG-be mother 3SG-PST.FOC/*PST 3SG-hug child

            'It was the mother that hugged the child (not the father).'

       d. * èkà   ké   á-ké   á-fát   áyín
            mother COMP 3SG-PST.FOC 3SG-hug child

            (Intended: 'It was the mother that hugged the child [not the father].')

This subject-object asymmetry in argument focus suggests a "that-trace effect" (Perlmutter 1971; Chomsky & Lasnik 1977) disallowing subject extraction over overt complementizers.

In summary, argument focus in Ibibio requires a special tense marker ("focus" *-ké* in past tense), and the neutral tense marker is illicit in such constructions. Focused arguments and *wh*-items undergo movement to HFocP in the complementizer domain, and land higher than the C head. As we discuss below, these properties of focus constructions are significant for differentiating between the two types of verb focus under consideration here: exhaustively focused verbs pattern much like argument focus constructions and involve phrasal movement to the left periphery, whereas contrastively focused verbs do not activate structure in the C system, and instead are derived in the inflectional domain via head movement.

4 Contrastive verb focus

4.1 Morphophonological properties

When verbs are contrastively focused, verb morphology expresses focus (Essien 1990a: 103–106; Akinlabi & Urua 2000; 2002; see Cook 2002 for verb focus in the closely related Efik).

(13)   a.   ákùn á-mà   á-dép ŋ-wèt   (input to 13b)
            akun 3SG-PST 3SG-buy NMLZ-write

            'Akun bought the book.'

b. ákùn á-ké   á-**dèé-dép**   ŋ̀-wèt   í-ké
    akun 3SG-PST.FOC 3SG-CON.FOC-buy NMLZ-write 3SG-PST.FOC
    í-yìp-pé-yìp
    3SG.CON.FOC-NEG-steal
    'Akun BOUGHT the book, she didn't STEAL it.'

Forms of focused verbs demonstrate interactions between phonology, morphology, and syntax. In affirmative forms, the focus component "takes the shape of a heavy (bi-moraic) syllable" (Akinlabi & Urua 2002: 156), which appears on the surface to be some type of prefixal "reduplicant." Vowel lengthening occurs on the "reduplicant," and the initial CV sequence of the verb root becomes a "reduplicative prefix" of the form CVV-P. This prefix bears a tone pattern (LH or HH) that is sensitive to the tone melody on the root. The -ATR vowels /i, ʉ, ʌ/ cannot be lengthened in Ibibio, and these change to [e, u, ɔ] in order to be lengthened. Finally, verb roots with underlyingly low tones become HL falling tones in contrastive reduplication. These properties can be seen in the examples of affirmative contrastively focused verbs in Table 1, which are given for each of the vowels and simple tones in Ibibio.

Table 1: Contrastive verb focus forms

Vowel (w/ tone)	Permissible syllable type	Verb	English gloss	Focused stem (affirmative)
[í]	CV(C)	dí	'come'	dìídí
[ì]	CV(C)	kpì	'cut'	kpìíkpî
[ɨ́]	CVC	tɨ́m	'pound'	tèétɨ́m
[ɨ̀]	CVC	nɨ̀m	'keep'	nèénɨ̂m
[é]	CV(C)	sé	'look'	sèésé
[è]	CV(C)	wèt	'write'	wèéwêt
[ú]	CV(C)	túúk	'touch'	tùútúúk
[ù]	CV(C)	fù	'be lazy'	fùúfû
[ʉ́]	CVC	bʉn	'keep many things'	bùúbʉ́n
[ʉ̀]	CVC	bʉm	'break'	bùúbʉ̂m
[ó]	CV(C)	bót	'mold'	bòóbót
[ò]	CV(C)	bòn	'begat'	bòóbôn
[ɔ́]	CVC	tɔ́k	'urinate'	tɔɔ́tɔ́k
[ɔ̀]	CVC	tɔ̀k	'verbally abuse'	tɔɔ́tɔ̂k
[ʌ́]	CVC	fʌk	'cover'	fɔɔ́fʌ́k
[ʌ̀]	CVC	tʌk	'grate'	tɔɔ́tʌ̂k
[á]	CV(C)	má	'love'	màámá
[à]	CV(C)	mà	'complete'	màámâ

Philip T. Duncan, Travis Major & Mfon Udoinyang

4.2 Morphosyntactic structure

Unlike argument focus, which recruits structure in the C domain, we claim that the derivation for verb focus is more local, that is, TP-internal:

(14) ákùn [$_{TP}$ á-ké   á-yèé-yîp   ŋ̀-wèt   ] í-ké
      akun   3SG-PST.FOC 3SG-CON.FOC-steal NMLZ-write   3SG-PST.FOC
      í-dép-pé-dép
      3SG-buy-NEG-buy

      'Akun STOLE the book, she didn't BUY it.'

Evidence for our claim comes from the position of contrastively focused verbs with respect to T^0. We take it that the presence or absence of "focus" -ké is a diagnostic of activation (or not) of the left periphery. Unlike argument focus, where "focus" -ké tense marker appears obligatorily, contrastively focused verbs can occur with the standard past tense -mà and without "focus" -ké:

(15) ímà á-mà   á-ɲèé-ɲímmé
      ima 3SG-PST 3SG-CON.FOC-agree

      'Ima AGREED (she didn't disagree).'

Thus, contrastive verb focus does not activate the left edge. Instead, the focused verb ɲééɲímmé 'AGREED' in (15) surfaces below the T^0 -mà.

To account for this, we posit a low focus projection that dominates VP, and propose that verbs undergo movement to LFoc^0 in contrastive verb focus. This is shown in the abbreviated tree in (16), which shows the derivation of (15):

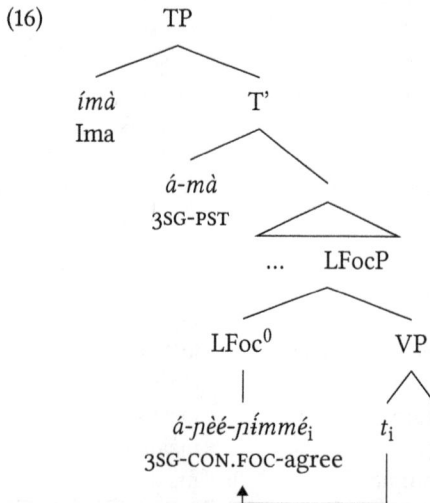

(16)

TP
- ímà / Ima
- T'
  - á-mà / 3SG-PST
  - ... LFocP
    - LFoc^0 : á-ɲèé-ɲímmé$_i$ / 3SG-CON.FOC-agree
    - VP : t_i

We argue that the contrastive verb focus "morpheme" is the product of the verb head-moving to LFoc^0 (see (2) above), and that the syntax provides input to phonology, which results in this special verb morphology. In the derivation in (16), LFoc^0 probes for V^0 (Chomsky 2000; 2001) and attracts it to itself. We take it that this probing and attraction is driven by an interpretable focus feature on LFoc^0, which V^0 values following head adjunction. Focus "reduplication" is a post-syntactic consequence that results from head raising. Interestingly, in Ibibio this low focus position is uniquely associated with contrastive semantics for verbs, which is sort of an unexpected restriction.[9] We stipulate—but leave for future investigation—that Ibibio LFoc^0 has a property such that it probes for features exclusive to verbs, and this disallows attracting phrasal units.

Negated verbs may offer insight into the syntactic structure of verb focus. As noted above, V raising produces a CV negative suffix, as seen in (17b).

(17) a. à-mà   á-fɔ́p   Affirmative
          2SG-PST 3SG-burn
          'You burned it.'

      b. ú-ké   ú-fɔ́p-pɔ́   Negative
          2SG-PST.FOC 2SG-burn-NEG
          'You didn't burn it.'

Instead of a phonologically reduced copy of the verb that appears in affirmative contrastive verb focus forms, negative focused verbs exhibit two full copies of the verb (irrespective of syllable type) with Neg intervening:

(18) a. ú-ké   ú-**fɔ́p-pɔ́-fɔ́p**   Neg + Contrastive Verb Focus
          2SG-PST.FOC 2SG-burn-NEG-burn
          'You didn't BURN it.'

      b. í-ké   í-**dép-pé-dép**   ŋ̀-wèt   á-ké   á-**yèé-yîp**
          3SG-PST.FOC 3SG-buy-NEG-buy NMLZ-write 3SG-PST.FOC 3SG-CON.FOC-steal
          'She didn't BUY the book, she STOLE it.'

Similar to our analysis of negated reciprocals above, we take it that the suffix closest to the verb attaches first as a result of verb raising. In (18), this is the negative suffix, either -pɔ́ (18a) or -pé (18b). Negation thus precedes contrastive focus, and the negated verb forms the input to the low focus position.

We propose (19) as the derivation of (18a):

---

[9]Belletti (2004) shows that, in Italian, low focus involving postverbal subjects is associated with new information.

(19)

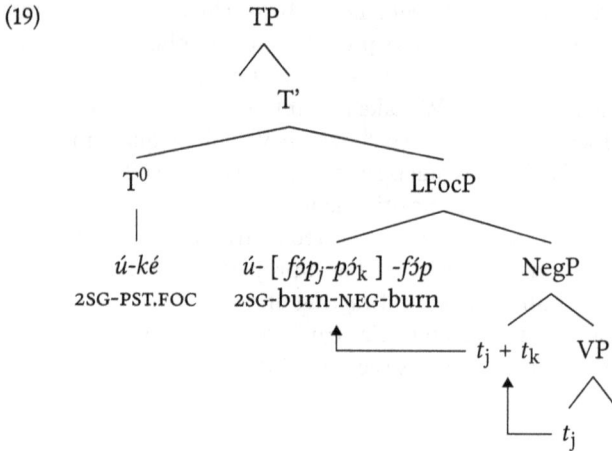

In the derivation of negative contrastive verb focus, LFoc^0 probes for V^0 (as in (16) above), but it attracts the morphologically complex verb that has first raised to Neg^0. The negative suffix is a consequence of V-to-Neg (similar to patterning of reciprocals), and the negative suffix + a full verb copy are a consequence of V-to-Neg-to-Foc.

Why is affirmative contrastive focus a heavy CVV "prefix" while negative contrastive focus retains a full copy? We tentatively propose (but leave for future analysis) the possibility that the grammar disprefers adjacent copies in contrastive focus constructions and instead prefers to dissimilate and maintain distinction. Support for this comes from other instances of contrastive focus in the language. Full reduplication exists elsewhere in Ibibio, as in (20) below, but when items are contrastively focused some strategy for differentiation is employed, as in (21):

(20)   a. ìtɔ́k

        '(a) race'

      b. ìtɔ́k ìtɔ́k

        'hurriedly'

(21)   a. éwá ámì   a'. éwá ámì-ŋím̀mí

        'this dog'   'THIS dog (not that one)'

      b. éwá ókò   b'. éwá ókó-ŋóǹkó

        'that (visible) dog'   'THAT (visible) dog (not this one)'

      c. éwá ódò   c'. éwá ódò-ŋóǹdó

        'that (not visible) dog'   'THAT (not visible) dog (not this one)'

Thus, (phonologically) maintaining a distinction seems to be specific to contrastively focused items – either verbs or demonstratives – in Ibibio; identical adjacent items in non-contrastive constructions are permitted (20). The patterning of contrastively focused demonstratives in (21) could be explained in a way that is analogous to the narrative of contrastive verb focus we develop here; that is, if the syntax generates adjacent items that are phonologically identical then the phonological system resorts to a post-syntactic strategy to differentiate them.

In our analysis, then, verb focus morphology is a syntactic consequence of focused verbs undergoing V-to-LFoc movement. This enables us to provide a more unified account of both affirmative and negative contrastive verb forms, since the same derivation underlies both, despite their superficial dissimilarity. However, more work is needed in this area to determine what additional morphophonological processes generate the affirmative forms (such as those proposed by Akinlabi & Urua 2000; 2002). What we see as critically important is that the presence of intervening material (e.g. the negative suffix) blocks phonological reduction, though full copies of the verbs are present in the syntactic derivation of both affirmative and negative forms.

5 Exhaustive focus

A second type of focus construction in Ibibio corresponds to exhaustive focus, which is illustrated below in (22). As with argument focus – and unlike contrastive verb focus – "focus" *ké* surfaces obligatorily in exhaustive focus constructions.

(22) a. ìmá á-mà   á-fèɰɛ́ ítɔ̀k   (input to 22b,c)
         ima 3SG-PST 3SG-run race

         'Ima ran the race.'

      b. ìmá **kpɔ́t** á-ké   á-fèɰɛ́ ítɔ̀k   Subject exhaustive focus
         ima only 3SG-PST.FOC 3SG-run race

         'Only Ima ran the race (not Ekpe or Akun).'/*'Ima only ran the race (she didn't go to the party).'

      c. ítɔ̀k **kpɔ́t** ké   ìmá á-ké   á-fèɰɛ́   Object exhaustive focus
         race only COMP ima 3SG-PST.FOC 3SG-run

         'It was only the race that Ima ran.'

      d. èté â-ké-dép-pé   àkàrà   á-mà   á-kót
         man 3SG-PST.FOC-buy-REL bean.cake 3SG-PST 3SG-read
         ŋ̀-wèt   (input to 22e)
         NMLZ-write

         'The man who bought the bean cake read the book.'

      e. èté â-ké-dép-pé   àkàrà   **kpɔ́t** á-ké   á-kót   ŋ̀wèt
         man 3SG-PST.FOC-buy-REL bean.cake only 3SG-PST.FOC 3SG-read NMLZ-write

         'Only the man who bought the bean cake read the book (not Ima or

Akun).'/*'The man who bought the bean cake only read the book (he didn't read the magazine/he didn't sell the book).'[10]

The focus particle *kpɔ́t* 'only' acts as an exhaustive focus operator, and it appears to the right of the focused element. We posit that *kpɔ́t* heads its own phrasal projection, which is a high focus phrase in the complementizer domain.[11,12] Exhaustively focused XPs that are attracted by HFoc[0] thus land in Spec, HFocP (Rizzi 1997; Kayne 1998; É. Kiss 1998), which guarantees that *kpɔ́t* always follows it's focused constituent, as the examples in (22) show. The structure in (23) shows the derivation of (22b) along these lines.

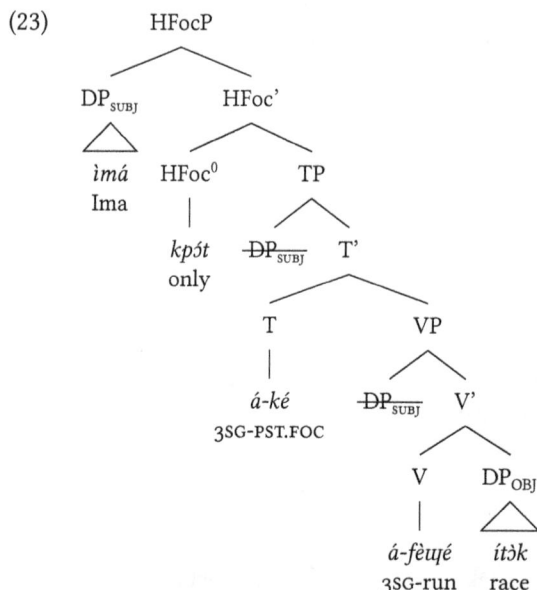

(23)

```
                    HFocP
                   /     \
            DP_SUBJ        HFoc'
             /\           /     \
           ìmá       HFoc⁰       TP
           Ima         |        /   \
                      kpɔ́t   D̶P̶_S̶U̶B̶J̶   T'
                      only          /    \
                                   T       VP
                                   |      /   \
                                 á-ké   D̶P̶_S̶U̶B̶J̶   V'
                              3SG-PST.FOC        /  \
                                                V    DP_OBJ
                                                |     /\
                                            á-fèɥé   ítɔk
                                            3SG-run  race
```

---

[10] An anonymous reviewer points out that this structure is ambiguous, and that it has the additional meaning 'The man who bought only the bean cake read the book.' We assume here that relative clauses of the form in (22d-e) involve raising-to-C, which accounts for the appearance of the relative suffix. We take it that this additional meaning is still compatible with movement to a high focus position, since the subject and relativized verb also undergo movement to the C domain. However, we leave a more precise account of relative clause structures for future investigation.

[11] Note, too, that the complementizer ké is required when an object is exhaustively focused, as in (22c), and that this complementizer appears after *kpɔ́t*. An overt C⁰ is illicit when subjects are exhaustively focused, which is reminiscent of the subject-object asymmetry observed in argument focus constructions due to the "that-trace effect" (see §3). It may be the case that *kpɔ́t* constructions do not require the type of Spec-Head configuration that we propose. However, what is most important for our analysis is that exhaustive focus in Ibibio recruits structure high in the left periphery.

[12] An alternative analysis could treat *kpɔ́t* as a focus-sensitive adjunct much like 'only' in English (this point was raised by an audience member of LSA 2015 and an anonymous reviewer). In such an account, *kpɔ́t* would not head a projection in the C domain; instead, it would adjoin to an XP that bears a focus feature. We take it that this is indeed a viable option, but at present it is difficult to distinguish with much certainty. Importantly, data suggest that *kpɔ́t*-focused constituents (including exhaustive verb focus) activate a left-peripheral focus projection in a way that parallels argument focus and wh-questions in the language. That is, exhaustive focus requires "focus" tense/aspect morphology (just like in cases of Ā-extraction), which is not a requirement of verb focus constructions that recruit the low focus projection.

When verbs are exhaustively focused in Ibibio, the entire TP is targeted for movement. Consequently, the exhaustive focus operator *kpɔ́t* always appears to the right edge of the TP, as seen in (24).[13]

(24) a. [HFocP [TP ìmá á-ké   á-fèɥè ítɔ̀k] **kpɔ́t**]
         ima 3SG-PST.FOC 3SG-run race   only

     'Ima only ran the race.'/*'Only Ima ran the race.'

   b. [HFocP [TP ékpê á-ké   á-kòt   ǹ-wèt   ] **kpɔ́t**]
         ekpe 3SG-PST.FOC 3SG-read NMLZ-write   only

     'Ekpe only read the book.'/*'Only Ekpe read the book.'

Moreover, exhaustive verb focus constructions bear an affinity to subject focus in that an overt complementizer is not permitted:

(25) * ìmá á-ké   á-fèɥé ítɔ̀k **kpɔ́t ké**
      ima 3SG-PST.FOC 3SG-run race only COMP

   (Intended: 'Ima only ran the race.')

Exhaustively focused verbs thus demonstrate a "that-trace effect," which is the same configuration for subject focus.

We propose the analysis for exhaustive TP focus shown in (26), where $HFoc^0$ probes for V^0 and pied-pipes (Ross 1967) TP.

(26)

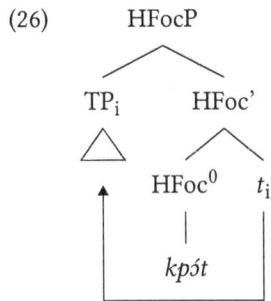

Our analysis of (24a) is given in (27):

---

[13] One anonymous reviewer notes that, with a change of tone, the second readings in (24) are possible. Thus, if the final tone of the verb complexes in (24a) and (24b) are high, the grammaticality judgments are reversed. We assume that the different readings have similar underlying structures. The fact that *kpɔ́t* can scope over the whole TP or the subject, but not the object, further supports our pied-piping analysis. It could be that the object is too deeply embedded inside TP to be focused in this construction.

(27)

```
                              HFocP
                   _____
                  TP_i                      HFoc'
            _____                  _____
          ìmá           T'              kpɔ́t      t_i
          Ima        _____          only
                   á-ké       VP
              3SG-PST.FOC   _____
                          á-fèʉ́é    ítɔ̀k
                          3SG-run   race
```

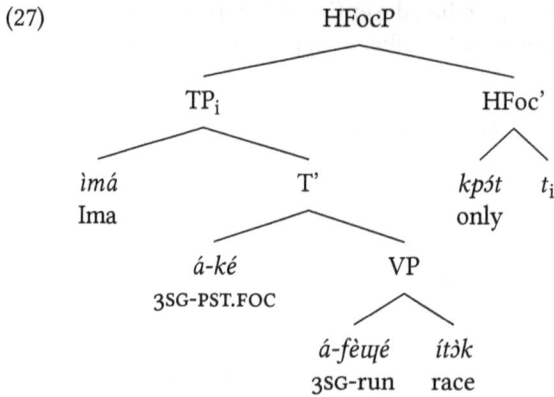

Exhaustive verb focus constructions thus require a different structural configuration than that of contrastively focused verbs. Exhaustive VP focus targets XPs for movement to the C layer, rather than being derived by head movement more local to VP. Exhaustively focused constituents move to Spec,HFocP and appear to the left of the exhaustive focus operator.

6 Double focus

Given the tree in (1), Ibibio should allow "real multiple focus" (Krifka 1992). That is, if there are truly two distinct focus projections, it should be able to activate both focus heads in a single clause; Ibibio shows that this can indeed happen.

Rizzi (1997: 298) noted for Italian that *wh*-questions are incompatible with focus constructions, since they compete for the same position:

(28) Italian

    a. * A chi IL PREMIO NOBEL dovrebbero dare?

       'To whom THE NOBEL PRIZE should they give?' (Rizzi 1997: 298)

    b. * IL PREMIO NOBEL a chi dovrebbeo dare?

       'THE NOBEL PRIZE to whom should they give?' (Rizzi 1997: 298)

In Ibibio, *wh*-questions allow movement to the left periphery, while contrastive verb focus is derived in the inflectional domain. As a result, Ibibio contrastive verb focus is compatible with *wh*-questions, as seen in (29) below.

(29) a. ǹsǒ ké (àfò) à-**dìá-díá**

       what COMP 2SG 2SG-CON.FOC-eat

       'What the hell are you EATING?'

    b. ǹsǒ ké (àfò) mmé-ú-ké-ú-dìá-**ʉ́á-díá**

       what COMP 2SG *mmé*-2SG-PST.FOC-2SG-CON.FOC-NEG-eat

       'What the hell didn't you EAT?'

In (29), the left edge HFoc and lower LFoc are both activated, allowing the *wh*-element *ǹsǒ* 'what?' to move to the C domain and the verb *diá* 'eat' to raise to the lower focus position. This type of double focus interestingly produces a *wh*-the-hell reading (Pesetsky 1987; den Dikken & Giannakidou 2002).

Ibibio also permits double focus (contrastive + exhaustive) with verbs probed for by both Foc heads:

(30) é-ké   é-bɔ́ɔ́-bwɔ́t   ákʌ́k   kpɔ́t
      3PL-PST.FOC 3PL-CON.FOC-borrow money only

'They only BORROWED money.' (Response to: 'Did they steal money?')

As with (29), our analysis can account for the simultaneity of these focus types since they correspond to distinct structural configurations.

We propose the (truncated) structure in (31) for double verb focus in Ibibio:

(31)   HFocP   Double verb focus

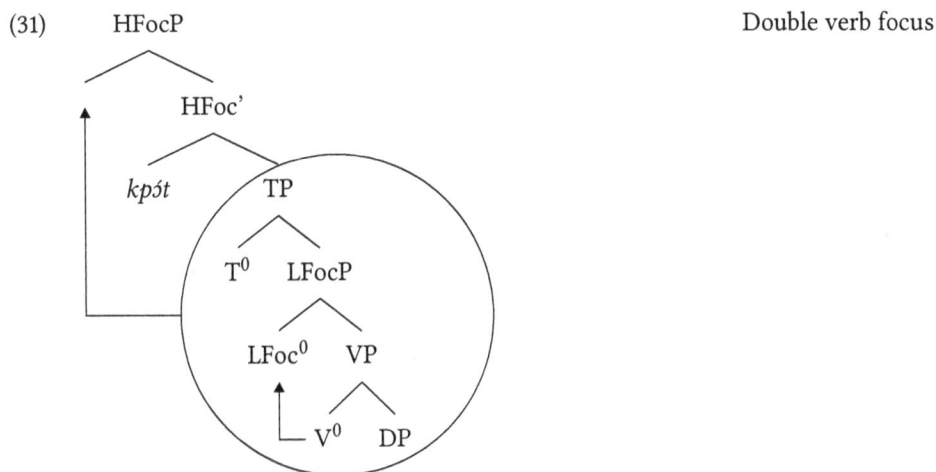

Here, the order in the derivation is critical, and the derivation of contrastive verb focus precedes exhaustive verb focus. Accordingly, LFoc^0 probes for V^0 and causes it to raise, which ensures the verb focus morphology unique to contrastively focused verbs. Following this, HFoc^0 also probes for V^0 and pied-pipes the whole TP to Spec,HFocP since exhaustive focus constructions require phrasal movement. This ensures that the contrastively focused verb along with the object DP surface to the left of the exhaustive focus operator. Our analysis of (30) is seen below in (32):

(32)   HFocP

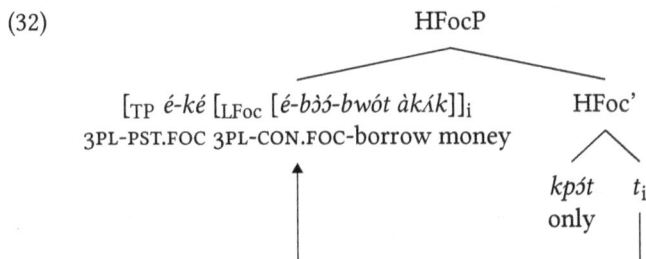

[TP *é-ké* [LFoc [*é-bɔ́ɔ́-bwót àkʌ́k*]]ᵢ   HFoc'
3PL-PST.FOC 3PL-CON.FOC-borrow money

kpɔ́t   *t*ᵢ
only

Again, in our proposal contrastively focused verbs must be derived prior to pied-piping of the TP for verb focus morphology to occur on the verb in a double verb focus construction.[14]

To summarize, in this section we presented data to show that Ibibio does allow double focus constructions, and that such constructions involve real multiple focus. Given the distinct structural configurations required for exhaustive and contrastive verb focus, our analysis comports rather nicely with these facts. Further, given that the different focus positions correspond to particular semantic interpretations when verbs are focused, our proposal also accounts for the scope effects present in double verb focus.

7 Conclusions

We have argued in this paper that Ibibio verb focus constructions are not unified. We motivated the existence of two types of syntactically-driven focus constructions involving verbs in Ibibio: verb raising to a low focus position in the inflectional domain corresponds to contrastive focus, and TP pied-piping to the C layer corresponds to exhaustive focus. Since these focus types are structurally distinct, both Foc probes can target V. Thus, double verb focus is permitted in Ibibio (Krifka 1992), and exhaustively focused verbs always take wide scope (Krifka 1992; Kiss 1998) over contrastively focused ones. From a typological perspective, Ibibio verb focus constructions are significant in that they provide independent evidence for a low focus position associated with a "specialized" semantic interpretation (Belletti 2004). The low focus position in Ibibio is rather unique, however, in that it seems to exclusively target verbs and not, say, NPs. Further exploration into Ibibio contrastive verb focus could thus yield interesting theoretical insights into the nature of low focus and what is possible cross-linguistically.

---

[14]Our analysis predicts that exhaustive focus always takes wide scope over contrastive focus, which is indeed borne out:

(i)   a.   ìyó, ékpê [$_{\text{HFocP}}$ [$_{\text{TP}}$ á-ke   á-kót   ŋ̀-wèt   ] kpɔ́t]
           no ekpe   3SG-PST.FOC 3SG-read NMLZ-write only

'No, Ekpe only [read the book] (not the magazine/he didn't even do his laundry/*he did not take it away).'

      b.   ìyó, ékpê [$_{\text{HFocP}}$ [$_{\text{LFocP}}$ á-ke   á-kòó-kót   ŋ̀-wèt   ] **kpɔ́t**]
           no ekpe   3SG-PST.FOC 3SG-CON.FOC-read NMLZ-write only

'No, Ekpe only [READ the book] (he did not take it away/*he didn't even do his laundry/*not the magazine).'

Thus, (i.b) only corresponds to the interpretation where reading (not doing something else to) the book is the only thing that Ekpe did; it cannot mean that some object other than the book was read.

Abbreviations

1	1st person	NEG	negation
2	2nd person	NMLZ	nominalizer
3	3rd person	OBJ	object
COMP	complementizer	PERF	perfective
CON	contrastive	PL	plural
COND	conditional	PST	past
FOC	focus	SG	singular
IMPF	imperfective	S/SUBJ	subject
INDF	indefinite		

Ibibio is tonal, and tones are marked in the following manner:

- V́   high tone
- V̀   low tone
- V̂   falling tone (note that tones are marked on either vowels or syllabic nasals in the data).

Acknowledgements

We would like to thank our fellow participants in the 2014 Field Methods in Linguistic Description class and the 2014 Research in Field Linguistics seminar at KU, and audience members at both ACAL 45 and LSA 2015 for helpful comments and discussions. We are especially grateful to Harold Torrence and Jason Kandybowicz for their many insights and critiques. Edopeseabasi Udoinyang also graciously provided examples and judgments that informed the final version of this paper. Finally, we thank two anonymous reviewers for their help in suggesting improvements. Unless otherwise noted, the data used in this paper are from Mfon and Edopeseabasi and reflect their judgments.

References

Akinlabi, Akinbiyi & Eno E. Urua. 2000. Tone in ibibio verbal reduplication. In H. Ekkehard Wolff & Orin D. Gensler (eds.), *Proceedings of the 2nd World Congress of African Linguistics Leipzig 1997*, 280–291. Köln: Rüdiger Köppe.

Akinlabi, Akinbiyi & Eno E. Urua. 2002. Foot structure in the Ibibio verb. *JALL* 23. 119–160.

Baker, Mark C. 1985. The Mirror Principle and morphosyntactic explanation. *Linguistic Inquiry* 16(3). 373–415.

Baker, Mark C. 2008. On the nature of the antiagreement effect: Evidence from wh-in-situ in Ibibio. *Linguistic Inquiry* 39. 615–632.

Baker, Mark C. & Willie U. Willie. 2010. Agreement in Ibibio: From every head, to every head. *Syntax* 13(2). 99–132.

Belletti, Adriana. 2004. Aspects of the low IP area. In Luigi Rizzi (ed.), *The structure of CP and IP*, 16–51. Oxford: Oxford University Press.

Chomsky, Noam. 2000. Minimalist inquiries: The framework. In Roger Martin, David Michaels & Juan Uriagereka (eds.), *Step by step: Essays on minimalist syntax in honor of Howard Lasnik*, 89–156. Cambridge, MA: MIT Press.

Chomsky, Noam. 2001. Derivation by phase. In Michael Kenstowicz (ed.), *Ken Hale: A life in language*, 1–52. Cambridge, MA: MIT Press.

Chomsky, Noam & Howard Lasnik. 1977. Filters and control. *Linguistic Inquiry* 8. 425–504.

Cook, Thomas L. 2002. Focus in Efik. *JALL* 23. 113–152.

den Dikken, Marcel & Anastasia Giannakidou. 2002. From hell to polarity: "Aggressively non-D-linked" wh-phrases as polarity items. *Linguistic Inquiry* 33(1). 31–61.

Essien, Okon E. 1990a. *A grammar of the Ibibio language*. Ibadan: University Press Limited.

Essien, Okon E. 1990b. The aspectual character of a verb and tense in Ibibio. *Journal of West African Languages* 20. 64–72.

Holmberg, Anders & Christer Platzack. 1995. *The role of inflection in Scandinavian syntax*. Oxford: Oxford University Press.

Kayne, Richard S. 1998. Overt vs. Covert movement. *Syntax* 1(2). 128–191.

Kiss, Katalin É. 1998. Identificational focus versus information focus. *Language* 74(2). 245–273.

Krifka, Manfred. 1992. A compositional semantics for multiple focus constructions. In Joachim Jacobs (ed.), *Informationsstruktur und grammatik*, 17–53. VS Verlag: Opladen.

Perlmutter, David M. 1971. *Deep and surface structure constraints in syntax*. New York, NY: Holt, Rinehart & Winston.

Pesetsky, David. 1987. Wh-in-situ: Movement and unselective binding. In Eric Reuland & Alice G. B. ter Meulen (eds.), *The representation of (in)definiteness*, 98–130. Cambridge, MA: MIT.

Pollock, Jean-Yves. 1989. Verb movement, Universal Grammar, and the structure of IP. *Linguistic Inquiry* 20(3). 365–424.

Rizzi, Luigi. 1997. The fine structure of the left periphery. In Liliane Haegeman (ed.), *Elements of grammar: A handbook in generative syntax*, 281–337. Kluwer: Dordrecht.

Ross, John R. 1967. *Constraints on variables in syntax*. Cambridge, MA: MIT Doctoral dissertation.

Willie, Willie U. & Mfon. E Udoinyang. 2012. The missing component in Ibibio linguistic time. In Michael R. Marlo, Nikki B. Adams, Christopher R. Green, Michelle Morrison & Tristan M. Purvis (eds.), *Selected proceedings of the 42nd Annual Conference on African Linguistics*, 240–256. Somerville, MA: Cascadilla.

Chapter 18

More on have and need

Claire Halpert
University of Minnesota

Michael Diercks
Pomona College

This paper addresses recent work on the cross-linguistic patterns involving *have* and *need* predicates, focusing on the debate surrounding the claim that all languages that lack a transitive *have* also lack transitive *need* (Harves & Kayne 2012). In this paper, we move the discussion beyond these surface patterns, first by presenting new syntactic diagnostics to demonstrate that the Bantu language counter-examples to the proposed generalization discussed by Antonov & Jacques (2014) are true counter-examples to the original claim by Harves & Kayne (2012). From this perspective, we evaluate the relevance of these conclusions for Harves & Kayne (2012)'s lexical decomposition analysis of *need*. We conclude that although Bantu languages form a straightforward counter-example to the proposed Harves & Kayne (2012) typology, as Antonov & Jacques (2014) noted, there are in fact some deep similarities between the Bantu patterns and the proposals of Harves & Kayne (2012). In particular, we suggest that their observations about the role of case in the distribution of *have* and *need* verbs may in fact be amenable to the Bantu patterns, suggesting that their conclusions cannot yet be abandoned.

1 Overview of the Issues

Harves & Kayne (2012) survey a number of languages and propose an empirical generalization: all languages that lack a lexical verb of possession (*have*) likewise lack a transitive lexical verb *need*. Based on this apparent typological gap they propose a lexical decomposition analysis of *need*. In response, Antonov & Jacques (2014) provide a range of typological data showing that the typological generalization that Harves & Kayne (2012) rely on is not in fact surface-true, a conclusion this paper supports. The chart in Table 1 summarizes both Harves & Kayne (2012)'s original typological conclusions and the additions of Antonov & Jacques (2014) and this paper, listed in bold.

Claire Halpert & Michael Diercks. More on have and need. In Jason Kandybowicz, Travis Major, Harold Torrence & Philip T. Duncan (eds.), *African linguistics on the prairie: Selected papers from the 45th Annual Conference on African Linguistics*, 289–305. Berlin: Language Science Press. DOI:10.5281/zenodo.1251742

Table 1: Revised typology of possession and need, with additions in bold

	H-languages	B-languages
Languages with transitive 'need'	Czech, Slovak, Polish, Slovenian, Croatian, Servian (dialects), Belorussian, English, German, Yiddish, Luxemburgish, Dutch, Swedish, Norwegian, Icelandic, Spanish, Catalan, Basque, Paraguayan Guaraní, Purépecha (Tarascan), Mapudungun	**Zulu, Setswana, Kuria, Swahili, Otjiherero, Estonian, Moroccan Arabic, Algerian Arabic, Likpe, Ewe, Ayacucho Quechua**
Languages without transitive 'need'	Bulgarian, Serbian (standard), Lithuanian, French, Italian, Bellinzonese, Portuguese, Romanian, Farsi, Armenian, Albanian, Latin, Ancient Greek	Russian, Latvian, Sakha, Bhojpuri, Bengali, Hindi, Marathi, Irish, Welsh, Scots Gaelic, Georgian, Hungarian, Turkish, Korean, Peruvian Quechua (Cuzco, Cajamarca, Huallaga), Bolivian Quechua, Yucatec Maya, Tamil, Mohawk, Amharic

1.1 An empirical correction to Harves & Kayne (2012)

Harves & Kayne (2012) focus on what they claim is a significant typological gap in the cross-linguistic expression of possession and *need*, formalized in (1):

(1) **Harves-Kayne Generalization** (Strong version):   (Harves & Kayne 2012: 1)
    All languages that have a transitive verb corresponding to *need* are H-languages.

  The gap in their data occurs when we compare languages that use a transitive verb of possession, or H(ave)-languages, to languages that use a non-transitive strategy to express possession, or B(e)-languages. While possession in H-languages looks straight-forwardly transitive, involving a nominative-accusative case pattern, possession in B-languages does not: in B-language possessors are typically oblique, and possessees are nominative instead of accusative (unlike possessees in H-languages). H-languages may or may not have a transitive *need* verb, but Harves & Kayne (2012) crucially claim that B-languages never do.

(2) **H-language with transitive need: Czech**   (Harves & Kayne 2012: 4a, 5a)

    a. Mají   nové auto.
       have.3PL new car.ACC

       'They have a new car.'

    b. Tvoje děti   tě   potřebují.
       your children.NOM you.ACC need.3PL

       'Your children need you.'

(3) **H-language with non-transitive need: French**   (Harves & Kayne 2012: 6a, 7a)

    a. J' ai   une voiture.
       I have.1SG a   car

       'I have a car.'

    b. J' ai   besoin d' une voiture.
       I have.1SG need of a   car

       'I need a car.'

(4) **B-language with non-transitive possession: Latvian**   (Harves & Kayne 2012: 2b, 3c)

    a. Man   ir velosipēds.
       me.DAT is bicycle.NOM

       'I have a bicycle.'

    b. Man   vajag   dakšu.
       me.DAT need.3SG fork.GEN

       'I need a fork.'

Harves & Kayne (2012) argue that this crucial gap – the absence of B-languages with transitive *need* – follows directly from an incorporation account of transitive *need*: the derivation of the verb *need* involves incorporation of a nominal 'need' into an unpronounced (transitive, abstract) HAVE. Because 'need' incorporates, it does not require case (Baker 1988), which allows HAVE to assign accusative to the object. Languages that lack an overt *have* verb are assumed to lack abstract HAVE and are thus unable to do the necessary incorporation to create transitive *need*.

(5)

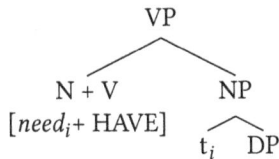

$$VP$$
$$N + V \qquad NP$$
$$[need_i + HAVE] \qquad t_i \quad DP$$

As noted by Antonov & Jacques (2014), a common pattern in Bantu languages contradicts the generalization in (1): the following examples show 3 languages that have transitive lexical verbs for *need* but construct predicative possession using a copular (*be*) construction followed by the preposition *with*.[1]

(6) Zulu: *be*-possession and transitive *need*

    a.   ngi- zo- ba ne-   mali.
           1SG- FUT- be with.AUG- 9money
           'I will have money.'

    b.   ngi- zo- dinga imali.
           1SG- FUT- need AUG.9money
           'I will need money.'

(7) Swahili: *be*-possession and transitive *need*

    a.   ni- li- kuwa na   nyumba.
           1SG- PST- be   with 9house
           'I had a house.'

    b.   ni- li- hitaji nyumba.
           1SG- PST- need 9house
           'I needed a house.'

(8) Kuria: *be*-possession and transitive *need*

    a.   Gati n- a- a-   re n-   eng'ɔɔmbe.
           1Gati FOC- 1S- REM.PST- be with- 9cow
           'Gati had a cow.' (remote past)

    b.   Gati n- a- a-   tun- ire   eng'ɔɔmbe.
           1Gati FOC- 1S- REM.PST- need- REM.PST 9cow
           'Gati needed a cow.' (remote past)

In addition to the languages shown here, initial evidence suggests that this pattern is well attested throughout the Bantu family. Herero, for example, expresses predicative possession using a *be (with)* construction, *na*, but has a transitive verb of need, *hepa*, that is distinct from the verb of wanting *vanga* (Nguako 2013). Setswana also uses a *be (with)* construction, *na (le)*, for predicative possession;[2] transitive *tlhoka* for 'need'; and *batla* for 'want'. We include these languages in table 1 on the basis of this preliminary evidence. Other languages, including Shona, Lubukusu, and Tiriki also lack a transitive verb *have* and express 'need' with a lexical verb; these differ, however, in that they seem to collapse *need* and *want* (relying on circumlocutions in sentences contrasting 'desiring'

---

[1] Antonov & Jacques (2014) give parallel data to ours here in Swahili and Zulu.
[2] Creissels (2013) observes, though, that in Setswana predicative possession patterns in some respects like a transitive verb. He remarks that this pattern is a departure from the general Bantu pattern in which predicative possession is completely indistinguishable from the comitative construction.

with 'needing').[3] No Bantu language that we examined expressed predicative possession via a transitive *have* verb.

It is clear from these Bantu examples that the generalization in (1) is not surface-true: these languages all have lexical verbs for *need* but lack a lexical verb *have*. Antonov & Jacques (2014) make this argument based on data like these from Swahili and Zulu, as well as similar data from a typologically diverse set of languages (including Arabic, Quechua, and Kwa languages). Our departure point is to investigate the issue in more syntactic depth to determine whether these apparent counter-examples hold up under further investigation and, if so, what the consequences are for the Harves & Kayne (2012) analysis of *need*.

We suggest in this paper that the resulting picture is more nuanced. While the Swahili and Zulu patterns indeed constitute true counter-examples to Harves & Kayne (2012)'s generalization in (1), Harves & Kayne (2012)'s revised generalization, discussed below in (10), and a more in-depth consideration of structural licensing suggests that their core intuitions may still have merit, at least with respect to the Bantu data. This conclusion contrasts with that of Antonov & Jacques (2014), who state on the basis of the typological evidence that Harves & Kayne (2012)'s "hypothesis is thus unlikely to be valid as an absolute universal." While their conclusion may ultimately be correct, we suggest that a revised conception of Harves & Kayne (2012)'s relevant generalization based on the Bantu evidence could potentially reveal a modified universal structural decomposition of *need* verbs. This proposal makes useful predictions about the structure of these predicates in the other languages in Antonov & Jacques (2014)'s study, setting the stage for future investigation.

While Antonov & Jacques (2014) establish a number of potential counter-examples to Harves & Kayne (2012)'s proposed typology,[4] Harves & Kayne (2012) themselves discuss one language that does not straightforwardly follow their generalization: Finnish is canonically described as a B-language but nonetheless has a transitive *need* verb with a NOM-ACC case pattern. Harves & Kayne (2012) point out that while Finnish uses the same *be* verb in existential, locative, predicational, and possessive sentences, possessives differ from the other constructions in taking an accusative – rather than a nominative – object:

---

[3]Kuria, illustrated in (8) and to which we do not return in this paper, appears at a glance to fall into this category: our consultant reports that the verb *ugu-tuna* 'INF-need' in Kuria can also have a reading of 'want.' Despite this apparent lexical overlap, it is possible to contrast *ugu-tuna* with an unambiguous verb of desire, *uku-igomba*, producing a sentence like *Gati **naigombere** imburi, si bono **natunire** en'gombe* 'Gati desired a goat, but he needed a cow.' This kind of sentence would be unlikely if *ugu-tuna* was lexically a verb of 'wanting' just as much as 'needing' (cf. English #*John desired a Porsche, but wanted a family sedan.*). We suspect, therefore, that Kuria's *ugu-tuna* verb is probably best classified as a true 'need' verb, with metaphorical extensions to notions of 'wanting' (cf. English *I need a beer right now*). On this basis we include Kuria in the languages added in Table 1. Due to this complication, however, we restrict the core examples discussed in the paper to Swahili and Zulu.

[4]See Kayne (2014), though, for a discussion of some problems with the evidence Antonov & Jacques (2014) give.

(9) **Finnish predicational vs. possessive *be***   (Harves & Kayne 2012: 14c, 13)

    a. Hän   on   vanha.
       he.NOM be.3SG old.NOM

       'He is old.'

    b. Minu- lla   on   häne-t.
       I-   ADESS be.3SG him-ACC

       'I have him.'

Harves & Kayne (2012) argue that the accusative case assignment in (9) crucially distinguishes Finnish from other B-languages: because Finnish expresses possession via an accusative-assigning (B)-verb, *need* may incorporate into accusative-assigning BE in this language to yield the transitive *need* pattern. They thus revise their generalization to reflect the importance of case-assignment patterns, as opposed to BE/HAVE distinctions:

(10) **Harves-Kayne Generalization** (revised):   (Harves & Kayne 2012: 15)
     All languages that have a transitive verb corresponding to *need* are languages that have an accusative-case-assigning verb of possession.

As we will see in the next section, even the revised generalization does not seem to capture the Bantu facts: the possessee in Swahili and Zulu possessive predication does not behave like a normal transitive direct object, but instead exhibits similar behavior to the 'objects' of copular, existential, and locative predication, which also involve *be*. In §3, we return to an aspect of the generalization in (10) without a clear connection to the Bantu data – case assignment patterns. We propose that the the Bantu exceptions to Harves & Kayne (2012)'s generalization(s) may in fact be linked to the exceptional behavior of Bantu languages with respect to syntactic case. Based on recent work on case in Bantu (e.g. Diercks 2012; Halpert 2012), we suggest that case-licensing of objects is independent of transitivity in these languages; transitive verbs and B-constructions have identical licensing properties. Given this pattern, a version of (10) that simply requires identical licensing properties between predicative possession and transitive verbs may be tenable.

2 The Bantu examples are true counter-examples

We have already established that the surface generalization in (1) cannot be upheld in the face of the patterns in Swahili and Zulu,[5] which are both B-languages that nonetheless have a lexical verb *need*. In this section, we demonstrate that possessees in these languages are not canonical transitive objects, which rules out a Finnish-style analysis for the Bantu facts.

As is common in the Bantu family, neither Zulu nor Swahili has overt case morphology, instead marking most grammatical relations on the verb itself via subject marking

---

[5]As well as the other Bantu languages discussed above. In addition, while we focus on Zulu and Swahili here, we note that Kuria exhibits identical behavior on all relevant diagnostics.

and object marking. This lack of case morphology means that we cannot simply use nominal morphology to evaluate Harves & Kayne (2012)'s generalizations. Instead, we focus on object marking and A-bar extraction as tests for transitive-object behavior. As the following patterns demonstrate, possessees in Zulu and Swahili show distinct properties from canonical transitive objects, suggesting that they are true counter-examples to the generalizations in (1)/(10) and not instances of covert canonical objects.

2.1 Object markers for *need* and *have*

Most Bantu languages can mark transitive objects on the verb via a morpheme that precedes the stem and follows other inflectional material (see Riedel 2009; Marten et al. 2007; Zeller 2012; Bax & Diercks 2012, a.o., for additional discussion). Abstracting away from particular analyses of object markers, we instead take their availability to be a canonical property of transitive objects. As Swahili shows in (11), *need* uses the normal pre-stem OM to pronominalize an object, just as the transitive verb *want* does, while predicative possession requires an exceptional enclitic morpheme to pronominalize an object. A pre-stem object marker (11d) is ungrammatical.

(11) Swahili

    a. Gati a- li- i-   taka.
        1Gati 1s- PST- 9o- want

        'Gati wanted it (a house).' (remote past)

    b. Gati a- li- i-   hitaji.
        1Gati 1s- PST- 9o- need

        'Gati needed it (a house).' (remote past)

    c. Gati a- li-   kuwa na- **yo.**
        1Gati 1s- PST- be   with- 9PRONOUN

        'Gati had it (a house).' (remote past)

    d. * Gati a- li- i-   kuwa na- (yo)
            1Gati 1s- PST- 9o- be   with- 9PRONOUN

The examples (12) illustrate the same pattern for Zulu:

(12) Zulu

    a. ngi- zo- **yi-** funa.
        1SG- FUT- 9o- want

        'I will want it (money).'

    b. ngi- zo- **yi-** dinga.
        1SG- FUT- 9o- need

        'I will need it (money).'

    c. ngi- zo- ba na- **yo.**
        1SG- FUT- be with- 9PRONOUN

        'I will have it (money).'

d. *ngi- zo- yi- ba na- (yo).
   1SG- FUT- 9O- be with (9PRONOUN)

These contrasts show that the canonical object marking patterns that are available for objects of transitive verbs are not available for possessees in predicative possession for Swahili and Zulu (see Antonov & Jacques 2014 for similar discussion). This pattern suggests that the Swahili and Zulu counter-examples are not instances of a transitive-like construction in disguise.

2.2 Object extraction for *need* and *have*

Extraction patterns provide an additional argument for distinguishing between possessee arguments and transitive objects. In Swahili, for example, the verb *need* shows the same patterns for object extraction as transitive verbs: an object operator can simply be A'-moved to the left periphery. In contrast, such dislocation in predicative possession requires a resumptive clitic:

(13) **Swahili object extraction**

a. Ni- li- ona ki- tabu amba- cho Gati a- li- nunua.
    1sgs- PST- see 7- book comp- 7REL 1Gati 1s- PST- buy

    'I saw the book that Gati bought.'

b. Ni- li- ona ki- tabu amba- cho Gati a- li- kuwa na- **cho**.
    1sgs- PST- see 7- book comp- 7REL 1Gati 1s- PST- be with- 7PRO.

    'I saw the book that Gati had.'

The requirement of a resumptive enclitic here is exceptional among instances of object extraction in Swahili. Notably, it is not exceptional for predicative possession in other Bantu languages. Zulu again shows the same patterns, distinguishing transitive object extraction, which requires object marking, from extraction of a possessee, which requires the enclitic:

(14) **Zulu object extraction**

a. y- imali-   ni   e- ngi- zo- yi- funa?
    COP- AUG.9money- what REL- 1SG- FUT- 9O- want

    'How much money will I want?'

b. y- imali-   ni   e- ngi- zo- yi- dinga?
    COP- AUG.9money- what REL- 1SG- FUT- 9O- need

    'How much money will I need?'

c. y- imali-   ni   e- ngi- zo- ba na- **yo**?
    COP- AUG.9money- what REL- 1SG- FUT- be with- 9PRONOUN

    'How much money will I have?'

d. *y- imali-   ni   e- ngi- zo- yi- ba na- (yo)?
    COP- AUG.9money- what REL- 1SG- FUT- 9O- be with- (9PRONOUN)

If Swahili and Zulu possessive constructions were transitive verbs disguised as B-constructions, we would expect parallel behavior between transitives and possessives, contrary to fact.

In fact, a closer parallel to the extraction properties of possessive constructions is extraction from a prepositional phrase, which also requires a resumptive enclitic pronoun:

(15) **Zulu PP extraction**

    a.   ubhuthi   e-   ngi- hamba na- **ye**   (u)- ng- uSipho.
          AUG.1brother REL- 1SG- go   with- 1PRONOUN (1s)- COP- AUG.1Sipho

          'The guy I'm going with is Sipho.'

    b.   ubhuthi e-ngi-khuluma nga- **ye** u- zo ba (ng)- umongameli.
          AUG.1br REL-1SG-speak INSTR- 1PRO 1s- FUT- be (COP)- AUG.1president

          'The guy who I'm talking about will be president.'

(16) **Swahili PP extraction**

    a.   mw- anafunzi ni- na- ye- enda na- **ye**   ni Gati.
          1-   student 1SG- PRES- 9REL- go   with- 1PRONOUN is 1Gati

          'The student who I'm going with is Gati.'

    b.   m- tu   ni- na- ye- zungumza na- **ye**   a- ta- kuwa
          1- person 1SG- PRES- 9REL- converse with- 1PRONOUN 1s- FUT- be

          rais.
          9president

          'The person who I'm talking to will be president.'

In short, A'-extraction in predicative possession patterns with extraction of obliques – and not with extraction of direct objects. This pattern is consistent with an analysis of the possessive constructions in Swahili and Zulu as a copula plus a prepositional phrase, exactly what it appears to be on the surface. This evidence therefore supports the conclusion that Swahili and Zulu are true B-languages (expressing possession via a basic copular construction), and therefore true counter-examples to the (1)/(10) generalization.

2.3 Predicative possession as a non-verbal construction

An additional parallel between predicative possession and other copular constructions in Bantu is found in the distribution of the *be* verb. The examples we have seen involve a *be* verb plus the preposition (some version of *na* or *ne* in all the languages considered here). More generally, the full verbal form appears only as needed to host overt tense morphology; in present tense constructions, for example, we find a reduced structure with only agreement and the preposition in many languages, as Zulu and Swahili show:

(17) a.   ngi- ne-   mali.   [Zulu]
            1SG- with.AUG- 9money

            'I have money.'

b. ni- na   nyumba.   [Swahili]
   1SG- with 9house
   'I have a house.'

This same pattern occurs in copular clauses, with the full copular verb (and inflection) only appearing in non-present tenses, as the examples above show in (15) for Zulu and in (16) for Swahili. Buell & de Dreu (2013) provide a detailed comparison of non-verbal predication in Zulu, demonstrating that possessive predication exhibits parallel behavior to other copular constructions, in line with what we have shown here.

2.4 Intermediate summary

What we have seen in this section is that, based on evidence from both object marking and object extraction, possessees in predicative possession constructions do not display canonical properties of transitive objects. Without overt accusative case-marking in Bantu languages, these canonical object properties are the best means to examine whether the revised generalization in (10) holds up in the face of the Bantu counter-examples. The kind of exceptional copula behavior of the *be*-possessive in Finnish does not extend to Swahili and Zulu, which appear to be truly copular-based constructions. This conclusion was bolstered by the observation that the *be*-verb in these contexts appears to pattern in normal ways for a copula, being null in the present tense. These facts thus allow us to move beyond Antonov & Jacques (2014)'s observation that Bantu languages form a surface counter-example to Harves & Kayne (2012)'s generalization to show that the counter-examples hold even on deeper syntactic measures of transitivity and objecthood.

3 The role of case

In the previous section, we concluded that Bantu languages like Zulu and Swahili constitute a robust counter-example to Harves & Kayne (2012)'s generalization about *have* and *need*. As we saw in (10), however, the revised version of their claim specifically refers to the case assignment properties of the relevant predicates, with the idea that languages where possessees receive ACC have transitive *need* (that assigns ACC to its direct object). Given the Bantu counter-examples, we can draw one of two possible conclusions. First, we might conclude that Harves & Kayne (2012)'s generalizations are empirically inaccurate and their resulting analysis of the decomposition of *need* is therefore untenable. A second alternative would be that Harves & Kayne (2012)'s revised generalization in (10) is on the right track, with the distribution of H- and B- languages relating to the the presence of transitive *need* based on the availability of Case-licensing.

This second alternative is not transparently correct: the surface forms show no evidence that objects of predicative possession and *need* are Case-licensed identically in Zulu and Swahili. We noted in the previous section that while Bantu languages show no obvious morphological case marking on nominals, evidence from structural diagnostics demonstrates clear syntactic distinctions between the objects of transitive predicates and possessees in predicative possession. In the following subsections we nonetheless return to the issue of Case and what role its presence (or absence) might play in the Bantu possession pattern.

3.1 Another test for *have* and *need*

As we saw above, *need* in Swahili and Zulu always patterns with transitive verbs – and not with *have* (i.e. BE + P) constructions. This raises a critical question, however: are *have* and *need* always syntactically different in Bantu? The short answer is *maybe not*: one morphosyntactic pattern in Zulu, augment distribution, in fact suggests that both types of object are licensed in the same way.

Zulu nouns are typically marked with an initial augment vowel that appears before the noun class prefix. This augment vowel can be dropped on some indefinites[6] in certain syntactic positions – in particular, immediately after the verb inside *v*P (Halpert 2012). We show in the data that follow that with respect to augment drop, *have*, *need*, and transitive verbs all behave in the same way in Zulu. As the data in (18) show, in the relevant contexts (triggering NPI readings in these examples) an augment may be dropped on the highest DP after a transitive verb. Unsurprisingly, *need* shows the same behavior in (19).

(18) Zulu: augment drop possible on highest DP after transitive verb

    a. ngi- bona u-muntu.
        1SG- see AUG-1person

        'I see someone/the person.'

    b. A- ngi- bon- i   muntu.
        NEG- 1SG- see- NEG 1person

        'I don't see anybody.'

(19) Zulu: augment drop possible on highest DP after *need*

    a. ngi- dinga i-mali.
        1SG- need AUG-9money

        'I need money.'

    b. A- ngi- ding- i   mali.
        NEG- 1SG- need- NEG 9money

        'I don't need any money.'

What distinguishes this test from those in the previous section is that, as (20) shows, the possessee in predicative possession behaves like a transitive object, allowing the augment to be dropped in the relevant syntactic contexts:

---

[6]While nonveridical environments are typically necessary for augment drop, Halpert (2012) demonstrates that there are additional, independent syntactic conditions under which the process is licensed, on which we focus here.

(20) **Zulu: augment drop possible on possessee with predicative possession *na***

    a.   ngi- **ne**-mali.   (na+imali)
         1SG- with.AUG-9money

         'I have money.'

    b.   A-   ngi- na   mali.
         NEG- 1SG- with 9money

         'I don't have any money.'

The behavior of the possessee in (20) is not unique to the possessive constructure, however; rather, it seems to be a property of the *na* preposition more generally that augment drop is permitted on its complement under the right structural conditions:

(21) **Zulu: preposition *na* allows augment drop when highest element in *v*P**

    a.   u-Mfundo   u- dlala i-bhola   **no-**   muntu. (na+umuntu)
         AUG-1Mfundo 1s- play AUG-5ball NA.AUG- 1person

         'Mfundo is playing soccer with someone/the person.'

    b.   u-Mfundo   a-   ka- dlal- i   **na- muntu** i-bhola.
         AUG-1Mfundo NEG- 1s- play- NEG NA- 1person AUG-5ball

         'Mfundo isn't playing soccer with anyone.'

    c.   *u-Mfundo   a-   ka- dlal- i   i-bhola   na- muntu.
         AUG-1Mfundo NEG- 1s- play- NEG AUG-5ball NA- 1person

Crucially, the *na* preposition contrasts with certain other prepositions in the language. While *na* PPs are essentially transparent with respect to the constraints on augment drop, some prepositions do not alternate, instead always requiring the no-augment version regardless of position or interpretation, as shown for *kwa-* and *ku-* below:

(22) **Zulu: prepositions *kwa-* and *ku-* prohibit augment on their complement**

    a.   u-Sipho   u- zo- pheka ukudla   **kwa-** zingane/ ***kwe-***   zingane.
         AUG-1Sipho 1s- FUT- cook   AUG.15food KWA- 10child/ *KWA.AUG- 10child

         'Sipho will cook food for the children.'

    b.   u-Sipho   u- zo- thumela imali   **ku-** bantwana.
         AUG-1Sipho 1s- FUT- send.APPL AUG.9money KU- 2child

         'Sipho will send money to the children'

Recall that there is no ACC-marking on transitive nominals in Zulu and that the complement of the preposition in predicative possession does not behave like a transitive object in many ways (triggering resumption under extraction, different object marking patterns). At the same time, we see here that the object of the possessive preposition *does* share underlying similarities with the transitive objects with respect to the distribution of augments. The apparent transparency of *na*[7] for the purposes of structurally-licensed augment-drop is *not* shared by all other prepositions in the language, which instead seem to simply replace the augment in all environments.

---

[7] And a few other prepositions in Zulu.

To summarize, the augment drop patterns in Zulu give us a test for possessees whose results diverge from those of the tests in the previous section, grouping the complements of *na* with transitive objects (and not with other prepositional complements). This discussion becomes particularly relevant for our concerns in light of Halpert (2012)'s proposal that augment drop is only permitted in positions where structural Case is assigned, as we discuss in the following subsection.

3.2 Case implications

The discussion in this section concerns the role of Case Theory in the Bantu language family. While we do not present a definitive account of Case in these languages, we show that the types of case-theoretic puzzles – and their proposed solutions – that emerge in the Bantu family suggest that Harves & Kayne (2012)'s revised approach to *have* and *need* in (10) may in fact be on the right track for these languages.

3.2.1 Existing proposals about Bantu case

Diercks (2012), building on a range of research (e.g. Harford Perez 1985; Ndayiragije 1999; Alsina 2001; Baker 2003; 2008), showed that a wide variety of constructions crosslinguistically among Bantu languages – including raising constructions, locative inversion, and *possible*-constructions, among others – do not behave in the familiar ways predicted by Case Theory, two examples of which are included below: the first shows a perception-verb raising construction that is equivalent of the ungrammatical English **John seems that fell*, in which the embedded subject has raised out of a tensed and agreeing clause, where it presumably should have been Case-licensed and rendered inactive (known as hyper-raising).

(23)   **Lubukusu hyper-raising**

    John a- lolekhana mbo ka- a-   kwa.
    1John 1s- seems   that 1s- PST- fell

    'John seems like he fell/John seems to have fallen.'

The example in (24), on the other hand, shows a noun phrase appearing as subject of a non-finite clause where there is no evidence of a Case-licenser (overt or covert) to license it.

(24)   **Swahili overt subject of infinitive**

    I- na- wezakana (*kwa) Maiko   ku- m- pig- i-   a Tegani simu.
    9s- PRES- possible   (*for) 1Michael INF- O- beat- APPL- FV 1Tegan 9phone

    'It is possible for Michael to call Tegan.'

Diercks concluded that these patterns indicate that Bantu languages simply lack abstract Case features, articulated in a macroparameter:

(25)   **Case Parameter:** Uninterpretable Case features are / **are not** present in a language.

Such a proposal raises the question of what (if any) prediction Harves & Kayne (2012)'s revised generalization makes about *have* and *need* in languages without Case. One possibility, discussed below, is that absent Case, incorporation of *need* is unrestricted by the absence of transitive HAVE.

Another approach to Case in Bantu emerged in the augment-drop discussion above. As we saw, Halpert (2012) argues against parameterizing Case in Bantu, attributing augment distribution patterns to Case-licensing. Crucially, this Case-licensing system is distinct from standard NOM-ACC licensing patterns: Halpert argues that augments and some prepositions give abstract Case to the nominals they mark and that abstract case is assigned to the highest element in *v*P. While it is unsurprising for prepositions to value Case features, the claim about Zulu is that only certain prepositions do so (as illustrated in the previous section). In addition, another surprising aspect of Halpert's proposal is that the augment, which is typically considered a DP-level prefix and not a preposition, also licenses nominals. Nominals without valuation in these ways are restricted to structural Case positions, which again differ in a standard NOM-ACC language, where T and v^0 are Case-licensers. Halpert proposes that Case is mediated by an intermediate phrase (LP), which licenses downward to the highest element in *v*P, accounting for patterns like those shown in §3.1. The result of this analysis is that Zulu Case, unlike ACC, is *not* connected to transitivity.

We do not attempt to resolve these differing approaches to Bantu Case here. Rather, we point out that the consistent thread throughout all preceding work on this issue is that Bantu Case is *not* business as usual. Whether one adopts a no-Case approach or a non-NOM/ACC approach, we argue in the next section that both in fact predict a similar pattern with respect to Harves & Kayne (2012)'s analysis of *have* and *need*.

3.3 Restating the generalization

We return now to the main problem that this Bantu data raises for Harves & Kayne (2012)'s account: predicative possession shows non-transitive behavior, despite the existence of transitive *need*. As discussed in the previous section, multiple proposals suggest that Case in Bantu is divorced from transitivity – either because there is no Case or because nominals are licensed by a projection above *v*P that is not linked to predicate type. This consensus holds even if we don't resolve the questions of Case-licensing in Swahili or Zulu (or Bantu more broadly) here.

We propose that on either approach, the Case properties of transitive objects and B-construction possessees are identical: either neither has Case, or both do (say, from Halpert's LP). Either way, this Case pattern is distinct from any traditional notion of accusative Case but uniform across predicative possession and transitive objects. The split that we demonstrated in section 2 between behavior of possessees and direct objects in syntactic tests for objecthood is expected because syntactic objecthood is divorced from structural case on either account. What we have available to us, then, is a modification of Harves & Kayne (2012)'s revised generalization in (10):

(26)   *Need*-Licensing Generalization:
       All languages that have a transitive verb corresponding to *need* are languages in
       which predicative possessees are licensed in the same manner as transitive objects.

Note that even if (26) accurately describes the current state of affairs, of course, it's not yet clear why it should be the case. The next subsection briefly discusses some ideas in this vein.

3.4 Thoughts on the derivation of *need*

Recall that for Harves & Kayne (2012), the role of ACC-assignment is closely tied to their proposed derivation of *need*: Transitive *need* occurs when the theme of a nominal *need* can get ACC Case. If the nominal *need* incorporates to a transitive *have*, the ACC from *have* is available for its theme.[8]

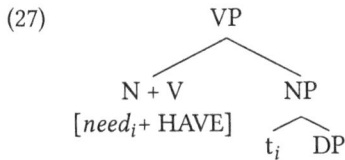

(27)

```
                VP
              /    \
        N + V        NP
    [needᵢ + HAVE]   /\
                   tᵢ  DP
```

We've argued, however, that transitivity has nothing to do with how themes are licensed in Bantu. The question that arises, of course, is: if our revised generalization regarding the relationship between *have* and *need* holds, how does a Case-less derivation of *need* fit into Harves & Kayne (2012)'s story? One possibility is that transitive *need* can be built directly by incorporating the nominal *need* into the (non-transitive) copular predicative possession construction. In other words, Harves & Kayne (2012)'s universal derivation for transitive *need* breaks down for the Bantu languages discussed here precisely because (accusative) Case-licensing is de-linked from transitivity. Transitive *have* is unnecessary for deriving *need* because the transitivity of *have* or HAVE is irrelevant for the licensing of the object of *need* due to the different Case-licensing properties of these languages. We suggest here, therefore, that transitive verbs can be derived from non-transitive components in this type of language if the incorporating nominal has its own theme: the theme can either be licensed by a higher head independent of transitivity of predicates (following Halpert 2012) or does not need to be licensed at all (Diercks 2012).

4 Conclusions

In this paper we have addressed recent discussion of the typological patterns surrounding the relationship between *have* and *need*. Following Antonov & Jacques (2014), we have shown that the typological generalizations proposed by Harves & Kayne (2012) do not hold up in the face of data from a variety of Bantu languages. Specifically, Zulu, Swahili and Kuria all are B-languages with lexical *need* verbs, contrary to the proposed generalization(s) of Harves & Kayne (2012). We moved beyond the evidence in Antonov & Jacques (2014) to provide new syntactic tests that show that the Zulu and Swahili counter-examples are in fact true counter-examples: B-possession is non-transitive while

---

[8]Under the assumption that incorporated nouns don't need Case, following Baker (1988)'s classic account: if transitive *have* is unattested elsewhere in the language, there's no base on which to build transitive *need*.

need patterns with other transitive verbs, ruling out the possibility that these languages are somehow covert H-languages.

While Antonov & Jacques (2014) conclude on the basis of similar evidence that the Harves & Kayne (2012) decompositional analysis of *need* is therefore incorrect and ought to be abandoned, we investigated a potential alternative route. In light of recent research suggesting deep differences between the properties of structural Case in Bantu and those of the languages discussed in Harves & Kayne (2012)'s original survey, we proposed the revised generalization in (26) that focuses not on *have* and *need* both assigning ACC case, but instead simply requires that *have* and *need* show the same structural licensing properties.

This proposal gives us a new set of empirical predictions. Antonov & Jacques (2014) discussed several additional languages (Estonian, Moroccan and Algerian Arabic; Likpe and Ewe from the Kwa family; and Ayacucho Quechua) that are surface counter-examples to Harves & Kayne (2012)'s generalizations. If our proposal is on the right track, these languages ought to show similar licensing properties between predicative possession and transitive *need*, even if they are not transparently related to ACC case on the surface. We see two potential outcomes of such investigations. The first is the same conclusion that Antonov & Jacques (2014) arrive at: if there are not underlying similarities in the licensing of objects of B-languages with a transitive lexical *need*, then Harves & Kayne (2012)'s generalization and our revised generalization proposed here may simply be inaccurate. If so, both versions should be abandoned, suggesting that we may not want a universal decomposition analysis of *need* after all.

Alternatively, we may find that the other exceptions to Harves & Kayne (2012)'s generalization noted by Antonov & Jacques (2014) are in fact rooted in underlying differences in structural licensing, as we have proposed for the Bantu languages discussed here. If this second possibility is borne out, then we may stand to uncover a deeper universal that underlies Harves & Kayne (2012)'s initial observations. In particular, if the predictions we discuss here are upheld, then Harves & Kayne (2012)'s generalizations (and our revision of them) point to some deep consistencies between languages (with with respect to the decomposition of *need*) that can be obscured by differences between languages with respect to structural licensing patterns. It is possible that this particular combination of traits that is problematic for Harves & Kayne (2012) – B-languages with transitive *need* – could ultimately be viewed as a diagnostic of underlying differences in structural licensing between Harves & Kayne (2012)'s languages and the 'exceptional' ones. These are of course empirical questions, meriting additional empirical investigation, though with potentially large theoretical import.

Acknowledgments

We would like to thank Johnes Kitololo, Justine Sikuku, Monwabisi Mhlophe, Mthuli Percival Buthelezi, and Tafadzwa Mtisi for lending their judgments to this project. Thanks also to Stephanie Harves, Richard Kayne, and Rodrigo Ranero, the audience at ACAL 45, and two anonymous reviewers for their helpful comments and suggestions.

References

Alsina, Alex. 2001. Is case another name for grammatical function? Evidence from object asymmetries. In William D. Davies & Stanley Dubinsky (eds.), *Objects and other subjects*, 77–102. Dordrecht: Kluwer Academic Publishers.

Antonov, Anton & Guillaume Jacques. 2014. Transitive NEED does not imply transitive HAVE: Response to Harves and Kayne 2012. *Linguistic Inquiry* 45(1). 147–158.

Baker, Mark C. 1988. *Incorporation*. Chicago, Illinois: University of Chicago Press.

Baker, Mark C. 2003. Agreement, dislocation, and partial configurationality. In Andrew Carnie, Heidi Harley & MaryAnn Willie (eds.), *Formal approaches to function in grammar*, 107–134. Amsterdam: John Benjamins.

Baker, Mark C. 2008. On the nature of the Antiagreement Effect: Evidence from wh-in-situ in Ibibio. *Linguistic Inquiry* 39(4). 615–632.

Bax, Anna & Michael Diercks. 2012. Information structure constraints on object marking in manyika. *Southern African Linguistics and Applied Language Studies* 30. 185–202.

Buell, Leston & Merijn de Dreu. 2013. Subject raising in Zulu and the nature of PredP. *The Linguistic Review* 30(3). 423–466.

Creissels, Denis. 2013. Control and the evolution of possessive and existential constructions. In Elly van Gelderen, Jóhanna Barðdal & Michela Cennamo (eds.), *Argument structure in flux. The Naples-Capri papers*, 461–476. Amsterdam: John Benjamins Publishing Company.

Diercks, Michael. 2012. Parameterizing case: Evidence from Bantu. *Syntax* 15(3). 253–286.

Halpert, Claire. 2012. Argument licensing & agreement in Zulu: MIT dissertation.

Harford Perez, Carolyn. 1985. *Aspects of complementation in three Bantu languages*. Madison, WI: University of Wisconsin-Madison dissertation.

Harves, Stephanie & Richard S. Kayne. 2012. Having 'need' and needing 'have'. *Linguistic Inquiry* 43(1). 120–132.

Kayne, Richard S. 2014. *Bisogna, need, and is To. The syntactic character of lexical gaps.* Handout, 8th Cambridge Italian Dialect Syntax-Morphology Meeting, Università di Padova. 15.

Marten, Lutz, Nancy Kula & Nhlanhla Thwala. 2007. Parameters of morpho-syntactic variation in Bantu. *Transactions of the Philological Society* 105(3). 253–338.

Ndayiragije, Juvénal. 1999. Checking economy. *Linguistic Inquiry* 30(3). 399–444.

Nguako, Nduvaa Erna. 2013. *The new otjiherero dictionary*. Bloomington, Indiana: Author-House.

Riedel, Kristina. 2009. *The syntax of object marking in Sambaa: A comparative Bantu perspective*. Leiden: Universiteit Leiden dissertation.

Zeller, Jochen. 2012. Object marking in Zulu. *Southern African Linguistics and Applied Language Studies* 30. 219–325.

Chapter 19

Structural transfer in third language acquisition: The case of Lingala-French speakers acquiring English

Philothé Mwamba Kabasele

University of Illinois at Urbana-Champaign, University of Calgary, Institut Superieur Pedagogique de la Gombe (RDC), University of KwaZulu-Natal

This paper tests the claims of Cumulative Enhancement Model, the 'L2 status factor', and the Typological Primacy Model in investigating how L1 Lingala, L2 French speakers express in English an event which took place and was completed in the past. The linguistic phenomena understudy informs us that English uses the simple past in a past-completed event while French and Lingala use the 'passé composé' and the remote or recent past, respectively. The study circumscribes the tense similarities and differences between the three languages.

The paper strives to answer the questions on which previously acquired language between the L1, L2, or both L1 & L2 overrides in L3 syntactic transfer. The paper aims to determine whether the L2 is the privileged source of syntactic transfer even when the L1 offers syntactic similarities with the L3. Finally, the study purports to determine whether subjects are more accurate when communicating in explicit mode than in implicit mode. That is, the study further aims to investigate whether subjects make less transfer errors in a task that promotes reliance on explicit knowledge than they do in task that promotes reliance on implicit knowledge.

The findings of the study show that subjects used the simple past tense in the context of a past-completed event. The use of the simple past tense in the context of a past-completed event might be attributed to transfer from the L1 or might be considered as a consequence of positive learning.

The results further show that subjects have transferred more explicit knowledge than implicit. And the results have ruled out the L2-status factor claim that the L2 is the privileged source of transfer in L3 acquisition.

1 Rationale

This paper tests the claims of the Cumulative Enhancement Model (CEM) by Flynn et al. (2004), the 'L2 status factor' by Bardel & Falk (2007), and the Typological Primacy Model

Philothé Mwamba Kabasele. Structural transfer in third language acquisition: The case of Lingala-French speakers acquiring English. In Jason Kandybowicz, Travis Major, Harold Torrence & Philip T. Duncan (eds.), *African linguistics on the prairie: Selected papers from the 45th Annual Conference on African Linguistics*, 307–323. Berlin: Language Science Press. DOI:10.5281/zenodo.1251744

(TPM) by Rothman (2010); Rothman (2011) in investigating how L1 Lingala L2 French speakers express in English an event which took place and was completed in the past.

The work aims to test the claims of those three models of L3 acquisition in terms of source of transfer and determine the factor, which takes precedence in determining the source of transfer when there is the potential for competition between multiple factors. The Cumulative Enhancement Model claims that previously acquired linguistic knowledge from both L1 and L2 positively impact the acquisition of any subsequent language. The 'L2 status factor' privileges and restricts the source of transfer from only the L2 while the Typological Primacy Model constrains transfer to the language that is perceived to be (psycho)-typologically closer to the L3.

The paper studies the population of twenty-five Lingala speakers who also speak French as L2 and who are learning English as L3, three languages of which two are Indo-European and one is a Bantu language. This is the first study, which combines those three languages in the context of third language acquisition.

The linguistic phenomena under study inform us that English uses the simple past to talk about an event which took place in the past and was completed in the past while French and Lingala use the 'passé composé' and the past (remote or recent past), respectively. For the sake of this study, the simple past (historical past) in French is not considered as a potential factor that can trigger transfer because as Rowlett (2007: 26) argues that changes in the spoken language in French have taken place in the use of the passé composé' in which the perfect is used instead of the past historic when talking about past completed event. Furthermore, with reference to the economy of cognitive design and linguistic architecture (Flynn et al. 2004; Rothman 2010) and in relation to the biological theory of language acquisition (Chomsky 2007), it is observed and documented that speakers of a language prefer the most economical linguistic option and this preference is hardwired into human cognition or better in the grammar of the language (Rothman 2010: 271). It is postulated in this paper that the L2-speaking French subjects would resort to the 'passé composé' to talk about a past completed event rather than the historical past (simple past) because the former is the option that is available to them and the parser would strongly and straightforwardly prefer the option which offers easier access.

Both French and English present some syntactic similarities in terms of form while they differ in terms of function. Their similarity is observed between the form of the 'present perfect tense' and the form of the 'passé compose' which are structured as 'AUX HAVE/AVOIR + PAST PARTICIPLE' in both languages. The differences are observed in their function; the 'passé composé' is used in French to talk about an event which took place and was completed in the past while the 'present perfect tense in English expresses an event that started in the past but has some implication in the present. Whereas, Lingala and English show some syntactic similarities in terms of both form and function because the simple past in both languages are used to talk about a past completed event and in terms of form both languages use inflectional morphemes to morpho-syntactically mark the past tense. The study circumscribes the similarities and differences, in tense, between the three languages.

The paper strives to answer the questions on which previously acquired language between the L1, L2, or both L1 & L2 overrides in L3 syntactic transfer. The paper aims to determine whether the L2 is the privileged source of syntactic transfer even when the L1 offers syntactic similarities with the L3. Finally, the study purports to determine whether subjects are more accurate when communicating in explicit mode than in implicit mode. That is, the study further aims to investigate whether subjects make less transfer errors in a task that promotes reliance on explicit knowledge than they do in task that promotes reliance on implicit knowledge. The predictions of the study permit to test the three models, specifically to test the descriptive and explanatory adequacies of the CEM, 'L2 status factor', and TPM.

Apart from the rationale and the conclusion, §2 is on the review of literature. §3 discusses the linguistic phenomenon that motivates the study. §4 provides the predictions and research questions of the study. §5 presents the design and methodology of the study. §6 is on the results while §7 presents the discussion on the findings of the paper.

2 Literature review

2.1 Transfer in L3 acquisition

Transfer in L3 varies depending on the domain and two languages are identified as source of transfer; the L1 or the L2. When a learner assumes that his L1 is closely related to the TL, there is a high likelihood for the L1 to trigger more transfer than when he assumes the opposite. Clearly, it is more probable to have less transfer when a learner assumes great linguistic distance between, say, his L1 and the TL in L3 acquisition. The speaker's perception of language similarity, which is psychological and does not necessarily reflect the actual linguistic distance between the languages, may trigger or constrain transfer in the acquisition of L3. Ringbom (2003) has restricted the importance of perceived typological distance in the transfer of lexis. When L2 and L3 offer a considerable number of common cognates, the speaker perceived both languages as similar and this psychotypological effect favors transfer.

2.2 Syntactic models in L3 acquisition

The three syntactic models in L3 acquisition agree upon the influence of, at least, one previously acquired language. They, however, depart from one another by the way they formulate their predictions.

2.2.1 Cumulative enhancement model (CEM)

The CEM (Flynn et al. 2004) claims that language learners rely on both their L1 and L2 cumulated linguistic knowledge when acquiring an additional language. This claim identifies language acquisition in a multilingual context as a cumulative process. The multilingual learner's reliance on the previously acquired linguistic knowledge is restricted to only transfer which has a noticeable rewarding impact in the learning process of the subsequent language. The previously acquired languages can positively contribute to the acquisition of a L3. The insistence of CEM on the sole beneficial effects of previous linguistic knowledge in the acquisition of an additional language implies a denial of negative transfer from previously acquired languages.

Flynn et al. (2004) ascertained that, "Language acquisition has a scaffolding effect" (Rothman 2010: 110). This means any previously acquired linguistic knowledge's role is twofold. It can either enhance the acquisition of any additional language or remain neutral. The impact of both L1 and L2 in the process of the acquisition of an additional language is relevant. The L2 contribution only supersedes that of L1 when, say, structure wise, the syntactic features which are in play are not available in the L1 linguistic system.

2.2.2 The L2 status factor

The 'L2 status factor' (Bardel & Falk 2007) privileges the L2; it argues that the L2 is the only linguistic system, which imposes its features onto the subsequent language. Bardel & Falk (2007) claim that the acquisition of the L3 is qualitatively different from those of the previously acquired languages because the linguistic knowledge of L2 plays a substantial role in facilitating the process (see also Hufeisen 1998; Cenoz & Jessner 2000; Cenoz 2001; 2003).

The claim, that the L2 is the strongest source of transfer in L3 acquisition stems from the findings of the studies by Bardel & Falk (2007) and Falk & Bardel (2011). The findings of this study were congruent with the claim that L2 is the strongest source of initial transfer in L3. In their recent paper, Falk & Bardel (2011), they studied the placement of object pronouns and their findings confirmed the privileged role of L2 in acquiring an L3.

2.2.3 Typological primacy model (TPM)

Rothman (2011: 233) stipulates, "Initial State transfer for multilingualism occurs selectively, depending on the comparative perceived typology of the language pairings involved or psychotypological proximity." The model argues that typological proximity or psychotypology constrains transfer to the L3. The prevailing role of typological similarity and its role as a crucial variable in the acquisition of an L3 are significant.

Transfer does not always happen in a facilitative fashion. TPM predicts that in a pair of previously acquired languages only the one, which offers typological proximity with the target language, serves as the source of transfer. TPM constrains transfer from two perspectives: the actual typological proximity or the perceived typological proximity, which is also called psychotypological proximity existing between the three grammars (García-Mayo & Rothman 2012: 19).

García-Mayo & Rothman (2012: 19) argue that, "At the initial state upon a limited amount of exposure to the target L3, the TPM proposes that the internal parser assesses relative typological proximity and selects which system should be transferred." The TPM is selective and conditionally non-facilitative. The parser selects the closest system to the TL. Any syntactic feature such as word order, tense similarity, or any other syntactic similarity depending on the case that is observed at the syntactic level may determine the selectivity of one of the competing previously acquired languages.

The criticism that is formulated against TPM addresses its apparent incapacity to predict the source of transfer when the languages at hand do not present any clear typological proximity. The TPM suggests that transfer can be non-facilitative when psychotypology conditions the transfer by matching and misanalysing the underlying syntax of L1 or L2. Should it be noted that TPM is not clear on the interpretation of 'typology'? The term is unclear and it lends itself to ambiguous interpretation. One can interpret it as referring to a specific linguistic structure, which is otherwise called for the sake of this paper 'local typology'; or one can also interpret it as referring to the whole language, which is called 'global typology'. For the sake of clarity in this study, I refer to typology as a specific linguistic structure or local typology.

3 The linguistic phenomenon

This section discusses and contrasts the use of the past tense, simple present, and the present perfect tense in the three aforementioned languages. The simple past exists in French, English, and Lingala while the form, "Aux (have/avoir) + past participle" exists only; form wise, in both French and English.

The present perfect tense in English is made up of the auxiliary "have" plus the past participle. This tense is similar in form to 'passé composé' in French, which is also made up of the auxiliary "avoir" (have) plus the past participle. The present perfect and the 'passé composé' tenses present the same formal paradigm but differ in terms of their function.

The present perfect tense is always used in English to talk about a past until now event while the 'passé composé' in French is often used to express a past-completed event. Syntactic change has taken place in French in which the 'passé composé' is used instead of the past historic to express a past-completed event. At this point, I can claim that the English present perfect tense is similar to French 'passé composé' with respect to form but it does not exist in Lingala. Therefore, different tenses are used to express the same idea but in a different language. For instance, in English, the present perfect tense is used with expressions like 'the first time', 'the second time', since, for, etc., while in French and Lingala the present and the immediate past are respectively used.

The simple past tense is used in English to talk about events which took place in the past and when the time period is completed. In French and Lingala the 'passé composé' and the past are respectively used. In Lingala, an appropriate past tense form needs to be selected depending on whether the event was completed in the recent past or in the distant past. Example (1) illustrates the case.

(1) English simple past
    Joe bought a car last year.

(2) French passé composé
     Joe a   acheté une voiture l'   année passé.
     Joe has bought a   car   the year past
     'Joe bought a car last year.'

(3) Lingala recent past
     Joe a-   somb -aki   mutuka mbula eleki.
     Joe 1pssva buy   rec.pst car   year   past
     'Joe bought a car last year.'

Tables 1 and 2 summarize tenses in these three languages.

Table 1: Past event that was completed in the past.

	Tense	Example	Gloss
English	Simple past	*Andy went to Paris last month.*	
French	Passé composé	*Andy est parti à Paris le mois passé.*	'Andy went to Paris last month.'
Lingala	Remote past	*Andy akendáká na Paris bambula eleka.*	'Andy went to Paris years ago.'
	Recent past	*Andy akendaki na Paris sanza eleki.*	'Andy went to Paris last month.'

Table 2: Past event with connection in the present.

	Tense	Example	Gloss
English	Present perfect	*Nathan has lived in Urbana since 2011.*	
French	Indicatif present (Simple present)	*Nathan vit à Urbana depuis 2011.*	'Nathan has lived in Urbana since 2011.'
Lingala	Past (Immediate past)	*Nathan afandi na Urbana banda 2011.*	'Nathan has lived in Urbana since 2011.'

In this paper, my attention is first focused on past-completed event whereby the simple past is used in English while the 'Passé composé' and remote/recent past are used in French and Lingala respectively. The linguistic phenomenon which is the focus of the predictions in this study informs us that both the 'present perfect' in English and the 'passé composé' in French present form similarities in terms of their syntactic structure which is "the auxiliary have + the past participle" but they diverge in terms of their function. The 'passé composé' is used to express a past-completed event while the 'present perfect tense' is used to express a past until now event. The 'passé simple' in French will not transfer because it is marked and is hardly used in spoken communication; it is a tense that is used by highly educated people in literary discourse.

Second, my interest is oriented to past until now event in which the present perfect tense is used in English while for the same event, French uses the simple present tense but Lingala uses the (immediate) past.

4 Predictions and research questions

The predictions of this paper are organized as such: Based on the TPM which claims that only the language with syntactic proximity with the TL serves as the source of transfer, the study posits that if subjects are tapping their linguistic knowledge from the L1 to talk about a past completed event in English they will use the simple past tense. This tense choice will be triggered by the local syntactic similarity in terms of form between the simple past in English and the remote/ recent past in Lingala in the context of a past-completed event.

Transfer occurs because subjects make an interlingual identification; they perceive and judge that the form of the syntactic structure of the remote/recent past in Lingala is similar to the form of the syntactic structure of the simple past tense in English. It is also the form of the syntactic structure of the simple past in English, which has invited the perception of the similarity between the forms of the sentences in both languages. Transfer is triggered by the psychotypological constraint, which enables subjects to perceive similarity between the two tenses. This similarity is observed at the level of form of the tenses. It is hence clear that the syntactic structure of a previously acquired language is susceptible to transfer as Jarvis (2010: 174) puts it, "only if it is perceived to have a similar counterpart in the recipient language." The perception of the similarity is not only observed on the surface level but subjects' perception of the similarity at the psychological level plays also a role for transfer to occur.

With reference to the "L2-status factor" model which claims that the L2 is the strongest source of transfer in L3 acquisition and that the L2 blocks any syntactic transfer from the L1 syntactic system, the study posits that if subjects are tapping their linguistic knowledge from the L2 to talk about a past completed event in English they will use the present perfect tense. As discussed earlier, the 'passé simple' in French will not transfer because it is marked and is hardly used in spoken communication. It is a tense that is used by highly educated people in literary discourse and it has been replaced by the 'passé composé'.

Based on the CEM which claims that learners rely on their cumulated linguistic knowledge from both L1 and L2 as source of transfer and that transfer is only positive or null;

the study posits that if subjects are tapping their linguistic knowledge from both L1 and L2 to talk about a past completed event in English they will use the simple past tense.

In light of the decisive factors, closeness between the L1 Lingala and L3 English (in form) but difference in 'form' between the L2 (passé compose) and L3 (simple past) and the aforementioned predictions, the work seeks to answer the following questions: Which previously acquired language between the L1, L2, or both L1 & L2 takes precedence in L3 syntactic transfer? Is the L2 the privileged source of syntactic transfer even when the L1 offers some syntactic similarities with the L3? Answers to these concerns will shed light on my study.

5 Design and methodology

5.1 Subjects

Twenty-five adult Congolese immigrants who live in the USA participated in the study. The average age when they started to be exposed to English is 15 years old and their average length of residence in the USA is 3 years. Most of them acquired French through instructional exposure at school and their average length of exposure through formal instruction in French is 4 years. They also formally learned English as a school subject.

All the subjects grew up in Kinshasa and attended school in the same setting. They are all native speakers of Lingala who also speak French as an official language. The latter is used as an official language and as the language of instruction from elementary school upward. French was also learned as a school subject whereby emphasis was made on the grammar of French. English was exclusively learned as a school subject. Subjects started taking English from ninth grade of high school up to twelfth grade. However, English was heavily taught structurally. Little attention was paid to other language basic skills. Therefore, students completed the high school program with very poor speaking, reading, writing, and listening skills. They all have at least a high school state diploma from the Democratic Republic of the Congo. Subjects are, however, exposed to English in the USA on a daily basis at work place, stores, and public places. They tend to interact in Lingala whenever they meet with other Congolese fellows.

Subjects with advanced level of proficiency in English could hold a long conversation of approximately ten minutes in English. They exhibited oral fluency but with a few grammatical errors. They could ask clarification questions and could answer questions on social life topics with certain ease. Intermediate proficiency level subjects could ask questions with hesitation and were able to hold an intelligible interaction despite some observed limitation they displayed in vocabulary. They made random language errors, which sometimes could lead to communication breakdown. Beginner subjects had limited English proficiency level. They had significant amount of difficulty in the four basic language skills. They were hesitant in their speech and their grammar was poor. Subjects were administered a cloze test to determine their proficiency level in English.

The control group was made up of five American native speakers of English. All the five subjects grew up in the USA and have been exposed to English since birth. They all have at least a high school degree and had taken at least a foreign language at school.

5.2 Task and procedure

I administered the interview and the written elicitation task to the subjects to collect the data of the study. The interview was always administered prior to the written elicitation task an each subject took both tasks on the same day. Subjects were interviewed in English and the interview, which was audio recorded elicited the data through oral mode of interaction and under time pressure. I used the smartphone Alcatel one touch to record the interviews. Whereas, the written elicitation task aimed to elicit data through the written mode of communication and allowed enough time to subjects to express themselves. Obviously, the interview elicited the data through the implicit mode while the written elicitation task did so through the explicit mode. All the questions were used only once in each task. They were never repeated in another task. All the interviews were recorded and then transcribed.

The interview was related to past-completed event. It aimed to elicit verb tense forms in the simple past (questions 1 and 3). The future (question 4) was used as a distractor in the study. The questions aimed to trigger a specific verb tense in the speech production of each subject. The simple past category had two questions while the future category had only one question. The question related to the future was a distractor. For the sake of this study, after analysis of the questions, only questions 1 and 3 were reported. Data related to question 2 would be incorporated in the larger project, which is related to this study. Question 4 was not reported because it was a distractor. The following are the interview questions: Tell me about something that you remember from your life in Congo? Tell me about your two big accomplishments in the last six months? Tell me about your first arrival in the USA? Tell me about something that you would like to do in six months? All the four interview questions were asked in the same order prior to handing out the written elicitation task to the subjects.

Later on in the analysis of the interview, three coders determined the obligatory contexts in which the simple past tense had to be used. I was the first coder. Then, two other coders who were native speakers of English contributed with their expertise. The native speakers were teachers of English who were trained as teachers of English to speakers of other languages or linguists. The coding was first done separately. And then, all the three coders came together to discuss some minor differences, which were observed.

However, the written elicitation task had 24 questions. The task was organized into a category of six items. The targeted category was the simple past tense and the present perfect tense; the future, the simple present and the present progressive were distractors. In this study, only the category of items that are related to the use of the simple past tense are reported and data related to the use of the present perfect tense will be reported in the other parts of the whole projects. All the instructions were given in English.

5.3 Proficiency test

The proficiency of the subjects was determined through the administration of the cloze test. The cloze test was an adaptation from the American Kernel Lessons that was drawn from the Advanced Students' Book by O'Neill et al. (1981). The cloze test provided blanks with three options of which subjects had to choose one in order to fill in the blank space with the option s/he deemed as the correct answer. The results of the test divided the subjects into three proficiency groups: beginning, intermediate, and advanced levels with the scores varying between 18 to 24, 25 to 29, and 30 to 37 respectively. Beside the cloze test, subjects were also administered the language learning history in order to elicit their language learning background, their personal data, and the family linguistic history.

6 Results

Discussing the results of the paper, the first task was the interview while the second was the written elicitation and the results are presented in tables, which quantify the former with respect to the category of items. The columns present the required context in which a given tense was expected to be used (this is the target tense), the prediction(s) to the category of items, i.e., the various tenses which were predicted, and finally the unexpected answers which were called "Other verbal forms".

The inferential statistics was conducted to compare the control group's use of the simple past and present perfect tense with the 3 proficiency groups that is, beginner, intermediate, and advanced groups in the context of past-completed event. Its goal was to determine whether the control group's use of the simple past and present perfect tense in the aforementioned contexts was significantly different from that of beginner, intermediate, and advanced groups respectively. Moreover, it also aimed to help draw sound decisions therefore on whether the use of the simple past and the present perfect tense by the 3 proficiency groups could be attributed to transfer or not.

Although the goal of this study was to examine the kinds of forms that subjects used in different circumscribed contexts rather than merely focusing on comparing the different groups in the study, I hope that inferential statistics will also contribute in inducing sound decisions on the interpretation of the results.

Table 3: Response types to interview eliciting the context of past completed event (Task 1).

	Simple past		Present perfect		Simple present		Other verbal forms	
	N	%	N	%	N	%	N	%
Beginner	66	64.7	0	0	36	35.2	0	0
Intermediate	140	79.0	0	0	35	19.7	2	1.1
Advanced	162	92.5	0	0	13	7.4	0	0
Control	41	95.3	2	4.6	0	0	0	0

A one-way ANOVA was conducted to compare the control group with the 3 proficiency groups with respect to the use of the simple past tense in the context of past-completed event whereby the use of the simple past tense expressed in percentage was the dependent variable and the groups the independent variables. The ANOVA reveals that there

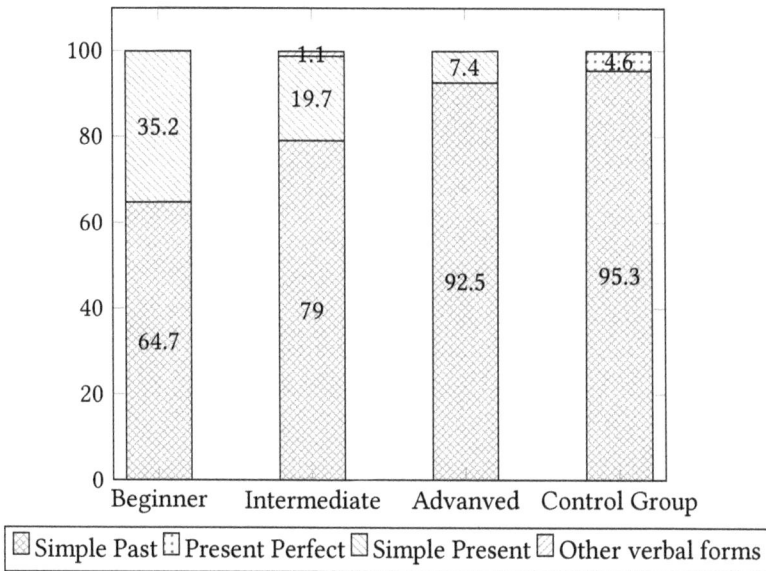

Figure 1: Interview eliciting the context of past completed event.

were no significant differences between the control group and the 3 proficiency groups [F (3, 29) = 2.36, p=.094]. A word of caution should be mentioned that given the small sample size in this study, I suspect that the small sample size might have impacted the statistical power to reach the significant difference between the control group and the 3 proficiency groups.

Table 4: Response types to the written elicitation task on past completed event (Task 2).

	Simple past		Present perfect		Simple present		Other verbal forms	
	N	%	N	%	N	%	N	%
Beginner	40	74	0	0	2	3.7	12	22.2
Intermediate	49	90.7	4	7.4	0	0	1	1.8
Advanced	41	97.6	1	2.3	0	0	0	0
Control	30	100	0	0	0	0	0	0

A one-way ANOVA was conducted to compare the control group with the 3 proficiency groups with respect to the use of the simple past tense in the context of past-completed event whereby the use of the simple past tense expressed in percentage was the dependent variable and the groups the independent variables. The ANOVA reveals that there

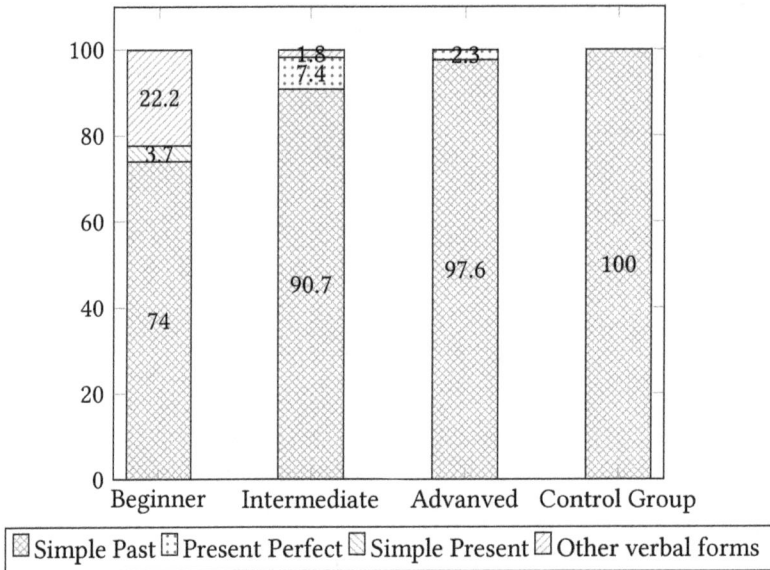

Figure 2: Written elicitation task on past completed event.

were no significant differences between the control group and the 3 proficiency groups [F (3, 29) =2.17, p=.11]. As mentioned earlier, the small sample size in this study might have impacted the statistical power to reach the significant difference between the control group and the 3 proficiency groups.

7 Discussion

Both the TPM and CEM predicted that subjects will use, to talk about past completed event, the simple past tense as a result of respectively transfer from the L1 which shows syntactic proximity with the TL and transfer from both the L1 and L2 as a result of cumulated knowledge. The "L2- status factor" predicted that subjects will use the present perfect tense in the aforementioned context.

In the present study, I investigated structural transfer in third language acquisition. In the interview and written elicitation tasks dealing with past-completed event the results showed that subjects used the simple past tense in the context of past-completed event. The results are contrasted with the predictions of the study in Table 5.

Referring to the context of past-completed event, the results raise the question of knowing whether the use of the simple past tense by the subjects in the context was due to transfer from the previously acquired languages or whether it was the result of successful acquisition of the tense in the L3. The results of the inferential statistics, which I take with reserve, in relation to the use of the simple past tense in the context of past completed event in both tasks, that is, the interview and the written elicitation

Table 5: Predictions and results of the study.

Context	L1 Transfer	L2 Transfer	L1 & L2 Transfer	English
Past completed event	Simple past (TPM)	Present perfect (L2 status factor)	Simple past (CEM)	Simple past

task fairly shows that there were no significant differences between the control and the 3 proficiency groups. In both the interview and the written elicitation task, the ANOVA showed respectively that there was no significant differences between the control group and the 3 proficiency groups [F (3, 29) = 2.36, p= .094] and [F (3, 29) = 2.17, p= .11]. However, because of the small sample size of the study, the inferential statistics is not taken into consideration because I suspect that the small sample size of the study might have affected the statistical power to reach the significant difference between the control group and the 3 proficiency groups, yet numerically the difference between those groups are obvious.

Referring to the descriptive statistics, specifically to the numerical results as they are depicted on table 5 and 6, there seem to be obvious differences between the control group and the 3 proficiency groups. It is likely that subjects are tapping their linguistic knowledge from the L1 to express in the TL an event, which took place in the past and was completed in the past. However, the possibility of interpreting the results as a consequence of learning from the input is still open because if the use of the simple past tense was solely attributed to transfer effects, we could expect to have more transfer with beginners than with advanced proficiency groups.

Considering the transfer option, the results suggest that when an L1 offers some syntactic similarities with the TL, its (L1) syntactic system becomes transparent and thus accessible to the learners. This finding challenges the claims of the L2 status factor, which postulate that the L2 blocks, the access to the syntactic system of the L1. I assume that the L2 blocks access to the L1 syntactic system only when the latter does not display any similarities with the syntactic system of the TL.

Should it be mentioned that it is not clear whether transfer from the L1 was due to the effects of previously cumulated linguistic knowledge or just a matter of syntactic proximity which was observed between the two linguistic systems. With reference to the numerical results on the aforementioned tables, I suspect that L1 transfer into the TL in this study was triggered by the syntactic proximity. The great number of simple past tense use by advanced learners in the context of past-completed event shows that there was positive transfer or positive learning as I will discuss it later in this section. However, the high use of the simple present tense by beginners at the rate of 35.2% and by intermediate learners at the rate of 19.7% implies that those learners are using the simple past tense but they just fail to inflect the verb with the appropriate past tense inflectional morpheme. The proficiency factor boosts and ameliorates the access to the syntactic system of the L1.

The other reading of the results attributes subjects' performance to learning. It is likely that the use of the simple past tense in the past-completed context may be due to learning. It might further be interpreted that subjects successfully learned the use of the simple past tense in past completed event context and that the occurrence of simple present tense use in this context might be just attributed to failure to append the simple past tense inflectional morpheme to the verb stem since subjects have not mastered the morphology inherent to the simple past tense yet.

Furthermore, contrasting their performance in interview versus written elicitation task with reference to subjects' use of the simple present tense in the context of past completed event, it is observed that in the interview whereby subjects had to resort to their implicit knowledge due to time pressure they made more omission errors than in the written elicitation task which required explicit knowledge. The rate of omission errors was decreasing and correlated with the level of proficiency: beginners 35.2%, intermediate 19.7%, and advanced 7.4%. Whereas, in the written elicitation task, beginners' rate of omission errors was relatively low, i.e., 3.7% while intermediate and advanced subjects did not make any omission error at all. The type of knowledge one resorted to can account for this difference. In the interview, subjects did not have enough time to think and readjust their speech as they were being interviewed while in the case of written elicitation task, subjects had more time to prepare their answers and to observe that there was an inflectional morpheme missing and they could self-correct their mistakes by appending the omitted simple past tense inflectional morpheme to the verb form.

Figure 1 depicts, in a stairs-like manner, how the use of the simple past tense correlates with the level of proficiency. Inversely, it also depicts how the occurrence of the simple past tense inflectional morpheme omission errors correlates with the same level of proficiency. This reinforces the option that subjects are at a learning stage whereby they have learned that the simple past tense should be used in the context of past-completed event but they are still struggling with inflecting the verb with the appropriate morphological marker, which will express and mark the simple past tense.

The use of the simple present tense in this context could be justified as the result of error of inflectional morpheme omission. This could imply that subjects made positive transfer but just failed to appropriately inflect the verbs in the past tense. Subjects need more time to reinforce the learning of function/use of the simple past tense which seems to be acquired but mostly to digest and control the appropriate morphological form to append in order to fully acquire the tense.

With reference to the prediction related to past-completed event, the use of the simple past tense by the subjects is the result of positive transfer. The use of the simple present tense in this context is considered as the result of error of the simple past tense inflectional morpheme omission.

In light of the research questions which sought to determine the language that takes precedence as source of syntactic transfer in L3 acquisition, the research question which aimed to determine whether the L2 syntactic system blocks the syntactic transfer even when the L1 offers some syntactic similarities with the L3, the interpretation of the results could be twofold. With reference to the inferential statistics, the latter did not have enough statistical power to determine the difference between the control group and the three proficiency groups. The statistical power was affected and weakened by the small sample size of the subjects. However, because of the small sample size in the study, which might have affected the statistical power, one can consider looking at the descriptive statistics, particularly the numerical results as they are presented on table 5 and 6. Numerically, it is obvious that there was transfer. Responding to the question 'Which previously acquired language between the L1, L2, or both L1 & L2 takes precedence in L3 syntactic transfer' the answer would be that transfer came from the L1.

Answering the second question which aimed to determine whether the L2 was the privileged source of syntactic transfer even when the L1 offers some syntactic similarities with the L3, the answer would be no. The L2 does not serve as the privileged source of transfer when the L1 offers syntactic similarity with the L3.

Finally, attempting to answer the question of knowing whether subjects have more and easy access to their implicit knowledge than the explicit knowledge and therefore transfer more explicit knowledge than the implicit one when tapping linguistic knowledge from a previously acquired linguistic system, the results have shown that subjects are more accurate when given the opportunity to use their explicit knowledge. This finding corroborates with those of previous studies whereby it was attested that subjects were more accurate when in explicit mode than in implicit one (Schmidt 2001; 1995; Leow 1998; Robinson 1997). It should, however, be noted that the erroneous use of the simple present tense in the context of past completed event was mostly observed in the context of implicit task. This shows and might imply that learners are linguistically unsecured when in implicit mode and thus they become inaccurate when they rely upon implicit knowledge in their use of the target language.

8 Conclusion

The findings of the study attribute the use of the simple past tense in the context of past-completed event to positive transfer. However, the possibility of attributing the results to positive learning is also to consider since inferential statistics did not reach any significance differences. The findings of inferential statistics were discarded because they were affected by the small sample size and thus could not determine significant difference between the control and the 3 proficiency groups.

The use of the simple present tense, in the context of past-completed event, which cannot be accounted for by transfer in this context is the result of omission of the simple past tense inflectional morpheme. This failure by the subjects to append the simple past inflectional morpheme to the verb to express the simple past tense shows that subjects have not fully acquired the morphology inherent to the simple past tense and this was mostly observed in implicit task.

The study has further shown that subjects were more accurate in using their explicit than implicit knowledge. They also made more positive transfer from explicit knowledge than from implicit one. The use of the simple past tense in the past completed event context could possibly suggest that the learners only know one way to discuss events that happened in the past using the simple past.

I envisage replicating this study with a representative number of subjects in order to avoid any negative implication on the statistical power. I will integrate the comprehension aspect of language transfer to have a full understanding of both production and comprehension. I further project to present a hierarchical matrix of potential factors which can trigger transfer and rank them in pairs, triplet or in quadruplet depending on the factors which will be controlled.

References

Bardel, Camilla & Yehuda Falk. 2007. The role of the second language in third language acquisition: The case of Germanic syntax. *Second Language Research* 23. 459–484.

Cenoz, Jasone. 2001. The effect of linguistic distance, l2 status and age on cross-linguistic influence in third language acquisition. In Jasone Cenoz, Britta Hufeisen & Ulrike Jessner (eds.), *Cross-linguistic influence in third language acquisition: Psycholinguistic perspectives*, 8–20. Clevedon: Multilingual Matters.

Cenoz, Jasone. 2003. The additive effect of bilingualism on third language acquisition: A review. *International Journal of Bilingualism* 7. 71–87.

Cenoz, Jasone & Ulrike Jessner (eds.). 2000. *English in Europe: The acquisition of a third language*. Clevedon: Multilingual Matters.

Chomsky, Noam. 2007. Of minds and language. *Biolinguistics* 1. 9–27.

Falk, Yehuda & Camilla Bardel. 2011. Object pronouns in German L3 syntax. Evidence for the L2 status factor. *Second Language Research* 27. 59–82.

Flynn, Suzanne, Claire Foley & Inna Vinnitskaya. 2004. The cumulative-enhancement model for language acquisition: Comparing adults' and children's patterns of development in first, second and third language acquisition. *International Journal of Multilingualism* 1. 3–17.

García-Mayo, Maria P. & Jason Rothman. 2012. L3 morphosyntax in the generative tradition: The initial stages and beyond. In Jennifer C. Amaro, Suzanne Flynn & Jason Rothman (eds.), *Third language acquisition in adulthood*, 9–32. Amsterdam: John Benjamins.

Hufeisen, Britta. 1998. L3 – Stand der Forschung – Was bleibt zu tun? In Britta Hufeisen & Beate Lindemann (eds.), *Tertiärsprachen. Theorien, Modelle, Methoden*, 169–183. Tübingen: Stauffenburg.

Jarvis, Scott. 2010. Comparison-based and detection-based approaches to transfer research. In Leah Roberts, Martin Howard, Muiris Ó Laoire & David Singleton (eds.), *EUROSLA Yearbook 10*, 169–192. Amsterdam: Benjamins.

Leow, Ronald P. 1998. Toward operationalizing the process of attention in second language acquisition: Evidence for Tomlin and Villa's (1994) fine-grained analysis of attention. *Applied Psycholinguistics* 19. 133–159.

O'Neill, Robert, Edwin T. Cornelius & Gay N. Washburn. 1981. *American kernel lessons, AKl: Advanced*. New York: Longman.

Ringbom, Hakan. 2003. *If you know Finnish as L2, there will be no major problem learning Swahili.* Paper presented at the International Conference on Trilingualism and Third Language Acquisition, Tralee, Ireland, September 4-6.

Robinson, Peter. 1997. Generalizability and automaticity of second language learning under implicit, incidental, enhanced, and instructed conditions. *Studies in Second Language Acquisition* 19(2). 223–247.

Rothman, Jason. 2010. On the typological economy of syntactic transfer: Word order and relative clause attachment preference in L3 Brazilian Portuguese. *International Review of Applied Linguistics* 48. 245–274.

Rothman, Jason. 2011. L3 syntactic transfer selectivity and typological determinacy: The typological primacy model. *Second Language Research* 27. 107–127.

Rowlett, Paul. 2007. *The syntax of French.* Cambridge: Cambridge.

Schmidt, Richard. 1995. Consciousness and foreign language learning: A tutorial on the role of attention and awareness in learning. In Richard Schmidt (ed.), *Attention and awareness in foreign language learning* (Technical Report 9), 1–64. Honolulu: University of Hawaii.

Schmidt, Richard. 2001. Attention. In Peter Robinson (ed.), *Cognition and second language instruction*, 3–32. Cambridge: Cambridge University Press.

Chapter 20

Adjectives in Lubukusu

Aggrey Wasike

University of Toronto

The lexical category of adjectives is proposed to be universal, but its realization varies across languages. In languages such as English, there is a clearly distinct category of adjectives. But in other languages the category of adjectives is not entirely distinct morphologically and syntactically from nouns and verbs. In this paper I show that there is a striking resemblance between adjectives and nouns in Lubukusu. In addition, stage-level predicate meanings are expressed by use of verbs rather than adjectives. Because of these facts, it is tempting to adopt an analysis that reduces Lubukusu adjectives to either nouns or verbs. However, I argue that there is not sufficient evidence to support such an analysis. Lubukusu has true adjectives in spite of the associated nominal and verbal characteristics. A verbal characteristic such as expressing adjectival meanings by use verbs is similar to languages such Mohawk and Vaeakau-Taumako. But there are significant differences between these languages and Lubukusu with regards to this verbal characteristic.

1 Introduction

This paper discusses adjectives in Lubukusu, a Bantu language spoken in Western Kenya. This discussion is particularly useful considering the fact that there is disagreement among linguists on the status of adjectives as a universal category. For linguists such as Mark Baker and R. M. W. Dixon, the lexical category of adjectives is universal (Baker 2001; 2003; Dixon & Aikhenvald 2004). But for R. M. W. Dixon in his earlier work and Chafe Wallace, the category of adjectives is not universal (Dixon 1982; Chafe 2012). Description and discussion of how adjectival meanings are expressed in different languages can help linguists draw a valid conclusions regarding the category of adjectives.

The lack of agreement on the status of adjectives as a universal category among linguists is attributed to cross-linguistic variation in the expression of adjectival meanings. Some languages express adjectival meanings by use of adjectives while others express similar meanings by use of verbs and nouns. Even those languages that have a distinct class of adjectives differ from each other in terms of the properties of adjectives: in some languages, adjectives "may share at least some of their morpho-syntactic behavior with nouns, in others they may have more in common with verbs, and still in others they may

Aggrey Wasike. Adjectives in Lubukusu. In Jason Kandybowicz, Travis Major, Harold Torrence & Philip T. Duncan (eds.), *African linguistics on the prairie: Selected papers from the 45th Annual Conference on African Linguistics*, 325–339. Berlin: Language Science Press.
DOI:10.5281/zenodo.1251746

be more or less independent of those other classes" (Chafe 2012: 1). Languages that have a distinct category of adjectives can also differ in terms of adjective inventory: some, such as English, have a large number of adjectives. In fact adjectives in English constitute an open class. But other languages have a closed set of adjectives. An example of such a language is Hausa which has approximately 12 adjectives (Whaley 1997).

As has already been pointed out, some languages lack a distinct category of adjectives. Instead they express adjectival meanings by use of either verbs or nouns. Examples of languages which use verbs to express adjectival meanings include Mohawk (Baker 2001), Seneca and other northern Iroquoian languages (Chafe 2012), Manipuri (Bhat 1994) and Mayali. To illustrate how a languages use verbs to express adjectival meanings consider sentences in (1) and (2) from Manipuri and Seneca respectively.

(1) a. Manipuri (Bhat 1994: 190)
    əy mabu   u-de
    I   him-ACC see-NEG(NFUT)

    'I did not see him.'

  b. phi ədu ŋaŋ-de
    cloth that red-NEG(NFUT)

    'That cloth is not red.'

(2) a. Seneca (Chafe 2012: 10)
    Tganöhso:t,   CIS-N.SG.AGT -building-upright-STA
    t-ka-nöhs-o:t-ø

    'The house there,'

  b. ganöhsasdë.   N.SG.AGT -building-big-STA
    ka-nöhs-astë-:

    'it was a big house.'

Notice that in these languages words that express adjectival meanings take inflectional morphology of verbs such as negation in (1).

An example of a language that uses nouns to express adjectival meanings is Quechua. In this language words that express adjectival meanings take nominal inflectional morphology such as case. This is illustrated in (3).

(3) a. Peru Quechua (Weber 1983: 6)
    rumi-ta   rikaa
    stone-ACC 1SG.see

    'I see a/the stone.'

  b. hatun-ta rikaa
    big-ACC 1SG-see

    'I see a/the big (one).'

Given the cross-linguistic variability illustrated above, it is understandable why linguists would fail to agree on whether the category of adjective is universal or not. Clearly, studying how adjectival meanings are expressed in languages that have not been studied yet is important as it can improve our understanding of adjectives.

In this paper, I show how adjectival meanings are expressed in Lubukusu. Questions that I seek to answer include, though not limited to the following: How are adjectival meanings expressed in Lubukusu? Is Lubukusu English-like, Mohawk-like or Quechua-like? How similar or different is Lubukusu from other languages? What nominal and verbal features do words that express adjectival meanings have? Why shouldn't Lubukusu adjectives be considered nouns?

I show that Lubukusu has pure adjectives like English, but it not exactly like English in all respects. This is because there are certain adjectival meanings that are expressed by use of verbs just like in Mohawk, Seneca, Mayali and Manipuri. Thus Lubukusu has a mixed adjectival system. I also show that that although adjectives are structurally similar to nouns, they constitute a lexical category that is distinct. Similarly, although certain adjectival meanings are expressed by use of verbs, it is cannot be true to argue that Lubukusu lacks adjectives.

This paper is organized as follows. §2 is a general description of adjectives in Lubukusu that recognizes two major subtypes of adjectives: basic adjectives and derived adjectives. §3 describes and discusses nominal features of adjectives focusing on morphological and syntactic features. §4 is a discussion of verbal features of adjectives. I show that only stage-level readings of predicates are expressed by use of verbs in Lubukusu. §5 is the conclusion.

2 Overview of adjectives in Lubukusu

Adjectives are nominal modifiers, and as illustrated in (4) they can occur in a Noun Phrase (NP) with other modifiers such as numerals, possessive pronouns, demonstratives, associative Prepositional Phrases (PP) and relative clauses.

(4) Lubukusu
ba[1]-ba-ana ba-taru ba-nge baa-bofu be lii-ria baa-kon-a ba-no
2-2[2]-person 2-three 2-mine 2.2-big of 5.5-respect 2.REL-sleep-FV 2-DEM
'these three big respectful children of mine who are sleeping'

Because of the constraints of space numerals, possessive pronouns, associative PPs and relative clauses are not discussed in this paper. I have also not discussed word in the NP. Instead I have focused on adjectives only, without reference to the other noun modifiers.

Adjectives in Lubukusu can be divided into two broad categories: basic adjectives and derived adjectives.

---

[2]Orthographic B or b is [β] when it is not preceded by a nasal sound
[2]In the sequence of these numerals here and in the rest of the paper, the first numeral is the pre-prefix (augment); the second numeral is class prefix

2.1 Basic adjectives

These are adjectives that are base generated and are not derived from other lexical categories. Basic adjectives describe size, color, quantity etc. and include -*bofu* 'big', -*titi* 'small', -*leyi* 'tall', -*imbi* 'short', -*balayi* 'wide', -*mali* 'black', -*wanga* 'white', -*besemu* 'red', -*kali* 'many', -*lendafu* 'stupid', -*kesi* 'clever', -*silu* 'stupid', -*kara* 'lazy', -*miliu* 'clean', -*nyalu* 'dirty', -*siro* 'heavy', -*angu* 'light', -*chou* 'big/fully grown', -*khulu* 'old', -*bisi* 'raw/ unripe', -*robe* 'ripe' etc.

2.2 Derived adjectives

Lubukusu has a very productive process of deriving adjectives from verbs. The process involves suffixing the root of the verb with the vowel -*e*[3]. In other words the final vowel of the verb root is replaced with the vowel -*e*. This suggests that -*e* is an 'adjectivizing' suffix. Derived adjectives ending in -*e* include-*funge* 'closed' (from *funga* 'close'), -*funule* 'open' (from *funula*[4] 'open'), -*funikhe* 'covered' (from *funikha* 'cover'), -*singe* 'washed' (from *singa* 'wash'), -*tekhe* 'cooked' (from *tekha* 'cook'), -*lekhule* 'free' (from *lekhula* 'free/let go'), -*khalange* 'fried' (from *khalanga* 'fry'), -*robe* 'ripe' (from *roba* 'become ripe'), -*simbe* 'busy' (from *simba* 'become busy'), -*lume* 'hard' (from *luma* 'become hard'), -*sye* 'ground' (from *sya* 'grind'), -*ake* 'weeded' (from *yaka* 'weed'), -*male* 'smeared' (from *mala* 'smear'), -*chichunge* 'sifted' (from *chichunga* 'sift'), -*osye* 'roasted' (from *yosya* 'roast') etc.

The derivation of adjectives from verbs with roots that end in liquids (/l/ & /r/) and the voiceless fricative (/x/) involve phonological processes that are different from -e final derived adjectives illustrated in the previous paragraph. To form adjectives from these verbs, the root final liquids and /x/ are changed into fricatives – either [f] or [s] and the final vowel is changed to [u] or [i]. Adjectives formed in this manner include: -*mesi* 'drunk' (from *mela* 'become drunk'), -*changalafu* 'insipid' (from *changalala* 'be dull, insipid, tasteless), -*randafu* 'brown' (from *randara* 'become brown', -*lendafu* 'stupid, slow' (from *lendala* 'be stupid, be slow thinking), -*angafu* 'mature' (from *angala* 'mature'), -*nyindafu* 'brave' (from *nyindala* 'brave'), -*labufu* 'dirty' (from *labukha*[5] 'become dirty'), *rundubafu* 'big' (from *rundubara* 'become big'), -*khalafu* 'sad' (from *khalala* 'be sad'), -*nefu* 'fat' (from *nera* 'become fat'), -*balakafu* 'dry' (from *balakala* 'dry'), -*kafu* 'stupid' (from *kala* 'be stupid/slow thinking'), -*khandyafu* 'proud' (from *khandyaba* 'walk proudly') etc.

In addition to the two types of derived adjectives exemplified above, there are derived adjectives that end in the suffix -*a*. These adjectives are fewer compared to the first two sub-types as they are restricted to occurring with only few nouns. Derived adjectives that end in -*a* include -*fumba* 'folding' (from *fumba* 'fold', in *endebe efumba* 'fold-

---

[3]Verbs that end in -*e* should not be confused with adjectives that are derived from verbs which also end in -*e*. The two are distinguishable even without reference to tonal patterns: derived adjectives have an augment and class prefix but verbs have subject agreement and verbal inflections such as tense.

[4]Verbs in Lubukusu in the imperative mood occur without any prefixes

[5]Orthographic kh- is [x]

ing chair'), *-chwisya* 'knotted' (from *chwisya* 'knot', in *kumukoye kumuchwisya* 'knotted rope'), *-chunula* 'unknotting' (from *chunula* 'unknot', in *kumukoye kumuchunula* 'unknotting rope', *-khalisya* 'crossing/shortcut' (from *khalisya* 'cross/shortcut', in *engila ekhalisya* 'short cut', *-kisa* 'hide' (from *kisa* 'hide', in *kumwinyawe kumwikisa* 'hide and seek game', *-kara* 'dribble' (from *kara* 'dribble', in *kumupira kumukara* 'dribbling ball game (=soccer)', *-chururusya* 'uninterrupted' (from *chururusya* 'let go uninterrupted' in *kumupira kumuchururusya* 'game where two people hit the soccer ball back and forth'). As already pointed out, adjectives in this subcategory are few. This may be due semantic reasons. For example only few objects can be described as folding[6], only few things can be described as knotting, only a handful on things can be described as dribbling etc. But it is also possible that these are noun-verb compounds rather than adjectives.

Up to this point we have seen that adjectives in Lubukusu can be formed from verbs. But the reverse is also possible: verbs can be formed from adjectives through a fairly productive process of suffixing *-a* to the root of the adjective. To briefly illustrate, adjective roots such, *-imbi* 'short', *-bofu* 'big', *-leyi* 'tall', and *-besemu* 'red' can be converted into the following verbs respectively: *imbia* 'become short', *bofua* 'become big', *lea* 'become tall' and *besema* 'become red'. The suffixation of *-a* to *-imbi* 'short' and *-bofu* 'big' to form a verb is clear and cannot be contested. These two examples show that the direction of conversion is from adjective to verb. I assume that this is also true in both *lea* 'become tall' and *besema'* even though these two examples involve additional phonological processes beyond suffixation of *-a*. In any case the roots *-imbi, -bofu, -leyi,* and *-besemu* are unequivocally adjectival, and conversion must be from adjective to verb.

To summarize this section, we have seen that Lubukusu has many adjectives, some of which can be classified as basic and others as derived. It is particularly instructive that the morphological process which forms adjectives from verbs is quite productive. It is therefore reasonable to conclude that the class of adjectives in Lubukusu is an open class. This differs from Bantu languages such as Chichewa which has "...very few 'pure' adjective stems..." (Mchombo 2004: 24). It also differs from Kiswahili which lacks a productive process of forming adjectives from verbs. For example Kiswahili lacks the noun + verb-derived-adjective equivalent of the Lubukusu *enyama endekhe* 'cooked meat'. In Kiswahili to say cooked meat, one must use a relative clause *-nyama iliyopikwa* 'meat that is cooked'.

Having provided a general description of adjectives in Lubukusu, we are now ready to tackle remaining issues that can challenge our conclusion that adjectives are indeed a separate and independent lexical category in Lubukusu. An examination of Lubukusu adjectives indicates that they do have what can be considered nominal features on the one hand and verbal features on the other. It is necessary to discuss these features and in the process explain how and why adjectives are neither nouns nor verbs.

---

[6]This contrasts with the adjective *-fumbe* 'folded' (from *fumba* 'fold') which is not as restricted semantically. Many things can be described as folded: *engubo efumbe* 'folded cloth', *ekaratasi efumbe* 'folded paper' etc.

3 Nominal features of adjectives in Lubukusu

By nominal features, I mean those features that are generally thought of as belonging to nouns. But instead of nouns being the bearers or associates of these features, it is adjectives that are. When adjectives carry many nominal features, it can be difficult to clearly and uniquely distinguish between nouns and adjectives, and it can be challenging to argue for the existence of a separate category of adjectives. In this section I examine and illustrate morphological and syntactic nominal features borne by or associated with the Lubukusu adjectives, beginning with morphological features.

3.1 Morphology of the adjective

Lubukusu adjectives must agree with the nouns that they modify. For this reason they have a morphological structure that similar to that of nouns. Like nouns, adjectives have the structure pre-prefix (augment)-class prefix-root. But it is the noun that determines the form of the pre-prefix and prefix borne by the adjective. The following data illustrates the structure of nouns, adjectives and agreement patterns in noun classes 1 to 11.

(5)   a.   o-mu-ndu o-mu-bofu
           1-1-person 1-1-big
           'big person'
      b.   ba-ba-ndu baa-bofu
           2-2-person 2.2-big
           'big people'

(6)   a.   ku-mu-sala ku-mu-bofu
           3-3-tree   3-3-big
           'big tree'
      b.   ki-mi-sala ki-mi-bofu
           4-4-tree   4-4-big
           'big trees'

(7)   a.   li-li-ino   lii-bofu
           5-5-tooth 5.5-big
           'big tooth'
      b.   ka-me-eno ka-ma-bofu
           6-6-tooth   6-6-big
           'big teeth'

(8)   a.   si-sy-uma sii-bofu
           7-7-bead   7.7-big
           'big bead'

b. bi-by-uma bii-bofu
   8.8-bead   8.8-big
   'big beads'

(9) a. e-n-dika   e-m-bofu
     9-9-bicycle 9-9-big
     'big bicycle'

   b. chi-n-dika   chi-m-bofu
      10-10-bicycle 10-10-big
      'big bicycles'

(10) a. lu-lu-ichi luu-bofu
      11-11-river 11.11-big
      'big river'

   b. chi-nj-ichi chi-m-bofu
      10-10-river 10-10-big
      'big rivers'

As shown in (5–10), the structure of adjective is similar to that of noun in each case both in terms of the number of morphemes and form of the morphemes. This is due to agreement requirements: the adjective must agree with the noun they modify. The adjective meets this requirement by copying or reduplicating the prefix form and structure of the noun it modifies. When a noun's prefixes are *o-mu* as in (5a), the adjective must also have *o-mu*; when a noun's prefixes are *ku-mu* as in (6a), the adjective must also have *ku-mu*. The only slight variations in the noun and adjective prefix structure can be found in (5b), (7a & b), (8a & b), and (9a & b), repeated here as (11), (12), (13) and (14) respectively.

(11) ba-ba-ndu baa-bofu
      1-1-person 1-1-big
      'big people'

(12) a. li-li-ino   lii-bofu
      5-5-tooth 5.5-big
      'big tooth'

   b. ka-me-eno ka-ma-bofu
      6-6-tooth   6-6-big
      'big teeth'

(13) a. si-sy-uma sii-bofu
      7-7-bead   7.7-big
      'big bead'

  b. bi-by-uma bii-bofu
      8.8-bead   8.8-big
      'big beads'

(14) a. e-n-dika   e-m-bofu
          9-9-bicycle 9-9-big
          'big bicycle'
      b. chi-n-dika   chi-m-bofu
          10-10-bicycle 10-10-big
          'big bicycles'

These are not counterexamples to the noun-adjective prefix similarity generalization since they can be explained phonologically. In (12b) the augment-noun prefix turns up as *ka-me* because the phonological process of vowel coalescence has taken place. In (14 & b), the nasal takes on different forms because it assimilates to the place of articulation of following stop. And finally in (11), (12a), and (13a & b), prefix haplology has taken place. Prefix haplology takes when identical prefixes such as *ba-ba* (class 2), *li-li* (class 5), *si-si* (class 7) and *bi-bi* (class 8) are followed by nominal root or adjectival root that begins with a consonant. In (11), *ba-ba* becomes *baa* because the root of the adjective begins with a consonant. This holds for (12) as well where *li-li* becomes *lii* because the adjective root is consonant initial. Prefix haplology is not limited to adjectives alone; it takes place in nouns as well. This is illustrated in the following data.

(15) a. baa-soreri (from ba-ba-soreri)
          2.2-boy
          'boys'
      b. lii-fumbi (from li-li-fumbi)
          5.5-cloud
          'cloud'

(16) a. sii-rekere (from si-si-rekere)
          7.7-village
          'village'
      b. bii-rekere (from bi-bi-rekere)
          8.8-village
          'villages'

For a detailed discussion of prefix haplology and how it is accounted for in phonological theory, see Mutonyi (2000).

I end this section by reiterating the nominal features borne by Lubukusu adjectives. Lubukusu adjectives bear class prefixes that agree with the noun they modify. In addition, they undergo prefix haplology just like nouns. But is this enough to conclude that Lubukusu adjectives are a sub-set of nouns rather than an independent lexical category?

Before answering this question, let us first examine the 'noun-ness' of adjectives at the level of syntax.

3.2 Syntactic function and position of Lubukusu adjectives

Lubukusu adjectives seem to occupy typical noun positions in the sentence without a modified noun. The typical noun positions which Lubukusu adjectives can occupy are subject position, object position and object of preposition position. To illustrate, consider the following sentences.

(17) a. O-m-bofu o-yu a-siim-a   o-mw-ana wewe.
     1-1-blind DEM-1 1-PRS-love-FV 1-1-child his/hers

     'That blind person loves his/her child.'

   b. Baa-tambi ba-a-sab-ang-a   byaa-khulya.
     2.2-poor 2-PRS-beg-HAB-FV 8.8-food

     'The poor usually beg for food.'

(18) a. Ku-mu-leeyi kw-a-funiikh-e.
     3-3-tall   3-PST-break-FV

     'The tall (one) broke.'

   b. Li-li-imbi lya-a-kw-a.
     5-5-short 5-PST-fall-FV

     'The short (one) fell.'

(19) a. Wafula a-a-yet-ang-a   baa-tambi.
     1.Wafula 1-PRS-help-HAB-FV 2.2-poor

     'Wafula usually helps the poor.'

   b. Mayi   a-a-kul-il-e   lii.bofu.
     Mother 1-PST-buy-ASP-FV 5.5-big

     'Mother bought the big (one).'

(20) a. Wafula a-a-r-a   sii-bofu khu-mesa.
     Wafula 1-PST-put-FV 7.7-big on.PRF-table

     'Wafula put the big (one) on the table.'

   b. Wafula a-a-r-a   sii-tabu khu-mu-bofu.
     Wafula 1-PST-put-FV 7.7-book 17-17-big

     'Wafula put the book on the big one.'

Thus Lubukusu adjectives can function as subject (17& 18), object (19) and object of preposition (20). These positions – subject position, object position and object of preposition – are noun positions and there is no doubt nor controversy about it. We are thus confronted yet again with data and facts that underscore the striking similarity between nouns and adjectives in Lubukusu. Does this mean that adjectives in Lubukusu are nouns? This is the question we turn to in the next section.

3.3 Are Lubukusu adjectives nouns?

In section 3.1, we saw that adjectives in Lubukusu have a structure that this similar to that of nouns. Like nouns they have a pre-prefix and a class prefix. In addition adjectives undergo prefix haplology just like nouns. And in section 3.2, we saw that Lubukusu adjectives take typical noun functions of subject, object and object of preposition. These striking similarities raise the possibility that adjectives are just a sub-type of nouns. If this is indeed the case, then it will not be justifiable to retain adjective as s separate lexical category in Lubukusu grammar.

I argue that the nominal features of adjectives that we have seen in previous sections are not sufficient to make the lexical category of adjective in Lubukusu irrelevant. One piece of evidence which shows that adjectives and nouns in Lubukusu are indeed separate lexical categories comes from NPs that contain both a noun and adjective. These NPs show unambiguously that nouns and adjectives are generated in different positions, suggesting that nouns are not adjectives and vice versa.

Nouns in Lubukusu precede adjectives in the NP and as we have already seen in previous sections, adjectives duplicate the prefix system of the nouns that they modify. Consider word order in the following simple Adjective-Noun structure.

(21) a. o-mu-soreri o-mu-leyi
          1-1-boy   1-1-tall

          'the/a tall boy'

      b. * o-mu-leyi o-mu-soreri
          1-1-tall   1-1-boy

          (Intended: 'the/a tall boy')

      c. ku-mu-sala ku-mu-leeyi
          3-3-tree   3-3-tall

          'the/a tall tree'

      d. * ku-mu-leyi ku-mu-sala
          3-3-tall   3-3-tree

          (Intended: 'the/a tall tree')

Clearly, the noun must precede the adjective in the NP. This is significant because it confirms that Lubukusu adjectives and nouns are base generated in different syntactic positions.

Notice once again that in (21) as in previous examples that the adjective duplicates the prefix structure of the noun: in (21a) the adjective duplicates the noun's *o-mu* prefix, while in (21c), the adjective copies the noun's *ku-mu* prefix. This type of agreement is referred to as concordial agreement in the Bantu literature. It is this concordial agreement that explains the rather surprising distribution facts of Lubukusu adjectives illustrated in (17–20) where adjectives seemed to function as subject, object and object of preposition. Adjectives in such cases contain enough nominal features of nouns (through the prefixes) and can allow for the dropping or omission of the associated nouns without affecting grammaticality.

Thus NPs such as those in (17–20) that occur without nouns do indeed have a noun underlyingly. This observation is supported by the fact that interpretation and comprehension of sentences (17–20) is only possible if one knows or has an idea about the nouns that the adjectives refer to. In other words, these sentences require an appropriate context: they cannot be uttered out of the blue.

The nouns in the underlying structure in (17–20) pass their nominal informationto the adjectival pre-prefix and prefix through agreement before they are dropped.

To summarize, I have argued that that there is no compelling reason, and there is no convincing evidence to support an analysis of Lubukusu adjectives as nouns. It is true that Lubukusu adjectives do indeed have nominal features but this is not entirely surprising. Lubukusu just happens to be a language (among many others perhaps) where adjectives share some features with nouns. This tendency by adjectives to share some of their morphosyntactic features with nouns has long been recognized in some world languages (Chafe 2012).

The conclusion of this section, then, is that nouns and adjectives exist in Lubukusu as separate lexical categories.

4 Verbal features of Lubukusu adjectives

A sub-set of adjectives or more broadly adjectival meanings show a relationship with verbs in Lubukusu. In particular some adjectival meanings are expressed by use of verbs rather than true adjectives. In (22) for example, the Lubukusu equivalents for 'happy', 'sad' and 'tall' which are unambiguously adjectives in English, are verbs as evidenced by the fact they bear subject agreement and tense.

(22)   a.   Wafula a-a-sangal-il-e.
          Wafula 1-PRS-happy-ASP-FV

          'Wafula is happy.'

   b.   Wafula a-a-suluny-e.
          Wafula 1-PRS-sad-FV

          'Wafula is sad.'

   c.   Wafula a-a-le-il-e.
          Wafula 1-PRS-tall-ASP-FV

          'Wafula has become tall.'

   Other examples of English adjectives whose equivalents in Lubukusu are verbs include the following: *lua* 'be tired', *chelewa* 'be late', *khalala* 'be sad', *meniukha* 'be shiny', *imbia* 'become short', *bia* 'become bad' etc.

   In general, the adjectival meanings that are expressed by use of verbs in Lubukusu are stage-level. These are either 'non-permanent', temporary states or continuing processes or states that are yet to reach their final state. For example *sangala* 'be happy' describes a temporary, transient state (in contrast to having a happy personality which is expressed by an adjective as will be illustrated below). Thus to say *Wafula aasangalile* 'Wafula is happy' means Wafula is happy now, but it doesn't mean that he will necessarily be happy later today or tomorrow. Similarly, *lea* 'be tall' does not designate a final state. It describes a process in progress. Thus to say *Wafula aaleile* 'Wafula has grown tall' means Wafula has grown taller from last time you saw him, and it doesn't suggest that he is done growing. In contrast, expressing the fact that Wafula is a tall person (as his final tall state) is an individual-level predicate. This in Lubukusu is expressed by an adjective as will be shown below.

Adjectival verbs such as *sangala* 'be happy' and *lea* 'become tall' occur only in predicative structures, and therefore they are translated in English as predicative adjectives. Notice that the equivalent English predicative adjectives are obligatorily preceded by BE in declarative sentences as well as in imperatives.

As already pointed out temporary states and on-going processes adjectival meanings in Lubukusu are expressed by use of verbs, but permanent final-state attributive adjectival meanings are expressed by use of adjectives. Adjectival meanings of this later type describe qualities of nouns that are enduring; qualities that are non-temporary. Where temporary states and on-going adjectival meanings have corresponding permanent attributive meanings, these are expressed by use of adjectives. To illustrate consider (23) where temporary states and their corresponding permanent states are provided.

(23) a. Wafula o-mu-sangafu
          Wafula 1-1-happy

          'happy Wafula' (Individual-level)

      b. Wafula a-a-sangal-il-e.
          Wafula 1-PRS-happy-ASP-FV

          'Wafula is happy.' (Stage-level)

      c. Ku-mu-sala ku-mu-leyi
          3-3-tree   3-3-tall

          'tall tree' (Individual level)

      d. Ku-mu-sala kw-a-le-il-e.
          3-3-tree   SA-PRS-tall-ASP-FV

          'The tree has become tall.' (Stage-level)

In (23a), there is some permanence to Wafula's happiness state. Here Wafula has a happy predisposition; he is naturally a happy person. In (23c) *kumuleyi* 'tall' is an attribute of *kumusala* 'tree': the tree has the attribute tall; it is an attribute that is not expected to change any time soon. Dixon is therefore correct when he observes that "...if a language has verbs derived from adjectives, then the adjective is preferred for describing a fairly permanent property and the verb for referring to a more transient state" (Dixon 2004: 32).

Notice that adjectives that express the attributive adjectival meanings (i.e. the true adjectives) in Lubukusu can be used predicatively. As illustrated in (24), when used predicatively, they retain their adjective forms and do not become verbs.

(24)   a. Wafula a-li o-mu-sangafu.
           Wafula 1-be 1-1-happy

           'Wafula is a happy person.'

      b. Ku-mu-sala ku-li ku-mu-leyi.
           3-3-tree   3-be 3-3-tall

           'The tree is tall.'

Thus attributive adjectives can be used as predicatively just like English. The most significant difference between English and Lubukusu (from the point of view of adjectives) is that Lubukusu (but not English) makes a distinction between the way it expresses temporary adjectival states or meanings on the one hand and permanent attributive qualities. The temporary states and on-going process adjectival meanings are expressed by verbs in Lubukusu, but they are expressed by adjectives in English.

A question that arises is whether verbs that express temporary and on-going processes are adjectives at some level or not. A straight forward way of determining this is showing that adjectival verbs differ in some significant way from regular verbs. This has been shown to be true in Mohawk and Vaeakau-Taumako. In these languages, verbs that are used to express adjectival meanings are different from regular verbs. For example Mohawk verbal adjectives contrast with regular verbs in not taking certain aspectual markers and future tense[7] (Baker 2001). In Austronesian languages such as Vaeakau-Taumako, verbal adjectives differ from regular verbs in their ability to occur without tense-aspect-mood marking (Naess & Hovdaugen 2011).

It is therefore reasonable to argue that adjectival verbs are adjectives in Mohawk and Vaeakau-Taumako at some level because they differ significantly from regular non-adjectival verbs.

In Lubukusu, there is no compelling reason to make a similar argument. This is because adjectival verbs that describe temporary non-final states and continuing processes are not different from regular verbs in terms of tense-aspect-mood marking. To illustrate consider the tense-aspect marking on *sangala* 'be happy' in the following data.

(25)   a. Wafula a-la-saangal-a
           Wafula 1-FUT-happy-FV

           Wafula will be happy today.

      b. Wafula a-kha-saangal-e
           Wafula 1-FUT-happy-FV

           'Wafula will be happy tomorrow/next week.'

---

[7]But see Chafe (2012) who found nothing significant that distinguishes 'adjectival verbs' from regular verbs in Seneca, a language that is related to Mohawk

c. Wafula a-li-saangal-a
   Wafula 1-FUT-happy-FV

   'Wafula will be happy sometime in the remote future.'

d. Wafula a-a-saangal-a
   Wafula 1-PST-happy-FV

   'Wafula was happy a long time ago.'

Clearly, *sangala* can occur with any tense and aspectual marker just like any regular verb. I take this to be evidence that Lubukusu adjectival verbs that describe temporary states and continuing processes are verbs and nothing more. They express adjectival meanings, but they are verbs in the true sense of the word.

What this means is that the Lubukusu adjective system is different from that of Mohawk and Vaeakau-Taumako in spite of the apparent similarities. Both languages and Lubukusu express some adjectival meanings by use of verbs. But while all verbal adjectives in Mohawk and Vaeakau-Taumako can be argued to be adjectives, the Lubukusu ones are not: they are true verbs.

5 Conclusion

In spite of the fact that words which express adjectival meanings in Lubukusu have nominal features on the one hand and verbal features on the other, there is enough strong evidence that support the existence of adjective as a distinct lexical category. Lubukusu adjectives have a prefix system that is identical to that of nouns, and the adjectives seem to function as subject and object, but this doesn't make them nouns. They remain adjectives and they acquire these features and functions by virtue of being modifiers of nouns. With regards to the adjectival meanings that are expressed by use of verbs, I showed that only stage-level predicate readings are expressed by use of verbs in Lubukusu. Individual-level predicate readings are expressed by use of adjectives. I also argued that 'adjectival verbs' in Lubukusu are real verbs. For this reason, Lubukusu is different from Mohawk and Vaeakau-Taumako where adjectival verbs have been argued to be adjectives at some level in the grammar. With regards to the existence of the lexical category of adjective, Lubukusu is like English (but unlike Mohawk and Vaeakau-Taumako): it has a distinct lexical category of adjective in its grammar. But this is not to suggest that Lubukusu and English have identical adjective systems. There are significant differences, one of which is that stage-level predicate readings in Lubukusu are expressed by use verbs, but in English it is adjectives that are used.

Acknowledgements

I would like to sincerely thank two anonymous reviewers for their useful detailed comments and suggestions. All errors and shortcomings are my own.

Abbreviations

Unless indicating person, numbers in glosses indicate noun class prefixes and pre-prefixes. Abbreviations follow Leipzig glossing conventions, with the following exceptions:

ASP	aspect	SA	subject agreement
FV	final vowel	STA	stative
HAB	habitual		

References

Baker, Mark C. 2001. *The atoms of language*. New York: Basic Books.

Baker, Mark C. 2003. *Lexical categories: Verbs, nouns, and adjectives*. New York: Cambridge University Press.

Bhat, D. N. S. 1994. The adjectival category. *Studies in Language Companion Series* 24.

Chafe, Wallace L. 2012. Are adjectives universal? The case of Northern iroquoian. *Linguistic Typology* 16(1). 1–39.

Dixon, R. M. W. 1982. *Where have all the adjectives gone and other essays in semantics*. Berlin: Mouton.

Dixon, R. M. W. 2004. Adjective classes in typological perspective. In R. M. W. Dixon & Alexandra Y. Aikenvald (eds.), *Adjective classes: A cross linguistic typology*, 1–49. Oxford: Oxford University Press.

Dixon, R. M. W. & Alexandra Y. Aikhenvald (eds.). 2004. *Adjective classes: A cross-linguistic typology*. Oxford: Oxford University Press.

Mchombo, Sam. 2004. *The syntax of Chichewa*. Cambridge: Cambridge University Press.

Mutonyi, Nasiombe. 2000. *Aspects of Bukusu morphology and phonology*. Columbus: Ohio State University Doctoral dissertation.

Naess, Åshild & Even Hovdaugen. 2011. *A grammar of Vaeakau-Taumako*. Berlin/Boston: Walter de Gruyter.

Weber, David J. 1983. *Relativization and nominalized clauses in Huallaga Quechua*. Berkeley: University of California Press.

Whaley, Lindsay J. 1997. *Introduction to typology: The unity and diversity of language*. Thousand Oaks, California: Sage Publications, Inc.

Chapter 21

Optional ergativity and information structure in Beria

Andrew Wolfe

SIL International

Tajeldin Abdalla Adam

Ergativity in Africa is rare; König (2008: 95–96) lists only twelve African languages that have been described as exhibiting ergative phenomena. Even more rarely does OPTIONAL ERGATIVE MARKING (OEM) appear, in which the use of an ergative marker may depend on information-structural or discourse-pragmatic considerations. McGregor (2010: 1631) lists a sole instance in Africa.

Previous literature on Beria, a Saharan language, describes a system of focus marking that shows ergative alignment, wherein one marker, =gu, focuses transitive actors (A) and another, =di, focuses either transitive patients (P) or intransitive single arguments (S) (Jakobi & Crass 2004: 151–154; Jakobi 2006).

Based on new data from texts and judicious elicitation, we suggest that this =gu functions as an optional ergative marker which speakers employ in diverse pragmatic and syntactic contexts, not simply for assigning argument focus to the A term (Lambrecht 1994) but also for identifying an A when the P term is in focus; for highlighting brand new A participants (Prince 1981) in sentence focus contexts; for disambiguating grammatical roles; and for marking the A of quotative constructions and embedded relative clauses.

We reanalyze =di as a specificational copula (Mikkelsen 2005), contrasting with the predicational copula =i. Speakers may use either of these copulas in cleft constructions in order to focus constituents other than transitive actors.

1 Introduction

1.1 Optional ergative marking in Africa

The term ERGATIVE describes any linguistic system in which the single or principal argument of an intransitive verb (S) patterns with the patient (P) of a transitive verb rather than with the actor (A) of the transitive verb. See Figure 1.

Andrew Wolfe & Tajeldin Abdalla Adam. Optional ergativity and information structure in Beria. In Jason Kandybowicz, Travis Major, Harold Torrence & Philip T. Duncan (eds.), *African linguistics on the prairie: Selected papers from the 45th Annual Conference on African Linguistics*, 341–358. Berlin: Language Science Press. DOI:10.5281/zenodo.1251748

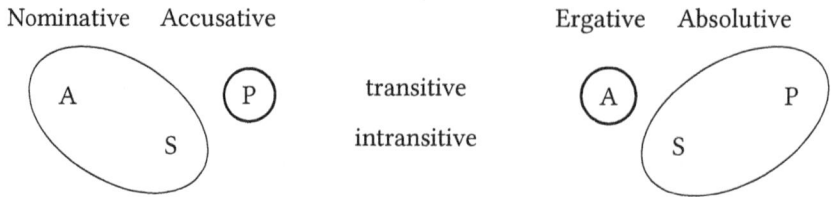

Figure 1: Ergative-absolutive vs. nominative-accusative (Dixon 1994; Payne 1997: 129–168)

In OPTIONAL ERGATIVE MARKING (or OEM; McGregor 2009; 2010; McGregor & Verstraete 2010), use or non-use of the ergative marker is conditioned by principles of information structure, discourse, or semantics. In the analysis below we follow the definition in McGregor (2009: 493):

> Optional ergative case-marking refers to the situation in which the ergative marker may be present or absent from the Agent NP without affecting the grammaticality or interpretation of the clause in terms of who is doing what to who. The term 'optional case-marking', like 'free variation', is potentially misleading, and […] does not mean that the marker is used randomly.

Only rarely does ergativity appear in descriptions of African languages. König (2008: 95–96) lists twelve languages with potential ergative phenomena, clustered in four families: West Nilotic, Kordofanian, Mande, and Chadic. McGregor (2010: 1631) offers only one of the West Nilotic languages from König's list, Shilluk, as the lone example of OEM from the over 2,000 languages in Africa.

1.2 Beria

Using new data from texts and elicitation, we propose adding Beria, a Saharan language of eastern Chad and western Darfur, to this short list of African languages known to exhibit OEM.

In Jakobi & Crass's (2004) grammar of the Kube dialect of Beria (henceforth J&C, 2004: 151–154; cf. Jakobi 2006), they present two enclitic focus markers, =gu and =di. They argue that these two focus markers follow an ergative distribution pattern: speakers employ =gu to mark focused A terms and =di to mark focused P and S terms. A third focus-marking strategy they characterize as a cleft construction, as it uses the copula =i. All three of these, =gu, =di and =i, encliticize to lexical NPs or free pronominals, though most participant reference tracking in natural discourse with unmarked pragmatics appears only in Beria's verbal cross-reference system, wherein suffixes indicate the person and number of A (agent / actor) arguments and prefixes indicate the person and number of P (patient / object) arguments.

The present study seeks to extend and refine Jakobi & Crass's analysis of =gu, =di and =i by examining contextualized discourse data with the tools of information structure (especially Prince 1981 and Lambrecht 1994). In a preliminary review of two texts from a local news broadcast genre, we describe a previously unrecognized usage of =*gu* in contexts with *sentence focus* (Lambrecht 1994: 233–235), i.e., where the entire sentence consists of new information. Specifically, we propose that in our data, this optional use of =*gu* only appears with *brand new* transitive-agent referents (Prince 1981: 233–237). We also confirm that =*gu* may also occur in contexts with *argument focus* (Lambrecht 1994: 228–233) on A.

In addition to cases where the A term features more prominently in its context, we delineate three specific constructions that feature a *less* prominent A argument, also marked with =*gu*. All of these occur in contexts where the speaker accords higher prominence to the P argument. This prominence on the P may be pragmatic, as with contexts where P is in argument focus or serves as the subject of a pseudo-passive, or it may be syntactic, as the head of a transitive relative clause. We also identify a quotative use of =*gu*.

Turning from =*gu*, we reanalyze =*di* and =*i* as two different copulas with distinct semantics, and recast each of their argument-focus usages as variations on the same cleft construction. Copular =*i*, which J&C consider a "copula of identification," we rebrand as a *predicational copula* (Mikkelsen 2005), and we call =*di* a *specificational copula*. In one documented difference between the two cleft constructions, OEM marker =*gu* appears on the A term in =*di* clefts but not in =*i* clefts. We suggest that this difference owes to the higher transitivity of the =*di* cleft, where the clause satisfies Hopper & Thompson's (1980: 252) high-transitivity criterion of the *individuation of O*.

2 Overview of key concepts and text sources

2.1 Information structure

Space considerations preclude an extensive review of the literature on information structure and related subdisciplines, where terminological choices and definitions vary widely. For present purposes it is helpful to highlight Lambrecht's (1994) definitions of focus as well as Prince's (1981) taxonomy of new information, both of which figure into the analysis below.

Lambrecht (1994: 211) offers a shorthand definition of *focus* as that which is "unpredictable" or "non-recoverable" in any utterance. As a corollary, every sentence has some element in focus. He delineates three domains of focus: predicate focus, argument focus, and sentence focus.

> The unmarked subject-predicate (topic-comment) sentence type [...], in which the predicate is in the focus and in which the subject (plus any other topical elements) is in the presupposition, will be said to have PREDICATE-FOCUS STRUCTURE; the iden-tificational type [...] in which the focus identifies the missing argument in a pre-supposed open proposition will be said to have ARGUMENT-FOCUS STRUCTURE; and the event-reporting or presentational sentence type, in which the focus extends

over both the subject and the predicate (minus any topical non-subject elements), will be said to have SENTENCE-FOCUS STRUCTURE. (Lambrecht 1994: 222).

Prince (1981) sketches out a taxonomy of discourse referents in terms of newness and givenness. New discourse referents may be either BRAND NEW, where the speaker asks the hearer to create a new entity in her mental representation; or UNUSED, where the speaker invokes a referent new to the discourse but assumed to be familiar to the hearer. Given discourse referents may be TEXTUALLY EVOKED, referred to previously in the discourse itself; or SITUATIONALLY EVOKED, which Prince primarily uses for the discourse participants themselves (first and second person). Between these new and given categories lie INFERABLE referents, whose existence the hearer is able to deduce by logical or cultural implication, as the presence of a "bus" in the discourse implies the existence of a "driver."

2.2 Text sources

New data analyzed below come from publicly available Radio Dabanga newscasts from March 18, 2013 and May 1, 2013, downloaded from the Radio Dabanga website (http://www.radiodabanga.org) the day following their broadcast. Based in the Netherlands, Radio Dabanga (henceforth RD) broadcasts daily Darfur-related news in Arabic and various languages of Darfur. The news anchor for the Beria portion of the broadcast, Tayiba Abdelkarim Abdul, is a well-respected native speaker of the Kube dialect. For the purposes of the broadcast, she translates from Arabic. Having been given the text well in advance of her studio time, she considers beforehand how best to render the meaning of each news piece as a whole into Beria. The final recording undergoes a light editing process before broadcast.

In general, the paragraph-by-paragraph translation method and the linguistic reputation of the translator notwithstanding, some interference from the source language cannot be ruled out. For present purposes, these concerns are mitigated by two factors: Arabic – even Darfuri Arabic – has no ergative case marking; and the second author of this study, as a native Kube Beria speaker, can critically evaluate the naturalness of the data in what concerns the conclusions below. Nonetheless, future studies will need to confirm the present findings with a more extensive data set that has no foreign-language origin. Accordingly, we qualify our conclusions below as preliminary while we work to assemble a larger, more diverse corpus.

Elicited data from the present study's second author appear marked with "TAA" below. In our discussions, elicitation never involved direct translation from English. Rather, we would discuss a pragmatic communicative context and ask what a native Beria speaker might say. Additionally, while recognizing the limitations of ungrammaticality judgments as linguistic evidence, in limited contexts below we deemed evaluations of infelicity important enough to the argument to include them.

3 Uses of =*gu*

3.1 A-argument focus constructions with =*gu*

Based on data like that given in (1)[1], J&C argue that =*gu* and =*di* are focus markers with complementary distribution, whose usage follows an ergative-absolutive alignment (2004: 151–154):

(1) a. (Focus markers with ergative alignment Jakobi 2006)

    bágʊ=ɔgɔ=gʊ   Ø:kú-gú-ɽ-í.   focused A: =*gu*

    wife-POSS.3SG=FOC$_{ERG}$ OJ:3:PFV:3-call-SJ:3-PFV

    'It's his wife who called him.' (Jakobi 2006: 136)

  b. náá=dɪ   nɛ-gɛr-g-ɪ.   focused P: =*di*

    PP:2SG=FOC$_{ABS}$ OJ:2-look.for-SJ:1SG-IPV

    'It's you I'm looking for.' (Jakobi 2006: 137)

  c. sʊltǎn=dɪ   Ø:nɪ-Ø-ɪ.   focused S: =*di*

    sultan=FOC$_{ABS}$ OJ:3:die-SJ:3-PFV

    'It's the sultan who has died.' (Jakobi 2006: 137)

The enclitic =*gu* only appears with transitive actors. When speakers want to focus patients or intransitive arguments, they invariably cliticize =*di* or =*i* to the focused noun phrase. In light of Beria's split-S verbal system (Mithun 1991; Dixon 1994: Chapter 4; see Jakobi 2011 for detailed analysis of the Beria facts), it bears noting that it is ungrammatical to use =*gu* with the S of even active intransitive verbs such as 'run' or 'leave,' which Beria codes with the A suffixes:[2]

(2) *Ai=gu suk=tu   hiri-g-í.

    1S=ERG market=DAT run-1SG.A-PFV

    'It was I who ran to the market.' (TAA)

  cf. *Ai-di suk-tu hirigí.*

(3) *Ai=gu sur-g-í.

    1S=ERG exit-1SG.A-PFV

    'It was I who left.' (TAA)

  cf. *Ai-di surgí.*

---

[1]We have reproduced J&C's examples as-is, with translation when in French. Note that they wrote before a working orthography was in place, so their examples use IPA transcription. Abbreviations from their work that do not follow the Leipzig Glossing Rules are listed in the Abbreviations section.

[2]New Beria examples are written in the working orthography approved by local administration (Faris 2006). High, [+ATR] vowels are represented with a circumflex diacritic: *û, î*. Mid, [+ATR] vowels remain unmarked, predictable from the presence of [+ATR] high vowels within the harmonic domain. Lexical tone is not written. Pluralization of both nouns and verbs uses the simplified orthographic convention of doubling the final letter of the word, capturing what is in actuality a complex system of tonal patterns. Imperfective verbs end in −*i* and perfective verbs in −*í*, reducing grammatical tone phenomena to an iconic visual form. Both rhotics are written *r*. Note that we have maintained a single representation for enclitics like =*gu* even though they harmonize for ATR with their host.

Because the label of ergative properly applies at the level of the particular grammatical construction, not of whole languages (Croft 2001: 132–171), it is unsurprising to find languages like Beria with both split-S and ergative alignments in operation in different components of the grammar. Note also that since =*gu* does not appear with S arguments, it indeed follows an ergative pattern and not a *marked nominative* one (König 2008: 138–203).

In fact, not even all clauses with two core arguments allow =*gu* on the more agentive argument. Certain low-transitive (Hopper & Thompson 1980) bivalent verbs such as 'have,' 'learn' and 'know' do not accept =*gu* but may use =*di* instead to focus the more agentive argument:

(4) *Ber=gu arabie kidí.   A arab tigo.
     3S=ERG car   3.A:have:PFV:SG 1s car have:1S.A:NEG

     'It is he who has a car. I don't have a car.' (TAA)

     cf. *Ber-**di** arabie kidí. Ai arabie tigo.*

(5) ɟàmâl=**dɪ**   àrmá   Ø:áwáá-ɽ-ɪ.
     Jamal=FOC_ABS Arabic OJ:3:learn-SJ:3-PFV

     'It's Jamal who has learnt Arabic.' (Jakobi 2006: 139)

(6) *Hawa=gu tir=egî.   ege=giní.   Maha ege=gino.
     Hawa=ERG name=1SG.POSS know=3A.PFV:AUX Maha know=3A.PFV:AUX:NEG

     'It was Hawa who learned (lit., 'knew') my name. Maha didn't learn it.' (TAA)
     cf. *Hawa-**di** tir-egî ege-giní. Maha ege-gino.*

Turning to information structure, among Lambrecht's three focus categories (see §2.1), J&C have already established the use of =*gu* for *argument focus*, with focus on the A term.[3] Within this usage, argument focus on the A can accomplish at least two distinct purposes: asserting the *identity* of the A term, or asserting its *role*. This becomes clear in negative assertions as in (7-8). In (7), the identity of the agent is corrected, whereas in (8) it is the clause's role assignments that are contradicted. Both contexts use =*gu*.

(7) Bur=do=**gu**   kana   tene sai=gi-n-o.   O   gie=i.
     boy=that=**ERG** NEG.PFV girl hit=3.A.PFV-AUX-NEG person other=COP_PR

     'It wasn't *that* boy that hit the girl. It was someone else.' (TAA)

(8) Bur=**gu** kana   tene sai=gi-n-o=ru,   tene=**gu**.
     boy=**ERG** NEG.PFV girl hit=3.A.PFV-AUX-NEG=CONJ girl=**ERG**

     'It wasn't that the *boy* that hit the *girl*. The *girl* hit the *boy*.' (TAA)

---

[3] They do not use Lambrecht's terms, but argument focus is clearly indicated in their work by cleft translations (Jakobi & Crass 2004: 151–153, examples 232–236 and 248; and in Jakobi 2006: 136, example 19). In the other four examples given of =*gu* (2004: 152, example 237; 2006: 137–138, examples 20, 21, and 26), it is unclear, based on the example and translation given, what the nature of the "focus" is. Some of these are treated below.

3.2 Sentence focus, brand new A construction

Not all uses of =*gu* entail argument focus, however. In both RD texts, the speaker uses =*gu* in contexts such as (9) where the remainder of the sentence is being asserted as new, not presupposed.

(9) barûgûî   yom_al_ahad=tu, oo   toûra kuni=gu,   arabie
     A.few.days.ago Sunday=on   person:PL armed INDF.PL=ERG vehicle

     tijari   ni   genî Gireda=re ji-e,   je   Jokhana=ru
     commercial INDF village Gireda=ABL COP_LOC.3-CVB PROG Jokhana=DAT

     si-r-ì=gi,   toûû   ki-si-n-e=ge,   bodo ajas=te
     go.IPFV.3-3A-IPFV=REL gun:PL 3.A.PFV-shoot-3.A-CVB=RSN that reason=ABL

     oo   wetti ku-nu-e,   ere   oo   sogodî gie noko=ru
     person:PL three 3A.PFV-kill:P.PL-CVB again person:PL ten   and one=DAT

     hiara=gine=ii   giníí.
     wounded=3A.PFV:AUX:CVB=COP_PR:PL 3A.PFV:say: PL

'Last Sunday some armed people(=ERG) opened fire on a commercial vehicle that was from the town of Gireda, going to Jokhana. Because of that they killed three people, and 11 people have been injured, they said.' [RD, 3/18/14, 5.1]

The news anchor does not expect the hearer to know there were people who opened fire on a commercial vehicle on the road from Gireda to Jokhana, nor does she merely assert that it was certain unnamed armed men who committed this deed; this is a news broadcast, and the entire utterance is unpredictable.

In the immediately following sentence, she restates and elaborates on the news just announced.

(10) oo   Ø-nuíí=gi   araa=gi ni   Radio Dabanga kerigi er
     person:PL 3.P-die:P.PL:PFV=these person:PL INDF Radio Dabanga within REL.PR

     k-î-í=gi   oo   toûra malisha hakuma=ru   tabi=gi
     3.A.PFV-say-PFV=REL person:PL armed militia government=DAT affiliated=REL

     dîî=ra   hirdee=ra   k-ori-e=gine=re
     camel:PL=CONJ horse:PL=CONJ 3.A.PFV-mount-CVB=3A.PFV:AUX:CVB=NFIN

     arabie tijari   yom_al_ahad tûî=gi   gardi genî Jokhana=re
     vehicle commercial Sunday   evening=this road village Jokhana=ABL

     ji-e=re   je   Gireda=r   ke-si-r-ì,   toûû
     COP_LOC.3-CVB=NFIN PROG Gireda=DAT VEN-go.IPFV.3-3A-IPFV gun:PL

     ki-si-n-e=ge,   bodo ajas=te   oo   wetti
     3.A.PFV-shoot-3.A-CVB=RSN that reason=ABL person:PL three

     ku-nu-e,   ere   oo   sogodî gie noko=ru
     3A.PFV-kill:P.PL-CVB again person:PL ten   and one=DAT

     hiara=giníí   giníí.
     wounded=3A.PFV:AUX:PL 3A.PFV:say: PL

'One of the relatives of the deceased told Radio Dabanga that the armed, government-affiliated militia people mounted on camels and horses and opened fire on a commercial vehicle on Sunday evening on the road coming from the village of Jokhana to Gireda. Because of that they killed three people and 11 people were injured, they said.' [3/18, 5.2]

This example well illustrates the optionality of the ergative marking as defined by McGregor and cited in §1.1: a "situation in which the ergative marker may be present or absent from the Agent NP without affecting the grammaticality or interpretation of the clause in terms of who is doing what to who" (McGregor 2009: 493). On the level of grammatical relations – and, in fact, even of sentence focus vs. argument focus – nothing changes between (9) and (10), yet =*gu* appears in (9) and not in (10). In both, 'armed people' (*oo toûra*) 'shot' (*toûû kisine*) a 'commercial vehicle' (*arabie tijari*) and 'killed' (*kunue*) people. In neither sentence is any one argument in focus. Everything that changes is irrelevant to the syntax of core arguments: the speaker adds the source of the information ('one of the relatives of the deceased'), expands on her description of the transitive agent (characterizing them as 'government-affiliated militia'), notes attendant action (transitive: they 'mounted camels and horses'), and shifts some minor details (mentioning the 'road' and changing the aspect of 'have been injured' to 'were injured').

No salient grammatical details change, but on a second repetition the once BRAND NEW identity and role of the transitive agent have become TEXTUALLY (Prince 1981: 233–237). All four of the non-quotative tokens of sentence-focus =*gu* occur with *brand new* transitive-agent participants.

3.3 Constructions with backgrounded A=*gu*, foregrounded P

Another distinct pragmatically marked construction with =*gu* appears in one token in the RD texts, which fits the pattern for neither A-argument focus nor sentence focus constructions:

(11) genîa   ha Sharq al Jabal hie=ru   Yara=ra   Nimra=ra   Dalma=ra
    villages Mt. Sharq al Jebel direction=LOC Yara=CONJ Nimra=CONJ Dalma=CONJ
    genîa=kî=ra,   oo   toûra malishat hakuma=ru   tabi
    villages=these=CONJ person:PL armed militia   government=DAT affiliated
    begî=gu a-we   gami=giníí.
    this=ERG go.3A.PL-CVB ambush=3A.PFV:AUX:PL

'The villages around Mt. Sharq al Jebel – Yara, Nimra, and Dalma – these villages too, these armed government-affiliated militiamen(=ERG) went and ambushed.' [3/18, 3.1]

Here the A is not new material but *textually evoked*, as shown by the deictic *begî* 'this, above.' In context this sentence immediately follows the description of another ambush by these militia, in the 'villages that lie to the northeast of Kutum' (line 2.1). The speaker marks continuity with the previous episode here not only through anaphoric participant reference (*begî*) but also with the lexical repetition of *gami-giníí* 'they ambushed' and *genîa* 'villages.' In other words, everything here is textually evoked except the names of the ambushed villages and the occurrence of a new incident in 'these villages, too' *genia-kî-ra*.

The new village names added to the list of 'villages ambushed by the Janjaweed' are the unrecoverable content in sentence (11). The speaker fronts the brand new P argument and demotes the textually evoked A argument in a sort of pseudo-passive construction. As noted by Zakaria Fadoul Khidir (2005: 80), Beria has no exact equivalent to the French passive construction because the presence of passive verbal morphology in Beria requires the total omission of an agentive lexical noun phrase. To express a demoted agent, the verbal morphology must remain the same but the constituent order changes to PAV and A gets marked with =*gu*.

Sentence (11) also exemplifies a phenomenon known to the literature as ERGATIVE HOPPING (Haviland 1979: 155, cited in Rumsey 2010: 1657) whereby an ergative-marked A term may simultaneously function as the S argument of an intransitive verb (here 'went and') that intervenes between the ergative-marked noun phrase and the bivalent verb that licenses it. Three tokens of =*gu* exhibit ergative hopping.

One of J&C's examples also falls into the pattern where P is promoted and constituent order is reversed:

(12) bɪɛ   kí=dî   ábā   égí=gú   Ø:sí-é-ɽ-î.
      house this=FOC~ABS~ father my=FOC~ERG~ OJ:3:build-PFV:3-SJ:3-PFV

      'It's this house that my father has built.' (Jakobi 2006: 138)

Although the situational context for utterance (12) is not given, it seems likely that the A term here is part of a presupposition 'my father built a house' or 'my father built something,' putting the A 'my father' in the pragmatic background (i.e., not in the focus domain) and focusing on the clefted P term 'this house.'

3.4 Quotative construction

Two separate quotative constructions account for the remaining tokens of =*gu* in the RD texts. In one of them, which is used in our data exclusively for *direct* reported speech, no verb of saying appears between the quoted agent and the quotation itself. The speaker uses =*gu* to signal to the hearer that she is transitioning from the A argument to a direct quotation, as in (13):

(13) ...genî=gi   kerigi oo   jii=gu,   "Ta-rdasin-e
      village=this within person:PL COP~LOC~.3:PL=ERG 1PL.P-come.together-CVB
      baa=ru   ere je   korekk=tu ba=gi   je   oû-d-í,"
      hand:PL=INS again PROG spade:PL=INS mine=this PROG dig-1PL.A-PFV
      gi-n-e   kîíí.
      3.A.PFV-say-CVB 3.A.PFV-say-PFV:PL

      '... the people who are in this village said, "We are coming together and we are digging this mine out with our hands, and again with spades."' [5/1, 4.3]

This "A – direct Quotation – quotative Verb" pattern satisfies Beria's default APV word order, with the quotation serving as the P. Quotative OEM constructions are well documented for at least two other languages (Rumsey 2010): Ku Waru (Trans-New Guinea) and Bunuba (non-Pama-Nyungan).

The existence of a quotative =*gu* construction sheds light on one of J&C's examples as well:

(14) bágâ   tɔ-gʊ-ɛ   ɟɪɪ   gɪnɛ, bɛr=gʊ   tɛbɪ
      millet:PL RV-scatter-3:SJ:CVB₁   LC:3:AFF:P SUB   PP:3=FOC₁ take:IMP
      gɪ-n-ɪ.
      PRF:3-say-3:SJ:AFF:PRF

      'Since the millet had been scattered, he said: "Take it!"' (Jakobi & Crass 2004: 152)

Without knowing the communicative context we cannot know for sure, but a direct quotative =*gu* reading here seems to fit more naturally than an argument focus reading.

The quotative construction appears in information-structurally diverse contexts: In (13) and the other RD token, the quoted speaker is a brand new referent and the utterance displays sentence focus whereas in (14), the quoted speaker is presumably textually evoked (by virtue of its pronominal reference) and the utterance thus has predicate focus.

3.5 Subordinate constructions with =*gu*

In the other quotative construction the quotation is introduced with a relative clause 'what A said.' In this relative clause, the A argument appears marked with =*gu*, as in (15; quotation omitted for space):

(15) o   wakil_amin_al-am   iga   Umam_al_Muttahida hifz_al_salaam
      person Undersecretary.General mission United.Nations   peacekeeping
      kî   tir-ogo   Hervé Ladsous gine_îrì, [o=kî=gu   er
      GEN name-3SG.POSS Hervé Ladsous is.called person=this=ERG REL.PR
      k-î-í]=gi,   ["..."] gine_kîí.
      3A.PFV-say-PFV.SG=REL ["..."] he.said

      'The UN Under-Secretary General for Peacekeeping, whose name is Hervé Ladsous, what this person said: [""], he said.' [5/1, 5.1]

In both such tokens in our data, a brand new participant enjoys an elaborated introduction from the speaker, which is topicalized at the beginning of the utterance. The speaker then proceeds to preface the participant's quoted speech act with the short relative clause 'what he said.' This relative clause uses a reduced noun phrase to refer to the quoted participant: 'this person' *o-kî* in (16), and in the other example even more simply 'he' *ber*. Such a reduced form of reference signals that the quoted participant has become an *evoked*, less prominent entity; critically it allows the speaker to pivot from the communicative purpose of introducing the participant to that of telling the hearer what it was that the participant said.

The ergative marking of A constituents embedded within relative clauses extends beyond quotative uses. In (16), *tene* 'girl' functions as both the patient of the verb *kidigarí* 'loves' in the embedded relative clause and as the single argument of the verb *karí* 'came' in the matrix clause. As the pivot, or shared argument between the two clauses, the P argument enjoys greater syntactic prominence than the A term.

(16) Tene [bur=gu ki-dig-a-r-í]=do   ka-r-í.
      girl boy=ERG PFV.3-love-PFV.3-3.SG-PFV:SG=that come-3.A-PFV:SG

      'The girl [that the boy loves] came.' (TAA)

3.6 Summary

Table 1 shows a taxonomy of =*gu* constructions identified to this point. Two of these constructions, shown at bottom – the disambiguation of roles shown in 'it wasn't that the *boy* hit the *girl*; the *girl* hit the *boy*' and the signaling of transition from quoted speaker to quoted speech – have no discernible function in assigning prominence, whether information-structural prominence or syntactic prominence. Rather, their only function is to disambiguate roles and constituents. This in itself provides the strongest argument for characterizing =*gu* as primarily a marker of ergativity and not as a marker of focus.

Common to the remaining constructions is the assignment of *marked prominence* to the A term of a transitive verb, whether higher prominence, as in the cases of sentence focus with a brand new A and of argument focus on A, or lower prominence, as in the cases of A embedded in relative clauses or of PAV word order (due to argument focus on P or to pseudo-passivization).

Table 1: Summary explanatory matrix of constructions in which A is marked with =gu

assigning prominence	higher prominence of A	main	argument focus on A (§3.1, (7))
			sentence focus on brand new A (§3.2)
	lower prominence of A	main (PAV)	clefted P with argument focus (=*di*), A in presupposed material (§3.3, (12))
			P as subject of pseudo-passive, evoked, demoted A (§3.3, (11))
		relative	P as pivot of clause linkage, A within relative clause (§3.5)
disambiguating	disambiguating roles (§3.1, (8))		
	quotative, signaling transition to speech complement (§3.4)		

This schema provides a clear account of all data points in our RD texts as well as elicited data, and may also elucidate examples given in previous literature that did not seem to express argument focus on the A term. One significant line of evidence remains unresolved, however: native speaker intuitions as to the function of =*gu*. The next section briefly turns to this before moving on to =*di* in §4.

3.7 Native speaker intuition: =*gu* as *deixis of role*

When Zakaria Fadoul Khidir, a native speaker of Kube Beria, discusses =*gu* under the category of "passive voice" (2005: 80; see §3.3 above), he glosses it as a "deictic" marker. While at first glance this does not seem to integrate easily with the analysis above, it well captures native speakers' intuitions about =*gu*, as the second author of this study attests and as is further confirmed by Amir Libiss (p.c.), a third Beria speaker.

Beria already has two sets of deictic markers, proximal =*kî* / =*gi* and distal =*to* / =*do* (Jakobi & Crass 2004: 126), both with wide syntactic distribution. These markers can even co-occur with =*gu*, as in the noun phrase *o-kî-gu* 'this person=ERG' in (15) above. Clearly =*gu* does not encode mere referential deixis.

At the same time, a deictic reading of =*gu* accords well with the broader social and cognitive purpose of deixis and demonstrative marking. If, as Diessel (2006: 463) argues, "demonstratives function to coordinate the interlocutors' joint focus of attention," =*gu* could be understood not perhaps as pointing at a referential entity per se, but as pointing at that entity's grammatical relation within the transitive clause. By using =*gu*, a speaker "points" and invites his hearer to focus attention on the agentive grammatical role played by the indicated referent. Deixis and argument focus perform related social and cognitive functions in terms of coordinating interlocutors' attention.

Of course, as argued at length above, =*gu* appears in more diverse constructions than just argument focus on the A term. Nevertheless this does not conflict with the singling out of A-argument focus as the prototypical use of =*gu*. By way of comparison, if asked to define the word 'that,' most English speakers would likely point – yet it is no less true that English 'that' has also been grammaticalized to serve in discourse-deictic functions and even as a relativizer. In fact, one would *expect* the evolution and grammaticalization of a deictic marker into such varied additional constructions (Diessel 2006, §4.2).

With this foundation laid, we propose DEIXIS OF ROLE as a descriptive term for the prototypical function of optional ergative marking in Beria. This not only incorporates native speaker insights about how Beria OEM works but it may provide fruitful directions for future OEM theorizing and research.

To fully comprehend the function of Beria's =*gu*, it is also necessary to understand other focus markers in its environment, especially =*di*, which was previously described as an absolutive focus marker (Jakobi & Crass 2004: 151–154; Jakobi 2006). §4 turns to this.

4 Copulas and clefts with =*di* and =*i*

J&C characterize =*di* as an absolute focus marker because of data such as in (1) above. To assign argument focus to the A term, Beria speakers use =*gu* but to focus P or S, they select =*di*. We reframe =*di*, however, as a previously unrecognized copula, which can then be employed in a cleft construction.

The strongest rationale for this shift is that Jakobi recognizes the existence of a "non-verbal predication marker" (2006: 138) =*di* sharing a presumed "common origin" with =*di* the absolute focus marker. These two are in fact formally identical, as shown in (17-18, cf. (1b) above):

(17) O   kese-r-ì=gi   Tayiba Abdelkarim Abdul=di.
      person speak-3A-IPFV.SG=REL Tayiba Abdelkarim Abdul=COP$_{SP}$.3

      'The person who is speaking is Tayiba Abdelkarim Abdul.' [5/1, 2.2]

(18) áɪ=dɪ.

      PP:1SG=PRED

      'It's me.' (Jakobi 2006: 138)

Furthermore, in argument focus constructions, =*di* shares common distribution with =*i*. Both =*di* and =*i* may focus S and P arguments but not A arguments. On the other hand, in our data, neither of these markers shows the complex and varied distribution summarized for =*gu* in Table 1 above.

As copular verbs, both =*di* and =*i* share a negative form, =*do*, while =*gu* has no negative form (cf. 7-8):

(19) ğǐm=d-ō.

      owl=IC-NEG

      'It's not an owl.' (J&C 2004: 101) (compare 23)

(20) O   arabie kidí=do   ber=d-o   kire=ego=di.
      person car   3.A:have:PFV:SG=REL 3S=COP$_{SP}$-NEG brother=3SG.POSS=COP$_{SP}$

      'The person who has a car is not him; it is his older brother.' (TAA)

Semantically, a clean division of labor exists between =*i* and =*di*. The first classifies or ascribes an attribute to the topic: X displays the characteristic Y (21-22), or X is a member of the set Y (23-24):

(21) mɪsā hɛrr=ɪ.

      pot full=IC:3:AFF

      'The pot is full.' (J&C 2004: 100)

(22) bɔɔ=égí   tákkʊrɛ=ɪ.

      ram:PL=1S.POSS very.fat=IC:3:AFF

      'My rams are very fat.' (J&C 2004: 100)

(23) gīmm=ī.
      owl=IC:3:AFF

      'It's an owl.' (J&C 2004: 100)

(24) tàmáṛā=ɪ.
      Tama.person=IC:3:AFF

      'It's a Tama.' (J&C 2004: 100)

The second marker predicates co-extensive reference between the two terms: X is fully described by Y and there are no other members in the set; see (17-18) above. Accordingly, following Mikkelsen (2005), we label =*i* a predicational copula, and =*di* a specificational copula. As she explains (2005: 1), predicational copulas "tell us something about the referent of the subject" whereas specificational copulas "says who or what the referent is."[4]

These semantics for =*di* and =*i* carry over into their corresponding versions of the cleft construction. In (12) above, for instance, the speaker presupposes 'a certain house exists which my father built' and, through the specificational cleft, he predicates that 'this is that house.' The two referents of 'this house' and 'the house that my father built' are co-extensive. In (25), by contrast, the speaker assumes 'a certain substance that the mother gave to the child' and then through an predicational cleft, clarifies the nature of that substance. What sort of thing is that which the mother has given the child? It is of the class of 'paste.'

(25) gʊʊ=ɪ   ɪà   ɟàá=r   Ø:kɛkk-ɪ.
      paste=COP.SG.ABS mother child=ADV OJ:3:give:SJ:3-PFV

      'It's paste that the mother has given to the child.' (Jakobi 2006: 139)

One complicating factor in this rendering of the facts is the presence of =*gu* in the =*di* cleft in (14) but not in the =*i* cleft in (25). We propose to resolve this complication with reference to Hopper & Thompson's (1980) scalar transitivity criteria. In §3.1, scalar transitivity already helped explain why low-transitive verbs 'have,' 'learn' and 'know' cannot occur with ergative-marked agents. If =*gu* correlates with high transitivity, then Hopper & Thompson's criterion of the individuation of O (1980: 252–253) may motivate the use or non-use of =*gu* in these two sub-constructions of the Beria cleft. The focused element of a =*di* cleft is invariably a referential, definite expression like 'this house' whereas in =*i* clefts it is a non-referential, indefinite class or attribute like 'paste.' In other words, the fronted P or O in a =*di* cleft is *individuated* whereas in a =*i* it is not.[5]

Distributional, morphological and semantic lines of evidence converge to support the assertion that =*di* is a copula. The only counterevidence we are aware of finds natural explanation in the dynamics of scalar transitivity.

---

[4] Jakobi & Crass (2004: 102–106) catalogue two other Beria copulas: locative/existential *ji* and comitative *bei*.

[5] In fact, the *individuation of O* may also be relevant to the quotative =*gu* construction (§3.4). Rumsey (2010) theorizes that the tendency of quotative OEM marking to apply more to direct reported speech than to indirect stems from this same *individuation of O* criterion, since the shift of voice and perspective involved in a direct speech act sets it off more sharply from the framing speech act; it is more clearly individuated than indirect reported speech.

5 Directions for further research

Directions for future research on OEM phenomena in Beria abound. As discussed in §2.2, the present study, which represents the first results of an ongoing program of Beria-language corpus collection and discourse analysis, necessarily offers only preliminary conclusions due to the small corpus size and its foreign-language source material. With a larger annotated corpus, a higher-resolution picture will emerge of what additional factors may influence speakers' choices of when to use =*gu*, potentially including animacy, discourse macrostructure, activation status, unexpectedness of agency, aktionsart, and zero anaphora of other core constituents, among others. More robust explorations of relative clauses, quotative constructions, topic chains, and ergative hopping will complement this fuller analysis.

Another open question is why Jakobi & Crass's two folk tale texts (2004: 185–192) include no instances of =*gu*, even in contexts with transitive predicates and newly introduced participants, such as in (26):

(26) sàgʊr tɛnɛ tɛbɪ-ɛ-ɽ-ɛ
      jackal girl take-PRF:3-3:SJ-CVB₁
      'a jackal took a girl, then...' (Jakobi & Crass 2004: 185)

We suggest that the lack of =*gu* here owes in part to the hearers' assumed familiarity with stock folk tale participants, which among the Beria speech community would perhaps better be classified as *unused* participants than *brand new* ones. This is consistent with the fact that J&C's storyteller omits, throughout the story, lexical noun phrases that would clarify the identity of referents for the benefit of uninitiated readers. J&C supply these identities in square brackets in their French translation – 21 times in the first four-page text alone. Considerations of genre and register may also be playing a role here: we expect to see =*gu* especially in other formal settings calling for precise speech, such as testimony in traditional courtroom proceedings or recitation of cultural history unfamiliar to hearers. At least, if anything, the lack of =*gu* in J&C's texts would seem to *strengthen* the *optional* ergativity analysis of =*gu* given above.

The diachronic origins of =*gu* also remain opaque. Descriptions of case marking for Western Saharan (WS) languages (surveyed in König 2008: 38–57) demonstrate similar optional case marking to Beria's: Core arguments go unmarked in default APV constituent order, and the presence of case marking is influenced by "syntactic, semantic and pragmatic factors" that are "yet to be adequately described" (Hutchison 1986: 193). While WS's "nominative" marker, *ye* in Kanuri-Kanembu and *i* in Teda-Daza, bears little formal resemblance to Beria's =*gu*, its usage as an optional marker on A terms is not unlike =*gu*. In fact, it is not certain that *ye / i* indeed functions as a nominative marker uniformly across WS. Hutchison (1986: 203–205) does establish that in some dialects of Kanuri, *ye* may mark an S term – though rarely, and only in narrative discourse when the subject switches – but in Keshirda Dazaga, for instance, Josiah Walters (p.c.) has yet found no tokens of an S marked with *i*. Possibly OEM is not uncommon in the Saharan family.

6 Conclusions

Close scrutiny of =*gu* data in Beria's Kube dialect yields much of interest to the typologist, discourse researcher, and Africanist alike. In the analysis of two radio news broadcasts and a handful of carefully elicited examples, we have teased apart as many as seven distinct constructions in which =*gu* marks only the A term of transitive clauses, and never P or S terms. Speakers employ =*gu* in these constructions to various communicative ends, including the disambiguation of roles and the assigning of either higher or lower prominence to a transitive agent. What brings unity to this diversity is the ergative nature of =*gu*: It is indeed foremost a case marker and not a focus marker. At the same time, it is essentially an *optional* ergative marker, the use of which varies according to syntactic and discourse-pragmatic principles. This makes it only the second such system described as such on the African continent.

Furthermore, we offered multiple lines of evidence showing that =*di*, which has been described as an absolutive focus marker, is in fact a previously unrecognized copula. We contrasted this specificational copula =*di* with the predicational copula =*i*. Both of these may be used in a clefted construction to focus an S or P argument. This reconfiguration may be summarized as in Table 2.

Table 2: Summary of reanalysis of Jakobi 2006

		Jakobi & Crass 2004; Jakobi 2006	
=gu	**focus**	focus marker, ergative	optional ergative marker
=di	**focus**	focus marker, absolutive	specificational cleft
		non-verbal predication marker	specificational copula
=i	**focus**	cleft construction	predicational cleft
		copula of identification	predicational copula

In addition, this analysis lends further support to multiple components of Rumsey's (2010) account of OEM phenomena in Ku Waru (Trans-New Guinea) and Bunuba (Non-Pama-Nyungan), especially in its reliance on scalar transitivity, particularly the *individuation of O*, in the description of a quotative OEM construction, and in the recognition of *ergative hopping* phenomena, in a language far removed from Ku Waru and Bunuba both geographically and genetically.

Finally, drawing from Khidir (2005) and Diessel (2006) we explored reframing Beria's OEM as a variety of deixis we called *deixis of role*, because in its prototypical usage =*gu* "points" to the grammatical role of the ergative-marked noun phrase, directing a listener's focus and attention to that agent role.

Much work remains to be done to understand Beria information structure as a whole, beginning with the assembly of a significantly larger and more diverse corpus, but the present study represents some basic steps forward toward this end. McGregor (2009: 1626) laments that the study of optional case marking suffers from "not enough data, not enough ideas." It is our hope that the present study makes a modest contribution toward addressing these lacunae.

Acknowledgements

We gratefully acknowledge insightful responses given after our initial presentation at ACAL, especially from Colleen Ahland, Michael Ahland and Malte Zimmermann, who pointed us in helpful directions for both clearer presentation and further literature review and engagement. Thanks also to Ryan Pennington, who tipped us off to a number of particularly valuable references. Special thanks to Josiah Walters who shared unpublished data from Keshirda Dazaga. We are grateful to Amir Libiss, another Kube speaker who reviewed our analysis and offered insights. Thanks finally to Deborah Morton for reviewing an early draft and offering a multitude of incisive comments. All mistakes are, of course, ours.

Abbreviations

Abbreviations follow the Leipzig Glossing Rules, except for the following:

A	agent of transitive verb or agentive single argument of intransitive verb	NFIN	non-final verb form
		O	object
		OJ	object marker
A_{IMPERS}	impersonal agent	P	Patient of transitive verb or patientive single argument of intransitive verb
ADV	adverbializer		
AFF	affirmative	PP	person pronoun
CONJ	conjunctive	PRED	verbless predicate
COP_{PR}	predicational copula	REL	relativizer
COP_{SP}	specificational copula	REL.PR	relative pronoun
COP_{LOC}	locative copula	RSN	reason clause
IC	identificational copula	RV	reduced valence
IPV	imperfective	SA	agent-like subject
LC	locative copula	SJ	subject marker
LM	lexical morpheme	SP	patient-like subject
MAN	manner	SUB	subordinator
MED	marker of medium verbs	V	verb
MID	middle voice	VEN	venitive

References

Croft, William. 2001. *Radical construction grammar*. Oxford: Oxford University Press.
Diessel, Holger. 2006. Demonstratives, joint attention, and the emergence of grammar. *Cognitive Linguistics* 17(4). 463–489.

Dixon, R. M. W. 1994. *Ergativity* (Cambridge Studies in Linguistics 69). Cambridge: Cambridge University Press.

Faris, David. 2006. *Beria-English English-Beria dictionary.* 2nd edn. Iriba, Chad: Association pour le Développement Économique et Social du département de Kobé (ADESK).

Haviland, John Beard. 1979. Guugu Yimidhirr. In R. M. W. Dixon & Barry J. Blake (eds.), *Handbook of Australian languages,* 27–180. Canberra: ANU Press.

Hopper, Paul J. & Sandra A. Thompson. 1980. Transitivity in grammar and discourse. *Language* 56(2). 251–99.

Hutchison, John P. 1986. Major constituent case marking in Kanuri. *Current approaches to African linguistics* 3. 191–208.

Jakobi, Angelika. 2006. Focus in an active/agentive alignment system – the case of Beria (Saharan). *ZAS Papers in Linguistics* 46. 129–42.

Jakobi, Angelika. 2011. Split-S in Beria. In Doris Löhr, Eva Rothmaler & Georg Ziegelmeyer (eds.), *Kanuri, Borno and beyond: Current studies on the Lake Chad region* (Topics in Interdisciplinary African Studies 22), 91–116. Cologne: Rüdiger Köppe Verlag.

Jakobi, Angelika & Joachim Crass. 2004. *Grammaire du beria (langue saharienne)* (Nilo-Saharan: Linguistic Analyses and Documentation 18). Cologne: Rüdiger Köppe Verlag.

Khidir, Zakaria Fadoul. 2005. *Bases et radicaux verbaux: Déverbatifs et déverbaux du beria (langue saharienne).* Köln: Rüdiger Köppe.

König, Christa. 2008. *Case in Africa.* Oxford: Oxford University Press.

Lambrecht, Knud. 1994. *Information structure and sentence form: Topic, focus, and the mental representation of discourse referents.* Cambridge: Cambridge University Press.

McGregor, William B. 2009. Typology of ergativity. *Language and Linguistics Compass* 3(1). 480–508.

McGregor, William B. 2010. Optional ergative case marking systems in a typological-semiotic perspective. *Lingua* 120. 1610–36.

McGregor, William B. & Jean-Christophe Verstraete. 2010. Optional ergative marking and its implications for linguistic theory. *Lingua* 120. 1607–1609.

Mikkelsen, Line. 2005. *Copular clauses: Specification, predication and equation.* Amsterdam: John Benjamins.

Mithun, Marianne. 1991. Active/agentive case marking. *Language* 67(3). 510–46.

Payne, Thomas Edward. 1997. *Describing morphosyntax.* Cambridge: Cambridge University Press.

Prince, Ellen. 1981. Toward a taxonomy of given-new information. In Peter Cole (ed.), *Radical pragmatics,* 223–55. New York: Academic Press.

Rumsey, Alan. 2010. 'optional' ergativity and the framing of reported speech. *Lingua* 120. 1652–76.

Part V

Semantics and pragmatics

Chapter 22

Two-place exceed comparatives in Luganda

M. Ryan Bochnak
University of Konstanz

Research on comparative constructions recognizes the need for both a 3-place ("phrasal") comparative operator, alongside a 2-place ("clausal") operator (e.g., Heim 1985; Bhatt & Takahashi 2011). Recent cross-linguistic work on comparatives has argued that exceed comparative constructions are phrasal comparatives, making use of a 3-place operator (e.g., Beck et al. 2009; Howell 2013 for Yorùbá). While certain exceed constructions in Luganda can indeed be analyzed in this way, I argue here for the idea that others involve a 2-place operator that compares two degrees directly. I treat nominalized adjectives as measure functions in the sense of Bartsch & Vennemann 1972 and Kennedy 1997: they map an individual to its maximal degree on a scale. This allows us to model possessed adjective nominalizations similar to Barker's (1995) analysis of relational nouns, although whereas for Barker a possessive DP denotes a predicate of individuals, in this case the resulting DP denotes a degree.

1 Introduction

Formal research on comparatives distinguishes between PHRASAL COMPARATIVES (1) and CLAUSAL COMPARATIVES (2), depending on the syntactic category of the standard phrase (complement of *than*; angled brackets represent ellipsis).

(1) Kim is taller than [$_{DP}$Lee].   PHRASAL

(2) Kim is taller than [$_{CP}$Lee is <del>tall</del>].   CLAUSAL

Along with their different syntax, phrasal and clausal comparatives are taken to have different semantic representations (Bhatt & Takahashi 2011; Heim 1985; Kennedy 1997: among others). While phrasal comparatives involve an operator with three argument positions, clausal comparatives involve an operator with two argument positions (see (3); the standard semantic analyses of these will be unpacked in §2).

(3) a. phrasal comparison ↔ 3-place comparative operator

   b. clausal comparison ↔ 2-place comparative operator

M. Ryan Bochnak. Two-place exceed comparatives in Luganda. In Jason Kandybowicz, Travis Major, Harold Torrence & Philip T. Duncan (eds.), *African linguistics on the prairie: Selected papers from the 45th Annual Conference on African Linguistics*, 361–375. Berlin: Language Science Press.   DOI:10.5281/zenodo.1251750

In this paper, I challenge the assumption that the syntax-semantics mapping in comparatives is necessarily as in (3), based on a study of *exceed*-comparison in Luganda (Bantu; JE15). Recent work has argued that *exceed*-comparatives are strictly phrasal and therefore make use of a 3-place comparative operator (Beck et al. 2009; Howell 2013 for Yorùbá). I too will argue that *exceed* comparatives in Luganda are syntactically phrasal comparatives, and that most *exceed* constructions can be analyzed as involving a 3-place operator. *Exceed* constructions in Luganda come in two varieties: the verb *okusinga* 'to exceed' can appear as the main verb as in (4), or in a subordinate (infinitive) form as in (5). In main verb *exceed* constructions, the gradable predicate appears in a nominalized form (with the noun class 14 prefix *bu-*), while in subordinate *exceed* constructions, the gradable predicate appears as the main predicate of the sentence (showing noun class agreement with the subject).

(4) Kizito **asinga** Kato obukulu.
 Kizito a-singa Kato o-bu-kulu
 Kizito NC1-exceed Kato AUG-NC14-old

 'Kizito is older than Kato.'
 lit.: 'Kizito exceeds Kato in oldness.' MAIN VERB EXCEED

(5) Kizito mukulu **okusinga** Kato.
 Kizito mu-kulu o-ku-singa Kato
 Kizito NC1-old AUG-NC15-exceed Kato

 'Kizito is older than Kato.'
 lit.: 'Kizito is old exceeding Kato.' SUBORDINATE EXCEED

However, I will argue that "subcomparatives" in Luganda are syntactically phrasal but make use of a 2-place "clausal"-like comparative operator. An example of this construction is given in (6), where the two arguments of *exceed* are delineated by square brackets, and are both DPs headed by nominalized gradable predicates. (A licit subcomparative in English is given in the translation line of (6).)

(6) [Obuwanvu bw' emmeeza] businga [obugazi bwayo].
 o-bu-wanvu bu-a e-N-meeza bu-singa o-bu-gazi bu-ayo
 AUG-NC14-long NC14-GEN AUG-NC9-table NC14-exceed AUG-NC14-wide NC14-POSS

 'The table's length exceeds its width.'

In order for this idea to go through, I will also need to provide an analysis of nominalized (NC14 *bu*-marked) adjectives in Luganda. To do this, I will build on the intuitions of Moltmann (2009) and Nicolas (2004) that nominalizations of gradable adjectives are relational, as well as on the standard degree-based analysis of gradable adjectives (Cresswell 1976; Kennedy & McNally 2005; von Stechow 1984: among others).

The consequences of this analysis are the following: (i) there is novel evidence for two-place comparatives for *exceed* languages, which has not previously been adduced; and (ii) at least some syntactically phrasal comparatives can receive a two-place comparative analysis, contra the mappings in (3). This paper proceeds as follows: §2 provides an overview of the phrasal vs. clausal distinction; §3 outlines a three-place operator analysis of phrasal comparatives in Luganda; in §4 I argue for the existence of a two-place operator in Luganda based on evidence from subcomparatives, and I consider two types of analyses for nominalized gradable predicates; §5 concludes.

2 The composition of comparatives

2.1 Phrasal comparatives

A phrasal comparative like (7) in English can be analyzed as involving the 3-place comparative operator in (8). The arguments of the operator are two individual arguments (the standard and target of comparison), and the gradable predicate that provides the scale for comparison. A gradable predicate is taken to denote a relation between an individual and a degree, as in (9).

(7) Kim is taller than [$_{DP}$Lee].

(8) **3-place *-er* for phrasal comparatives:**
$[\![-er_3]\!] = \lambda x \in D_e \lambda G \in D_{\langle d,\langle e,t\rangle\rangle} \lambda y \in D_e.\max(\lambda d.G(d)(y)) > \max(\lambda d'.G(d')(x))$

(9) $[\![tall]\!] = \lambda d\lambda x.\textbf{height}(x) \geq d$ (Cresswell 1976; Kennedy & McNally 2005)

A sample derivation of (7) is given in (10)-(11), assuming that DegP is the sister of A′ (Heim 2001), *than* is semantically vacuous, and the *than* phrase extraposes at PF.

(10)

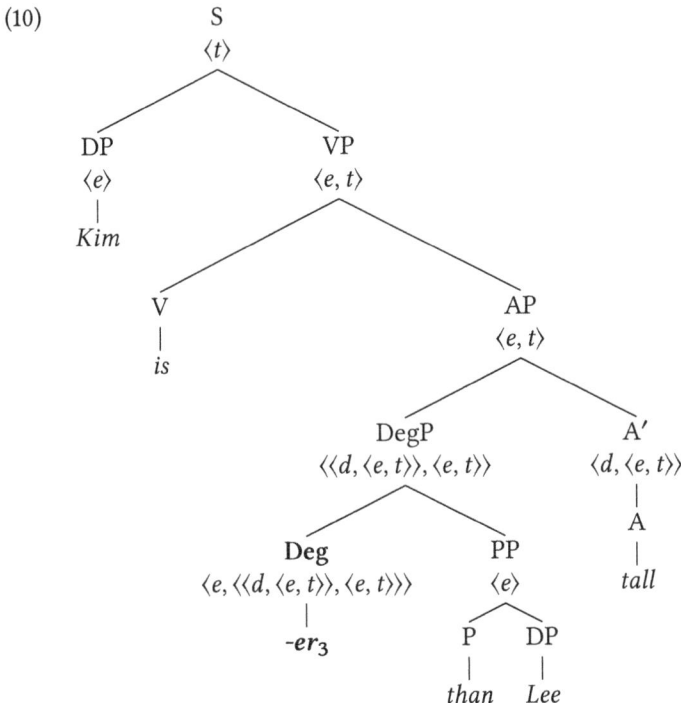

(11) a. $[\![\text{Deg}]\!] = [\![-er_3]\!] = \lambda x_{\langle e \rangle} \lambda G_{\langle d, \langle e, t \rangle \rangle} \lambda y_{\langle e \rangle} . \max(\lambda d . G(d)(y)) > \max(\lambda d' . G(d')(x))$

  b. $[\![\text{PP}]\!] = l$

  c. $[\![A']\!] = [\![\text{tall}]\!] = \lambda d \lambda x . \text{height}(x) \geq d$

  d. $[\![\text{DegP}]\!] = [\![\text{Deg}]\!]([\![\text{PP}]\!]) = \lambda G \lambda y . \max(\lambda d . G(d)(y)) > \max(\lambda d' . G(d')(l))$

  e. $[\![\text{VP}]\!] = [\![\text{AP}]\!] = [\![\text{DegP}]\!]([\![\text{AP}]\!]) = \lambda y . \max(\lambda d . \text{height}(y) \geq d) > \max(\lambda d' . \text{height}(l) \geq d')$

  f. $[\![S]\!] = [\![\text{VP}]\!]([\![\text{DP}]\!]) = 1$ iff $\max(\lambda d . \text{height}(k) \geq d) > \max(\lambda d' . \text{height}(l) \geq d')$

The truth conditions for the sentence can be paraphrased as "the maximal degree to which Kim is tall is greater than the maximal degree to which Lee is tall."

2.2 Clausal comparatives

Meanwhile, clausal comparatives like (12) are analyzed in terms of the two-place comparative operator in (13). The two arguments of two-place -er are both sets of degrees (type $\langle d, t \rangle$ functions), which are derived in syntax by movement.

(12) Kim is taller than [$_{CP}$Lee is <~~tall~~>].

(13) **2-place -er for clausal comparatives:**
  $[\![-er_2]\!] = \lambda D1 \in D_{\langle d, t \rangle} \lambda D2 \in D_{\langle d, t \rangle} . \max(D2) > \max(D1)$

A sample derivation of (12) is given in (14), assuming null operator movement within *than* phrase to derive a $\langle d, t \rangle$ function (this step not shown here; see Chomsky 1977), movement of DegP to derive another $\langle d, t \rangle$ function, and ellipsis within the *than* phrase.

(14)

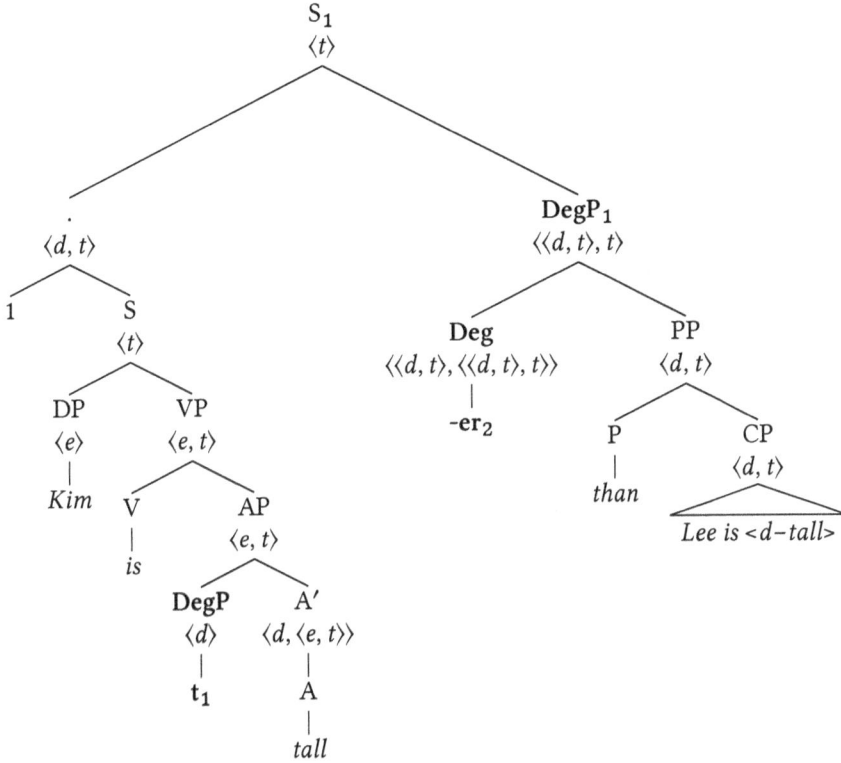

(15) a. $[\![PP]\!] = \lambda d'.\text{height}(l) \geq d'$

   b. $[\![-er_2]\!] = \lambda D1 \in D_{\langle d,t\rangle}\lambda D2 \in D_{\langle d,t\rangle}.\text{max}(D2) > \text{max}(D1)$

   c. $[\![DegP]\!] = [\![-er_2]\!]([\![PP]\!]) = \lambda D2.\text{max}(D2) > \text{max}(\lambda d'.\text{height}(l) \geq d')$

   d. $[\![A']\!] = [\![tall]\!] = \lambda d\lambda x.\text{height}(x) \geq d$

   e. $[\![VP]\!] = [\![AP]\!] = \lambda x.\text{height}(x) \geq d$

   f. $[\![S]\!] = \text{height}(k) \geq d$

   g. $[\![.]\!] = \lambda d.\text{height}(k) \geq d$

   h. $[\![S_1]\!] = [\![DegP]\!]([\![.]\!]) = \text{max}(\lambda d.\text{height}(k) \geq d) > \text{max}(\lambda d'.\text{height}(l) \geq d')$

Note that the exact same truth conditions are derived for 3-place and 2-place comparatives (compare (11f) and (15h)). With this background in place, we now turn to the analysis of *exceed* comparatives in Luganda.

3 A 3-place comparative operator in Luganda

Reviewing what we have already seen, comparatives in Luganda are formed using the verb *(oku)singa* 'exceed', where the direct object of *(oku)singa* is a DP naming the standard of comparison. *Exceed* comparatives in Luganda come in two varieties. In (16), the *exceed* verb is the main verb, with a gradable predicate in nominalized form with the NC14 *bu*-prefix. In (17), the *exceed* verb phrase is in a subordinate (infinitive) form marked with the NC15 *ku*-prefix, while the gradable predicate is the main predicate.

(16)   Kizito **asinga**   Kato obukulu.
        Kizito a-singa   Kato o-bu-kulu
        Kizito NC1-exceed Kato AUG-NC14-old

        'Kizito is older than Kato.'
        lit.: 'Kizito exceeds Kato in oldness.'   MAIN VERB EXCEED

(17)   Kizito mukulu **okusinga**   Kato.
        Kizito mu-kulu o-ku-singa   Kato
        Kizito NC1-old   AUG-NC15-exceed Kato

        'Kizito is older than Kato.'
        lit.: 'Kizito is old exceeding Kato.'   SUBORDINATE EXCEED

Comparatives with *(oku)singa* can be used in quality comparisons (above), as well as amount comparisons, as shown in (18)-(19).[1]

(18)   Charlotte **yasinga**   Rita okuwandiika   amabaluwa.
        Charlotte a-a-singa   Rita o-ku-wandiika a-ma-baluwa
        Charlotte NC1-PST-exceed Rita AUG-NC15-write AUG-NC6-letter

        'Charlotte wrote more letters than Rita.'
        lit.: 'Charlotte exceeds Rita in writing letters.'   MAIN VERB EXCEED

(19)   Charlotte yawandiika   amabaluwa   **okusinga**   Rita.
        Charlotte a-a-wandiika a-ma-baluwa   o-ku-singa   Rita
        Charlotte NC1-PST-write AUG-NC6-letter AUG-NC15-exceed Rita

        'Charlotte wrote more letters than Rita.'
        lit.: 'Charlotte wrote letters, exceeding Rita.'   SUBORDINATE EXCEED

Given that the object of *(oku)singa* is a DP, this looks like phrasal comparison. Let us propose that *(oku)singa* has the semantics of three-place comparative *-er₃* as in (20), where the direct object of *(oku)singa* (i.e., the standard of comparison) is an individual-denoting DP. Evidence for a degree-based analysis for Luganda comes from the fact that both the main verb and subordinate *exceed* constructions pass Kennedy's (2007a) tests for explicit comparison, including acceptability in crisp judgment contexts, and the ability to be formed with absolute-standard gradable predicates (see Bochnak 2013 for these tests). This proposal thus makes Luganda similar to other *exceed* languages, such as Yorùbá, which has also been argued to use a 3-place operator (Beck et al. 2009; Howell 2013).

(20) $[\![(oku)singa_3]\!] = [\![-er_3]\!] =$
        $\lambda x \in D_e \lambda G \in D_{\langle d, \langle e,t \rangle \rangle} \lambda y \in D_e . \max(\lambda d.G(d)(y)) > \max(\lambda d'.G(d')(x))$

---

[1] I assume a covert adjective *ma-ngi* 'many' is present in (18)-(19) to derive the amount comparison reading. The adjective may also appear overtly, but not shown here due to space. See Bochnak 2013.

The proposed structure and derivation of the main verb *exceed* comparative in (16) is given in (21)-(22).[2]

(21) *Kizito asinga Kato obukulu.*
      'Kizito exceeds Kato in oldness.'

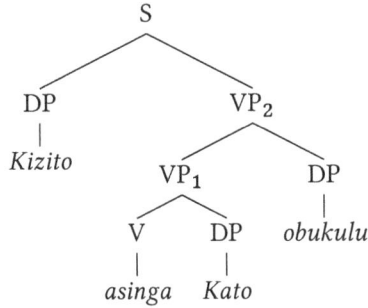

```
                        S
          ┌─────────────┴─────────────┐
         DP                          VP₂
          │                  ┌─────────┴─────────┐
       Kizito              VP₁                   DP
                     ┌──────┴──────┐              │
                     V            DP           obukulu
                     │             │
                  asinga          Kato
```

(22) a. $[\![asinga]\!] = \lambda x \lambda G \lambda y.\max(\lambda d.G(d)(y)) > \max(\lambda d'.G(d')(x))$

      b. $[\![obukulu]\!] = \lambda d \lambda x.\mathbf{old}(x) \geq d$

      c. $[\![VP_1]\!] = \lambda G \lambda y.\max(\lambda d.G(d)(y)) > \max(\lambda d'.G(d')(Kato))$

      d. $[\![VP_2]\!] = \lambda y.\max(\lambda d.\mathbf{old}(y) \geq d) > \max(\lambda d'.\mathbf{old}(Kato) \geq d')$

      e. $\boxed{[\![S]\!] = 1 \text{ iff } \max(\lambda d.\mathbf{old}(Kizito) \geq d) > \max(\lambda d'.\mathbf{old}(Kato) \geq d')}$

This analysis derives the intuitively correct truth conditions for the comparative: (16) is true if and only if the maximal degree to which Kizito is old is greater than the maximal degree to which Kato is old. It thus provides a straightforward derivation of main verb *exceed* constructions parallel to English phrasal comparatives. However, note that I have assigned a semantics for nominalized *bu-kulu* 'NC14-old' identical to that of gradable adjectives in English (cf. 9). If the underlying semantics of the gradable adjective stem *-kulu* 'old' is the same as gradable adjectives in English, this means that the nominalization morphology *bu-* is semantically vacuous. This assumption will be revised later on in §4, but for now it allows us to straightforwardly derive the truth conditions for the comparative with the semantic tools familiar from English.

For subordinate *exceed* constructions, let us assume the same three-place comparative operator semantics for *(oku)singa* in (20). Given the (simplified) structure for (17) as in (23), the semantic derivation proceeds as in (24).

(23) *Kizito mukulu okusinga Kato.*
      'Kizito is old, exceeding Kato.'

---

[2]See Bochnak 2013 for arguments for the syntax proposed here.

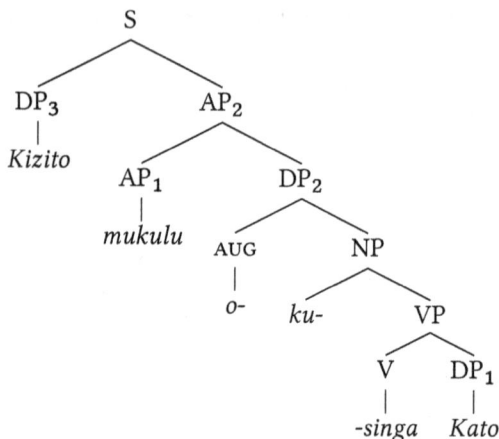

(24) a. $[\![\textit{-singa}]\!] = \lambda x \lambda G \lambda y.\max(\lambda d.G(d)(y)) > \max(\lambda d'.G(d')(x))$

b. $[\![DP_2]\!] = \lambda G \lambda y.\max(\lambda d.G(d)(y)) > \max(\lambda d'.G(d')(Kato))$

c. $[\![\textit{mukulu}]\!] = \lambda d \lambda x.\mathbf{old}(x) \geq d$

d. $[\![AP_2]\!] = \lambda y.\max(\lambda d.\mathbf{old}(y) \geq d) > \max(\lambda d'.\mathbf{old}(Kato) \geq d')$

e. $\boxed{[\![S]\!] = 1 \text{ iff } \max(\lambda d.\mathbf{old}(Kizito) \geq d)) > \max(\lambda d'.\mathbf{old}(Kato) \geq d')}$

Parallel truth conditions are thus derived for (16) and (17), and indeed these constructions appear to have the same truth conditions.[3] Note once again the assumption that nominalization morphology (this time *ku-* on the verb phrase) is semantically vacuous.

In sum, both main verb and subordinate *exceed* comparatives in Luganda receive a straightforward analysis as three-place phrasal comparatives by borrowing the familiar tools from English and other better-studied languages. This seems like a nice result, given that other *exceed* languages have also been analyzed in this way.[4] Furthermore, it has been noted for other languages that only three-place comparatives exist (e.g., Bhatt & Takahashi 2011 on Hindi/Urdu). That is, there is no reason to expect that a language necessarily uses both 3-place and 2-place comparison. However, in the next section I present evidence for the existence of two-place comparatives in Luganda, and propose an analysis involving a two-place version of the *exceed* verb.

---

[3] Again, they are both acceptable in crisp judgment contexts and are productive will gradable predicates of all scale structures (Bochnak 2013). However, my consultants seem to have a preference for subordinate *exceed* constructions, in that they are almost always offered first as translations of English. The corresponding main verb versions are nevertheless always accepted by speakers when offered by the researcher. I have no explanation for this apparent preference.

[4] In an LFG-based analysis, Beermann et al. (2005) likewise propose a common semantics for comparison between English and Luganda, despite their different syntactic structures.

4 A 2-place comparative operator in Luganda

One of the tests for diagnosing clausal (2-place) comparatives is the availability of multiple standards of comparison (Lechner 2001; Merchant 2009; Bhatt & Takahashi 2011). For instance, (25) contains three standards of comparison following *than*. The idea is this: the apparent phrasal surface form of comparatives like *Kim is taller than Lee* is the result of ellipsis applying to an underlyingly clausal complement of *than*, where the standard has moved out of the ellipsis site. Multiple standards can appear after *than* so long as they have all moved out of the ellipsis site.[5]

(25) Kim read more books on Tuesday than Lee magazines on Thursday.

Multiple standards in Luganda, however, are not licensed, either in main verb (26) or subordinate (27) *exceed* constructions.[6]

(26) * [Charlotte] [ku mande] yasinga   [Rita] [ku lw'okubiri] okuwandiika
Charlotte ku mande a-a-singa   Rita ku lw'okubiri o-ku-wandiika
Charlotte LOC Monday NC1-PST-exceed R   LOC Tuesday   AUG-NC15-write
amabaluwa   amangi.
a-ma-baluwa   a-ma-ngi
AUG-NC6-letter AUG-NC6-many

Intended: 'Charlotte wrote more letters on Monday than Rita wrote
on Tuesday.'   MAIN VERB

(27) * Charlotte yawandiika   amabaluwa   mangi   ku mande okusinga
Charlotte a-a-wandiika a-ma-baluwa ma-ngi   ku mande o-ku-singa
Charlotte NC1-PST-write AUG-NC6-letter NC6-many LOC Monday AUG-NC15-exceed
[Rita] [ku lw'okubiri].
Rita   ku lw'okubiri
Rita   LOC Tuesday

Intended: 'Charlotte wrote more letters on Monday than Rita wrote
on Tuesday.'   SUBORDINATE

A second test for the availability of clausal comparatives comes from SUBCOMPARATIVES: comparisons based on two different dimensions. An English example is given in (28). In this case, the complement of *than* has overt clausal syntax.

(28) The table is longer than it is wide.

---

[5]See Lin (2009) for arguments that comparatives with multiple standards in Chinese are still phrasal in nature, and not the result of ellipsis from a clausal source. In other words, the ability to have multiple standards does not necessarily entail that there is an underlying clausal source, so this test does not provide strong evidence for diagnosing clausal comparatives.

[6](26)-(27) contain the adjective *ma-ngi* 'many'; cf. footnote 1 and (18)-(19). Its presence/absence does not affect the grammaticality of these sentences.

Versions of these types of comparisons are possible using the Luganda main verb *exceed* construction, as shown in (30). However, the constituents forming the comparison are not full clauses. Rather, the subject and object of *okusinga* are headed by nominalized gradable adjectives (bolded in 30), which name the two dimensions of comparison. These nominalizations appear in a possessive construction, the general form of which is given in (29), where GEN is the genitive particle.[7]

(29)   possessed adjective nominalizations = [*bu*-adj + GEN + possessor]

(30)   **Obuwanvu**   bw'   emmeeza   businga   **obugazi**   bwayo.
       o-bu-wanvu   bu-a   e-N-meeza   bu-singa   o-bu-gazi   bu-ayo
       AUG-NC14-long NC14-GEN AUG-NC9-table NC14-exceed AUG-NC14-wide NC14-POSS

       'The table's length exceeds its width.'

I suggest that this is a case of 2-place comparison in Luganda, despite the fact that these are not syntactically clausal comparatives (i.e., no clausal syntax in the standard). To see how this would work, we need an analysis of possessed nominalized adjectives. I consider two styles of analysis here, which both deliver the desired result.

The first style of analysis I will call the RELATIONAL ANALYSIS, following the intuitions of Moltmann (2009) and Nicolas (2004) that nominalized properties like *length* are inherently relational. That is, a nominalized adjective like *bu-wanvu* ('NC14-long' ≈ 'length'/'longness') relates an individual to its length. Given that gradable adjectives are also standardly taken to denote relations between individuals and degrees (Cresswell 1976; Heim 2001; Kennedy & McNally 2005), it seems at first blush that the assumption we made in §3 that nominalization is vacuous is a reasonable one. However, rather than assuming that nominalizing *bu-* is vacuous, I propose it has the function of reversing the argument relations of a gradable adjective; the difference between the gradable adjective and its nominalized form is thus given in (31)-(32).

(31) $[\![\text{-}wanvu]\!] = [\![long]\!] = \lambda d \lambda x.\textbf{length}(x) \geq d$ $\qquad\qquad$ $\langle d, \langle e, t \rangle \rangle$

(32) $[\![bu\text{-}wanvu]\!] = \lambda x \lambda d.\textbf{length}(x) \geq d$ $\qquad\qquad$ $\langle e, \langle d, t \rangle \rangle$

This change of argument structure means that a nominalized adjective expects an individual as its first argument, which will be the possessor x of the property. After saturating the individual argument position, we are left with a set of degrees that x's length is greater than or equal to. Thus, the DP *obuwanvu bw'emmeeza* (≈ 'the length of the table') denotes the set of degrees in (33).

(33) $[\![obuwanvu\ bw'emmeeza]\!] = \lambda d.\textbf{length}(t) \geq d$

For a compositional analysis, I follow the syntax of possession proposed by Barker (1995). On Barker's analysis, the possessive DP is headed by a possessive D head POSS, which is null in English. For non-relational nouns (e.g., *table*), POSS introduces the possessive relation π, as shown in (34). For inherently relational nouns, POSS is still present,

---

[7]Note that *bu-* on GEN,POSS, and *-singa* are inflectional prefixes for agreement with a NC14 noun.

but simply denotes the identity function ($\lambda R.R$). Barker's analysis of possessed relational nouns in English in outlined in (35)-(36).

(34) $[\![\text{POSS}]\!] = \lambda P \lambda y \lambda z.\pi(y, z) \wedge P(z)$

(35)

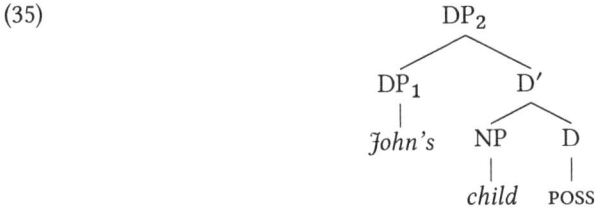

(36) a. $[\![child]\!] = \lambda x \lambda y.\text{child}(x, y)$
      b. $[\![\text{POSS}]\!] = \lambda R.R$
      c. $[\![John's\ child]\!] = \lambda y.\text{child}(j, y)$

I propose for Luganda that the genitive particle *-a* is the overt spell-out of Barker's POSS. The analysis for the possessive nominalized adjective *obuwanvu bw'emmeeza* 'the length of the table' is thus given in (37)-(38), whereby the nominalized adjective denotes a relational noun, and the result of applying the possessor is a (characteristic function of a) set of degrees of length.

(37)

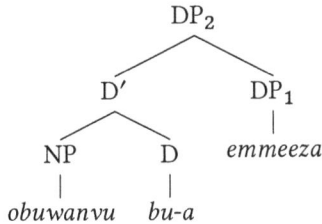

(38) a. $[\![obuwanvu]\!] = \lambda x \lambda d.\text{length}(x) \geq d$
      b. $[\![-a]\!] = [\![\text{POSS}]\!] = \lambda R.R$
      c. $[\![obuwanvu\ bwa]\!] = \lambda x \lambda d.\text{length}(x) \geq d$
      d. $[\![obuwanvu\ bw'emmeezza]\!] = \lambda d.\text{length}(t) \geq d$

Now let's return to the exceed comparative we want to analyze, namely (30). Under the analysis of possessed adjective nominalizations proposed here, the subject and object of *okusinga* 'exceed' both denote sets of degrees. But these are exactly the arguments that a 2-place comparative operator expects (cf. 13). If we submit that *okusinga* has a 2-place variant as in (39), the analysis of (30) can proceed straightforwardly as in (40)-(41).

(39) $[\![(oku)singa_2]\!] = [\![-er_2]\!] = \lambda D1 \in D_{\langle d,t \rangle} \lambda D2 \in D_{\langle d,t \rangle}.\text{max}(D2) \succ \text{max}(D1)$

(40)

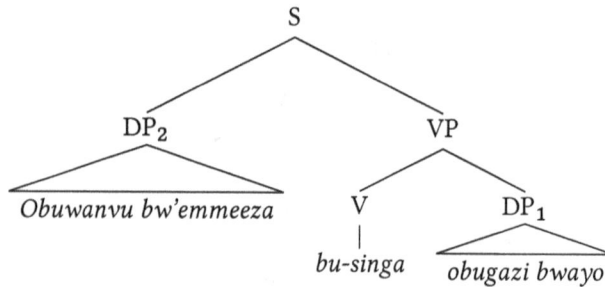

(41) a. $[\![V]\!] = [\![(oku)singa_2]\!] = [\![-er_2]\!] = \lambda D1 \in D_{\langle d,t\rangle}\lambda D2 \in D_{\langle d,t\rangle}.\max(D2) > \max(D1)$
      b. $[\![DP_1]\!] = \lambda d.\text{width}(t) \geq d$
      c. $[\![VP]\!] = \lambda D2.\max(D2) > \max(\lambda d.\text{width}(t) \geq d)$
      d. $[\![DP_2]\!] = \lambda d.\text{length}(t) \geq d$
      e. $\boxed{[\![S]\!] = 1 \text{ iff } \max(\lambda d.\text{length}(t) \geq d) > \max(\lambda d.\text{width}(t) \geq d)}$
          = "the maximal degree to which the table is long is greater than the maximal degree to which it is wide"

I refer to the second style of analysis for adjective nominalizations as the MEASURE FUNCTION analysis. The idea is that instead of denoting relations, nominalized gradable adjectives instead denote measure functions directly, i.e., functions from individuals to the maximal degree to which they hold a property (Kennedy 2007b). Under this analysis, the denotation of *obuwanvu* 'length' would be modeled as in (42).

(42) $[\![obuwanvu]\!] = \lambda x.\text{length}(x)$ type $\langle e, d\rangle$

Such an analysis has the following consequences. First, in the genitive construction, a possessed nominalized adjective denotes a degree (instead of a set of degrees), as in (43).

(43) $[\![obuwanvu\ bw'emmeezza]\!] = \text{length}(t)$

Second, we require a modified lexical entry for 2-place *exceed*, reflecting this type difference. Under this analysis, *okusinga* compares two degrees directly, as in (44). The derivation in (40) proceeds in the same was as before; it's only the type of the arguments of the comparative operator that are different. Also note that there are no maximality operators within the semantics of *oksuinga* under this analysis: maximality comes for free from the measure function itself.

(44) $[\![-singa_2]\!] = \lambda d \in D_d\lambda d' \in D_d.d' > d$

Third, if we continue to assume a relational (type $\langle d, \langle e, t \rangle \rangle$) analysis for gradable adjectives, then the nominalizing *bu-* morphology now has the function of turning the gradable adjective into the corresponding measure function, as in (45).[8]

(45) $\llbracket bu\text{-}\rrbracket = \lambda G \in D_{\langle d, \langle e, t \rangle \rangle} \lambda x.\mathbf{m}_G(x)$
where $\mathbf{m}_G$ is the measure function associated with a gradable predicate G

Finally, the measure function analysis allows for a more straightforward analysis of nominalized adjectives in argument position, an example of which is given in (46).

(46) Obuwanvu   bwa   Lydia bwe   wunyisa.
o-bu-wanvu bu-a   Lydia bu-e   wunyisa
AUG-NC14-tall NC14-GEN Lydia NC14-CLEFT surprise

'Lydia's height is surprising.'

Intuitively, it is Lydia's maximal degree of height that is surprising, not any smaller degree of height. Once again, the measure function analysis of nominalized adjectives gets maximality for free, whereas the relational analysis must posit an ad hoc maximality operator to turn the $\langle d, t \rangle$ expression into a degree.[9]

Summarizing, I take evidence from subcomparatives to indicate that Luganda has a two-place version of the comparative operator, alongside a three-place variant. There are two plausible analyses of nominalized gradable adjectives that allow for a straightforward analysis of two-place *exceed* comparatives like (30). While I do not come down definitively in favor of either the relational or measure function analysis for nominalized gradable adjectives, examples like (46) may point towards the measure function analysis.

5 Conclusion

I have argued for the existence of (at least) two versions of *(oku)singa* qua comparative operator in Luganda, namely those in (47)-(48).[10]

(47) 3-place comparative:
$\llbracket (oku)singa)_3 \rrbracket = \lambda x \lambda G \lambda y.\max(\lambda d.G(d)(y)) > \max (\lambda d'.G(d')(x))$

---

[8] Alternatively, if we take as a starting point a measure function analysis of gradable adjectives (Bartsch & Vennemann 1972; Kennedy 2007b), then we maintain that *bu-* is semantically vacuous:

(i) $\llbracket \text{-}wanvu_A \rrbracket = \llbracket obuwanvu_N \rrbracket = \lambda x.\mathbf{length}(x)$

[9] Of course, this also involves making the non-trivial assumption that predicates like *wunyisa* 'surprise' can be predicates of degrees. See Castroviejo & Schwager (2008) and Moltmann (2009) for discussion of related issues.

[10] Which version of the 2-place operator in (48) we choose depends on whether we adopt the relational or measure function analysis of nominalized gradable adjectives.

(48) 2-place comparative:

$\llbracket(oku)singa_2\rrbracket = \lambda D1\lambda D2.max(D2) > max(D1)$

or

$\llbracket(oku)singa_2\rrbracket = \lambda d\lambda d'.d' > d$

Significantly, Luganda has a 2-place *exceed* comparative despite having only syntactically "phrasal" standards. This results in an important consequence for theories of comparatives cross-linguistically, namely that having only syntactically phrasal standards does not necessarily entail the absence of 2-place comparatives. Meanwhile, the right analysis for nominalization depends on our starting assumptions about the underlying meaning of gradable adjectives and the semantic type of possessed adjective nominalizations.

Acknowledgments

I thank Kisuule Magala Katende for his patience and enthusiasm for working with me on his language. I also thank Karlos Arregi, Chris Kennedy, Jason Merchant, two anonymous reviewers, as well as audiences at the University of Chicago, UC Berkeley, ACAL 45 at the University of Kansas, and the Semantics of African, Asian, and Austronesian Languages at the University of Tübingen for comments and criticisms. The usual disclaimers apply.

Abbreviations

AUG	augment		NC#	noun class
CLEFT	cleft		POSS	possessive
GEN	genitive marker		PST	past
LOC	locative			

References

Barker, Chris. 1995. *Possessive descriptions*. Stanford, CA: CSLI Publications.

Bartsch, Renate & Theo Vennemann. 1972. The grammar of relative adjectives and comparison. *Linguistische Berichte* 20. 19–32.

Beck, Sigrid, Sveta Krasikova, Daniel Fleischer, Remus Gergel, Stefan Hofstetter, Christiane Savelsberg, John Vanderelst & Elisabeth Villalta. 2009. Crosslinguistic variation in comparative constructions. In Jeroen van Craenenbroeck & Johan Rooryck (eds.), *Linguistic Variation Yearbook*, vol. 9, 1–66. Philadelphia: John Benjamins. DOI:10.1075/livy.9.01bec

Beermann, Dorothee, Jonathan Brindle, Lars Hellan, Solomon Telda, Janicke Furberg, Florence Bayiga & Yvonne Otoo. 2005. A comparison of comparatives. In Miriam Butt & Tracy Holloway King (eds.), *Proceedings of LFG05*, 42–53. Stanford, CA: CSLI Publications.

Bhatt, Rajesh & Shoichi Takahashi. 2011. Reduced and unreduced phrasal comparatives. *Natural Language and Linguistic Theory* 29. 581–620.

Bochnak, M. Ryan. 2013. *Cross-linguistic variation in the semantics of comparatives.* Chicago: University of Chicago dissertation.

Castroviejo, Elena & Magdalena Schwager. 2008. Amazing DPs. In Tova Friedman & Satoshi Ito (eds.), *Proceedings of Semantics and Linguistic Theory (SALT) XVIII*, 176–193. Ithaca, NY: CLC Publications.

Chomsky, Noam. 1977. On wh-movement. In Peter Culicover, Thomas Wasow & Adrian Akmajian (eds.), *Formal syntax*, 71–132. New York: Academic Press.

Cresswell, Max J. 1976. The semantics of degree. In Barbara Partee (ed.), *Montague Grammar*, 261–292. New York: Academic Press.

Heim, Irene. 1985. Notes on comparatives and related matters. Ms. University of Texas at Austin.

Heim, Irene. 2001. Degree operators and scope. In Caroline Féry & Wolfgang Sternefeld (eds.), *Audiatur Vox Sapientiae*, 214–239. Berlin: Akademie-Verlag.

Howell, Anna. 2013. Abstracting over degrees in Yoruba comparison constructions. In Emmanuel Chemla, Vincent Homer & Grégoire Winterstein (eds.), *Proceedings of Sinn und Bedeutung 17*, 271–288. Paris. Talk presented at Sinn und Bedeutung 17.

Kennedy, Christopher. 1997. *Projecting the adjective: The syntax and semantics of gradability and comparison.* University of California, Santa Cruz dissertation.

Kennedy, Christopher. 2007a. Modes of comparison. In Malcolm Elliott, James Kirby, Osamu Sawada, Eleni Staraki & Suwon Yoon (eds.), *Chicago Linguistic Society (CLS) 43.* Chicago: Chicago Linguistic Society.

Kennedy, Christopher. 2007b. Vagueness and grammar: The semantics of relative and absolute gradable adjectives. *Linguistics and Philosophy* 30(1). 1–45. DOI:10.1007/s10988-006-9008-0

Kennedy, Christopher & Louise McNally. 2005. Scale structure, degree modification and the semantics of gradable predicates. *Language* 81(2). 345–381. DOI:10.1353/lan.2005.0071

Lechner, Winfried. 2001. Reduced and phrasal comparatives. *Natural Language and Linguistic Theory* 19(4). 683–735.

Lin, Jo-wang. 2009. Chinese comparatives and their implicational parameters. *Natural Language Semantics* 17. 1–27.

Merchant, Jason. 2009. Phrasal and clausal comparatives in Greek and the abstractness of syntax. *Journal of Greek Linguistics* 9. 134–164.

Moltmann, Friederike. 2009. Degree structure as trope structure: A trope-based analysis of positive and comparative adjectives. *Linguistics and Philosophy* 32. 51–94.

Nicolas, David. 2004. The semantics of nouns derived from gradable adjectives. In Cécile Meier & Matthias Weisgerber (eds.), *Proceedings of Sinn und Bedeutung 8*, 197–207.

von Stechow, Arnim. 1984. Comparing semantic theories of comparison. *Journal of Semantics* 3. 1–77. DOI:10.1093/jos/3.1-2.1

Chapter 23

Temporal remoteness and vagueness in past time reference in Luganda

M. Ryan Bochnak
University Konstanz

Peter Klecha
The Ohio State University

In this paper, we point out that past time operators (PTOs) in Luganda, a language that makes three past time remoteness distinctions, are vague and context-dependent, and provide an analysis whereby PTOs contain context-sensitive measure functions akin to gradable adjectives. We call the relevant PTOs RECENT, INTERMEDIATE, and DISTANT, respectively. Luganda PTOs give rise to borderline cases, where it is difficult to decide whether a past reference time (RT) counts as 'recent', 'intermediate' or 'distant'. What counts as 'recent', 'intermediate' or 'distant' is context dependent; e.g., there are contexts where REC is acceptable with an RT of a few weeks ago, and contexts where DIST is acceptable for an RT of a few minutes ago. We assume that like tenses in English, PTOs in matrix clauses in Luganda restrict the relation between utterance time (UT) and RT. However, while English past tense presupposes that RT precedes UT (e.g. Kratzer 1998), Luganda PTOs additionally encode as part of their meaning a vague, context-dependent measure function that compares the length of a time interval to a contextual standard.

1 Introduction

So-called 'graded tense' systems are cross-linguistically quite common (Comrie 1985; Dahl 1983; Mithun 1999; Nurse 2008). Such systems make use of multiple morphemes that make more fine-grained distinctions than simply 'past' or 'future'. Rather, they encode varying degrees of remoteness (e.g., recent vs. distant) from a reference point. Languages with such systems vary with respect to what distinctions are made, and how many.

However, grammaticalized temporal remoteness morphemes have only recently begun to attract attention within formal semantics (see e.g., Cable 2013 for Gĩkũyũ, Hayashi 2011 for South Baffin Inuktitut; Mucha 2014 for Medumba). We aim to expand upon this discussion here by investigating the paradigm of graded past tenses in Luganda (Bantu;

M. Ryan Bochnak & Peter Klecha. Temporal remoteness and vagueness in past time reference in Luganda. In Jason Kandybowicz, Travis Major, Harold Torrence & Philip T. Duncan (eds.), *African linguistics on the prairie: Selected papers from the 45th Annual Conference on African Linguistics*, 377–391. Berlin: Language Science Press. DOI:10.5281/zenodo.1251752

JE15). Luganda has three remoteness categories for past time reference. We refer to these as RECENT (1), INTERMEDIATE (2), and DISTANT (3). They are bound morphemes that are obligatory on verbs with past time reference, i.e., a speaker must choose one of these three forms for finite clauses with past time reference.

(1) **Nzinye** (ku matya).
1SG.dance.REC.PST (LOC morning)

'I danced (this morning).' RECENT PAST

Template (REC.PST): AGR-∅-ROOT-**ie**

(2) **Nazinye** (jjo).
1SG.dance.INT.PST (yesterday)

'I danced (yesterday).' INTERMEDIATE PAST

Template (INT.PST): AGR-a-ROOT-**ie**

(3) **Nazina** (luli).
1SG.dance.DIST.PST (another.time)

'I danced (the other day).' DISTANT PAST

Template (DIST.PST): AGR-a-ROOT-**a** (modulo irregular verbs)

The boundaries of the temporal delineations are often described in the literature as being quite precise, e.g., up to 4 hours ago; one day ago. In this connection, it is quite common for authors to use labels such as 'hesternal' or 'hodiernal'. Despite such characterizations, it is also often reported that the use of these morphemes can be rather flexible and context-sensitive (e.g., Hyman 1980 on Bamileke; Sharman 1956 on ChiBemba). Our primary objective in this paper is to show that the temporal remoteness morphemes[1] (TRMs) in Luganda display the hallmarks of vagueness found elsewhere in unrelated phenomena across languages (e.g., certain nouns and gradable adjectives); in other words, in certain contexts, even native speakers with full knowledge of the facts are unable to determine which TRM should be used. We provide an analysis of TRMs in Luganda that takes into account the properties of vagueness we observe. In doing so, we also compare the behavior of temporal operators cross-linguistically with that of relative and absolute gradable adjectives.

The paper proceeds as follows. In §2 we describe in more detail the use of TRMs in Luganda. In §3 we outline the behavior of vague expressions in general, and in §4 we show that Luganda TRMs indeed display the properties of vague expressions. Our analysis is presented in §5, and in §6 we draw a comparison between types of temporal operators on one hand and gradable adjectives on the other. §7 concludes and hints at areas for further research.

---

[1]Following Cable (2013), we use the term 'temporal remoteness morphemes' so as not to prejudge their analysis as true tenses or something else, e.g., modifiers of events as Cable argues for Gĩkũyũ. We do, however, analyze them as tenses in §5.

2 Temporal remoteness morphemes in Luganda

Recall that Luganda has three remoteness categories in the past tense paradigm, which we label as RECENT, INTERMEDIATE, and DISTANT past in (1)-(3).[2] Ashton et al. (1954: 122–123) characterize these morphemes in the following way: the recent past "expresses the completion of an action and/or state entered upon within the immediate past"; the intermediate past "expresses an action actually finished and accomplished as an action, but confined or limited ..., roughly speaking, to the past twelve hours"; and the distant past "denotes an action in the past, but is indefinite as to the exact time. ... It corresponds to a Past Aorist." We spend time in this section going into more detail about the semantics and use of these morphemes.[3]

First, we argue that these morphemes are not aspectual, since they can freely combine with predicates of all Aktionsarten without coercing any aspectual interpretation. Witness (4)-(7).

(4) Statives:
    a. Babilie abadde   lubuto.
       B.   3SG.be.REC.PST NC11.pregnant.woman
       'Babilie was just pregnant.'
    b. Babilie yabadde   lubuto.
       B.   3SG.be.INT.PST NC11.pregnant.woman
       'Babilie was pregnant (a little while ago).'
    c. Babilie yali   lubuto.
       B.   3SG.be.DIS.PST NC11.pregnant.woman
       'Babilie was pregnant (a long time ago).'

(5) Activities:
    a. Kato azinye.
       K.   3SG.dance.REC.PST
       'Kato just danced.'
    b. Kato yazinye.
       K.   3SG.dance.INT.PST
       'Kato danced (a little while ago).'

---

[2]Our data come from elicitation sessions with two native speakers of Luganda, bilingual in English, living in the United States. All elicitation sessions were conducted in English, and involved a mix of translation tasks and felicity judgements of grammatical sentences in particular contexts.

[3]Note that we restrict ourselves here to the three "simple" past time markers in matrix clauses. We also do not talk about so-called "special" and "compound" tenses of Luganda (see Kisubika-Musoke 1986). Grammars such as Ashton et al. (1954) have also cited future TRMs which similarly divide future time into nearer and more distant time zones. However, our consultants have indicated to us that these forms are not colloquial, and the commonly used future forms do not carry temporal remoteness inferences, so we do not discuss these here.

    c. Kato yazina.
       K.   3SG.dance.DIS.PST
       'Kato danced (a long time ago).'

(6) Accomplishments:

    a. Kato addusse   mairo biri.
       K.   3SG.run.REC.PST mile three
       'Kato just ran three miles.'

    b. Kato yaddusse   mairo biri.
       K.   3SG.run.INT.PST mile three
       'Kato ran three miles (a little while ago).'

    c. Kato yadduka   mairo biri.
       K.   3SG.run.DIS.PST mile three
       'Kato ran three miles (a long time ago).'

(7) Achievements:

    a. Ensuwa   eyatisse.
       AUG.NC9.pot NC9.break.REC.PST
       'The pot just broke.'

    b. Ensuwa   yeyatisse.
       AUG.NC9.pot NC9.break.INT.PST
       'The pot broke (a little while ago).'

    c. Ensuwa   yeyatika.
       AUG.NC9.pot NC9.break.DIST.PST
       'The pot broke (a long time ago).'

Second, certain TRMs in Luganda asymmetrically entail others. In particular, the intermediate past appears to be usable in any context where the recent past is. For instance in (8)-(9), the intermediate past is possible both with *tano emabega* 'five hours ago' and *satu emabega* 'three hours ago', while the recent past is possible only with the latter.

(8) Nzinye   saawa {satu/#tano} emabega.
     1SG.dance.REC.PST hour {three/five} behind
     'I danced {three/five} hours ago.'   (RECENT PAST)

(9) Nazinye   saawa {satu/tano} emabega.
     1SG.dance.INT.PST hour {three/five} behind
     'I danced {three/five} hours ago.'   (INTERMEDIATE PAST)

The distant past cannot as easily be used in contexts where the intermediate or recent past can, but there is some evidence that it is the most general past, and that the inference of 'distance' is due to scalar implicature. For instance, a question with a the recent or intermediate past gives rise to an inference that the speaker has at least some knowledge about the temporal location of the event at issue – but a question with the distant past gives rise to no such inference. The contexts below are adapted from Cable (2013), who finds the same thing for Gĩkũyũ.

(10) Context: You have known Kato for a long time, but have never been to his house. You are finally invited over and you see that he often buys very old things for fun. He tells you he bought an old Apple computer from 1985 just a few hours before you arrived. You see his TV, which is also quite old, but you can't tell if he just recently bought it, or if he's actually had it since the 80's.

   a. Eno   TV wagigguladi?
       this.NC9 TV 2SG.SUBJ-NC9.OBJ-buy-DIS.PST-when

      'When did you buy this TV?'

   b. Naagigguzze   jjo.
       1SG.SUBJ.NC9.OBJ.buy.INT.PST yesterday

      'I just bought it yesterday.'

(11) Same context as above.

   a. Eno   TV wagigguzzedi?
       this.NC9 TV 2SG.SUBJ.NC9.OBJ.buy.INT.PST.when

      'When did you buy this TV?' (Suggests it happened recently)

   b. Naagiggula   luli.
       1SG.SUBJ.NC9.OBJ.buy.DIS.PST another.time

      'I bought it a while ago.' (Sounds contradictory)

   c. Speaker notes that one might precede the answer in 11b by saying "What makes you think I bought it recently?".

Crucially, the speaker notes that (11a) can be challenged, by saying something like "What makes you so sure I just bought it?", whereas (10a) *cannot* be challenged similarly, i.e., with something like "What makes you so sure I bought it a long time ago?". Thus we conclude that the inference of temporal distance that is produced by what we call the distant past is an implicature. But note that this implicature is vague and context-sensitive in exactly the same way that the semantic inferences of the recent and intermediate past are vague and context-sensitive. Thus for the following discussion we will not distinguish between implicatures and semantic inferences when discussing vagueness and context-sensitivity.

3 Vagueness in natural language

Certain expressions in natural language display *vagueness*, for instance certain 'scalar' nouns like *heap*, and relative gradable adjectives like *tall*. Vague expressions are those where the criteria of application are not clear-cut and can shift in different contexts of use. Here we outline three properties of vague expressions and sentences that contain them (Fine 1975; Kamp 1975; Fara 2000; Kennedy 2007).

First, CONTEXT DEPENDENCE: what counts as a heap or tall varies from context to context. Consider the sentence in (12).

(12)   Tom is tall.

In a context where Tom has a height of 165 cm, and is in the second grade, (12) is intuitively true. Meanwhile, in a context where Tom has a height of 165 cm and is a professional basketball player, (12) is intuitively false. Crucial here is the COMPARISON CLASS, namely the set of objects against which Tom's height is compared in order to judge whether (12) counts as true or not.

Second is the existence of BORDERLINE CASES. That is, there are certain cases where it's hard to judge whether a vague predicate holds or not. For instance, consider a context where Tom is a 12-year-old boy. Is (12) true or false? This case seems harder to judge one way or the other, compared with the previous contexts we considered where the judgements were more clear-cut.

The third property of vague expressions is that they give rise to the sorites paradox. Consider (13).

(13)   P1: 1,000,000 grains of sand is a heap of sand.
        P2: A heap of sand less one grain is still a heap of sand.
        C: #One grain of sand counts as a heap of sand.

If we accept P1 & P2, then with enough iterations of P2 we should also accept C. Nevertheless, the intuition is that C does not hold, resulting in a paradox.

There are various proposals on the market for how vagueness comes about, and we do not wish to take a stand on this issue here.[4] However, we would like to highlight the following passage from Kennedy (2007: p. 42): "[V]agueness comes from epistemic uncertainty about where we actually draw the line and metalinguistic resistance to treating highly similar objects differently relative to the property expressed ...Whether this analysis extends to an account of vagueness in other categories is an issue that must be addressed in future work." It is this last point that we aim to address in this paper, namely whether these properties of vagueness manifest themselves in temporal operators in natural language.

4 Vagueness in the Luganda past paradigm

In this section we show that Luganda TRMs display the same properties of vagueness that we find in vague nouns and adjectives. First, a methodological point: we presented discourse contexts to the consultant in English, which does not have TRMs, because we

---

[4]See Fara 2000, Grinsell 2012, Soames 1999 and Williamson 1994 for various proposals.

wanted to avoid prejudicing the response given by the consultants by having a TRM in the prompt.[5]

Context-dependence: for many events, the restrictions on when certain TRMs can be used more or less follows the pattern described in Ashton et al. (1954). However, what counts as recent or distant can vary across contexts. For instance, the recent past can be used to talk about a time months prior to the utterance time (UT), as in (14). Likewise, the distant past can be used to talk about a time only a few minutes prior to UT, as in (15).[6] Thus, the notions of what counts as recent or distant can vary with the context, much like what counts as tall varies across contexts.

(14) a. Context: You plant your crops every year in February. It is now April, and I ask you what you planted this year. You tell me that you planted maize.

     b. Nsimbye   kasooli.
        1SG.plant.REC.PST maize

        'I planted maize.'

(15) a. Context: We are at a party, and I ask you why you are not dancing to the song that's playing. You tell me that you danced a few songs ago.

     b. Nazina   luli.
        1SG.dance.DIST.PST another.time

        'I danced a while ago (to another song).'

In other words, the use of a particular TRM seems to depend on a relevant comparison class, just like for predicates like *tall*. Here is a first stab at characterizing the relevant comparison class for TRMs: in (14) the comparison class is time intervals between UT and previous crop plantings, while in (15) the comparison class is time intervals between UT and previous songs.

Borderline cases: there are also cases where it is difficult to decide whether an event counts as 'recent', 'intermediate' or 'distant'. There is an interesting contrast here between TRMs in Luganda and gradable adjectives. Namely, for gradable adjectives, a speaker can refuse to make a judgment (e.g. "I'm not sure whether Bill would count as tall or not"). However, verbs in Luganda naming past events are *obligatorily* marked with TRMs - a speaker always has to choose one. Consider the following responses to the question "What have you been doing?"

(16) Nzinye   saawa {satu/?nnya/#tano} emabega.
     1SG.dance.REC.PST hour {three/four/five}   behind

     'I danced {three/four/five} hours ago.'   (RECENT PAST)

(17) *Nazinye saawa {satu/nnya/tano} emabega.*
     'I danced {three/four/five} hours ago.'   (INTERMEDIATE PAST)

---

[5]See AnderBois & Henderson (2015) for comments on choosing elicitation language in semantic fieldwork.
[6]One of our consultants finds (15) not completely natural, but does accept it.

(18) #*Nazina saawa {satu/nnya/tano} emabega.*
      'I danced {three/four/five} hours ago.'   (DISTANT PAST)

According to our consultants, in the context in (16), the use of the recent past is definitely fine for '3 hours ago', definitely excluded for '5 hours ago', but borderline for '4
hours ago'.[7]

Sorites sequences: Luganda TRMs also give rise to sorites paradox effects, just like
scalar nouns and gradable adjectives. Consider the party scenario in (19), and the subsequent sentences offered and rejected by our consultant to describe the scenario in
(20)-(23).[8]

(19) Context: You are at a party, and they play the following songs (in order):
      Twist and Shout
      YMCA
      Dancing Queen
      Sweet Caroline
      Gangnam Style
      Blue Suede Shoes
      Don't Stop Believing
      Macarena
      Rollin' in the Deep
      Zamboni Driver

(20) a. Context as in (19). Peet comes to the party late, just as Zamboni Driver is
          finishing. He is always really interested in the music they play, so you want
          to tell him what songs were played.

      b. Baakubye   Twist and Shout.
          3PL.play.INT.PST Twist and Shout

          'They played Twist and Shout.'

      c. Observation: Speaker uses INT.PST discourse-initially in this scenario.

(21) a. Context: same as above

      b. # Baakuba   Twist and Shout.
            3PL.play.DIST.PST Twist and Shout

          'They played Twist and Shout.'

      c. Speaker's comment: "Sounds like it's a different party, another day."

(22) a. Context: same as above

      b. # Bakubye   Twist and Shout.
            3PL.play.REC.PST Twist and Shout

          'They played Twist and Shout.'

---

[7]Given the variable nature of context dependency and borderline cases, we imagine that judgments could
also vary somewhat between speakers.

[8]We have performed this activity with only one of our consultants so far (Kisuule Magala Katende).

c. Speaker's comment: "That's like they just played it. That's like a couple of minutes ago. ... Just missed it."

(23) a. Context: Immediately after uttering (20b)

b. Baaziza-ko   YMCA.
3PL.add.INT.PST-PART YMCA

'Then they played YMCA.'
('They added on YMCA.')   (offered by speaker)

c. Observation: Speaker uses INT.PST again for event immediately following the first

(24) a. Context: Immediately after uttering (20b) and (23b)

b. *Baazizako Dancing Queen.*
'Then they played Dancing Queen.'   INT.PST
Judgment: Accepted by speaker

c. *Baazizako Sweet Caroline.*
'Then they played Sweet Caroline.   INT.PST
Judgment: Accepted by speaker
⋮

d. *Baazizako Zamboni Driver.*
'Then they played Zamboni Driver.'   INT.PST
Judgment: Accepted by speaker

e. Speaker's comment: "If you just played it, you would say *bazaako* [REC.PST]. ... When you are coming towards the end, it has to be *bazaako*. ... Because it's more recent than the other ones."

f. Peet: "Can you be really sure about where you would switch?"
Speaker: "No, the time difference is in your mind. ... There is no obvious timeline to stop it."

A similar effect is observed in the following OCD friend scenario in (25)-(27).

(25) a. Context: Your (crazy) friend wants to know what songs were played on the radio in the last few days in order. Being an indulgent friend, you tell him what songs were played.

b. Baakuba   Twist and Shout.
3.SG.play.DIST.PST Twist and Shout

'They played Twist and Shout.'

c. Speaker's comment: "That's another day. That's not today."

(26) a. Context: Immediately after uttering (25b)

b. Baakuba   YMCA.
3.SG.play.DIST.PST YMCA

'They played YMCA.'

(27) a. Context: Immediately after uttering (25b)

  b. # Baakubye   YMCA.
      3.SG.play.INT.PST
      'They played YMCA.'

  c. Speaker's comment: "No. It would be very awkward. ... You never know
      when you switch to *baakubye* [INT.PST]. But that should be within a day or
      something like that. ... There's no clear place where you would stop to apply
      it [the distant past form]."

Thus, we seem to have evidence that sorites sequences behave like expected for sentences containing vague expressions. Small differences in time don't prompt speakers
to suddenly switch TRMs, and speakers are not sure when exactly it is appropriate to
switch TRMs in these listing contexts.[9]

In sum, sentences containing TRMs in Luganda behave like sentences containing other
vague expressions (in English).

5 Analysis

Following Kennedy (1997; 2007), we take simple relative gradable adjectives like *tall*,
which in their positive (i.e., bare) forms are vague, to denote **measure functions**, i.e.,
functions from an object to a *degree*, an abstract unit of measurement. The denotation of
tall on this basis is given below.

(28) $[\![\,tall\,]\!] = \lambda x.\textbf{height}(x)$ type $\langle e, d \rangle$

The above says that *tall* maps an individual to her height. Any simple adjective phrase,
however, should ultimately denote something of type $\langle e, t \rangle$; i.e., should map an individual
to true or false, depending on her height. So some assumption must be made about how
the type of a bare adjective shifts when in its positive form. Kennedy's proposal is an
abstract morpheme POS which has the following interpretation.

(29) $[\![\,POS\,]\!] = \lambda G_{\langle e,d \rangle}.\lambda x.G(x) \geq s(G)$ type $\langle\langle e, d \rangle, \langle e, t \rangle\rangle$

Following Kennedy (2007), the function s is a contextually provided one which takes
a measure function and returns the degree that that function would have to map an
individual to in order for that individual to 'stand out', in terms of that property, in the
context. If *tall* combines with POS rather than a degree modifier, the result is a vague
predicate.

(30) $[\![\,POS\ tall\,]\!] = \lambda x.\textbf{height}(x) > s$ type $\langle e, t \rangle$

---

[9]It has been suggested to us that these effects might be obviated if the list is given out of order. We have
not been able to test this idea yet.

Thus a sentence like *John is tall*, which includes the positive form of an adjective, is true iff John's height stands out in the context, i.e., if it exceeds the determined standard.

On Kennedy's account, borderline cases arise because speakers are unsure about where the cut-off is for 'standing out'. Cases like the Sorites Paradox arise because given a context that contains any two objects that have gradable property *G* to very slightly varying degrees, neither one can 'stand out' with respect to the other.

Note that the reason that *tall* is not simply given the denotation in (30) above is that it may instead combine with degree modifiers or measure phrases, which do not necessarily involve comparison of superiority. However, Luganda TRMs do not compose with anything like degree modifiers, and so we need not commit to any account of the positive form of gradable adjectives.[10] We provide denotations for the Luganda TRMs below which build in the vagueness witnessed in the positive morpheme above.

Our denotations are built upon the following measure functions, which relate time intervals to degrees.

(31)   **close**(t, t') assigns to a time t' a degree on a scale of closeness to t

(32)   **far**(t, t') assigns to a time t' a degree on a scale of distance from t

We embed our analysis in a theory of tense which says that, like tenses in English, TRMs in Luganda in matrix clauses constrain the relation between an evaluation time and a reference time (RT), where that evaluation time is, at least in matrix contexts, utterance time (Reichenbach 1947; Klein 1994). However, cf. Cable (2013; 2015) for a different view of TRMs in Gĩkũyũ. Following Heim (1994) and Kratzer (1998) we assume that temporal operators constrain the relation between RT and UT by placing presuppositions on the reference of a temporal pronoun which corresponds to RT. Following Cable (2013) and others, we assume that TRMs do not denote this pronoun itself, but adjoin to such pronouns. Note that these are all assumptions, and moreover our analysis does not crucially hinge on any of them.

(33) $[\![\text{REC.PST}]\!]^{t} = \lambda t' : \textbf{close}(t, t') > \textbf{s(close)} \ \& \ t' < t \ . \ t'$
       Presupposition: the degree of closeness of t' to t exceeds a contextual standard

(34) $[\![\text{INT.PST}]\!]^{t} = \lambda t' : \textbf{far}(t, t') < \textbf{s(far)} \ \& \ t' < t \ . \ t'$
       Presupposition: the degree of far-ness of t' to t is less than a contextual standard
       Implicature: the degree of closeness of t' to t is less than a contextual standard

(35) $[\![\text{DIST.PST}]\!]^{t} = \lambda t' : t' < t \ . \ t'$
       Implicature: the degree of far-ness of t' to t exceeds a contextual standard.[11]

---

[10] A reviewer suggests that temporal adverbs might be treated as degree modifiers under this view. We leave this intriguing suggestion for future work.

[11] Crucially the scalar implicature generated by comparison to the other tenses carries the same vagueness and context-dependence that those tenses do.

In the denotations above, t' corresponds to RT, i.e., the temporal pronoun that the TRMs adjoin to, while t corresponds to the evaluation time, which in matrix contexts is UT.[12]

Each of these morphemes is a partial identity function on RT, presupposing two things about it: First, that it is in the past relative to UT ($t' < t$), and second, its distance from t, denoted by the measure function and the comparative operator (> or <).

Our analysis of these TRMs makes them comparable to the positive forms of relative gradable adjectives like *tall*. So our analysis captures the vagueness associated with these expressions. Note that this analysis does not commit us to one view of vagueness over another; since our analysis equates these expressions with positive gradable adjectives, whatever account can be made of gradable adjectives can be extended to TRMs.

6 Accounting for crosslinguistic variation: scale type and vagueness

Why are Luganda TRMs vague while English tenses are not? We suggest it is for the same reason that *relative* gradable adjectives are vague in their positive forms, while *absolute* gradable adjectives are not. Absolute adjectives, like **full**, are still perfectly gradable (36), but fail the tests described above for vagueness.

(36) This cup is more full than that one.

For example, for (37) to be true, the degree of fullness exhibited by the cup must simply be the maximum; there is no contextually determined standard.

(37) This cup is full.

Likewise, such adjectives do not have borderline cases or give rise to Sorites Paradoxes.[13] Kennedy (2007) attributes this to the differences between these adjectives in terms of their *scale structure*. In other words, while there is an inherent upper-bound to fullness, there is no inherent upper-bound for height. So for an object to 'stand-out' on the fullness scale it simply must occupy the highest point on said scale, while the same cannot be said for the height scale. Instead, since such scales lack obvious 'milestones' for determining what stands out, interlocutors must appeal to context. This in turn gives rise to vagueness.

English past tense is like an absolute gradable adjective; it does not exhibit vagueness because it does not depend upon context (not in the same way as a relative gradable adjective, anyway). We therefore predict that no language with a single past tense like English should exhibit vagueness either. We also predict that, if any languages with graded tense systems like Luganda actually do differentiate them in a rigid, diurnal way,

---

[12] The same may also be true for embedded contexts; see Cable (2013)

[13] Note that, as Kennedy (2007) discusses, such adjectives may give rise to *imprecision*, e.g., in a case where a cup which is not strictly speaking full is called 'full' in a particular context; this is different from vagueness. See Kennedy 2007 for more discussion.

as Luganda was described to do by Ashton et al. (1954), then we also predict that those graded tense systems should not exhibit vagueness either. And finally, we predict that any graded tense system which is context dependent like Luganda's should also be vague.

7 Conclusion and future research

Contrary to descriptions like that of Ashton et al. (1954), the graded tense system of Luganda exhibits context dependence and vagueness. This finding expands the empirical domain for work on vagueness, which so far has been focused mostly on adjectives and other lexical categories.

Many questions remain. For example, Cable (2013) argues against treating TRMs in Gĩkũyũ as tenses, relying on data from adverbials and embedding. Tenses, according to Klein (1994), relate reference time to utterance time, while the relation between reference time and the event described by the verb is mediated by aspect. According to Cable, TRMs in Gĩkũyũ behave like neither tense nor aspect according to these definitions, instead relating utterance time directly to the event described by the verb. It remains to be seen whether Luganda TRMs are like those in Gĩkũyũ in this regard. This question is left for future research.

Abbreviations

1, 2, 3	first, second, third person	OBJ	object
AGR	agreement	PART	particle
AUG	augment	PST	past
DIST	distant	REC	recent
INT	intermediate	SG	singular
LOC	locative	SUBJ	subject
NC	noun class		

Acknowledgements

We thank Kisuule Magala Katende and Waiswa Nkwanga for their patience and enthusiasm for working with us on their language. We also thank audiences at the University of Chicago, the University of Potsdam, SWAMP at University of Michigan, the 40th Berkeley Linguistics Society, ACAL 45 at the University of Kansas, and two anonymous reviewers for comments and criticisms. The usual disclaimers apply.

References

AnderBois, Scott & Robert Henderson. 2015. Linguistically establishing discourse context: Two case studies from Mayan languages. In M. Ryan Bochnak & Lisa Matthewson (eds.), *Methodologies in semantic fieldwork*, 207–232. New York: Oxford University Press.

Ashton, Ethel O., Enoch M. K. Mulira, E. G. M. Ndawula & Archibald N. Tucker. 1954. *A Luganda Grammar*. New York: Longmans, Green & Co.

Cable, Seth. 2013. Beyond the past, present, and future: Towards the semantics of 'graded tense' in Gĩkũyũ. *Natural Language Semantics* 21. 219–276.

Cable, Seth. 2015. Graded tenses in complement clauses: Evidence that the future is not a tense. In *NELS 45*.

Comrie, Bernard. 1985. *Tense*. New York: Cambridge University Press.

Dahl, Östen. 1983. Temporal distance: Remoteness distinctions in tense-aspect systems. *Linguistics* 21(1). 105–122.

Fara, Delia Graff. 2000. Shifting sands: An interest-relative theory of vagueness. *Philosophical Topics* 28. 45–81. Originally published under the name "Delia Graff". DOI:10.5840/philtopics20002816

Fine, Kit. 1975. Vagueness, truth and logic. *Synthese* 30. 265–300.

Grinsell, Timothy. 2012. Social choice theory and linguistic vagueness. Paper presented at *Semantics and Linguistic Theory (SALT) XXII*.

Hayashi, Midori. 2011. *The structure of multiple tenses in Inuktitut*. University of Toronto dissertation.

Heim, Irene. 1994. Comments on Abusch's theory of tense. In Hans Kamp (ed.), *Ellipsis, tense, and questions*, 143–170. Amsterdam: University of Amsterdam.

Hyman, Larry M. 1980. Relative time reference in the Bamileke tense system. *Studies in African Linguistics* 11(2). 227–237.

Kamp, Hans. 1975. Two theories of adjectives. In Edward Keenan (ed.), *Formal semantics of natural language*, 123–155. Cambridge: Cambridge University Press.

Kennedy, Christopher. 1997. *Projecting the adjective: The syntax and semantics of gradability and comparison*. University of California, Santa Cruz dissertation.

Kennedy, Christopher. 2007. Vagueness and grammar: The semantics of relative and absolute gradable adjectives. *Linguistics and Philosophy* 30(1). 1–45. DOI:10.1007/s10988-006-9008-0

Kisubika-Musoke, E. M. 1986. *Tense formation in Luganda and some problems related to learning English*. Kampala: Uganda Bookshop.

Klein, Wolfgang. 1994. *Time in language*. New York: Routledge.

Kratzer, Angelika. 1998. More structural analogies between pronouns and tenses. In *Proceedings of Semantics and Linguistic Theory (SALT) 8*. Ithaca, NY: CLC Publications.

Mithun, Marianne. 1999. *The Languages of Native North America*. New York: Cambridge University Press.

Mucha, Anne. 2014. Past interpretation and "graded tense" in Medumba. Ms. University of Potsdam.

Nurse, Derek. 2008. *Tense and aspect in Bantu.* New York: Oxford University Press.

Reichenbach, Hans. 1947. The tenses of verbs. In Hans Reichenbach (ed.), *Elements of symbolic logic*, 287–298. New York: The Macmillan Company.

Sharman, J. C. 1956. The tabulation of tenses in a Bantu language (Bemba: Northern Rhodesia). *Africa* 26. 29–46.

Soames, Scott. 1999. *Understanding truth.* Oxford: Oxford University Press.

Williamson, Timothy. 1994. *Vagueness.* London: Routledge.

Chapter 24

Focus marking in Kuria

Meredith Landman
Pomona College

Rodrigo Ranero
University of Maryland, College Park

This paper examines focus marking in Kuria. We propose an account of the syntax/semantics of the prefix /ne-/. This prefix displays a varied syntactic distribution, posing a puzzle as to what semantically unifies all of its uses. In focus constructions, /ne-/ obligatorily appears on a fronted (i.e. focused) phrase, whereas in simple declaratives, /ne-/ obligatorily appears pre-verbally. Following previous analyses of similar markers in Bantu (Schwarz 2007 for Kikuyu and Abels & Muriungi 2008 for Kiitharaka), we analyze /ne-/ uniformly as a focus marker that arises in a focus phrase in the left periphery. We support this account of /ne-/ by presenting novel data that suggest that even when /ne-/ occurs pre-verbally, it still marks focus (VP focus or sentential focus.) We also show how /ne-/ differs syntactically from similar markers in other languages. For example, Kuria allows for the focus marker to appear internal to the focused constituent, in contrast with data from Kiitharaka (Abels & Muriungi 2008) and other languages (see Hartmann & Zimmermann 2009 for Guruntum). This paper thus discusses a range of data patterns relating to the Kuria prefix /ne-/, offering insight into a syntax/semantic puzzle as well as cross-linguistic variation in the realization of focus.

1 Introduction

Kuria (Narrow Bantu E.43) is an understudied language spoken in Kenya and Tanzania. In this paper, we investigate the syntax and semantics of the Kuria morpheme /ne-/, which in the literature has been labeled a focus marker (Cammenga 2004; Mwita 2008). In declaratives, this morpheme obligatorily occurs pre-verbally, as in (1):[1,2]

---

[1] The morpheme /ne-/ displays predictable allomorphy, surfacing as either [ne] or as [n], and it is possible that it is /n-/ that is in fact underlying.

[2] In the declaratives presented in this paper, /ne-/ is obligatory only in the remote past and remote future tenses; /ne-/ does not appear in the immediate past or immediate future tenses—see also Mwita 2008, who reports that /ne-/ must appear in 11 out of 22 TAM combinations. It is unclear to us why /ne-/ is absent in certain tenses; this may be due to phonological, syntactic, or semantic/pragmatic conditioning, and we do not attempt an account of this pattern here.

Meredith Landman & Rodrigo Ranero. Focus marking in Kuria. In Jason Kandybowicz, Travis Major, Harold Torrence & Philip T. Duncan (eds.), *African linguistics on the prairie: Selected papers from the 45th Annual Conference on African Linguistics*, 393–412. Berlin: Language Science Press. DOI:10.5281/zenodo.1251754

(1) Ichi-ng'iti *(n-)cha-a-it-ir-e   ege-toocho.
     10-hyena (FOC-)10SA-PST-kill-PRF-FV 7-rabbit
     'The hyenas killed the rabbit.'

Previous analyses of Kuria /ne-/, as well as similar morphemes in other Bantu languages, treat these items in different ways: Some view them as focus markers (see Cammenga 2004 and Mwita 2008 for Kuria, Schwarz 2007 for Kikuyu, and Abels & Muriungi 2008 for Kiitharaka), while others see them as assertion or polarity markers (see Bergvall 1987 for Kikuyu and Eslinger 2013 for Kuria). We argue here, based on original data, that /ne-/ is in fact a focus marker, and we propose an extension of Schwarz's (2007) syntactic account of Kikuyu to Kuria, by which /ne-/ heads a Focus Phrase projection in the left periphery of the clause.[3] Thus, our aims in this paper are twofold: first, empirically, to document an array of patterns related to Kuria /ne-/, which illustrate the language's strategy for focus realization, and, second, from a theoretical perspective, to show that an extension of a previous syntactic analysis of a similar morpheme in a related language (i.e., Schwarz's account of Kikuyu) can capture the Kuria data.

The remainder of this paper is organized as follows. In §2, we present the basic syntactic distribution of /ne-/. In §3, we present evidence for analyzing /ne-/ semantically as a focus marker. In §4, we propose a syntactic account of /ne-/, extending Schwarz (2007)'s account of Kikuyu to Kuria. In §5, we compare focus marking in Kuria with what has been observed for focus marking in other languages, discussing how Kuria fits into a crosslinguistic typology of focus marking. In §6, we document a number of additional patterns regarding /ne-/, articulating several issues regarding /ne-/ for future research. Finally, §7 concludes our paper.

2 The basic distribution of /ne-/

Kuria displays default SVO word order, with some freedom of object ordering in ditransitive and tritransitive constructions. As shown in (1), in declaratives, /ne-/ obligatorily appears pre-verbally and only once per clause (parallel to Kikuyu; see Schwarz 2007: 142).[4,5]

---

[3]Mwita (2008) suggests that some cases involving pre-verbal /ne-/ are due to grammaticalization, and therefore lose the focus meaning. We argue here that because some instances of pre-verbal /ne-/ involve focus, the simplest synchronic analysis is to take all instances of pre-verbal /ne-/ as instantiating focus.

[4]This also holds for embedded declaratives, e.g. clauses embedded by a bridge verb such as 'say':

(i) N-eng'we a-a-gamb-er-e   iga gati *(n-)a-a-ha-y-e   umw-igia ege-tabo.
    FOC-who SA-PST-say-PRF-FV COMP 1.Gati FOC-3SG.SA-PST-give-APPL.PRF-FV 1-teacher 5-book
    'Who said that Gati gave the teacher a book?'

[5]See, however, §5.1, in which we observe some phrase-internal instances of /ne-/.

In *wh*-questions and focus constructions, that is, constructions that involve a fronted constituent, /ne-/ obligatorily precedes the fronted constituent. For example, in the *wh*-questions in (2), /ne-/ precedes the fronted *wh*-phrase; note that here /ne-/ cannot also occur pre-verbally:

(2)   a. *(N-)ke   (*n-)ge-it-ir-e   ege-toocho?
          (FOC-)what (FOC-)SA-kill-PRF-FV 7-rabbit
          'What killed the rabbits?'
     b. *(N-)ke   ichi-ng'iti (*n-)cha-a-it-ir-e?
          (FOC-)what 10-hyena (FOC-)10SA-PST-kill-PRF-FV
          'What did the hyenas kill?'

Similarly, in (information) focus constructions, e.g. answers to *wh*-questions, as in (3), /ne-/ appears on the fronted, focused phrase; here too, /ne-/ cannot also appear pre-verbally:

(3)   a. *(N-)ichi-ng'iti (*n-)cha-a-it-ir-e   ege-toocho.
          (FOC-)10-hyena (FOC-)10SA-PST-kill-PRF-FV 7-rabbit
          'THE HYENAS killed the rabbit.'
     b. *(N-)ege-toocho ichi-ng'iti (*n-)cha-a-it-ir-e.
          (FOC-)7-rabbit   10-hyena (FOC-)10SA-PST-kill-PRF-FV
          'The hyenas killed THE RABBIT.'

Note that alongside (3a), the alternative word order in (4) is also possible, where the subject precedes the constituent marked with /ne-/; as far as we can tell, there is no difference in interpretation or contextual appropriateness between (3a) and (4).

(4)   Ichi-ng'iti *(n-)ege-toocho (*n-)cha-a-it-ir-e.
      10-hyena (FOC-)7-rabbit   (FOC-)10SA-PST-kill-PRF-FV
      'The hyenas killed THE RABBIT.'

It is not possible for /ne-/ to appear post-verbally, thus, attempting to focus an *in-situ* object is ungrammatical:

(5)   Ichi-ng'iti cha-a-it-ir-e   (*n-)ege-toocho.
      10-hyena 10SA-PST-kill-PRF-FV (FOC-)7-rabbit
      (Intended meaning: 'The hyenas killed THE RABBIT.')

To summarize this section, in declaratives, /ne-/ obligatorily appears pre-verbally, while in *wh*-questions and focus constructions, /ne-/ obligatorily precedes the fronted constituent.[6] We see the varied distribution of this morpheme as raising two questions for a uniform account of its different uses. First, is /ne-/ truly a focus marker? Second, where does /ne-/ originate syntactically? We put forward answers to these questions in the next two sections. Specifically, in §3, we present evidence that /ne-/ semantically is uniformly a focus marker, and in §4, we show that Schwarz's (2007) syntactic account of Kikuyu can be extended to Kuria, so that in all cases, /ne-/ heads a Focus Phrase projection in the left periphery of the clause.

3 Diagnosing focus

In this section, we present evidence that /ne-/ behaves like a focus marker, across its different uses. Following the alternative semantics approach to focus (Rooth 1985; 1992), we assume that 'focus indicates the presence of alternatives that are relevant for the interpretation of linguistic expressions' (Krifka 2008). This definition encompasses different types of focus, e.g. signaling new information, correction, contrast, etc. We elicited data from three types of contexts in which focus marking would be expected, and found that /ne-/ consistently marks focused constituents, across syntactic categories. Specifically, following in part Hartmann & Zimmermann (2009)'s work on focus marking in Gùrùntùm, we looked at the following four focus contexts in Kuria, all of which involve morphological marking with /ne-/: (i) question-answer congruence, (ii) corrective focus, (iii) contrastive focus, and (iv) association with focus sensitive operators such as Kuria *bene* 'only'. In the following subsections, we consider each type of focus context in turn.

3.1 Question-answer congruence

In felicitous answers to *wh*-questions, /ne-/ obligatorily appears on the phrase corresponding to the *wh*-phrase. Consider, e.g. the object *wh*-question in (6). A felicitous an-

---

[6] A reviewer asks whether /ne-/ also appears in copular constructions, as in Kikuyu (Schwarz 2007). A nasal morpheme does indeed appear in copular constructions, as in (ii) below, but investigating the distribution of this morpheme and whether it is the same as /ne-/ goes beyond the scope of this paper:

(i) Gati n-omo-reri.
     1.Gati N-1-doctor
     'Gati is a doctor.'

Note also that the negative counterpart to /ne-/, /te-/, which we discuss in §6.2, also appears in copular constructions:

(ii) Gati t-omo-reri.
      1.Gati T-1-doctor
      'Gati is not a doctor.'

swer to this question is one where the object bears /ne-/, as in (7); answers in which /ne-/ appears on the subject, as in (8), are grammatical but infelicitous in this context.[7]

(6) Q: N-ke   ichi-ng'iti cha-a-it-ir-e?
       FOC-what 10-hyena 10SA-PST-kill-PRF-FV

'What did the hyenas kill?'

(7) A1: N-ege-toocho ichi-ng'iti cha-a-it-ir-e.
        FOC-7-rabbit 10-hyena 10SA-PST-kill-PRF-FV

'The hyenas killed THE RABBIT.'

(8) A2: #N-ichi-ng'iti cha-a-it-ir-e   ege-toocho.
        FOC-10-hyena 10SA-PST-kill-PRF-FV 7-rabbit

(Intended meaning: 'They hyenas killed THE RABBIT.')

Consider also subject *wh*-questions and their answers, as in (7). A felicitous answer to a subject *wh*-question exhibits a fronted subject DP bearing /ne-/, as in A1; if other phrases bear /ne-/, the answer is infelicitous, as in (10).

(9) Q: Who ate mangoes?
     A1: N-omo-onto a-a-rey-e   ama-yembe.
         FOC-1-person 1SA-PST-eat.PRF-FV 6-mango

'SOMEONE ate mangoes.'

(10) A2: #N-ama-yembe omo-onto a-a-rey-e.
         FOC-6-mango   1-person 1SA-PST-eat.PRF-FV

(Intened meaning: 'SOMEONE ate mangoes.')

---

[7]We have conflicting judgments from our speaker regarding whether pre-verbal /ne-/ as in (iv) below is felicitous in contexts where we would expect the object to bear /ne-/. For example, (iv) below is sometimes judged as infelicitous and sometimes as felicitous as an answer to (6); however, (7) is consistently offered by our speaker as the first and best answer to the question in (6).

(i) A3: #Ichi-ng'iti n-cha-a-it-ir-e   ege-toocho.
        10-hyena   FOC-10SA-PST-kill-PRF-FV 7-rabbit

'The hyenas killed the rabbit.'

/Ne-/ marking in answers to *wh*-questions holds not only for object and subject *wh*-questions, but also for adjuncts, such as PPs and adverbials. For example, (11) illustrates a focused PP, and (12) illustrates a focused AdvP.[8],[9]

(11) Q: Where will Gati see the owl?
    A: **N-ko-mesa**   gati umw-iti a-ra-maah-e.
       FOC-on-17.table 1.Gati 3-owl   3SG.SA-FUT-see-FV
    'Gati will see the owl ON THE TABLE.'

(12) Q: How did Chacha drink the chai?
    A: **M-bongo**   chacha a-a-nyoy-e   i-chaahe.
       FOC-quickly 1.Chacha 3SG.SA-PST-drink.PRF-FV 8-chai
    'Chacha drank the chai QUICKLY.'

In answers to VP-oriented *wh*-questions, /ne-/ must occur pre-verbally, as the question-answer pair in (13)-(14) shows; we take this to indicate that pre-verbal /ne-/ is also a focus marker, in this case marking VP focus.[10],[11]

(13) Q: **N-ke**   gati a-a-korr-e.
       FOC-what 1.Gati 3SG.SA-PST-do.PRF-FV
    'What did Gati do?'

---

[8]PP adjuncts canonically appear at the end of the sentence and manner adverbs are relatively free in their positioning.

[9]A reviewer asks whether in this case the PP S O V ordering is obligatory. We note that a postverbal object is also possible, as in (v):

    (i) Q: Did you see the frog on the table or on the floor?
        A: **N-ko-mesa**   naa-mah-er-e   i-kjoora.
          FOC-on-17.table 1SG.SA-PST-see-PRF-FV 9-frog
        'I saw the frog ON THE TABLE.'

The PP S O V ordering in (8) above might be evidence for a TopP below FocP, although this matter needs further investigation.

[10]The example in (vi) below, in which the object bears /ne-/, is occasionally judged by our speaker as a felicitous reply to the VP-oriented question in (13); thus, objects appear to project focus to VP in Kuria, as has been observed for English (Selkirk 1984):

    (i) ?N-i-chaahe a-a-nyoy-e.
        FOC-8-chai 3SG.SA-PST-drink.PRF-FV
        'He DRANK CHAI.'

[11]Note that while fronting the nominalized version of a verb is grammatical in Kuria, as in (vii) below, this construction is infelicitous as an answer to a VP *wh*-question:

    (i) #N-oko-ria ama-ako b-a-rey-e.
        FOC-15-eat 6-fruit 3PL.SA-PST-eat.PRF-FV
        (Intended meaning: 'They ATE FRUITS.')

This contrasts with data reported for Kikuyu (see Schwarz 2007); see §5.2 below.

(14) A: N-a-a-nyoy-e   i-chaahe.
        FOC-3SG.SA-PST-drink.PRF-FV 8-chai
        'He DRANK CHAI.'

Answers to questions in which sentential focus is expected, e.g. answers to questions such as 'What happened?', also require pre-verbal /ne-/, as (15) shows; thus, preverbal /ne-/ also marks sentential focus.[12] Attaching /ne-/ to any other constituent, e.g. the object, as in (16), would be infelicitous:

(15) Q: What happened?
      A1: Gati n-a-a-it-ir-e   ama-siisi.
          Gati FOC-3SG.SA-PST-kill-PRF-FV 6-ant
      'Gati killed ants.'

(16) A2: #N-ama-siisi gati   a-a-it-ir-e.
        FOC-6-ant   1.Gati 3SG.SA-PST-kill-PRF-FV
      (Intended meaning: 'Gati killed ants.')

Summarizing this subsection: (i) /ne-/ consistently marks focus expressions in answers to *wh*-questions across categories; and (ii) pre-verbal /ne-/ marks VP focus as well as sentential focus.

3.2 Corrective focus

Corrective focus contexts are those in which a (focused) phrase serves as a correction to a like phrase already introduced into the discourse. Consider, e.g. the dialogue in (17) below; in (18), speaker B corrects the VP from speaker A's utterance. In this context, /ne-/ may not occur on any phrase other than the corrected VP, as the infelicitous (19) shows:[13]

(17) A: M-ba-a-gurr-i   i-nyamu.
        FOC-3PL.SA-PST-sell.PRF-FV 9-cat
        'They sold the cat.'

(18) B: Aʔa, m-ba-a-gi-sirr-i.
        ŋo,   FOC-3PL.SA-PST-9OM-lose.PRF-FV
        'No, they LOST it.'

(19) C: #Aʔa, n-i-nyamu ba-a-sirr-i.
        no,   FOC-9-cat 3PL.SA-PST-lose.PRF-FV
        (Intended meaning: 'No, they LOST the cat.')

---

[12] A reviewer notes that this instance of sentential focus looks identical to what we called a declarative in (1). We wish to emphasize that this is a context where sentential focus would be expected, and so we take /ne-/ to be indicating focus here.

[13] A reviewer asks if something is focused in (17). We assume that the appearance of /ne-/ in this instance shows sentential focus.

Compare the dialogue in (20) and (21), where, in (21), B corrects the object DP from A's utterance in (20); in this case, the corrected DP object bears /ne-/:[14]

(20)　A: Ichi-ng'iti n-cha-a-it-ir-e　　　　　ege-toocho.
　　　　　10-hyena FOC-10SA-PST-kill-PRF-FV 7-rabbit
　　　　　'The hyenas killed the rabbit.'

(21)　B: Aʔa, n-in-chage　cha-a-it-ir-e.
　　　　　no, FOC-9-zebra 10SA-PST-kill-PRF-FV
　　　　　'No, they killed the ZEBRA.'

Corrective focus contexts thus provide further evidence that phrases bearing /ne-/ are focused.

3.3 Contrastive focus

Contrastive focus contexts are those in which a phrase is presented in contrast with one or more like phrases already introduced into the discourse. Consider for example (22), where the contrastively focused VP in the conjoined clause bears /ne-/:[15]

(22)　Chacha n-a-a-gorr-e　　　　　i-indwi, na　gati
　　　　　1.Chacha FOC-3SG.SA-PST-buy.PRF-FV 9-lion　and 1.Gati
　　　　　n-a-a-gurr-i　　　　　　i-indwi.
　　　　　FOC-3SG.SA-PST-sell.PRF-FV 9-lion
　　　　　'Chacha bought a lion and Gati SOLD a lion.'

Similarly, in (23), the contrastively focused DP in the conjoined clause bears /ne-/:[16]

(23)　Chacha n-a-a-gorr-e　　　　　i-nyamu, na　gati　n-i-indwi
　　　　　1.Chacha FOC-3SG.SA-PST-buy.PRF-FV 9-cat　　and 1.Gati FOC-9-lion
　　　　　a-a-gorr-e.
　　　　　3SG.SA-PST-buy.PRF-FV
　　　　　'Chacha bought a cat and Gati bought a LION.'

---

[14]As with question-answer congruence, we have conflicting judgments regarding whether pre-verbal /ne-/ is felicitous in object-focused contexts. Thus, (viii) below is occasionally judged as felicitous for corrective focus on the object:

　(i)　Aʔa, n-cha-a-it-ir-e　　　　　in-chage.
　　　　　no, FOC-10SA-PST-kill-PRF-FV 9-zebra
　　　　　'No, they killed a ZEBRA.'

[15]A reviewer asks how we can tell that /ne-/ in the second conjunct in (22) marks VP focus. The alternative would be to claim that nothing is marking VP focus in the second conjunct and it is just another case of sentential focus (i.e., a declarative). Given that in this contrastive context we expect VP focus in the second conjunct, we conclude that it is /ne-/ that marks focus.

[16]A reviewer asks whether the appearance of /ne-/ in the first conjunct means that it is an instance of focus. We assume that all sentences in this tense bear focus, and that the first conjunct is an instance of default or sentential focus.

Since /ne-/ appears on a contrastively focused phrase in these examples, they thus also indicate that /ne-/ is a focus marker.

3.4 Focus sensitive operators

Finally, we consider focus sensitive operators analogous to English *only*, which have been shown to associate with phrases bearing focus (see e.g. Rooth 1992; 1996). In Kuria, focus sensitive operators such as *bene* 'only' associate with phrases bearing /ne-/. Consider e.g. (24) below, which is felicitous given the context:

(24) Context: *We are discussing the methods used by students to protest dining hall food two weeks ago at school. There was only one method they used to protest and I specify it as such.*
M-ba-a-tan-er-a   g-oko-rekeera ama-geena bene.
FOC-3PL.SA-PST-protest-PRF-FV by-15-throw   6-stone   only
'They only PROTESTED BY THROWING ROCKS.'

Bene may also associate with a focused DP, in which case *bene* displays noun class agreement morphology, as evidenced by (25) (which is felicitous in a different context):[17]

(25) N-i-nswi   i-nyene ba-a-ta-rey-e.
FOC-9-fish 9-only   3PL.SA-PST-NEG-eat.PRF-FV
'They only didn't eat FISH.'

That Kuria *bene* associates with phrases bearing /ne-/ also indicates that /ne-/ is a focus marker.

3.5 Summary of focus diagnostics

Summarizing this section, we have shown that /ne-/ appears on just those phrases that are in focus, based on four types of focus constructions: (i) question-answer congruence; (ii) corrective focus; (iii) contrastive focus; and (iv) association of phrases bearing /ne-/ with focus sensitive operators.

4 Analysis

Having established that /ne-/ is semantically a focus marker, we turn now to its syntax. Extending Schwarz (2007)'s account of Kikuyu to Kuria, we analyze /ne-/ as heading a Focus Phrase (FocP) projection in the left periphery of CP (Rizzi 1997), as in (26).[18]

---

[17] A reviewer asks whether this is the only reading for this sentence or whether any scope interactions exist; this is indeed the only reading available for the sentence.

[18] A TopP projection is observed in the tree, since we will argue for this position below.

(26) Position of *ne*

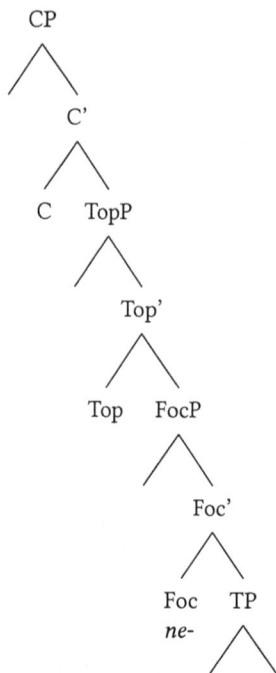

```
        CP
       /  \
          C'
         /  \
        C   TopP
           /  \
             Top'
            /  \
          Top  FocP
              /  \
                Foc'
               /  \
             Foc   TP
             ne-  /  \
```

Following Schwarz, we derive the different constructions that /ne-/ occurs in via movement of phrases bearing /ne-/ into [Spec, FocP].[19] For example, in a sentence with a fronted object, the object raises to [Spec, FocP], as (27) illustrates.[20] Here, topicalization of the subject is optional.

(27) Object focus

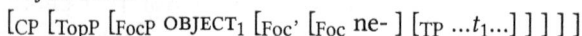

[CP [TopP [FocP OBJECT₁ [Foc' [Foc ne-] [TP ...t₁...]]]]]

---

[19] We, like Schwarz (2007), are noncommittal with respect to how /ne-/ combines morphologically with the constituent in [Spec, FocP]. Schwarz (2007: 144) notes two possibilities for Kikuyu *ne*: (i) *ne* itself heads FocP, and cliticizes to whatever is in the specificer of FocP, and (ii) the focus feature is spelled out phonologically as *ne*, and surfaces to the left edge of whatever occupies [Spec, FocP]. For concreteness, we adopt the first possibility, and position /ne-/ as heading the focus phrase in the trees throughout.

[20] A reviewer asks what the trigger for movement is in our analysis. While we do not spell out in detail the mechanics of movement, our account is compatible with a Minimalist analysis (Chomsky 2000; 2004), whereby A-bar movement is the result of an Agree operation between a head bearing an uninterpretable feature (such as [wh], [Foc]) and a Goal which carries a matching feature. Furthermore, when the Probe has the [EPP] property, this property is satisfied via internal merge of the Goal, which merges in the Spec position of the Probe. While extending the Agree operation to account for A-bar movement in addition to A movement is not uncontroversial—see the discussion in Horvath 2007 for instance—the present analysis is compatible with accounts that take Agree and [Foc] features to drive syntactic movement.

In the case of sentential focus, again following Schwarz (2007), TP moves up into [Spec, FocP], while the subject is obligatorily topicalized, as in (28).[21]

(28)   Sentential focus

$[_{CP} [_{TopP}$ SUBJECT$_2 [_{Top'} [_{FocP} [_{TP1} ...t_2...] [_{Foc'} [_{Foc}$ *ne-* $] [_{TP} ...t_1...]]]]]$

In the case of VP focus, VP moves to [Spec, FocP], while the subject is obligatorily topicalized, again following Schwarz:

(29)   VP focus

$[_{CP} [_{TopP}$ SUBJECT$_2 [_{Top'} [_{FocP} [_{VP1} ...t_2...] [_{Foc'} [_{Foc}$ *ne-* $] [_{TP} ...t_1...]]]]]$

Summarizing the analysis, we have extended Schwarz's account of Kikuyu to Kuria, so that in all of its uses, /ne-/ heads a Focus Phrase in the left periphery of the clause. We turn first to a comparison of /ne-/ to morphological marking of focus in other languages (§5), and then to further data regarding the distribution of /ne-/ (§6).[22,23]

---

[21] A reviewer asks whether movement of the subject out of the TP, which itself has moved to [Spec, FocP] in (28) constitutes a violation of Rizzi 2010's Criterial Freezing: "In a criterial configuration, the Criterial Goal is frozen in place." We believe that it does not, on the following grounds. Rizzi states that "In the criterial configuration, only the element carrying the crucial feature is frozen in place, while the other elements of the phrase pied-piped to the Spec of the Criterial Probe remain available for movement, and can be subextracted, if no other syntactic principle is violated..." Although Rizzi does not specifically discuss examples in which a TP moves to the specifier of a Criterial Probe, we hypothesize that in these cases the subject is still available for movement, as observed in example (28).

[22] An alternative account of /ne-/ might analyze it as a cleft construction. For example, Bergvall (1987) treats Kikuyu /ne-/ as an assertion marker that heads TP, which would correctly account for the position of pre-verbal /ne-/. To account for clauses involving fronted phrases, Bergvall proposes a bi-clausal cleft analysis: The matrix clause has a null expletive subject, and /ne-/ appears before a null copula, followed by a relative clause. We see this type of account as problematic for Kuria on several counts. First, if these sentences are clefts, we might expect that idiomatic readings should not be possible (e.g. in English *It was the bucket that he kicked* lacks the idiomatic reading). However, idiomatic readings are preserved in Kuria, as the example in (ix) illustrates:

(i)   N-i-bara   chonesi a-a-gey-e.
FOC-9-wild 1.Johnes 3SA-PST-go.PRF-FV

'Johnes went INTO THE WILD.' ~ 'Johnes did something completely unexpected.'

Second, as Schwarz (2007) points out, clefts are not expected to occur in multiple *wh*-questions, such as *Who killed what?* However, we do find such data in Kuria:

(ii)   N-eng'we a-it-ir-e   (*n-)ke?
FOC-who SA-kill-PRF-FV FOC-what

'Who killed what?'

Third, /ne-/ appears in non-assertive contexts, e.g. yes/no questions, which differ tonally from declaratives but are otherwise identical (see Mwita 2008 for a discussion of Kuria tonology).

[23] A reviewer asks whether an analysis along the lines of Horvath (2007), according to which an exhaustivity operator merges with some phrase and then is attracted by a higher head, would also account for the Kuria pattern. While the full consequences of extending Horvath's analysis to Kuria is an issue for future research (especially with regards to phrase-internal focus marking; see §5.1), we do not see how Horvath's account can be extended to Kuria for the following reason: Horvath justifies the exhaustivity operator based on

5 Crosslinguistic comparison

In this section, we compare focus marking in Kuria to focus marking in other languages, thereby placing the Kuria data in a crosslinguistic context.

5.1 Phrase-internal focus

In contrast with related Bantu languages (Abels & Muriungi 2008 on Kiitharaka) and other language families (Hartmann & Zimmermann 2009 for Gùrùntùm), Kuria permits phrase-internal focus marking. Consider first the following examples, which show that /ne-/ can appear on the head noun in a fronted DP, (30), or on the determiner, (31):

(30) Q: Which owls did Johnes see, these owls or those owls?
    A: **N-imi-iti**   ge-no chonesi a-a-roch-e.
       FOC-4-owl 4-this 1.Johnes 3SG.SA-PST-see.PRF-FV

    'Johnes saw THESE OWLS.'

(31) Q: Which owls did Johnes see, these owls or those owls?
    A: Imi-iti **n-ge-no**   chonesi a-a-roch-e.
       4-owl FOC-4-this 1.Johnes 3SG.SA-PST-see.PRF-FV

    'Johnes saw THESE OWLS.'

In contrast with (30) and (31), if the determiner is kept constant and the nouns in the two possible answers provided by the question differ, marking the determiner with /ne-/ becomes infelicitous:

(32) Q: What did the children like, this lion or this rhinoceros?
    A1: **N-i-huuburia** e-no b-a-tanch-er-e.
        FOC-9-rhino 9-this 3PL.SA-PST-like-PRF-FV

    'They liked this RHINOCEROS.'

(33) A2: #I-huuburia **n-e-no**   ba-a-tanch-er-e.
       9-rhino   FOC-9-this 3PL.SA-PST-like-PRF-FV

    (Intended meaning: 'They liked this RHINOCEROS.')

As a reply to questions that require a possessive DP as an answer, /ne-/ may also appear phrase internally. Possessive DPs exhibit the following surface structure:

(34) [Possessed DP Associative Marker Possessor DP]

---

the empirical observation that information focus remains in-situ in Hungarian, while contrastive/identificational focus undergoes overt movement. Since no such asymmetry exists in Kuria (i.e., both types of focus are expressed in the same way, with /ne-/), we do not see that positing an exhaustivity operator is justified for Kuria.

The morpheme can attach to the possessed DP on the left edge of the phrase, or on the associative marker. Consider first (35) below, where a question offers two alternative answers in which the possessor DP is kept constant. Attaching /ne-/ to the left-edge of the fronted phrase is the only felicitous reply in this context:

(35)   Q: What did Boke eat, Gati's ugali or Gati's chapati?
       A1: N-iri-chabati re   gati   a-a-rey-e.
           FOC-5-chapati 5.ASSOC 1.Gati 3SG.SA-PST-eat.PRF-FV
       'He ate Gati's CHAPATI.'

(36)   A2: #Iri-chabati **ne**-re   gati   a-a-rey-e.
           5-chapati   FOC-5.ASSOC 1.Gati 3SG.SA-PST-eat.PRF-FV
       (Intended meaning: 'He ate Gati's CHAPATI.')

However, compare (35) with (37) below. Here, the question asks for the identity of the possessor. As the second answer, (38), shows, only attaching /ne-/ to the associative marker is felicitous in this context:

(37)   Q: Whose ugali did Sammy eat?
       A1: #N-ubu-kima bo   gati   a-a-rey-e.
           FOC-14-ugali 14.ASSOC 1.Gati 3SG.SA-PST-eat.PRF-FV
       (Intended meaning: 'He ate GATI's ugali.')

(38)   A2: Ubu-kima n-obo   gati   a-a-rey-e.
           14-ugali   FOC-14.ASSOC 1.Gati 3SG.SA-PST-eat.PRF-FV
       'He ate GATI'S ugali.'

As a reply to the question in (37) above, we might have expected that marking the possessor DP with /ne-/ would have been the only felicitous reply. However, it is ungrammatical (in any context) to mark the possessor DP with /ne-/, as (39) shows:[24]

(39)   *Ubu-kima bo   **n-gati**   a-a-rey-e.
       14-ugali   14.ASSOC FOC-1.Gati 3SG.SA-PST-eat.PRF-FV
       (Intended meaning: 'He ate GATI's ugali.')

Based on these examples, we wish to highlight the fact that /ne-/ may attach to different subconstituents of a focused phrase, depending on the context. Therefore, a potential analysis treating the appearance of /ne-/ on different subconstituents of a focused phrase to a semantically vacuous morphological operation would be undesirable. For now, we leave the mechanics by which the focus marker appears phrase internally for future research, although we can shed doubt on /ne-/ being base-generated phrase internally given examples like (40) below, which show that marking /ne-/ on both the possessed DP and the associative phrase is ungrammatical:

---

[24]The ban on this type of construction was also noted for Kiitharaka by Abels & Muriungi (2008). We hypothesize that the correct analysis of the surface structure of a possessive DP is one in which the associative marker and the possessor DP form a single morphophonological unit that cannot be broken up by the /ne-/ morpheme. Therefore, the ban against marking the possessor DP with /ne-/ might not be related to semantics at all.

(40) *N-ubu-kima n-obo   gati a-a-rey-e.
      FOC-14-ugali FOC-14.ASSOC 1.Gati 3SG.SA-PST-eat.PRF-FV

      (Intended meaning: 'He ate Gati's ugali.')

5.2 VP fronting

As reported by Schwarz (2007), VP focus in Kikuyu involves fronting an infinitival verb, while a fully inflected form remains in base position (see his example 15B). This construction is also possible in Kuria, but does not trigger VP focus. Instead, fronting an infinitival verb is felicitous only as a reply to a question expressing incredulity. Therefore, this construction can only be used to express a *verum* interpretation. Consider first the following question-answer pairing, in which marking the VP with /ne-/ triggers VP focus, as expected:

(41) Q: What did they do, eat fruits or drink water?
      A1: **M-ba-a-rey-e**   ama-ako.
          FOC-3PL.SA-PST-eat.PRF-FV 6-fruit

      'They ATE FRUITS.'

(42) A2: #N-oko-ria ama-ako ba-a-rey-e.
          FOC-15-eat 6-fruit   3PL.SA-PST-eat-PRF-FV

      (Intended meaning: 'They ATE FRUITS.')

However, as a reply to the follow-up question observed below, only example (43) is felicitous:

(43) Q: Did they really?
      A: E,   n-oko-ria ama-ako ba-a-rey-e.
         yes, FOC-15-eat 6-fruit 3PL.SA-PST-eat.PRF-FV

      'Yes, they DID eat fruits.'

These data indicate that in Kuria, *verum* focus in the remote past is marked via fronting of an infinitival verb and predicate doubling. Further, these data show that Kuria differs from Kikuyu with respect to the use of preverbal /ne-/ and the expression of *verum* focus: In Kikuyu, preverbal /ne-/ is used for *verum* focus, while fronting the infinitival verb and predicate doubling is akin to the use of preverbal /ne-/ in Kuria (what Schwarz 2007 calls "narrow focus on the verb"). Although we leave an analysis of constructions such as (31) for future research, we note the typological difference between Kikuyu and Kuria with regards to the realization of VP and *verum* focus.[25]

---

[25]The examples in (42) and (43) are parallel to data from other languages discussed in Aboh (2006) and Aboh & Dyakanova (2009), where they are called "predicate fronting with doubling". We refer the reader to these papers for further examples of this type of construction crosslinguistically and thank an anonymous reviewer for bringing these papers to our attention.

6 Additional patterns regarding /ne-/

In this section, we document some additional patterns regarding the syntactic distribution of /ne-/, and in doing so articulate some puzzles for future research with respect to focus marking in Kuria. Specifically, in §6.1, we observe certain contexts which appear to involve focus, but lack /ne-/, and in §6.2, we discuss the complementary distribution between /ne-/ and the negative marker /te-/.

6.1 Focus but no /ne-/

We have identified at least three contexts in which a phrase is semantically focused, while /ne-/ is absent, which we discuss in the following subsections.

6.1.1 TAM

In certain TAM combinations, /ne-/ does not appear pre-verbally in certain contexts (as also observed by Mwita 2008). Consider, e.g. the question-answer pairing in the immediate past below (cf. the remote past, in which /ne-/ does appear, as in, e.g. (1)):

(44)   Q: What did Gati and Johnes just do?
    A: Ba-rey-e   omo-gate.
       3PL.SA-eat.PRF-FV 3-bread
       'They just ATE BREAD.'

The morpheme may only appear pre-verbally in this tense as a reply to questions showing incredulity, expressing a *verum* focus interpretation. This context, similar to the previously discussed VP nominalization cases in the remote past, is exemplified below in (45):

(45)   Follow up Q: *Did they really?*
    A: **M**-ba-rey-e   omo-gate.
       FOC-3PL.SA-eat-PRF.FV 3-bread
       'They DID just eat bread.'

We presently have no explanation for why /ne-/ only appears in *verum* focus contexts in certain TAM combinations, as illustrated above, and why *verum* focus in certain TAM combinations is not expressed via fronting of the infinitival verb and doubling.

6.1.2 Focus in relative clauses

Relative clauses provide another context in which /ne-/ does not appear pre-verbally. Even in answer to an echo question context that forces a focus interpretation on the verb, /ne-/ may not appear, as the question-answer pair in (46) shows:

(46) Q: The teacher who did WHAT drank water?
       A: Umw-arimu ora   (*n-)a-a-giy-er-e.
           1-teacher   1.who (FOC-)3SG.SA-PST-march-PRF-FV
       'The teacher who MARCHED.'

We might account for the restriction on /ne-/ in this context to the absence of a FocP projection in the left periphery of relative clauses. However, it remains a puzzle how phrases with no morphological marking are interpreted as being focused. We leave this issue for future research.[26]

6.1.3 Multiple *wh*-phrases

Since we assume that congruent answers to *wh*-questions involve semantic focus, we would expect all replies to *wh*-questions to bear /ne-/; this, however, is not the case. Consider the multiple *wh*-question-answer pairing below; notice that only the phrase that answers the *wh*-phrase marked with /ne-/ in the question can bear /ne-/ in the answer; the in-situ constituent cannot also bear /ne-/:

(47) Q: N-eng'we a-it-ir-e   (*n-)ke?
           FOC-who SA-kill-PRF-fv (FOC-)what
       'Who killed what?'

(48) A1: **M-boke**   a-it-ir-e   igi-siisi.
           FOC-1.Boke 3SG.SA-kill-PRF-FV 7-ant
       'Boke killed ANTS.'

(49) A2: #N-igi-siisi boke   a-it-ir-e.
           FOC-7-ant   1.Boke 3SG.SA-kill-PRF-FV
       (Intended meaning: 'BOKE killed ANTS.')

Examples like these again raise the question of how semantic focus is expressed and interpreted in Kuria; if structural restrictions ban the appearance of multiple instances of /ne-/ in a clause, how are phrases with no morphological marking interpreted as being focused? We leave further discussion of this matter for future research.

6.2 The complementary distribution of /ne-/ and /te-/

While /ne-/ appears in positive sentences, its apparent negative counterpart, /te-/, appears in exactly the same position in negative sentences:

(50) Aba-saacha **te-ba-a-mah-er-e**   eng'-ombe.
       2-man   NEG.FOC-3PL.SA-PST-see-PRF-FV 9-cow
       'The men did not SEE THE COW.'

---

[26] A reviewer notes that a fuller paradigm related to the unavailability of /ne-/ in relative clauses might show this is due to island effects.

The two are in complementary distribution, never co-occurring on the same phrase or in the same clause. /Te-/ appears to express both negation as well as focus. Like /ne-/, /te-/ attaches to focused phrases, such as the question-answer pairing below:

(51) Q: Was it the men who saw the cow?
   A: A:, *(t-)aba-saacha (*m-)ba-a-mah-er-e   eng'-ombe.
     no, NEG.FOC-2-man (FOC-)3PL.SA-PST-see-PRF-FV 9-cow
   'It was not THE MEN who saw the cow.'

Also like /ne-/, focus sensitive semantic operators such as *bene* 'only' may associate with /te-/. The example below is felicitous if the speaker is commenting on the methods used by student protesters:

(52) **Te-ba-a-giy-ir-e**   bene.
   NEG-FOC-3PL.SA-PST-march-PRF-FV only
   'They did not only MARCH.'

The complementary distribution of /ne-/ and /te-/ in Kuria suggests to us that the two are closely related in their syntax and semantics, though we do not presently have an explanation for this connection. Mwita (2008) attributes the incompatibility of /ne-/ with /te-/ to negation itself being "inherently focused". However, this approach would not account for the fact that /ne-/ can co-occur with a different negation marker, /ta-/, which immediately precedes the verb root in contexts such as the following:[27]

(53) Q: What won't they do?
   A: **M-ba-taa-r-e**   ege-eki.
     FOC-3PL.SA-NEG.FUT-eat-FV 5-cake
   'They will not EAT THE CAKE.'

A connection between the morphological marking of focus and negation has not, to our knowledge, been studied in detail in the Bantu literature on focus realization. While Schwarz (2007) and Abels & Muriungi (2008) acknowledge the incompatibility of the focus morpheme with a negation morpheme in Kikuyu and Kiitharaka, respectively, they do not propose an account of the pattern.[28] We leave the issue for future research as well.

7 Conclusion

In this paper, we have presented a range of novel data regarding the syntax and semantics of the Kuria morpheme /ne-/. We have argued that our data support analyzing the morpheme /ne-/ as a focus marker, and we have shown that an analysis in the spirit of

---

[27] /Te-/ and /ta-/ may not both appear on the verb stem.
[28] A similar connection between focus and negation manifests in English do-support, suggesting a cross-linguistic connection between focus and negation. E.g. in English, *do*-support is obligatory in negated sentences (e.g. *They *(did) not leave*) as well as *verum* focus sentences (e.g. *They *(DID) leave*).

Schwarz (2007) captures the syntactic distribution of /ne-/. This paper thus contributes to our understanding of focus strategies in Bantu specifically, as well as across languages more generally. Furthermore, we have articulated the following puzzles regarding the realization of focus, not only for Kuria but across the Bantu family. First, we have documented patterns that involve phrase-internal focus marking, which have not previously been reported in the Bantu literature. Second, we have shown how VP focus differs in Kuria in comparison with other Bantu languages like Kikuyu. Finally, we have observed the complementary distribution of focus and negation in Kuria, a connection that may have implications for the analysis of focus in Kuria specifically, as well as focus across languages more generally.

Acknowledgements

Authors are listed alphabetically. Special thanks to Johnes Kitololo for his judgments and patience, to Michael Diercks for extensive input and advice, and to Adele Eslinger, whose paper on Kuria /ne-/ for the Spring 2013 Field Methods course at Pomona College, taught by Michael Diercks, provided a starting point for this work. Thanks also to Mary Paster, Jesse Harris, the participants of the 2014 mini-symposium on African languages at Pomona, the participants of ACAL 2014, and two anonymous reviewers for many helpful questions and comments. This paper builds on the second author's undergraduate thesis at Pomona College. Any mistakes are our responsibility.

Abbreviations

Glosses are as follows:

FOC	focus	SA	subject agreement
PST	past	NEG	negation
PRF	perfective	COMP	complementizer
FUT	future	ASSOC	associative marker
FV	final vowel	APPL	applicative.

In the orthographic conventions used throughout, an intervocalic <b> represents a voiced bilabial fricative [β], an intervocalic <g> a voiced velar fricative [ɣ], <ng'> a velar nasal [ŋ], <ny> a palatal nasal [ɲ], <y> a palatal glide [j], <r> an alveolar tap [ɾ], <rr> a voiced alveolar trill [r], and <ch> a voiced alveo-palatal affricate [ʧ]. Numbers indicate Bantu noun class. For ease of comprehension, when one morpheme's presence is to be noticed in an utterance, it appears in bold; when two morphemes are to be noticed, the second one is underlined. We do not transcribe tone in our data; see Mwita (2008) and Marlo et al. (2014; 2015) for discussion of Kuria tone.

References

Abels, Klaus & Peter Muriungi. 2008. The focus marker in Kiitharaka: Syntax and semantics. *Lingua* 118. 687–731.

Aboh, Enoch O. 2006. When verbal predicates go fronting. *ZAS Papers in Linguistics* 46. 21–48.

Aboh, Enoch O. & Marina Dyakanova. 2009. Predicate doubling and parallel chains. *Lingua* 119. 1035–1065.

Bergvall, Victoria Lee. 1987. *Focus in Kikuyu and Universal Grammar*. Cambridge: Harvard University Doctoral dissertation.

Cammenga, Jelle. 2004. *Igikuria phonology and morphology: A Bantu language of southwest Kenya and northwest Tanzania*. Köln: Rudiger Koppe Verlag.

Chomsky, Noam. 2000. Minimalist inquiries: The framework. In Roger Martin, David Michaels & Juan Uriagereka (eds.), *Step by step: Essays on minimalist syntax in honor of Howard Lasnik*, 89–156. Cambridge, MA: MIT Press.

Chomsky, Noam. 2004. Beyond explanatory adequacy. In Adriana Belletti (ed.), *Structures and beyond: The cartography of syntactic structures*, vol. 3, 104–131. New York: Oxford Univerity Press.

Eslinger, Adele. 2013. *The mystery Nasal*. Ms. Pomona College.

Hartmann, Katharina & Malte Zimmermann. 2009. *Morphological focus marking in Gùrùntùm (West Chadic)*.

Horvath, Julia. 2007. Separating 'focus movement' from focus. In Simin Karimi, Vida Samiian & Wendy Wilkins (eds.), *Phrasal and clausal architecture*, 108–145. Amsterdam: John Benjamins.

Krifka, Manfred. 2008. Basic notions of information structure. *Acta Linguistica Hungarica* 55. 243–276.

Marlo, Michael R., Leonard Chacha Mwita & Mary Paster. 2014. Kuria tone melodies. *African Linguistica* XX. 277–294.

Marlo, Michael R., Leonard Chacha Mwita & Mary Paster. 2015. Problems in Kuria H tone assignment. *Natural Language and Linguistic Theory* 33. 251–265.

Mwita, Chacha. 2008. *Verbal tone in Kuria*. Los Angeles: University of California Doctoral dissertation.

Rizzi, Luigi. 1997. The fine structure of the left periphery. In Liliane Haegeman (ed.), *Elements of grammar: A handbook in generative syntax*, 281–337. Kluwer: Dordrecht.

Rizzi, Luigi. 2010. On some properties of Criterial Freezing. In Phoevos Panagiotidis (ed.), *The complementizer phase: subjects and operators*, 17–32. Oxford: Oxford University Press.

Rooth, Mats. 1985. *Association with focus*. Amherst: University of Massachusetts Doctoral dissertation.

Rooth, Mats. 1992. A theory of focus interpretation. *Natural Language Semantics* 1. 75–116.

Rooth, Mats. 1996. Focus. In Shalom Lappin (ed.), *The handbook of contemporary semantic theory*, 271–297. London: Basil Blackwell.

Schwarz, Florian. 2007. *Ex-situ focus in Kikuyu*. Focus Strategies in African Languages: The Interaction of Focus, Grammar in Niger-Congo & Afro-Asiatic. Walter de Gruyter.

Selkirk, Elisabeth. 1984. *Phonology and syntax*. Cambridge, Massachusetts: MIT Press.

Chapter 25

A corpus study of the Swahili demonstrative position

Mohamed Mwamzandi

Synchronic studies on Swahili adnominal demonstratives have not addressed the interplay between syntactic position and pragmatic function of these structures. This study shows how referential givenness of discourse entities may explain Swahili word order variation in Swahili adnominal demonstratives. Class 1 (animate nouns) demonstratives are examined in the two attested word orders: NP+DEM and DEM+NP. A close analysis of dataset extracted from the Helsinki Corpus of Swahili reveals that the two structures have distinct pragmatic values. The NP+DEM order is used for active topics while the DEM+NP order reactivates semiactive/inactive topics. This study reveals how the syntax-pragmatics interplay may explain distinct structures viewed as semantic equivalents by native speakers.

1 Introduction

This paper exploresword order variation in Swahili adnominal demonstratives via corpus analysis. The term "adnominal demonstrative" is used in the literature to distinguish demonstratives that co-occur with nouns from stand-alone pronominal demonstratives. While an adnominal demonstrative forms a constituent with an adjacent noun, a pronominal demonstrative is a noun phrase in its own right. More specifically, I analyze the pragmatic use of Swahili demonstratives as outlined by Fillmore (1975; 1982; 1997). Thereafter, I present a qualitative and quantitative analysis of the pre and postnominal position of the Swahili demonstrative. I focus on the relationship that exists between cognitive level of the hearer on discourse entities and the choice of referring expressions (Chafe 1987; Ariel 1988; 1991; 2001; Gundel et al. 1993).

Swahili has various proximal and distal demonstrative forms that obligatorily agree with the nominal class of the noun they modify as exemplified in Table 1.

Notice that the hV- stem is used for the proximal demonstrative while the -*le* stem is used for the distal demonstratives. Further, the agreement affix varies with noun class hence *yu*- and *wa*- for class 1 and 2 and *u*- and *i*- for class 3 and 4.

Besides the semantic distinction of distal and proximal demonstratives, there are two demonstrative constructions that vary in their word order: NP + DEM as seen in (1) and DEM + NP as seen in (2).

Mohamed Mwamzandi. A corpus study of the Swahili demonstrative position. In Jason Kandybowicz, Travis Major, Harold Torrence & Philip T. Duncan (eds.), *African linguistics on the prairie: Selected papers from the 45th Annual Conference on African Linguistics*, 413–429. Berlin: Language Science Press. DOI:10.5281/zenodo.1251756

Table 1: Proximal and distal demonstrative forms of the first four noun classes.

Noun class	Proximal Dem	Distal Dem
1	*hu-yu*	*yu-le*
2	*ha-wa*	*wa-le*
3	*hu-u*	*u-le*
4	*hi-i*	*i-le*

(1) [Msichana yule]   a-li-ingia.
    1.girl   1.DIST.DEM 1.SM-PST-enter
    'That girl entered.'

(2) [Yule   msichana] a-li-ingia.
    1.DIST.DEM 1.girl   1.SM-PST-enter
    'That girl entered.'

The distal demonstrative *yule* 'that' is postnominal in (1) but prenominal in (2). The general tendency in studies on the demonstrative position in Bantu is to claim that the postnominal demonstrative (1) is the unmarked form reserved for the basic gestural function, while the prenominal demonstrative (2) is an innovation aimed at marking definite reference (Ashton 1944; Carstens 1991; 2008; Tamanji 2006). Amidu (2006) points out that both the pre and postnominal demonstrative positions as seen in (1) and (2) can be referential (anaphoric due to previous mention) but does not discuss the pragmatic implications of these demonstratives.

In my analysis, I first discern the adnominal demonstrative function as gestural, anaphoric, or recognitional (Fillmore 1975; 1982; 1997; Himmelmann 1996; Diessel 1999). Thereafter, I qualitatively and quantitatively analyze the pragmatic function of the Swahili demonstrative position. I posit that the postnominal demonstrative as seen in (1) indicates that the intended referent is "active" (Chafe 1987). On the other hand the prenominal demonstrative as seen in (2) indicates that the intended referent is "semi-active" or "inactive". "Semiactive" referents are those discourse entities reintroduced in the discourse after topic shift (change of topic) as well as discourse entities within the conversational context. Topic in this study is what an utterance is about. "Inactive" topics are (re)introduced in the discourse after a long gap of absence or are familiar to the interlocutors.

It is important to note here that Chafe's (1987) activation states as outlined above do not make specific claims on the relationship that exists between activation level and forms of referring expressions. To tackle this absence of matching activation level with forms of referring expression, I invoke the Accessibility Hierarchy (Ariel 1988; 1991; 2001) and the Givenness Hierarchy (Gundel et al. 1993) cognitive theories which associate referential choice with "referential givenness": The awareness level of interlocutors to discourse entities (Gundel & Fretheim 2006). These two cognitive hierarchies rank demonstrative expressions as mid-accessibility markers. Pronouns are ranked higher than demonstratives while explicit NPs are ranked lower.

A few things on the scope and limitations of this study are worth mentioning. In this study, I examine class 1 (animate nouns) proximal (*hu-yu*) and distal (*yu-le*) demonstratives. Class 1 is chosen because of the relative prominence and sustainability of animate nouns as opposed to inanimate nouns in discourse (Givón 1976; 1983). The applicability of the results is therefore limited to class 1 demonstratives though an extension of the findings to other noun classes is plausible. Further, this study does not look at the distribution of referential demonstratives. Referential demonstratives such as *huyo* are formed by suffixing the "O" of reference to the proximal demonstrative and then deleting the final vowel of the demonstrative (Ashton 1944). While the referential demonstrative is mainly used in discourse to mark definiteness, the use of a proximal/distal demonstrative is not limited to this function (See §2.2.1). Due to its difference in form and functional limitation, the distribution of the referential demonstrative is left out for future research.

The organization of the rest of the paper is as follows. In §2 I explain the methodology. In §3 I present and discuss the results of the study. §4 presents the conclusion and theoretical implications.

2 Methodology

In this section, I explain extraction of the dataset from the Helsinki Corpus of Swahili in §2.1. I then discuss how the dataset was coded in §2.2.

2.1 Extraction of the dataset from the corpus

The source of data in this study is the Helsinki Corpus of Swahili (HCS) which has 14 annotated corpora. The corpora contain current newspaper articles as well as excerpts of literary texts, education and science material written in the mid to late 20th century. Due to the absence of annotations on anaphora resolution in the corpora, I limit the analysis to the HCS books (cf. Mitkov 1994). The HCS books sub-corpus has 1,055,425 words in 71 documents. The documents are mainly Swahili literary texts and education manuscripts.

To obtain the dataset, four queries were made in the HCS. Due to limitations associated with functionality of corpus software, the queries asked for all nouns adjacent to demonstratives whether the demonstrative and the adjacent noun formed a syntactic unit or not. Thus, a manual postediting process aimed at eliminating all the DEM+NP collocations that did not form a syntactic unit was done. Most of these cases were ditransitive verbs with a demonstrative adjacent to both the direct object and the oblique argument as seen in (3).

(3) Njoo u-m-pat-i-e [kijana huyu] [maji ya kunywa].
come 2SG-OM-get-APPL-IMP teenager PROX.DEM water of drinking

'Come and give this teenager some water to drink.'

In (3), the proximal demonstrative *huyu* is modifying the direct object *kijana* 'teenager' but was also displayed by the HCS concordancer as a prenominal demonstrative modifying the indirect object *maji ya* kunywa 'drinking water'. Other cases that were eliminated include pronominal identification demonstratives in which the copula introducing the demonstratum was deleted; and adnominal demonstratives from poems whose pre or postnominal position may be driven by metrical requirements. Table 2 shows the number of adnominal demonstratives before and after disambiguation.

Table 2: Adnominal demonstratives before and after postediting.

And-Dem	And-Dems before disambiguation	And-Dems after disambiguation	Difference
Prenominal proximal	133	109	24
Postnominal proximal	135	124	11
Prenominal distal	140	126	14
Postnominal distal	114	75	39
Total	522	434	88

Each of the disambiguated demonstrative expression was then displayed in its narrow context (in the HCS of Swahili concordancer) as well as its wider context (in the original text) for contextual and statistical analysis.

2.2 Coding the data

Each demonstrative expression was coded for the following variables: dem-type (proximal, distal), dem-function (gestural, anaphoric, recognitional), dem-position (prenominal, postnominal) and the activation state (active, semiactive, inactive). Anaphoric demonstratives were further coded for referential distance. While coding for dem-type and dem-position was straightforward after displaying the queries in their wider context, coding for the dem-function, referential distance and activation state needs further elaboration. Each of these variables is explained in turn in §2.2.1, §2.2.2 and §2.2.3.

2.2.1 Demonstrative function

Adnominal demonstratives as referring expressions have mostly been analyzed by looking at the demonstrative function: gestural, anaphoric, and recognitional. Coding for these demonstrative functions is explained below.

'Gestural' here does not necessarily mean actual pointing but rather situations which need 'pointing' of some sort to establish reference. In the dataset there are instances such as (4) where a cue word may indicate that the demonstrative in question is gestural.

(4) [Yule   bwana] u-na-mu-on-a: Mzalamo yule?
     DIST.DEM person 2SG-PRS-OM-see-FV Zaramo   DIST.DEM

'Do you see that person: is he a Zamoro (ethnic community)?'

In (4), the demonstrative expression *yule bwana* 'that person' was coded gestural because the verb *on-a* 'see' draws the attention of the hearer to a potential discourse entity within the conversational context. Only first mentions of referents within conversational contexts were coded as gestural. Subsequent mentions were coded as anaphoric.

Anaphoric demonstratives track discourse entities across clauses (intra-sentential) (5) as well as across sentences (inter-sentential) (6) (Botley & McEnery 2000).

(5) A-li-po-fik-a   kwa [mzee   Malongo], [mzee   yule]
     SM-PST-when-arrive-FV at   old.man Malongo   old.man DIST.DEM

a-ka-shangaa.
SM-SEQ-surprise

'When he (Kiliilo) arrived at mzee Malongo's home, that old man (Malongo) was surprised (to see him).'

(6)   a. U-ki-vuka   bahari saba, ku-na   [chewa]ᵢ mkubwa.
          2SG-COND-cross seas   seven, 17SM-be grouper big

'If you cross the seven seas, there is a grouper (type of fish).'

      b. [Chewa   huyu]ᵢ a-ki-vuta   pumzi
          1grouper this   1SM-COND-breath air

'When this grouper is breathing...'

In (5), the NP *mzee Malongo* in the matrix clause is the antecedent of the demonstrative expression *mzee yule* 'that mzee' in the embedded clause. In (6a), the noun *chewa* 'grouper' is the antecedent of the demonstrative NP *chewa huyu* 'this grouper' in (6b). Demonstratives used to track referents in intra and intersentential contexts were coded as anaphoric.

Demonstratives used recognitionally indicate common knowledge and therefore do not have a co-specification element in the surrounding situation or preceding discourse (Diessel 1999). This is illustrated in (7).

(7) [Huyu   Juma] ka-shindw-a   ku-ku-tunz-a.
     PROX.DEM Juma SM.PRF-defeat-FV INF-OM-take.care-FV

'This Juma has failed to provide for you.'

In (7) the proximal demonstrative *huyu* indicates that *Juma* is the man the speaker and the hearer all know. The demonstrative expression here is not anaphoric since the referring expression *Juma* has no apparent antecedent in the preceding discourse. It is also not gestural because the referent *Juma* is not physically present in the conversational context.

Although recognitional demonstrative expressions are overwhelmingly used in first mentions to indicate common knowledge, there are instances where subsequent mentions via a demonstrative expression may mark the referent as familiar at that point of discourse. This is illustrated in (8).

(8) Kumbe [yule   mtu mweupe] amba-ye a-li-kuwa a-me-nusur-ik-a
    INTJ   DIST.DEM man white   COMP-REL SM-AUX   SM-PERF-save-STV-FV
    ku-ua-w-a   na wenyeji
    INF-kill-pass-FV by natives

'Alas, that white man who had escaped being killed by the natives … '

In (8), the referential distance between the adnominal demonstrative and its antecedent was 118 clauses. The writer is aware of the "referential problem" (Auer 1984) caused by topic shift and therefore adds more information to the adnominal demonstrative in form of a restrictive clause to ensure successful identification of the referent. Following Himmelmann (2006: 230), in addition to first mention of discourse entities to indicate common knowledge, I also coded demonstrative expressions as recognitional if the gap of absence after previous mention was too long to warrant "additional anchoring or descriptive information to make the intended referent more accessible".

2.2.2 Referential discourse

Referential distance has been described as the most important diagnostic tool for measuring referential givenness. Givón (1983: 36), for example, explains that the effect of referential givenness on accessibility correlates with other factors such as interference from other possible discourse entities since "a high referential distance would show - all other things being equal - more interfering topics in the preceding register." Interfering topics are other topics mentioned other than the immediate topic before its previous mention in the discourse.

Since the finite clause is the locus for topic update, referential distance in this study is the number of finite clauses from the relevant adnominal demonstrative expression to a co-specifying explicit NP to its left (cf. Kameyama 1998; Poesio et al. 2004; Taboada & Zabala 2008). The clause as the 'locus for topic update' implies that it is at the clause level that more information about the topic is added. Example (9) illustrates how coding for referential distance with the finite clause as the unit of analysis was done. Notice that each of the clauses in (9a-c) contains new information about the topic (*mjumbe* 'messenger'). The letter *u* stands for 'utterance' – the minimal unit of analysis in discourse, in this case, the finite clause (cf. Grosz et al. 1995).

(9) a. (u1) mjumbe wa tano alipotakikana, (u2) alitokea bila ya ajizi. (u3) Mjumbe
        huyu alikuwa Ridhaa
        [Mjumbe]   wa tano a-li-po-tak-ik-an-a,
         messenger of fifth SM-PST-when-want-STV-RECP-FV
        When the call for the fifth messenger was made,

b. a-li-toke-a   bila   ya ajizi
   SM-PST-appear-FV without of fail

   he came forth without fail.

c. [Mjumbe   huyu]   a-li-kuwa   Ridhaa.
   messenger PROX.DEM SM-PST-AUX Ridhaa

   This messenger was Ridhaa.

The ref-distance in (9) was coded as 2, that is, there are two finite clauses before the subsequent mention of the topic *mjumbe* in (9c).

2.2.3 Activation states

Depending on the referential distance between the adnominal demonstrative under consideration and its antecedent, the adnominal demonstrative in question was coded as active, semi-active or inactive. A question that arises under this description adapted from Chafe (1987) is: What is the number of intervening utterances that qualify a discourse entity to be active/semiactive/inactive?

The intended referent of an active referent is within the immediate consciousness of the discourse participants. Thus, an adnominal demonstrative expression was coded as 'active' if there was an apparent antecedent in the preceding utterance as is the case in (10).

(10) a. Mtu   wa pili   ku-kut-an-a   na-ye   a-li-kuwa [mzee].
         person of second INF-meet-RECP-FV with-3SG SM-PST-AUX old.man

         'The second person to meet me was an old man.'

      b. [Mzee   huyu]   a-li-kuwa   a-ki-peleka ng'ombe wake mtoni.
         old.man PROX.DEM SM-PST-AUX SM-IPFV-take cows   his   river-LOC

         'This old man was taking his cows to the river.'

In (10a) the NP *mzee* 'old man' is an apparent antecedent of the adnominal expression *mzee huyu* 'this old man' in (10b). The adnominal demonstrative expression *mzee huyu* 'this old man' in (10b) was therefore coded as active.

Semiactive referents in this study were of two types: situational (in conversational context) and textual (in discourse texts). Consequently, all gestural adnominal demonstratives were coded as semiactive. In discourse texts, a referent was coded as semiactive if there was an intervening topic(s) between the previous explicit mention of the antecedent NP to the adnominal demonstrative expression under consideration. This is illustrated in (11) and (12).

(11) Mbele ya-ngu ku-li-kuwa   bado watu wawili [yule   mzee]   na
      in.front POSS-1SG LOC17-PST-AUX still people two   DIST.DEM old.man and
      [msichana mmoja].
      girl   one

      'In front of me, there were still two people remaining, that old man and one girl.'

(12) [Msichana huyu],   a-li-ye-kuwa   bado a-me-weka kitambaa
     girl   PROX.DEM SM-PST-REL-AUX still SM-PRF-put handkercheif

'This girl, who still had a handkercheif placed ... '

In (11), yule mzee 'that old man' and *msichana mmoja* 'a girl' are the potential topics for the following utterance. A potential topic is a referent within an utterance that can be chosen by the speaker to be the center (topic) of the next utterance (cf. Grosz et al. 1995). In the following 4 utterances (not presented above), the *mzee* 'old man' is established and continued as the topic. In (12), the demonstrative expression *msichana huyu* 'this girl' reintroduces the girl mentioned in (11). The adnominal demonstrative *msichana huyu* 'this girl' in (12) was therefore coded as semiactive because of the interfering topic, *mzee* 'old man'.

All recognitional demonstratives were coded as "inactive" because their identification depends on retrieval of the discourse participants from the memory (see §2.2.1).

3 Results and discussion

In this section, I discuss the relevance of the demonstrative function in explaining the demonstrative position in §3.1. I then discuss the relationship that exists between the demonstrative position and activation states (active, semiactive, inactive) in §3.2.

3.1 Demonstrative function and position

Of the 434 adnominal demonstratives in the dataset, gestural demonstratives were 52, anaphoric 308 and recognitional 74. The frequencies of dem-type (proximal and distal) in both the pre and postnominal position are presented in Table 3.

Table 3: Dem-function and dem-position in proximal and distal demonstratives.

	Gestural			Anaphoric			Recognitional		
	Pre	Post	Total	Pre	Post	Total	Pre	Post	Total
Proximal	38	9	47	49	110	159	22	5	27
Distal	2	3	5	83	66	149	41	6	47

The pragmatic value of the demonstrative position for each of the demonstrative functions will be discussed in turn.

3.1.1 Gestural demonstratives

Table 3 above shows that the proximal gestural demonstratives in prenominal position were 38 and 9 in postnominal. There were 2 distal gestural demonstratives in prenominal position and 3 in postnominal. These frequencies show that, first, the proximal demonstrative is mostly used as the deictic expression for the gestural function. The total frequency of proximal gestural demonstratives is 47 while the total frequency of the distal gestural demonstratives is 5. This frequency difference is significant (X^2 (1,N=52)=33.92, p < 0.001). Second, the gestural demonstratives have a higher frequency count in prenominal position than postnominal. The total number of prenominal demonstratives is 40 while in the postnominal position the total number is 12. This frequency difference is also significant (X^2 (1,N=52)=15.08, p < 0.001).

The difference in the demonstrative position for the gestural demonstratives can be explained by recalling the grammaticalization of the Swahili prenominal demonstrative to express definite reference (Ashton 1944; Givón 1976; Carstens 1991; 2008). In their paper on definite reference in English, Clark & Marshall (1981: 38), mention PHYSICAL COPRESENCE (presence in conversational contexts) as one of the reasons which license definite reference in English. Based on the contextual analysis of the corpus data, I posit that the prenominal demonstratives are mostly used to point to definite referents due to PHYSICAL COPRESENCE as seen in (4) repeated here as (13).

(13) [Yule   bwana] u-na-mu-on-a: Mzalamo yule?
      DIST.DEM person 2SG-PRS-OM-see-FV Zaramo   DIST.DEM

      'Do you see that person: is he a Zamoro (ethnic community)?'

Based on the high frequency of gestural demonstratives in prenominal position, it can be deduced that the prenominal position is mainly used to mark the referents as accessible (semi-active) in conversational contexts. The examples in (14) and (15) further illustrate this.

(14) Huyu   kondoo tu-m-pelek-e   kwa Mfalme Ndevu.
      PROX.DEM sheep   1PL-OM-take-IMP to   King   Ndevu

      'This sheep, let us take her to King Ndevu.'

(15) Mfalme a-ki-m-pat-a   kondoo huyu   a-ta-furahi   sana.
      King   SM-SBJV-OM-get-FV sheep   PROX.DEM SM-FUT-happy very

      'If the King gets this sheep, he will be very happy.'

In (14), because the discourse participants are all aware of the sheep's presence within the conversational context, the prenominal demonstrative in *huyu kondoo* 'this sheep' marks the referent as definite due to PHYSICAL COPRESENCE. In (15), however, the postnominal position of the demonstrative marks the previously mentioned *kondoo* 'sheep' as anaphoric. As it will be seen in §3.1.2, the unmarked position for anaphoric demonstratives is postnominal.

3.1.2 Anaphoric demonstratives

The distribution of the 308 anaphoric demonstratives was as follows. There were 49 proximal demonstratives in prenominal position but 110 in postnominal position (X^2

(1,N=159)=23.40, p<0.001). The distal demonstratives were 83 in prenominal position but 66 in postnominal position, p>0.05. These results show that for the anaphoric demonstratives the proximal demonstrative has a higher frequency in postnominal position than in prenominal. When contrasted with the distal postnominal demonstrative, the proximal postnominal demonstrative frequency is also significantly higher (X^2 (1,N=176)=11.00, p<0.001). In the prenominal position, the distal demonstrative has a significantly higher frequency than the proximal demonstrative (X^2 (1,N=132)=8.76, p<0.005).

In order to further explore the frequency tendencies of the anaphoric demonstratives, the referential distance of the anaphoric demonstrative expressions in the dataset was analyzed. The results are presented in §3.1.3.

3.1.3 The effect of referential distance on the anaphoric demonstrative position

In measuring the referential distance, the number of finite clauses between an adnominal demonstrative and a co-referential NP to its left was counted and recorded in a database. The raw data was then log transformed to reduce the skewness of the data distribution. After log-transformation, the Shapiro-Wilk test revealed that the data distribution for the distal and proximal prenominal demonstratives was normal, p>0.05. The skewness of the distal and proximal postnominal demonstrative data was greatly reduced but not completely eliminated, p<0.05.[1]

Table 4 and Table 5 report the descriptive statistics of the demonstrative position for the raw and log-transformed data respectively. The number in parentheses is the standard deviation while the number outside the parentheses is the mean referential distance.

Table 4: Mean referential distance and standard deviation of raw data.

Dem_Type	Prenominal	Postnominal
Proximal	5.55 (5.39)	5.25 (5.06)
Distal	7.40 (6.55)	5.29 (4.35)

Table 5: Mean referential distance and standard deviation of log-transformed data.

Dem_Type	Prenominal	Postnominal
Proximal	1.34 (0.87)	1.25 (0.92)
Distal	1.70 (0.77)	1.30 (0.89)

---

[1] The statistical operations conducted in this study assume normal distribution. Log transformation of the variables enhances normal distribution, hence reducing the influence of outliers on the results (Baayen 2008).

The mean referential distance of the prenominal demonstratives is higher than that of postnominal demonstratives. A non-repeated measures ANOVA with ref-distance as the dependent variable and dem-type and dem-position as the independent variables reveal that there is a significant main effect of ref-distance on dem-type ($F(1,308)=6.09$, $p<0.05$) and dem-position ($F(1,308)=5.90$, $p<0.05$). There was no significant interaction between dem-type and dem-position, $p>0.05$.

Further, a planned comparison using the t.test reveals that the mean ref-distance of the distal prenominal demonstrative is higher that of the proximal prenominal demonstrative, $p<0.05$. The nonparametric Wilcoxon test applied to compare the median of the distal prenominal demonstrative and the distal postnominal demonstrative indicates that the medians of these two vectors and their distributions are different. Hence, the mean referential distance of the distal prenominal demonstrative is also higher than that of the postnominal distal demonstratives, $p<0.05$. However, there is no significant difference between the mean ref-distance of the proximal pre and postnominal demonstratives. These statistics show that:

1. The difference in referential distance between the proximal and distal postnominal demonstrative is not significant.

2. The distal prenominal demonstrative tends to be separated from its antecedent by longer referential distance than the distal postnominal demonstrative as well as the proximal pre and postnominal demonstrative.

3. The difference in referential distance between the proximal pre and postnominal demonstratives is not significant.

I illustrate these observations with examples from the corpus.

These statistics show that the proximal demonstrative is frequently used in postnominal position when the referential distance is short (See example (15)). The insignificant difference in referential distance between the proximal and distal postnominal demonstratives further suggests that there are cases when a distal postnominal demonstrative may be used after a short referential distance as seen in (16).

(16) a. Adili a-li-po-taka   ku-ingia ndani,
          Adili SM-PST-when-want INF-enter inside

          'When Adili was about to go inside (the house), '

      b. a-li-ona   [mtu] a-me-simama mlango-ni
          SM-PST-see person SM-PRF-stand door-LOC

          'he saw a person standing at the door ... '

      c. Adili a-li-dhani   [mtu   yule]   a-li-kuwa   bawabu.
          Adili SM-PST-assume person DIST.DEM SM-PST-AUX security.officer

          'Adili thought that the person was a security officer.'

The referent *mtu* 'person' introduced in (16b) is continued in (16c). The postnominal position of the demonstrative in (16c) marks the referent as 'active'. The use of the post-nominal distal demonstrative *yule* 'that' instead of the proximal demonstrative *huyu* 'this' has a special effect of marking the "narrative distance" (Leonardo 1987; Wilt 1987), that is, the author is narrating events from a third person's perspective. In the third person's perspective style of narration, the narrator is not involved in the events of the story.

Further, the results show that the distal prenominal demonstrative is separated from its antecedent by long referential distance as illustrated in (17).

(17) [Yule   msichana] a-li-ingi-a.
     DIST.DEM girl   SM-PST-enter-FV
     'That girl entered.'

In (17), the demonstrative expression *yule msichana* reintroduces the girl as the topic after 45 clauses.

It is important to mention here that most corpus generalizations are based on statistical tendencies (See Mwamzandi 2014 for more examples). In general, anaphoric proximal and distal demonstrative are used postnominally after a short referential distance to mark the intended referent as active. Anaphoric distal demonstrative are used prenominally after topic shift to mark the referent as semiactive.

3.1.4 Recognitional demonstratives

The frequency of recognitional proximal demonstratives in prenominal position was 22, and 5 in postnominal position (X^2 (1,N=27)=10.70, p < 0.01). In prenominal position, the frequency of distal demonstratives was 41, and 6 in postnominal position (X^2 (1,N=47)=26.06, p < 0.001). The difference between the recognitional demonstratives in pre and postnominal positions is statistically significant (X^2 (1,N=74)=36.54, p < 0.001). It can be inferred from the results that a demonstrative is preferred in prenominal position if used recognitionally.

Contrary to Himmelmann's (1996) claim that only one of the demonstratives, mostly the distal demonstrative, is preserved for the recognitional function across languages, both the distal and proximal demonstratives can be used for this function in Swahili as seen in (18) and (19).

(18) [Yule   mtoto wako] a-na-ye-fundisha Chuo Kikuu,
     DIST.DEM child your   SM-PRS-REL-teach university
     'That child of yours who teaches at the university, ...'

(19) Hii   ni kazi ya majirani   zetu, hasa   [huyu   mjukuu   wa
     9PROX.DEM is 9work of neighbours our   especially PROX.DEM grandchild of
     Ndenda].
     Ndanda
     'This is the work of our neighbours, especially this grandchild of Ndenda.'

In (18), the speaker uses the distal demonstrative *yule* 'that' to signal familiarity. However, in (19) the proximal demonstrative *huyu* 'this' signals not only "larger situation" familiarity (Hawkins 1978) but also "community membership", that is, the referent (mjukuu wa Ndenda) lives within the speaker's neighborhood (Clark & Marshall 1981). The use of the distal demonstrative expression *yule mjukuu wa Ndenda* in (19) instead of the proximal demonstrative *expression huyu mjukuu wa Ndeda* eliminates the "community membership" implication.

3.2 Activation states

In this section, I discuss the effect of the active, semiactive and inactive activation states on the form of the adnominal expression in the following paragraphs in turn.

As mentioned earlier, subsequent mentions of referents via anaphoric demonstrative expressions if the referent was a continued topic were coded as active. Table 6 presents the frequencies of the demonstrative expressions coded as active.

Table 6: Demonstrative expressions coded as active.

	Prenominal	Postnominal	Total
Proximal	42	88	130
Distal	32	47	79

A few things can be said about these frequencies. First, the frequencies show that the proximal demonstrative is used more frequently than the distal demonstrative if the activation state of the intended referent is active (X^2 (1,N=209)=12.45, p < 0.001). Second, there is a higher frequency of proximal demonstrative in postnominal position than in prenominal position if the activation state of the intended referent is active (X^2 (1,N=130)=16.28, p < 0.001). Third, though insignificant, the frequency of the distal demonstrative in postnominal position is higher than in prenominal position if the activation state of the intended referent is active, p > 0.05. These results corroborate the statistics I presented on the effect of referential distance on demonstrative position of anaphoric demonstratives in §3.1.3.

All gestural demonstratives as well as demonstratives used anaphorically after topic shift were coded as semi-active. Table 7 and Table 8 present the frequencies of the gestural and anaphoric semi-active demonstratives.

Table 7: Semiactive gestural demonstratives.

	Prenominal	Postnominal	Total
Proximal	38	9	47
Distal	2	3	5

Table 8: Semiactive anaphoric demonstratives.

	Prenominal	Postnominal	Total
Proximal	7	22	29
Distal	51	19	70

I have discussed the significance of the gestural demonstrative frequencies in pre and postnominal position in §3.1.1. Here I discuss the frequencies of the anaphoric demonstratives coded as semiactive. First, the frequencies of the anaphoric semiactive demonstratives show that the distal demonstrative is used more frequently than the proximal demonstrative (X^2 (1,N=99)=16.98, p < 0.001). Second, the frequency of proximal postnominal demonstrative is higher than proximal prenominal demonstratives (X^2 (1,N=29)=7.76, p < 0.01). Third, the frequency of distal demonstrative in prenominal position is higher than postnominal (X^2 (1,N=70)=14.63, p < 0.001).

As for inactive activation state, all first mentions of familiar referents and subsequent mentions of discourse entities after a long referential distance via adnominal demonstrative expressions were coded as inactive. Table 9 presents the frequencies of the adnominal demonstratives coded as inactive.

Table 9: Inactive adnominal demonstratives.

	Prenominal	Postnominal	Total
Proximal	22	5	27
Distal	41	6	47

I have also discussed the significance of these frequencies in §3.1.4. In summary, the prenominal position is used more frequently than postnominal if the referent is inactive.

4 Conclusion and theoretical implications

The observation that pre and postnominal demonstratives can be used as referring expressions for discourse entities has ramifications on the analysis of Swahili demonstrative expressions in pragmatics as well as syntax. In pragmatics, it has been observed cross-linguistically that activation level of topics may be represented via different forms of referring expressions (Gundel et al. 1993; Ariel 1988; 1991; 2001). In Swahili, the demonstratives co-occur with the noun to mark different activation levels of referents. The results of this study show that postnominal demonstratives are high accessibility markers, prenominal demonstratives are mid-accessibility markers, and prenominal demonstratives followed by a restrictive clause are low accessibility markers.

This functional role of the demonstrative position independently motivates a syntactic analysis of the Swahili demonstrative in pre and postnominal position (Carstens 1991;

2008). In the postnominal position, the unmarked order of Swahili noun modifiers is: N>POSS>DEM>Quantifier (20) (cf. Rugemalira 2007).

(20) eneo langu   hili   lote
      area 5AGR.POSS.1SG PROX.DEM all
      'all this area of mine'

Of these three types of modifiers, only the demonstrative may occur prenominally. The functional distinction of the demonstrative in pre and postnominal position as observed in this study rules out the possibility of these demonstratives orders being manifestation of a single abstract syntactic structure. The different N + DEM/DEM + N constructions correspond to different discourse needs.

Acknowledgements

I thank Dr. Laurel Stvan, Dr. Jason Kandybowicz and Dr. Jeffrey Witzel for their input on earlier versions of this paper. I also thank the ACAL reviewers for their comments and recommendations.

Abbreviations

Unless indicating person, numbers in glosses indicate noun class. Abbreviations follow Leipzig Glossing Rules, with the following exceptions:

FV	final vowel	SEQ	sequential
INTJ	interjection	SM	subject marker
OM	object marker	STV	stative

References

Amidu, Assibi A. 2006. *Pronouns and pronominalization in Swahili grammar*. Rüdiger Köppe Verlag: Köln.

Ariel, Mira. 1988. Referring and accessibility. *Journal of Linguistics* 24(1). 65–87.

Ariel, Mira. 1991. The function of accessibility in a theory of grammar. *Journal of Pragmatics* 16(5). 443–463.

Ariel, Mira. 2001. Accessibility theory: An overview. In Ted Sanders, Joost Schilperoord & Wilbert Spooren (eds.), *Text representation: Linguistic and psycholinguistic aspects*, 29–87. Amsterdam/Philadelphia: John Benjamins.

Ashton, Ethel O. 1944. *Swahili grammar (including intonation)*. London: Longmans, Green & CO LTD.

Auer, Peter. 1984. Referential problems in conversation. *Journal of Pragmatics* 8.5-6. 627–648.

Baayen, Harald R. 2008. *Analyzing linguistic data: A practical introduction to statistics using R.* Cambridge University Press: New York.

Botley, Simon & Mark Anthony McEnery. 2000. *Corpus based and computational approaches to discourse anaphora.* Amsterdam/Philadelphia: John Benjamins.

Carstens, Vicki May. 1991. *The morphology and syntax of determiner phrases in Kiswahili.* UCLA dissertation.

Carstens, Vicki May. 2008. DP in Bantu and Romance. In Cecile De Cat & Demuth Katherine (eds.), *The Bantu-romance connection,* 131–166. Amsterdam/Philadelphia: John Benjamins.

Chafe, Wallace L. 1987. Cognitive constraints on information flow. In Russel S. Tomlin (ed.), *Coherence and grounding in discourse. Typological studies in language,* vol. II, 21–52. Amsterdam: John Benjamins.

Clark, Herbert H. & Catherine R. Marshall. 1981. Definite reference and mutual knowledge. In Aravind K. Joshi, Bonnie L. Webber & Ivan A. Sag (eds.), *Elements of discourse understanding,* 10–64. Cambridge: Cambridge University Press.

Diessel, Holger. 1999. *Demonstratives: Form, function and grammaticalization.* John Benjamins: Amsterdam/Philadelphia.

Fillmore, Charles J. 1975. *Santa Cruz lectures on deixis, 1971.* Bloomington: Indiana University Linguistics Club.

Fillmore, Charles J. 1982. Towards a descriptive framework for spatial deixis. In Robert J. Jarvella & Wolfgang Klein (eds.), *Speech, place and action: Studies in deixis and related topics,* 31–59. Chichester/New York/Brisbane/Toronto/Singapore: John Wiley & Sons LTD.

Fillmore, Charles J. 1997. *Lectures on deixis.* CSLI Publications: Stanford, California.

Givón, Talmy. 1976. Topic, pronoun, and grammatical agreement. In Charles N. Li (ed.), *Subject and topic,* 149–188. New York: Academic Press.

Givón, Talmy (ed.). 1983. *Topic and continuity in discourse* (Typological studies in language 3). Amsterdam/Philadelphia: John Benjamins.

Grosz, Barbara J., Aravind K. Joshi & Scott Weinstein. 1995. Centering: A framework for modeling the local coherence of discourse. *Computational Linguistics* 21(2). 203–225.

Gundel, Jeanette K. & Thorstein Fretheim. 2006. Topic and focus. In Laurence R. Horn & Gregory Ward (eds.), *The handbook of pragmatics,* 175–196. Malden, USA: Blackwell Publishing.

Gundel, Jeanette K., Nancy Hedberg & Ron Zacharski. 1993. Cognitive status and the form of referring expressions in discourse. *Language* 69(2). 274–307.

Hawkins, John A. 1978. *Definiteness and indefiniteness.* Groom Helm: London.

Himmelmann, Nikolaus P. 1996. Demonstratives in narrative discourse: A taxonomy of universal uses. In Barbara Fox (ed.), *Studies in anaphora,* 205–254. John Benjamins: Amsterdam/Philadelphia.

Himmelmann, Nikolaus P. 2006. Language documentation: What is it and what is it good for? In Jost Gippert, Nikolaus P. Himmelmann & Ulrike Mose (eds.), *Essentials of language documentation,* 1–30. Berlin: Mouton de Gruyter.

Kameyama, Megumi. 1998. Intrasentential centering: A case study. In Marilyn A. Walker, Aravind K. Joshi & Ellen F. Prince (eds.), *Centering theory in discourse*, 89–112. New York: Oxford University Press.

Leonardo, Robert. 1987. Response to Wilt: Discourse distances and the Swahili demonstratives. *Studies in African Linguistics* 18(1). 97–105.

Mitkov, Ruslan. 1994. An intergrated model for anaphora resolution. Proceedings of the 15th International Conference on Computational Linguistics. Kyoto, Japan. In.

Mwamzandi, Mohamed. 2014. *Swahili word order choices*. University of Texas at Arlington. Ph.D dissertation.

Poesio, Massimo, Rosemary Stevenson, Barbara Di Eugenio & Janet Hitzeman. 2004. Centering: A parametric theory and its instantiations. *Computational Linguistics* 30(3). 309–63.

Rugemalira, Josephat M. 2007. The structure of the Bantu noun phrase. *SOAS Working Papers in Linguistics* 15. 135–148.

Taboada, Maite & Loreley Hadic Zabala. 2008. Deciding on units of analysis within Centering Theory. *Corpus Linguistics & Linguistic Theory* 4(1). 63–108.

Tamanji, Pius N. 2006. *Concord and DP structure in Bafut. Afrikanistik online.*

Wilt, Timothy. 1987. Discourse distances and the Swahili demonstratives. *Studies in African Linguistics* 18(1). 81–95.

Name index

Language index

Subject index